# Social Network Mining, Analysis, and Research Trends:

## Techniques and Applications

I-Hsien Ting
*National University of Kaohsiung, Taiwan*

Tzung-Pei Hong
*National University of Kaohsiung, Taiwan*

Leon S.L. Wang
*National University of Kaohsiung, Taiwan*

Information Science
REFERENCE

| Managing Director: | Lindsay Johnston |
| Senior Editorial Director: | Heather Probst |
| Book Production Manager: | Sean Woznicki |
| Development Manager: | Joel Gamon |
| Development Editor: | Myla Harty |
| Acquisitions Editor: | Erika Gallagher |
| Typesetters: | Lisandro Gonzalez |
| Print Coordinator: | Jamie Snavely |
| Cover Design: | Nick Newcomer, Greg Snader |

Published in the United States of America by
Information Science Reference (an imprint of IGI Global)
701 E. Chocolate Avenue
Hershey PA 17033
Tel: 717-533-8845
Fax: 717-533-8661
E-mail: cust@igi-global.com
Web site: http://www.igi-global.com

Library of Congress Cataloging-in-Publication Data

Social network mining, analysis, and research trends: techniques and applications / I-Hsien Ting, Tzung-Pei Hong and Leon S.L. Wang, editors.
    p. cm.
 Includes bibliographical references and index.
 Summary: "This book covers current research trends in the area of social networks analysis and mining, sharing research from experts in the social network analysis and mining communities, as well as practitioners from social science, business, and computer science"--Provided by publisher.
 ISBN 978-1-61350-513-7 (hardcover) -- ISBN 978-1-61350-514-4 (ebook) -- ISBN 978-1-61350-515-1 (print & perpetual access)  1. Online social networks. 2. Data mining.  I. Ting, I-Hsien. II. Hong, Tzung-Pei, 1963- III. Wang, Leon Shyue-Liang, 1955-
 HM742.S6288 2012
 302.30285--dc23
                          2011038347

British Cataloguing in Publication Data
A Cataloguing in Publication record for this book is available from the British Library.

All work contributed to this book is new, previously-unpublished material. The views expressed in this book are those of the authors, but not necessarily of the publisher.

# Table of Contents

**Section 1**
**Introduction and Surveys of Social Networks Mining and Analysis**

## Section 2
## Measures, Methods and Techniques in Social Networks Mining and Analysis

# Detailed Table of Contents

## Section 1
## Introduction and Surveys of Social Networks Mining and Analysis

In recent years there is a vast and rapidly growing amount of multimedia content available online. Web 2.0 and online social networks have dramatically influenced the growing amount of multimedia content due to the fact that users become more active producers and distributors of such multimedia context. This work conceptualizes and introduces the concept of social multimedia mining as a new emerging research area that combines web mining research, multimedia research and social media research. New challenges in multimedia research, social network analysis research as well as trends and opportunities in research areas of social and communication studies and more specific in politics, public relations, public administration, marketing and advertising are discussed in this chapter.

Similarity breeds connections, the principle of homophily, has been well studied in existing sociology literature. Several studies have observed this phenomenon by conducting surveys on human subjects. These studies have concluded that new ties are formed between similar individuals. This phenomenon has been used to explain several socio-psychological concepts such as segregation, community development, social mobility, etc. However, due to the nature of these studies and limitations because of involvement of human subjects, conclusions from these studies are not easily extensible in online social media. Social media, which is becoming the infinite space for interactions, has exceeded all the expectations in terms of growth, for reasons beyond human comprehension. New ties are formed in social media in the same way that they emerge in the real world. However, given the differences between real-world and online social media, do the same factors that govern the construction of new ties in the real world also govern the construction of new ties in social media? In other words, does homophily exist in social media? In this chapter, the authors study this highly significant question and propose a systematic approach by studying two online social media sites, BlogCatalog and Last.fm, and report our findings along with some interesting observations.

This chapter describes techniques for sociocognitive inquiry based on conceptual grid elicitation and analysis using web-based tools, such as WebGrid, which are designed to elicit conceptual models from those participating in a networked community. These techniques provide an interactive web-based experience with immediate payback from online graphic analysis, that provides an attractive alternative to, or component of, conventional web-based surveys. In particular, they support targeted follow-up studies based on passive data mining of the by-products of web-based community activities, allowing the phenomena modeled through data mining to be investigated in greater depth. The foundations in cognitive sociology and psychology are briefly surveyed, a case study is provided to illustrate how web-based conceptual modeling services can be customized to integrate with a social networking site and support a focused study, and the implications for future research are discussed.

# Chapter 4

This chapter presents a state of the art of research on the discovery of Web communities, in a general sense. For this purpose, the authors discuss various notions of communities and their related assumptions: hypertextual communities, tag communities and semantic-based communities.

**Section 2**
**Measures, Methods and Techniques in Social Networks Mining and Analysis**

In recent years, a considerable amount of research has focused on the study of graph structures arising from technological, biological and sociological systems. Graphs are the tool of choice in modeling such systems since they are typically described as sets of pairwise interactions. Important examples of such datasets are the Internet, the Web, social networks, and large-scale information networks which reach the planetary scale, e.g., Facebook and LinkedIn. The necessity to process large datasets, including graphs, has led to a major shift towards distributed computing and parallel applications, especially in the recent years. MapReduce was developed by Google, one of the largest users of multiple processor computing in the world, for facilitating the development of scalable and fault tolerant applications. MapReduce has become the de facto standard for processing large scale datasets both in industry and academia. In this chapter, the authors present state of the art work on large scale graph mining using MapReduce. They survey research work on an important graph mining problem, estimating the diameter of a graph and the eccentricities/radii of its vertices. Thanks to the algorithm they present in the following, the authors are able to mine graphs with billions of edges, and thus extract surprising patterns. The source code is publicly available at the URL http://www.cs.cmu.edu/~pegasus/.

## Chapter 6

*Qiang Shen, Aberstwyth University, UK*
*Tossapon Boongoen, Royal Thai Air Force Academy, Thailand*

In the wake of recent terrorist atrocities, intelligence experts have commented that failures in detecting terrorist and criminal activities are not so much due to a lack of data, as they are due to difficulties in relating and interpreting the available intelligence. An intelligent tool for monitoring and interpreting intelligence data will provide a helpful means for intelligence analysts to consider emerging scenarios of plausible threats, thereby offering useful assistance in devising and deploying preventive measures against such possibilities. One of the major problems in need of such attention is detecting false identity that has become the common denominator of all serious crime, especially terrorism. Typical approaches to this problem rely on the similarity measure of textual and other content-based characteristics, which are usually not applicable in the case of deceptive and erroneous description. This barrier may be overcome through link information presented in communication behaviors, financial interactions and social networks. Quantitative link-based similarity measures have proven effective for identifying similar problems in the Internet and publication domains. However, these numerical methods only concentrate on link structures, and fail to achieve accurate and coherent interpretation of the information. Inspired by this observation, the chapter presents a novel qualitative similarity measure that makes use of multiple link properties to refine the underlying similarity estimation process and consequently derive semantic-rich similarity descriptors. The approach is based on order-of-magnitude reasoning. Its performance is empirically evaluated over a terrorism-related dataset, and compared against several state-of-the-art link-based algorithms and other alternative methods.

## Chapter 7

*Kathy J. Liszka, University of Akron, USA*
*Chien-Chung Chan, University of Akron, USA*
*Chandra Shekar, University of Akron, USA*

Microblogs are one of a growing group of social network tools. Twitter is, at present, one of the most popular forums for microblogging in online social networks, and the fastest growing. Fifty million messages flow through servers, computers, and cell phones on a wide variety of topics exchanged daily. With this considerable volume, Twitter is a natural and obvious target for spreading spam via the messages, called tweets. The challenge is how to determine if a tweet is a spam or not, and more specifically a special category advertising pharmaceutical products. The authors look at the essential characteristics of spam tweets and what makes microblogging spam unique from email or other types of spam. They review methods and tools currently available to identify general spam tweets. Finally, this work introduces a new methodology of applying text mining and data mining techniques to generate classifiers that can be used for pharmaceutical spam detection in the context of microblogging.

    *Arkaitz Zubiaga, NLP & IR Group, UNED, Spain*
    *Víctor Fresno, NLP & IR Group, UNED, Spain*
    *Raquel Martínez, NLP & IR Group, UNED, Spain*

The lack of representative textual content in many resources suggests the study of additional metadata to improve classification tasks. Social bookmarking and cataloging sites provide an accessible way to increase available metadata in large amounts with user-provided annotations. In this chapter, the authors study and analyze the usefulness of social annotations for resource classification. They show that social annotations outperform classical content-based approaches, and that the aggregation of user annotations creates a great deal of meaningful metadata for this task. The authors also present a method to get the most out of the studied data sources using classifier committees.

    *Michael Farrugia, University College Dublin, Ireland*
    *Neil Hurley, University College Dublin, Ireland*
    *Diane Payne, University College Dublin, Ireland*
    *Aaron Quigley, University College Dublin, Ireland*

Social scientists have been studying and refining their network data collection instruments for the last number of decades. Data collection in this field traditionally consists of manually conducting interviews and questionnaires on a population of interest to derive a list of ties between the members of the population and which can later be studied from a sociological perspective. Great care and considerable resources are often required during the research design and data collection phases in order to ensure that the final data set is well focused, unbiased and representative of the selected population. Nowadays electronic network data is becoming widely available and easier to access and this data brings with it a number of advantages over manually collecting data. The ease of data collection, lower cost, large scale, temporal information and the elimination of respondent bias and recall problems are all concrete benefits of electronic data. With these clear advantages, could electronic data be a solution to problems encountered with manual data collection? Electronic data is often available as a bi-product of other processes (such as phone call logs and email server logs), so often the data is not collected with the explicit purpose of being studied from a social network perspective. This aspect shifts the design decisions on electronic data to a later processing stage once the data is available, rather than before the data is collected. This shift introduces a different set of decisions and processes when dealing with electronic data collection. What are the best ways to process and interpret the data to achieve valid insights into the 'real' social network that the social scientist is interested in? In this chapter, the authors will discuss the differences between manual data collection and electronic data collection to understand the advantages and the challenges brought by electronic social network data. They will discuss in detail the processes that are used to transform electronic data to social network data and the procedures that can be used to validate the resultant social network.

# Chapter 10

Previous chapters focused on the models of static networks, which consider a relational network at a given point in time. However, real-world social networks are dynamic in nature; for example, friends of friends become friends. Social network research has, in recent years, paid increasing attention to dynamic and longitudinal network analysis in order to understand network evolution, belief formation, friendship formation, and so on. This chapter focuses mainly on the dynamics and evolutional patterns of social networks. The chapter introduces real-world applications and reviews major theories and models of dynamic network mining.

# Chapter 11

Contemporary companies try to build customer relationship management systems based on the customer social relations and behavioral patterns. This is in correspondence with the current trend in marketing that is to move from broadcast marketing operation to a one-to-one marketing. The key issue in this activity is predicting to which products or services a particular customer was likely to respond to. In order to build customer relationship management systems, companies have to learn to understand their customer in the broader social context. The key hypothesis in this approach is that the predictors of behavior in the future are customers behavior patterns in the past. This is a form of human behavioral modeling. The individual customer behavior patterns can be used to build an analytical customer profile. This will be described in section "Introduction" and "Customer profiling". Based on this profile a company might target a specific customer with a personalized message. In section "Critical examples" the authors will focus in particular on the importance of the customer social relations, that reflects referrals influence on the marketing response. In the end in section "Market of analytical profiles" they will discuss the potential business models related to market exchange of analytical profiles.

# Chapter 12

Most existing personalized search systems do not consider group profiling. Group profiling can be an efficient retrieval mechanism, where a user profile is inferred from the profile of the social groups to which the user belongs. The authors propose an XML search system called DemoFilter which employs the concept of group profiling. DemoFilter simplifies the personalization process by pre-defining various categories of social groups and then identifying their preferences. Social groups are characterized based on demographic, ethnic, cultural, religious, age, or other characteristics. DemoFilter can be used for various practical applications, such as Internet or other businesses that market preference-driven products. In the ontology, the preferences of a social group are identified from published studies about the social group. They experimentally evaluate the search effectiveness of DemoFilter and compare it to an existing search engine.

## Section 3
## Applications and Case Studies in Social Networks Mining and Analysis

This chapter presents six examples of organization-related social network mining: 1) interorganizational and sentiment networks in the Deepwater BP Oil Spill events, 2) intraorganizational interdepartmental networks in the Savannah College of Art and Design (SCAD), 3) who-to-whom email networks across the organizational hierarchy the Ford Motor Company's automotive engineering innovation: "Sync® w/ MyFord Touch", 4) networks of selected individuals who left that organization, 5) semantic associations across email for a corporate innovation in that organization, and 6) assessment of sentiment across its email for innovations over time. These examples are discussed in terms of motivations, methods, implications, and applications.

The complex network approach developed in statistical physics seems particularly well-suited to analyzing large networks. Progress in the study of complex networks has been made by looking for shared properties and seemingly universal dynamics, thus ignoring the details of networks individual nodes, links, or sub-components. Researchers now need to assess the differences in the processes that take place on complex networks. The author first discusses briefly the theoretical understanding of evolutionary laws governing the emergence of these universal properties (small-world and scale-free networks) and recent evolutions in the field of network analysis. Using data on two empirical networks, a transaction network in the venture capital industry and an interfirm alliance network in a major sector of the bio-pharmaceutical industry, the author then demonstrates that networks can switch from one 'universal' structure to another, but each in its own way. This chapter highlights the need of knowing more about networks, as 'more is different'.

## Chapter 15

*Kon Shing Kenneth Chung, University of Wollongong, Australia*

This chapter presents a theoretical model based on social network theories and the social influence model for understanding how knowledge professionals utilise technology. In particular, the association between egocentric network properties (structure, position and tie) and information and communication technology (ICT) use of individuals in knowledge-intensive and geographically dispersed settings is explored. A novel triangulation methodology is adopted where in-depth interviews and observation techniques were utilised to develop constructs for the conceptual model which were then vetted by domain-level experts. A reliable and validated social network-based questionnaire survey is also developed to operationalise the model. Results show that task-level ICT use is significantly associated with degree centrality and functional tie-diversity; and communication-level ICT use is negatively associated with efficiency. The implications of these associations for knowledge-intensive work mean that it is important to consider the professional social network characteristics of potential users of the technology for designing ICT-enabled organisations.

## Chapter 16

*Armelle Brun, Nancy Université, France*
*Sylvain Castagnos, Nancy Université, France*
*Anne Boyer, Nancy Université, France*

Recommender systems aim at suggesting to users items that fit their preferences. Collaborative filtering is one of the most popular approaches of recommender systems; it exploits users' ratings to express preferences. Traditional approaches of collaborative filtering suffer from the cold-start problem: when a new item enters the system, it cannot be recommended while a sufficiently high number of users have rated it. The quantity of required ratings is not known a priori and may be high as it depends on who rates the items. In this chapter, the authors propose to automatically select the adequate set of users in the network of users to address the cold-start problem. They call them the "delegates", and they correspond to those who should rate a new item first so as to reliably deduce the ratings of other users on this item. They propose to address this issue as an opinion poll problem. The authors consider two kinds of delegates: mentors and leaders. They experiment some measures, classically exploited in social networks, to select the adequate set of delegates. The experiments conducted show that only 6 delegates are sufficient to accurately estimate ratings of the whole set of other users, which dramatically reduces the number of users classically required.

## Chapter 17

*Shintaro Okazaki, Universidad Autónoma de Madrid, Spain*
*Jaime Romero, Universidad Autónoma de Madrid, Spain*
*Sara Campo, Universidad Autónoma de Madrid, Spain*

The objective of this chapter is to identify a market maven segment among advergamers on a mobile-based social networking site (SNS). A real online campaign with a multiplayer game is designed for Procter & Gamble's Pringles, after which online surveys are conducted via mobile device. Finite mixture models are employed to identify clusters. The estimation results suggest four clusters. The majority group belongs to Clusters 1 (67%) and 2 (21%), while Clusters 3 (6.8%) and 4 (4.8%) exhibit the propensity of market mavens. Specifically, the members of Cluster 3 are likely to have been actively engaged in information search, purchased the sponsor brand, and disseminated their brand knowledge of the brand, mainly through personal conversation after the game play. By contrast, the members of Cluster 4 are unlikely to have sought information, nor to have purchased the brand after the game, but are very likely to have spread their brand knowledge through word-of-mouth. Furthermore, they did so via not only personal conversation but also SNS functions (i.e., messaging, blog, and discussion board). Given this, Clusters 3 and 4 could be labeled as traditional and innovative market mavens, respectively. Our findings suggest that online marketers should identify and incentivize market mavens by branded entertainment so that they can then disseminate information, encourage followers, and generate a viral chain of word-of-mouth.

**Chapter 18**

*Johann Stan, Alcatel-Lucent Bell Labs, France*
*Myriam Ribière, Alcatel-Lucent Bell Labs, France*
*Jérôme Picault, Alcatel-Lucent Bell Labs, France*
*Lionel Natarianni, Alcatel-Lucent Bell Labs, France*
*Nicolas Marie, Alcatel-Lucent Bell Labs, France*

In this book chapter the authors address two main challenges for building compelling social applications. In the first challenge they focus on the user by addressing the issue of building dynamic interaction profiles from the content they produce in a social system. Such profiles are key to find the best person to contact based on an information need. The second challenge presents their vision of "object-centered sociality", which allows users to create spontaneous communities centered on a digital or physical object. In each case, proof-of-concept industrial prototypes show the potential impact of the concepts on the daily life of users. The main contribution of this chapter is the design of conceptual frameworks for helping users to take maximum advantage from their participation in online communities, either in the digital web ecosystem or real-life spontaneous communities.

**Chapter 19**

*Valentina Hlebec, University of Ljubljana, Slovenia*
*Maja Mrzel, University of Ljubljana, Slovenia*
*Tina Kogovšek, University of Ljubljana, Slovenia*

Some studies (e.g., Kogovšek & Hlebec, 2008, 2009) have shown that the name generator and the role relation approaches to measuring social networks are to some extent comparable, but less so the name generator and the event-related approaches (Hlebec, Mrzel, & Kogovšek, 2009). In this chapter, the composition of the social support network assessed by both the general social support approach and the event-related approach (support during 15 major life events) is analyzed and compared. In both cases, the role relation approach is used. In addition, in both approaches a more elaborate (16 possible categories ranging from partner, mother, father, friend to no one) and a more simple (6 possible categories ranging from family member, friend, neighbor to no one) response format is applied and compared. The aim of the chapter is to establish, in a controlled quasi-experiment setting, whether the different approaches (i.e. the general social support and the event-related approach) produce similar social networks regardless of the response format (long vs. short).

# Foreword

It is my great honor to get the chance to read this excellent book before its publication. This book, co-edited by three world-class specialists in the field of Social Network Analysis and Mining, Professors I-Hsien Ting, Tzung-Pei Hong and Leon S.L. Wang, responds to an urgent need for excellent books on this important and emerging research frontier: Social Network Analysis and Mining.

This edited book treats this important theme comprehensively and presents an international forum for the synergy of new developments from multiple research disciplines related to social networks and data mining. It fuses diverse techniques from multiple disciplines, stimulates many new ideas, and promotes technical innovations and applications.

This book contains 19 original and high-quality chapters authored by highly reputed researchers in the field of social network analysis and mining as well as practitioners from social science, business and computer science. The book is organized into three sections. The first section includes four innovative chapters that give a flavor of the introduction and survey about the state-of-art of current researches in social network analysis and mining. The second section covers eight chapters that propose new measures, methods and techniques in social networks analysis. The last one includes seven chapters that present applications and case studies in which the techniques of social networks analysis and mining have been applied.

The research results presented in these chapters are original and interesting. I would like to congratulate the editors for their excellent work as well as the authors for their wonderful contributions.

In my opinion, the techniques for social networks analysis and mining collected in this book are valuable and readers will find they are innovative and inspiring. They are especially valuable for students, researchers and practitioners who are working on social network analysis, social network mining, and web mining.

*Jiawei Han*
*Urbana, Illinois, USA, June 2011*

*Jiawei Han*, *Professor of Computer Science, University of Illinois at Urbana-Champaign. He has been researching into data mining, information network analysis, database systems, and data warehousing, with over 500 journal and conference publications. He has chaired or served on many program committees of international conferences, including PC co-chair for KDD, SDM, and ICDM conferences, and Americas Coordinator for VLDB conferences. He is currently the founding Editor-In-Chief of ACM Transactions on Knowledge Discovery from Data and as the Director of Information Network Academic Research Center supported by U.S. Army Research Lab. He is a Fellow of ACM and IEEE, and received 2004 ACM SIGKDD Innovations Award, 2005 IEEE Computer Society Technical Achievement Award, and 2009 IEEE Computer Society Wallace McDowell Award. His book "Data Mining: Concepts and Techniques" (2nd ed., Morgan Kaufmann, 2006) has been adopted as a textbook worldwide.*

# Preface

The history of social networks analysis is more than hundred years old, dating from around 1900, and originating mostly in the research areas of sociology. During this period, the studies of social networks analysis focused on small groups and small social networks. However, it has become harder and harder to manually analyze larger and more complex social networks, such as the World Wide Web. Therefore, strong computer ability and information technologies have become very important tools for social networks analysis and the field itself is therefore now moving from sociology to computer science.

Data Mining has claimed it could be the most suitable technique to deal with large amounts of data and therefore the subject of social networks mining has become a very popular issue in the area of computer science. Issues related to Social Networks Analysis and Mining include social networks data collection and preprocessing, social networks extraction and construction, algorithms and methods for mining social networks, visualization and representation, applications, etc.

As such, the objective of this book is aim to cover current, state-of-the-art, research trends in the area of social networks analysis and mining. It will be a useful reference book for academics and practitioners seeking research in this emerging area. Currently, there are few good quality books addressing this subject specifically, making this publication valuable to researchers.

The book "Social Networks Analysis and Mining: Techniques and Applications" is targeted at both academic researchers and practicing professionals in the fields of information science, engineering, computer science, statistics, management, anthropology, biology, communication studies, economics, geography, organizational studies, social psychology, and sociolinguistics, and others.

This book contains nineteen original and high quality chapters authored by leading researchers of social network analysis and mining communities as well as practitioners from social science, business and computer science. The book is organized into three sections. The first section includes four innovative chapters that give a flavor of the introduction and survey about the state-of-art of current researches in social network analysis and mining. In the second section eight chapters have been included to propose new measures, methods and techniques in social networks analysis. The last section includes seven chapters to present applications and case studies in which the techniques of social networks analysis and mining have been applied. Since the chapters are written by many researchers with different backgrounds around the world, the topics and content covered in this book provides insights which are not easily accessible otherwise.

While social networks analysis and mining clearly falls in the emerging category because of recency, it is now beginning to reach popularity and more books on this topic becomes desirable. It is hoped that this book will provide a reference to researchers, practitioners, students in both social networks analysis and social networks mining communities and others, for the benefit of more creative ideas.

We are grateful to all authors for their contributions and the referees for their vision and efforts. We would like to express our thanks to IGI Global and National University of Kaohsiung for realizing this book project.

*I-Hsien Ting*
*Tzung-Pei Hong*
*Leon S.L. Wang*
*June 2011*

# Section 1
# Introduction and Surveys of Social Networks Mining and Analysis

# Chapter 1
# Social Multimedia Mining:
## Trends and Opportunities in Areas of Social and Communication Studies

**Georgios Lappas**
*Technological Educational Institution of Western Macedonia, Greece*

## ABSTRACT

*In recent years there is a vast and rapidly growing amount of multimedia content available online. Web 2.0 and online social networks have dramatically influenced the growing amount of multimedia content due to the fact that users become more active producers and distributors of such multimedia context. This work conceptualizes and introduces the concept of social multimedia mining as a new emerging research area that combines web mining research, multimedia research and social media research. New challenges in multimedia research, social network analysis research as well as trends and opportunities in research areas of social and communication studies and more specific in politics, public relations, public administration, marketing and advertising are discussed in this chapter.*

## INTRODUCTION

Web mining is the use of data mining techniques to extract information from web documents. Although data mining is a well established field, the application of data mining techniques on web data is not an easy convertible task as web data, unlikely the well described and organized data in various databases are usually semi-structured data (Lappas, 2008). With the rapid development of the internet, web mining has now become a very popular research area for many different disciplines.

In the age of Web 2.0 as users actively communicate, interact, and share content on the web, it become a very interesting research field the use of web mining techniques for online social network analysis. (Ting, 2008). Existing online social networks offer now a large variety of different types of multimedia data and metadata from textual to complex visual content, from tags to video content and from photos to sound content to name a few.

DOI: 10.4018/978-1-61350-513-7.ch001

On the one hand, the use of an evolving number of ubiquitous capture devices and on the other hand, the evolving number of social media sites as well as the increasing number of user involvement with those media, is leading to an unpredicted amount of web delivered multimedia content and applications. Social media such as wikis, blogs, forums, microblogs, vlogs, media sharing sites, virtual worlds, collaboration sites, and social networks offer a large variety of multimedia data. Moreover, the field of online social networks like Facebook, MySpace, Linkedin and the field of multimedia sharing content like YouTube, Flickr is already converging in various platforms, offering users' the opportunity to both sharing content and forming groups of social networks. As a result, multimedia content on the web can stimulate even more web mining researchers for mining interesting and usable information from this content. Mining such multimedia content from online social networks, also presents new challenges and existing opportunities for multimedia research (Boll, 2007; Naamarn, 2010), as well as research opportunities in a number of various disciplines as internet computing, social computing, marketing, business, pattern recognition, artificial intelligence, establishing that the research interest is interdisciplinary.

Herrera-Viedma and Pasi (2006) denote that due to the complexity of web research there is a requirement for the use of interdisciplinary approaches like statistics, databases, information retrieval, decision theory, artificial intelligence, cognitive social theory and behavioral science. Multimedia data increase the complexity of web research and such research around multimedia data on social media is a relatively new area. As a relatively new area, there is a lot of confusion when comparing research efforts from different point of views and therefore there is a need for surveys that record and aggregate efforts done by independent researchers, provide definitions and explain structures and taxonomies of the field from various points of view.

In this work, we will focus on emerging trends in mining multimedia data from social media in some research areas of communication studies (like political science, public relations, public administration, advertising and marketing research).

This work is organized as follows: definitions and new terms are introduced in the next section, a survey in the literature for existing applications of multimedia mining in online social networks in the above research areas of communication studies will collect, organize and present various different approaches, trends and existing opportunities.

This work is differentiated from other surveys and related work as it combines and conceptualizes theory from multimedia mining, web mining and social media, introducing the *social multimedia mining* concept described in next section. At the same time, this article provides social network mining research perspective, multimedia mining research perspective as well as social and communication science research perspectives so that to familiarize

A.  Multimedia and online social network mining researchers to consider areas of interest in social and communication science as potential areas of research and applications;
B.  Social and Communication science researchers to consider current trends in multimedia and online social network mining for empowering their web and online social network research activities.

## SOCIAL MULTIMEDIA MINING

The web by itself may be considered as the largest existing multimedia application. The web provides an era where multimedia research agenda and multimedia applications are rapidly changing. New terms using the word multimedia appear in the literature revealing the emerging research interest in working with multimedia data from the web. Such new terms are related in the literature with:

- *"Internet Multimedia Mining"* (2009), where the research difficulty and focus is on forming a good dataset for algorithm developing, system prototyping and performance evaluation.
- *"Social Multimedia"* (Naamarn, 2010) and *"Social Multimedia Computing"* (Tian, et. al, 2010) are other two new terms related to multimedia content from online social media. The hybrid of multimedia and social media created a new research area called "social multimedia". Naamarn (2010) defines the term as the *"online sources of multimedia content posted in settings that foster significant individual participation and that promote community curation, discussion and re-use of content"* Tian et. al. (2010) expanded Naamarn's (2010) basic definition expressing *"social multimedia" as multimedia resources and applications designed to be disseminated through social interaction or be used to capture social activity and interaction"*.
- *"Social Multimedia Computing"* denotes the more focused multidisciplinary research and application field between social sciences and multimedia technology (Tian et. al. 2010).

Some examples of social multimedia provided by Tian et. al. (2010) may be: a) asynchronous multimedia conversations, where users may respond to other users' video contributions, a feature introduced in YouTube videos; b) aggregating behavioral data on a video, like click and pause, may reveal video's more interesting scenes or objects. Although the two examples are used by Tian et. al. (2010) to demonstrate that social multimedia support new types of user interaction, changing the way we communicate and collaborate, it is clear from the second example that part of social multimedia may be also related to mining multimedia content from online social networks. Our aim in this chapter is to focus on research that combines

multimedia research, social multimedia research and web mining research and to study this field as a new interdisciplinary field being part of the social multimedia field, multimedia research field and web mining field.

Combining multimedia research, social multimedia research and web mining research, new fascinating fields of research are emerging. Building on the above terms we introduce new terms to better capture the emerging research opportunities in interdisciplinary research:

- *"Multimedia Web Mining"* defines the *use of data mining techniques for mining multimedia data from the web and from social media in order to discover useful information patterns*.
- *"Intelligent Multimedia Web Mining"* may be an expansion of the above term in order to emphasize *the use of artificial intelligence techniques for mining multimedia data from the web and from social media in order to discover useful information patterns*.
- *"Social Multimedia Mining"* defines *the use of web mining techniques for discovering useful information patterns from multimedia content from social media*. "Social Multimedia Mining" may be part of "Multimedia Web Mining" and part of "Social Multimedia Computing" focusing on mining tasks related to multimedia data, user participatory data and social networking data. These mining tasks will be further analyzed in next section.

As mentioned earlier, web mining is a harder task than data mining. Similarly social multimedia mining is much harder than web mining due to many existing problems in the interpretation of the extracted data from visual data. The problem in multimedia research is known as the semantic gap problem (Smeulders et. al., 2000), which yet makes content analysis from multimedia data a very complicated task. Moreover, the available metadata found in social media are not always accurate. There is a lot of misleading, inaccurate, wrong and noisy metadata (Naamarn, 2010). The above limitations, the existing open problems in multimedia research, as well as the need for precision in mining results from vast volumes of social multimedia data, create premises that social multimedia mining is a hard task and can be a very excited new research area. As current social media research is naturally evolved from efforts to improve information seeking and sense making on the Web (Chi, 08), social multimedia mining may enhance both information seeking and sense making.

Our focus on this chapter is on social multimedia mining in areas of social and communication studies. In the following sections new trends on our focused field are reviewed and organized into application areas of study, whereas opportunities and research issues are identified and discussed.

## THE THREE TYPES OF SOCIAL MULTIMEDIA MINING

Web mining is divided into three mining categories according to the different sources of the target data:

A.  Web content mining focus on the discovery of knowledge from the content of web pages and therefore the target data consist of multivariate type of data contained in a web page as text, images, multimedia etc

B.  Web usage mining focus on the discovery of knowledge from user navigation data when visiting a website. The target data are requests from users recorded in special files stored in the website's servers called log files.

C.  Web structure mining deals with the connectivity of websites and the extraction of knowledge from hyperlinks of the web.

The above taxonomy is now broadly used in web mining and has the origins from Coley et. al (1997) who introduced web content mining and web usage mining and Kosala and Blockeel (2000), who added web structure mining.

Web mining taxonomy is heavily related to the web 1.0 environment dominated by broadcast media developed by professional designers for passive users. Most of web content mining researchers for instance focus on text data processing and few on other multimedia data (Ting, Wu, 2009). Participatory Web 2.0, user-generated content and explosion of multimedia content provided a new web environment for mining that is not fully covered by the above web mining taxonomy. There can be two different scopes of study of social multimedia mining according to the different sources of the multimedia target data: data related to the multimedia content and data related to social activity around the multimedia data. Similarly with the web mining taxonomy, this article suggests the following taxonomy of social multimedia mining:

**Social Multimedia Content Mining:** Where the emphasis is on mining content from captured multimedia data from social networks. Such data may be images, video content, text, tags, sounds etc. Social multimedia content mining compared to traditional multimedia content analysis may add improved content analysis as a result of the additional social media metadata.

**Social Multimedia Activity Mining:** Where the emphasis is on activities of people or a group around multimedia data from social networks. Such data are usually derived by visitors' activities on social networks as responses around multimedia activities for instance behavioral responses of visitors to image and video files, user comments, user tagging, user clicks on multimedia objects, viewing metadata, like hood metadata and other behavioral data etc.

**Social Multimedia Relations Mining:** Where the emphasis is on mining relations among people or a group and multimedia is the medium for how

*Figure 1. Interrelations between the three types of Social Multimedia Mining*

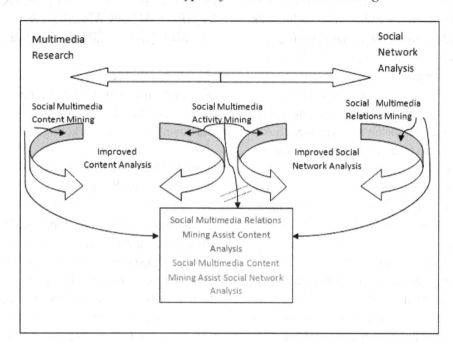

they connect and transfer information. Such data may be related with visitor's preferences, profiles, links, social participatory and relations with other visitors in various social networking sites.

Compared to web mining taxonomy social multimedia activity mining may be considered being in accordance to web usage mining. This article suggest the "activity" term instead of the "usage" term as activity is closer to the participatory nature in social media, whereas the term usage denotes a more passive role of the user. Similarly, social multimedia relations mining may be considered being in accordance with web structure mining. Although the structure term may be also well used here, as it is related to web links that construct web pages and web communities, this article suggests the "relation" term as it brings interrelated in various social media users and multimedia medium on the first line.

We can examine the three types of Social Multimedia Mining under the scope of two main research areas in social multimedia mining: Multimedia research and Social Network Analysis research.

Figure 1 shows the relations of the three types of Social Multimedia Mining with Multimedia Research and Social Network Analysis. Content mining in social media is closer to traditional multimedia research, whereas mining relations in social media is closer to social network analysis research. Social Multimedia Activity Mining stands between the two disciplinary research fields. Mining behavioral and other activity data may lead to interesting patterns examined under both scope of research. For instance, mining behavioral data on video streams like pause and click may reveal video's most interesting scenes (Tian, et. al., 2010), whereas analyzing comments on YouTube derive interestingness in conversations in social media (De Choundhury et. al., 2009).

Although researchers originated in the two edges of the arrows may still perform research as usual related only to their discipline, this article suggests that combining social multimedia activity mining with each of the other two types may lead to improved content analysis and improved social network analysis respectively. This suggestion complies also with Ting and Wu (2009) suggestion that the three web mining techniques do not work alone in online social networks.

Combining social multimedia activity mining with social multimedia content mining, the semantic inference of multimedia content analysis may be improved by behavioral data and annotation data. For instance the behavioral (pause, clicks) and annotation data (tags, comments) by users on a video from a soccer game may improve content analysis to both identify game highlights and the semantic of these highlights (goals, opportunities, red cards, penalties, injuries, game conflicts etc). Recent works (Davis et. al., 2009, Yamamoto et. al., 2008) focuses on the extraction of video semantics using user activity, establishing the importance of user activity data in semantic inference.

Similarly, social multimedia relations mining combined with behavioral and annotation data may lead to better analyze groups and behaviors of the group by segmenting groups according to common behavioral data or other activity data.

Also interesting is the combination of social multimedia content mining and social multimedia relations mining with or without combining social multimedia activity mining, leading to powerful cross-disciplinary research. For instance, semantic inference from noisy photos may become easier after eliminating noise by identifying more photos from a related social group; likewise social network analysis may be assisted by integrating images, icons, faces, and user logos in various social media or by using typical face recognition techniques (Luo and Huang, 2009) or by extracting visual appearance of people from videos or photos and by comparing them with appearances in other networking sites may reveal the type of relationship and participation in social networks. Future powerful search engines may combine all three types of social multimedia mining may aiming to more accurate and meaningful search results by mining and combining all available multimedia type of data (content, behavioral and relational data).

## SOCIAL MULTIMEDIA MINING IN RESEARCH AREAS OF COMMUNICATION STUDIES

In next sections we sketch trend and opportunities of social multimedia mining research in the areas of political science, public relations, e-government, and advertising and marketing.

### Social Multimedia Mining and Political Science

Web mining in political science has been used to estimate the size of political web graphs (Ackland, 2005), to map political parties network on the web (Ackland, and Gibson, 2004) and to investigate the U.S. political Blogosphere (Ackland, 2005b). Political web linking is also studied by Foot et. al. (2003) during U.S. Congressional election campaign on the web. Mori et al (2006) use a clustering method, which automatically extracts labels from web context to describe relations among entities in political social networks. Their work has been used for the discovery of relevant terms that relate a politician to a location. Web linkage mining using artificial immune system to retrieve the list of URLs that have relevant information on political issues in Malaysia is used for analyzing political social networks (Nasir et. al., 2009). From the web mining perspective, current applications to e-politics are mainly web structure driven applications. These applications are rather beneficial to parties and politicians than to the society. Web mining applications empowering e-democracy by improving politics, political transparency and political participation in decision-making, have not been identified in web mining literature. The emergence of social media provides new premises for e-democracy.

Social Media held the promise for better citizen participation in politics enhancing the potential of e-democracy. During election campaigns we experience politicians and their campaign staff to become much innovative in the use of new media.

Obamachine (Carpenter, 2010) refers to the excellent use of social media in Obama's campaign. Web 2.0 features provides opportunities for parties and candidates to gain marginal advantage from their opponents, as well as provides opportunities for individuals to become citizen-campaigners capable of assuming a more direct or organized role in a campaign (Gibson, 2009), elevating hopes for the growth of "bottom-up" campaigns. First studies of parties experimenting with web 2.0 (Kalnes, 2009) showed that although Web 2.0 offers a weak pluralizing effect in party communication, it enhanced participatory democracy by lowering the threshold for the involvement of the party grassroots and other sympathizers with the party. The effect of web 2.0 in campaigning appears already in a number of studies (Gibson and McAllister, 2009; Jackson and Lilleker 2009; Jaeger et.al. 2010; Kalnes 2009; Lilleker et. al 2010, Lappas et. al, 2010), offering interesting findings on the use of web 2.0 in the political arena.

Specific new Web 2.0 environments like Facebook, Youtube, Twitter, My Space and Second Life have attracted parties and politicians and their use in politics become the focus of research in a number of studies. Facebook adoption diffused rapidly in the US between 2006 and 2008 Congressional Elections generated interest among researchers for studying the Facebook phenomenon in these elections contests (Robertson et. al. 2009, Williams and Gullati 2007, 2009a, 2009b). Campaigning on YouTube was first used during 2006 and 2008 US elections (Church 2010, Gulati and Williams 2010; Klotz, 2010; Wallsten, 2010). Twitter recently gained attention for its usage in political campaigns. Williams and Gullati (2010) studied the use of Twitter by members of Congress, whereas Tumasjan et. al (2010) proposed a challenging approach to use the tweets for predicting election results in the context of German federal elections. Shamma et. al. (2009,2010) reason about the content of the US 2008 presidential election debates by analyzing the content and volume of Twitter messages.

In a previous study (Lappas et. al. 2010) we used behavioral data from users on parties Facebook sites during the April 09-June10 period in Greece. This period is loaded with campaign information, spanning two electoral campaigns (European Parliament Elections in June 09, National Elections in October 09) and the outbreak of the Greek Financial Crisis (Spring 10). Working with Facebook "Likes" and "Comment" features we identified interesting patterns like that the citizen-campaigning effect (Gibson, 2009) may be more evident in crisis periods and periods that call for political changes than in election campaign periods. During elections most of the users participate in a positive and enthusiastic manner. Crisis periods are more amenable to generating "bottom-up" campaigns. Parties however, seem reluctant to increase their online communication responding to increases in citizen participation on their Facebook sites. Parties are trying rather to retain their control by employing a tight "top-down" communication strategy, without responding or engaging with users' initiatives. The battle between "top down" and "bottom up" campaigns is more pronounced during crisis periods. We also identified that the average "likes" from users on party posts seems to be a quantitative indicator that better reflects the underlying enthusiasm of voters and can be used as a predictor indicator for the outcome election result.

Social media increasingly provide massive amounts of multimedia information during campaigns from users, groups and social communities. The challenge in future political campaign research is to exploit this mass of multimedia information provided by social media in order to formalize the structure behind the parties' communities and discover campaign patterns, trends, and dynamics. Social Multimedia Mining may provide the tools for this task.

In another area of political science, the area of soft diplomacy, social media can be an invaluable support mechanism because it allows people to share cultural experiences and political views, which can help break down social and cultural barriers (Olson et. al, 2010). As soft diplomacy aims that a person can shape another's preferences to the point that the two seek shared objectives (Nye, 2004), social multimedia mining may identify people with common preferences or shared objectives for enhancing and strengthening common policies.

Overall, social multimedia mining in politics may be used for user modeling, for providing personalized services to user or group of users, for extracting interesting political data, for predicting election outcomes, for connecting the user with social networks that share common political interests, for providing the user with decision-making processes related to the user interests, and for enhancing political communication according to user political interests.

## Social Multimedia Mining and Public Relations

The term PR2.0 has been widely used to denote the use of web 2.0 tools for public relations and communication activities. Social media and social networking seem to be an ideal environment for modern public relations. Today the area of public relations is heavily mediated. Traditional public relations of the previous decade were heavily relied on the three communication channels: TV, Radio, and Newspaper. Over the last decade, Internet has dramatically increased media complexity for public relations. Social media and social networks have geometrically added on the media complexity as new social media channels are invented every while, challenging the area of public relations and communication studies for more creativity in a more complex communication environment.

As more social media and social networking sites are emerging, the need for trusted interconnectivity between social networking sites seems to be an open research problem. Users need to provide accounts, passwords, profiles and other data in every social network that they participate.

Social networks connect services (Ko et. al., 2010) let third-party sites develop social applications without having to build their own social network. These SNCSs may increase access to and enrich user data to the social web and although they currently present several security and privacy problems they expect to further break down the garden walls of the social networking sites. Public relations and communications studies have major interest and benefits from an interconnected social web for improved relationship practices, campaign strategies and other related activities.

Social multimedia mining may play an important role either in building such interconnectivity between social networking sites or in mining user data in the social web for providing services and applications to users. Human Flesh Search as an advertising and public relations platform is suggested by Wang et. al. (2010). HFS is a new web phenomenon that lacks a precise definition, with so far definition trials vary from rather negative definitions as "finding and punishing people who publish material that web users consider inappropriate" to more modest like "a new web phenomenon that refers to searches that are conducted with help from human users". From a technical research perspective HSF shares many common characteristics with emerging social search engines. HFS research is related to the machine learning, data mining and social science field shifting traditional social theory from the offline behavior the development of new social theories focusing on online behavior and social intelligence (Wang, et. al., 2007). Social multimedia mining may assist HFS research and the creation of precise advertising and public relations platforms. Detailed description for HFS can be found in Wang's et. al. article (2010).

Web mining for emotion on MySpace is researched by Thelwall et. al. (2010) for exploring emotion differences based on gender. This research, partially based on content mining in social networks, revealed the interesting pattern that females are likely to give and receive more positive comments than are males, but there is no difference for negative comments. It is thus possible that females are more successful social network site users partly because of their greater ability to textually harness positive affect.

Social multimedia mining may also assist in the succession of virtual communities, establishing reliable social networks, vital for public relations. This can be done by overcoming the start-up paradox problem that appears in the early times of social networks life circle, where these social communities have few members to generate content and few content to generate new members (Kraut,et. al, 2010). Social multimedia content mining and social multimedia relations mining may be ideal tool to find both appropriate content and reliable new members, establishing a successful startup of a new social network group.

## Social Multimedia Mining and Online Public Administration (E-Government)

The major characteristics of e-government systems are related to the use of technology to deliver services electronically focusing on citizens needs by providing adequate information and enhanced services to citizens to support political conduct of government. Latest UN Global E-Government Readiness Report (2008) focuses in e-government initiatives directed at improving operational efficiency through the integration of back-office functions. Whilst such initiatives, if successful, will deliver benefits to citizens, the primary purpose is to improve the effectiveness of government and governmental agencies.

In practice, the e-government dimension of an institution is usually implemented gradually. E-government maturity models (Irani, et. al. 2006; Yannas and Lappas, 2007) describe the online stages an organization goes through time, becoming more mature in using the web for providing better services to citizens. The maturity stages start from the organization's first attempt to be online aiming

at publishing useful to citizens information and move to higher maturity stages of being interactive, making transactions and finally transforming the functionality of the organization to operate their business and services electronically through the web. E-government systems as slower adopters of new ideas and technologies, are still trying to maturing the shift to the social media age. One reason may be that governments are still reluctant to adopt new ideas that will have significant impact on their policies and will redefine government boundaries with the public. Social media may transform the democratic process lowering the boundaries between community and government and although it seems that democracy is shifting to a more participatory form, governmental agencies still want to have the overall control on their policies. On the other hand it is not yet clear how governmental agencies can incorporate social media technology-driven participation into the act of governing (Bertot, et. al., 2010). E–deliberation platforms like www.opengov.gr provided promises of citizen-participation into government decisions, as it provides a forum for commenting on law sketches before they come to parliament and become new laws. At the end of the e-deliberation, Greek government provides a summary report on what were the major comments from citizens based on some qualitative analysis, without actually providing any positive or negative feedback to that comments, or seem to taking any action. The lack of feedback processes to citizen participation, like answering why a specific action proposed by participants should be taken or not, and the lack of legislations that actual incorporate public participation into the government policy, might result to governmental deaf ears on public participation making governmental policies as usual.

Social media hold great promise in their ability to transform governance by increasing government's transparency, by creating new ways of democratic participation, pressures for new institutional structures, and processes and frameworks for open and transparent government (Bertot, et. al., 2010). However, social multimedia mining in e-government still lacks research initiatives due to late adoption of social media by governmental agencies. E-government agencies are still heavily relied on web 1.0 websites.

Moreover, E-Government literature reveals few early web mining attempts. Riedl (2003) states that by using interviews and web mining the actual access to information by citizens should be tracked, analyzed and used for the redesign of e-government information services. Fang and Sheng (2005) present a web mining approach for designing better web portal for e-government. Hong and Lee (2005) propose an intelligent web information system of government based on web usage mining to help disadvantaged users make good decisions-making for their profit improvements. Panagis et. al (2008) follow the design trends to create the so-called 'citizen-oriented websites' where content and services are organised around the anticipated needs of web visitors. Their method used graph mining for mining the recurrent design solutions of e-government services. From the web mining perspective, applications to e-government are web usage driven applications using citizen's logs. The few web mining approaches in e-government common research efforts (Riedl, 2003; Fang and Sheng, 2005; Panagis, et. al. 2008) are concentrated in the redesign process of the site according to knowledge extracted by the site visitors. Citizen logs may be also used for providing customized services and implementing recommendation systems for citizens.

The area of e-government thus, may be considered as an unexplored field for web mining (Zhou and Le, 2007; Lappas, 2008). The main challenge in e-government research is to match citizen's particular interests. Surprisingly, web mining has not been integrated so far into e-government applications. While governmental organizations are striving for providing better services to citizens, the

challenge for web mining and social multimedia mining is to meet these needs.

Prospective web mining research for e-government is related to personalization of e-government services to meet user (or group of users) needs, citizen modelling to identify similar needs by group of citizens, filtering approaches (collaborative, content-based, or rule based filtering) for predicting citizen needs, and recommendation agents for gathering citizens actions on the site and providing them with what they need.

As more governmental agencies will adopt social media, social multimedia mining offers new opportunities in e-government research. Areas where social multimedia mining may assist governmental processes may be:

A.  Provide solutions to public participation in e-deliberation platforms by creating mining mechanism to automate feedbacks. Such mining mechanism will mine data from multimedia forms of participation like comments, video content and video usage from popular public videos, click on likes (or agree, or disagree buttons, etc), in order to better organize, respond, decide, provide feedback and form policies, enhancing democracy by taking real care on public participation.

B.  Providing crowd-sourced solutions by identifying on social media local experts and talents, through which public knowledge may transform government innovation.

C.  Empowered by social multimedia mining methods e-government systems may provide improved customized and recommendation services to citizens. Such services, result to user satisfaction, quality of services, support in citizen's decision-making, and finally leads to social benefits. However, gaining these benefits, citizens much rely on the organization's willingness, knowledge and ability to move on the level of using social multimedia mining.

On the other hand social multimedia mining may also assist community as through HFS research and social multimedia mining may expose governmental corruption and corrupted politicians, increasing governmental transparency.

It is author's belief that in the future many applications related to social multimedia mining will emerge for e-government, placing at the top of the e-government maturity models the social multimedia mining approach, denoting the maximum ability of an organization to deliver quality services to citizens.

## Social Multimedia Mining in Advertising and Marketing Research

Social media is already perceived as a challenging medium for business. Thus, advertisement and marketing research on social media attracts already lots of researchers. This section highlights some opportunities offered by social multimedia mining in the area. More details on business, marketing, advertising and social media may the reader find in many related textbooks.

Surma and Furmanek, (2010) provide evidence that mining social networks results to improvement in marketing responses. Jin et. al. (2009) provide a ranking methodology for companies on the web based on social network mining. Perhaps the area of travel marketing (hotel marketing, location and places suggestions) has been influenced more than other marketing areas from social media. The reason is that travelers are very willing to share their travel experiences in social media offering rich multimedia data (comments, photos, videos, maps, tags, etc) about locations, hotel services, sightseeing, local markets and other traveling data. Social multimedia mining for travel marketing may provide challenging research and business opportunities in the tourism industry. Current research examples mining travel data from social media deal with building location overviews (Hao et. al. 2009), city landmarks (Ji et. al., 2009) web-scale landmark recognition engine (Zheng et. al., 2009) travel assistant from images (Jing, et. al. 2006) and systems mining Flickr aiming to identify representative landmark photos (Abbasi, et. al 2009; Chen, et. al. 2009; Crandall et. al. 2009; Kennedy and Naaman, 2008).

Another promising application area for social multimedia mining is online advertising. With the explosion of vlogs (video+blogs) and vlogging (video+blogging) (Gao et. al, 2010) social multimedia mining may use behavioral data, user preferences and social networks to better target individuals and groups of people for marketing and advertisement.

Online advertisement is rapidly growing overtaking advertisements in traditional media. Social media offer new channels for marketing and advertisement and new challenges for social multimedia mining research for successful business. Again, interconnectivity between social networking sites (Ko et. al., 2010) offers, like in public relations research described above, a very challenging area both for social multimedia mining and for advertising and marketing strategies.

## CONCLUSION

The combination of web mining, multimedia research and social media research yields to a new excited research field, which was conceptualized and introduced in this chapter as the social multimedia mining field. Social multimedia mining is already a very active field of research despite the lack of a name and/or a theoretical framework. The aim of this chapter was to conceptualize and provide a theoretical framework of the new research field, to review current research approaches and to discuss the dynamics and opportunities of the new research field. After introducing and conceptualizing the social multimedia mining field, the chapter focused on current research trends that are related to the areas of social and communication studies. Research opportunities in the social and communication areas have been also discussed on close relation to the current research trends.

More research opportunities in social multimedia mining are emerging from the vast and rapidly growing amount of multimedia content available online. As current search engines are reaching their limitations on effectiveness and accuracy, intelligent web search for retrieving vital information has become one of the most important research issues on the web offering research opportunities for many disciplines. Moreover, the participatory web 2.0 phenomenon provides vast volumes of new data and alters dramatically the way business, government, policies, enterprises, organizations operate and perform. Thus, social multimedia mining becomes a new exciting evolving research field that attracts already the attention of an astonishingly diverse set of researchers from many fields as well as marketers, businesspeople, policymakers and practitioners for mining and discovering vital information. The author believes that social multimedia mining has an important role to play to improve information retrieval, identify behavioral patterns, improve multimedia semantics, improve social network analysis, and discover interesting online, offline, group and social network patterns. As new methods and innovative approaches in social media are still emerging, social multimedia mining has the potential to become a very popular and rapidly growing research area in the next years.

# REFERENCES

Abbasi, R., Chernov, S., Nejdl, W., Paiu, R., & Staab, S. (2009). *Exploiting Flickr Tags and Groups for Finding Landmark Photos.* In proceedings of the 31st European Conference on Information Retrieval Research. Springer-Verlag, Berlin, Heidelberg, pp. 654-661.

Ackland, R. (2005). *Estimating the Size of Political Web Graphs.* Retrieved from http://acsr.anu.edu.au/ staff/ackland /papers/ political webgraphs.pdf.

Ackland, R. (2005b). *Mapping the U.S. Political Blogosphere: Are Conservative Bloggers More Prominent?* Retrieved from http://acsr.anu.edu.au/ staff/ackland/papers/ polblogs.pdf.

Ackland, R., & Gibson, R. (2004). Mapping Political Party Networks on the WWW. *Australian Electronic Governance Conference*, April 14-15, Melbourne, Australia.

Bertot, J. C., Jaeger, P. T., Munson, S., & Glaisyer, T. (2010). Social Media Technology and Government Transparency. *IEEE Computer Society*, *43*(11), 53–59.

Boll, S. (2007). Multitube-where web 2.0 and multimedia could meet. *IEEE MultiMedia*, *14*(1), 9–13. doi:10.1109/MMUL.2007.17

Carpenter, C. (2010). The Obamachine: Technopolitics 2.0. *Journal of Information Technology & Politics*, 7(2), 216–225. doi:10.1080/19331681003765887

Chen, W.-C., Battestini, A., Gelfand, N., & Setlur, V. (2009). *Visual Summaries of Popular Landmarks from Community Photo Collections.* In proceedings of the 17th ACM International Conference on Multimedia. New York: ACM, pp. 789-792.

Chi, E. H. (2008). The Social Web: Research and Opportunities. *Computer*, (Sept): 88–91. doi:10.1109/MC.2008.401

Church, S. H. (2010). YouTube Politics: You Choose and Leadership Rhetoric During the 2008 Election. *Journal of Information Technology & Politics*, 7(2), 124–142. doi:10.1080/19331681003748933

Cooley, R., Mobasher, B., & Srivastava, J. (1997). Web Mining: Information and Pattern Discovery on the World Wide Web. *9th International Conference on Tools with Artificial Intelligence(ICTAI '97).* New Port Beach, CA, USA, IEEE Computer Society, 558-567.

Crandall, D., Backstrom, L., Huttenlocher, D., & Kleinberg, J. (2009). *Mapping the World's Photos.* In proceedings of the 18th International conference on World Wide Web. ACM, New York, USA.

Davis, S. J., Burnett, I. S., & Ritz, C. H. (2009). Using Social Networking and Collections to Enable Video Semantics Acquisition. *IEEE MultiMedia, 16*(4), 52–61.

De Choudhury, M., Sundaram, M., John, A., & Seligmann, D. D. (2009). *What Makes Conversations Interesting? Themes, Participants, and Consequences of Conversations in Online Social Media.* In proceedings of the 18th International conference on World Wide Web. ACM, New York, USA.

Fang, X., & Sheng, O. R. L. (2005). Designing a Better Web Portal for Digital Government: A Web-Mining Based Approach. *Proceedings of the 2005 National Conference on Digital Government Research*, May 15-18, Atlanta, pp. 277-278.

Foot, K., Schneider, S., Dougherty, M., Xenos, M., & Larsen, E. (2003). Analyzing Linking Practices: Candidate Sites in the 2002 U.S. Electoral Web Sphere. *Journal of Mediated Communication, 8*(4). Retrieved from http://jcmc.indiana.edu/vol8/issue4/foot.html.

Gao, W., Tian, Y., Huang, T., & Yang, Q. (2010). Vlogging: A Survey of Video Blogging Technology on the Web. *ACM Computing Surveys, 42*(4), 1–57. doi:10.1145/1749603.1749606

Gibson, R. K. (2009). New Media and the Revitalisation of Politics. *Representation, 45*(3), 289–299. doi:10.1080/00344890903129566

Gibson, R. K., & Mcallister, I. (2009). Crossing the Web 2.0 Frontier? Candidates and Campaigns Online in the Australian Federal Election of 2007. *Paper presented at the 2009 ECPR General Conference,* Potdam, Germany.

Gullati, G. J. J., & Williams, C. B. (2010). Congressional Candidates' Use of YouTube in 2008: Its Frequency and Rationale. *Journal of Information Technology & Politics, 7*(2), 93–109. doi:10.1080/19331681003748958

Hao, Q., Cai, R., Wang, X. J., Yang, J. M., Pang, Y., & Zhang, L. (2009). *Generating Location Overviews with Images and Tags by Mining User-generated Travelogues.* In *Proceedings of the 17th ACM International Conference on Multimedia.* New York: ACM. pp. 801-804.

Herrera-Viedma, E., & Pasi, G. (2006). Soft Approaches to Information Retrieval and Information Access on the Web: An Introduction to the Special Topic Section. *Journal of the American Society for Information Science and Technology, 57*(4), 511–514. doi:10.1002/asi.20305

Hong, G. H., & Lee, J. H. (2005). Designing an Intelligent Web Information System of Government Based on Web Mining. *Lecture Notes in Computer Science, 3614*, 1071–1078. doi:10.1007/11540007_138

Internet Multimedia Mining. (2009). *The 1st International Workshop on Internet Multimedia Mining in conjunction with IEEE International Conference on Data Mining.* December 6, Miami, Florida.

Irani, Z. Al-Sebie, & M., Elliman, T. (2006). Transaction Stage of e-Government Systems: Identification of its Location & Importance. *Proceedings of the 39th Hawaii International Conference on System Sciences*, January 4-7, Hawaii, USA.

Jackson, N., & Lilleker, D. (2009). Building an Architecture of Participation? Political Parties and Web 2.0 in Britain. *Journal of Information Technology & Politics, 6*(3-4), 232–250. doi:10.1080/19331680903028438

Jaeger, P. T., Paquette, S., & Simmons, S. N. (2010). Information Policy in National Political Campaigns: A Comparison of the 2008 Campaigns for President of the United States and Prime Minister of Canada. *Journal of Information Technology & Politics*, 7, 67–82. doi:10.1080/19331680903316700

Ji, R., Xie, X., Yao, H., & Ma, W.-Y. (2009). *Mining City Landmarks from Blogs by Graph Modeling*. In *proceedings of the 17ᵗʰ ACM international conference on multimedia* (pp. 105–114). New York: ACM.

Jin, Y., Matsuo, Y., & Ishizuka, M. (2009). Ranking Companies on the Web Using Social Network Mining. In Ting, I.-H., & Wu, H.-J. (Eds.), *Web Mining Applications in E-commerce and E-services, Studies in Computational Intellligence 172* (pp. 169–179). Heidelberg, Germany: Springer-Verlag. doi:10.1007/978-3-540-88081-3_8

Jing, F., Zhang, L., & Ma, W.-Y. (2006). *Virtualtour: An Online Travel Assistant Based on High Quality Images*. In *proceedings of the 14ᵗʰ ACM international conference on multimedia* (pp. 599–602). New York, USA: ACM.

Kalnes, O. (2009). Norwegian Parties and Web 2.0. *Journal of Information Technology & Politics*, 6(3), 251–266. doi:10.1080/19331680903041845

Kennedy, L. S., & Naaman, M. (2008). *Generating Diverse and Representative Image Search Results for Landmarks*. In *proceedings of the 17ᵗʰ international conference on World Wide Web* (pp. 297–306). New York: ACM.

Klotz, R. (2010). The Sidetracked 2008 YouTube Senate Campaign. *Journal of Information Technology & Politics*, 7(2), 110–123. doi:10.1080/19331681003748917

Ko, M. N., Cheek, G. P., Shehab, M., & Sandhu, R. (2010). Social-Networks Connect Services. *IEEE Computer Society*, 43(8), 37–43.

Kosala, R., & Blockeel, H. (2000). Web Mining Research: A Survey. *ACM*, 2(1), 1–15.

Kraut, R., Maher, M. R., Olson, J., Malone, T. W., Pirolli, P., & Thomas, J. C. (2010). Scientific Foundations: A Case for Technology-Mediated Social-Participation Theory. *IEEE Computer Society*, 43(11), 22–28.

Lappas, G. (2008). An Overview of Web Mining in Societal Benefit Areas. *Journal of Online Information Review*, 32(2), 179–195. doi:10.1108/14684520810879818

Lappas, G., Kleftodimos, A., & Yannas, P. (2010). Greek Parties and Web 2.0. *paper presented at Elections, Campaigning, and Citizens Online Workshop*, Oxford Internet Institute, Oxford, UK, 15-16 September, available at: http:// drupals. humanities.manchester.ac.uk/ ipol/sites/default/ files/ ecco/Lappas.pdf.

Lilleker, D. G., Pack, M., & Jackson, N. (2010). Political Parties and Web 2.0: The Liberal Democrat Perspective. *Politics*, 30(2), 103–112. doi:10.1111/j.1467-9256.2010.01373.x

Luo, D., & Huang, H. (2009). *Link Prediction of Multimedia Social Network via Unsupervised Face Recognition*. In ACM Multimedia Proceedings, ACM Press, pp. 805-808.

Mori, J., Tsujishita, T., Matsuo, Y., & Ishizuka, M. (2006). Extracting Relations in Social Networks from the Web Using Similarity Between Collective Contexts. *Lecture Notes in Computer Science*, 4273, 487–500. doi:10.1007/11926078_35

Naamarn, M. (2010). Social Multimedia: highlighting opportunities for search and mining of multimedia data in social media applications. *Multimedia Tools and Applications*, http://www. springerlink.com/ content/v836432078k27014/

Nasir, A. N. M., Selamat, A., & Selamat, M. H. (2009). Web Mining for Malaysia's Political Social Networks using Artificial Immune System. *Lecture Notes in Computer Science*, 5465, 137–146. doi:10.1007/978-3-642-01715-5_12

Nye, J. (2004). *Soft Power: The Means to Success in World Politics*. New York: Public Affairs.

Olson, G., Mark, G., Churchill, E., & Rotman, D. (2010). Technology-Mediated Social Participation: New Missions for a Sociotechnical Infrastructure. *IEEE Computer Society*, *43*(11), 37–43.

Panagis, Y., Sakkopoulos, E., Tsakalidis, A., Tzimas, G., Sirmakessis, S., & Lytras, M. (2008). Techniques for mining the design of e-government services to enhance end-user experience. *Int. J. Electronic Democracy*, *1*(1), 32–50. doi:10.1504/IJED.2008.021277

Riedl, R. (2003). Design Principles for E-Government Services. *Proceedings eGov Day*, February 13-14, Vienna, Austria.

Robertson, S. P., Vatrapu, R. K., & Medina, R. (2009). *The Social Life of Social Networks: Facebook Linkage Patterns in the 2008 U.S. Presidential Election*. In the *Proceedings of the 10th International Digital Government Research Conference*, Puebla, Mexico, May 17-20, 2009.

Shamma, D. A., Kennedy, L., & Churchill, E. F. (2009). Tweet the Debates: Understanding Community Annotation of Uncollected Sources. In *proceedings of the 1st SIGMM workshop on Social Media*, ACM, New York, USA, pp 3-10.

Shamma, D. A., Kennedy, L., & Churchill, E. F. (2010). Statler: Summarizing media through short-messages services. In *proceedings of the 2010 ACM conference on Computer Supported Cooperative Work (CSCW 2010)*. ACM, New York, USA.

Smeulders, A., Worring, M., Santini, S., Gupta, A., & Jain, R. (2000). Content-based Image Retrieval at the End of the Early Years. *IEEE Transactions on Pattern Analysis and Machine Intelligence*, *22*(12), 1349–1380. doi:10.1109/34.895972

Surma, J., & Furmanek, A. (2010). Improving Marketing Response by Data Mining in Social Network, *in Proceedings of the International Conference on Advances in Social Networks Analysis and Mining (ASONAM 2010)*, Aug 09-11, Odense, Denmark, pp.446-451, 2010, 2010

Thelwall, M., Wilkinson, D., & Uppal, S. (2010). Data Mining Emotion in Social Network Communication: Gender Differences in MySpace. *Journal of the American Society for Information Science and Technology*, *61*(1), 190–199.

Tian, Y., Srivastava, J., Huang, T., & Contractor, N. (2010). Social Multimedia Computing. *IEEE Computer Society*, *43*(8), 27–36.

Ting, I.-H. (2008). *Web Mining Techniques for On-line Social Networks Analysis*. In *Proceedings of the 5th International Conference on Service Systems and Service Management (ICSSSM'08)*. pp. 696-700, June 30-July 2, 2008

Ting, I.-H., & Wu, H.-J. (2009). Web Mining Techniques for On-line Social Networks Analysis: An Overview. In Ting, I.-H., & Wu, H.-J. (Eds.), *Web Mining Applications in E-commerce and E-services, Studies in Computational Intellligence 172* (pp. 169–179). Heidelberg, Germany: Springer-Verlag. doi:10.1007/978-3-540-88081-3_10

Tumasjan, A., Sprenger, T. O., Sandner, P. G., & Welpe, I. M. (2010). Predicting Elections with Twitter: What 140 Characters Reveal about Political Sentiment, In *Proceedings of the 4th International AAAI Conference on Weblogs and Social Media*, pp. 178-185.

UN Global E-Government Readiness Report. (2008). *From E-Government to Connected Governance*. Available on http://www2.unpan.org/egovkb/global_reports/08report.htm

Wallsten, K. (2010). "Yes We Can": How On-line Viewership, Blog Discussion, Campaign Statements, and Mainstrem Media Coverage Produced a Viral Phenomenon. *Journal of Information Technology & Politics*, *7*(2), 163–181. doi:10.1080/19331681003749030

Wang, F.-Y., Carley, K. M., Zeng, D., & Mao, W. (2007). Social Computing: From Social Informatics to Social Intelligence. *IEEE Intelligent Systems*, *22*(2), 79–83. doi:10.1109/MIS.2007.41

Wang, F.-Y., Zeng, D., Hendler, J. A., Zhang, Q., Feng, Z., & Gao, Y. (2010). A Study of the Human Flesh Search Engine: Crowd-Powered Expansion of Online Knowledge, *IEEE. Computers & Society, 43*(8), 45–53.

Williams, C. B., & Gulati, G. J. J. (2007). Social Networks in Political Campaigns: Facebook and the 2006 Midterm Elections, *paper presented at the 2009 Annual Meeting of the American Political Science Association*, Chicago, Illinois, August 30- September 2.

Williams, C. B., & Gulati, G. J. J. (2009a). Facebook Grows Up: An Empirical Assessment of its Role in the 2008 Congressional Elections, *paper presented at the 2009 Annual Meeting of the Midwest Political Science Association*, Chicago, Illinois, April 2-5.

Williams, C. B., & Gulati, G. J. J. (2009b). *Social Networks in Political Campaigns: Facebook and Congressional Elections 2006, 2008*. Paper presented at the 2009 Annual Meeting of the American Political Association, Toronto, Canada, September 3-6.

Williams, C. B., & Gulati, G. J. J. (2010). *Communicating with Constituents in 140 Characters or Less: Twitter and the Diffusion of Technology Innovation in the United States Congress*. Paper presented at the 2010 Annual Meeting of the Midwest Political Science Association, Chicago, Illinois, April 22-25.

Yamamoto, D., Masuda, T., Ohira, S., & Nagao, K. (2008). Video Scene Annotation Based on Web Social Activities. *Multimedia. IEEE, 15*, 22–32. doi:10.1109/MMUL.2008.67

Yannas, P., & Lappas, G. (2007). Evaluating Local E-Government: An Analysis of Greek Prefecture Websites. In *Proceedings of the 2nd IEEE International Conference on Digital Information Management (ICDIM 07),* October 28-31, Lyon, France, pp. 254-259.

Zheng, Y.-T., Zhao, M., Song, Y., Adam, H., Buddermeier, U., Bissacco, A., et al. (2009). *Tour the World: Building a Web-scale Landmark Recognition Engine*. In proceedings of the 2009 IEEE computer society conference on computer vision and pattern recognition, pp. 1085-1092.

Zhou, P., & Le, Z. (2007). A Framework for Web Usage Mining in Electronic Government, *in IFIP International Federation for Information Processing: Vol. 252. Integration and Innovation Orient to E-Society* (pp. 487–496). Boston: Springer.

# Chapter 2
# A Study of Homophily on Social Media

**Halil Bisgin**
*University of Arkansas at Little Rock, USA*

**Nitin Agarwal**
*University of Arkansas at Little Rock, USA*

**Xiaowei Xu**
*University of Arkansas at Little Rock, USA*

## ABSTRACT

*Similarity breeds connections, the principle of homophily, has been well studied in existing sociology literature. Several studies have observed this phenomenon by conducting surveys on human subjects. These studies have concluded that new ties are formed between similar individuals. This phenomenon has been used to explain several socio-psychological concepts such as segregation, community development, social mobility, etc. However, due to the nature of these studies and limitations because of involvement of human subjects, conclusions from these studies are not easily extensible in online social media. Social media, which is becoming the infinite space for interactions, has exceeded all the expectations in terms of growth, for reasons beyond human comprehension. New ties are formed in social media in the same way that they emerge in the real world. However, given the differences between real-world and online social media, do the same factors that govern the construction of new ties in the real world also govern the construction of new ties in social media? In other words, does homophily exist in social media? In this chapter, the authors study this highly significant question and propose a systematic approach by studying two online social media sites, BlogCatalog and Last.fm, and report our findings along with some interesting observations.*

DOI: 10.4018/978-1-61350-513-7.ch002

# INTRODUCTION

Originally proposed by Lazarfeld and Merton (1954), the term *homophily* refers to the concept that similar individuals are assumed to associate with each other more often than with others. Since then hundreds of studies have been performed as summarized in (McPherson, Smith-Lovin, & Cook, 2001) that extensively investigated the phenomenon of homophily. Over the years, sociologists have studied the human population on numerous sociodemographic dimensions including race, gender, age, social class, and education and have concluded that friends, co-workers, colleagues, spouses, and other associations tend to be more similar to each other than randomly chosen members of the same population. This phenomenon has been widely used to explain certain sociological concepts like segregation, social mobility, etc.

All these studies have one thing in common, that is all of them were conducted in a physical world scenario by surveying a group of human subjects. Often these subjects belonged to a specific geographical location. These subjects were studied over a set of sociodemographic dimensions as mentioned above. Their ties were subject to social influence. For example, parents had to approve their kids' friends, individuals usually acquainted with those either in the same workplace, schools, etc. that inherently favored the conclusions of the study. Lack of a platform where individuals can explore relations outside their geographical locations, outside their social circles, outside their workplace or schools etc., made it difficult to generalize the results.

Homophily was categorized by Lazarfeld and Merton (1954) into status homophily and value homophily. Status homophily takes into consideration the social status of individuals, implying that individuals with similar social status tend to associate with each other. Value homophily defines similarity based on what people think, implying that individuals who think alike tend to associate

with each other regardless of the differences in their social status. However, results from both the categories were concluded on a small-scale experiment involving human subjects in a physical world scenario.

Often on social media, information such as age, gender, education, and social status is either unavailable or untrustworthy. Moreover, individuals share their interests, likes, dislikes, opinions, perspectives, thoughts, etc. Due to the absence of sociodemographic dimensions, it is difficult to assume that homophily that was studied on sociodemographic dimensions. Interests of individuals are one of the strongest factors to evaluate homophily in the virtual world. These factors were often neglected in the studies conducted in the physical world. Precisely due to this reason it is difficult to evaluate status homophily in the virtual world. Authors in (Kossinets & Watts, 2009) study a university campus social network and conclude that social ties are often influenced by triadic and focal closures.

Another major difference between studies conducted in the physical and virtual worlds is the scale of the study. Millions of individuals could be easily studied in the virtual world as compared to the physical world. This makes the results much more conclusive and generalizable. Next, we summarize the differences between the physical and virtual worlds in Table 1.

Inspired by the differences between physical and online world, in this chapter we study the existence of homophily in online social networks. Specifically, we make the following contributions:

1.  We study the differences between real world and online/virtual world interactions;
2.  Based on the differences highlighted above, we investigate the question whether creation of new ties in the online world is inspired by homophily. In other words, we investigate whether individuals in the online world are likely to become friends if they share similar interests;

*Table 1. Differences between physical and online/virtual world scenarios*

| Physical World | Online/Virtual World |
|---|---|
| Sociodemographic dimensions such as age, gender, education, and social status used to study homophily. | Sociodemographic dimensions are often not available or could not be trusted. |
| Physical locality such as geographical proximity and organizational locality such as workplace, schools play significant role in governing new tie. | Interactions between individuals span all geographical barriers across different time zones. Geographical or organizational proximity do not govern construction of ties. |
| User interests, opinions, thoughts, perspectives, and preferences were often ignored in studies conducted in physical world scenario. | Individuals on social media are defined by what they write/share. Interests, opinions, thoughts, perspectives, and preferences are the significant dimensions that could govern new ties. |
| Construction of ties in physical world is often regulated by social status or class. | Construction of ties in virtual world are beyond social status and class. |
| Studies conducted in physical world were often limited to a particular geographical area constraining the scale of the study. | Millions of individuals could be easily studied in virtual world as compared to physical world. This makes the results much more conclusive and generalizable. |

3.    We propose a systematic methodology using three independent techniques (dyadic, community-based, random rewired model) to analyze ties in online social networks;

4.    We study three online social networks, Blogcatalog and Last.fm, using the proposed methodology to analyze the factors that govern the construction of new ties and simultaneously the efficacy of the proposed methodology;

5.    We present our findings for the three online social networks and bearing upon the analysis envisage possible explorations to study potential factors that influence the decision of creating new ties and the evolution of social networks at large; and

6.    Data collected from this research is made publicly available after anonymization due to its efficacy for various interdisciplinary research endeavors.

This chapter is organized as follows: the next section describes the related work. Section on 'Data Collection' describes the data collection strategy from three online social networks: viz., BlogCatalog and Last.fm. Sections on 'Analyzing Dyadic Relations', 'Analyzing Community Structures', and 'Random Rewired Analysis' present our methodology including three independent techniques, dyadic, community based, and random rewired model, respectively, to examine homophily and test the hypothesis that individuals with similar interests are more likely to create ties with each other. Last section concludes our findings and outlines possible factors that influence the decision of creating new ties.

## RELATED WORK

There has been a significant body of work studying homophily using real world data. This involved conducting surveys with human subjects and then evaluating their responses (Hoyt & Babchuk, 1983; Lazarfeld & Merton, 1954; Verbrugge, 1977). As mentioned in the beginning of the chapter, often choices for constructing new ties in the real world are influenced by several factors, such as demographics, geographical and organizational locality, etc. In this chapter, we studied online social networks where such factors do not play much of a role. This differentiates our work from the existing works mentioned above. However, to the best of our knowledge there have been very few studies that involved analysis of large online social networks to investigate homophily. Next, we summarize these works and point out the essential differences.

Authors in (McPherson, Smith-Lovin, & Cook, 2001) discuss the similarity between individuals and ties. Authors study the various sociodemographic characteristics and the role they play in determining construction of new ties. This article investigates the sources of homophily such as social structures and cognitive processes. The article also studied the influence from geographical and organizational locality factors. However, authors did not consider the interests of individuals in governing the ties. Authors also proposed the need for further study to investigate the principle of homophily. Similarly, Singla & Richardson (2008) study the instant messaging data and concluded that friends tend to share similar demographic characteristics. However, interests of these users were not included in the study. In another study (Gilbert & Karahalios, 2009) authors consider a set of 35 Facebook users and proposed a regression model for predicting the friendship on Facebook. The features mainly consisted of user demographics and interactions, but did not include their interests. Moreover, the results from a survey of 35 users are not easily extensible, when compared to the datasets used in our work.

Authors in (Crandell, Cosley, Huttenlocher, Kleinberg, & Suri, 2008) study the LiveJournal and Wikipedia data and used activities such as user edits to evaluate the similarity between individuals. This is quite different from the research conducted in this chapter, which looks at the interests of the users to investigate homophily. In another work by Adamic and Adar (2003), the authors study the homepages of users and model friendship using hyperlinks between the homepages. While one can link to the webpages of several individuals, this does not make the person friends with all of them.

Extensive literature exists (Fortunato, 2009) that suggest the emergence of communities due to shared interests among the members, which is also leveraged by several community extrac-

tion approaches. In principle, there are three dominant approaches used by computational social network analysis scholars for community extraction: network-centric, content-centric and hybrid approaches (Agarwal and Liu, 2009). Network-centric approaches leverage network structural properties to identify communities within a social network. Since the fundamental assumption is that the members of a community tend to interact more often with each other as compared to the members of other communities, the network is partitioned into clusters with lower between cluster edges and higher within cluster edges (Hagen and Kahng, 1992; Shi and Malik, 2000; Luxburg, 2007; Clauset et al., 2004; Dhillon et al., 2007). Variations of the above network partitioning approaches address the dynamic nature of social networks (Ning et al., 2007; Chi et al., 2007a; Chi et al., 2007b). Content-centric approaches rely on the assumption that the members of a community tend to talk about similar topics due to similarity of their interests. Communities thus are extracted based on the similarity of content available in the form of blog post texts or profile information of the individuals (Li et al., 2007; Brooks and Montanez, 2006). Hybrid approaches leverage both content and network information to extract communities. The central tenet behind such an approach is: a set of blogs that are highly linked and tend to share similar content, reflect tighter communities (Java et al., 2008). In our analysis, we use two most widely studied community extraction approaches, Fast Modularity (Clauset et al., 2004) and Graclus (Dhillon et al., 2007) to examine if similarity of interests is the latent process behind emergence of communities in online social networks. More details are given later in the Section on 'Analyzing Community Structures'.

The communities identified by the above approaches are different from special interest groups or focus groups (such as "Windows Interest Groups", etc.) that are intentionally created by like-minded individuals with a set of objectives and desired expectations. Such groups find significant applications in recommender systems (Pazzani, 1999) and demographic filtering (Aïmeur et al., 2006; Jagersberger and Waldhör, 2008). In this work, however, we focus on community formation as a more natural self-evolving process without a pre-conceived bias. For this reason, we differentiate our analysis and do not include such communities in this study. However, as a future research direction, it would be interesting to explore special interest communities and compare and contrast our findings with such communities.

## DATA COLLECTION

Two online social networks were used to perform the analysis, BlogCatalog[1] and Last.fm[2]. Blog-Catalog is a blogging portal where bloggers can submit their blogs, tags, categories, and specify their friends. This data was obtained from Social Computing Data Repository (Zafarani & Liu, 2009). The second data set was constructed by crawling Last.fm. Last.fm is a social networking website where users can specify the genre of music they like and connect with others. It hosts a huge community of users and their taste in music. Users specify their friends on Last.fm. This link structure was used to crawl data in a breadth-first fashion. The crawler was forcefully terminated after 279,678 users were crawled. Crawler collected both the network information and the music genre(s) the user likes. While BlogCatalog has a very broad spectrum of interests a user could have, on the other hand Last.fm has a very narrow focus on user interests.

### Data Pre-Processing

Users in BlogCatalog are required to label their blog(s) by using system-defined tags. There were 344 total tags found in the dataset. Two default tags i.e., *Personal* and *Blogging* were removed which could be considered as noise. Thus, we ac-

cepted the remaining 342 tags as ground truth of tags or interests. Out of 88,784 users in this site, 79,115 users had valid labels for their blogs. In other words, the result of tag validation process, which was a superset of the friendship network, has been considered as our initial step.

Last.fm data had more challenging noise issues when compared to BlogCatalog. Namely, there was no system defined tagging procedure, which resulted in a high variety of user-defined labels. This required standardization of user-defined tags/ genres with respect to a ground truth. Therefore, we assumed a genre reference from Wikipedia where we had 1496 types of music listed. Like the 342 tags in BlogCatalog, we adopted 1496 genres for tag validation. In this case, as a superset of a social network to be mined, 64,805 users passed the tag validation stage among the crawled dataset of 279,678 users.

After discarding the noisy tags (in BlogCatalog) and unrecognized tags (in Last.fm), those users that did not have a single valid tag were removed from the dataset. This resulted in social networks consisting of 78,445 and 54,987 users for BlogCatalog and Last.fm, respectively. The social network datasets obtained from BlogCatalog and Last.fm after pre-processing contain 1,848,245 and 214,628 links respectively. Statistics of both the datasets have been summarized in Table 2.

## ANALYZING DYADIC RELATIONS

This section describes our first technique to examine homophily at a finer granularity based on dyadic relations. Specifically, we study the ties of individuals and analyze the overlap in the interests of the individuals for both the social networks. We compute the percentage of ties that share common interests and divide the ties in two groups, (a) ties with no common interests and (b) ties with one or more common interests. Table 3 presents the results for both the datasets. Clearly from Table 3, it can be observed that for Blogcatalog data

*Table 2. Summary of BlogCatalog and Last.fm networks.*

| Statistics | BlogCatalog | Last.fm |
|---|---|---|
| Number of Nodes | 78,445 | 54,987 |
| Number of Links | 1,848,245 | 214,628 |
| Link Density[3] | 0.00060 | 0.00 |
| Average Degree | 23.56 | 3.9 |
| Attribute Name | Category | Genre |
| Size of Attribute Domain | 342 | 1,496 |
| Average number of interests per node | 2.49 | 10.63 |

*Table 3. Overlap in interests for individuals sharing ties in Blogcatalog and Last.fm datasets.*

| | Blogcatalog | Last.fm |
|---|---|---|
| **0 interests in common** | 84.06% | 23.25% |
| **1 or more interests in common** | 15.94% | 76.75% |

over 84% of the ties do not share a single interest, which indicates that individuals do not consider interests before they form the ties. However, the same analysis on Last.fm data yields different result. It seems that over 76% of the ties have at least one interest in common. Deeper analysis showed that in Last.fm individuals have a large number of various forms of interests (as also shown in Table 2, average number of interests per node is 10.63 for Last.fm as compared to 2.49 for Blogcatalog). We investigated into this apparently higher value of interest overlap for Last.fm data by examining the normalized similarity score between pair-wise individuals connected with a tie by computing Jaccard similarity coefficient, as defined below,

$$J(A,B) = \frac{|A \cap B|}{|A \cup B|} \qquad (1)$$

where A and B represent the set of interests of two individuals that share a tie and $0 \leq J(A,B) \leq 1$ is defined as the Jaccard similarity coefficient between the two sets, A and B. We then averaged

the Jaccard similarity score for all the ties, which was found to be 0.04 for Blogcatalog and $5 \times 10^{-7}$ for Last.fm. This shows that there is even lesser similarity in terms of interests between individuals who create ties in Last.fm as compared to Blogcatalog. This demonstrates that since individuals on Last.fm have varied and large numbers of interests, they are rarely common between individuals who share a tie.

We further analyze the distribution of the Jaccard similarity coefficient between the individuals sharing a tie. We binned the similarity scores into equal-sized bins of 0.1 from 0 to 1 and plotted the frequency of the ties that fall into the bins. The results for Blogcatalog and Last.fm are shown in Figure 1 (a) and Figure 1 (b), respectively. Clearly Figure 1 (a) and Figure 1 (b) show that over 86% of ties in Blogcatalog dataset and over 73% ties in Last.fm dataset connect individuals with similarity less than 0.1. This analysis shows that very often individuals that share a tie do not share interests, hence contradicting the assumption that homophily influences creation of new ties.

*Figure 1. Distribution of Jaccard similarity coefficient in equal-sized bins of 0.1 for (a) Blogcatalog dataset and (b) Last.fm dataset.*

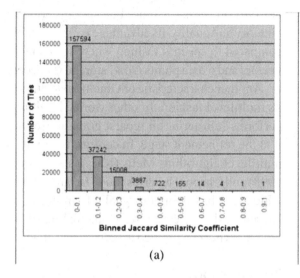

(a)

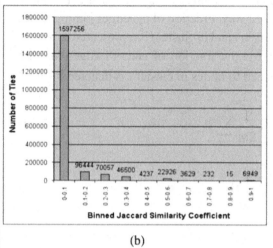

(b)

## ANALYZING COMMUNITY STRUCTURES

This section describes our second technique to examine homophily at a community structure level. It has been well studied that similar groups of people come together to form communities. This has been the underlying phenomenon for the vast literature on community extraction as mentioned in the related work section. The micro-level processes of creating new ties based on their similarity gives rise to macro patterns of associations, also known as communities. This concept has been extensively used in discovering communities in online social networks. We study some of the most widely used community extraction algorithms and analyze whether the extracted communities actually shared similarities. Next, we briefly describe the community extraction algorithms used in our work, Fast Modularity (Clauset et al., 2004) and Graclus (Dhillon et al., 2007).

## Community Extraction Algorithms

*Fast Modularity:* Unlike other methods, Fast Modularity can extract communities from very large networks due to its hierarchical fashion (Clauset et al., 2004). It tries to optimize a modularity value during the procedure in an agglomerative way. If we let $v$ and $w$ denote vertices, and $A_{vw}$ represents the entry in the adjacency matrix with $m$ edges, Clauset et al. defines the modularity function, $Q$ as follows,

$$Q = \frac{1}{2} \sum_{vw} [A_{vw} - k_v k_w] \delta(c_v, c_w) \qquad (2)$$

where, $k_v$ denotes degree of $v$ and $c_v$ represents the cluster that $v$ belongs to. The *Kronecker delta* function, $\delta(i, j)$ is also defined as below,

$$\delta(i, j) = \begin{cases} 1 & if\ i = j \\ 0 & otherwise \end{cases} \qquad (3)$$

The procedure adopts a bottom-up approach by assuming every node as a community at the beginning and merges the communities if they contribute in Q. Formally; they define following two quantities, which make us represent Q in a more explicit way. Fraction of the edges joining nodes in cluster *i* and in cluster *j* is represented by $e(i, j)$ whereas the fraction of ends of edges that are attached to nodes in cluster *i* is denoted by $a_i$

$$e_{ij} = \frac{1}{2m} \sum_{vw} A_{vw} \delta(c_v, i)\delta(c_w, j) \tag{4}$$

$$a_i = \frac{1}{2m} \sum_v k_v \delta(c_v, i) \tag{5}$$

It's clear that $\delta(c_v, c_w)$ can be expressed as $\sum_i \delta(c_v, i)\delta(c_w, j)$. Then it turns out to be,

$$\begin{aligned}
Q &= \frac{1}{2m} \sum_{vw} [A_{vw} - \frac{k_v k_w}{2m}] \sum_i \delta(c_v, i)\delta(c_w, j) \\
&= \sum_i \left[ \frac{1}{2m} \sum_{vw} A_{vw} \delta(c_v, i)\delta(c_w, j) \right] \\
&- \sum_i \left[ \frac{1}{2m} \sum_v k_v \delta(c_v, i) \frac{1}{2m} \sum_w k_w \delta(c_w, j) \right] \\
&= \sum_i e_{ii} - a_i^2
\end{aligned} \tag{6}$$

$Q$ is recomputed as the cluster configuration is changed due to agglomeration. Configuration corresponding to the maximum value of Q is selected as the best partitioning result.

*Graclus:* Spectral clustering has been a well-studied partitioning method for graphs. However, its computational cost has led people to improve this approach. Graclus algorithm is a result of those studies where Dhillon *et al.* tried to model their problem in an equivalent form (Dhillon et al., 2007). In particular, instead of working with an eigenvalue-based approach, they have utilized a *k-means* approach. More specifically, Graclus is based on a *kernel k-means* clustering which has

been showed that its performance is much better than spectral clustering methods. It outperforms not only in terms of time, but also in terms of memory and quality. Its advantage is considerable compared to spectral fashion where for *k* eigenvectors and n data points *O(nk)* storage is needed.

Another characteristic of Graclus algorithm is its multilevel fashion. In other words, it initially performs a clustering on a coarse graph and refines it in the refinement stage. In contrast to previous multilevel algorithms Metis (Karypis & Kumar, 1998) and Chaco (Hendrickson & Leland, 1995), which are based on the goal of optimization Kernighan-Lin objective (Kernighan & Lin, 1970), Graclus is not constrained to equal-sized clusters.

## Methodology

Here, we present the experiment methodology to study homophily with respect to community formation. We extract the communities from the social network datasets and investigate whether creation of these ties was influenced by the similarity of interest(s). Towards this direction, we first identify the communities and then extract the interests of these communities.

## Community Structure Detection

We applied the two clustering algorithms, viz., Graclus and Fast Modularity, to obtain communities for each social network dataset. Graclus extracts communities using a multilevel approach whereas Fast Modularity uses a completely different approach of splitting the network as explained previously. Graclus requires the total number of clusters *a priori* whereas Fast Modularity automatically computes the number of clusters. Graclus tries to partition the data into equal-sized clusters, whereas Fast Modularity could partition the data into highly uneven cluster distribution. After careful analysis of data, it was found that the optimal number of clusters for BlogCatalag and Last.fm was 31 and 20, respectively. Cluster dis-

*Figure 2. Distribution of cluster sizes (a) Graclus on BlogCatalog dataset (b) Graclus on Last.fm dataset (c) Fast Modularity on BlogCatalog dataset (d) Fast Modularity on Last.fm*

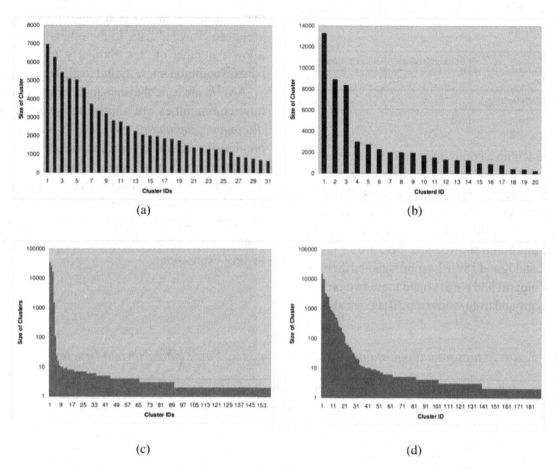

(a)

(b)

(c)

(d)

tributions obtained from both clustering methods on both datasets are illustrated in Figure 2 (a) and Figure 2 (d). It can be observed Fast Modularity generates large number of highly uneven-sized clusters with several clusters having size less than 100, whereas clusters obtained through Graclus are comparatively fewer and sufficiently large.

## Shared Interests Acquisition

Next we compare the extracted community to the whole population or the entire dataset with respect to the interests, as specified by the individuals using categories and tags. To extract representative interests of communities as well as the entire population we utilize frequent pattern mining

algorithm. An a priori algorithm (Bodon, 2003) was implemented to find out frequently occurring itemsets for each cluster (also the community) as well as whole population from each dataset with a minimum support of 1% of the cluster size. For this step we considered the clusters mentioned in Table 4.

## Experimental Results

This section presents the results of community aspect of the homophily phenomenon. We compute the overlap between the interests of the communities and the entire population for all the datasets. We analyze the results using qualitative and quantitative metrics. Most common interests

*Table 4. Number of clusters for random rewired models of BlogCatalog and Last.fm for Graclus and Fast Modularity considered for interests acquisition.*

|  | BlogCatalog | Last.fm |
|---|---|---|
| **Graclus** | 31 | 20 |
| **Fast Modularity** | 5 | 20 |

shared within a community and the ones that are more prominent in the population need to be compared regarding the previous steps. Therefore, we first fixed the frequent items of populations as ground truth with respect to their frequencies. A priori algorithm showed that there are 79 tags in BlogCatalog and 189 in Last.fm satisfied the minimum support and we assumed these two ordered sets as ground truth whose top 20 tags are showed in Table 5 and Table 6. The processed 76 groups also gave tags in an order, which are specific to that community. Whereas in some clusters, there are more crowded lists, in the others we notice a lower number of tags. Similarly, groups may contain common interests, but in different orders.

A valid measure that can quantitatively prove how communities are similar to others is the *discounted cumulative gain (DCG)* method. As previously mentioned, regarding the ground truth, relevance scores are assigned to every 5 labels in the list. Depending on the list sizes of two social media sites, scorings start from 36 and 16 for BlogCatalog and Last.fm, respectively. What *DCG* does is to calculate information gain by the following expression.

*Table 5. Top 20 tags from BlogCatalog and clusters found by Fast Modularity and Graclus*

| BLOGCATALOG | Fast Modularity | Graclus |
|---|---|---|
| Entertainment | Sports | Technology |
| Art | Travel | Internet |
| Technology | Technology | Lifestyle |
| Internet | Entertainment | Art |
| Marketing | Real Estate | Entertainment |
| Health | Finance | Writing |
| Travel | Music | Marketing |
| Music | Business | Music |
| Lifestyle | Art | Photography |
| Business | Internet | Family |
| Writing | Marketing | Computers |
| Development and Growth | Lifestyle | News and Media |
| Humor | Health | Business |
| Photography | Christian | Travel |
| Small Business | Christianity | Political |
| Political | News and Media | Humor |
| News and Media | Film | Health |
| Family | Writing | Small Business |
| Sports | Political | Development and Growth |
| Shopping | Photography | Society |

*Table 6. Top 20 tags from Last.fm and clusters found by Fast Modularity and Graclus*

| LAST FM | Fast Modularity | Graclus |
|---|---|---|
| rock music | rock music | pop music |
| electronic music | indie music | dance music |
| indie music | electronic music | rock music |
| experimental music | folk music | soul music |
| pop music | pop music | electronic music |
| folk music | indie rock | indie music |
| jazz | experimental music | pop rock |
| alternative rock | electronica | hip hop music |
| electronica | alternative rock | jazz |
| indie rock | classic rock | alternative rock |
| industrial music | jazz | singer-songwriter |
| dance music | dance music | soundtrack |
| classic rock | singer-songwriter | folk music |
| singer-songwriter | progressive rock | funk |
| progressive rock | industrial music | chillout |
| chillout | hard rock | country music |
| hard rock | psychedelic music | electronica |
| soundtrack | blues | house music |
| psychedelic music | indie pop | reggae |
| trip-hop | punk rock | disco |

$$DCG_p = rel_1 + \sum_{i=2}^{p} \frac{rel_i}{\log_2 i} \qquad (7)$$

where, $i$ denotes the rank position and $rel_i$ represents the relevance score of the specific item.

Since the ground truth lists have the maximum information gain, we call value obtained from those *ideally discounted cumulative gain, IDCG.* If one takes the ratio of *DCG* and *IDCG*, the outcome will be the normalized *DCG,* denoted by *nDCG.*

$$nDCG = \frac{DCG}{IDCG} \qquad (8)$$

We took 76 processed clusters into account to calculate *nDCG* in order to measure the similarity between any group and the general site tendency. Due to the fact that label list may differ from group to group, we used the overlapping tags through all calculations preserving the rankings and relevance scores. Although there exist tags that appear in partitions, but not in the bigger set and vice versa, the amount of overlapping patterns led for a reliable comparison. As a matter of fact, our results show that any group of people constituting a community has a very high similarity with the population they come from. The table below summarizes similarity values acquired from both clustering algorithm results for both social media sites.

## RANDOM REWIRED ANALYSIS

Both the community extraction algorithms, viz., Graclus and Fast Modularity, recognize a group of individuals as a community if they have more links

*Table 7. nDCG statistics.*

| | BlogCatalog | | Last.fm | |
|---|---|---|---|---|
| | $\bar{x}$ | σ | $\bar{x}$ | σ |
| **Graclus** | 0.95 | 0.05 | 0.98 | 0.01 |
| **Fast Modularity** | 0.96 | 0.04 | 0.98 | 0.008 |

amongst them as compared to the whole population. Now results from the previous section show that different communities have highly similar interests. This indicates that individuals connect with each other regardless of the interest(s). To further examine this, we performed another study. We broke all the ties that were created by the individuals in both datasets, viz., BlogCatalog and Last.fm, and created new ties following the BA model (Albert and Barabasi, 2002). Network Workbench tool was used to create the random rewiring (Team, NWB, 2006). The new random networks were constrained to the same set of nodes and approximately the same number of ties correspondingly in the two original datasets. The network characteristics for the random rewired dataset for BlogCatalog and Last.fm are shown in Table 6.

We followed the same experiment methodology as explained previously in the "analyzing community structure" section. For both the random rewired datasets, we ran Graclus and Fast Modularity to identify communities. Note that clustering parameters were kept exactly the same as with the original dataset in the "analyzing community structure" section. The cluster distribution for the random rewired datasets for BlogCatalog and Last.fm using both Graclus and Fast Modularity

are shown in Figure 3 (a) and Figure 3 (d). The cluster distribution for random rewired dataset is very similar to the original dataset as shown in Figure 2 (a) and Figure 2 (d). We observed a very similar power law distribution, where there are several clusters with very few cluster members and very few clusters with large numbers of cluster members. Clusters with less than 100 members were ignored for further analysis, similar to the "analyzing community structure" section. Table 9 shows the clusters that were considered for the interest acquisition step. Once the communities were extracted, we identify the communities' interests using the approach mentioned in analyzing community structure section and computed the overlap between communities' interests and interests of the whole population for both BlogCatalog and Last.fm. We analyzed the top-$k$ interests of individuals in a community and the entire population using tag clouds for varying $k$. Due to space constraints we display the tag clouds obtained using Fast Modularity clustering approach for the random rewired datasets for BlogCatalog and Last.fm in Figure 4 and Figure 5 for $k$=50. Fast Modularity clustering approach generates the clusters of sizes with maximum variation unlike Graclus where clusters are approximately equal-sized. It can be observed from these tag

*Table 8. Summary of random rewired models of BlogCatalog and Last.fm networks.*

| Statistics | BlogCatalog | Last.fm |
|---|---|---|
| Number of Nodes | 78,445 | 54,987 |
| Number of Links | 1,878,849 | 214,628 |
| Link Density | 0.00061 | 0.00014 |
| Average Degree | 23.95 | 3.9 |

*Figure 3. Distribution of cluster sizes obtained using (a) Graclus on Random Rewired model of Blog-Catalog dataset, (b) Graclus on Random Rewired model of Last.fm dataset, (c) Fast Modularity on Random Rewired model of BlogCatalog dataset, and (d) Fast Modularity on Random Rewired model of Last.fm dataset.*

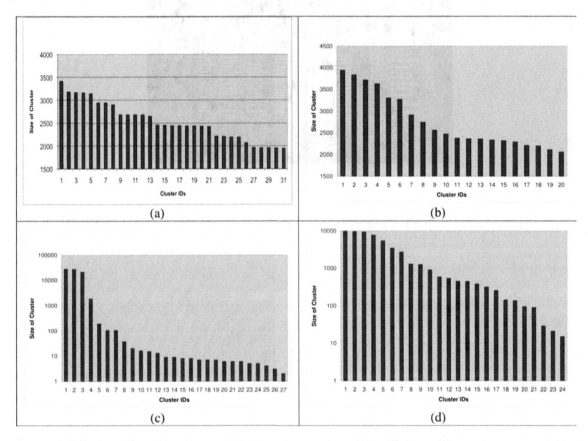

clouds that the interests of different communities are not very different from the whole population as indicated in Table 5 and Table 6.

Due to the visualization limitations of tag clouds, we compared the interests of different communities with the whole population using

*Table 9. Number of clusters for Random Rewired models of BlogCatalog and Last.fm for Graclus and Fast Modularity considered for Interests Acquisition.*

| | BlogCatalog | Last.fm |
|---|---|---|
| Graclus | 31 | 20 |
| Fast Modularity | 7 | 19 |

*nDCG* measure as explained in analyzing community structures section. We report the mean *nDCG* values and the (Crandell et al., 2008) variance results in Table 10. It can be observed from the *nDCG* values that there is a high similarity in interests between different communities and the whole population. These results are quite similar to what we obtained from original BlogCatalog and Last.fm datasets where creation of ties was not random. This clearly demonstrates that creation of ties in online communities does not depend on the interest(s) or is rather a random process. This research has raised more questions than it has answered. We need to further investigate the factors that influence the creation of new ties in

*Figure 4. Top 50 Tags from BlogCatalog Clusters (a) Biggest Cluster (b) Smallest Cluster*

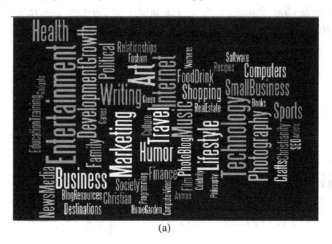

(a)

(b)

online communities, which is discussed more in the next section as future research direction.

## CONCLUSION AND FUTURE RESEARCH DIRECTIONS

In this chapter, we studied the principle of homophily in the context of online social networks. Although the existence of homophily has been studied in the real world, its existence in online social media is questionable due to the differences pointed out earlier in the chapter. We proposed a systematic approach to study two online social media networks BlogCatalog and Last.fm leveraging three independent methodologies: dyadic, community-based, and random rewired analysis.

Analysis based on dyadic relations demonstrated that often the users that share a tie in online social network do not share interests. For community structure analysis, we specifically extracted communities using two of the most widely used community discovery algorithms based on network ties. The emerging communities had very similar

*Table 10. nDCG Statistics comparing Communities with the whole Population for Random Rewired model of BlogCatalog and Last.fm networks.*

|                 | BlogCatalog |        | Last.fm |        |
|-----------------|-------------|--------|---------|--------|
|                 | $\bar{x}$   | σ      | $\bar{x}$ | σ    |
| Graclus         | 1.00        | 0.00   | 0.95    | 0.01   |
| Fast Modularity | 0.98        | 0.02   | 0.92    | 0.03   |

*Figure 5. Top 50 Tags from Last.fm Clusters (a) Biggest Cluster (b) Smallest Cluster*

(a)

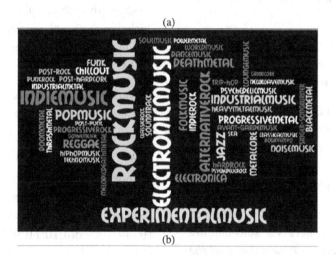

(b)

interests not only to each other but also to the whole population. This implies that the communities that are evolved based on dense emergence of ties within a specific group of individuals do not have distinctive interests, indicating that the ties that are constructed are not governed by homophily. Further, a random rewired network for these two online social networks showed very similar analysis, suggesting a random process behind creation of new ties. This study has raised several interesting questions, such as, what are the real factors behind construction of new ties in online social media, are the real-world ties also influenced by the online social media due to the inevitable penetration of social media in our day-to-day lives, how do these ties evolve which needs a longitudinal study, among others.

Further, it would be desirable to explore other dimensions (such as, geographic location, ties, demographics) for investigating the homophily phenomenon, depending upon their availability in online social media.

## ACKNOWLEDGMENT

This research was funded in part by the National Science Foundations Social-Computational Systems (SoCS) Program within the Directorate for Computer and Information Science and Engineering Division of Information and Intelligent Systems (Award numbers: IIS - 1110868 and IIS - 1110649) and the U.S. Office of Naval Research (Grant number: N000141010091).

# REFERENCES

Adamic, L. A., & Adar, E. (2003). Friends and neighbors on the web. *Social Networks, 25*(3), 211–230. doi:10.1016/S0378-8733(03)00009-1

Agarwal, N., & Liu, H. (2009). *Modeling and Data Mining in Blogosphere* (Vol. 1). Morgan & Claypol Publishers. A · eur, E., Brassard, G., Fernandez, J., & Mani Onana, F. (2006). Privacy preserving demographic filtering. *Proceedings of the ACM Symposium on Applied Computing (SAC '06)*, (pp. 872-878).

Albert, R., A. L. (2002). Statistical mechanics of complex networks. *Reviews of Modern Physics, 74*(1), 47–97. doi:10.1103/RevModPhys.74.47

Bodon, F. (2003). A fast apriori implementation. *Proceedings of the IEEE ICDM Workshop on Frequent Itemset Mining Implementations (FIMI' 03), volume 90 of CEUR Workshop Proceedings.* Melbourne, Florida, USA.

Brooks, C., & Montanez, N. (2006). Improved annotation of the blogosphere via auto-tagging and hierarchical clustering. *Proceedings of the Fifteenth International Conference on World Wide Web*, (pp. 625–632). New York.

Chi, Y., Song, X., Zhou, D., Hino, K., & Tsend, B. (2007a). Evolutionary spectral clustering by incorporating temporal smoothness. *Proceedings of the 13th ACM SIGKDD international conference on Knowledge discovery and data mining*, (pp. 153–162).

Clauset, A., J., N. M., & Moore, C. (2004). Finding community structure in very large networks. *Physical Review E: Statistical, Nonlinear, and Soft Matter Physics, 70*(6), 66–111. doi:10.1103/PhysRevE.70.066111

Crandell, D., Cosley, D., Huttenlocher, D., Kleinberg, J., & Suri, S. (2008). *Feedback effects between similarity and social influence in online communities* (pp. 160–168). ACM.

Dhillon, I., Guan, Y., & Kulis, B. (2007). Weighted graph cuts without eigenvectors: A multilevel approach. *IEEE Transactions on Pattern Analysis and Machine Intelligence*, 1944–1957. doi:10.1109/TPAMI.2007.1115

Gilbert, E., & Karahalios, K. (2009). Predicting tie strength with social media. *Proceeding of the 27th international conference on Human factors in computing systems* (pp. 211-220). New York: ACM.

Girvan, M., & Newman, M. E. (2002). *Community structure in social and biological networks, 99* (12), 7821.

Hagen, L., & Kahng, A. (1992). New spectral methods for ratio cut partitioning and clustering. *IEEE Transactions on Computer-Aided Design of Integrated Circuits and Systems, 11*(9), 1074–1085. doi:10.1109/43.159993

Hendrickson, B., & Leland, R. W. (1995). *A multi-level algorithm for partitioning graphs.* Supercomputing.

Hoyt, D. R., & Babchuk, N. (1983). Adult kinship networks: The selective formation of intimate ties with kin. *Social Forces, 62*(1), 84–101.

Jagersberger, A., & Waldh, K. (2008). Dynamic Packaging using a Cluster-based Demographic Filtering Approach. In P. O'Connor, W. Hken, & U. Gretzel, (eds). *Information and Communication Technologies in Tourism*, 186-197. New York: Springer.

Java, A., Joshi, A., & Finin, T. (2008). Detecting communities via simultaneous clustering of graphs and folksonomies. *Proceedings of the Tenth Workshop on Web Mining and Web Usage Analysis (WebKDD)*. ACM.

Karypis, G., & Kumar, V. (1998). A fast and high quality multilevel scheme for partitioning irregular graphs. *SIAM Journal on Scientific Computing*, *20*(1), 359–392. doi:10.1137/S1064827595287997

Kernighan, B. W., & Lin, S. (1970). An efficient heuristic procedure for partitioning graphs. *The Bell System Technical Journal*, *49*(1), 291–307.

Kossinets, G., & Watts, J. D. (2009). Origins of homophily in an evolving social network. *American Journal of Sociology*, *115*(2), 405–450. doi:10.1086/599247

Kumar, R., Novak, J., Raghavan, P., & Tomkins, A. (2005). On the bursty evolution of blogspace. *World Wide Web (Bussum)*, *8*(2), 159–178. doi:10.1007/s11280-004-4872-4

Lazarfeld, P. F., & Merton, R. K. (1954). A substantive and methodologies analysis. *Freedom and control in modern society*, *18*, 66.

Li, B., Xu, S., & Zhang, J. (2007). Enhancing clustering blog documents by utilizing author/reader comments. *Proceedings of the 45th Annual Southeast Regional Conference*, (pp. 94–99). New York

Lin, Y. R., Sundaram, H., Chi, Y., Tatemura, J., & Tseng, B. L. (2007). Blog community discovery and evolution based on mutual awareness expansion. *Proceedings of the IEEE/WIC/ACM international conference on web intelligence*, 48-56.

Luxburg, U. (2007). A tutorial on spectral clustering. *Statistics and Computing*, *17*(4), 395–416. doi:10.1007/s11222-007-9033-z

McPherson, M., Smith-Lovin, L., & Cook, J. M. (2001). Birds of a feather: Homophily in social networks. *Annual Review of Sociology*, *27*(1), 415–444. doi:10.1146/annurev.soc.27.1.415

Ning, H., Xu, W., Chi, Y., Gong, Y., & Huang, T. (2007). *Incremental spectral clustering with application to monitoring of evolving blog communities*. Paper presented at the SIAM International Conference on Data Mining.

Pazzani, M. (1999). A Framework for Collaborative, Content-Based and Demographic Filtering. *Artificial Intelligence Review*, *13*(5-6), 393–408. doi:10.1023/A:1006544522159

Shi, J., & Malik, J. (2000). Normalized cuts and image segmentation. *IEEE Transactions on Pattern Analysis and Machine Intelligence*, *22*(8), 888–905. doi:10.1109/34.868688

Singla, P., & Richardson, M. (2008). Yes, there's a correlation: -from social networks to personal behavior on the web.

Team, N. W. B. (2006). *Network Benchmark Tool*. Retrieved from http://nwb.slis.indiana.edu

Verbrugge, L. M. (1977). The structure of adult friendship choices. *Social Forces*, *56*(2), 576–597.

Zafarani, R., & Liu, H. (2009). *Social computing data repository at ASU*. Retrieved from http://socialcomputing.asu.edu.

Zhou, Y., & Davis, J. (2006). Community discovery and analysis in blogspace. *Proceedings of the 15th international conference on World Wide Web* (p. 1018). ACM.

## KEY TERMS AND DEFINITIONS

**Homophily:** Is the tendency of individuals to associate and bond with similar others.

**Link Density:** Is defined as the number of actual links divided by the maximum possible number of links in the social network.

## ENDNOTES

[1]    www.blogcatalog.com

[2]    www.last.fm

[3]    Please see the key terms at the end of this chapter

# Chapter 3
# Sociocognitive Inquiry

**Brian R. Gaines**
*University of Victoria, Canada*

**Mildred L. G. Shaw**
*University of Calgary, Canada*

## ABSTRACT

*This chapter describes techniques for sociocognitive inquiry based on conceptual grid elicitation and analysis using web-based tools, such as WebGrid, which are designed to elicit conceptual models from those participating in a networked community. These techniques provide an interactive web-based experience with immediate payback from online graphic analysis, that provides an attractive alternative to, or component of, conventional web-based surveys. In particular, they support targeted follow-up studies based on passive data mining of the by-products of web-based community activities, allowing the phenomena modeled through data mining to be investigated in greater depth. The foundations in cognitive sociology and psychology are briefly surveyed, a case study is provided to illustrate how web-based conceptual modeling services can be customized to integrate with a social networking site and support a focused study, and the implications for future research are discussed.*

## INTRODUCTION

There are many significant aspects of social networks that can only be partially modeled through passive data mining techniques, partly because a high proportion of the members of the network are primarily recipients making infrequent contributions, and partly because many community beliefs and values are tacit, and implicitly embedded in

DOI: 10.4018/978-1-61350-513-7.ch003

its *habitus* (Bourdieu, 1989; Gaines, 2003). In order to extend the models developed through passive data mining and to address issues that may be very relevant to the community but have not been adequately covered through its normal processes, some form of *active inquiry* exploring the sociocognitive structure may be required.

Sociocognitive inquiry provokes network activity through the introduction of materials and processes that generate additional data. Asking provocative questions or initiating new topics are common techniques for provoking natural community activity used by moderators and others with social capital in the network. Questionnaires provide a more structured technique for obtaining specific data from members but can be unattractive because they require time and effort to complete, usually have no immediate payback to the individuals completing them, and do not allow the emergence of topics beyond those originally conceived in the questionnaire design.

This chapter presents computer-based *conceptual modeling* techniques (Gaines & Shaw, 1989; Gaines & Shaw, 2010) as a means of exploring the sociocognitive structure of networked communities on the Internet in a way that is socially acceptable and supportive of the communities and those studying them. It demonstrates how the modeling process is itself interesting and stimulating, and how the ongoing online analysis provides an immediate payback to individual members by reflecting back to them their personal conceptual models.

It describes and illustrates techniques for comparing models, and the graphic output presenting individual models, pairwise comparisons, and sociocognitive networks derived from them that can be analyzed by standard social network analysis techniques. It exemplifies the way in which the technology may be used to support networked communities, and discusses the issues involved in using it in this way, and the outcomes both in targeted studies and in long-term community support. It shows how active sociocognitive inquiry can enhance and complement existing social mining techniques, and be used to follow-up preliminary models from data mining with more detailed models based on, and refining, that research.

## BACKGROUND

Empirical study of social networks has been based primarily on behavioral data, on observing what and how members of a community are interacting. However social action also has cognitive connotations of being interpreted as *meaningful*. For example, Weber (1968, p.4) defines *action* as human behavior to which the acting individual attaches subjective meaning, and *social action* as that whose subjective meaning takes account of the behavior of others. Weber's definition captures the cognitive aspects constitutive of all social interaction, but is not in itself sufficient to guarantee that the interaction will take place in the context of a social group or community. One person could be acting socially with respect to one or more others, without those others being aware of it, attributing similar meaning, or reciprocating.

Gilbert (1992, p.153) captured the essential cognitive nature of social interaction in a community, drawing upon Simmel's (1910, p.374) notion that members' consciousness of being a unity is what constitutes that unity, and proposing that "*We* refers to a set of people each of whom shares, with oneself, in some action, belief, attitude, or other such attribute." That is cognitive commonality is constitutive of a social group or community. Again, the commonality does not guarantee the existence of the social group—there could be commonality among people who have never met but share a culture—but is what constitutes the *meaning* of membership to those in a social group or community.

Cognitive commonality is itself a difficult notion, with connotations of collective cognition (Gaines, 1994; Resnick, Levine, & Teasley, 1991), collective rationality (Gaines, 2010; Goldberg, 2010), organizational knowledge (Gaines, 2003; Weick, 1995) and the extent to which we do actually use what we regard as shared concepts in the same way (Shaw & Gaines, 1989). Hattiangadi (1987, p.15) notes that "our understanding of language is approximate—I do not believe that we ever do understand the *same* language, but only *largely similar* ones." A miracle of human social existence is that we manage to "muddle through" despite major lack of cognitive commonality (Fortun & Bernstein, 1998). Computer tools for eliciting conceptual models intrinsically have the same issues as those of a human learner coming to calibrate their cognition against the norms of their communities, and can only lead to approximate models with which we can, hopefully, muddle through in an improved fashion.

In social network mining the behavioral data generated through social interaction provides us with structural information about the network but often what we wish to ascertain are the cognitive commonalities underlying that interaction. What is the *meaning* of that interaction for those participating, what are common underlying *beliefs* and *values*, what *roles* are people playing, perhaps in providing access to relevant *uncommon* knowledge relating to individual experience, expertise, and so on.

In some cases a textual analysis of the discourse (Berry & Castellanos, 2008; Feldman & Sanger, 2007) may provide the cognitive models of interest but, often, the basis of the social interaction is tacit, either because it is presupposed and taken for granted by the participants, or because a substantial part of the community is not taking part in the overt interaction even though they embody the cognitive foundations of that community.

Those members in moderator roles may become aware that issues are not being adequately addressed by the community, and attempt to rectify this by provoking particular discussion and engaging more of the community. They may also attempt to use more structured techniques such as surveys through questionnaires.

Web-based surveys have become widely used in recent years (Couper & Miller, 2008) but studies suggest they are not as effective as conventional techniques (Heerwegh & Loosveldt, 2008; Manfreda, Bosnjak, Berzelak, Haas, & Vehovar, 2008). However, the majority of such studies focus on market research and public opinion surveys where the data collected is primarily of interest to those collecting it, there may be little sense of community among the participants, and the survey methodologies have largely been based on the conversion of paper-based surveys to HTML. That is, the user may well find them of *slight interest*, having little of the *expected interactivity* of web-based experiences, and failing to provide the *flow experience* (Gaines, Chen, & Shaw, 1997) and *instant gratification* (Greenfield, 2008) characteristic of well-designed web services and expected by experienced web users.

Recent studies have begun to focus on issues that characterize effective web experience in social networking applications, such as *interactivity* (Bolton & Saxena-Iyer, 2009), *flow experience* (Hoffman & Novak, 2009), *peer discourse* (Dhar & Chang, 2009), *sense of community* (Scarpi, 2010), and so on, and to model the *personality factors* (Brüggen & Dholakia, 2010) of active participants. Conceptual modeling tools supporting a web-based community must enable a moderator to address topics that are core to the interests of the community in such a way as to provide rich experience that takes advantage the interactivity of the web to provide immediate paybacks for members' engagement both as individuals and as community supporters.

WebGrid (Gaines & Shaw, 2007) is a web-based conceptual modeling service based on Kelly's (1955)*conceptual grids* derived from *personal construct psychology* (Gaines & Shaw, 2010). Manual modeling techniques were computerized in the 1970s (Shaw, 1980) and ported to the web in 1994 (Gaines, 1995) as tools for knowledge modeling in expert system development (Gaines & Shaw, 1993a, 1993b). The tools readily integrate with survey methodologies and have the merit of providing instant online conceptual models in graphic form enabling participants to view their own models and compare them with those of others in the community, together with overall socionets of cognitive relations between members, and consolidated conceptual models that show the sociocognitive structure of the community.

The next section outlines the socio-psychological foundations of the method and its links with theories of social action, and the following section provides a case history illustrating their application.

## PERSONAL CONSTRUCT PSYCHOLOGY

Kelly's (1955) *personal construct psychology* provides a framework for conceptual modeling based on Dewey's pragmatic instrumentalism that models the future-orientation characterizing living systems. Dewey (1910) saw our conceptual systems as forming in order to be able to anticipate a world that had sufficient coherence in time for such anticipation to be reasonably effective and provide evolutionary advantage. Hume (1888) had noted that there is no logical rationale for it to be possible to anticipate future events, and hence it is an empirical phenomenon that the world we live in often exhibits patterns that enable future experience to be anticipated from past experience. As Dewey (1911) notes: "While there is no a priori assurance that any particular instance of continuity will recur, the mind endeavors to regulate future experience by postulating recurrence. So far as the anticipation is justified by future events, the notion is confirmed. So far as it fails to work the assured continuity is dropped or corrected."

Kelly based his constructivist psychology on Dewey's insights, taking anticipation as the generative principle underlying all psychological phenomena, that "a person's processes are psychologically channelized by the ways in which he anticipates events" (Kelly, 1955, p.46), and deriving all other aspects of psychological processes as corollaries of this fundamental postulate. His first corollary is that of *construction*, that "a person anticipates events by construing their replications", where: "By construing we mean 'placing an interpretation': a person places an interpretation upon what is construed. He erects a structure, within the framework of which the substance takes shape or assumes meaning. The

substance which he construes does not produce the structure; the person does" (Kelly, 1955, p.50).

Kelly uses a *templet* metaphor for our constructive processes: "Man looks at his world through transparent patterns or templets which he creates and then attempts to fit over the realities of which the world is composed. The fit is not always very good. Yet without such patterns the world appears to be such an undifferentiated homogeneity that man is unable to make any sense out of it. Even a poor fit is more helpful to him than nothing at all." (Kelly, 1955, p.8-9).

One can use the more common term, concept, in place of templet providing one notes that: fitting a templet or concept to experience may be not only a classification but also the setting of appropriate parameters in a *model* or *theory*, and the derivation of its consequences; and that fitting a templet or concept can be an *action* changing the world to induce the fit, not just a passive process of perception of whether an templet or concept fits an experience. Dewey and Kelly accommodate within the term anticipation: *prediction* of what may happen; *action* to make something happen; *imagination* of what might happen or be made to happen; and *preparation* for eventualities that may well never happen.

Kelly's (1955, p.56-64) "organization" and "dichotomy" corollaries focus on the relations between templets/concepts, that fitting one implies that some others are entailed by it and also fit, and some others are negatively entailed, or opposite to it, and do not. He saw a triple of concepts with two in opposition but entailing a common superordinate as a fundamental psychological structure that he termed a *construct*. He saw the relations of entailment and opposition as fundamental constraints upon the meanings being imposed on experience, noting that "no construct ever stands entirely alone; it makes sense only as it appears in a network" (Kelly, 1955, p.304).

The network of constructs used by an individual in a certain role is constitutive of that role and of the individual's actions in behaving in that role

(Shaw, 1985). Kelly models social action in terms of two more corollaries to his fundamental postulate. His "commonality corollary: to the extent that one person employs a construction of experience which is similar to that employed by another, his psychological, processes are similar to those of the other person" (Kelly, 1955, p.90) captures the cognitive commonalities that constitute a culture. His "sociality corollary: to the extent that one person construes the construction processes of another, he may play a role in a social process involving the other person." (Kelly, 1955, p.95) captures the capability to understand another's culture within the framework one's own.

## CONCEPTUAL GRIDS

Kelly developed a method for eliciting the construct system of a person in a particular role or domain that focused on the dimensions of opposition of the constructs significant to acting within that role, the distinctions critical to anticipation in that domain. His method involves the selection of a range of stereotypical elements of experience characterizing the domain, and then eliciting the constructs used to classify those experiences in terms of their similarities and differences. He terms the matrix of elements classified by the constructs a *conceptual grid*, and describes how the network of relations between the constructs can be derived from it as a conceptual model, and how grids may be compared to derive relations between the conceptual models of different people (Kelly, 1955, p.297-308). Kelly's (1955, ch.5) "Role Construct Repertory Test" is a conceptual grid in which the elements are various roles significant in the life of the person being tested, such as "your mother" or "the most interesting person whom you know personally," and his generic conceptual grid has come to be called a "repertory grid" in much of the literature.

His grid technique for eliciting conceptual models became widely used in a wide variety of disciplines such as education (Pope & Keen, 1981), clinical psychology (Kirkcaldy, Pope, & Siefen, 1993), management studies (Tan, Tung, & Xu, 2009; Wright & Cheung, 2007), consumer preferences (Earl, 1986), market research (David & Dale, 2000; Heine, 2009), knowledge modeling (Gaines & Shaw, 1993a; Shaw & Gaines, 1983), expert system development (Boose, 1986; Gaines & Shaw, 1993b) and modeling industrial and scientific communities (Gaines & Shaw, 1994; Shaw & Gaines, 1991a).

Shaw (1978, 1980) computerized conceptual grid elicitation and analysis in the mid-1970s and developed algorithms for their automatic interactive elicitation guided by online analysis, and for their comparison in such a way as to model the cognitive relationships between individuals in a sociocognitive network (Shaw, 1979; Shaw & Gaines, 1989). In 1994, as interactive forms became available on the web, Shaw's conceptual grid tools were reprogrammed as web services (Gaines, 1995; Gaines & Shaw, 1997; Shaw & Gaines, 1996) and have been extensively used to develop conceptual models of distributed online communities.

Conceptual grid services, such as WebGrid 5 (Gaines & Shaw, 2009), now utilize CSS and Javascript to make the elicitation and analysis processes highly customizable and readily integrated with other social network services, and the servers are completely script-driven so that all aspects of the interaction, such as the vocabulary or language used, can be modified for the purposes of particular communities and applications. This enables conceptual modeling to be integrated seamlessly with other activities on social network sites, and be made an integral component of survey methodologies. Since multimedia representations of the elements being construed can be readily incorporated, ongoing analysis is used to prompt the user with suggestions related to their previous entries, and continuously updated conceptual models are available throughout the elicitation,

*Figure 1. Initial screen of conceptual grid elicitation*

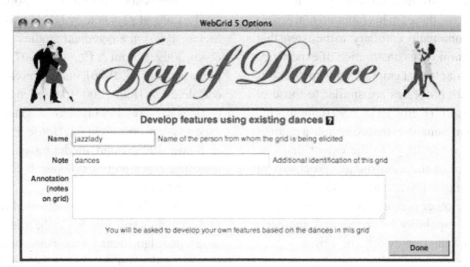

the interactivity and instant gratification expected of the web is well supported.

Details of the psychological foundations, methodology, technology and a range of applications are available elsewhere (Gaines & Shaw, 2009) and are best illustrated for the purposes of this chapter by a brief example as presented in the next section.

## WEBGRID IN ACTION

To illustrate conceptual grid elicitation and analysis we will use an example from a ballroom dance community that coordinates its activities through a web site providing it with an event calendar, bulletin board, interactive blog, photo archives, and so on. The organizing committee wished to poll all members' opinions on some controversial issues regarding the form, content and timing of events but knew from past experience that the response rate would be low and unrepresentative. The webmaster, whose nickname on the community web site was *pasoman*, decided to try and engage more members by incorporating conceptual modeling in an area of general interest in the survey.

He used a generally available WebGrid server and entered an initial grid whose elements were the ten standard international ballroom dances. He used the server's option to register a cache in order to manage the collection of grids from others based on the elements in his grid. He also used the option to customize the styling of the elicitation dialog in such a way that it appeared to be an integral part of the community's web site. He embedded the survey questions of the poll in the dialog in the same way. He then linked the community web site to a url provided by the WebGrid server with a request to all members to respond to the survey, sending the request out by email and through leaflets distributed at the dances also.

Figure 1 shows the first screen of the conceptual grid elicitation being filled in by a member whose nickname on the web site was *jazzlady*.

When she has entered her nickname she clicks "Done" and is taken to the screen shown in Figure 2 where she is presented with three of the dances and asked to distinguish between them. She selects "slow foxtrot" as different from "cha cha" and "jive" because it is very much more difficult to learn, and enters the distinguishing terms "poor dance to learn as a beginner" and "good dance to learn as a beginner."

*Figure 2. Eliciting a distinguishing construct by comparing elements*

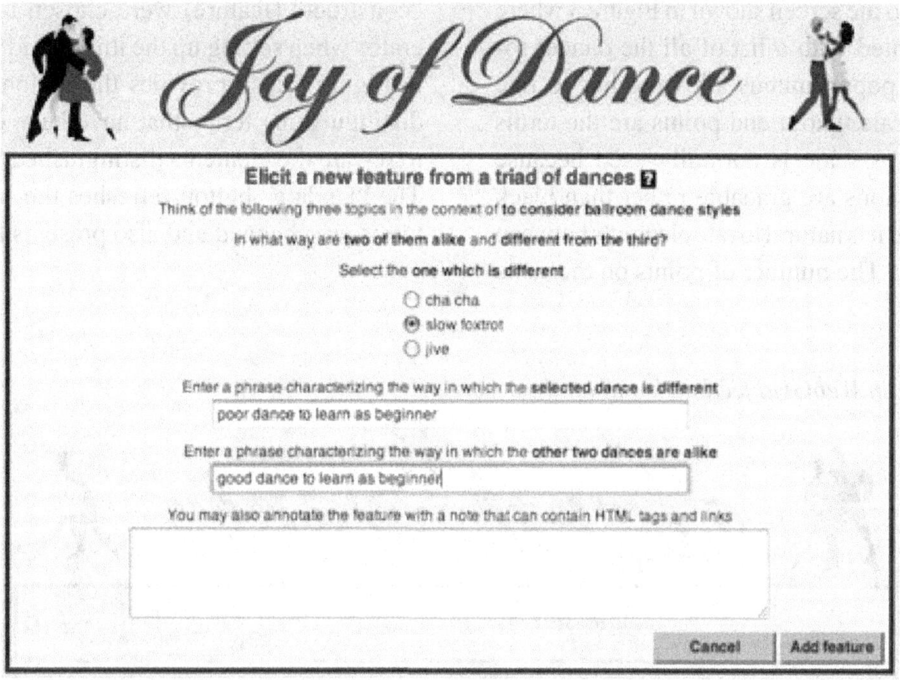

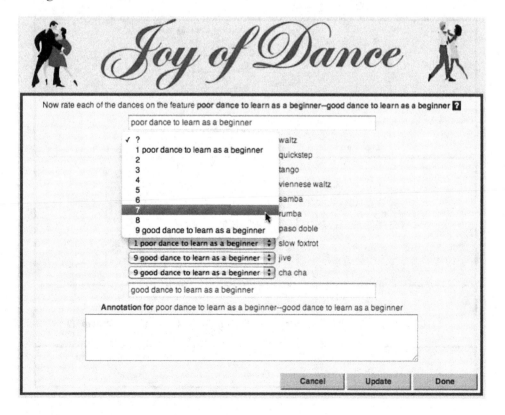

*Figure 3. Rating all the elements*

When she clicks on the "Add feature" button she is taken to the screen shown in Figure 3 where she is presented with a list of all the dances together with popup menus allowing her to rate them on a scale whose end points are the terms she entered. A scale is normally used because most distinctions are gradable rather than black and white and it is natural to rate elements between the extremes. The number of points on the scale and the terms used for "element" (dance) and "construct" (feature) were chosen by the moderator when setting up the initial grid. The screen in Figure 3 also provides the option to edit the distinguishing terms that have been entered and to re-rate the elements distinguished in Figure 2. The "Update" button refreshes the screen if the terms are changed and also presents the element

*Figure 4. Main WebGrid feedback and analysis screen*

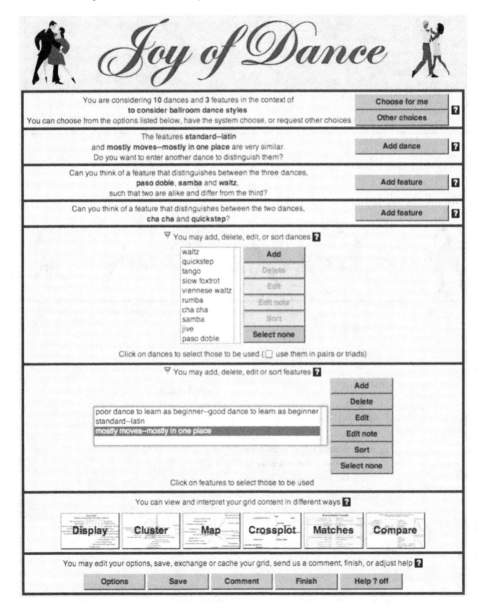

list sorted by the ratings so that the user can see if the rank order is what she intended.

When she clicks "Done" she is taken to a screen similar to that of Figure 2 where she is presented with a new set of elements and asked to enter another construct. After she has entered three constructs she is taken to the screen of Figure 4 which is the main feedback and analysis screen in WebGrid. The centre two sections are lists of the elements and constructs with buttons enabling selected ones to be deleted, edited, and so on. Above them is a variable number of sections generated through the ongoing analysis. For example, if two constructs are very similar the user will be prompted to enter a new element that differentiates between them. Below is a set of analysis options, and below that a set of general options.

To illustrate a conceptual grid, Figure 5 shows the screen when jazzlady clicks on the "Display" button to see the three constructs she has entered.

Figure 6 shows the screen when she is ready to finish after entering another seven constructs. She has also entered two more elements: "bolero" to reduce a match between the constructs "standard—latin and "keep flat —rise and fall", and

"west coast swing" because she enjoys dancing it. There are five options at the top, two of them being based on the online analysis that the elements "tango" and "paso doble", and the constructs "standard—latin" and "mostly moves—mostly in one place", are highly matched. Such matches prompt the entry of additional constructs and elements, respectively, and are what encourages the ongoing elicitation process as the conceptual grid is developed.

At any time during the elicitation process the user can click on one of the analysis buttons and see the conceptual model resulting from the grid that has been entered so far. Figure 7 shows a hierarchical cluster model of jazzlady's construct system generated when she clicks on the "Cluster" button.

In her construct clusters at the top she can see that she uses the constructs, "standard—latin", "heel leads—ball flat", "mostly moves—mostly in one place" and "travels—travels less" to make similar distinctions. In general her constructs are different significant dimensions of the way she construes similarities and differences in the dances of her community.

*Figure 5. Display of initial grid when three constructs have been elicited*

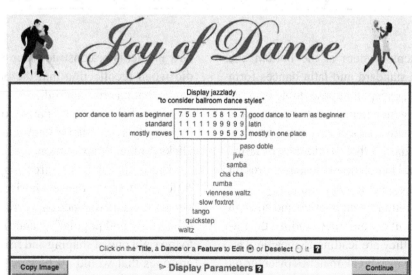

*Figure 6. Main WebGrid screen after eleven constructs have been elicited*

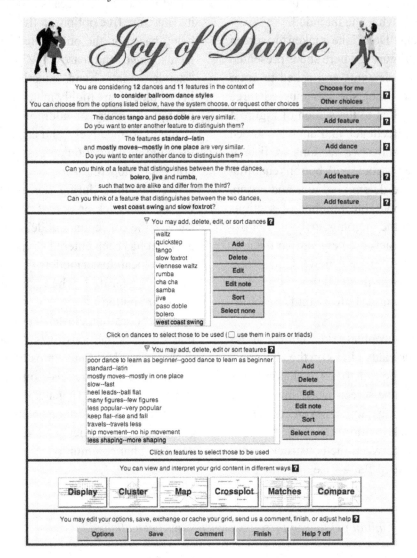

In her element clusters at the bottom she can see that the standard and latin dances form separate clusters, except that paso doble is in the standard cluster which makes sense because it is more similar in many respects to tango (which is classed as "standard") than to the other "latin" dances. In general her element clusters represent those she would expect in her community.

The graphic output is interactive and she can click on an element or construct to adjust the ratings if she feels they are leading to meaningless matches. She can also break matches by entering new elements or constructs, for example, as she did when recollecting that the bolero is a latin dance that has rise and fall,

Figure 8 shows an alternative conceptual model of jazzlady's construct system generated when she clicks on the "Map" button.

There appear to be three major dimensions differentiating the dances: horizontally, the latin versus standard distinction; vertically one of ease of learning and popularity; and from bottom left to top right one of shaping and rise and fall. These are ones that would all be recognized by other

*Figure 7. Hierarchical cluster model of the construct system*

dancers in her community, and the dances are located in a meaningful way in relation to these dimensions.

Figure 9 shows a comparison of jazzlady's construct system with that of pasoman generated when she clicks on the "Compare" button.

WebGrid has taken each construct in jazzlady's system, found the closest match in that of pasoman, and sorted the grids in order of declining matches. At the top right she can see that she and pasoman use the top eight dance constructs "heel leads—ball leads", "standard—latin", and so on, in much the same way, and that what she construes as a "poor dance to learn as a beginner" he construes as "tough to learn basic", and "travels" as "progressive". It seems reasonable that rise and fall is associated with soft dances, and that very popular dances are easy to learn, but pasoman appears to have no construct matching jazzlady's

"many figures—few figures" which contrasts the Viennese waltz with all the other dances.

Jazzlady has enjoyed thinking about the dances that she enjoys in her ballroom dancing, has developed models to explore how she construes them, and has identified the relations between the distinctions she makes in her conceptual framework and those of others. Her experience in doing so has had the usual rich interaction and immediate gratification she expects from the web. She has incidentally learnt to use the WebGrid functionality and would be happy to undertake another grid elicitation on the more controversial topics and choices about which the organizing committee would like to survey members, or to answer those questions directly as part of her WebGrid interaction.

*Figure 8. Principal components model of the construct system*

## PAYBACKS TO INDIVIDUALS AND THE COMMUNITY

The paybacks to individuals in the WebGrid elicitation process come through the ongoing feedback suggesting relations between their constructs and elements using their own terminology, the instant conceptual analysis in graphic form, and the comparisons with others in graphic form. There is also a payback to the community as a whole through the promotion of discussion on the web and the analysis of the entire collection of grids that have been elicited.

Rep 5 (Gaines & Shaw, 2009), the suite of conceptual modeling tools of which WebGrid is part, also contains RepSocio, a tool for analyzing multiple grids. Figure 10 shows a sociocognitive network derived by comparing ten conceptual grids elicited by WebGrid in the same way as that of jazzlady. The measure of overall match

between conceptual models shown at the top right of the comparison in Figure 9 is asymmetric since one person may have constructs that correspond to all those of another but not vice versa. Hence pairwise comparison of a set of grids results in a weighted directed graph.

The socionets tool displays this weighted directed graph, allowing a threshold to be specified such that an edge will only be displayed if the match it represents is at or above that threshold. In Figure 10 the threshold control is at the bottom left and enables a minimum match to be typed in, or the match adjusted by clicking on the arrows to left and right of it to lower the threshold and increase the number of edges shown, or raise it and reduce them. The check box specifies whether the edge weights will be shown on the graph. The graph shown has the threshold set at the highest level at which all nodes are connected.

*Figure 9. Comparison of two construct systems*

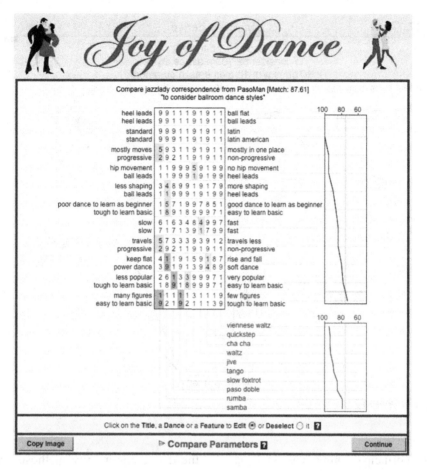

We term the graph a sociocognitive network rather than a social network because it represents the shared meanings (Batchelder, 2002; Fuhse, 2009) between participants in a social network rather than their behavioral interactions. Socio-cognitive network models provides additional information to behavioral studies and, together, the two types of structure provide a multi-dimensional model (Chopra & Wallace, 2000; Krackhardt, 1987) of the social network. For example, the strong mutual linkage of loretta and wallflower in Figure 10 does not indicate they are interacting strongly, but that, if they did so, they would understand one another, at least on the topic of the relations between different dances. The links in a sociocognitive network may correspond to the shared meanings of those who are already

interacting, or the potential or power to interact of those who have not so far done so. Shaw and Gaines (1991b) demonstrated a pre-web system of networked personal computers, *RepGrid-Net*, at CHI'91 designed to allow participants at a conference to discover like-minded participants with whom they were not acquainted based on the elicitation of a sociocognitive network.

RepSocio can also provide a consensual conceptual model for the entire community using a Procrustes analysis technique (Gower & Dijksterhuis, 2004) where everyone's constructs are ranked in terms of the average best match in all other grids. The top ranked constructs are then combined in a conceptual grid that models the distinctions common across the community, termed a *mode* or *consensus grid* (Shaw, 1980).

*Figure 10. Sociocognitive network based on comparisons of conceptual grids*

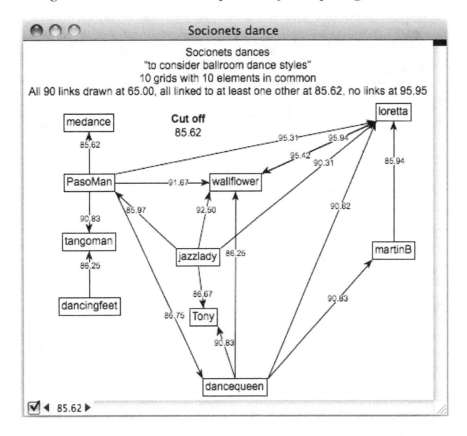

Figure 11 shows a principal components analysis of such a consensus grid derived from ten participants in the dance community study.

It can be seen that there are two major dimensions agreed across the community: one representing the "standard—latin" distinction; and the other the "fast—slow" distinction. These are the primary parameters that a ballroom dance DJ uses in putting a program of dances together, providing a balanced mixture of standard and latin dances, and ensuring that fast and slow dances are interlaced so that not too many of the same type occur closely in sequence. The way the dances themselves cluster in Figure 11 would also make sense to any member of the community.

What is missing from a consensual picture is the idiosyncratic conceptual structures of those individuals or special-interest groups that go beyond the normal consensus, for example, in the dance community of those concerned with the techniques necessary to pass medal tests, or the flair necessary to win competitions. Such sub-cultures can also be derived through use of the RepSocio analyses.

## FUTURE RESEARCH DIRECTIONS

Since the commercialization of the World Wide Web in 1995 the growth of the web and Internet has followed an exponential trajectory and become an integral part of everyday life in western society (Gaines, 2006). There are special interest communities on the web nowadays that did not previously exist, and they operate through new modes of social interaction that are difficult to model within our existing human sciences. These communities create by-products that are generally

*Figure 11. A consensus conceptual model based Procustes analysis of multiple conceptual grids*

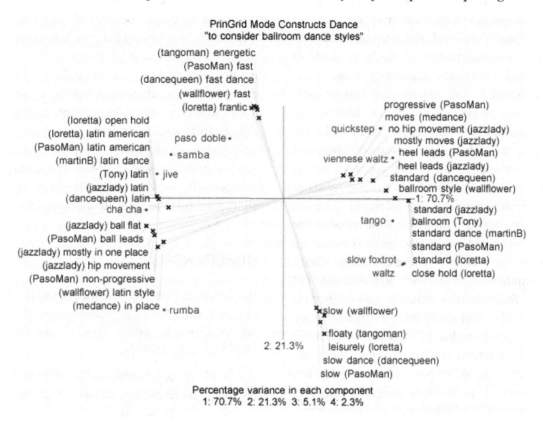

Percentage variance in each component
1: 70.7%  2: 21.3%  3: 5.1%  4: 2.3%

publically available to those who are not part of the community and may be unaware that it exists, and these artifacts are readily accessible as knowledge sources through the powerful search technologies that have co-evolved with the web.

The success of Google's search engine is based on its use of social linkages between web materials to enhance keyword search, and its PageRank (Langville & Meyer, 2006) web mining techniques are analogous to human information retrieval techniques (Griffiths, Steyvers, & Firl, 2007). However, the socio-cognitive foundations of web mining techniques are currently very weak. We do not have adequate theories of communities, their meaning formation processes, and the way that these generate and constrain social action. There is a wealth of relevant material, such as that of Simmel, Dewey, Weber, Kelly, Bourdieu, Gilbert, Weick, Hattiangadi and Goldberg, already cited,

and others such as Mead (1934), Schutz (1943), Wolff (1976) and Tuomela (2007), whose collective works provide a rich framework integrating human meaning, culture and society, but there is, as yet, no comprehensive account that draws on these to provide theoretical foundations on which to base models of web-based communities and associated data mining and modeling techniques.

Thus, one very important future direction for the research area reported in this chapter is to encourage the development of stronger theoretical foundations for human socio-cognitive activities, for example, by making web data mining tools readily accessible to empirical social scientists. Web-based communities provide a rich, instrumented resource of, often post-modern, socio-cognitive phenomena, and collaboration between tool developers, empirical researchers in the human sciences, and theorists developing accounts of human social action could advance the differing research agendas of all those involved.

At a technical level, the integration of conceptual modeling tools with social networking technologies is already beginning to take place, as illustrated in this chapter, but web technology cannot, as yet, support all the functionality that is required for some of the major tools. For example, Rep 5 includes the RepNet conceptual network modeling tools that support *concept mapping* (Gaines & Shaw, 1995) and *semantic network* development and inference (Gaines, 2009), integrated with and complementing the conceptual grid tools. These network modeling tools require interactive graphics similar to those of computer-based drawing applications, but support for interactive drawing in web clients is still primitive and unreliable. When interactive scalable vector graphics (SVG, Campesato, 2004) are fully supported by the mainstream browsers it will be possible to port conceptual network modeling tools to the web, integrate them with the conceptual grid elicitation, and text analysis tools, and provide an even richer environment for sociocognitive inquiry.

Thus, another important future direction for the research area reported in this chapter is to encourage the development of increasingly more effective web-based conceptual modeling tools, to make them an integral component of social networking technology, and to promote standards for the interchange and reuse of the resulting conceptual models.

## CONCLUSION

Sociocognitive inquiry is a framework for targeted studies of the cognitive structures underlying social network activity. It is based on a family of techniques for eliciting conceptual models from web communities through their direct participation in an interactive web-based experience that has immediate payback to those individuals participat-

ing. It complements techniques for passive data mining of the by-products of web-based community activities, allowing the phenomena modeled through data mining to be investigated in greater depth, and provides an attractive alternative to, or component of, conventional web-based surveys. This chapter has outlined the relevant background in cognitive sociology and psychology, provided a case study to illustrate how web-based conceptual modeling services can be customized to integrate with social networking sites, and highlighted some significant directions for future research.

## REFERENCES

Batchelder, E. (2002). Comparing three simultaneous measurements of a sociocognitive network. *Social Networks*, *24*(3), 261–277. doi:10.1016/S0378-8733(02)00007-2

Berry, M. W., & Castellanos, M. (Eds.). (2008). *Survey of Text Mining II: Clustering, Classification, and Retrieval*. New York: Springer.

Bolton, R., & Saxena-Iyer, S. (2009). Interactive services: a framework, synthesis and research directions. *Journal of Interactive Marketing*, *23*(1), 91–104. doi:10.1016/j.intmar.2008.11.002

Boose, J. H. (1986). *Expertise Transfer for Expert System Design*. Amsterdam: Elsevier.

Bourdieu, P. (1989). *The Logic of Practice*. Cambridge: Polity.

Brüggen, E., & Dholakia, U. M. (2010). Determinants of participation and response effort in web panel surveys. *Journal of Interactive Marketing*, *24*(3), 239–250. doi:10.1016/j.intmar.2010.04.004

Campesato, O. (2004). *Fundamentals of SVG Programming*. Hingham, MA: Charles River Media.

Chopra, K., & Wallace, W. A. (2000). Modeling relationships among multiple graphical structures. *Computational & Mathematical Organization Theory*, *6*(4), 361–379. doi:10.1023/A:1009658313423

Couper, M. P., & Miller, P. V. (2008). Web survey methods. *Public Opinion Quarterly, 72*(5), 831–835. doi:10.1093/poq/nfn066

David, M., & Dale, L. (2000). Repertory grid technique, an interpretive research framework. *European Journal of Marketing, 34*(7), 816–834. doi:10.1108/03090560010331261

Dewey, J. (1910). *How We Think*. Boston: Heath. doi:10.1037/10903-000

Dewey, J. (1911). Causation. In P. Monroe (Ed.), *A Cyclopedia of Education (Dewey Middle Works 6)* (pp. 38). New York: The Macmillan company.

Dhar, V., & Chang, E. A. (2009). Does chatter matter? The impact of user-generated content on music sales. *Journal of Interactive Marketing, 23*(4), 300–307. doi:10.1016/j.intmar.2009.07.004

Earl, P. E. (1986). *Lifestyle Economics: Consumer Behavior in a Turbulent World*. New York: St. Martin's Press.

Feldman, R., & Sanger, J. (Eds.). (2007). *The Text Mining Handbook: Advanced Approaches in Analyzing Unstructured Data*. Cambridge: Cambridge University Press.

Fortun, M., & Bernstein, H. J. (1998). *Muddling Through: Pursuing Science and Truths in the 21st Century*. Washington: Counterpoint.

Fuhse, J. A. (2009). The meaning structure of social networks. *Sociological Theory, 27*(1), 51–73. doi:10.1111/j.1467-9558.2009.00338.x

Gaines, B. R. (1994). The collective stance in modeling expertise in individuals and organizations. *International Journal of Expert Systems, 7*(1), 21–51.

Gaines, B. R. (1995). Porting interactive applications to the web *4th International World Wide Web Conference Tutorial Notes* (pp. 199-217). Sebastopol, CA: O'Reilly.

Gaines, B. R. (2003). Organizational knowledge acquisition. In Holsapple, C. W. (Ed.), *Handbook on Knowledge Management: 1* (pp. 317–347). Berlin: Springer.

Gaines, B. R. (2006). The learning curves underlying convergence. *Technological Forecasting and Social Change, 57*(1-2), 7–34. doi:10.1016/S0040-1625(97)00078-4

Gaines, B. R. (2009). Designing visual languages for description logics. *Journal of Logic Language and Information, 18*(2), 217–250. doi:10.1007/s10849-008-9078-1

Gaines, B. R. (2010). Human rationality challenges universal logic. *Logica Universalis, 4*(2), 163–205. doi:10.1007/s11787-010-0019-9

Gaines, B. R., Chen, L. L.-J., & Shaw, M. L. G. (1997). Modeling the human factors of scholarly communities supported through the Internet and World Wide Web. *Journal of the American Society for Information Science American Society for Information Science, 48*(11), 987–1003. doi:10.1002/(SICI)1097-4571(199711)48:11<987::AID-ASI3>3.0.CO;2-Y

Gaines, B. R., & Shaw, M. L. G. (1989). Comparing the conceptual systems of experts *Proceedings of the Eleventh International Joint Conference on Artificial Intelligence* (pp. 633-638). San Mateo, California: Morgan Kaufmann.

Gaines, B. R., & Shaw, M. L. G. (1993a). Basing knowledge acquisition tools in personal construct psychology. *The Knowledge Engineering Review, 8*(1), 49–85. doi:10.1017/S0269888900000060

Gaines, B. R., & Shaw, M. L. G. (1993b). Eliciting knowledge and transferring it effectively to a knowledge-based systems. *IEEE Transactions on Knowledge and Data Engineering, 5*(1), 4–14. doi:10.1109/69.204087

Gaines, B. R., & Shaw, M. L. G. (1994). Using knowledge acquisition and representation tools to support scientific communities *AAAI'94: Proceedings of the Twelfth National Conference on Artificial Intelligence* (pp. 707-714). Menlo Park, California: AAAI Press/MIT Press.

Gaines, B. R., & Shaw, M. L. G. (1995). Concept maps as hypermedia components. *International Journal of Human-Computer Studies*, *43*(3), 323–361. doi:10.1006/ijhc.1995.1049

Gaines, B. R., & Shaw, M. L. G. (1997). Knowledge acquisition, modeling and inference through the World Wide Web. *International Journal of Human-Computer Studies*, *46*(6), 729–759. doi:10.1006/ijhc.1996.0122

Gaines, B. R., & Shaw, M. L. G. (2007). *WebGrid evolution through four generations 1994-2007* (No. TR-2007-WG): http://cpsc.ucalgary.ca/~gaines/reports/.

Gaines, B. R., & Shaw, M. L. G. (2009). *Rep 5 Manuals*: Centre for Person-Computer Studies, http://repgrid.com.

Gaines, B. R., & Shaw, M. L. G. (2010). Computer aided constructivism. In P. Caputi & L. Viney (Eds.), *Constructivist Methods* (pp. to appear). New York: Wiley.

Gilbert, M. (1992). *On Social Facts*. Princeton, N.J.: Princeton University Press.

Goldberg, S. (2010). *Relying on Others: An Essay in Epistemology*. Oxford: Oxford University Press.

Gower, J. C. (1966). Some distance properties of latent root and vector methods used in multivariate analysis. *Biometrika*, *53*, 325–338.

Gower, J. C., & Dijksterhuis, G. B. (2004). *Procrustes Problems*. Oxford: Oxford University Press. doi:10.1093/acprof:oso/9780198510581.001.0001

Greenfield, S. (2008). *I.D.: The Quest for Meaning in the 21st Century*. London: Hodder & Stoughton.

Griffiths, T. L., Steyvers, M., & Firl, A. (2007). Google and the mind. *Psychological Science*, *18*, 1069–1076. doi:10.1111/j.1467-9280.2007.02027.x

Hattiangadi, J. N. (1987). *How is Language Possible?: Philosophical Reflections on the Evolution of Language and Knowledge*. La Salle: Open Court.

Heerwegh, D., & Loosveldt, G. (2008). Face-to-face versus web surveying in a high-Internet-coverage population. *Public Opinion Quarterly*, *72*(5), 836–846. doi:10.1093/poq/nfn045

Heine, K. (2009). Using personal and online repertory grid methods for the development of a luxury brand personality. *Electronic Journal of Business Research Methods*, *7*(1), 25–38.

Hoffman, D. L., & Novak, T. P. (2009). Flow online: lessons learned and future prospects. *Journal of Interactive Marketing*, *23*(1), 23–34. doi:10.1016/j.intmar.2008.10.003

Hume, D. (1888). *A Treatise of Human Nature*. Oxford: Clarendon Press.

Kelly, G. A. (1955). *The Psychology of Personal Constructs*. New York: Norton.

Kirkcaldy, B., Pope, M., & Siefen, G. (1993). Sociogrid analysis of a child and adolescent psychiatric clinic. *Social Psychiatry and Psychiatric Epidemiology*, *28*(6), 296–303. doi:10.1007/BF00795911

Krackhardt, D. (1987). Cognitive social structures. *Social Networks*, *9*(2), 109–134. doi:10.1016/0378-8733(87)90009-8

Langville, A. N., & Meyer, C. D. (2006). *Google's PageRank and Beyond: The Science of Search Engine Rankings*. Princeton, N.J.: Princeton University Press.

Manfreda, K. L., Bosnjak, M., Berzelak, J., Haas, I., & Vehovar, V. (2008). Web surveys versus other survey modes: a meta-analysis comparing response rates. *International Journal of Market Research*, *50*(1), 79–104.

Mead, G. H. (1934). *Mind, Self & Society From the Standpoint of a Social Behaviorist*. Chicago: University of Chicago Press.

Pope, M. L., & Keen, T. R. (1981). *Personal Construct Psychology and Education*. London: Academic Press.

Resnick, L. B., Levine, J. M., & Teasley, S. D. (1991). *Perspectives on Socially Shared Cognition*. Washington: American Psychological Association. doi:10.1037/10096-000

Scarpi, D. (2010). Does size matter? An examination of small and large web-based brand communities. *Journal of Interactive Marketing*, *24*(1), 14–21. doi:10.1016/j.intmar.2009.10.002

Schütz, A. (1943). The problem of rationality in the social world. *Economica*, *10*(38), 130–149. doi:10.2307/2549460

Shaw, M. L. G. (1978). Interactive computer programs for eliciting personal models of the world. In Fransella, F. (Ed.), *Personal Construct Psychology 1977* (pp. 59–67). London: Academic Press.

Shaw, M. L. G. (1979). Conversational heuristics for eliciting shared understanding. *International Journal of Man-Machine Studies*, *11*, 621–634. doi:10.1016/S0020-7373(79)80012-7

Shaw, M. L. G. (1980). *On Becoming a Personal Scientist: Interactive Computer Elicitation of Personal Models of the World*. London: Academic Press.

Shaw, M. L. G. (1985). Communities of knowledge. In Epting, F., & Landfield, A. W. (Eds.), *Anticipating Personal Construct Psychology* (pp. 25–35). Lincoln, Nebraska: University of Nebraska Press.

Shaw, M. L. G., & Gaines, B. R. (1983). A computer aid to knowledge engineering *Proceedings of British Computer Society Conference on Expert Systems* (pp. 263-271). Cambridge: British Computer Society.

Shaw, M. L. G., & Gaines, B. R. (1989). Comparing conceptual structures: consensus, conflict, correspondence and contrast. *Knowledge Acquisition*, *1*(4), 341–363. doi:10.1016/S1042-8143(89)80010-X

Shaw, M. L. G., & Gaines, B. R. (1991a). Extending electronic mail with conceptual modeling to provide group decision support *COCS'91: Proceedings of Conference on Organizational Computing Systems* (pp. 153-158). New York: ACM Press.

Shaw, M. L. G., & Gaines, B. R. (1991b). Supporting personal networking through computer networking *Proceedings of CHI'91: Human Factors in Computing Systems* (pp. 437-438). New York: ACM Publications.

Shaw, M. L. G., & Gaines, B. R. (1996). WebGrid: knowledge elicitation and modeling on the web. In Maurer, H. (Ed.), *Proceedings of WebNet96* (pp. 425–432). Charlottesville, VA: Association for the Advancement of Computing in Education. doi:10.1007/978-1-4471-0351-6_21

Simmel, G. (1910). How is Society Possible? *American Journal of Sociology*, *16*(3), 372–391. doi:10.1086/211904

Slater, P. (Ed.). (1976). *Dimensions of Intrapersonal Space* (*Vol. 1*). London: John Wiley.

Slater, P. (Ed.). (1977). *Dimensions of Intrapersonal Space* (*Vol. 2*). London: John Wiley.

Tan, F. B., Tung, L.-L., & Xu, Y. (2009). A study of web-designers' criteria for effective business-to-consumer (b2c) websites using the repertory grid technique. *Journal of Electronic Commerce Research*, *10*(3), 155–177.

Tuomela, R. (2007). *The Philosophy of Sociality: The Shared Point of View*. Oxford: Oxford University Press.

Weber, M. (1968). *Economy and Society: An Outline of Interpretive Sociology*. New York: Bedminster Press.

Weick, K. E. (1995). *Sensemaking in Organizations*. Thousand Oaks, CA: Sage.

Wolff, K. H. (1976). *Surrender and Catch: Experience and Inquiry Today*. Dordrecht: Reidel.

Wright, R. P., & Cheung, F. K. K. (2007). Articulating appraisal system effectiveness based on managerial cognitions. *Personnel Review*, *36*(2), 206–230. doi:10.1108/00483480710726118

## ADDITIONAL READING

A good entry point for the background sociological literature is Gilbert's (1992) book *On Social Facts* which, while primarily targeted on her arguments for treating collectives as individuals, also surveys the relevant sociological literature. The collective stance she advocates is a useful framework for data mining in social networks and the extended web version of (Gaines, 1994) illustrates its applicability to many aspects of information technology. Good introductions to collective sense-making and knowledge processes in organization are provided in (Weick, 1995) and (Gaines, 2003).

An open access WebGrid 5 service is accessible at http://gigi.cpsc.ucalgary.ca:2000

For those primarily interested in using the tools described, or implementing similar ones:

Relevant papers and reports are available http://cpsc.ucalgary.ca/~gaines/reports/

The psychological foundations and computational algorithms underlying the WebGrid software have not been detailed in this paper because the focus has been on their application to sociocognitive inquiry. The psychological background is still best provided by Kelly's (1955) book on *Personal Construct Psychology*. A concise introduction with a computational slant is provided in (Gaines & Shaw, 2010). WebGrid development is described in (Gaines & Shaw, 2007). The algorithms for conceptual grid elicitation, clustering, matching, sociocognitive network production and consensus mode grids are in (Shaw, 1980), and those for principal components analysis in (Gower, 1966; Slater, 1976, 1977).

The software manuals and tutorials for Rep 5 and WebGrid are accessible at http://repgrid.com

## KEY TERMS AND DEFINITIONS

**Community:** A collection of agents each of whom construes themselves as a member of the community, and usually manifesting other common construing constituting the *culture* of the community.

**Concept Network:** Concepts do not stand alone but are embedded in a network of logical relations with other concepts: *entailment*, that fitting one concept implies that others also fit; and *opposition*, that fitting one concept implies that others do not fit.

**Concept:** A templet that an agents fits to a new experience in order to be able to match it to past experiences and hence anticipate unknown aspects of the new experience from known aspects of the old.

**Conceptual Grid:** A matrix for an individual or community of the concepts that they have fitted to a set of elements of experience, often termed a *repertory grid*.

**Construct:** A minimal concept network that Kelly saw as the basic psychological structure with which we classify experience in which two concepts in opposition both entail a third constituting their range of applicability or *relevance*.

**Construe:** The constructive process of making experience meaningful, often termed *cognition*.

**Meaning:** The conceptual structure that an agent fits to an experience and interprets as making that experience meaningful.

**Rep 5:** A suite of conceptual modeling tools based on personal construct psychology.

**Sociocognitive Network:** A weighted directed graph with agents as nodes that models the commonality of construing between them.

**Sociocognitive:** Pertaining to the construing of a community, its sub-communities and its members.

**WebGrid:** A component of Rep 5 that provides a user interface to many of the tools through a web client, allowing them to be used both locally and over an intranet or the Internet.

# Chapter 4

# Community Discovery:
## From Web Pages to Social Networks

**Damien Leprovost**
*University of Bourgogne, France*

**Lylia Abrouk**
*University of Bourgogne, France*

**David Gross-Amblard**
*University of Bourgogne, France*

## ABSTRACT

*This chapter presents a state of the art of research on the discovery of Web communities, in a general sense. For this purpose, the authors discuss various notions of communities and their related assumptions: hypertextual communities, tag communities and semantic-based communities.*

## COMMUNITY DISCOVERY: FROM WEB PAGES TO SOCIAL NETWORKS

During the past ten years, the Web has turned into an open collaborative system, often called Web 2.0, where anyone can provide information to others using publishing tools such as forums, blogs and wikis. The Web 2.0 also contains social web sites like Myspace, Facebook or Flickr, where people can annotate third-party information with tags. Various kinds of people use these collaborative systems, ranging from simple visitors to experts of a discussion topic.

From the huge amount of the resulting web pages one can observe emerging structures, forming communities of topics. Similarly, social networks enable to build communities of people, according to their friendship or common interests. A natural challenge for the next decade is to discover and exploit these communities.

This survey presents a state of the art of Web communities emergence, and is organized as follows. The first section discusses the concept of communities and their related assumptions, and presents our analysis method. The subsequent

DOI: 10.4018/978-1-61350-513-7.ch004

sections support the resulting classification: hypertextual communities, tag-based communities, social networks and semantic communities. The last section concludes.

## Communities and Social Networks

What is a community? Indeed, community is an ambiguous term with over 120 definitions noted by Poplin (1979). According to the Wikipedia entry[1] on communities, "*A community is a group of interacting organisms sharing a populated environment. In human communities, intent, belief, resources, preferences, needs, risks, and a number of other conditions may be present and common, affecting the identity of the participants and their degree of cohesiveness*". In this survey, we consider that a community is a virtual group of interacting entities (a web page, a user, etc.) sharing something or having something in common, each entity being identified in some way (by an URL or a UID). From there, we can distinguish between web pages communities and social networks. More specifically, a social network is a social structure made up of individuals (or organizations) called nodes, which are connected by one or more specific types of interdependency, such as friendship, kinship, common interest, financial exchange, emotional relationships, knowledge, and so on. Hence, a social network is a specific type of community, where relations are explicit, declared (or assumed) by its members.

## First Movement: From Implicit to Explicit Communities

As illustrated by the social network example, there is a historical and natural movement on the Internet from implicit communities to explicit ones. This operation of community discovery is the hard goal of many organizations. We can illustrate this proposition by two scenarios:

- **Web pages community discovery:** due to its openness, the Web allowed a huge number of users for producing content, according to a agreed format, HTML. Hence users or organizations first produced content, regardless of its classification or accessibility. Since group of web pages addressing the same topics were hard to find, a first step toward expliciting communities was registration: that is the effort of declaring a web site to an authority, like DMOZ[2], Lycos[3], or Yahoo! Directory[4]. A second step was the use of automatic content analysis to identify topics of interest. Finally, a great success was obtained by combining this content analysis with the examination of explicit web links between pages (Kleinberg, 1998; Brin & Page, 1998).

- **Social community discovery:** as a communication artifact, the Internet naturally hosts social communications. Being part of a thematic mailing list is an example of an explicit community. Similarly, several systems ask users to fulfill detailed profiles to find their matching partners. These approaches, not covered in the present survey, suffer from the hindrance of profile typing, often neglected by users. More recently, registering on a social network, applying for a group and making its friendship relations explicit are other examples. But systems like Facebook[5] are actively analyzing this explicit social graph to discover and suggest new friends to a given user. This way, the social network is expanding from a hidden, implicit state to an explicit one.

The evolution of these notions of communities therefore illustrates a movement from implicit communities to explicit ones. It is not a transformation, but rather the continuous inclusion of unknown or not understood preexisting elements.

## Second Movement: From Structural to Semantic Communities

A second point of view is to classify communities according to the key features that lead to their detection. This classification suggests that the evolution of the community notion have been influenced by heterogeneity concerns. Indeed, an interesting parallel can be drawn with the evolution of database integration techniques, where several types of heterogeneity were identified such as: structural heterogeneity (managing files without a common storage format), schematic heterogenicity (merging databases with distinct schemas) or semantic heterogeneity (comparing data with close meanings, like synonyms). Similarly, the structural heterogeneity of information on the Internet was severely reduced by the global acceptance of the unifying HTML format and HTTP protocol. Basic thematic communities can then emerge, as their content is now uniformly accessible. Based on the unifying format and one of its key components, the hyperlink, hypertextual communities can be analyzed. The on-going deployment of XHTML and XML is tackling the schematic mismatch between pages: for example the RSS or ATOM formats are becoming the de-facto standard for news aggregation. Each of these formats can be translated into the other in a transparent way. Finally ontology-based languages and techniques lead to a better understanding of pages content, and reduce semantic ambiguities like language mismatches, synonymy and so forth.

The chosen layout for this survey follows this second movement: we begin by purely structural analysis of web pages and end by semantic-based analysis. In each section, we distinguish between the explicit and implicit information provided by pages or users.

## Hypertext Communities

Hypertext communities are the oldest concept of Web communities that have been formulated,

long before the advent of dynamic content, and notions like social Web, collaborative Web, etc. These communities are communities of Web pages, but their analysis can also apply to communities of people linking to each other. We can distinguish between purely topological methods and content-based topological methods.

### Purely Topological Methods

Selman et al. (1997) introduce the notion of the referral Web: they consider that the Web major issue not to "find information" but rather to devise "who has the best information". This assumption is indeed the major growing problem of Web. They construct a social community by finding co-occurrences of names on Web pages, which transcribe a social relationship. From this network, they allow to find experts who are able to satisfy at best any query.

Analysis of communities in this first setting relies on the existence of hyperlinks between pages. Various techniques analyze the topology of links to define so-called hubs and authorities (as (Kleinberg, 1998 & Dourisboure, 2007), or exploits the maximum flow passing through web links to determine the inner edges of a community (for example (Flake, 2000 & Imafuji, 2002).

Gibson, Kleinberg and Raghavan (1998, 2002) develop a notion of hyperlinked communities on the WWW through an analysis of the link topology. These communities can be viewed as containing a core of central pages, called "authoritative pages", linked together by "hub pages". They propose an algorithmic formulation of this notion of authorities and hubs, called HITS. It consist in an iterative discovery algorithm that crawls a provided set of web pages and analyzes their hypertext links. A *hub page* is a page that links to many pages. An *authority page* is a page that is linked by many hubs. HITS can be considered as the first major definition of web communities. In this approach, only links between pages are used, but not their content. It is therefore a purely topological approach. According to this, a community can be seen as a set of hub pages and authority pages, linked together, about one topic. It is not strictly a community, but rather a nebulous set: HITS gives a principal community but also surrounding communities related to this principal, from pages that have a similar topic to the principal community.

Based on Kleinberg's approach, Flake et al. (2000) propose a new formal definition of a community as a set of web pages $S$ that are more interlinked from inside $S$ than from outside. They rely on hubs and authorities detected by HITS as the starting point of their community discovery. A community $S$ is first a hub page. Then, pages that can be reached in one hop are considered for addition in $S$. A new page is added if its addition to $S$ does not increase the shortest path between each page in $S$ beyond a preset threshold.

The authors pinpoint the need to compute point-to-point shortest paths throughout the graph, which is a strong requirement at the Web scale. They use the classical max flow - min cut theorem, which proves that the maximum flow of a network between two ends is identical to the minimum cut. It thus becomes possible to analyze the graph sequentially, and to realize the desired partitioning. The authors propose an algorithm called Incremental Shortest Augmentation (ISA) to this end. However, this Manichean approach does not allow for assessing the relative proximity to a community.

Following the work of G. Flake et al, Imafuji et al. (2002) identify the main weaknesses of this previous method, which is its sensitivity to the starting vertices. The authors propose to consider the origin of a community as a mobile vertex, which is moved in order to reduce the influence of massively linking pages and to avoid unnecessary iterations. Based on the same assumptions as the work of Flake et al., this contribution can be seen as a technical improvement of the previous method, but still with a Manichean flavor.

Girvan et al. (2002) highlight the community structure between pages. The communities are

described as dense clusters, which are linked together by looser connections, called *bridges*, forming meta-communities. They argue that the knowledge of these relationships between communities allows for a better understanding of the latter. Based on the work of Freeman [Fre77], they generalize the concept of "*vertex betweenness*", as a measure of the centrality and influence of a node in a network, to the concept of "*edge betweenness*", as the number of shortest paths that pass through those bridges. They propose an algorithm that removes edges with the highest edge betweenness, in order to isolate communities, thereby revealing the bridges ("*axis cowards*") that bind communities together, creating the meta-community structure. This approach breaks with the binary vision of dense and loose communities. Indeed, endless levels of imbrications of (meta-) communities can be envisioned. The main obstacle to this method is that it requires a complete knowledge of the network to assess its structure, and that it suffers a $\Omega(n^3)$ running time.

Ino et al. (2005) define a stricter concept of web communities than Flake et al.'s. Indeed, Flake et al. define an internal node of the graph of a community as a node having at least as many edges to the inside of the community as to the outside. But it is possible in many cases to find numbers of nodes of the frontal community that can be stated as being both inside and outside the community. The authors call FLG communities (for Flake, Lawrence and Giles) those communities resulting from this definition. Then they distinguish between two types of communities, based on stricter definitions:

- IKN-weak communities, which are FLG communities where any node has at least as much edges to the outside of community than to the inside.
- IKN communities, which are IKN-weak communities where any interior node has strictly more edges to the inside of a community that to the outside.

This definition of IKN communities reduces the border ambiguity of FLG communities. From a computational point of view, the existing solution proposed by Flake et al. using a maximum flow algorithm can be adapted to explore IKN-weak communities. However, the discovery of IKN communities is NP-complete.

Lozano et al. (2006) propose a method for detecting communities across large networks. To avoid computing on a complete graph, which is an obvious impediment, the authors use a divide-and-conquer method. Starting from the graph, vertices are split into two random subgraphs. Then, vertices are exchanges from one graph to another in order to reduce a *stress* function, which is a function of the number of inward and outward edges between the subgraphs. Once the stress is minimized, the algorithm is applied recursively on each subgraph. When the stress reaches a stable state, the obtained decomposition represents the intended communities. The main advantage of this method is that it discovers the graph gradually, during computation, which is a suited property for a potentially infinite network. Its main limitation is the dependency of this method to its starting point: if the dense communities are still well identified, the "hierarchy of communities" resulting from the recursive application of the method depends directly from the starting point of computation.

## Content-Based Topological Methods

Dourisboure et al. (2007) aim to detect and classify communities on the Web, following a hypertext-oriented approach. In this case, a community is defined as a dense subgraph of the overall graph. Specifically, communities are almost-dense bipartite graphs, structured in centers and fans. A subject or topic is identified for centers, and fans refer to these centers. To detect these communities, the authors propose an extraction algorithm in two steps: definition of similarity, and refinement. The first step consists in analyzing the Web graph. For each pair of vertices joined by an edge,

their content is analyzed to determine their degree of similarity.

This value is recorded on the concerned arc. For each arc addition, an iterative refinement is operated. It aims at removing arcs of low degree, to increase the average level of the community. Once the subgraph is virtually isolated from the rest of the graph and there are no more arcs to remove, the stated maximum refinement is reached and iteration stops. Once communities are extracted in this way, the authors partition the results, to reconcile each subgraph to a given subject. They are interested also in possible duplication of parts of different sub-bipartite graphs, to highlight communities that share their centers, or their fans. Their operating tool is publicly available.

In this classification of hypertext relations on the Web, the ability to detect interactions between communities (sharing center or fans) can provide valuable information that could prove useful in interpreting the future development of communities. A shared center could then be explained as a merge before or after a split, shared fans as a possible vector for transfer of community, etc. However, by the nature of the cleaning algorithm, this method is very effective to detect and classify dense communities, but cope poorly with sparse or less closed communities.

Yolum et al. (2003) propose a definition of Web communities close to the sociological view. They also define referral systems, as a network where elements share recommendations about other elements.

## Tag Communities

Tag communities are tag-based clusters of documents or users, depending of the tagging activity of users. It is often associated with notions of taxonomy or folksonomy. This type of annotation often suffers from a significant lack of structure, which can be a hindrance to direct interpretation, and requires more semantic understanding. Most approaches of tag communities discovery improve on techniques to compute the similarity of resources (Cattuto, 2008 & Kim, 2009).

Cattuto (2008) and al. seek to highlight a community structure by the work of the tagging activity of users. They compute a measure of resource distance based on the collective tagging activity. Starting from each unrelated distinct tag, they aim at computing tag-clouds around them using methods such as TF-IDF on a set of resources annotated by the same starting tag.

An interesting aspect of this work is that it highlights relationships between tags, that do not exist initially. That boils down to generating an early semantic relationship between tags, and this without any semantic analysis, thus without a knowledge base. We see this as an emerging understanding of the "knowledge base of the Web".

Kim and al. (2009) focus on tag systems of musical resources. They provide a statement of unequal work on these resources, where a minimum of songs concentrates a maximum of tags, leaving a vast majority of resources with little or no tag. It is therefore proposed to solve this problem of lack of information by automatic propagation of tags resources, exploiting the similarity of the artists responsible for these resources. To compute similarities between artists, the authors propose four methods of filling matrix similarity: collaborative filtering, social tags (redundant shared tags), web documents (artists similarity through Google eyes), and content analysis. Then, they use the detected similarities to propagate tags on the resources that are lacking.

The authors propose several types of semantic research, both internal (through user activity) and external (interpretation of Google results). Besides the advantage of combining the results in order to complete the analysis, this work also compares response profiles of each method, to judge their relative relevance. Thus, the authors found that the interpretation of user activity seems a more faithful witness, when their numbers are sufficient, although this character may seem at first glance unreliable because non-objective. A search of

the nearest neighbor seems a reliable method for interpreting the obtained similarity matrix, but it may be necessary to implement a limit. Indeed, it is possible that a resource is far from all of its peers, can we then say that it is semantically close to the resource, which it is closest mathematically?

## Semantic Communities

Following the recent formalisms of the Semantic Web, Semantic-based community is a new step in the conceptualization of communities. Due to a semantic analysis of content, users or resources are clustered according to their proximity in the used ontologies. In this way, some techniques use semantic analysis of relationship in a social network (Jung, 2007), or extract their own ontology from the target network ([HMNT09]).

Jung et al. (2007) define a semantic social network as a three-layered model, based as a stack of strongly interlinked networks:

- **A Social network:** relating people on the basis of common interests;
- **An Ontology network:** relating ontologies on the basis of explicit import relationships or implicit similarity;
- **A Concept network:** relating concepts on the basis of explicit ontological relationships or implicit similarity.

Haase et al. (2004) propose peer-to-peer routing strategies in a system where every peer describes his content, relative to a common ontology, shared by all peers in the network. A peer knows about the expertise of other peer's, through their messages or given explicitly. In this way, they are able to properly forward query to the righteous peer. However, the entire analysis is based on a joint use of a single ontology, which must be specific to the intended domain, and commonly adopted by peers.

Amer Yahia et al. (2009) define the notion of a Social Content Site, as a traditional content site (a website on which users manipulate contents), which has integrated social network features. They define this notion as a significant new trend on the Web, and propose to tackle the new challenge of information management and discovery over such sites. SocialScope is the name of an architecture proposal for exploiting information form Social Content Sites. Its purpose is to obtain data from social content sites, extract relevant information and then, use it to improve community comprehension. At its core is the social content graph, which represents users, objects, and various connections among them. Information in the graph may be locally owned (e.g., destinations in Y!Travel), externally integrated (e.g., friendship connection obtained from Facebook) or derived (e.g., links describing similarities between users). Social-Scope is organized into three layers: Information Discovery which incorporates social information from remote sites, Content Management which provides social content subgraphs relevant to a given user and query, and Information Presentation which provides a comprehensive result exploration framework.

Presented as a kind of standard, SocialScope aims at providing a generic way to manage social information. But rather than considering communities as the goal of the analysis, they are used as a way to recommend content to users, considering a given query. This approach may be reductive for the notion of community, because here it is objective and absolute, and not dependent on any analysis criterion.

## CONCLUSION

The collaborative Web aims at transforming users into contributors. One of the main aspects of this new Web is a social network to connect persons, generally based on people interests. Several techniques are used to create communities. We presented in this survey a state of the art of Web communities emergence. We defined the concept of a community and the evolution of the community notions from implicit to explicit ones. Our classification is based on the evolution from the structural to the semantic Web.

The main benefit of all approaches is to improve user experience: from a user who adapts to the Web, to the Web that adapts to the user. And more, it allows taking maximum advantage of new information derived from the behavior of users. This means time savings for people, efficiency gain for companies (with better customer targeting), and so on.

Future development of community emergence should slash the void between heterogeneous systems, in order to consider the user activity is as a global task on the Web, not only on focused domains.

## ACKNOWLEDGMENT

This work was partially funded by the French National Research Agency (ANR) grant Neuma (http://www.neuma.fr), by the European Research Council under the European Community's Seventh Framework Programme (FP7/2007-2013) / ERC grant Webdam, agreement 226513 (http://webdam.inria.fr), and by the Bourgogne Regional councils JCE grant.

## REFERENCES

Alani, H., Dasmahapatra, S., O'Hara, K., & Shadbolt, N. (2002). Identifying communities of practice through ontology network analysis. *IEEE Intelligent Systems*, *18*(2), 18–25. doi:10.1109/MIS.2003.1193653

Amer-Yahia, S., Lakshmanan, L., & Yu, C. (2009). SocialScope: Enabling Information Discovery on Social Content Sites. *CIDR'09: Proceedings of the biennial Conference on Innovative Data Systems Research.*

Brin, S. & Page, L. (1998). The anatomy of a large-scale hypertextual Web search engine. *Computer Networks and ISDN Systems, 30*(1–7), pp. 107–117.

Cattuto, C., Baldassarri, A., Servedio, V., & Loreto, V. (2008). Emergent Community Structure in Social Tagging Systems. [ACS]. *Advances in Complex Systems, 11*(04), 597–608. doi:10.1142/S0219525908001817

Dourisboure, Y., Geraci, F., & Pellegrini, M. (2007). Extraction and classification of dense communities in the Web. *WWW '07: Proceedings of the 16th international conference on World Wide Web*, pp. 461-470.

Flake, G., Lawrence, S., & Giles, C. (2000). Efficient identification of Web communities. *KDD '00: Proceedings of the sixth ACM SIGKDD international conference on Knowledge discovery and data mining*, pp. 150-160.

Gibson, D., Kleinberg, J., & Raghavan, P. (1998). Inferring Web communities from link topology. *HYPERTEXT '98: Proceedings of the ninth ACM conference on Hypertext and hypermedia: links, objects, time and space--structure in hypermedia systems*, pp. 225-234.

Girvan, M., & Newman, M. (2002). Community structure in social and biological networks. *Proceedings of the National Academy of Sciences of the United States of America, 99*(12), 7821–7826. doi:10.1073/pnas.122653799

Haase, P., Siebes, R., & van Harmelen, F. (2004). Peer selection in peer-to-peer networks with semantic topologies. In Bouzeghoub, M.,( ed).*: Proc. of the Int. Conf. on Semantics in a Networked World (ICNSW '04). Volume 3226 of Lecture Notes in Computer Science., Springer-Verlag*, pp. 108–125.

Imafuji, N., & Kitsuregawa, M. (2002). Effects of maximum flow algorithm on identifying Web community. *WIDM '02: Proceedings of the Fourth International Workshop on Web Information and Data Management*, pp. 43-48.

Ino, H., Kudo, M., & Nakamura, A. (2005). Partitioning of Web Graphs by Community Topology. *WWW '05: Proceedings of the 14th international conference on World Wide Web.*

Jung, J. J., & Euzenat, J. (2007). Towards semantic social networks. *ESWC '07: Proceedings of the 4th European conference on The Semantic Web: Research and Applications*, pp. 267–280.

Kim, J., Tomasik, B., & Turnbull, D. (2009). Using Artist Similarity to Propagate Semantic Information. *ISMIR '09: 10th International Conference on Music Information Retrieval.*

Kleinberg, J. (1998). Authoritative sources in a hyperlinked environment. *SODA '98: Proceedings of the ninth annual ACM-SIAM symposium on Discrete algorithms*, pp. 668–677.

Lozano, S., Duch, J., & Arenas, A. (2006). Community detection in a large social dataset of European Projects. *Workshop on Link Analysis, Counterterrorism and Security (SIAM on Data mining).*

O'Hara, K., Alani, H., & Shadbolt, N. (2002). Identifying Communities of Practice: Analysing Ontologies as Networks to Support Community Recognition. *Proc. Conf. Int'l Federation Information Processing (IFIP), World Computer Congress.*

Poplin, D. E. (1979). *Communities: A Survey of Theories and Methods of Research* (2nd ed.). New York: MacMillan Publishing Co., Inc.

Selman, B., Kautz, H., & Shah, M. (1997). Referralweb: Combining social networks and collaborative filtering. *Communications of the ACM*, (March): 1997.

Staab, S., Domingos, P., Mika, P., Golbeck, J., Ding, L., & Finin, T. (1993). Social networks applied. *IEEE Intelligent Systems, 20*(1), 80–93. doi:10.1109/MIS.2005.16

Yolum, P., & Singh, M. P. (2003). Dynamic communities in referral networks. *Web Intelligence and Agent Systems, 1*(2), 105–116.

Yoshii, K., Goto, M., Komatani, K., Ogata, T., & Okuno, H. (2006). *ISMIR'06: 7th International Conference on Music Information Retrieval,* pp. 296-301.

## KEY TERMS AND DEFINITIONS

**Betweenness:** As a Centrality measure, Betweenness computes the node importance within the graph by taking into account the node's neighbor connectivity. It describes the number of indirectly connected nodes, through node's direct links.

**Bridge:** A bridge is an edge that links two identifiable subsets of a graph.

**Centrality:** This measure is used to determine the relative importance of a node within the graph. "Betweenness", "Closeness", and "Degree" are all measures of centrality.

**Centralization:** The centralization is the difference between the number of links for each node divided by the maximum possible sum of differences. The measure computes how the network is centralized around a core of few nodes.

**Closeness:** Another centrality distance, the closeness measures the proximity of a node from the rest of the network, by the inverse of the sum of the shortest distances between each individual and every other person in the network.

**Clustering Coefficient:** The probability that two nodes that are connected to another, are also connected together. A Higher clustering coefficient means a denser network.

**Degree:** The number of edges to other nodes in the network.

**(Individual-Level) Density:** The degree a respondent's ties know one another/ proportion of ties among an individual's nominees. Network or global-level density is the proportion of ties in a network relative to the total number possible (sparse versus dense networks).

**Flow Betweenness Centrality:** The degree with which the node contributes to increase the maximum flow between all other network nodes.

**Local Bridge:** An edge is a local bridge if its nodes are not linked to any common node. But unlike a bridge, a local bridge is a part of a cycle.

**Path Length:** Path Length of a pair of node is the distance between them in the network. Average path-length is the average of these distances between all pairs of nodes.

**Radiality:** The degree with which a network can access information from outside, and provides information and new influences in his own.

**Reach:** The degree with which any node can reach any other node of the network.

**Structural Cohesion:** The minimum number of nodes that, if removed from a group, would disconnect the group.

**Structural Equivalence:** Measuring the similarity of nodes' link set, to other nodes of the network. Nodes do not need to be directly connected to be structurally equivalent.

**Structural Hole:** Static holes that can be strategically filled by connecting one or more link to link together other points. Linked to ideas of social capital: if you link to two people who are not linked you can control their communication.

## ENDNOTES

[1]  http://en.wikipedia.org/wiki/Community, visited March 9, 2011

[2]  http://www.dmoz.org

[3]  http://www.lycos.com

[4]  http://dir.yahoo.com

[5]  http://www.facebook.com

# Section 2
# Measures, Methods and Techniques in Social Networks Mining and Analysis

# Chapter 5
# Large Scale Graph Mining With MapReduce:
## Diameter Estimation and Eccentricity Plots of Massive Graphs with Mining Applications

**Charalampos E. Tsourakakis**
*Carnegie Mellon University, USA*

## ABSTRACT

*In recent years, a considerable amount of research has focused on the study of graph structures arising from technological, biological and sociological systems. Graphs are the tool of choice in modeling such systems since they are typically described as sets of pairwise interactions. Important examples of such datasets are the Internet, the Web, social networks, and large-scale information networks which reach the planetary scale, e.g., Facebook and LinkedIn. The necessity to process large datasets, including graphs, has led to a major shift towards distributed computing and parallel applications, especially in the recent years. MapReduce was developed by Google, one of the largest users of multiple processor computing in the world, for facilitating the development of scalable and fault tolerant applications. MapReduce has become the de facto standard for processing large scale datasets both in industry and academia.*

*In this chapter, the authors present state of the art work on large scale graph mining using MapReduce. They survey research work on an important graph mining problem, estimating the diameter of a graph and the eccentricities/radii of its vertices. Thanks to the algorithm they present in the following, the authors are able to mine graphs with billions of edges, and thus extract surprising patterns. The source code is publicly available at the URL http://www.cs.cmu.edu/~pegasus/.*

DOI: 10.4018/978-1-61350-513-7.ch005

## INTRODUCTION

The total digital output is expected to exceed 1.2 ZetaBytes in 2010 (Blake, 2010). The New York Stock Exchange generates about one terabyte of new trade data per day and Facebook hosts approximately 10 billion photos, taking up one PetaByte of storage (White, 2009). It has become apparent that as the amount of data generated increases at this unprecedented rate, scalability of algorithms is crucial. In recent years, MapReduce (Dean et al., 2008) and Hadoop (Hadoop Wiki, 2010), its open source implementation, have become the *de facto* standard for analyzing large datasets. Despite its limitations, the MapReduce framework stands out for making the programmer's life who uses MapReduce to develop applications easy. Specifically, from the programmer's perspective, MapReduce is just a library imported at the beginning of the program, like any other common library. MapReduce takes care of the parallelization and all its details including distributing the data over the cluster and fault tolerance. In the next Section we provide more details on MapReduce and Hadoop. According to (Hadoop Users, 2010) over 70 major companies over the world use Hadoop. Furthermore, innovative commercial ideas like Amazon's Elastic Compute Cloud (EC2) where users can upload large data sets and rent processor time in a large Hadoop cluster have proved successful. Besides companies, MapReduce and Hadoop have become also the *de facto* standard for research. Several universities including Carnegie Mellon University, Cornell and Berkeley are using Hadoop clusters for research purposes. Projects include text processing, analysis of large astronomical datasets and graph mining. Currently, (Pegasus CMU, 2010) provides an open source Hadoop-based library for performing important graph mining operations.

In this Chapter, we survey state-of-the-art work related to estimating the diameter in massive graphs using MapReduce. The interested reader is urged to study the original publications

(Kang et al., 2010a), (Kang et al., 2010b) which we survey in this Chapter for the full details of the algorithms described in the following. The outline of this Chapter is as follows: in Section 2 we provide a brief description of MapReduce and Hadoop, an open source package which includes a freely available implementation of MapReduce. Furthermore, we present the necessary background for the proposed method HADI (HAdoop DIameter). In Section 3 we present HADI and in Section 4 we show certain applications of our method. In Section 5 we provide future research directions. Finally, in Section 6 we conclude. For the interested reader, we provide at the end of the Chapter additional reading material.

## BACKGROUND

In this section we provide the necessary background: the MapReduce framework, basic graph theoretic definitions and the Flajolet-Martin method for counting distinct elements in a multiset.

### MapReduce

While the PRAM model (Jaja, 1992) and the bulk-synchronous parallel model (BSP) (Valiant, 1990) are powerful models, MapReduce has largely "taken over" both industry and academia (Hadoop Users, 2010). In few words, this success is due to two reasons: first, MapReduce is a simple and powerful programming model which makes the programmer's life easy. Secondly, MapReduce is publicly available via its open source version Hadoop. MapReduce was introduced in (Dean et al, 2008) by Google, one of the largest users of multiple processor computing in the world, for facilitating the development of scalable and fault tolerant applications. In the MapReduce paradigm, a parallel computation is defined on a set of values and consists of a series of *map*, *shuffle* and *reduce* steps. Let $(x_1,.., x_n)$ be the set of values, *m* denote the mapping function which takes a value x and returns a pair of a key k and a value *u* and *r* the reduce function.

1. In the map step a mapping function *m* is applied to a value $x_i$ and a pair $(k_i, u_i)$ of a key $k_i$ and a value $u_i$ is generated.
2. The shuffle step starts upon having mapped all values $x_i$ for i=1 to n to pairs. In this step, a set of lists is produced using the key-value pairs generated from the map step with an important feature. Each list is characterized by the key k and has the form $L_k = \{k: u_1, .., u_{j(k)}\}$ if and only if there exists a pair $(k, u_i)$ for i=1 to j.
3. Finally in the reduce step, the reduce function *r* is applied to the lists generated from the shuffle step to produce the set of values $(w_1, w_2, \ldots)$.

To illustrate the aforementioned abstract concepts consider the problem of counting how many times each word in a given document appears. The set of values is the ``bag-of-words'' appearing in the document. For example, if the document is the sentence ``The dog runs in the forest'', then $\{x_1, x_2, x_3, x_4, x_5, x_6\}$={*the, dog, runs, in, the, forest*}. One convenient choice for the MapReduce functions is the following and results in the following steps:

- The map function *m* will map a value *x* to a pair of a key and a value. A convenient choice for *m* is something close to the identity map. Specifically, we choose m(x) =(x,$), where we assume that the dollar sign $ a especially reserved symbol.
- The shuffle step for our small example will produce the following set of lists: (the:$,$), (dog:$), (runs:$), (in:$), (runs:$), (forest:$)
- The reduce function *r* will process each list defined by each different word appearing in the document by counting the number of dollar signs $. This number will also be the

count of times that specific word appears in the text.

Hadoop -as already mentioned- implements MapReduce and was originally created by Doug Cutting. Even if Hadoop is well known for MapReduce it is actually a collection of subprojects that are closely related to distributed computing. For example HDFS (Hadoop filesystem) is a distributed filesystem that provides high throughput access to application data and HBase is a scalable, distributed database that supports structured data storage for large tables (column-oriented database). Another subproject is Pig, which is a high-level data-flow language and execution framework for parallel computation (Gates, 2009). Pig runs on HDFS and MapReduce. For more details and other subprojects, the interested reader can visit the website that hosts the Hadoop project (Hadoop Wiki 2010).

Karloff, Suri and Vassilvitskii in (Karloff et al. 2010) in their fundamental paper towards understanding which problems can be solved efficiently in MapReduce present a formal computation model for MapReduce and compare it to the popular PRAM model. There are three main aspects of the MapReduce complexity class (*MRC*) are the following:

- **Memory:** The input to any mapper and any reducer should be sublinear in the size of the data.
- **Machines:** The total number of machines should also be sublinear in the data size.
- **Time:** Both map and reduce functions run in time polynomial with respect to the original input size.

Clearly, the requirements are well grounded. For example, if the memory requirement did not hold, then we could use a single reducer to solve the problem. However, this is against the parallel programming paradigm in which we are interested in. Furthermore, imagine requiring a superlinear number of machines, for example for $n^2$ machines where n is the size of the Web graph. This is unrealistic and this is why we require a sublinear number of machines. Similarly, the third requirement is in accordance to Complexity theory where a polynomial time algorithm implies an efficient solution. The algorithm we present in Section 4 is in accordance with this model of computation. For the details of the *MRC* complexity class, the interested reader is encouraged to study the (Karloff et al. 2010) paper.

## Graph Theoretic Definitions

In this Section we define terms that the familiar reader can skip safely. The radius r(v) of a node v in a graph is defined to be the distance between v and a reachable node farthest away from v. The diameter d(G) of a graph G is the maximum radius over all nodes v, i.e., $d(G) = \max_v r(v)$. Since the radius and the diameter are susceptible to outliers (e.g., long chains), we define the effective radius and diameter as follows:

- **Effective Radius:** For a node v in a graph G, the effective radius $r_{eff}(v)$ of v is the 90th-percentile of all the distances from v.
- **Effective Diameter:** The effective diameter $d_{eff}(G)$ of a graph G is the minimum number of hops in which 90% of all connected pairs of nodes can reach each other.

## Related Work

We briefly present related works on algorithms for radius and diameter computation, as well as on large graph mining.

*Computing Radius and Diameter*: The typical algorithms to compute the radius and the diameter of a graph include Breadth First Search (BFS) and Floyd's algorithm (Cormen et al., 1990). Both approaches are prohibitively slow for large graphs, requiring $O(n^2 + nm)$ and $O(n^3)$ running time, where n and m denote the number of nodes and

edges, respectively. For the same reason, related BFS or all-pair shortest-path based algorithms like (Bader et al., 2008), (Ferrez et al., 1998), (Sinha et al., 1998) cannot handle large graphs. To the best of our knowledge, HADI –our proposed method- is the first academic method that scales to huge graphs with billions of edges.

*Large Scale Graph Mining*: Atrbox keeps a large collection of academic papers which use MapReduce to perform large scale graph mining tasks (Atrbox 2010). Furthermore the Hadoop related web pages (Hadoop Users 2010) and (Hadoop Wiki 2010) show different organizations and applications of MapReduce, including large scale graph mining applications. The PEGASUS project (Pegasus project CMU 2010) is a valuable source of code and large scale graph mining applications. Examples include counting of triangles (Tsourakakis et al., 2009a), (Tsourakakis et al., 2009b), (Tsourakakis et al., 2009c), (Tsourakakis, 2010), (Tsourakakis et al., in press) and GIM-V (Kang et. al., 2009) an important primitive for common operations on large graphs.

## Counting Distinct Elements in a Multiset

Flajolet and Martin in (Flajolet et al., 1985) consider the following problem: assume we are given a multiset M. How many distinct elements, call that number n, does M have? For example the multiset M={1,1,5,1} has n=2 distinct elements. The main idea of their algorithm is surprisingly simple and effective. However, the analysis of their algorithm is subtle and the interested reader is urged to read their excellent paper. In the next few lines, we reveal the intuition behind their algorithm.

Let's assume that we have a hash function $h:M \rightarrow \{0,1,\ldots,2^L-1\}$ which is "good" in the sense that it hashes the elements of the multiset sufficiently uniformly over the allowed range of values. Observe that duplicates will have the same hash value always. Let $y = \Sigma_{k \geq 0} bit(y,k) 2^k$ and let if y>0 otherwise if y=0, the set $\rho(y)$=L. Their algorithm first initializes a bitmask of length L with zeros and then goes over the multiset and hashes each element x. Let h(x) be the hash value, which is a random binary string. We find the index of the least significant bit of the hashed value which is 1, i.e., $\rho(h(x))$ and then we flip the corresponding bit of the bitmask from 0 to 1 (if it is already 1 we leave it as is). Now observe that by our assumption about the "goodness" of the hash function the pattern 0 in the first bit (position 0) has probability 1/2. The pattern 00 has probability 1/4 and the pattern 10...0 has probability equal to $2^{-k-1}$ where k is the number of zeros. Therefore we expect that the first bit of the i-th bitmask will be accessed in expectation $n/2^i$ times. Since we flip the bits, when i is significantly smaller that $\log_2(n)$ we expect with high probability to see ones. When i is significantly larger than $\log_2(n)$ we expect to see zeros and when i is at the range of $\log_2(n)$ we expect to see a mix of ones and zeroes. That is the region that will tell us something interesting concerning the number of distinct elements. Flajolet and Martin showed that under the assumption of uniform hashing the expected value of the leftmost zero position R in the bitmask is E[R]=$\log_2(\varphi n)$ and that the variance is 1.12 where $\varphi$=0.77351. In practice since the variance can be really large -recall that the variance is 1 bit, and thus it can be significantly off from the correct value- we typically take several hash functions and average out the error.

## PROPOSED METHOD

Our proposed method, HADI (HAdoop Diameter), is based on the ingenious idea of Flajolet and Martin: we reduce the problem of diameter and radii estimation to counting distinct elements in appropriately defined multisets and then we show

how we can implement this idea in the MapReduce framework.

## Main Idea

The first key observation is that if we keep expanding iteratively the neighborhood of a vertex v it stabilizes as soon as we make r(v) hops. In other words, the number of distinct vertices reachable from node v within r(v) steps is exactly the same with the number of distinct elements reachable within r(v)+1 steps. We maintain K Flajolet-Martin bitstrings b(h,i) for each node i and for each hop h. This bitstring encodes the number of nodes reachable from node i within h hops and is used to estimate the radii (and hence the diameter) using the Flajolet-Martin main theorem. At the h-th iteration each node updates its bitstring using the bitstrings of its neighbors in the following way: *b(h,i) = b(h-1,i) BIT-OR { b(h-1,j) for all edges (i,j) in G}* Furthermore, the number of neighbors of node i reachable within at most h hops N(h,i) is estimated using the K bitstrings that we use (recall that in the Flajolet-Martin algorithm we need to average out the effect of the large variance by using several bitstrings) and the Flajolet-Martin theorem, i.e.,

$$N(h,i) = \frac{1}{0.77351} 2^{\frac{1}{k}\Sigma_{(i-1)}^{K} b_l(i)}$$

where $b_l(i)$ is the position of the leftmost 0 bit of the l-th bitstring of node i. Algorithm 1 shows the main idea for the diameter and radii estimation. Observe that given the radii of the nodes, it is easy to estimate the diameter. Also, the Algorithm outputs the effective diameter and radii given that in practice large graphs have long chains and thus the diameter and the radii are not insightful. It is worth pointing out that the parameter K is typically set ro 32 and MaxIter is set to 256 since real graphs have small effective diameter typically.

*Complexity Analysis:* The running time of Algorithm 1 is O(dm) where d is the diameter of the graph and m is the number of edges. Furthermore it requires O(nlogn) space. The algorithm runs efficiently on graphs with several millions of edges but in order to be able to handle huge graphs with billions of edges, we have to parallelize the algorithm. In the next section we present the details of the parallelization of the algorithm in the MapReduce framework.

---

**Algorithm 1** Computing Radii and Diameter

---

**Input:** Input graph G and integers $MaxIter$ and $K$
**Output:** $r_{eff}(i)$ of every node $i$, and $d_{eff}(G)$
1: **for** $i = 1$ to $n$ **do**
2:   $b(0, i) \leftarrow$ NewFMBitstring$(n)$;
3: **end for**
4: **for** $h = 1$ to $MaxIter$ **do**
5:   $Changed \leftarrow 0$;
6:   **for** $i = 1$ to $n$ **do**
7:     **for** $l = 1$ to $K$ **do**
8:       $b_l(h, i) \leftarrow b_l(h - 1, i)$BIT-OR$\{b_l(h - 1, j) | \forall j$ adjacent from $i\}$;
9:     **end for**
10:     **if** $\exists l$ s.t. $b_l(h, i) \neq b_l(h - 1, i)$ **then**
11:       increase $Changed$ by 1;
12:     **end if**
13:   **end for**
14:   $N(h) \leftarrow \sum_i N(h, i)$;
15:   **if** $Changed$ equals to 0 **then**
16:     $h_{max} \leftarrow h$, and break for loop;
17:   **end if**
18: **end for**
19: **for** $i = 1$ to $n$ **do** {estimate eff. radii}
20:   $r_{eff}(i) \leftarrow$ smallest $h'$ where $N(h', i) \geq 0.9 \cdot N(h_{max}, i)$;
21: **end for**
22: $d_{eff}(G) \leftarrow$ smallest $h'$ where $N(h') \geq 0.9 \cdot N(h_{max})$;

---

## IMPLEMENTATION DETAILS

HADI is a disk-based algorithm since it is targeted to handle huge, disk-resilient graphs. HADI saves two types of information to the distributed file system (Hadoop Distributed File System, abbreviated as HDFS):

- *Edge* has the format of (from, to)

- *Bitstring* has the format (vertex id,flag,bit string$_1$,..,bitstring$_K$) where K is the number of bitstrings we use per each vertex. The flag encodes (if it is equal to 1) that the bitstring has been changed.

*HADI-naïve:* Let's consider first a naïve implementation of HADI. The main idea of HADI-naive is to use the bitstrings file as a logical "cache" to machines which contain edge files. The bitstring update operation requires that the machine which updates the bitstrings of node i should have access to (a) all edges adjacent from i, and (b) all bitstrings of the adjacent nodes. To meet the requirement (a), it is needed to reorganize the edge file such that edges with a same source id are grouped together. That can be done by using an Identity mapper which outputs the given input edges in (source id, destination id) format. The most simple yet naive way to meet the requirement (b) is sending the bitstrings to every machine which receives the reorganized edge file. Thus, HADI-naïve iterates over two-stages of MapReduce. The first stage updates the bitstrings of each node and sets the "Changed" flag bit if at least one of the bitstrings of the node is different from the previous bitstring. The second stage counts the number of changed nodes and stops iterating when the bitstrings stabilized, as illustrated in the swim-lane diagram of Figure 1.

HADI: Now we can describe the efficient version of HADI. HADI copies only the necessary bitstrings to each reducer. The main idea is to replicate bitstrings of node j exactly x times where x is the in-degree of node j. The replicated bitstrings of node j is called the partial bitstring and is denoted by .

The replicated used to update b(h,i), the bitstring of node i where (i,j) is an edge in the graph. HADI runs in three stages, each of which is a MapReduce job, until all bitstrings of all nodes stop changing. Algorithms 2, 3, 4 describe the three stages of HADI. We use h for the current iteration number, starting from h=1.

*Figure 1. HADI- naïve*

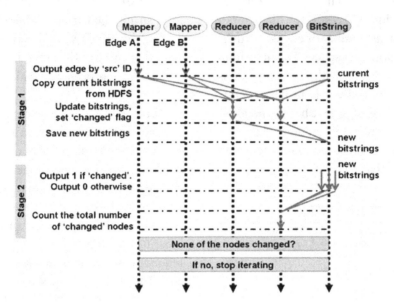

*Stage 1:* We generate (key, value) pairs, where the key is a node id i and the value is the partial bitstrings 's where j ranges over all the neighbors adjacent from node i. To generate such pairs, the bitstrings of node j are grouped together with edges whose destination id is j. Notice that at the very first iteration, bitstrings of nodes do not exist; they have to be generated on the fly, and we use the Bitstring Creation Command for that. Notice also that line 22 of Algorithm 2 is used to propagate the bitstrings of one's own node. These bitstrings are compared to the newly updated bitstrings at Stage 2 to check convergence.

*Stage 2:* Bitstrings of node i are updated by combining partial bitstrings of itself and nodes adjacent from i. For the purpose, the mapper is the Identity mapper (output the input without any modification). The reducer combines them, generates new bitstrings, and sets flag by recording (a) whether at least a bitstring changed or not, and (b) the current iteration number h and the neighborhood value N(h,i) (line 9). This h and N(h,i) are used to calculate the effective radius of nodes after all bitstrings converge, i.e., don't change. Notice that only the last neighborhood N(h_{last},i)

and other neighborhoods N(h',i) that satisfy need to be saved to calculate the effective radius. The output of Stage 2 is fed into the input of Stage 1 at the next iteration.

*Stage 3:* The last stage computes the number of changed nodes and sums up the neighborhood values of all nodes in order to calculate N(h), i.e., the total number of node pairs reachable within

*Figure 2. Toy Graph*

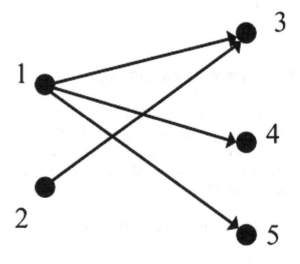

---

**Algorithm 2** HADI Stage 1

**Input:** Edge data $E = \{i, j\}$,
    Current bitstring $B = \{(i, b(h-1, i))\}$ or
    Bitstring Creation Command $BC = \{(i, cmd)\}$
**Output:** Partial bitstring $B' = \{(i, b(h-1, j))\}$

1: Stage1-Map(key $k$, value $v$);
2: **if** $(k, v)$ is of type B or BC **then**
3:    Output$(k, v)$;
4: **else if** $(k, v)$ is of type E **then**
5:    Output$(v, k)$;
6: **end if**
7:
8: Stage1-Reduce(key $k$, values $V[]$);
9: $SRC \leftarrow []$;
10: **for** $v \in V$ **do**
11:   **if** $(k, v)$ is of type BC **then**
12:     $\hat{b}(h-1, k) \leftarrow$ NewFMBitstring();
13:   **else if** $(k, v)$ is of type B **then**
14:     $\hat{b}(h-1, k) \leftarrow v$;
15:   **else if** $(k, v)$ is of type E **then**
16:     Add $v$ to $SRC$;
17:   **end if**
18: **end for**
19: **for** $src \in SRC$ **do**
20:   Output$(src, \hat{b}(h-1, k))$;
21: **end for**
22: Output$(k, \hat{b}(h-1, k))$;

---

**Algorithm 3** HADI Stage 2

**Input:** Partial bitstring $B = \{(i, \hat{b}(h-1, j))\}$
**Output:** Full bitstring $B = \{(i, b(h, i))\}$

1: Stage2-Map(key $k$, value $v$); // Identity Mapper
2: Output$(k, v)$;
3:
4: Stage2-Reduce(key $k$, values $V[]$);
5: $b(h, k) \leftarrow 0$;
6: **for** $v \in V$ **do**
7:   $b(h, k) \leftarrow b(h, k)$ BIT-OR $v$;
8: **end for**
9: Update $flag$ of $b(h, k)$;
10: Output$(k, b(h, k))$;

---

**Algorithm 4** HADI Stage 3

**Input:** Full bitstring $B = \{(i, b(h, i))\}$
**Output:** Number of changed nodes, Neighborhood $N(h)$

1: Stage3-Map(key $k$, value $v$);
2: Analyze $v$ to get $(changed, N(h, i))$;
3: Output(key_for_changed, $changed$);
4: Output(key_for_neighborhood, $N(h, i)$);
5:
6: Stage3-Reduce(key $k$, values $V[]$);
7: $Changed \leftarrow 0$;
8: $N(h) \leftarrow 0$;
9: **for** $v \in V$ **do**
10:   **if** k is key_for_changed **then**
11:     $Changed \leftarrow Changed + v$;
12:   **else if** k is key_for_neighborhood **then**
13:     $N(h) \leftarrow N(h) + v$;
14:   **end if**
15: **end for**
16: Output(key_for_changed, $Changed$);
17: Output(key_for_neighborhood, $N(h)$);

---

## HADI AT WORK: EXPERIMENTAL RESULTS

HADI is a valuable mining tool for large graphs. In this section we describe several patterns that are revealed via using HADI. We start from a fundamental question, what is the effective diameter of the Web? Thanks to Yahoo!, such a dataset was provided to the CMU data mining group and using HADI the following answer was given:

*The effective diameter of the Yahoo! Web Graph in the year 2002 is between 7 or 8.*

Furthermore, HADI reveals the eccentricity distribution which as can be seen in Figure 4 is multimodal.

This phenomenon doesn't occur in smaller scale networks with several million of edges. Figure 5 shows the radius plot for the US Patent. The eccentricity plot is bimodal and the outsider, core and whisker vertices are evident.

Given this distribution a natural question to ask is what are the common properties of vertices with roughly the same radius, if any. Indeed, after checking vertices which belong to the first mode, we found that these vertices belong in disconnected components. The vertices which belong

h hops. We use only two unique keys which correspond to the two calculated values.

## AN EXAMPLE OF HADI

Figure 2 shows a toy graph and Figure 3 shows how HADI runs on this algorithm. Each column of Figure 3 corresponds to a MapReduce job, and specifically from left to right the i-th column corresponds to Stage i, i=1,2,3.

*Figure 3. HADI running on the toy graph of Figure 2. Each column corresponds to the stage described in the previous subsection.*

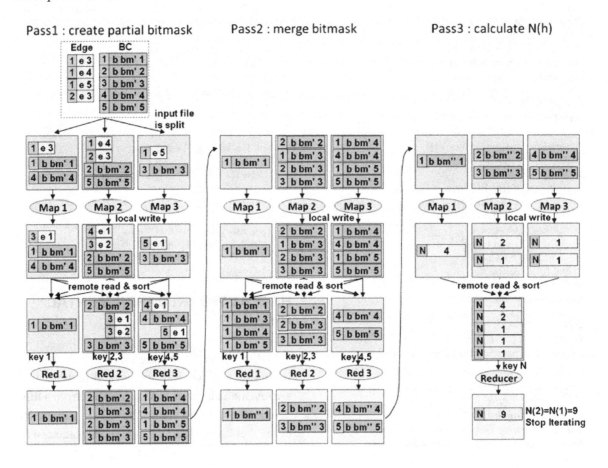

*Figure 4. Radius plot for the Yahoo Web Graph (1.4 Billion vertices, 6.6 Billion edges). Observe that the radius distribution has several modes. The effective diameter lies between 7 and 8.*

*Figure 5. Radius plot for US Patent Graph (6 Million vertices, 16 Million edges). Observe that the radius distribution is bimodal.*

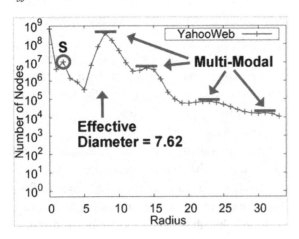

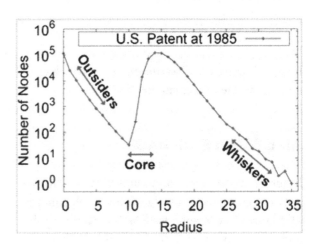

*Figure 6. Radius plot for several connected components of the Patent graph in 1985. In red is shown for the giant connected component and the other colors show other disconnected components. Notice that the first mode has disappeared which corresponds to vertices belonging to several disconnected components.*

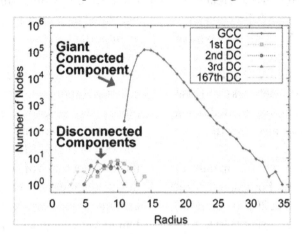

*Figure 7. Radius plot of the giant component of the Yahoo! Web Graph. The only vertex with radius 5 is "google.com".*

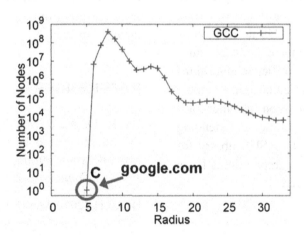

to the "dip" are typically core nodes in the giant component and the vertices which belong to the second mode are in their vast majority well-connected nodes in the giant component. Figure 6 shows the radii distribution for the nodes of the giant components in red color and the nodes of the few largest remaining components. Notice that the first mode disappears exactly because it consists of nodes from the disconnected components that we omit here.

Figure 7 shows a striking pattern, all nodes of the giant component of the Yahoo! Web graph have radius 6 or more except for one node, which after inspection, is the web site "www.google.com". This is somehow surprising since besides the dominant Google web site, there are other important web sites such as Amazon's, eBay etc.

## FUTURE RESEARCH DIRECTIONS

In the following, we propose several research directions with respect to the large scale graph mining using distributed computing:

1.  GIM-V is a primitive developed by Kang, Tsourakakis and Faloutsos in (Kang et. al., 2009) which is frequently used in many applications. A natural research direction is the development of a BLAS/ARPACK type of library for large scale matrix computations. This will provide us significant insight in the spectra of real world networks and also an insight in the clustering of nodes via the second eigenvector, also known as the Fiedler vector.

2.  HADI is a mining tool whose capabilities can be further enhanced. For example as it was shown in (Kang et al., 2010b) temporal patterns can be extracted using HADI. Can we find other interesting applications of HADI?

3.  An important framework was introduce in (Karloff et al., 2010) for MapReduce. Unfortunately several algorithms which are implemented in PEGASUS do not follow the sublinear constraints of the MapReduce class. Can we develop efficient algorithms under this model which count triangles, clusterings, diameter estimation and other common graph mining operations? Extending and improving the PEGASUS library for performing large scale graph mining has a lot of space for research.

## CONCLUSION

In this chapter we surveyed state of the art work on the diameter and radii estimation problem using MapReduce. The choice of MapReduce is well-justified: it has become the *de facto* standard for distributed computing in both academia and industry. Even if there exist several other powerful models for distributed computing, MapReduce due to its simplicity offers the programmer the ability to use MapReduce as a simple library that is imported at the beginning of the program, like any other library. However, implementing several graph algorithms becomes non-trivial, not to mention the characterization of what can be and what cannot be efficiently computed. In this Chapter we presented the first piece of work which addresses an important problem in such a large scale, at least from an academic perspective. Estimating the diameter and the radii distribution provides us an effective mining tool for detecting central nodes, outliers and several other applications which the interested reader can find in (Kang et al., 2010a) and (Kang et al., 2010b). Our method is based on the ingenious idea of Flajolet-Martin for counting distinct elements in a multiset since the diameter estimation problem reduces in the former problem as we explained. Upon careful optimization of the implementation, our algorithm can run on the Yahoo! Web graph the largest graph ever to be analyzed (again, from an academic perspective). Finally, we presented new research directions with respect to graph mining and distributed computing using MapReduce.

## REFERENCES

Bader, D. A., & Madduri, K. (2008) A graph-theoretic analysis of the human protein-interaction network using multicore parallel algorithms. In *Parallel Computing*, 2008.

Blake, H. (2010, May 04), *Digital universe to smash 'zettabyte' barrier for first time*. The Telegraph, Retrieved from http://www.telegraph.co.uk/.

Chierichetti, F., Kumar, R., & Tomkins, A. (2010). *Max-Cover in MapReduce. Proceedings of the 19th international conference on world wide web*, (pp. 231-240)

Cormen, T. Leiserson, C., & Rivest, R. (1990) *Introduction to Algorithms*. Cambridge, MA: The MIT Press.

Dean, J., & Ghemawat, S. (2008). Mapreduce: simplified data processing on large clusters. *Communications of the ACM, 51*(1), 107–113. doi:10.1145/1327452.1327492

Ferrez, J.-A., Fukuda, K., & Liebling, T. (1998) Parallel computation of the diameter of a graph. *Proc. 12th Annual International Symposium on High Performance Computing Systems and Applications (HPCS'98),* Kluwer.

Flajolet, P., & Martin, G.N. (1985) Probabilistic counting algorithms for database applications. *Journal of Computer and System Sciences.*

Gates, A., Natkovich, O., Chopra, S., Kamath, P., Narayanamurthy, S., Olston, C., et al. (2009) Building a high-level dataflow system on top of map-reduce: the pig experience. Proc. V*LDB Endow. 2* (2), 1414-1425.

Hadoop Related Papers. (2010). Retrieved from: http://atbrox.com/2009/10/01/ mapreduce-and-hadoop-academic-papers/

Hadoop Users. (2010). Retrieved from: http://wiki. apache.org/hadoop/PoweredBy

Hadoop Wiki. (2010). Retrieved from: http:// hadoop.apache.org/

JaJa. J. (1992). *An introduction to parallel algorithms.* Redwood City, CA: Addison Wesley Longman Publishing Co., Inc.

Kang, U., Tsourakakis, C., Appel, A., Leskovec, J., & Faloutsos, C. (2010a). *Hadi: Mining radii of large graphs.* ACM Transactions on Knowledge Discovery from Data.

Kang, U., Tsourakakis, C., Appel, A., Leskovec, J., & Faloutsos, C. (2010b) *Radius plots for mining TeraByte scale graphs: Algorithms, patterns, and observations.* SIAM International Conference on Data Mining.

Kang, U., Tsourakakis, C., & Faloutsos, C. (2009) *Pegasus: A peta-scale graph mining system - implementation and observations* IEEE International Conference on Data Mining.

Karloff, H., Suri, S., & Vassilvitskii, S. (2010) *A Model of Computation for MapReduce,* ACM-SIAM Symposium on Discrete Algorithms.

Pegasus project. CMU (2010). Retrieved from: http://www.cs.cmu.edu/~pegasus

Sinha, B. P., Bhattacharya, B. B., Ghose, S., & Srimani, P. K. (1986). *A parallel algorithm to compute the shortest paths and diameter of a graph and its VLSI implementation* (In, I. E. E. E., Trans.). Comput.

Tsourakakis, C. (2008). *Fast counting of triangles in large real networks without counting: Algorithms and laws,* ICDM. *IEEE Computer Society, 2008,* 608–617.

Tsourakakis, C. (2010). (in press). Counting triangles in real-world networks using projections. *Knowledge and Information Systems.*

Tsourakakis, C., Drineas, P., Michelakis, E., Koutis, I., & Faloutsos, C. (2009a). *Spectral counting of triangles in power-law networks via element-wise Sparsification.* ASONAM '09. *Advances in Social Networks Analysis and Mining, 2009,* 66–71.

Tsourakakis, C., Drineas, P., Michelakis, E., Koutis, I., & Faloutsos, C. (2011) *Spectral counting of triangles via element-wise sparsifcation and triangle-based link recommendation.* In Journal of Social Network Analysis and Mining 2011, in press.

Tsourakakis, C., Kang, U., Miller, G., & Faloutsos, C. (2009b) *DOULION: counting triangles in massive graphs with a coin,* KDD '09: Proceedings of the 15th ACM SIGKDD international conference on Knowledge discovery and data mining (New York, NY, USA), ACM, 2009, 837-846.

Tsourakakis, C., Kolountzakis, M., & Miller, G. L. (2009c) *Approximate triangle counting,* CoRR, *abs/0904.3761.*

Valiant, L. (1990). A bridging model for parallel computation. *Communications of the ACM, 33*(8), 103–111. doi:10.1145/79173.79181

White, T. (2009). *Hadoop: The definitive guide* (1st ed.). CA, USA: O'Reilly Media.

## ADDITIONAL READING

The interested reader is urged to read the following literature to get acquainted with the state of the art results on graph mining: for estimating the diameter and the radii distribution in large networks, see (Kang et al., 2010a), (Kang et al., 2010b).

For programming primitives and a graph mining library, see (Kang et al., 2009). Chierichetti, Kumar and Tomkins proposed an efficient implementation of the Max-Cover problem for the MapReduce framework in (Chierichetti et al., 2010).

Apache Pig is also worth mentioning. It is a platform for analyzing large data sets that consists of a high-level language for expressing data analysis programs (Gates, 2009). A list of papers related to graph mining can be found in (Hadoop Related Papers, 2010).

# Chapter 6
# Social Network Inspired Approach to Intelligent Monitoring of Intelligence Data

**Qiang Shen**
*Aberstwyth University, UK*

**Tossapon Boongoen**
*Royal Thai Air Force Academy, Thailand*

## ABSTRACT

*In the wake of recent terrorist atrocities, intelligence experts have commented that failures in detecting terrorist and criminal activities are not so much due to a lack of data, as they are due to difficulties in relating and interpreting the available intelligence. An intelligent tool for monitoring and interpreting intelligence data will provide a helpful means for intelligence analysts to consider emerging scenarios of plausible threats, thereby offering useful assistance in devising and deploying preventive measures against such possibilities. One of the major problems in need of such attention is detecting false identity that has become the common denominator of all serious crime, especially terrorism. Typical approaches to this problem rely on the similarity measure of textual and other content-based characteristics, which are usually not applicable in the case of deceptive and erroneous description. This barrier may be overcome through link information presented in communication behaviors, financial interactions and social networks. Quantitative link-based similarity measures have proven effective for identifying similar problems in the Internet and publication domains. However, these numerical methods only concentrate on link structures, and fail to achieve accurate and coherent interpretation of the information. Inspired by this observation, the chapter presents a novel qualitative similarity measure that makes use of multiple link properties to refine the underlying similarity estimation process and consequently derive semantic-rich similarity descriptors. The approach is based on order-of-magnitude reasoning. Its performance is empirically evaluated over a terrorism-related dataset, and compared against several state-of-the-art link-based algorithms and other alternative methods.*

DOI: 10.4018/978-1-61350-513-7.ch006

## INTRODUCTION

Most criminal and terrorist organisations form flexible networks of loosely related individuals and sub-organisations (units). These networks are often embedded within legitimate society and they evolve over time to attain their concealment. However, organised crime and terrorist activity does leave a trail of information, such as captured communications and forensic evidence, which can be collected by police and intelligence organisations. Whilst experienced intelligence analysts can suggest plausible scenarios based on such information, promptly identifying potential organisations that pose a threat, the amount of intelligence data possibly relevant may well be overwhelming for human examination. Automated hypothetical (re-) construction of the organisations and activities that may have generated the intelligence data obtained, therefore, presents an important and challenging research for crime prevention and detection.

The effectiveness of initial automated decision-support systems, such as COPLINK (Chen et al., 2003) and the Universal Situational Awareness (USA) system (Rubin and Lee, 2003), is crucially dependent upon the experience of the user/analysts as the potential threats are identified only by the analysts. This vulnerability has been addressed by systems such as those reported in (Keppens et al., 2005) and (Shen et al., 2006), which automatically generate plausible scenarios when given a limited amount of real or hypothesised evidence. These systems also provide the user with the means to analyse such scenarios and offer helpful information that may enhance efforts for crime reduction. However, the problem of identity disambiguation which is commonly encountered in intelligence data analysis (Badia and Kantardzic, 2005; Wang et al., 2006) has not been addressed thus far. In fact, a modest resolution typically used within the existing crime investigation systems is to assume that the identities of any instances (e.g., person, object, place, and organisation) involving in a reasoning process are globally unambigu-

ous. However, this simple ignorance of possible identity aliases drastically reduces the degree of this approach's flexibility and actual utilisation within the real world. The quality of generated crime scenarios may be enhanced through the resolution of duplicated references. This additional mechanism helps to reveal an unforeseen scenario that may be overlooked otherwise (Fu et al., 2010; Fu and Shen, 2010).

In the context of terrorism and organised crimes, such a task is not straightforward as most duplications are subject to deception. Holders of a false identity intend to avoid accountability and to leave no traces for law enforcement authority. Identity fraud is intentionally committed with a view to perpetrating another crime from the most trivial to the most dreadful imaginable. Especially in the case of terrorism, it is widely utilised to provide financial and logistical support to terrorist networks that have set up and encourage criminal activities to undermine civil society. Tracking terrorist activities undoubtedly requires authentic identification of criminals and terrorists. Particularly to the September 11 terrorist attacks, tragic consequences could have been prevented to a certain extent if U.S. authorities had been able to discover the use of deceptive identity, e.g., multiple dates of birth and alias names. In such circumstance, identity verification and name variation detection systems (e.g., (Blienko et al., 2003; Torvik et al., 2004)) that rely solely on the inexact search of textual attributes are partially effective. Nevertheless, these methods will fail to disclose the unconventional truth where highly deceptive identities (e.g., 'Usama bin Laden' and 'The prince') refer to the same person.

The aforementioned dilemma may be overcome through social network analysis (SNA) (Ting et al., 2010; Wasserman and Faust, 1994) or link analysis (Getoor and Diehl, 2005), which seeks to discover knowledge based on the relationships in data about people, places, things, and events. Intuitively, despite using distinct false identities, each terrorist normally exhibits unique relations with other entities involved in legitimate activities found in any open or modern society via making use of mobile phones, public transportation and financial systems. This network based methodology has proven effective for identity problems (Boongoen et al., 2010; Pantel, 2006) by exploiting link information instead of content-based information, which is typically unreliable due to intentional deception and translation error (Wang et al., 2005). Recently, it has also been employed by Argentine intelligence organisations for analysing Iranian-Embassy telephone records. This specific investigation aims to make a circumstantial case that the Iranian Embassy had been involved in the July 18, 1994 terror bombing of a Jewish community centre (Porter, 2008).

This chapter presents an innovative model of qualitative link analysis, which is effective for detecting deceptive names or aliases in intelligence data. The underlying analysis is conducted on a social network representation of relations amongst references of real-world entities, which has been effectively exploited for link prediction (Liben-Nowell and Kleinberg, 2007; Murata and Moriyasu, 2008) and author-name resolution (Reuther and Walter, 2006) problems. However, many advanced link-based techniques suffer from the inaccuracy of quantitative description and misled interpretation which is usually caused by a few observations with unduly high values. The new approach introduced here takes on board qualitative reasoning (Forbus, 1996; DeKleer and Brown, 1984) in general, and the orders-of-magnitude model (Raiman, 1991) in particular, such that the deficiency with the numerical models can be alleviated. While a number of existing link-based techniques such as SimRank (Jeh and Widom, 2002) and Random-Walks (Fouss et al., 2007; Minkov et al., 2006) are generally inefficient, the qualitative model is simple and scales up to a large data set. This is achieved by aggregating multiple SNA measures in accordance with their relevance (i.e., significance).

The proposed model derives a qualitative similarity description from multiple link characteristics, such as connected-triple (CT) (Reuther and Walter, 2006) and uniqueness (UQ) (Boongoen et al., 2010) measures, each of which is expressed using the absolute order-of-magnitude (AOM) model (Piera, 1995). In essence, these properties are perceived at different precision levels and hence, are gauged in accordance to values represented by distinct orders of magnitude. With different sets of measurement labels (i.e., landmarks), such scales differ by at least one qualitatively important order of magnitude. In particular, a semi-supervised method is provided for the selection of data-driven landmarks, which may be more reliable than those human-directed ones. For any pair of entities within a link network, their link-based similarity is calculated by combining the corresponding qualitative descriptors, each assigned with a possibly different degree of relevance. This weight-alike parameter is also expressed by a qualitative descriptor defined in an AOM space. Since label sets adopted for different properties are usually defined in a dissimilar universe of discourse and of unequal granularity, they are homogenised onto a common scale on which references of distinct label sets can be uniformly manipulated and integrated. Then, these homogenised descriptors are aggregated using the qualitative equivalence of the numerical weighted summation, following the work of (Agell et al., 2000).

The rest of this chapter is organised as follows. Section 2 and Section 3 introduce the basic concepts of social network inspired approach to false identity detection and absolute order-of-magnitude model, upon which the present research is developed. Following that, Section 4 describes link properties and order-of-magnitude based similarity evaluation. Section 5 presents the semi-supervised method for designing landmarks, which is data-driven and more robust than the human-directed counterpart. The performance evaluation of this qualitative link-based similarity measure, through applications for detecting the use of false identity, is detailed in Section 6. The chapter is concluded in Section 7, with the perspective of further work.

## SOCIAL NETWORK INSPIRED APPROACH TO FALSE IDENTITY DETECTION

### False Identity and Alias Name Detection

Identity is a set of characteristic descriptors unique to a specific person, which can be principally categorized into three types of attributed, biographical and biometric identity, respectively (Clarke, 1994; Wang et al., 2006). Initially with attributed identity, a person can be identified using descriptions of name, details of parents, date and place of birth. In addition, biographical identity constituted from personal information over a life span (e.g. criminal, educational and financial history) can also be exploited for such purpose. Comparing to biometric identity like fingerprints and DNA features, the first two types are greatly subject to deception as they are much easier to falsify.

The main focus of this research is to discover the possibility of attributed identity being falsely or deceptively specified, especially for the case of personal names. According to the study of identity deception of Wang et al. (2006), name deception or the use of false names is the practice commonly adopted by all investigated criminal cases. In particular, such illegitimate act can be accomplished by employing one of the following falsified formats:

- Partly deceptive name, either false first or family name.
- A completely different name.
- Dropping, adding or abbreviating middle name.
- Abbreviation and add-on to first or last name.

- Similar pronunciation, but with different spelling.
- Name swap via transposing first and last names.

### Approaches to Detecting Duplicates and Similar Objects

Discovering duplicates and similar data objects has been a major subject in the fields such as information retrieval, database and natural language processing. A seminal work is the theory of record linkage (Fellegi and Sunter, 1969) in which records of two files are matched, based on the distance between two corresponding feature vectors, during the merge of databases. This research has been further pursued within the area of database for de-duplication and data cleaning tasks (Blienko et al., 2003; Buechi et al., 2003; Kalashnikov et al., 2005). With the purpose of grouping similar publications, citation systems such as Citeseer (Lawrence et al., 1999) apply similar ideas using text similarity measured on publication details. In natural language processing systems, coreference resolution has been formalised with the analogous intuition of determining whether two expressions in natural language refer to the same entity in the world. Applications of machine learning techniques (Soon et al., 2001) to this problem prove to be efficient by making use of text-based properties, such as string similarity and syntactic functions.

In order to tackle the problem of alias names, the 'content-based' approach has been adopted by Bilenko and Mooney (2003) and several other authors (Bagga and Baldwin, 1998; Mann and Yarowsky, 2003; Ng et al., 2003), using text-based comparison and learning techniques. Recently, Torvik et al. (2004) developed an unsupervised query system, which accepts an author's name as an input and returns a list of scientific articles being ranked in decreasing certainty of whether or not an article was authored by the same person. Essentially, articles are ranked by performing a pairwise textual similarity of title, journal name, coauthor names, subject headings, and affiliation.

A drawback commonly encountered with these methods originates from their requirements of domain-specific rules/grammars for comparison, and of a typically vast amount of computational time and space (Calado et al., 2006). Such methods are therefore restricted in their potential applications and in worst circumstances, as they may be misleading. This is particularly the case within the domains of intelligence data analysis (Boongoen et al., 2010; Pantel, 2006; Wang et al., 2005) and online resources (Lin et al., 2006), where objects are falsely specified or they are of incomparable types.

Accordingly, the 'social network inspired' approach (or 'link analysis') to this problem has been proposed to underpin the accountability for unstructured information: probabilistic models of word usage in terms of surrounding words (Gale et al., 1992; Ginter et al., 2004), object-relation networks and link analysis (Bhattacharya and Getoor, 2007; Chan and Franklin, 1998; Hiro et al., 1996; Mitchell, 2006). In particular, link analysis has proven effective for a wide range of domains, including personal name resolution in publication databases (Klink et al., 2006; Sun et al., 2005; Tong et, 2006), web-page similarity (Hou and Zhang, 2003: Lin et al., 2006), email address resolution (Holzer et al., 2005), personal name resolution in emails (Minkov et al., 2006), citation matching (Pasula et al., 2003), data cleaning (Kalashnikov et al., 2005), collaborative recommendation (Fouss et al., 2007), alias detection in spam emails and terrorism-related datasets (Boongoen et al., 2010; Hsiung et al., 2005).

## Problem Formulation

Link analysis can be conducted on a social network representation of relations amongst references of real-world entities. This has been effectively exploited for link prediction in (Liben-Nowell and Kleinberg, 2007; Murata and Moriyasu, 2008)

and author-name resolution in (Reuther and Walter, 2006). The underlying link network is specified as an undirected graph $G = (V, E)$, which is composed of two sets, the set of vertices $V$ and that of edges $E$, respectively. Let $X$ and $R$ be the sets of all references and their relations in the dataset. Then, vertex $v_i \in V$ denotes a reference $x_i \in X$ and each edge $e_{ij} \in E$ linking $v_i, v_j \in V$ corresponds to a relation $r_{ij} \in R$ between references $x_i, x_j \in X$.

The current research concentrates on the analysis of a social network whose edges correspond to 'co-occurrence' relations amongst references. In other words, a relation $r_{ij} \in R$ determines the fact that references $x_i, x_j \in X$ appear together in a specific observation. It is bi-directional such that $r_{ij}$ is equivalent to $r_{ji}, \forall r_{ij}, r_{ji} \in R$. As such, edges in $G$ are undirected and any $e_{ij}, e_{ji} \in E$ are equivalent. Note that this paradigm is simple (semantics-less) and efficient regarding its information acquisition and analysis. It can be effectively extended to the highly semantics-embedded cases, where both direction and type of examined relations are exhibited within a directed graph (e.g., the semantic network of email communication (Minkov et al., 2006) and the citation network of scientific publications (Pasula et al., 2003)).

In addition, each edge $e_{ij} \in E$ possesses statistical information $f_{ij} \in \{1, \ldots, \infty\}$, representing the frequency of any relation occurring between references $x_i$ and $x_j$ within the underlying dataset. By representing the multiplicity of each link as a frequency count, the graph terminology used in this paper becomes simple (i.e., no parallel edges), without losing any potential link information (Wasserman and Faust, 1994). Let $O$ be the set of real-world entities each being referred to by at least one member of set $X$, a pair of references $(x_i, x_j)$ are aliases when both references correspond to the same real-world entity:

*Figure 1. Relations between author references and publications, presented in: (a) database table format and (b) graphical format.*

(a) relations in database table

| publications | author names |
|---|---|
| paper$_1$ | A and B |
| paper$_2$ | A, C and D |
| paper$_3$ | A and D |
| paper$_4$ | B and E |
| paper$_5$ | C and D |

(b) relations in a graph format

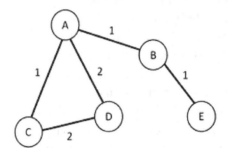

$x_i \equiv o_k \wedge x_j \equiv o_k, o_k \in O$. In practice, disclosing an alias pair in a graph $G$ is to find a couple of vertices $(v_i, v_j)$, whose similarity $s(v_i, v_j)$ is significantly high. Intuitively, the higher $s(v_i, v_j)$ is, the greater the possibility of vertices $v_i$ and $v_j$, and hence the corresponding references $x_i$ and $x_j$, which constitute the actual alias pair becomes.

To illustrate this framework, the link network of publication data, similar to that exploited in (Reuther and Walter, 2006), is discussed here. Effectively, a set of author references (i.e., names) and their relations can be represented as the graph shown in Figure 1, where

$$X = \{A, B, C, D, E\}, R = \{r_{AB}, r_{AC}, r_{AD}, r_{BE}, r_{CD}\}$$

and $r_{ij}$ denotes the fact that references $x_i$ and $x_j$ co-occur as authors of a specific publication (i.e., co-author). In addition, the edge $e_{AD}$ is presented with $f_{AD} = 2$ since references $A$ and $D$ are co-authors of two different papers (i.e., *paper$_2$* and *paper$_3$*). However, the frequency statistics $f_{AC}$ of the edge $e_{AC}$ is 1 as references $A$ and $C$ have only one joint publication, *paper$_2$*. Effectively, given $O$ as the set of real-world author entities, a pair of references, such as $(A, B)$, may be hy-

pothesized, based on their similarity, as the alias pair (i.e., $A \equiv o_k \wedge B \equiv o_k, o_k \in O$).

## Link-Based Similarity Measures

Unlike the content-based approach in which appearances and other characteristic features of references are directly compared, the relation-based analysis makes use of the link-based similarity measured upon link patterns between studied references. Due to this perspective and increasing volume of network-alike information (online resources, publication repository, phone and credit-card usages, for instance), several link-based similarity methods have been introduced to evaluate the similarity between information objects: Co-citation (Small, 1973), SimRank (Jeh and Widom, 2002), Connected-Triple (Klink et al., 2006), PageSim (Lin et al., 2006) and a variety of random walk methods (Fouss et al., 2007; Minkov et al., 2006; Tong et al., 2006). See more details in (Getoor and Diehl, 2005; Liben-Nowell and Kleinberg, 2007).

Initially, many existing link-based similarity measures have concentrated exclusively on the numerical count of shared neighboring objects. Let a vertex $v_i$ in the graph $G$ represent an entity of interest (e.g., a paper in a publication network) and $N_{v_i}$ be a set of vertices (i.e., entities) directly linked to $v_i$, called neighbors of $v_i$. The similarity between $v_i$ and $v_j$ is then determined by the cardinality of $N_{v_i} \cap N_{v_j}$. In essence, the higher the cardinality is, the higher the similarity of these entities becomes. This 'cardinality' perspective has been adopted by several well-known methods, some of which are outlined below.

- **SimRank (SR).** With the principal objective of finding similar publications given their citation relations, the SimRank algorithm (Jeh and Widom, 2002) relies on the cardinality of shared neighbors that are iteratively refined to a fixed point. In each iteration, the similarity $s(v_i, v_j)$ of any pair of vertices $v_i, v_j \in V$ is approximated as follows:

$$s(v_i, v_j) = \frac{C \sum_{p=1}^{|N_{v_i}|} \sum_{q=1}^{|N_{v_j}|} s(N_{v_i}^p, N_{v_j}^q)}{|N_{v_i}| |N_{v_j}|} \quad (1)$$

where individual neighbors of vertices $v_i$ and $v_j$ are denoted as $N_{v_i}^p$ and $N_{v_j}^q$, for $1 \le p \le |N_{v_i}|$ and $1 \le q \le |N_{v_j}|$. The constant $C \in [0,1]$ is a decay factor that represents the confidence level of accepting two non-identical entities as similar. Note that $s(v_i, v_j) = 0$ when $N_{v_i} = \varnothing$ or $N_{v_j} = \varnothing$.

- **PageSim (PS).** Within a different domain, the PageSim algorithm (Lin et al., 2006) was developed to capture similar web pages based on associations implied by their hyperlinks. In essence, the similarity $s(v_i, v_j)$ is dictated by the coherence of ranking scores $R(v_g, v_i)$ and $R(v_g, v_j)$ propagated to them from any other vertex $v_g \in V$. It is noteworthy that ranking scores are explicitly generated using the page ranking scheme, PageRank (Brin and Page, 1998), of the well-known Google search engine.

Given a link network $G = (V, W)$, let $P(v_i)$ denote the PageRank score of a vertex $v_i \in V$. Its value can be estimated from the following iterative refinement:

$$P(v_i) = \lim_{k \to \infty} P_k(v_i) \quad (2)$$

$$P_k(v_i) = (1 - \beta) + \beta \sum_{v_j \in V, w_{i,j} \in W} P_{k-1}(v_j) \times Dist(v_j, v_i) \quad (3)$$

where $\beta$ is a dampening factor that is usually set to 0.85 (Brin and Page, 1998), and $P_0(v_i), \forall v_i \in V$ is initially set to 1. In addition, $Dist(v_j, v_i)$ can be found by:

$$Dist(v_j, v_i) = \frac{|w_{j,i}|}{\sum_{v_x \in V, v_x \neq v_j} |w_{j,x}|} \quad (4)$$

Having achieved this, the score $R(v_i, v_j)$ propagated from $v_i \in V$ to $v_j \in V$ can be calculated as follows:

$$R(v_i, v_j) = \sum_{p \in PATH(v_i, v_j, r)} d \times P(v_i) \times PDist(p, v_i, v_j) \quad (5)$$

where $d \in (0, 1]$ is a decay factor, $r$ is the maximum path length, and $PDist(p, v_i, v_j)$ is defined by the following equation with $v_{x+1}$ denoting the vertex adjacent to $v_x$ in path $p$, along the direction from $v_i$ to $v_j$:

$$PDist(p, v_i, v_j) = \prod_{v_x \in P, v_x \neq v_j} \frac{|w_{x,x+1}|}{\sum_{v_y \in V, v_y \neq v_x} |w_{x,y}|} \quad (6)$$

Effectively, the similarity measure can be defined as

$$s(v_i, v_j) = \sum_{v_g \in V, v_g \neq \{v_i, v_j\}} \frac{\min(R(v_g, v_i), R(v_g, v_j))^2}{\max(R(v_g, v_i), R(v_g, v_j))} \tag{7}$$

- **Connected-Triple (CT).** With the same neighbor-based intuition, this approach evaluates the similarity of objects in accordance to their overlapping social context (Klink et al., 2006). This measurement is based on the social network $G = (V, E)$ in which objects of interest and their relations are represented by the sets of vertices $V$ and edges $E$, respectively. The similarity of any two objects can be estimated by counting the number of the Connected-Triples that they are part in. Formally, a Connected Triple, $Triple = \{V_{Triple}, E_{Triple}\}$, is a subgraph of $G$ where

$$V_{Triple} = \{v_1, v_2, v_3\} \subset V$$

and $E_{Triple} = \{e_{v_1 v_2}, e_{v_1 v_3}\} \subset E$, with $e_{v_2 v_3} \notin E$

Figure 2 presents an example of a social network in which object $A$ and object $B$ are justified similar due to the fact that there exists a Connected-Triple link connecting them together, $V_{Triple} = \{A, B, D\}$ and $E_{Triple} = \{e_{AD}, e_{BD}\}$, with $e_{AB} \notin E$.

Despite their simplicity, the aforementioned cardinality-based measures are greatly sensitive to noise and often generate a large proportion of false positives (Klink et al., 2006). This shortcoming emerges because these methods exclusively concern with the cardinality aspect of link patterns without taking into account the underlying characteristics of a link itself. As the first attempt to extend this approach by addressing such characteristics, Boongoen and Shen (2010) suggested the 'uniqueness measure' of link patterns as an additional criterion to the cardinality in order to crystalise the estimation of similarity values. The resultant mechanism proved effective over the terrorism-related data collection (Hsiung et al., 2005).

Given a graph $G = (V, E)$ in which objects and their relations are represented with the sets of vertices $V$ and edges $E$, respectively, a uniqueness measure $UQ_{ij}^k$ of vertices $v_i, v_j \in V$ can be approximated from each joint neighbor $v_k \in V$ as follows:

$$UQ_{ij}^k = \frac{f_{ik} + f_{jk}}{\sum_m f_{mk}} \tag{8}$$

where $f_{ik}$ is frequency of the edge $e_{ik}$ connecting vertices $v_i, v_k \in V$. To summarize the uniqueness of joint link patterns $UQ_{ij}$, the ratios estimated for each shared neighbor are aggregated by

$$UQ_{ij} = \frac{1}{n} \sum_{k=1}^{n} UQ_{ij}^k \tag{9}$$

where $k = 1 \ldots n$ and $n$ is the number of common neighbors between vertices $v_i, v_j$.

## ABSOLUTE ORDER-OF-MAGNITUDE (AOM) REASONING

The absolute order-of-magnitude (AOM) model (Piera, 1995) operates on a finite set of ordered

*Figure 2. A social network with Connected-Triple.*

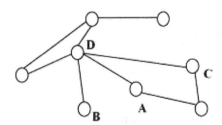

labels or qualitative descriptors, achieved via a partition of the real number line $\Re$. Each element of the partition represents a basic qualitative class to which a label is associated. The number of labels selected to express each variable of a real problem is subject to both the characteristics and the precision level that is required to support comprehension and communication. In practice, multiple label sets with dissimilar granularities are typically utilised to define domain attributes qualitatively.

Despite the intuition that the number of labels is not fixed, the most conventional partitions are symmetric. That is, the partition of the underlying domain typically has $n$ positive and $n$ negative labels, which is formally represented by $OM(n)$, and referred to as the AOM model of granularity $n$. The partition of the real line into $2n + 1$ labels is dictated by the set of $2n - 1$ landmarks. In essence, landmarks are domain dependent and determined by either subjective justification of human experts or learning from data. For instance, the $OM(3)$ model is built on the following set of landmarks: $\{-\beta, -\alpha, 0, \alpha, \beta\}$. Figure 3 illustrates the resulting partition into seven qualitatively distinct order-of-magnitude labels, which are the most commonly used: Negative Large (NL), Negative Medium (NM), Negative Small (NS), Zero (0), Positive Small (PS), Positive Medium (PM) and Positive Large (PL) (Olmo et al., 2007).

## Order of Magnitude Space

An order of magnitude (OM) space $S$ defined for a qualitative variable is the combination of the ordered label set $S_l$ and the interval-like treatment of such labels. For instance, the value of one variable is expressed by the set of basic labels $S_l = \{B_1, \ldots, B_n\}$ with $B_1 < \ldots < B_n$ denoting its qualitative order, meaning that $\alpha < \beta, \forall \alpha \in B_i, \beta \in B_j, i < j$. The corresponding OM space $S$ is formally described as $S = S_l \cup \{[B_i, B_j] \mid B_i, B_j \in S_l, i < j\}$. In effect, the label $[B_i, B_j]$ with $i < j$ is defined as the union of the elements within the set $\{B_i, B_{i+1}, \ldots, B_j\}$. In addition, the order in $S_l$ induces the partial order $\leq_p$ in $S$, which represents 'being more precise than' or 'being less general than':

$$[B_i, B_j] \leq_p [B_x, B_y] \Leftrightarrow [B_i, B_j] \subset [B_x, B_y] \quad (10)$$

where $[B_i, B_i] = \{B_i\}$. According to Figure 4, the least precise label is $[B_1, B_n]$, denoted by '?'. This manipulation of ordered labels allows reasoning and analysis with single or combined labels that may reflect uncertainty of one agent on another agent's judgement.

It is possible to define qualitative equality, termed q-equal, in an $OM(n)$ space $S$. Given $O, P \in S$, $O$ and $P$ are q-equal or $O \approx P$, if

*Figure 3. The $OM(3)$ absolute partition.*

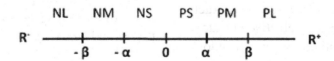

**Qualitative labels:**
NL = ( -∞, -β ]; NM = ( -β, -α ]; NS = ( -α, 0 )
0 = {0}
PS = ( 0, α ); PM = [ α, β ); PL = [ β, +∞)

*Figure 4. Graphical illustration of the partial order relation $\leq_p$ in an order-of-magnitude space $S$.*

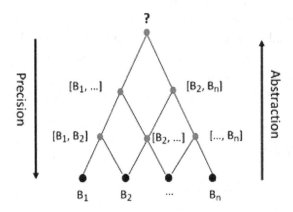

there is a $Q \in S$ such that $Q \leq_p O$ and $Q \leq_p P$. This effectively implies that $O$ and $P$ encompass, in part or in full, common basic elements. In addition, for presentational simplicity, $\forall O \in S$, the sets $B_O = \{B \in S_l - \{0\}, B \leq_p O\}$ and $B_O^* = \{B \in S_l, B \leq_p O\}$ are termed the 'base of O' and the 'enlarged base of O', respectively.

## Qualitative Algebra of AOM

At the outset, the mathematical structure of the AOM model, called Qualitative Algebra or Q-algebra, was initially defined as the unification of sign and interval algebra over a continuum of qualitative partitions of the real line (Trave-Massuyes and Piera, 1989). However, although being superior to the sign algebra, such qualitative operators still suffer significantly from producing ambiguous and indeterminate outcomes. The notion of 'qualitative expression of a real operator' has been introduced to restrain this problem (Agell et al., 2000). In particular, qualitative operators are considered as multidimensional functions defined in an AOM space. The Cartesian product of $S^1, S^2, \ldots, S^k$ (where $k$ is the number of variables of a given problem domain, $S^i$ is an $OM(n)$ space, $i = 1 \ldots k$) is adopted to express the out-

come of a real operator in $\Re^k$ qualitatively, which is reflected onto the resulting qualitative space $S'$

Given a real operator $\omega$ defined on $\Re^k$ involving $k$ real variables with each taking values in $\Re$, the corresponding qualitative abstraction of $\omega$, denoted as $[\omega]$, is specified on $S^k$ with values in $S'$ as follows:

$$[\omega](X_1, X_2, \ldots, X_k) = [\omega(X_1, X_2, \ldots, X_k)]_{S'} \quad (11)$$

where $X_i \in S^i, i = 1 \ldots k$ and

$$\omega(X_1, X_2, \ldots, X_k) = \{\omega(x_1, x_2, \ldots, x_k), x_i \in X_i\}.$$

Inherently, $[\omega]$ assigns to each $k$-tuple element of $(X_1, X_2, \ldots, X_k)$ a qualitative description of the subset enclosing all underlying numerical results of applying $\omega$ over all real values in $X_1, X_2, \ldots, X_k$

To simplify this, it is feasible to generate the qualitative operator, $[\omega]$, from the basic ordered labels of an OM space, $S, S^i = S, \forall i = 1 \ldots k$. For any $[\omega]$ and $X_1, X_2, \ldots, X_k \in S$:

$$[\omega](X_1, X_2, \ldots, X_k) = \bigcup_{B_i \in B_{X_i}^*} [\omega](B_1, B_2, \ldots, B_k)$$

$$(12)$$

According to Equation 11, the qualitative operator $[\omega]$ can be generalized as follows:

$$[\omega](X_1, X_2, \ldots, X_k) = \bigcup_{B_i \in B_{X_i}^*} [w(B_1, B_2, \ldots, B_k)]_{S'}$$

$$(13)$$

It is noteworthy that the $[\omega]$ operator presented above is compatible only to variables specified in the same order of magnitude space. To enhance the applicability of this terminology, the utilisation of this qualitative operator is further introduced to multi-granularity domains via the homogenisation of references, which has been successfully applied to realistic problems like credit risk prediction (Agell et al., 2000) and marketing segmentation (Olmo et al., 2007). This intuitive technique is extensively used in the current research, which will be thoroughly discussed in the following sections.

## ORDER-OF-MAGNITUDE BASED LINK ANALYSIS

This section introduces a novel order-of-magnitude based link analysis in which multiple link properties are combined to improve the quality of estimated link-based similarity measures.

### Link Properties

Link analysis makes use of the link-based similarity that is measured upon link patterns between studied references. According to this perspective and in response to the increasing volume of network-like information (such as online resources, publication repository, phone and credit-card usages), several link-based similarity methods have been introduced to evaluate the similarity between information objects: e.g., SimRank (Jeh and Widom, 2002) and PageSim (Lin et al., 2006). Despite notable achievement, these techniques are computationally inefficient, comparing to

those simple methods developed for social network analysis (SNA) (Wasserman and Faust, 1994). In order to boost the performance of the SNA methodology whilst maintaining its efficiency, a new aggregated model is proposed here to provide a systematic framework for combining multiple link properties and consequently deriving an accurate conclusion. Specifically, the property measures of cardinality (CT) and uniqueness (UQ) are employed in the present research to illustrate the potential of such approach. Details of these measures have been given in Section 2.

### Link Based Similarity Evaluation

A common drawback of those numerical measures previously discussed is the inability to achieve coherent and natural interpretation through existing seemingly fine-grained scales. Exploring a link network with crisp numerically-valued criteria is typically considered inflexible comparing to the use of interval and linguistic descriptors. Specifically, a wrong interpretation of a property measure may occur if there exists an unduly high property value within a link network. A more accurate and naturally expressive measure is to exploit qualitative labels like highly, moderately or poorly certain.

In order to overcome this important shortcoming, measures of link properties like cardinality and uniqueness are gauged in accordance with property-specific order-of-magnitude (OM) spaces. Subsequently, the link-based similarity value is derived by combining these qualitative descriptors, each assigned with a possibly different degree of relevance. Homogenising of references in multi-granularity OM spaces (Agell et al., 2000) is applied to this aggregation process in such a way that values measured in distinct scales can be analogously manipulated.

## OM Spaces for Link Properties

At the outset, measures of link properties, originally in quantitative terms, are translated into elements of ordered label sets. Formally, let $P^i$ and $L^i$ be the set of intervals partitioned on the real line and that of the corresponding qualitative labels, defined for measures of the link property $i$ on the discourse $U^i$. That is, $P^i = \{p_1^i, \ldots, p_{n^i}^i\}$ and $L^i = \{l_1^i, \ldots, l_{n^i}^i\}$, where $n^i$ is the number of intervals/labels and $l_1^i < \ldots < l_{n^i}^i$ denotes the qualitative orders of magnitude specified for property $i$. Without causing confusion, for simplicity, intervals partitioned on real number line are termed partitions. They are non-overlapped over the discourse $U^i$, and their crisp boundaries are determined by one or two members of the landmark set $M^i = \{m_1^i, \ldots, m_{n^i-1}^i\}$. Each partition $p_j^i$ is qualitatively expressed by the label $l_j^i, \forall j = 1 \ldots n^i$, and its interval is defined by lower bound $\alpha_j^i$ and/or upper bound $\beta_j^i$ such that $\alpha_j^i, \beta_j^i \in M^i$ and $\alpha_j^i \leq \beta_j^i$. Intuitively, the number of labels should be small enough so as not to impose useless precision onto analysts, but it must be rich enough to allow meaningful assessment and discrimination of measurement (Herrera et al., 2000). In fact, average human beings can reasonably manage to bear in mind seven or so items/labels (Miller, 1956).

For the current research with $i \in \{CT, UQ\}$, as a simple example, measures of the cardinality property over the discourse $U^{CT} = [0, \infty)$ may be described using a member of the label set of three qualitative labels

$$(n^{CT} = 3), L^{CT}$$
$$= \{l_1^{CT} = Small, l_2^{CT} = Medium, l_3^{CT} = Large\}$$

In particular, given the landmark set

$$M^{CT} = \{m_1^{CT} = 2, m_2^{CT} = 6\},$$

members of the partition set are then specified as $P^{CT} = \{p_1^{CT} = [0, 2], p_2^{CT} = (2, 6], p_3^{CT} = (6, \infty)\}$. Likewise, for the uniqueness measure, its values can be defined on the universe of discourse $U^{UQ} = [0, 1]$, which may be expressed using the ordered set of five qualitative descriptors $(n^{UQ} = 5), L^{UQ} = \{l_1^{UQ} = VeryLow, l_2^{UQ} = Low, l_3^{UQ} = Moderate, l_4^{UQ} = High, l_5^{UQ} = VeryHigh\}$. Using the set of landmarks ($M^{UQ} = \{m_1^{UQ} = 0.1, m_2^{UQ} = 0.3, m_3^{UQ} = 0.6, m_{\leq 4}^{UQ} = 0.8\}$), the corresponding partition set can be defined as

$$P^{UQ} = \{p_1^{UQ} = [0, 0.1], p_2^{UQ} = (0.1, 0.3], p_3^{UQ} = (0.3, 0.6], p_4^{UQ} = (0.6, 0.8], p_5^{UQ} = (0.8, 1]\}$$

## Similarity Measure via Aggregation of Properties

Relying on one particular link property, as with existing link-based methods, for justifying the similarity between any two objects in a link network may lead to false interpretation and perhaps revolting consequences. The more rational alternative is to integrate all available link properties in order to refine the similarity measure. Fortunately, the link-based similarity between any two vertices $v_a, v_b \in V$ in the link network can be estimated through the aggregation of qualitative descriptors each corresponding to a particular link property $i$. In particular, each property $i$ can be assigned with a different degree of relevance (e.g., importance) $RV^i$, which may be given by domain experts in accordance with their past experiences or estimated from past data if such expertise is not readily available. Similar to measures of link properties previously emphasised, relevance can be naturally expressed using the order-of-magnitude label set $L^{RV}$, such as

$$L^{RV} = \{None, +, ++, +++\}$$

or $L^{RV} = \{0, 1, 2, 3\}$. In the discussion above, the relevance degrees of cardinality $RV^{CT} \in L^{RV}$ and uniqueness properties $RV^{UQ} \in L^{RV}$ are subjectively set to 2 and 1, respectively.

*Table 1. Homogenised Landmarks*

| Landmarks | CT | UQ |
|---|---|---|
| Original | 2, 6 | 0.1, 0.3, 0.6, 0.8 |
| Step1 | 0, 4 | -0.2, 0, 0.3, 0.5 |
| Step2 | -4, 0, 4 | -0.5, -0.3, -0.2, 0, 0.2, 0.3, 0.5 |
| Step3 | -4, -2, -1, 0, 1, 2, 4 | -0.5, -0.3, -0.2, 0, 0.2, 0.3, 0.5 |
| Homogenised | -3, -2, -1, 0, 1, 2, 3 | -3, -2, -1, 0, 1, 2, 3 |
| *Irrelevant* | -3, -2, -1, 1, 2 | -3, -2, 1 |

However, since label sets defined for different properties are usually of unequal granularity, they have to be homogenised onto a common scale on which references of distinct label sets can be uniformly manipulated and integrated. Following the work of Agell et al. (2000), the procedure below will be used in this work:

- *Step 1*: Convert each set of landmarks $M^i$ into a symmetric arrangement. Given a central landmark $m_c^i \in M^i$, translate each landmark $m_t^i, t = 1 \ldots n^i - 1$ to the new landmark $sm_t^i$ in the symmetric scale using $sm_t^i = m_t^i - m_c^i$. Note that the central landmark is now 0 in the new scale.

- *Step 2*: Obtain a fully symmetric pattern by adding missing landmarks, so that one absolute landmark can be found on both positive and negative sides of 0. This is done because landmarks appearing on both positive and negative sides may be dissimilar in general. These newly added elements are of balancing purpose only, they will not be used to represent values and will be deliberately marked as irrelevant.

- *Step 3*: Modify the landmark sets for each property further by adding new landmarks on both side of 0, in such a way that all landmark sets have the same cardinality. Similar to Step 2, new elements are irrelevant with respect to each particular property and are simply to support the unification mechanism.

In accordance to the landmarks of two link properties given earlier, Table 1 summarises the results achieved at each step of the homogenisation process.

Following the terminology of AOM algebra, with the property-specific relevance degrees previously clarified, order-of-magnitude based similarity measure (OMS) can be estimated from measures of any $n$ properties using the qualitative expression of a real weighted summation operator $[\omega]$:

$$
\begin{aligned}
OMS &= [\omega]\big(x_1, \ldots, x_n, RV_1, \ldots, RV_n\big) \\
&= \Big[\omega\big(x_1, \ldots, x_n, RV_1, \ldots, RV_n\big)\Big]_{S^{Sum}}
\end{aligned}
$$

(14)

where $X_i \in S^H$ is the qualitative measure of link property $i, i = 1 \ldots n$, expressed on the homogenized scale $S^H$, $RV_i$ is its corresponding relevance degree, $S^{Sum}$ is the resulting order-of-magnitude space of this summarization and $\omega$ is defined as

$$
\begin{aligned}
\omega\big(X_1, \ldots, X_n, RV_1, \ldots, RV_n\big) &= \omega\big(x_1, \ldots, x_n, rv_1, \ldots, rv_n\big) \\
&= x_1 rv_1 + \ldots + x_n rv_n
\end{aligned}
$$

(15)

where $x_i \in X_i, rv_i \in RV_i, i = 1 \ldots n$.

Specific to the two link property measures used here: CT and UQ, with their relevance degrees being $RV^{CT}$ and $RV^{UQ}$ and the homogenized scale $S^H$ being {-3, -2, -1, 0, 1, 2, 3}, the previous equations can be employed as follows:

$$OMS = [\omega](CT, UQ, RV^{CT}, RV^{UQ})$$
$$= [\omega(CT, UQ, RV^{CT}, RV^{UQ})]_{S^{Sum}} \quad (16)$$

Following this,

$$OMS = [\omega(2ct + uq)]_{S^{Sum}} \quad (17)$$

where $ct \in M^{CT}$, and $M^{CT}$ is the set of relevant landmarks of CT in the homogenized scale $S^H$ : $M^{CT} = \{0, 3\}$. Likewise, $uq$ is a member of $M^{UQ}$, with $M^{UQ} = \{-1, 0, 2, 3\}$. Effectively, the resulting order-of-magnitude space $S^{Sum}$ is established upon landmark values of this qualitative operation, which are {-1, 0, 2, 3, 5, 6, 8, 9}. To obtain a coherent interpretation of similarity measures within the $S^{Sum}$ space, a set of qualitative labels $L^{OMS}$, as partitions of $S^{Sum}$, is chosen to express the different orders of magnitude of the similarity values. For instance,

$$L^{OMS} = \{Low(OMS < 2), Medium(2 \leq OMS \leq 6), High(OMS > 6)\}$$

Note that a more or less refined label sets may be used depending on the precision level required.

## SEMI-SUPERVISED METHOD TO DESIGNING LANDMARKS

Designing an appropriate set of landmarks $M^i$ for a link property $i$ is non-trivial and proves to be critical towards the quality of generated similarity measures. A simple approach is to rely on human experts, who select suitable landmark values in accordance with their personal intuition and judgment. This is not usually effective regarding the availability of experts and the diverse nature of different problem domains. In addition, human input may be rather subjective and inconsistent. As a result, a data-driven mechanism that can be used to obtain an appropriate $M^i$ is specifically discussed here.

For a link property $i$, a density graph is formulated to represent the proportion of entity pairs (i.e., $(v_x, v_y), v_x, v_y \in V$), each with a different property measure $i_{xy}$. Let $D : [0, i_{\max}] \to [0, 1]$ be the density function (where $i_{\max}$ denotes the maximum value of $i_{xy}$), which is formally defined as

$$D(t) = \frac{N(t)}{\sum\limits_{\forall r \in [0, i_{\max}]} N(r)} \quad (18)$$

where $N(t)$ denotes the number of entity pairs $(v_x, v_y)$ whose property measure

$$i_{xy} \geq t, t \in [0, i_{\max}].$$

Figure 5 presents the density function of cardinality property (i.e., $i = CT$) derived from the Terrorist dataset (Hsiung et al., 2005), where $CT_{\max} = 113$ (and the magnified presentation of $D(t), t \in \{7, 113\}$ is included for better interpretation).

With this function, the following set of heuristics can be articulated especially to help data analysts to assess a proper set of landmarks $M^i$ for link property $i$:

- Let $M^i = \{m_1^i, m_2^i, \ldots, m_{n^i}^i\}$ be an appropriate landmark set for property $i$, where $m_g^i \leq i_{\max}, \forall g \in \{1 \ldots n^i\}$ and $m_h^i \leq m_{h+1}^i, \forall h \in \{1 \ldots n^i - 1\}$.

*Figure 5. Example of density function derived from Terrorist dataset.*

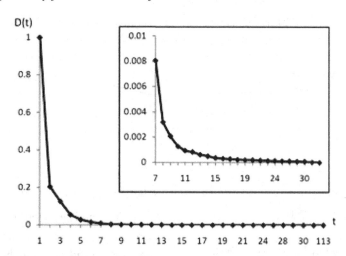

- Each pair of adjacent landmarks (i.e., $m_h^i$ and $m_{h+1}^i$) encapsulates all property values $i_{xy} \in [m_h^i, m_{h+1}^i)$ whose density $D(i_{xy})$ can be perceived at a particular order of magnitude. Note that orders of magnitude utilized in this research are of $\alpha \times 10^z$, where $z \in \{-1, -2, \ldots, -\infty\}$ and $\alpha \in (0, 10)$. According to Figure 5, $M^{CT}$ of the Terrorist dataset is {4, 7, 10, 23} such that $D(CT_{xy})$ is expressed in five different orders of magnitude of
    - $10^{-1}$ where $CT_{xy} < 4$
    - $10^{-2}$ where $4 \leq CT_{xy} < 7$
    - $10^{-3}$ where $7 \leq CT_{xy} < 10$
    - $10^{-4}$ where $10 \leq CT_{xy} < 23$
    - $10^{-5}$ where $CT_{xy} \geq 23$

This semi-supervised method is effective to assist analysts in designing appropriate landmarks and descriptive labels, based on quality measures of the particular link network being studied. Unlike human-directed alternatives, it is data oriented and capable of being adapted to a variety of problems.

## PERFORMANCE EVALUATION

For performance evaluation, similarity estimates acquired from the proposed approach are compared with those derived by other link-based and related techniques, for the task of finding aliases in the 'Terrorist' dataset (Hsiung et al., 2005). This is a link dataset manually extracted from web pages and news stories regarding terrorism. Each entity presented in this network corresponds to the name of a person, place and organisation, while a link denotes an association between objects through reported events. Statistically, this network contains 4,088 entities, 5,581 links and 919 alias pairs (i.e., false identities). Figure 6 shows an example of this link network in which names 'Bin laden' and 'Abu abdallah' truly refer to the same real-world person.

### Efficiency of Semi-Supervised Method

Initially, it is important to examine the effectiveness of the proposed semi-supervised method for modeling a landmark set. By following the heuristics previously prescribed, appropriate landmark values are:

*Figure 6. Example of Terrorist link dataset.*

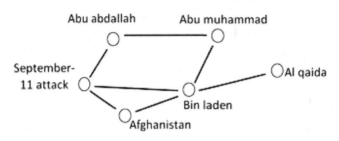

- $M^{CT} = \{4, 7, 10, 23\}$
- $M^{UQ} = \{0.05, 0.12, 0.27, 0.43, 1\}$

With these data-oriented landmarks, Table 2 compares the number of disclosed alias pairs successfully detected by different methods, where $K$ denotes the number of entity pairs with the highest similarity measures (details of homogenization for semi-supervised landmarks are not included due to save space). Note that $OMS$ and $OMS^H$ represent order-of-magnitude based similarity measures, with semi-supervised and human-directed landmarks, respectively. In addition, $QT$ denotes a simple integration of numerical $CT$ and $UQ$ measures, where relevance degrees $RV^{CT}$ and $RV^{UQ}$ (2 and 1, respectively) similar to those of $OMS$ and $OMS^H$ are employed.

These results indicate that the $OMS$ measure with semi-supervised landmarks usually outperforms both human-directed landmarks $OMS^H$ and the quantitative evaluation $QT$. Given $K$ being *400*, the precision of OMS is $80/400$, which

*Table 2. Number of alias pairs disclosed by each method*

| $K$ | $OMS$ | $OMS^H$ | $QT$ |
|---|---|---|---|
| **400** | 80 | 57 | 41 |
| **600** | 115 | 91 | 60 |
| **800** | 146 | 110 | 75 |

is better than $57/400$ of $OMS^H$ and $41/400$ of $QT$. This trend has been similarly observed when the values of K are 600 and 800, respectively. These results indicate that the qualitative aggregation of link properties (i.e., $OMS$ and $OMS^H$) provides a more accurate similarity measure than the quantitative counterpart (i.e., $QT$). Also, the use of data-dependent landmarks obtained from the aforementioned semi-supervised framework can further boost the accuracy of the measure and hence, the detection.

## Comparison with Alternative Link-Based Methods

The performance of the OMS method is further generalized by evaluating against the following state-of-the-art link-based measures and other alternative techniques:

- Basic property measures that are exploited to construct the proposed OMS methods: numerical CT and UQ.
- Advanced link-based similarity techniques: SimRank (SR) and PageSim (PS).
- String-matching measure: Jaro (JR), (Jaro, 1995), which is employed to illustrate the effectiveness of the text-based approach and also to set the base-line performance for the underlying tasks. This distance-based metric relies on the number and order of the common characters between strings $p = a_1 ..., a_K$ and $q = b_1 ..., b_L$.

Particularly, a character $a_i \in p$ is *common with q* when there is $b_j \in q, b_j = a_i$ such that $i - H \leq j \leq i + H$ and

$$H = \frac{\min(|p|, |q|)}{2} \qquad (19)$$

where $|p|$ denotes the length of string $p$.

Let $p' = a'_1 \ldots a'_{K^*}, (K^* \leq K)$ be the sequence of characters in $p$ that are common with $q$, in the same order that they appear in $p$ and $q' = b'_1 \ldots b'_{L^*}, (L^* \leq L)$ be the similar sequence of characters in $q$ that are common with $p$, *transposition for p'* and $q'$ is specified as the cardinality of positions $i$ where $a'_i \neq b'_i$. Effectively, the Jaro similarity metric for strings $p$ and $q$ is defined as follows:

$$Jaro(p, q) = \frac{1}{3}\left(\frac{|p'|}{|p|} + \frac{|q'|}{|q|} + \frac{|p'| - T_{p',q'}}{|p'|}\right) \qquad (20)$$

where $T_{p',q'}$ is a half of transposition for $p'$ and $q'$.

- Computational linguistic method that is developed for the discovery of morphologically related words in an unannotated corpus (Baroni et al. 2002). To justify the similarity $s(p_1, p_2)$ of any word pair ( $p_1$ and $p_2$ ), this technique combines the corresponding appearance-based and semantic-based similarity measures ( $\Lambda(p_1, p_2) \in [0,1]$ and $\Phi(p_1, p_2)$, respectively):

$$s(p_1, p_2) = w_\Lambda \Lambda(p_1, p_2) + w_\Phi \Phi(p_1, p_2) \qquad (21)$$

where $w_\Lambda, w_\Phi \in [0,1]$ and $w_\Lambda + w_\Phi = 1$. In particular, the semantic similarity of $\Phi(p_1, p_2)$ is determined by the frequency of co-occurrence between $p_1$ and $p_2$. For the present evaluation, Jaro (JR) is used to estimate the appearance-based similarity, and the ultimate result can be achieved using a simple arithmetic average (i.e., $w_\Lambda = w_\Phi = \frac{1}{2}$ ).

Figure 7 shows the evaluation results summarized over the number of actual alias pairs disclosed by the examined methods: OMS (Orders-of-magnitude similarity), SR (SimRank; Jeh and Widom, 2002), PS (PageSim; Lin et al., 2006), JR (Jaro string-matching measure; Jaro, 1995) and MOP (Morphology based model; Baroni et al., 2002). Again, $K$ denotes the number of retrieved name pairs, i.e., $K$ pairs with the highest similarity degrees estimated by each technique.

According to this statistical analysis, the qualitative framework (OMS) usually outperforms the string-matching technique (JR), the morphological based model (MOP), and those complex link-based techniques (SR and PS). In addition to this improvement, the new approach offers the potential of coherent human interpretation and communication. For any automated information awareness system, the generation of false positives is a serious issue (Popp and Yen, 2006). To this point, an explanatory capability of the qualitative method can help to verify the disclosed results and mitigate this problem. That is, it provides natural language-like explanations of why specific name pairs may have been selected. In so doing, the approach allows intelligence analysts to better validate the results, with a possible suggestion of further investigation. The integration of this identity disambiguation module and a scenario synthesising system (Shen et al., 2006) may increase the likelihood of successfully detection and promptly counteracting terrorists' malicious acts.

## CONCLUSION

This chapter has presented a novel qualitative link-based similarity measure, which can be efficiently employed for intelligence data analysis,

*Figure 7. Evaluation results of OMS and other alternative techniques.*

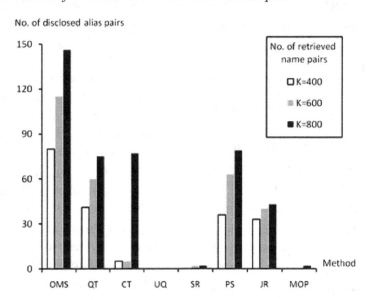

disclosing the use of false identity typically appearing in terrorists and criminals' activities. Unlike the existing numerical similarity estimation that concentrates solely on the link structures, the qualitative method also includes underlying link properties such as uniqueness in order to purify the similarity description. In addition, qualitatively distinct order-of-magnitude labels incorporate semantics towards similarity justification and allow coherent interpretation and reasoning that is hardly feasible with pure numerical terms. Technically, measures of link properties are gauged in accordance with property-specific order of magnitude spaces, whose dissimilar scales are subsequently homogenized to permit the unification of their values. In essence, the similarity descriptor is achieved via aggregating property values regarding to their relative degrees of relevance.

Empirically, this qualitative approach consistently outperforms numerical similarity measures over a terrorism-related dataset. However, the crisp distinctions amongst qualitative descriptors can encounter important limitations in data and knowledge modeling, such as ad-hoc definition of operators and unnatural semantic interpreta-

tion (Shen and Leitch, 1993). It is interesting to investigate how fuzzy sets may be incorporated in the qualitative mechanism in this work. Initial research following this idea shows that the use of fuzzy representation can provide flexible and interpretable semantics of order-of-magnitude labels, while being supported with mathematically-sound operations (Shen and Boongoen, 2011).

A future challenge beyond the present research is to include temporal information such that the resulting system is effective and adaptive to changes. This up-to-date concept (see Hong et al., 2009 for example) may form a stronger basis for authorities to tackle typical and new deceptive schemes, supported with reasoning maintenance systems that work under uncertain situations (Shen and Zhao, 2011). In addition, it is also interesting to observe the effectiveness of different aggregation techniques, e.g., OWA (Ordered Weighted Averaging; Yager, 1988) and its data-dependent variant (Boongoen and Shen, 2010; Boongoen et al., 2011), for the task of combining multiple SNA measures. To compare the possible performances of such different qualitative approaches, methods proposed in (Fu and Shen, 2011) may be utilized.

# REFERENCES

Agell, N., Rovira, X., & Ansotegui, C. (2000). Homogenising references in orders of magnitude spaces: An application to credit risk prediction. In *Proceedings of International Workshop on Qualitative Reasoning* (pp. 1-8).

Badia, A., & Kantardzic, M. M. (2005). Link analysis tools for intelligence and counterterrorism. In *Proceedings of IEEE International Conference on Intelligence and Security Informatics* (pp. 49-59).

Bagga, A., & Baldwin, B. (1998). Entity-based crossdocument coreferencing using the vector space model. In *Proceedings of Annual Meeting of Association for Computational Linguistics*, (pp. 79-85).

Baroni, M., Matiasek, J., & Trost, H. (2002). Unsupervised discovery of morphologically related words based on orthographic and semantic similarity. In *Proceedings of the ACL-02 workshop on Morphological and phonological learning* (pp. 48-57).

Bhattacharya, I., & Getoor, L. (2007). Collective entity resolution in relational data. *ACM Transactions on Knowledge Discovery from Data, 1*(1).

Bilenko, M., Mooney, R., Cohen, W., Ravikumar, P., & Fienberg, S. (2003). Adaptive name matching in information integration. *IEEE Intelligent Systems, 18*(5), 16–23. doi:10.1109/MIS.2003.1234765

Boongoen, T., Shang, C., Iam-On, N., & Shen, Q. (2011) Extending data reliability measure to a filter approach for soft subspace clustering. To appear in *IEEE Transactions on Systems, Man and Cybernetics, Part B: Cybernetics.*

Boongoen, T., & Shen, Q. (2010). Nearest-neighbor guided evaluation of data reliability and its applications. *IEEE Transactions on Systems, Man and Cybernetics. Part B, 40*(6), 1622–1633.

Boongoen, T., Shen, Q., & Price, C. (2010). Disclosing false identity through hybrid link analysis. *AI and Law, 18*(1), 77–102.

Brin, S., & Page, L. (1998). The anatomy of a large-scale hypertextual web search engine. *Computer Networks and ISDN Systems, 30*(1-7), 107-117.

Buechi, M., Borthwick, A., Winkel, A., & Goldberg, A. (2003). Cluemaker: A language for approximate record matching. In *Proceedings of Eighth International Conference on Information Quality* (pp. 207-223).

Calado, P., Cristo, M., Goncalves, M. A., de Moura, E. S., Ribeiro-Neto, B. A., & Ziviani, N. (2006). Link-based similarity measures for the classification of web documents. *Journal of the American Society for Information Science and Technology, 57*(2), 208–221. doi:10.1002/asi.20266

Chan, S., & Franklin, J. (1998). Symbolic connectionism in natural language disambiguation. *IEEE Transactions on Neural Networks, 9*(5), 739–755. doi:10.1109/72.712149

Chen, H., Schroeder, J., Hauck, R., Ridgeway, L., Atabakhsh, H., & Gupta, H. (2003). Coplink connect: information and knowledge management for law enforcement. *Decision Support Systems, 34*(4), 271–285. doi:10.1016/S0167-9236(02)00121-5

Clarke, R. (1994). Human Identification in Information Systems: Management Challenges and Public Policy Issues. *IT and People, 7*(4), 6–37. doi:10.1108/09593849410076799

De Kleer, J., & Brown, J. S. (1984). A qualitative physics based on confluences. *Artificial Intelligence, 24*, 7–83. doi:10.1016/0004-3702(84)90037-7

Fellegi, I., & Sunter, A. (1969). Theory of record linkage. *Journal of the American Statistical Association, 64*, 1183–1210. doi:10.2307/2286061

Forbus, K. (1996). *Qualitative Reasoning. CRC Handbook of Computer Science and Engineering.* CRC Press.

Fouss, F., Pirotte, A., Renders, J. M., & Saerens, M. (2007). Random-walk computation of similarities between nodes of a graph with application to collaborative recommendation. *IEEE Transactions on Knowledge and Data Engineering, 19*(3), 355–369. doi:10.1109/TKDE.2007.46

Fu, X., Boongoen, T., & Shen, Q. (2010). Evidence directed generation of plausible crime scenarios with identity resolution. *Applied Artificial Intelligence, 24*(4), 253–276. doi:10.1080/08839511003715154

Fu, X., & Shen, Q. (2010). Fuzzy compositional modeling. *IEEE Transactions on Fuzzy Systems, 18*(4), 823–840. doi:10.1109/TFUZZ.2010.2050325

Fu, X., & Shen, Q. (2011). Fuzzy complex numbers and their application for classifiers performance evaluation. *Pattern Recognition, 44*(7), 1403–1417. doi:10.1016/j.patcog.2011.01.011

Gale, W. A., Church, K. W., & Yarowsky, D. (1992). A method for disambiguating word senses in large corpora. *Computers and the Humanities, 26*, 415–439. doi:10.1007/BF00136984

Getoor, L., & Diehl, C. P. (2005). Link mining: a survey. *ACM SIGKDD Explorations Newsletter, 7*(2), 3–12. doi:10.1145/1117454.1117456

Ginter, F., Boberg, J., Jarvinen, J., & Salakoski, T. (2004). New techniques for disambiguating in natural language and their application to biological text. *Journal of Machine Learning Research, 5*, 605–621.

Herrera, F., & Herrera-Viedma, E. (2000). Linguistic decision analysis: steps for solving decision problems under linguistic information. *Fuzzy Sets and Systems, 115*, 67–82. doi:10.1016/S0165-0114(99)00024-X

Hiro, K., Wu, H., & Furugori, T. (1996). Word-sense disambiguation with a corpus-based semantic network. *Journal of Quantitative Linguistics, 3*, 244–251. doi:10.1080/09296179608599631

Holzer, R., Malin, B., & Sweeney, L. (2005). Email alias detection using social network analysis. In *Proceedings of International Workshop on Link Discovery* (pp. 52-57).

Hong, T. P., Wu, Y. Y., & Wang, S. L. (2009). An effective mining approach for up-to-date patterns. *Expert Systems with Applications, 36*, 9747–9752. doi:10.1016/j.eswa.2009.02.029

Hou, J., & Zhang, Y. (2003). Effectively finding relevant web pages from linkage information. *IEEE Transactions on Knowledge and Data Engineering, 15*(4), 940–951. doi:10.1109/TKDE.2003.1209010

Hsiung, P., Moore, A., Neill, D., & Schneider, J. (2005). Alias detection in link data sets. In *Proceedings of International Conference on Intelligence Analysis.*

Jaro, M. A. (1995). Probabilistic linkage of large public health data files. *Statistics in Medicine, 14*(5-7), 491–498. doi:10.1002/sim.4780140510

Jeh, G., & Widom, J. (2002). SimRank: A measure of structural-context similarity. In *Proceedings of the ACM SIGKDD International Conference on Knowledge Discovery and Data Mining* (pp. 538-543).

Kalashnikov, D. V., & Mehrotra, S. (2006). Domain-independent data cleaning via analysis of entity-relationship graph. *ACM Transactions on Database Systems, 31*(2), 716–767. doi:10.1145/1138394.1138401

Keppens, J., Shen, Q., & Schafer, B. (2005). Probabilistic abductive computation of evidence collection strategies in crime investigation. In *Proceedings of International Conference on Artificial Intelligence and Law* (pp. 215-224).

Klink, S., Reuther, P., Weber, A., Walter, B., & Ley, M. (2006). Analysing social networks within bibliographical data. In *Proceedings of International Conference on Database and Expert Systems Applications* (pp. 234-243).

Lawrence, S., Giles, C. L., & Bollacker, K. D. (1999). Autonomous citation matching. In *Proceedings of International Conference on Autonomous Agents* (pp. 392-393).

Liben-Nowell, D., & Kleinberg, J. (2007). The link-prediction problem for social networks. *Journal of the American Society for Information Science and Technology, 58*(7), 1019–1031. doi:10.1002/asi.20591

Lin, Z., King, I., & Lyu, M. R. (2006). Pagesim: A novel link-based similarity measure for the world wide web. In *Proceedings of IEEE/WIC/ACM International Conference on Web Intelligence* (pp. 687-693).

Mann, G., & Yarowsky, D. (2003). Unsupervised personal name disambiguation. In *Proceedings of International Conference on Computational Natural Language Learning* (pp. 33-40).

Miller, G. (1956). The magical number seven, plus or minus two: Some limits on our capacity for information processing. *Psychological Review, 63*(2), 81–97. doi:10.1037/h0043158

Minkov, E., Cohen, W. W., & Ng, A. Y. (2006). Contextual search and name disambiguation in email using graphs. In *Proceedings of International ACM SIGIR Conference on Research and Development in Information Retrieval* (pp. 27-34).

Mitchell, M. (2006). Complex systems: Network thinking. *Artificial Intelligence, 170*, 1194–1212. doi:10.1016/j.artint.2006.10.002

Murata, T., & Moriyasu, S. (2008). Link prediction based on structural properties of online social networks. *New Generation Computing, 26*, 245–257. doi:10.1007/s00354-008-0043-y

Ng, H. T., Wang, B., & Chan, Y. S. (2003). Exploiting parallel texts for word sense disambiguation: an empirical study. In *Proceedings of Annual Meeting of the Association for Computational Linguistics* (pp. 455-462).

Olmo, C., Sanchez, G., Prats, F., Agell, N., & Sanchez, M. (2007). Using orders of magnitude and nominal variables to construct fuzzy partitions. In *Proceedings of IEEE International Conference on Fuzzy Systems* (pp. 1-6).

Pantel, P. (2006). Alias detection in malicious environments. In *Proceedings of AAAI Fall Symposium on Capturing and Using Patterns for Evidence Detection* (pp. 14-20).

Pasula, H., Marthi, B., Milch, B., Russell, S., & Shpitser, I. (2003). Identity uncertainty and citation matching. *Advances in Neural Information Processing Systems, 15*, 1425–1432.

Piera, N. (1995). *Current trends in qualitative reasoning and applications. Monografia CIMNE, 33*. Barcelona: International Center for Numerical Methods in Engineering.

Popp, R. L., & Yen, J. (2006). *Emergent information technologies and enabling policies for counter-terrorism*. Wiley. doi:10.1002/047178656X

Porter, G. (Jan 25, 2008). Crying (iranian) wolf in argentina. *Asia Times Online*

Raiman, O. (1991). Order of magnitude reasoning. *Artificial Intelligence, 51*(1-3), 11–38. doi:10.1016/0004-3702(91)90107-U

Reuther, P., & Walter, B. (2006). Survey on test collections and techniques for personal name matching. *International Journal on Metadata. Semantics and Ontologies, 1*(2), 89–99. doi:10.1504/IJMSO.2006.011006

Rubin, S., & Lee, G. (2003). A natural language interface for an intelligent universal situational awareness (USA) system. In *Proceedings of IEEE International Conference on Fuzzy Systems* (pp. 1261-1267).

Shen, Q., Keppens, J., Aitken, C., Schafer, B., & Lee, M. (2006). A scenario-driven decision support system for serious crime investigation. *Law Probability and Risk, 5*, 87–117. doi:10.1093/lpr/mgl014

Shen, Q., & Leitch, R. (1993). Fuzzy qualitative simulation. *IEEE Transactions on Systems, Man, and Cybernetics, 23*(4), 1038–1061. doi:10.1109/21.247887

Shen, Q., & Zhao, R. (2011). A credibilistic approach to assumption-based truth maintenance. *IEEE Transactions on Systems, Man, and Cybernetics. Part A, Systems and Humans, 41*(1), 85–96. doi:10.1109/TSMCA.2010.2064298

Shen. Q., & Boongoen, T. (2011) Fuzzy orders-of-magnitude based link analysis for qualitative alias detection. To appear in *IEEE Transactions on Knowledge and Data Engineering.*

Small, H. (1973). Co-citation in the scientific literature: A new measure of the relationship between two documents. *Journal of the American Society for Information Science American Society for Information Science, 24*, 265–269. doi:10.1002/asi.4630240406

Soon, W. M., Ng, H. T., & Lim, D. C. Y. (2001). A machine learning approach to coreference resolution of noun phrases. *Computational Linguistics, 27*(4), 521–544. doi:10.1162/089120101753342653

Sun, J., Qu, H., Chakrabarti, D., & Faloutsos, C. (2005). Relevance search and anomaly detection in bipartite graphs. *ACM SIGKDD Explorations Newsletter, 7*(2), 48–55. doi:10.1145/1117454.1117461

Ting, I. H., Wu, H. J., & Ho, T. H. (2010). *Mining and Analysing Social Networks.* Heidelberg, Germany: Springer-Verlag.

Tong, H., Faloutsos, C., & Pan, J. Y. (2006). Fast random walk with restart and its applications. In *Proceedings of International Conference on Data Mining* (pp. 613-622).

Torvik, V., Weeber, M., Swanson, D. W., & Smalheiser, N. R. (2004). A probabilistic similarity metric for medline records: a model of author name disambiguation. *Journal of the American Society for Information Science and Technology, 56*(2), 140–158. doi:10.1002/asi.20105

Trave-Massuyes, L., & Piera, N. (1989). The orders of magnitude models as qualitative algebras. In *Proceedings of International Joint Conference on Artificial Intelligence* (pp. 1261-1266).

Wang, G. A., Atabakhsh, H., Petersen, T., & Chen, H. (2005). Discovering identity problems: A case study. In *Proceedings of IEEE International Conference on Intelligence and Security Informatics* (pp. 368-373).

Wang, G. A., Chen, H., Xu, J. J., & Atabakhsh, H. (2006). Automatically detecting criminal identity deception: an adaptive detection algorithm. *IEEE Transactions on Systems, Man and Cybernetics. Part A, 36*(5), 988–999.

Wasserman, S., & Faust, K. (1994). *Social network analysis: methods and applications.* Cambridge, UK: Cambridge University Press.

Yager, R. R. (1988). On ordered weighted averaging aggregation operators in multi-criteria decision making. *IEEE Transactions on Systems, Man, and Cybernetics, 18*, 183–190. doi:10.1109/21.87068

# Chapter 7
# Detecting Pharmaceutical Spam in Microblog Messages

**Kathy J. Liszka**
*University of Akron, USA*

**Chien-Chung Chan**
*University of Akron, USA*

**Chandra Shekar**
*University of Akron, USA*

## ABSTRACT

*Microblogs are one of a growing group of social network tools. Twitter is, at present, one of the most popular forums for microblogging in online social networks, and the fastest growing. Fifty million messages flow through servers, computers, and cell phones on a wide variety of topics exchanged daily. With this considerable volume, Twitter is a natural and obvious target for spreading spam via the messages, called tweets. The challenge is how to determine if a tweet is a spam or not, and more specifically a special category advertising pharmaceutical products. The authors look at the essential characteristics of spam tweets and what makes microblogging spam unique from email or other types of spam. They review methods and tools currently available to identify general spam tweets. Finally, this work introduces a new methodology of applying text mining and data mining techniques to generate classifiers that can be used for pharmaceutical spam detection in the context of microblogging.*

## INTRODUCTION

Social networking, in its many forms, is overtaking email in popularity for communication. Facebook[1] and Twitter[2] are leading the race, but many other notable sites exist and are very popular. Twitter, identi.ca[3] and bentio.com[4] are known as open microblogging services. They operate under free software licenses, providing a public application interface (API) for accessing and mining the messages posted by registered users. The parallel to text messaging is short message content but that's where the similarity ends. In general, the audience and subject content are of a totally different nature. People subscribe to sites like Twitter so they can post about topics such as "I'm waiting

DOI: 10.4018/978-1-61350-513-7.ch007

for a flight and I'm bored" to "the new Android minifigs rock."

Given the public, open-nature of sites like Twitter, it's not surprising that spammers have found new, fertile ground for distributing their unsolicited messages, catching users unaware. Twitter lets users post messages, called tweets. These can be saved in their personal profile and forwarded to others in their circle of friends. The information may be kept private among the list, or by default, remain public and unrestricted. Spammers use a variety of techniques to exploit Twitter for nefarious purposes.

In this chapter, we discuss how Twitter is used, the open API, and present some statistics about tweets in general. From there, we focus on a specific type of spam, those that are classified as pharmaceutical spam. It turns out that while it accounts for a significant and increasing percentage of traditional email spam, it only accounts for a small percentage of Twitter spam. Nonetheless, there are many dangers associated with these illegal scams and feel that identifying tweets engaging in this type of spam should be taken seriously and addressed in these early stages. Our contribution is a new classification scheme specifically targeting pharmaceutical spam that appears specifically in microblog messages. The decision strategy and data mining techniques used in this work take into account the unbalanced nature of the data set. A broader decision set is used, classifying a post as strongly identified as pharmaceutical spam, yes, maybe, and no.

## BACKGROUND

When email became a popular form of communication, junk mail flowing through the United States Postal Service morphed into spam messages flowing through Internet Service Providers. It is well known that spam is more than an annoyance dealt with over morning coffee. It consumes massive amounts of bandwidth, spreads malware, entices

users to phishing sites, and offers products for sale that are either illegal or fake. We start by discussing Twitter as a medium for this undesirable activity and specific aspects that spammers use to mount successful campaigns. Then we focus on the pharmaceutical industry and the difference between traditional spam techniques and adaptations for intruding into the microblog world.

## The Nature of Spam

Unwanted solicitations, better known as spam, are not new. Fighting spam is a never ending battle as spammers are relentless. Original anti-spam methods included keyword analysis, honeypots, and black lists (mxLogic, 2004). Honeypots are a reactive approach analyzing spam email and blocking identical messages for clients. Alone, this is not good enough to combat spam, but it does increase effectiveness when combined with other approaches. Challenge-response is a variation of white listing where a new sender not on a recipient's personal white list must answer a question that presumably only a human could answer. This is meant to deter spammers who would not find it feasible to do this manually. The way around this today is via botnets that infiltrate machines and hijack accounts that are already white listed. Email header analysis is another technique for identifying spam emails by checking the IP address against the domain in an attempt to identify IP spoofing attempts. Other analysis includes tracking the amount of email sent from an IP address. Bayesian statistical filtering, pioneered by (Sahimi et al., 1998) is still probably the most effective technique in the email spam fighting toolbox. This is still a popular and widely implemented tool.

On the horizon of the social networking revolution, spammers lay in wait, devising new ways to score a hit on unsuspecting victims. Their intent is malicious including monetary theft, identity theft, fake merchandise and malware propagation. (Stringhini et al., 2010) set up a honeypot to study the new landscape of spam in social networks.

What they did not find is a clear pattern of behavior. Different bot campaigns operate completely different. Some campaigns leverage many bots, each creating a small number of posts per day to avoid drawing attention to them. Other campaigns employ a few bots, each making a large number of posts. Content varied as well. Spammers attempt to avoid detection by posting what seem to be a proportionally large number of credible looking messages in order to dilute the number of overall spam posts. Other significant honeypot work is found in (Lee et al., 2010). They deploy honeypots on MySpace and Twitter and monitor messages to identify spamming behavior. They differentiate tweeters as legitimate, spammers and promoters. They concentrate on user profiles as opposed to the actual posts. Two general properties are used for classification: user profile (e.g., whether a user possesses a *verified account badge*, something Twitter uses to validate that a users is who they claim to be) and tweet activity, including the number of URLs in posts, unique URLs used, mentions, and unique mentions. Using the Weka classifier, they conclude that honeypots are an effective way to identify spammers by predictable and observable behaviors.

After the stunning take down of Apple's new social media website, Ping, within twenty-four hours of its launch, the media took notice. Spammers saturated the site with survey spam, promising free iPods and iPhones (Elmer-DeWitt, 2010). One wonders at the sense of this, an entire site populated almost entirely of spammers while legitimate users sit on the sidelines, literally locked out from subscribing to and using the service.

## The Nature of Twitter

Measuring popularity of this social network is easy. Six months after Twitter was introduced, people were sending tweets at the rate of 5,000 per day. Three years later, in February 2010, tweets per day reached 50 million[5]. This is certainly startling enough to take notice and spammers have done just that.

Twitter is about holding a conversation in some shared social context. Participants can follow other users or they can follow a topic of interest. A posted message, or tweet, is limited to 140 characters, an average of ten words. It's about shooting off a thought asynchronously. Twitter allows you to follow other people's tweets and for others to follow you. However, the social network created by these links is not bidirectional. Someone may follow you without you following them back, unlike making friends on Facebook.

There are several different mechanisms used in tweets. Figure 1 (a) shows a normal tweet with no embellishments. It's a simple message post with an avatar and timestamp. Most tweets are simple posts, but tweets can also be reused through a process called *retweeting*. This is a convenient way to share information without retyping it. It is accomplished by inserting the tag:

*RT @username*

The username indicates the original author of the tweet. Figure 1(b) shows what a retweet looks like once posted, to a follower. A small grey box with arrow to the right of the avatar picture is the visual that a user sees.

Similar to this feature are replies and mentions. Placing @username at the beginning of a tweet followed by a message is called a reply. Placing it anywhere else in a tweet is called a mention. Twitter collects these and sends them to the user so they know what is being discussed. Spammers take advantage of these to get attention without having to be followed and to give the spammer credibility.

Hash tags are not actually part of Twitter. They are a user invented feature to help organize tweets into categories. These are identified using the symbol # to mark a topic. Conversations that catch on become trending topics. A website called hashtags.org keeps track of the most popular hash

*Figure 1. Example tweets*

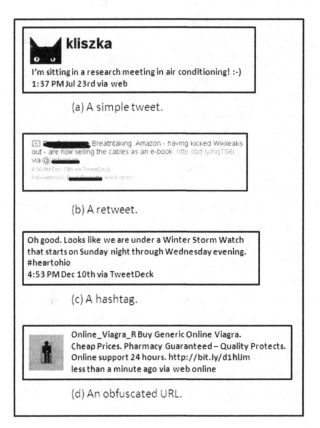

tags and trends on Twitter and several other social networking sites. Figure 1(c) shows a sample trending tweet using #heartohio as a hash word. Spammers lure users into reading their posts by adding the hash tag for a popular topic in the message

It is very common to include URLs in tweets. This causes problems where the URL contains a significant number of characters since tweets are limited to 140. Various URL "shortening" services are available for free online[67]. Figure 1(d) shows an example where http://bit.ly/d1hiJm expands to http://e.freewebhostingarea.com/403.html. The point of spam advertising and phishing is to lure people to a site for nefarious purposes; therefore a URL is a key element of the tweet. An obfuscated URL makes it impossible for a user to determine the authenticity of the site before clicking on it.

## Previous Work

There is a small sector of research in spam targeting Twitter. The nature of tweets is significantly different than email in both content and delivery. Abuse of automated agents using the Twitter API is discussed in (Mowbray 2010). One technique allows spammers to generate followees automatically in anticipation that in some cases the social link will be reciprocated. Another interesting angle is the social network profile. (Benevenuto et al., 2010) applies machine learning techniques to identify potential spammers by the number of followers, friends, age of the account, average tweets per day and so forth. (Yardi et al., 2010) also focus on network structure based on followers versus followees. (Wang, 2010) also uses a social graph technique. They define reputation as the ratio of friends to followers. Spammers are identified by sending a larger than normal number of duplicate or remarkably similar tweets. Behavioral content features studied are trending topics, replies, and mentions. They also search tweets for the presence of a URL. A number of classification algorithms are compared with the naïve Bayesian classifier outperforming k-nearest neighbor, neural networks, and support vector machines. They conclude that analysis based on content features proves tricky and will continue to become more difficult as legitimate businesses start leveraging the popularity of Twitter to promote themselves. Moh and Murmann (2010) introduce trust metrics in addition to adding a finer-grained list of attributes identifying spammers.

Hijacking legitimate users' accounts is a method that avoids detection based on abnormal profiles. This has the negative effect of luring followers into clicking on the URLs contained in the post because of a trust relationship. Indeed, the click-through rate is higher on Twitter than normal email (Grier et al. 2010).

Blocky[8] is a grass roots effort rallying the power of users to identify spammers manually. Users "vote" by reporting another tweeter. If enough votes are tallied, the spam tweeter is added to a black list. Two drawbacks limit this system. First, is determining the true nature of spam. A phishing link present in a tweet is clearly spam but classification of a tweet for herbal remedies linked to a health food store may be subject to debate. Second, add an estimated 300,000 new accounts generated daily and the task simply becomes daunting[9].

## FUNDAMENTAL PROCESS AND TOOLS

### Pharmaceuticals

According to Symantec, pharmaceutical spam accounts for over 65% of all email spam (Kako-Batt, 2010). This outpaces phishing attempts for Nigerian scams and Rolex watches. A leader in the anti-spam war, Symantec is particularly concerned with pharmaceutical advertising for two reasons. The first is to make sure the false positive rate is as close to zero as possible. Deleting spam is annoying, but missing a legitimate email to refill a life-saving medication is not a tolerable event. The second concern is to keep the false negative rate also low. Pharmaceutical advertisements are rarely legitimate. They peddle medications that are most likely illegal, depending on the country the consumer is ordering them from. Prescriptions by a licensed physician prevent people from self-medicating and harming themselves. In addition, medications that are shipped are fake more often than not. For those with legitimate prescriptions seeking a cheaper product, it is equally dangerous to receive meds that are not effective. In the last scenario, the scammers simply abscond with the money and no product is delivered at all.

In (Liszka et al. 2010) we apply text mining techniques to preprocess Twitter data to be used by data mining tools to generate classifiers for spam tweet detection. A simple method was applied for labeling spam training tweets based on 65 pharmaceutical discriminating words selected manually. Results show that the J48 decision tree classifier may be used as an effective tool for detecting pharmaceutical spam.

We have adopted a list of common terms related to panhandling medical drugs derived from (WordPress, 2010; Vaughn, 2010; Surfer, 2010). We have also combed through tweets and our own email inboxes in search of new terms. In all, a collection of 131 words have been selected for our experiments. We further categorize our words into two sets, primary and secondary. The primary word set contains blatantly pharmaceutical references. For example, these cover tweets such as: *which is best viagra livetra cialis - Men's Health: Buy Levitra ...: Men's Health: Buy Levitra... Buy Cialis Online* http://bit.ly/99TMxs. This post contains the words of interest, *levitra* and *cialis*. The secondary word set was derived from observing the nature of the posts. There are some that do not specify a product, but use advertising phrases such as *cheapest supplements – Mastercard accepted* and *Lose that weight for good*. The obfuscated URL takes you to a phishing site or a questionable pharmaceutical web site. We classify these as pharmaceutical spam. In all, we have identified 86 primary words in our list and 45 words in our secondary list.

## The Nature of Tweets

Twitter allows access to the data via an Application Programming Interface (API) that consists of three parts: two REST APIs and a streaming API[10]. The Twitter REST API methods give access to core Twitter data including update timelines, status data, and user information. We use the *search* method to collect real time tweets. Among the timeline resources provided by the REST API we have used the *statuses/public_timeline* resource. This returns the 20 most recent statuses and retweets (if any) from non-protected users. The data is available in a variety of formats. We use the *json*[11] format (JavaScript Object Notation). Twitter is rate-limited, restricting the number of requests to 150 per hour. Requests are anonymous based on the IP of the host.

*cURL*[12] is a tool used to transfer data from or to a server, using one of the supported protocols. It is designed to work without user interaction. We use a PHP script to download tweets using the timeline resource and the cURL library to make calls to the Twitter API.

Tweets are short messages and mostly contain short words and emoticons. In order to mine useful information the tweets undergo a pretreatment process. We treat this step independently from spam identification, but rather a generic process for any research of interest on the microblogging data and content. Figure 2 shows the process of cleaning tweets used in typical natural language processing and text mining systems (Jackson

& Moulinier, 2007; Kao & Poteet, 2007). This includes identifying emoticons, tokenizing the tweets with space, tab and newline as delimiters. Next, we identify tokens with punctuations and control characters and remove them. We replace hyperlinks with the string "URL" and store the hyperlinks for other research purposes.

## Decision Logic and Unbalanced Data

Spam detection in any context, email or social networking, is considered a classification problem. We use J48 and Random Tree of the Weka data mining software (Witten & Frank, 2005; Hall et al., 2009) to generate decision tree classifiers for detecting tweets as pharmaceutical spam or not. Then we apply a new heuristic, a decision matrix, to classify tweets in finer granularity than a simple yes/no.

Following the step of tweets preprocessing which cleanses and transforms each tweet into a set of tokens, we need to assign class labels to tweets as spam or non-spam which will be used as training examples for classifier learning programs. This is done based on the presence of spam words in a tweet. We consider spam words as those contained in the two aforementioned pharmaceutical word lists. To evaluate the performance of classifiers generated by learning algorithms, an independent testing dataset of 5000 tweets is selected randomly, the content of each tweet is checked and a class label of spam or non-spam is assigned manually.

One challenge of applying data mining tools to spam tweet detection is that the majority of tweets in our training sets are non-spam (i.e., directly related to pharmaceutical content). In other words, the class distribution of spam versus non-spam is highly skewed. It is called an imbalanced class problem in data mining, where instances of one class is many more than the other in the training dataset. Consequently, in our case, high accuracy of classification results can be obtained simply by classifying all tweets as non-spam. However, high

*Figure 2. Preprocessing tweets*

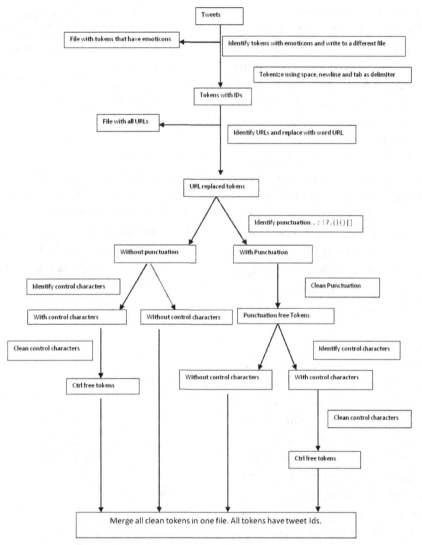

classification accuracies are misleading and not meaningful under such circumstances.

Solutions to deal with imbalanced data sets of classification problems have been proposed (Chawla et al., 2004; Weiss, 2004). Many positive results have been reported based on applying improved sampling methods and using more appropriate metrics, other than classification accuracy, for evaluating the performance of classification algorithms with imbalanced data (Weiss, 2004; He and Garcia, 2009). Two popular methods for improved sampling are up-sampling

(over-sampling) of the minority class and down-sampling (under-sampling) of the majority class. In both cases, the basic idea is to alter class distribution of training data by increasing instances of the minority class or by reducing instances of the majority class such that an approximately balanced class distribution is obtained in the training dataset. Alternatively, algorithms based on cost-sensitive learning by taking into account of misclassification costs in the learning process may accomplish similar effects as using improved sampling methods (Breiman et al., 1984; Elkan, 2001). In fact, there is no clear winner

among the three methods: up-sampling, down-sampling and cost-sensitive learning, as found in previous researches (Breiman et al., 1984; Drummond and Holte, 2003; McCarthy et al., 2005).

Alternative metrics other than classification accuracy for effective evaluation of classifier performance include: Receiver Operating Characteristic (ROC) graphs derived from signal detection theory for measuring tradeoffs between hit rate and false alarm rate of binary diagnostic systems (Egan, 1975; Swets, 1988; Provost and Fawcett, 1997), precision-recall curves and F-measures used in studies of Information Retrieval systems (Van Rijsbergen, 1979), and sensitivity-specificity analysis in medical diagnostic systems. Basic definitions of these measures are reviewed in the following.

The class labels used by binary classifiers are usually regarded as positive and negative, which could stand for: yes or no, spam or non-spam, and so on. Typically, positive class refers to the target instances under study. In highly skewed class distribution, the positive class usually refers to the minority class, which is the target of main interest. As an example, in spam tweet detection, the positive class refers to spam tweets.

Performance of binary classifiers are evaluated in terms of the following counts: TP (True Positive), TN (True Negative), FN (False Negative), and FP (False Positive) as shown in Table 1 where TP is the number of positive instances predicted correctly by a classifier, TN is the number of negative instances predicted correctly, FN is the number of positive instances that are predicted as negative, and FP is the number of negative instances predicted as positive.

The total number of instances used for evaluation is the sum of TP + TN + FN + FP, and the accuracy of classification is defined as the ratio (TP + TN) / (TP + TN + FN + FP). From this definition, it is clear that accuracy is not a good measure for the performance of classifiers when

*Table 1. Confusion matrix of binary classification.*

| | | PREDICTED | |
|---|---|---|---|
| | | Positive Class | Negative Class |
| ACTUAL | Positive Class | TP | FN |
| | Negative Class | FP | TN |

the class distribution is highly skewed. For example, if we have 0.1% of positive instances, then we can achieve 99.9% of classification accuracy simply by predicting all instances to be negative. Under such circumstances, the following measures are more appropriate and informative for evaluating performance of binary classifiers:

$$recall = \frac{TP}{TP + FN},$$

$$precision = \frac{TP}{TP + FP},$$

$$F\text{-}measure = \frac{2 \times recall \times precision}{recall + precision} = \frac{2 \cdot TP}{2 \cdot TP + FN + FP},$$

$$sensitivity = \frac{TP}{TP + FN} = recall,$$

$$specificity = \frac{TN}{FP + TN}.$$

In this work, we use the down-sampling method to create balanced training data for Weka decision tree classifiers *J48* and *RandomTree*. J48 is an open source implementation of *C4.5* (Quinlan, 1993), and *RandomTree* is based on the idea of randomly selecting features to split nodes in the process of building a decision tree. In addition, we develop a decision matrix to refine the predicted binary outputs of decision tree classifiers with a heuristic derived from human experts' observations of spam tweets. It has been noted that human interaction with domain knowledge in learning from imbalanced data can be effective (Kohavi, 1998). We refine the typical binary class labels of *Yes/No* into four categories: SY (Strongly Yes), Y (Yes), MB (Might Be), and N (No). Table 2 shows the decision matrix used to capture the heuristic of our categorization. In Table 2, the columns *TreeP* and *TreeS* are Boolean values denoting the predictive results, 1 means positive, of decision tree

classifiers generated by Weka. Classifier TreeP is generated based on training data with words on the Primary list as data attributes, and classifier TreeS is generated from training data with attribute words on the Secondary list. Column *C(P)* is the frequency count of Primary words occurring in a tweet, and *C(S)* is the frequency count of occurrence of Secondary words. The decision labels are assigned manually.

We further reduce the decision logic shown in Table 2 by applying the rule learning program Blem2 (Chan and Santhosh, 2003), which is based on the rough set theory (Pawlak, 1982). The result

*Table 2. A decision matrix for refining categories.*

| TreeP | TreeS | C(P) | C(S) | Decision |
|-------|-------|------|------|----------|
| 1 | 1 | 1 | >1 | SY |
| 1 | 1 | >1 | 1 | SY |
| 1 | 1 | 1 | 1 | SY |
| 1 | 1 | >1 | >1 | SY |
| 1 | 0 | 1 | 0 | Y |
| 1 | 0 | 1 | 1 | SY |
| 1 | 0 | 1 | >1 | SY |
| 1 | 0 | >1 | 0 | SY |
| 1 | 0 | >1 | 1 | SY |
| 1 | 0 | >1 | >1 | SY |
| 0 | 0 | 0 | 0 | N |
| 0 | 0 | 1 | 0 | MB |
| 0 | 0 | >1 | 0 | Y |
| 0 | 0 | 0 | 1 | N |
| 0 | 0 | 1 | 1 | Y |
| 0 | 0 | >1 | 1 | SY |
| 0 | 0 | 0 | >1 | MB |
| 0 | 0 | 1 | >1 | Y |
| 0 | 0 | >1 | >1 | SY |
| 0 | 1 | 0 | 1 | N |
| 0 | 1 | 1 | 1 | Y |
| 0 | 1 | >1 | 1 | SY |
| 0 | 1 | 0 | >1 | MB |
| 0 | 1 | 1 | >1 | Y |
| 0 | 1 | >1 | >1 | SY |

*Table 3. Reduced decision matrix generated by Blem2.*

| TreeP | TreeS | C(P) | C(S) | Decision |
|-------|-------|------|------|----------|
| 1 | * | >1 | * | SY |
| 1 | * | 1 | 1 | SY |
| 0 | * | >1 | 1 | SY |
| 1 | * | 1 | >1 | SY |
| 0 | * | >1 | >1 | SY |
| 0 | * | 1 | 1 | Y |
| 1 | * | 1 | 0 | Y |
| 0 | * | 1 | >1 | Y |
| 0 | * | >1 | 0 | Y |
| * | * | 0 | >1 | MB |
| 0 | * | 1 | 0 | MB |
| * | * | 0 | 1 | N |
| * | * | 0 | 0 | N |

is shown in Table 3 where the wild character '*' denotes "don't care" condition. It is interesting to note that the column TreeS becomes superfluous, and it can be removed from conditions of the rule table; furthermore, it implies that it is unnecessary to generate classifiers from the secondary words list.

## EXPERIMENTAL RESULTS

### Experiment Setup

We used a publicly available dataset for our sample space, provided for research purposes under Creative Commons license from Choudhury[13]. This data set contains more than 10.5 million tweets collected from over 200,000 users in the time period from 2006 through 2009. In addition, we use a second dataset of 500,000 tweets collected in October and November 2010.

Some observations are in order. In both the older and more recent dataset, roughly 3% of all tweets contain words from the primary and secondary lists. In the older set the 10 most frequently appearing words in the primary list are {medical, medicine, pregnancy, supplement, pill, meds, pharma, prescription, remedies, pharmacy} and in the newer dataset, they are {medical, medicine, viagra, pill, pregnancy, meds, remedies, pharmacy, supplement, medication}. We see that *pharma* and *prescription* still rank high in the new tweets, but are replaced by *Viagra* and *medication*. As a general observation, the more generic words consistently rank high, while the drug specific names (xanax, cialis, valium, prozac, codeine, percocet, etc.) lag behind. This is, perhaps, because these are commonly misspelled to mislead any type of keyword filtering attempt, as is commonly seen in email.

Among the old tweets, the ten most frequently occurring words on the secondary list are {buy, order, brand, price, weight, lose fat, cheap, diet, shipping} and in the newer tweet data set, they are {buy, order, weight, fat, lose, price, diet, cheap, shipping, brand}. The time differential between tweet posts does not appear to have any significant difference in the composition.

Two experiments were conducted using the J48 and Random Tree learning algorithms of Weka to generate tree classifiers. We used downsampling method to create balanced training data sets in both experiments. The data set for the first experiment consists of 46,533 of tweets randomly selected from the 10.1 millions tweets collected by Choudhury et al., and the data set for the second experiment consists of 1,079 tweets randomly selected from the 500K tweets collected by us. The 86 words on the primary list are used as attributes to represent all training tweets. The class labels of training tweets were assigned automatically based on the presence of primary words. Default settings of J48 and RT (Random Tree) and 10-fold cross-validation were applied during training. An independent testing data set consists of 4,956 tweets randomly selected from the 10.1 million collection. The class labels were manually assigned to testing tweets after screening over the content manually. This is a labor intensive process; however, it provides a more reliable validation data set. The class distribution of our independent testing set is 178:4778, which is about 1:24 of spam over non-spam or about 3.73% of tweets in the testing data are spam. Interestingly, this ratio is close to the 3% of tweets containing the primary and secondary words in the 10.1 million tweets collection.

## Results

There are four classifiers used in two experiments. Classifiers J48 and Random Tree (RT) are generated by Weka tools, and classifiers DL(J48) and DL(RT) are based on the combination of J48 and RT with the decision matrix of Table 3, respectively. The manual labeled testing set of 4956 tweets is used to evaluate performance of the classifiers in both experiments.

Tables 4 shows the confusion matrices (contingency tables) computed from the first experiment using 46,533 training tweets randomly selected from the collection of 10.1 million tweets.

From the confusion matrices shown in Table 4 and Table 5, we can compute the following measures: accuracy, recall, precision, F-measure, sensitivity, and specificity. Table 6 shows the evaluation results of the four classifiers from experiment 1 (D1) and experiment 2 (D2) where classifiers DL(J48) and DL(RT) have the same results in both experiments.

It is clear from Table 6 that high classification accuracy does not translate directly into high performance in terms of other measures. Performance of the Random Tree classifiers RT is almost identical even when they are generated from dif-

*Table 4. Confusion matrices computed from first experiment*

| J48 classifier | | |
|---|---|---|
| | Y | N |
| y | 72 | 106 |
| n | 45 | 4733 |
| RT classifier | | |
| | Y | N |
| y | 72 | 106 |
| n | 46 | 4732 |
| DL(J48) and DL(RT) classifiers | | |
| | Y | N |
| y | 115 | 63 |
| n | 96 | 4682 |

*Table 5. Confusion matrices computed from second experiment*

| J48 classifier | | |
|---|---|---|
| | Y | N |
| y | 38 | 140 |
| n | 32 | 4746 |
| RT classifier | | |
| | Y | N |
| y | 72 | 106 |
| n | 45 | 4733 |
| DL(J48) and DL(RT) classifiers | | |
| | Y | N |
| y | 115 | 63 |
| n | 96 | 4682 |

*Table 6. Performance measures of the four classifiers.*

| Measures | J48 | | RT | | DL(J48) and DL(RT) | |
|---|---|---|---|---|---|---|
| | D1 | D2 | D1 | D2 | D1 | D2 |
| accuracy | 0.9695 | 0.9653 | 0.9693 | 0.9695 | 0.9679 | 0.9679 |
| recall | 0.4045 | 0.2135 | 0.4045 | 0.4045 | 0.6461 | 0.6461 |
| precision | 0.6154 | 0.5429 | 0.6102 | 0.6154 | 0.5450 | 0.5450 |
| F-measure = 2*TP/(2*TP+FP+FN) | 0.4881 | 0.3065 | 0.4865 | 0.4881 | 0.5913 | 0.5913 |
| sensitivity = tp | 0.4045 | 0.2135 | 0.4045 | 0.4045 | 0.6461 | 0.6461 |
| specificity = 1-fp | 0.9906 | 0.9933 | 0.9904 | 0.9906 | 0.9799 | 0.9799 |
| sensitivity*specificity | 0.4007 | 0.2121 | 0.4006 | 0.4007 | 0.6331 | 0.6331 |
| # of nodes in resulting tree | 57 | 17 | 97 | 73 | - | - |
| # of spam words selected | 28 | 8 | 48 | 36 | - | - |

ferent training data sets, D1 and D2. However, performance of J48 is notably worse when it is generated from D2. One reason is that the independent testing dataset was created using the same sample space as D1. In other words, Random Tree learning algorithm is more stable than the J48 algorithm with respect to learning from different sample spaces. This may be related to the feature selection measure used in J48, since the tree sizes resulted from J48 are smaller than those of RT trees in both experiments. It implies that J48 trees tend to under-fitting the data. The spam words picked by J48 are consistently the highest frequency words, for both the new and old tweet set. The same is almost true for Random Tree. In one case (the last experiment where they used the 1079 tweets), J48 picked 8 words, which were the 8 highest frequency and RT picked 36 of the 40 highest. RT is clearly more thorough.

It is interesting to see that classifiers DL(J48) and DL(RT) based on our decision logic have identical performance, they are independent of the performance of underlying tree classifiers, and the improvement of performance is significantly noticeable in most measures with small tradeoffs in precision and specificity.

## CONCLUSION

Pharmaceutical spam presents a danger to an unsuspecting public. Fake drugs, illegal prescriptions and phishing attempts are at the heart of most of these messages which have evolved from email to microblog posts. We introduced a new decision logic for identifying pharmaceutical related spam tweets harvested from Twitter. Four classifiers were used to identify pharmaceutical spam tweets. Classifiers J48 and Random Tree (RT) are generated by Weka tools, and classifiers DL(J48) and DL(RT) are based on the combination of J48 and RT with the decision matrix. Given the highly imbalanced data set, results are very promising. Additional attributes in the decision logic may increase the effectiveness and reduce false positives even further. Tweets that do not include words on the primary list but contain multiple words on the secondary list may be more accurately classified if only a small subset of tweet profile attributes is included. As spammers evolve their techniques, more work is necessary to protect users and identify dangerous posts quickly and accurately.

# REFERENCES

Benevenuto, F., Magno, G., Rodrigues, T., & Almeida, V. (2010). *Detecting spammers on Twitter, Collaboration, Electronic messaging.* Anti-Abuse and Spam Conference, CEAS, July.

Breiman, L. (2001). Random forests. *Machine Learning, 45*(1), 5–32. doi:10.1023/A:1010933404324

Brieman, L., Friedman, J., Olshen, R., & Stone, C. (1984). *Classification and Regression Trees.* Belmont, CA: Wadsworth International Group.

Chan, C.-C., & Santhosh, S. (2003). Blem2: Learning Bayes' Rules From Examples Using Rough Sets (pp 187–190). *NAFIPS 2003, 22nd Int. conf. of the North American Fuzzy Information Processing Society,* July 24–26, Chicago, Illinois.

Chawla, N. V., Japlowicz, N., & Kolcz, A. (2004). Editorial: special issue on learning from imbalanced data sets. *SIGKDD Explorations, 6*(1), 1–6. doi:10.1145/1007730.1007733

Drummond, C., & Holte, R. C. (2003). C4.5, class imbalance, and cost sensitivity: why under-sampling beats over-sampling. *Workshop on Learning from Imbalanced Data Sets II, ICML,* Washington DC.

Egan, J. P. (1975). *Signal detection theory and ROC analysis. Series in Cognition and Perception.* New York: Academic Press.

Elmer-DeWitt, P. (2010). *Apple's Ping is a spam magnet, CNN Money.com.* Retrieved September 2010 from http://tech.fortune.cnn.com/2010/09/03/apples-ping-is-a-spam-magnet/

Grier, C., Thomas, K., Paxson, V., & Zhang, M. (2010). @spam; the underground on 140 characters or less, *CCS '10, Proceedings of the 17th ACM conference on Computer and Communications Security* (pp. 27–37), October 4–8, 2010, Chicago, Illinois.

Hall, M., Frank, E., Holmes, G., Pfahringer, B., Reutemann, P., & Witten, I. H. (2009). The WEKA Data Mining Software: An Update. *SIGKDD Explorations, 11*(1). doi:10.1145/1656274.1656278

He, H., & Garcia, E. A. (2009, September). Learning from imbalanced data. *IEEE Transactions on Knowledge and Data Engineering, 21*(9), 1263–1284. doi:10.1109/TKDE.2008.239

Jackson, P., & Moulinier, I. (2007). *Natural Language Processing for Online Applications. Text Retrieval, Extraction and Categorization,* 2nd revised edition. John Benjamins Publishing Company, Amsterdam/Philadephia, 2007. ISBN: 978-90-272-49920.

Kako-Batt, Y. (2010). *Pharmacy spam: pharmaceutical websites fall into two distinct operations.* Retrieved December 1, 2010, from http://www.symantec.com/connect/blogs/ pharmacy-spam-pharmaceutical-websites- fall-two-distinct-operations

Kao, A., & Poteet, S. R. (2007). *Natural Language Processing and Text Mining.* Springer-Verlag, 2007.

Kohavi, R. (1998). Data mining with MineSet: what worked, what did not, and what might. In *Workshop on Commercial Success of Data Mining.* Fourth International Conference on Knowledge Discovery and Data Mining.

Lee, K., Caverlee, J., & Webb, S. (2010). Uncovering social spammers: social honeypots + machine learning. *SIGIR 2010, Special Interest Group on Information Retrieval* (pp. 435–422), July 19–23, 2010, Geneva, Switzerland.

Liszka, K., Chan, C., Shekar, C., & Wakade, S. (2010). Mining pharmaceutical spam from Twitter. *International Conference on Intelligent Systems and Applications (ISDA 2010),* November 2010, pp. 813-817.

McCarthy, K., Zabar, B., & Weiss, G. (2005). Does cost-sensitive learning beat sampling for classifying rare classes? *Proceedings of UBDM 2005*, August 21, Chicago, Illinois, USA, pp. 69 – 77.

Moh, T. S., & Murmann, A. (2010). Can you judge a man by his friends? - Enhancing spammer detection on the Twitter microblogging platform using friends and followers. *Information Systems, Technology and Management. Communications in Computer and Information Science, 54*(4), 210–220. .doi:10.1007/978-3-642-12035-0_21

Mowbray, M. (2010). The twittering machine. *Journal of Applied Statistics, 17*(2), 211–217.

mxLogic (2004). *Spam classification techniques*. Retrieved October 2010 from http://wp.bitpipe.com/resource/ org_1094140501_975/MX_Logic_Spam% 20Classification%20Techniques.pdf

Provost, F., & Fawcett, T. (1997). Analysis and visualization of classifier performance: comparison under imprecise class and cost distributions. *Proceedings of the Third International Conference on Knowledge Discovery and Data Mining (KDD 1997)*, Huntington Beach, CA, pp. 43 – 48.

Quinlan, J. R. (1993). *C4.5: Programs for Machine Learning*. San Francisco, CA: Morgan Kaufmann Publishers.

Sahimi, M., Dumais, S., Heckerman, D., & Horvitz, E. (1998). A Bayesian approach to filtering junk e-mail, *Learning for Text Categorization: Papers from the 1998 Workshop*. AAAI Technical Report WS-98-05.

Stringhini, G., Kruegelm, C., & Vigna, G. (2010). A study on social network spam. *GSWC 2010, The Fifth Annual Graduate Student Workshop on Computing*, (pp. 43 – 44), October 8, 2010, Santa Barbara, California.

Surfer Beware. (2010). *Spam filters word list*. Retrieved July 2010 from http://www.surferbeware.com/ spam/spam-spam-filter.htm

Swets, J. (1988). Measuring the accuracy of diagnostic systems. *Science, 240*, 1285–1293. doi:10.1126/science.3287615

Van Rijsbergen, C. A. (1979). *Information retrieval* (2nd ed.). London: Butterworths.

Vaughn's Summaries. (2010). *Email spam filter word list*. Retrieved July 2010 from http://www.vaughns-1-pagers.com/ internet/spam-word-list.htm

Wang, A. (2010). Don't follow me: Twitter spam detection. *Proceedings of 5th International Conference on Security and Cryptography (SECRYPT)*, July 2010, Athens, Greece.

Weiss, G. M. (2004). Mining with rarity: a unifying framework. *SIGKDD Explorations, 6*(Issue 1), 7–19. doi:10.1145/1007730.1007734

Witten, I. H., & Frank, E. (2005). *Data Mining: Practical Machine Learning Tools and Techniques* (2nd ed.). San Francisco: Morgan Kaufmann Publishers.

Wordpress, (2010). *Spam words*. Retrieved July, 2010, from http://codex.wordpress.org/Spam_Words

Yardi, S., & Romerao, D., Schoenebeck, & G., Boyd, D. (2010). Detecting spam in a Twitter network. *First Monday, 15*(1).

## KEY TERMS AND DEFINITIONS

**Data Mining:** The process of applying machine learning tools to extract useful patterns from large amount of data.

**Decision Tree Classifier:** A procedure or decision algorithm for assigning objects with different categories that is represented in the format of trees.

**Imbalanced Class Problem:** In a problem domain where instances of one class is many more than the other. For example, most credit card transactions are not fraudulent and most network traffic is not intrusive.

**Microblogging:** The act of exchanging short messages through social networking platforms such as Twitter.

**Pharmaceutical Spam:** Unwanted pharmaceutical advertising messages or solicitations.

**Text Mining:** The process of applying natural language processing and data mining tools to extract information from large collection of unstructured messages or documents.

**Twitter:** A popular free and open microblogging service for holding a conversation in some shared social context. Participants can follow other users or they can follow a topic of interest. A posted message, or tweet, is limited to 140 characters, an average of ten words.

## ENDNOTES

1   http://facebook.com
2   http://twitter.com
3   http://identi.ca
4   http://bentio.com
5   http://blog.twitter.com/2010/02/measuring-tweets.html
6   http://bit.ly/, last access December 2010.
7   http://tinyurl.com, last access December 2010.
8   http://blocky.elliottkember.com/
9   http://twitter.com
10  http://dev.twitter.com/doc
11  http://www.json.org/
12  http://curl.haxx.se/docs/manpage.html
13  http://www.public.asu.edu/~mdechoud/datasets.html

# Chapter 8
# Exploiting Social Annotations for Resource Classification

**Arkaitz Zubiaga**
*NLP & IR Group, UNED, Spain*

**Víctor Fresno**
*NLP & IR Group, UNED, Spain*

**Raquel Martínez**
*NLP & IR Group, UNED, Spain*

## ABSTRACT

*The lack of representative textual content in many resources suggests the study of additional metadata to improve classification tasks. Social bookmarking and cataloging sites provide an accessible way to increase available metadata in large amounts with user-provided annotations. In this chapter, the authors study and analyze the usefulness of social annotations for resource classification. They show that social annotations outperform classical content-based approaches, and that the aggregation of user annotations creates a great deal of meaningful metadata for this task. The authors also present a method to get the most out of the studied data sources using classifier committees.*

## INTRODUCTION

Resource classification is the task of labeling resources with their corresponding categories from a predefined taxonomy. Resource classification is of vital importance for information management and retrieval tasks, and for assisting the semi-automatic development of categorized directories.

In the case of web pages, it is also essential to focused crawling, and to topic-specific web link analysis, among others. It can also help improve search results when it is applied to organizing ranked results.

To carry out this kind of tasks automatically, the textual content is commonly used to represent the resource to classify. Many times, the lack of representative content makes it insufficient, though (Qi & Davison, 2009). In this way, social

DOI: 10.4018/978-1-61350-513-7.ch008

bookmarking sites present an accessible way to get additional descriptive metadata.

Social bookmarking is a Web 2.0 based phenomenon that allows users to describe web contents by annotating them with different kinds of metadata in a collaborative and aggregated way. Websites like Delicious[1], StumbleUpon[2], LibraryThing[3] and Diigo[4], among others, allow their users to add information to a web page, collecting hundreds of thousands of annotations per day (Heymann et al., 2008). As a result, a global community of volunteer users creates a huge repository of described resources that can ease their subsequent retrieval. Until now, the use of social annotations for resource classification tasks has remained relatively unexamined. The little work performed so far has shown the suitability of social tags for this kind of tasks. Nonetheless, the study of the optimal representation based on social tags, and the use of social annotations other than social tags, are still unexplored.

In this chapter, we study and analyze the use of metadata extracted from social bookmarking and cataloging sites to classify a set of annotated resources. We perform the experiments with two different types of resources: web pages and books. We find two types of social annotations to be applicable and useful for resource classification: tags and comments provided by end users. We propose a way to represent each kind of annotation, and we present a method to outperform their results by means of combining different data using classifier committees.

Next, in Section Background, we describe the nature of social annotations and the existing types. We continue in Section Related Work presenting earlier research in the literature. After that, we detail the settings of our experiments as well as the datasets we used, to continue in Section Results with the analysis of the results. We discuss them in Section Discussion. Finally, we conclude with our thoughts and future work.

## BACKGROUND

Social bookmarking and cataloging sites allow users to save and annotate their favorite resources, sharing them with the community. These annotations are provided in a collaborative way, so that it makes possible a large amount of metadata to be available for each resource. Going into further details on these metadata, different kinds of user-generated annotations can be defined:

- **Tags:** Keywords defining and characterizing a resource are known as tags. In collaborative tagging systems, each user $u_i$ can post a resource $r_j$ with a set of tags $T_{ij} = \{t_1,...,t_p\}$, with a variable number $p$ of tags. After $k$ users posted $r_j$, it is described with a weighted set of tags $T_j = \{w_1 t_1,...,w_n t_n\}$, where $w_1,...,w_n \leq k$. The resulting organization from users' tagging activity is known as a folksonomy. In most of the social bookmarking systems, there are no constraints on the keywords users can set as tags. The use of tags was originally suggested to make easier the later search and retrieval of relevant documents. Most of the research in this field has focused on the study of dataset properties (Ramage et al., 2009), the analysis of usage patterns of tagging systems (Golder & Huberman, 2006), and the discovery of hidden semantics in tags (Yeung et al., 2008). Incorporating social annotations with document content and other sources of information is a natural idea (Zhou et al., 2008), especially when trying to improve information management tasks.

- **Notes or descriptions:** Free text describing a resource is known as a note or description.

- **Reviews:** A review is a free text valuating a web page. Even though this kind of annotations can initially look subjective and non-descriptive, users tend to mix descriptive texts with opinions.

- **Ratings:** Valuations indicating to what extent users like or dislike a resource, commonly by means of punctuations from one to five.
- **Highlights:** Highlights are only applicable when the resources are web pages, by selecting the most relevant part or parts of the bookmarked web page.

Most of the annotations described above in this Section seem to be really interesting for topical resource tasks. Nonetheless, it is obvious that 'Ratings' cannot contribute to this kind of classification, since they do not provide topical information. For this reason, in the process of creation of our dataset we based on all the social annotations but ratings. Thus, we consider three families grouping the remaining data: 'Tags', 'Notes & Reviews' (grouped as 'Comments'), and 'Content'. In our experiments, 'highlights' were not considered due to their low representativity over the web pages, as we point out later, so that they are not listed above. Moreover, they are not available when the resources are books.

## Nature of Social Annotations

Every annotation becomes social when it is available either on a public Internet website or a private network where a community is involved. Any user of the website can then access these annotations. Not all the annotations are provided in the same way, though. The site itself may define some constraints, mainly by setting who is able to annotate each resource. In this sense, two kinds of annotations can be distinguished (Smith, 2008):

- **Simple Annotations:** Users describe their own resources, such as photos on Flickr.com, news on Digg.com or videos on Youtube.com, but nobody else annotates others' resources. Usually, the author of the resource is who annotates it. This means no more than one user tags a resource.

- **Collaborative Annotations:** Many users annotate the same resource, and every person can tag and describe it with their own tags and reviews in their own vocabulary. The collection of tags assigned by a single user creates a smaller folksonomy, also known as personomy. As a result, several users tend to post the same resource. For instance, CiteULike.org, LibraryThing.com and Delicious are based on collaborative annotations, where each resource (papers, books and URLs, respectively) can be annotated and tagged by all the users who considered it interesting.

These terms are usually applied to tagging systems. Tags present high likelihood to coincide across users. This feature makes the aggregation of tags especially strong rather than simple tagging systems. Notwithstanding this, the collaborative idea can also be applied to any other annotations, as different users use to provide their own annotations (e.g., reviews) to the same resource.

In this chapter, we rely on collaborative annotations in social bookmarking and cataloging systems, taking advantage of the strength of the aggregated annotations provided by large amounts of users.

## Related Work

Up to now, little work has been done on analyzing the usefulness of social tags specifically for web page organization tasks, but no enough attention has been paid to other kind of social annotations.

Noll & Meinel (2008a) present a study of the characteristics of social annotations provided by end users, in order to determine their usefulness for web page classification. The authors matched user-supplied tags of a page against its categorization by the expert editors of the ODP. They analyzed at which hierarchy depth matches occurred, concluding that tags may perform better for broad categorization of documents rather than for more specific categorization. The study also points out that since users tend to bookmark and tag top level web documents, this type of metadata will target classification of the entry pages of websites, whereas classification of deeper pages might require more direct content analysis. They observed that tag noise (the opposite of popular tags) provides helpful data for information retrieval and classification tasks in general. In a previous work, the same authors (Noll & Meinel, 2007) suggested that tags provide additional information about a web page, which is not directly contained within its content.

Also, Noll & Meinel (2008b) studied three types of metadata about web documents: social annotations (tags), anchor texts of incoming hyperlinks, and search queries to access them. They concluded that tags are better suited for classification purposes than anchor texts or search keywords.

The above works had shown the usefulness of social tags for web page organization tasks but, to the best of our knowledge, different tag representations, and social annotations other than tags have not been applied.

In Ramage et al. (2009) the inclusion of tagging data improved the performance of two clustering algorithms when compared to content-based clustering. They found that tagging data was more effective for specific collections than for a collection of general documents.

In a previous work (Zubiaga et al., 2009a), we presented a preliminary study on the use of social annotations for web page classification, applied to the top level of the ODP categorization scheme, where social tags and comments show high performance against textual content. In this chapter, we extend this work by analyzing the usefulness of social annotations for other kinds of resources.

## MAIN FOCUS OF THE CHAPTER

### Datasets

Our experiments require large collections of resources with both a considerable number of annotations and categorization data within standard and consolidated taxonomies. As an approach, we looked for popular resources on social tagging sites[5]. Next, we introduce the two datasets we use in our experiments, made up by sets of categorized web pages and books, which include social annotations provided by users of well-known social tagging sites.

### Web Pages Dataset

As a starting point for the dataset of web pages, we monitored the recent feed of Delicious looking for popular bookmarked URLs during December 2008 and January 2009. This yielded an initial list of 94,130 unique URLs. As we decided to consider the Open Directory Project (ODP) as a categorization scheme for the web pages, we looked for all the available matches between this list and URLs making up the ODP. We found that 12,616 URLs had a category assigned in ODP. As a few of them had two categories assigned, we randomly selected one of them.

Then, with this final list of URLs with their corresponding ODP category data, we fetched the page content for each of the URLs. In addition to the page content and the corresponding categorization of this set of pages, we gathered the following data from social bookmarking sites:

- *Bookmark data from Delicious:* Delicious is a social bookmarking site where each user can annotate with tags and describe with notes their preferred web pages. When gathering information from this site, we saved the following data for each web page:

○ *Number of users* bookmarking it, what is always equal or higher than 100.

○ *Top 10 list of tags* annotated by users, along with their corresponding weights, referring to the number of users.

○ *Notes provided by users.* This is optional, though, and not all the users fill in this field. Within our dataset, we found that roughly 10% of the bookmarks have a note attached to it.

○ *The Full Tag Activity (FTA).* This includes an exhaustive list of users bookmarking each page, with the tags provided by each of them, so that a list of top tags larger than 10 can be inferred. We refer to each of the annotations made by different users for a URL as a bookmark. Note that the FTA is limited by the system to the 2,000 last users, whereas the top 10 list provides data corresponding to all the users, even when more than 2,000 bookmarked it. In our dataset, 957 web pages were saved by more than 2,000 users, with an average user count of 5,329.

• *Reviews from StumbleUpon:* StumbleUpon is a social bookmarking site intended to help users discover new web pages. By navigating over the pages suggested by the site, it allows users to rate and describe them. On this site, we looked for reviews provided by users to our list of URLs, and we found that 9,919 of them have review information.

• *Highlights from Diigo:* Diigo is another social bookmarking site, with a new feature that allows users to highlight and add sticky notes to web pages. We looked in this site for highlight data available for our URLs, but only 1,920 of the documents in our dataset were provided highlight infor-

mation, so that we decided not to use this information in our study due to its low availability.

Summarizing, our final dataset is composed by 12,616 unique URLs with their corresponding ODP categorization, page content and incoming anchor texts, along with a set of social annotations including tagging data, notes and reviews.

We rely on the hierarchical structure of the Open Directory Project, a human-edited web directory, as the categorization scheme. Particularly, we experiment the classification by using the top level of the hierarchy, which is made up by 17 categories.

For this dataset, this is how we group the available data:

• *Content:* We consider the textual content of a web page as we crawled it from the Web.

• *Comments:* We merge notes from Delicious and reviews from StumbleUpon.

• *Tags:* We use tags annotated by users on Delicious.

The dataset is available as a benchmark[6].

## Books Dataset

For the second dataset, which is made up by books, we started by gathering a set of popular works from LibraryThing. In this process, we found a set of 65,929 popular books. In the next step, we looked for classification labels assigned by experts to these books. We fetched their classification for both the Dewey Decimal Classification (DDC) and the Library of Congress Classification (LCC) systems. The former is a classical taxonomy that is still widely used in libraries, whereas the latter is used by most research and academic libraries. We found that 27,299 books were categorized on DDC, and 24,861 books have an LCC category assigned to it. In total, there are 38,149 books with category data from either one or both category schemes.

Then, we fetched the following data from social cataloging sites for each of the books:

- Bookmark data from LibraryThing:
  - *Number of users* bookmarking it, what is always equal or higher than 100.
  - The *Full Tag Activity (FTA)*, which is similar to Delicious.
  - *Reviews:* a free text with user comments on the book.
- *Reviews from GoodReads:* similar to the reviews on LibraryThing.
- *Product descriptions and reviews from Amazon.* Product descriptions are usually formal descriptions and reviews provided by editorials. Reviews, on the other hand, are provided by end users.
- *Synopses from Barnes&Noble.* The synopsis of each book includes a brief summary of the content of the book.

For this dataset, this is how we group the available data:

- *Content:* as we do not have the textual content of the books, we consider the product reviews and the synopses as a summary of their content.
- *Comments:* we merge user reviews from LibraryThing, GoodReads and Amazon for the comments.
- *Tags:* we use tags annotated by users on LibraryThing.

## Support Vector Machines

Regarding the algorithm we use for the classification tasks, we rely on our study in Zubiaga et al. (2009b). We analyzed the suitability of several variants of Support Vector Machines (SVM) (Joachims, 1998) to topical web page classification

tasks, considering them as multiclass problems. We concluded that supervised approaches outperform semi-supervised ones, and that considering the task as a single multiclass problem instead of several smaller binary problems performs better. Thus, we use supervised multiclass SVM for our experiments. Even though the traditional SVM approach only works for binary classification tasks, multiclass classification approaches have also been proposed and used in the literature (Weston & Watkins, 1999; Hsu & Lin, 2002). We use the freely available and well-known "svm-light"[7] in its adapted multiclass version named "svm-multiclass", with the linear kernel and the default parameters suggested by the author for text classification tasks.

A multiclass SVM classifier for k classes defines a model with a set of hyperplanes in the training phase, so that they separate the documents in a class from the rest (Crammer & Singer, 2002). In the test phase, when making predictions for each new document, the classifier is able to establish a margin for each class. These margins refer to the reliability of the document to belong to each of the classes. The bigger is the margin, the more likely is the document to belong to the class. As a result, the class maximizing the margin value will be predicted by the classifier.

To evaluate the resource classification performance using different training set sizes, we randomly select 6 different runs for each of the training sets. We present the accuracy based on the average of the 6 runs, in order to get more realistic results. The accuracy represents the proportion of correct predictions among the whole test set.

## Experiments

### Tag-Based Classification

Previous works suggest that tags could be used to classify web documents, and show encouraging results while using them (Noll & Meinel, 2008a; Aliakbary et al., 2009; Zubiaga et al.,

2009a). Going further, we would like to resolve the following issues: which is the best way to exploit these metadata? And do they outperform the content-based classification even when classifying into narrower categories? Are they also useful for classifying resources other than web pages? Next, we propose, evaluate and compare several approaches for tag-based representation relying on these data:

- *Ranked Tags (Top 10):* tags corresponding to the top 10 list of a resource are assigned a value in a rank-based way. The first-ranked tag is always set the value 1, 0.9 for the second, 0.8 for the third, and so on. This approach respects the position of each tag in the top 10, but the different gaps among tag weights are ignored.
- *Tag Fractions (Top 10):* taking into account both the number of users who bookmarked a resource and the top list of tags, it is possible to define the fraction of users assigning each tag. A tag would have been annotated by the 100% of the users when its weight matches the user count of a resource, getting a value of 1 as the fraction. According to this, a value from 0 to 1 is set to each tag in the top 10. Thus, for the tag i in a resource annotated by $p$ users, the value would be defined as $wi / p$.

- *Unweighted Tags (Top 10 and FTA):* the only feature considered for these two representations are the occurrence or non-occurrence of a tag in the top 10 list or the full tag activity of a resource, depending on whether we rely on the top 10 of tags or the FTA, respectively. These approaches ignore tags' weights, and assign a binary value to each feature in the vector.
- *Weighted Tags (Top 10 and FTA):* the weight for each of the tags of a resource ({w1,...,wn}, as described above) is considered as it is in these two approaches, relying on the top 10 list of tags and the FTA, respectively. Now, by definition, the weights of the tags are fully respected, although the amount of users bookmarking a resource is ignored. Note that different orders of magnitude are mixed up now, since the count of bookmarking users range from 100 to higher values.

Note that for the approaches above relying on the FTA, the dimensionality of the vectors is reduced, in order to relax the computational cost while maintaining the representativity. The reduction consists of tags appearing only in a document.

Next, we present the results of the experiments for all the datasets and classification schemes.

The results in Table 1, Table 2 and Table 3 show the marked inferiority of the ranked and fraction-

*Table 1. Accuracy results for tag-based web page classification*

| Web Page Classification - ODP | | | | | | | |
|---|---|---|---|---|---|---|---|
| | Training Set Size | | | | | | |
| | 600 | 1400 | 2200 | 3000 | 4000 | 5000 | 6000 |
| Tag Fractions | 0.456 | 0.470 | 0.473 | 0.475 | 0.474 | 0.474 | 0.476 |
| Tag Ranks | 0.466 | 0.477 | 0.490 | 0.496 | 0.496 | 0.501 | 0.488 |
| Unweighted Tags (Top 10) | 0.503 | 0.515 | 0.519 | 0.522 | 0.527 | 0.520 | 0.524 |
| Unweighted Tags (FTA) | 0.523 | 0.552 | 0.557 | 0.563 | 0.561 | 0.566 | 0.569 |
| Weighted Tags (Top 10) | 0.510 | 0.574 | 0.604 | 0.620 | 0.634 | 0.641 | 0.652 |
| Weighted Tags (FTA) | **0.526** | **0.590** | **0.616** | **0.636** | **0.645** | **0.654** | **0.665** |

*Table 2. Accuracy results for tag-based book classification (DDC)*

| Book Classification - DDC | Training Set Size | | | | | | |
|---|---|---|---|---|---|---|---|
| | 3000 | 6000 | 9000 | 12000 | 15000 | 18000 | 21000 |
| Tag Fractions | 0.719 | 0.717 | 0.720 | 0.721 | 0.727 | 0.721 | 0.724 |
| Tag Ranks | 0.791 | 0.783 | 0.778 | 0.782 | 0.788 | 0.787 | 0.797 |
| Unweighted Tags (Top 10) | 0.756 | 0.763 | 0.753 | 0.766 | 0.759 | 0.759 | 0.758 |
| Unweighted Tags (FTA) | 0.624 | 0.622 | 0.628 | 0.629 | 0.629 | 0.628 | 0.624 |
| Weighted Tags (Top 10) | 0.858 | 0.861 | 0.862 | 0.865 | 0.866 | 0.866 | 0.864 |
| Weighted Tags (FTA) | **0.861** | **0.864** | **0.864** | **0.867** | **0.869** | **0.869** | **0.868** |

*Table 3. Accuracy results for tag-based book classification (LCC)*

| Book Classification - LCC | Training Set Size | | | | | | |
|---|---|---|---|---|---|---|---|
| | 3000 | 6000 | 9000 | 12000 | 15000 | 18000 | 21000 |
| Tag Fractions | 0.739 | 0.740 | 0.741 | 0.743 | 0.741 | 0.738 | 0.746 |
| Tag Ranks | 0.783 | 0.790 | 0.788 | 0.783 | 0.789 | 0.795 | 0.790 |
| Unweighted Tags (Top 10) | 0.759 | 0.772 | 0.764 | 0.771 | 0.763 | 0.770 | 0.763 |
| Unweighted Tags (FTA) | 0.654 | 0.660 | 0.661 | 0.661 | 0.658 | 0.655 | 0.661 |
| Weighted Tags (Top 10) | 0.852 | 0.854 | **0.856** | 0.858 | 0.858 | 0.855 | 0.858 |
| Weighted Tags (FTA) | **0.853** | **0.857** | **0.856** | **0.861** | **0.861** | **0.857** | **0.861** |

based approaches. These two representations do not seem to be a good way to carry out a topical classification task.

On the other hand, it is clear that the approaches considering weights are far better than the unweighted approaches, what shows the relevance of considering the agreement between users, rather than just whether or not a tag appears annotated in a resource.

Among the weighted approaches, the difference is not so clear, but the use of the FTA instead of just the top 10 list of tags gets slightly better results. This suggests that the tags in the top 10 are the most relevant for the classification task, as they have been annotated by a bigger number of users, but the tags in the tail only considered in the FTA also provide some useful information.

This suggests considering the full tag activity, so that annotations of users differing from the most common behaviors may also be helpful. When the computational cost matters, though, it could be enough to consider just the top 10 tags to reduce it.

Other ideas like a possible removal of useless or harmful tags set by misbehaving users remain as an open issue, though.

## Comparing Data: Content vs. Comments vs. Tags

With the experiments above we found the best approach to represent resources using tags for classification tasks. Once we had these results, we compared the usefulness of tags as against to the

*Table 4. Accuracy results for different data inputs on web page classification*

| Web Page Classification - ODP | | | | | | | |
|---|---|---|---|---|---|---|---|
| | Training Set Size | | | | | | |
| | 600 | 1400 | 2200 | 3000 | 4000 | 5000 | 6000 |
| Content | 0.518 | 0.561 | 0.579 | 0.588 | 0.595 | 0.604 | 0.610 |
| Comments | 0.520 | 0.578 | 0.602 | 0.618 | 0.630 | 0.639 | 0.646 |
| Weighted Tags (FTA) | 0.526 | 0.590 | 0.616 | 0.636 | 0.645 | 0.654 | 0.665 |

*Table 5. Accuracy results for different data inputs on book classification (DDC)*

| Book Classification - DDC | | | | | | | |
|---|---|---|---|---|---|---|---|
| | Training Set Size | | | | | | |
| | 3000 | 6000 | 9000 | 12000 | 15000 | 18000 | 21000 |
| Content | 0.767 | 0.792 | 0.802 | 0.809 | 0.809 | 0.815 | 0.817 |
| Comments | 0.777 | 0.808 | 0.820 | 0.831 | 0.833 | 0.839 | 0.840 |
| Weighted Tags (FTA) | 0.861 | 0.864 | 0.864 | 0.867 | 0.869 | 0.869 | 0.868 |

*Table 6. Accuracy results for different data inputs on book classification (LCC)*

| Book Classification - LCC | | | | | | | |
|---|---|---|---|---|---|---|---|
| | Training Set Size | | | | | | |
| | 3000 | 6000 | 9000 | 12000 | 15000 | 18000 | 21000 |
| Content | 0.767 | 0.789 | 0.798 | 0.803 | 0.806 | 0.807 | 0.810 |
| Comments | 0.780 | 0.803 | 0.816 | 0.823 | 0.827 | 0.828 | 0.833 |
| Weighted Tags (FTA) | 0.853 | 0.857 | 0.856 | 0.861 | 0.861 | 0.857 | 0.861 |

other data inputs. Thus, we compare the results of tags to comments and content.

Table 4, Table 5 and Table 6 show the results of the comparison of the three approaches. Our results show that both social annotations, tags and comments, improve the content-based baseline in either classification schemes.

Comparing the behavior of the social annotations, the results show higher performance for the approach using tag information than using comments. The use of comments outperforms the content-based classification, though.

## Using Classifier Committees

Even though the tag-based representation outperforms the other two approaches, all of them offer encouraging results and look good enough to try to combine them and improve even more the classifier's performance. Though, what if a classifier is getting right while the others are making a mistake? Could we combine the results to get the most out of them?

An interesting approach to combine classifiers is known as classifier committees (Sun et al., 2004). Classifier committees rely on the predictions of various classifiers, and combine them by means of a decision function, which serves to define the weight and/or relevance of each classifier in the final prediction.

An SVM classifier outputs a margin for each resource over each class in the taxonomy, meaning the reliability to belong to that class. The class with the largest positive margin for each resource is then selected as the classifier's prediction. Thus, combining SVM classifiers' predictions could be done by means of adding up their margins or reliability values for each class. Each resource will then have a new reliability value (i.e., the sum of margins) for each class. Nonetheless, in this case, since each of the three classifiers work with different type of data, the range of the margins they output differs. To solve this, we propose the normalization of the margins based on the maximum margin value outputted by each classifier ($max(mi)$):

$$m'_{ijc} = m_{ijc} / \max(m_i)$$

where $m_{ijc}$ is the margin by the classifier i between the resource $j$ and the hyperplane for the class $c$, and $m'_{ijc}$ is its value after normalizing it.

The class maximizing this sum will be predicted by the classifier. Then, the sum of margins between the class $c$ and the resource $j$ using a committee with $n$ classifiers could be defined as:

$$S_{jc} = \sum_{i=1}^{n} m_{ijc}$$

If the classifiers are working over $k$ classes, then the predicted class for the resource $j$ would be defined as follows:

$$C_j^* = \arg\max_{i=1..k} S_{ji}$$

The results of the experiments using classifier committees are shown in Table 7, Table 8, and Table 9. Note that the table also includes the tag-based classifier's results, enabling the comparison of the results by the classifier committees against the best of the simple classifiers. In most of the cases, when different classifiers are combined, the errors of a classifier can be corrected by the rest, as these results show. It is worth to note that a classifier with the highest accuracy does not have to be the best on committees. The gaps among the margins outputted for the ideal class and the rest are also relevant for a classifier to perform well at committees.

Making different combinations among the classifiers has outperformed the best non-combining approach in all cases for the web page classification task. Either of the committees performs better than using only tags in this case. Among the committees, the best results are always for the one that includes the three kinds of metadata. Merging the outputs of the classifiers based on tags, comments and content yielded the highest performance, outperforming any of the combinations where only two kinds of metadata are

*Table 7. Accuracy results of classifier committees for the web page classification*

| Web Page Classification - ODP | | | | | | | |
|---|---|---|---|---|---|---|---|
| | Training Set Size | | | | | | |
| | 600 | 1400 | 2200 | 3000 | 4000 | 5000 | 6000 |
| **Tags** | 0.526 | 0.590 | 0.616 | 0.636 | 0.645 | 0.654 | 0.665 |
| **Content + Comments** | 0.554 | 0.604 | 0.627 | 0.643 | 0.651 | 0.660 | 0.670 |
| **Content + Tags** | 0.560 | 0.623 | 0.651 | 0.669 | 0.681 | 0.690 | 0.700 |
| **Comments + Tags** | 0.555 | 0.621 | 0.650 | 0.671 | 0.681 | 0.691 | 0.702 |
| **Content + Comments + Tags** | **0.572** | **0.634** | **0.661** | **0.679** | **0.690** | **0.700** | **0.709** |

*Table 8. Accuracy results of classifier committees for the book classification (DDC)*

| Book Classification - DDC | Training Set Size | | | | | | |
|---|---|---|---|---|---|---|---|
| | 3000 | 6000 | 9000 | 12000 | 15000 | 18000 | 21000 |
| Tags | **0.861** | 0.864 | 0.864 | 0.867 | 0.869 | 0.869 | 0.868 |
| Content + Comments | 0.778 | 0.803 | 0.814 | 0.821 | 0.823 | 0.827 | 0.830 |
| Content + Tags | 0.823 | 0.842 | 0.845 | 0.849 | 0.851 | 0.852 | 0.852 |
| Comments + Tags | 0.857 | **0.866** | **0.868** | **0.872** | **0.875** | **0.876** | **0.876** |
| Content + Comments + Tags | 0.824 | 0.843 | 0.847 | 0.852 | 0.855 | 0.856 | 0.856 |

*Table 9. Accuracy results of classifier committees for the book classification (LCC)*

| Book Classification - LCC | Training Set Size | | | | | | |
|---|---|---|---|---|---|---|---|
| | 3000 | 6000 | 9000 | 12000 | 15000 | 18000 | 21000 |
| Tags | **0.853** | 0.857 | 0.856 | 0.861 | 0.861 | 0.857 | 0.861 |
| Content + Comments | 0.800 | 0.823 | 0.834 | 0.844 | 0.854 | 0.865 | 0.892 |
| Content + Tags | 0.808 | 0.828 | 0.840 | 0.848 | 0.859 | 0.868 | 0.896 |
| Comments + Tags | 0.848 | **0.863** | **0.873** | **0.879** | **0.888** | **0.896** | **0.917** |
| Content + Comments + Tags | 0.812 | 0.833 | 0.844 | 0.854 | 0.864 | 0.872 | 0.900 |

considered. Among the double-committees, the performance is higher when tags are considered; this means that tags seem to be the most helpful for committees, and not only as a single classifier.

Regarding the book classification task, the classifier committees require bigger training sets to outperform the best non-combining approach. This does not happen for the smallest training sets, but there is a clear outperformance of the combining approaches in the largest training sets. As opposed to the web page classification, it is slightly better to combine the outputs of only comments and tags, without considering content. It obtained better results rather than the triple-committee. In this case, content does not seem to be as helpful as for web pages when it comes to combining classifiers. The underperformance of content as against to tags in much bigger for books than for web pages, so that it is likely that

the content-based approach is not providing good margin values. However, considering product reviews and synopses as a summary of books' content may not be enough.

## DISCUSSION

Our analysis on the use of social annotations for automated classification shows that both social tags and comments are representative enough to perform the task. Nonetheless, other type of social annotations like highlights and ratings do not seem to be useful at present; highlights are not popular enough yet, as we showed that most of the web documents remain unannotated and cannot be represented, whereas ratings do not provide useful information, at least for topical classification. Both using social tags and comments have shown outperforming results against the content-based approach. Among these two types of social annotations, tags show the best results. In this case, relying on a detailed representation considering the full tag activity seems to be the optimal approach.

Moreover, we conclude that none of the three kinds of data is refusable, since all of them may provide positive results when dealing with classifier committees, particularly with web pages. Combining the outputs outperforms the non-combining approaches in most cases. Thus, we conclude that tags are the annotations that best fit the expert-based categorization scheme, as well as the best contributors for classifier committees.

## FUTURE RESEARCH DIRECTIONS

It has been shown the high usefulness of social tags when it comes to automated classification, and it also has been shown that considering the weights of tags as users' consensus is also really helpful. Though, all the tags have been considered in the same way, without any semantic or linguistic processing. Grouping together synonymous tags, and detecting the usefulness of each tag, being able to rule out useless tags, could help improve this kind of tasks.

## CONCLUSION

In this chapter, we have studied and analyzed the application of different annotations from social bookmarking and cataloging sites to the automated classification task. As a Gold Standard, we rely on the top level category schemes of the Open Directory Project for web pages, and the Dewey Decimal Classification (DDC) and the Library of Congress Classification (LCC) for books. We have found that social tags and comments, among the existing social annotations, are representative enough to perform this kind of task. Our experiments show encouraging results for the use of social annotations, outperforming the use of textual content. Finally, we conclude with social tags as the best representation approach, especially by relying on aggregated tagging data for a resource.

## REFERENCES

Aliakbary, S., Abolhassani, H., Rahmani, H., & Nobakht, B. (2009). Web page classification using social tags. *IEEE International Conference on Computational Science and Engineering, 4* (pp. 588-593. Vancouver, BC, Canada. IEEE Computer Society 2009.

Crammer, K., & Singer, Y. (2002). On the algorithmic implementation of multiclass kernel-based vector machines. *Journal of Machine Learning Research, 2*, 265–292.

Golder, S., & Huberman, B. A. (2006). The structure of collaborative tagging systems. *Journal of Information Science, 32*(2), 198–208. doi:10.1177/0165551506062337

Heymann, P., Koutrika, G., & Garcia-Molina, H. (2008). Can social bookmarking improve web search? *WSDM '08: Proceedings of the international conference on Web search and web data mining* (pp. 195-206). New York: ACM.

Hsu, C.-W., & Lin, C.-J. (2002). A comparison of methods for multi-class support vector machines. *IEEE Transactions on Neural Networks, 13*(2), 415–425. doi:10.1109/72.991427

Joachims, T. (1998). Text categorization with support vector machines: Learning with many relevant features. *European Conference on Machine Learning* (pp. 137–142). Berlin: Springer.

Noll, M. G., & Meinel, C. (2007). Authors vs. readers: A comparative study of document metadata and content in the WWW. *Proceedings of the 2007 ACM symposium on Document engineering* (pp. 177-186). Winnipeg, Manitoba, Canada: ACM.

Noll, M. G., & Meinel, C. (2008a). Exploring social annotations for web document classification. *Proceedings of the 2008 ACM symposium on Applied computing* (pp. 2315-2320). Fortaleza, Ceara, Brazil: ACM.

Noll, M. G., & Meinel, C. (2008b). *The metadata triumvirate: Social annotations, anchor texts and search queries. Web Intelligence and Intelligent Agent Technology* (pp. 640–647). Sydney, Australia: IEEE CS Press.

Qi, X., & Davison, B. D. (2009). Web page classification: Features and algorithms. *ACM Computing Surveys, 41*(2), 1–31. doi:10.1145/1459352.1459357

Ramage, D., Heymann, P., Manning, C. D., & Garcia-Molina, H. (2009). Clustering the tagged web. *Proceedings of the Second ACM International Conference on Web Search and Data Mining* (pp. 54-63). Barcelona, Spain: ACM.

Smith, G. (2008). *Tagging: people-powered metadata for the social web.* Berkeley, California, United States: New Riders.

Sun, B.-Y., Huang, D.-S., Guo, L., & Zhao, Z.-Q. (2004). *Support vector machine committee for classification. Advances in Neural Networks – ISNN 2004* (pp. 648–653). Dalian, China: Springer.

Weston, J., & Watkins, C. (1999). Multi-class support vector machines. Proceedings of the 1999 European Symposium on Artificial Neural Networks (pp. 219-224). Bruges, Belgium: D-Facto.

Yeung, C. M. A., Gibbins, N., & Shadbolt, N. (2008). Web search disambiguation by collaborative tagging. *Proceedings of the Workshop on Exploring Semantic Innotations in Information Retrieval at ECIR'08* (pp. 48-61).

Zubiaga, A., Fresno, V., & Martínez, R. (2009b). Is unlabeled data suitable for multiclass SVM-based web page classification? *SemiSupLearn '09: Proceedings of the NAACL HLT 2009 Workshop on Semi-Supervised Learning for Natural Language Processing* (pp. 28-36). Morristown, NJ: ACL.

Zubiaga, A., Martínez, R., & Fresno, V. (2009a). Getting the most out of social annotations for web page classification. *DocEng'09: Proceedings of the 9th ACM symposium on Document engineering* (pp. 74-83). New York: ACM.

## ADDITIONAL READING

Babinec, M. S., & Mercer, H. (2009). *Metadata and open access repositories.* Philadelphia, PA: Taylor & Francis.

Baca, M., & Getty Research Institute. (2008). *Introduction to metadata.* Los Angeles, CA: Getty Research Institute.

Bonino, S. (2009). *Social tagging as a classification and search strategy: A smart way to label and find web resources.* Saarbrcken, Germany: VDM Verlag Dr. Mll.

Caplan, P. (2009). *Metadata fundamentals for all librarians.* New Delhi: Indiana Pub. House.

Foulonneau, M., & Riley, J. (2008). *Metadata for digital resources: Implementation, systems design and interoperability. Chandos information professional series.* Oxford: Chandos.

Gartner, R., L'Hours, H., & Young, G. (2008). *Metadata for digital libraries: State of the art and future directions.* Bristol: JISC.

Golder, S., & Huberman, B. A. (2006). The structure of collaborative tagging systems. *Journal of Information Science, 32*(2), 198–208. doi:10.1177/0165551506062337

Granitzer, M., Lux, M., & Spaniol, M. (2008). *Multimedia semantics: The role of metadata.* Berlin: Springer.

Heymann, P., Koutrika, G., & Garcia-Molina, H. (2008). Can social bookmarking improve web search? *WSDM '08: Proceedings of the international conference on Web search and web data mining* (pp. 195-206). New York: ACM.

Hider, P. (2009). *Information resource description: Creating and managing metadata*. London: Facet.

Hillmann, D. I., Guenther, R., Hayes, A., Library of Congress., & Association for Library Collections & Technical Services. (2008). *Metadata standards & applications*. Washington, D.C: Library of Congress.

International Conference on Metadata and Semantics Research, Sartori, F., Sicilia, M.-A., & Manouselis, N. (2009). *Metadata and semantic research: Third international conference*, MTSR 2009, Milan, Italy, October 1-2, 2009: proceedings. Berlin: Springer.

Lanius, L., & Vermont. (2009). *Embracing Metadata: Understanding MARC and Dublin Core [workshop]*. Montpelier, VT: Vermont Dept. of Libraries.

Mittal, A. C. (2009). *Metadata management*. Delhi, India: Vista International Pub. House.

Noll, M. G., & Meinel, C. (2008a). Exploring social annotations for web document classification. *Proceedings of the 2008 ACM symposium on Applied computing* (pp. 2315-2320). Fortaleza, Ceara, Brazil: ACM.

Peters, I. (2009). *Folksonomies. Indexing and Retrieval in Web 2.0 (Knowledge & Information: Studies in Information Science)*. Berlin, Germany: De Gruyter/Saur.

Ramage, D., Heymann, P., Manning, C. D., & Garcia-Molina, H. (2009). Clustering the tagged web. *Proceedings of the Second ACM International Conference on Web Search and Data Mining* (pp. 54-63). Barcelona, Spain: ACM.

Smith, G. (2008). *Tagging: people-powered metadata for the social web*. Berkeley, CA: New Riders.

Taylor, A. G., & Joudrey, D. N. (2009). *The organization of information*. Westport, CT: Libraries Unlimited.

Turrell, A. (2008). *Augmenting Classifications and Search with Tags to Create Usable Content- and Product-Based Websites*. Baltimore, MD: University of Baltimore.

Wu, X., Zhang, L., & Yu, Y. (2006). Exploring social annotations for the semantic web. *WWW '06: Proceedings of the 15th international conference on World Wide Web* (pp. 417-426). New York: ACM.

Zhou, D., Bian, J., Zheng, S., Zha, H., & Giles, C. L. (2008). Exploring social annotations for information retrieval. *Proceedings of the 17th international conference on World Wide Web* (pp. 715-724). Beijing, China: ACM.

Zubiaga, A., Martínez, R., & Fresno, V. (2009a). Getting the most out of social annotations for web page classification. *DocEng'09: Proceedings of the 9th ACM symposium on Document engineering* (pp. 74-83). New York: ACM.

## KEY TERMS AND DEFINITIONS

**Collaborative Tagging:** Many users tag the same item, and every person can tag it with their own tags in their own vocabulary. The collection of tags assigned by a single user creates a smaller folksonomy, also known as personomy. As a result, several users tend to post the same item. For instance, CiteULike, LibraryThing and Delicious are based on collaborative tagging, where each resource (papers, books and URLs, respectively) could be tagged (therefore annotated) by all the users who considered it interesting.

**Folksonomy:** As a result of a community tagging resources, the collection of tags defined by them creates a tag-based organization, so-called folksonomy. A folksonomy is also known as a community-based taxonomy, where the classification scheme is plain, there are no predefined tags, and therefore users can freely choose new words as tags. A folksonomy is basically known as weighted set of tags, and may refer to a whole collection/site, a resource or a user. A summary of a folksonomy is usually presented in the form of a tag cloud.

**Personomy:** Personomy is a neologism created from the term folksonomy, and it refers to the weighted set of tags of a single user/person. It summarizes the topics a user tags about.

**Simple Tagging:** Users describe their own resources or items, such as photos on Flickr, news on Digg or videos on Youtube, but nobody else tags another user's resources. Usually, the author of the resource is who tags it. This means no more than one user tags an item. In many cases, like in Flickr and Youtube, simple tagging systems include an attachment to the resource, and not just a reference to it.

**Social Bookmarking:** Delicious, Stumble-Upon and Diigo, amongst others, are known as social bookmarking sites. They provide a social means to save web pages (or other online resources like images or videos) as bookmarks, in order to retrieve them later on. In contrast to saving bookmarks in user's local browser, posting them to social bookmarking sites allows the community to discover others' links and, besides, to access the bookmarks from any computer to the user itself. In these systems, bookmarks represent references to web resources, and do not attach a copy of them, but just a link. Note that social bookmarking sites do not always rely on social tags to organize resources, e.g., Reddit is a social bookmarking approach to add comments on web pages instead of tags. The use of social tags in social bookmarking systems is a common approach, though.

**Social Cataloging:** They are quite similar to social bookmarking sites in that resources are socially shared but, in this case, offline resources like music, books or movies are saved. For in-stance, LibraryThing allows to save the books you like, Hulu does it for movies and TV series, and Last.fm for music-related resources. As in social bookmarking sites, tags are the most common way to annotate resources in social cataloging sites.

**Social Tagging:** A tagging system becomes social when its tag annotations are publicly visible, and so profitable for anyone. The fact of a tagging system being social implies that a user could take advantage of tags defined by others to retrieve a resource.

**Tagging:** Tagging is an open way to assign tags or keywords to resources or items (e.g., web pages, movies or books), in order to describe them. This enables the later retrieval of the resources in an easier way, using tags as resource metadata. As opposed to a classical taxonomy-based categorization system, they are usually non-hierarchical, and the vocabulary is open, so it tends to grow indefinitely. For instance, a user could tag this chapter as social-tagging, research and chapter, whereas another user could use web2.0, social-bookmarking and tagging tags to annotate it.

## ENDNOTES

[1] http://delicious.com

[2] http://www.stumbleupon.com

[3] http://www.librarything.com

[4] http://www.diigo.com

[5] Golder and Huberman found that after about 100 users tagged a specific web page, the distribution of its top tags tends to converge (Golder & Huberman, 2006). Thus, we considered 100 users as a threshold for a bookmarked resource to be popular.

[6] http://nlp.uned.es/social-tagging/socialod-p2k9/

[7] http://svmlight.joachims.org

# Chapter 9
# Social Network Construction in the Information Age:
## Views and Perspectives

**Michael Farrugia**
*University College Dublin, Ireland*

**Neil Hurley**
*University College Dublin, Ireland*

**Diane Payne**
*University College Dublin, Ireland*

**Aaron Quigley**
*University College Dublin, Ireland*

## ABSTRACT

*Social scientists have been studying and refining their network data collection instruments for the last number of decades. Data collection in this field traditionally consists of manually conducting interviews and questionnaires on a population of interest to derive a list of ties between the members of the population and which can later be studied from a sociological perspective. Great care and considerable resources are often required during the research design and data collection phases in order to ensure that the final data set is well focused, unbiased and representative of the selected population.*

*Nowadays electronic network data is becoming widely available and easier to access and this data brings with it a number of advantages over manually collecting data. The ease of data collection, lower cost, large scale, temporal information and the elimination of respondent bias and recall problems are all concrete benefits of electronic data. With these clear advantages, could electronic data be a solution to problems encountered with manual data collection?*

DOI: 10.4018/978-1-61350-513-7.ch009

*Electronic data is often available as a bi-product of other processes (such as phone call logs and email server logs), so often the data is not collected with the explicit purpose of being studied from a social network perspective. This aspect shifts the design decisions on electronic data to a later processing stage once the data is available, rather than before the data is collected. This shift introduces a different set of decisions and processes when dealing with electronic data collection. What are the best ways to process and interpret the data to achieve valid insights into the 'real' social network that the social scientist is interested in?*

*In this chapter, the authors will discuss the differences between manual data collection and electronic data collection to understand the advantages and the challenges brought by electronic social network data. They will discuss in detail the processes that are used to transform electronic data to social network data and the procedures that can be used to validate the resultant social network.*

## INTRODUCTION

Generally speaking one's social circle, or more specifically one's social network, includes friends, family, colleagues and acquaintances. Social connectedness however, is a psychological term which describes the duration, frequency, familiarity and reciprocal nature of the relationships people have with others in this circle or network. Both our social network and how connected we feel to people within it are important aspects of one's social wellbeing. Our social circle and how we perceive our degree of social connectedness can be subjective and possibly difficult to articulate.

Classically, social scientists interested in such social networks and connectedness would perform small scale data collection studies. Such data collection traditionally consisted of observation or manually conducting interviews and questionnaires on a population of interest, to derive a list of ties between the members of the population which can later be studied from a sociological perspective. Clearly, this is a time consuming and expensive process. In addition, the ability to document networks and our connectedness over the course of time is limited by the frequency of the data collection activities. The realisation that both human memory and our perception of social connectedness are limited implies that any data collected through such manual processes will

inherently contain errors. Regardless of all these problems, such data collection methods have represented the gold standard for some time.

By contrast, consider the rapid expansion of technologies which collect data either explicitly or implicitly about our social networks and connectedness. Social networking services have become part of most people's daily lives. These services support people's connections and interactions while keeping an electronic trace of all these activities. There is also a wealth of electronic data that is available as a bi-product of other processes (sales, travel, phone call logs and email server logs). Within this data are the digital footprints of activity from which social networks and our connectedness can be deduced. In such cases the data is not collected with the explicit purpose of being studied from a social network perspective. This aspect shifts the design decisions on electronic data to a later processing stage once the data is already available, rather than the data collection stage before the data is collected. This shift introduces a different set of decisions and processes when dealing with electronic data collection.

When considering electronic data, from which we wish to extract both social networks and information on connectedness, there are a number of problems to consider. Firstly, records may relate to an entity relevant to the business (customer, caller, traveller, recipient). These entities must be resolved into the actors within our social network. Next, methods to relate the actors must be determined based on relevant context provided within the domain in question. For instance, actors may be linked in an online store if one sends another a gift or if two people travel together. Finally, it is important to differentiate between relationships of different strength. One cannot possibly have equal relationships to all 500 friends on a social networking site. In this case, identifying the strong and weak relationships is important for a better network understanding.

In this chapter we will discuss the differences between manual data collection and electronic data collection to understand the advantages and the challenges brought by electronic social network data. We will discuss in detail the processes that are used to transform electronic data to social network data and the procedures that can be used to validate the resultant social network.

The rest of this chapter is arranged as follows: We first give a brief overview of manual social network data collection to orient the reader who is not familiar with the general practices in this area. In the second section, we describe electronic data collections and give some examples of studies that make use of this kind of data. Following this, we compare the two types of data collection and then proceed to explain the processes involved in electronic data collection. As part of the process involved we describe the steps of actor identification, tie inference, tie strength measurement and network validation. We conclude this chapter by giving some recommendations on future research related to network construction.

## MANUAL SOCIAL NETWORK DATA COLLECTION

Similar to most other data collection methods in the field of sociology, manual data collection in social networks is based predominantly on survey methods (interviews and questionnaires), behavioural observation (ethnographic studies) and text extraction from archives or diaries (Marsden, 1990). The process of data collection in social science has been the subject of many research papers that specifically tackle the question of how best to obtain relational data. We will only outline the most common approaches here and refer the reader to more comprehensive work such as the textbook by Wasserman and Faust (Wasserman & Faust, 1994), and work by Marsden (Marsden, 1990, 2005), Scott (Scott, 2000) and Scott and Carrington's recent book "The Sage Handbook of Social Network Analysis" (Carrington & Scott, 2011).

Social network data can either be collected through an *ego-centric approach* or through a *network centric approach*. Typically network centric data collection involves only small populations such as school classes or organisations where the population and environment is small enough to be tractable and the network boundary relatively easy to define. Generally all the members of the population are known beforehand which enables the researcher to provide the respondent with a whole list of network members. Therefore, the most common approach to collect network centric data is to use a roster approach and *self-report* questionnaires. The respondent then specifies all those network members with whom a tie exists. Apart from establishing the presence of a tie, the respondent may be asked to rank the relationship (quantify it) or else define some properties of the relationship.

In a large population, manual network centric data collection is impractical due to the large number of ties to be considered: $n \times (n-1)/2$, where $n$ is the number of actors in the network.

Ego centric data collection tries to overcome this scale problem by concentrating on specific actors called *egos* and their relationships with their neighbours called *alters*. In this approach a representative number of people from a population are chosen and asked to name other people (alters) with whom they have a tie characteristic according to the nature of the study. The participants are sometimes also asked to identify ties between alters and attributes of the alters (e.g. gender, nationality).

The most common technique to collect ego centric data is to use a *name generator* and a name interpreter (Burt, 1984). The challenges in collecting ego centric network data are firstly to choose the appropriate egos from where to start sampling the network. Once the egos are identified then the challenge is to ask the appropriate questions that will best elicit alters of interest based on the research question. The name generator is effectively a questionnaire whose aim is to derive the names of alters from an ego's network for a certain type of relationship. After the name generator is used, the *name interpreter* questionnaire is used to obtain more information on the attributes of the alters, the types, and the intensities of the ties. There is also the possibility of using multiple name generators and name interpreters in a single questionnaire. Due to the complexity of the questionnaire often an interviewer administers the questionnaire to collect the data rather than simply sending it by mail.

In general, with regard to both network centric data collection and ego centric data collection, there can be a number of constraints that are imposed because of the research context. In particular, the design of the network questionnaire and the formulation of the network survey questions face three challenges: accessibility, validity and research resource constraint with regard to time and money For example, sometimes the social phenomena may not easily be studied. Accessing "hidden networks" such as drug users or sex workers pose particular problems, in terms of identifying the actors in the network. Snowball sampling is a technique which allows the researcher to build up the sample, whereby existing network members recruit other members from among their acquaintances. Likewise, political networks are often difficult to access and interviewees may be

reluctant to give frank and open responses. In such instances the researcher is required to provide re-assurance in the interview process that the data collected will be used in strict confidence. Another issue is the validity of the responses when measuring existing social ties. In the case of political networks, there may be a likelihood of strategic responses being given, whereas with friendship networks, social desirability may play a role in the network ties identified (Torenvlied & VanSchuur, 1994).

The researcher(s) should also recognise the constrains due to time limits within which it is feasible to collect the network data during interviewing, so that the goal of obtaining reliable results is achieved without frustrating the respondent. Problems with data collection arise when there are a large number of network actors and as a result, potentially a large number of relations in the data set. For example, Torenvlied et al suggest that "policy influence networks for example, realistically can include more than fifty actors, implying the existence of 2450 potential directed relations"(Torenvlied & VanSchuur, 1994). A typical constraint imposed is limiting the number of alters that an ego can name when reporting ties. The issue of time constraints may also need to be balanced with respect to the need to collect data on different types of ties between actors, as well as collecting data on the direction of ties between actors in the network. From the outset, a clearly specified research design is required to minimise many of these challenges associated with ego-centric and network-centric manual data collection.

While the two approaches to data collection yield different results and are usually analysed differently, it is possible if an ego network is sampled extensively, that the data will eventually match a whole network sample close enough to enable network centric analysis. An example of this type of strategy can be seen in Kirke's study (Kirke, 1996) on a youth population in Dublin, where an initial ego centric data collection method yielded sufficient information to enable a whole network view of the data. This is often seen in electronic data collection when a crawler starts from an ego and gradually collects data to cover a percentage of the whole population.

## ELECTRONIC DATA COLLECTION

One of the most significant advances in social network data collection since the authoritative paper by Marsden (Marsden, 1990), is the explosion of electronic network data that became available to researchers. This surge in data availability coupled with developments in computing power and new algorithms, generated interest in networks from other fields, such as physics, computer science, mathematics, statistics and biology. The extent of this interest is highlighted by the creation of research branches such as Computational Social Science (Lazer et al., 2009) and Complex Systems, where networks are a central aspect of study.

Although studies using electronically gathered data are on the increase, this type of data collection has not been readily embraced by social science fields such as sociology, economics and political science (Lazer, et al., 2009). In fact, the most recent work by Marsden on social network data collection (Marsden, 2005) does not give much attention to electronic data collection.

A data collection method that is gaining traction in sociology is running surveys and questionnaires on the internet using web forums to facilitate their distribution and possibly reach a wider audience (Matzat & Snijders, 2010; Vehovar, Lozar Manfreda, Koren, & Hlebec, 2008). These approaches generally convert manual data collection questionnaires into online forms. The disadvantage of online surveys is that they are completely reliant on self report data and cannot be supplemented with interviews. When we refer to electronic data collection, we are not referring to these approaches but to other electronic data that is not collected with the explicit intent to be analysed for social network purposes.

In this section we will give some examples of studies that use electronically collected network data to explore the social implications of the data. We will draw comparisons between the two types of data collection and hope to shed some light on the reasons why there has been a hesitancy to adopt electronic network data by social scientists.

### Communication Data

The most common types of electronic communication data available are email (Kossinets & Watts, 2006), phone call data (Akoglu & Dalvi; Cebrian, Pentland, & Kirkpatrick, 2010; Onnela et al., 2007), and instant messengers such as MSN (Leskovec & Horvitz). This type of data is often used as a means to represent social communication. Interaction and communication patterns are often of interest to sociologists in different contexts such as the diffusion of ideas, information flow, advice relationships and provision of social support.

Communication data sets generally contain detailed timing information and extend to millions of nodes and edges. For instance, in a phone call network, the time and duration when the calls are made need to be accurately tracked for billing purposes. This makes these networks ideal to study large scale dynamics of networks. Also, the rich nature of communication data facilitates the study of tie strength in evolving networks (Akoglu & Dalvi; Onnela, et al., 2007).

Most work on real phone call data is motivated by the phone call industry and therefore the research questions posed are usually relevant to the phone business, such as trying to develop predictive measures to determine future calls (Akoglu & Dalvi) and trying to identify people leaving the network (Dasgupta et al.).

### Friendship Networks

Today, our ability to maintain a social circle is supported by a variety of Social Networking Services (Boyd & Ellison, 2008). These services offer interactive web based environments for enabling people to connect and maintain social connections, thus supporting the mirroring of real communities into virtual "friendship networks". Initially, online social networks were the playgrounds of young people, from early teens to mid-twenties but that changed rapidly (Wellman & Haythornthwaite, 2002). With the ongoing niche stratification of the social network space, there are many social network services targeting specific audiences, e.g. Eons for those aged 50+, LinkedIn for maintaining and creating professional ties (Licoppe & Smoreda, 2005). It is therefore possible to envision a spread of social network services with people being members of multiple services over to course of their life. In recent years, social networks have exploded in popularity and diversity, with rough estimates indicating online social networks are a regular part of hundreds of millions of people's online lives. Specific features of online social networks enable people to:

- Create online personal profiles
- Form connections with friends with have also created personal profiles, i.e. have a large circle of friends on a social network
- Easily update their profiles to share what is happening in their lives with their friends, i.e. profile updates and blog updates
- Share content, such as photographs and videos
- Engage in shared conversations between multiple groups of friends, e.g. share comments about shared photographs
- Communicate privately
- Create and engage in online interest groups
- Play games together e.g. Farmville and playfully interact, e.g. giving each other virtual flowers

Social network sites are commonly used to reinforce existing relationships, rather than build new friendships. As a result, they represent an interesting insight into our social networks and connectedness. Social network services provide the potential for the social scientist to collect large amounts of network and connectedness information. However, in practice, concerns about privacy, data protection and justifiable user apprehension limit the scale of what a social scientist can legally and ethically obtain.

Internet social networking sites provide an interesting platform for the social scientist because the data in these systems is intrinsically social. Ties between individuals in social networking sites are created as part of the core functionality of the service. Although ties are explicitly defined, not all ties are equal. With the increase in user growth and platform evolution the purpose and usage of the social networking sites extended beyond the original friendship based message boards to, gaming platforms, advertising and marketing activities and other business focused interaction. A Facebook member with a thousand or more friends cannot possibly have the same types of ties with all thousand friends. With such an overloaded and abused definition of tie, the issue of determining tie strength (becomes a key network construction processing task. We therefore return to discuss this issue in more detail later in this chapter.

In the early days of Facebook, when the site was only limited to college students, Mayer and Puller (Mayer & Puller, 2007) studied Facebook friendship networks from 10 different university social networks. They use the friendship data to characterise the structure of friendship networks, in particular the segmentation of social ties by race, socioeconomic background and ability.

Lewis et al (Lewis, Kaufman, Gonzalez, Wimmer, & Christakis, 2008) constructed a Facebook social network with the intention of making the dataset public and available for researchers. In the paper the authors describe the features of the dataset and outline the differences between data collected from social network sites and other social network data sources. Unfortunately due to privacy concerns the social network is currently not available. This highlights the important issue of privacy for the researcher collecting and using any type of electronic data that is not collected with the exclusive intent of being used for research purposes.

## Web Data

Web page data with the intricate linking structure between web pages creates a natural network that has been extensively studied in various studies that look at the topological structure of the web (Barabasi & Albert, 1999; Gibson, Kleinberg, & Raghavan). The links between web pages and blogs also provides a rich dataset for studying community formation and structure (Lada A. Adamic & Glance; Gibson, et al.) and patterns of information diffusion (Gomez Rodriguez, Leskovec, & Krause).

In a study that tries to characterise the polarity and diversity of opinion between blogs supporting different political parties, Adamic and Glance (Lada A. Adamic & Glance) examine the degree of interaction between different party blogs and highlight differences in the two different community structures. In their study, they also observe how the blogs interact (through linking) with mainstream media sites. This study brings to mind a similar study by Valdis Krebs on political book purchases on Amazon (Krebs, 2000).

## MMOG

Massive online multiplayer games (MMOG's) bring together a large community of users to inhabit an online virtual world and play a game together to achieve goals and interact within the game environment. The largest of such games like World of Warcraft have millions of players who log in daily to the environment to play and interact with other players. MMOGs typically promote cooperation between players to achieve goals that cannot otherwise be achieved individually, such as killing large monsters.

From an academic perspective these games create a virtual society where all the interactions,

actions and activities taking place in the society are recorded. Perhaps more than any other data source, MMOG data provides an excellent proxy for behaviour and actions in a society that has well established goals and reward schemes but which allows for different ways to achieve those goals (Bainbridge, 2007).

In a recent study, Szell and Thurner (Szell & Thurner, 2010) use data from an MMOG game to study human communication networks. The researchers use the communication data from the game in the form of chat logs, forum messages and private messages to test well established hypotheses on social network dynamics. Using the data from the MMOG they empirically test the hypotheses of triadic closure, weak ties and social balance. Based on the positive obtained results when comparing virtual with non virtual communities, the authors make a strong argument that online game communities can serve as a model of human societies. In another study (Kawale, Pal, & Srivastava) using MMOG data, researchers use models of social influence to predict players who are likely to churn and stop playing the game or move to play a different game.

## COMPARING ELECTRONIC AND MANUAL DATA COLLECTION

Electronic data collection cuts down on the time, effort and costs a researcher spends in the field administering questionnaires, interviews or observing behaviour. This increased accessibility and availability of data provides a tangible benefit whenever electronic data is available for the particular research question.

Another advantage of electronic data is the amount of data that can be collected. The scale at which electronic data can be collected is orders of magnitude greater than any data that can be collected manually. While the largest manual datasets can reach up to a few thousand records, electronic datasets can have millions of records.

This increase in scale can contribute to the attainment of more statistically significant results in the larger datasets. The issues of scale and ease of data collection are major obstacles for social scientists to collect data from a network centric perspective. The sheer number of questions that need to be asked becomes prohibitively large as the population increases. Automatically collected data sets can often provide a network perspective without the burden of exhaustive questions to survey participants.

Most electronic data sets contain time stamp information that can accurately determine the time when events occur. This additional data facilitates the collection of longitudinal social network data without having to run surveys multiple times or spend years observing people's behaviour. Moreover, the time stamp information can be very detailed, sometimes down to milliseconds, thus allowing networks of different time granularity to be constructed without having to repeat the data collection.

The reliability of reported data during interviews is known to suffer from accuracy problems due to the difficultly in recalling past events (Bernard, Killworth, Kronenfeld, & Sailer, 1984). This problem however is not applicable to electronic data, as electronic data does not rely on human memory and data is automatically collected.

While often there are benefits to be gained from using electronic data, there are also some drawbacks. Firstly, not all data can be collected from electronic data sources. The primary reason is that when an explicit type of relationship is being studied (e.g. HIV infection through injecting drug users), then it is often difficult to use a generic data set that is not collected purposely for measuring the specific tie. Also, certain populations of interest are difficult to track in electronic data sources.

With electronic data one tends to ask the questions *after* the data is collected, rather than start with the questions and proceed towards collecting data to answer those questions. In contrast, in manual data collection the design decisions are taken *before* the data is collected, when designing the name generator and interpreter. The control and level of information that is obtained from electronic data is therefore dependent on what is available and on the interpretation the data is given after it is collected.

An often neglected difference between the two data collection methods is the issue of privacy and ethical clearance. When conducting manual data collection, there are clear rules and well established ethical procedures that need to be followed. With electronic data, this important aspect of the research process is still not fully explored. The processing, usage and reporting of data collected through electronic channels needs to be guarded more closely by privacy and data protection considerations.

It is important to note that both manual and electronic methods of data collection form an incomplete representation of the actual ties that exist in the real social network. For example, while the data collector may be able to form a full log of all email communication that occurs through a particular server, it is possible that two actors in the network email each other through a different server and thus a "sends-email-to" tie that exists in reality is missed by the data collection process. The same can be said for population sampling in manual social network data collection. In order to summarise these various points, the properties of manual and electronic data collection are listed in Table 1.

## UNDERSTANDING NETWORKS

When describing and discussing networks it is often useful to categorise and describe the network based on the patterns of connection that the network exhibits. On a structural level, networks can be categorized by the graph theoretic properties that describe the type of graph structure used to represent the network. Descriptions such as

*Table 1. Comparison between electronic and manual data collection*

| Manual Data Collection | Electronic Data collection |
| --- | --- |
| Data collection involves surveys, questionnaires or interviews | Data is typically available automatically as a bi-product of a separate process |
| Relatively small scale | Scale of data can extend to millions of records |
| Network centric data is difficult to collect, therefore most data is collected using ego-centric methods | Network centric data is as easily accessible as ego centric data. |
| Longitudinal data is laborious to collect and limited in possible data collection points | Time stamped data is easily available |
| Human recall is prone to error | Electronic memory is accurate |
| Relationships are well defined | Relationships need to be interpreted from the data |
| Data is collected with the intent of research. Research questions formulated first, data is collected after | Data is available and questions are made to fit the data available. Data is collected first, research questions formulated afterwards |
| Well established ethics procedures and guidelines | Less well-developed ethical procedures. Privacy Considerations |

direction, weighting, tie structure (hypergraph etc) and mode (one-mode or two-mode graph) are examples of graph theoretic descriptions of networks.

In recent years, the physics community has been very active in studying and categorising networks based on their statistical properties and patterns of connection (Albert & Barabasi, 2002; Dorogovtsev & Mendes, 2002; Newman, 2001). Research advances in this area established the now popular terms, scale free networks (Barabasi & Albert, 1999) and small world networks (Watts & Strogatz, 1998). Networks can also be described based on the process used to collect the network data, thus distinguishing between whole networks and ego networks.

Describing networks using topological properties, patterns of connection or the data collection process are all useful descriptors of the network. However, all these descriptions isolate the network structure from the meaning behind the network. These descriptive measures focus on the actual patterns of connection and the universality of network structure, irrespective of the meaning of the ties in the network. It would be beneficial to formulate a structure and differentiation of network ties to assist with the understanding of network construction.

## Network Relevance

One can argue that a tie exists between each individual in the world. The fact that we are living on the same planet and globally breathing the same air may be sufficient to create a link between all 7 billion people living on earth. Ties are easy to define and if one wants, it is possible to link two people on opposite sides of the world through a number of ties.

Consider two people, one is sitting at a diner having breakfast in San Francisco and the other is sitting at a cafe in Rome. One can purport that a tie exists between these two people because they both use Google as their search engine. Moreover, in the last two days they both ran a search query for Lady Gaga. Additionally, their coffees are coming from the same plantation in Colombia.

Taken out of context and without a problem formulation, these links might seem useless and possibly exaggerated. However, if one were to put a valid research question on such ties then they can become *relevant*. For instance, if one was studying the distribution network of coffee around the world, or the network of influence of search results, the links between the two people on opposite sides of the world become relevant to the research question.

If one were to consider all of his/her different ties one would easily come to the conclusion that there is not only one 'real' social network but many different, possibly overlapping, networks. Even one particular network can be made up of different layers of ties that together form the network. The ties and corresponding social networks are relevant depending on the process being studied. If one were studying the transmission of sexually transmitted diseases (STDs), the ties with one's family might not be relevant, whereas if one were studying the social support network of the same person, the family ties are possibly very important (De Choudhury, Mason, Hofman, & Watts).

A tie that is relevant for one actor might not be relevant for another actor. For instance, if one were building a network for intelligence purposes, a family link between two actors is usually indicative of a path of information transmission or collaboration. However, in the case of the world's most wanted criminal, Osama Bin Laden, this does not apply. Bin Laden's family is a wealthy family with global investments who are not connected to him in any way apart from the blood ties. Even though Bin Laden's links with the family are present and 'real', they are not relevant to the network of his alleged criminal activities.

The reconfiguration and redefinition of the network based on new, incoming information is an important feature in applications such as intelligence and disease transmission networks. Such dynamic problem environments might quickly need to reconstruct the network based on new incoming information.

With the extent of electronic data available nowadays, we are no longer experiencing a lack of information, but possibly an excess of information. Most electronic data sources are derived from logs that are designed to record extra information for completeness. As was discussed in the previous section and illustrated in this section, the challenge with electronic data is to filter out the noise and extra information to leave only the information relevant to the research question (Garton, Haythornthwaite, & Wellman, 1997).

## Understanding Network Ties

Since ties define networks, understanding ties is an important step in understanding networks. In this section we differentiate between two types of ties, *implicit ties* and *explicit ties*. This tie distinction will serve as a grounding structure in the process of network construction from electronic data.

Explicit ties are ties that are purposely gathered in a data collection process. For example, it is straight-forward to automatically keep a log of email communications and thus observe a tie between two actors, defined on the basis that they have emailed each other in the past. Explicit ties such as sends-email-to, co-authors-with, travels-with etc are readily available through such data collection processes. They can be explained usually by an event in the real world and are often quantifiable and unambiguous.

Implicit ties on the other hand are those ties whose manifestation in the real world is not reflected in a single observable instance that leads to the conclusion that such a tie exists. Social ties such as friendship and partnership are typical examples of implicit ties. These ties are usually not defined by a single event but by a sequence of possibly different events that lead to the creation, strengthening or dissolution of that tie.

As explicit ties are associated with a particular observation, the weight of the tie can easily be calculated by enumerating the number of times the observation occurs. A researcher can, for example, quantify the number of times an email is sent from A to B to add a strength to the tie. Conversely quantifying the strength of a friendship and even more so associating a numeric value is much more difficult, if not perhaps unreasonable. Similarly it is easy to associate a temporal element to explicit ties, particularly when the data is in electronic form and the start time and possibly the duration of the tie are known. On the other hand,

*Figure 1. Social Network Construction Process*

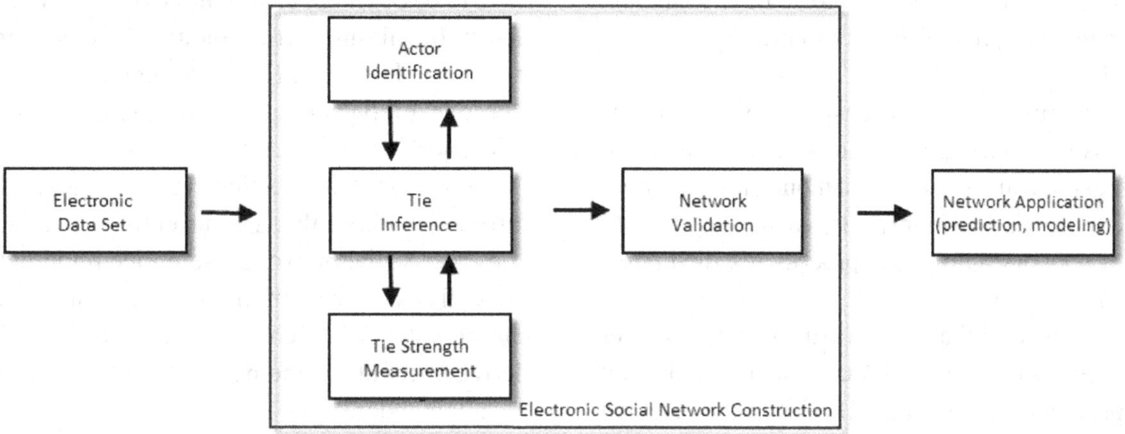

with implicit ties one cannot exactly quantify the time when a friendship starts, how long it lasts and when it ends.

The distinction between types of ties has been documented by other authors before. Getoor and Diehl (Getoor & Diehl, 2005), distinguish between predicting *friendships*, predicting *events*, and predicting *semantic relationships* (e.g. advisor-of). O'Madadhain et al (O'Madadhain, Hutchins, & Smyth, 2005) distinguishes between *persistent* relationships (e.g. friendships, affiliations, web links) and *discrete events* (meetings, publications, communications, transactions). In sociology the terms *behavioural observations* (e.g. events and interactions) and *cognitive observations* (e.g. friendship, love) are often used to differentiate between these types of ties (Eagle, Pentland, & Lazer, 2009).

From these definitions one can note that it is usually easier to collect explicit relationships rather than implicit relationships, particularly because most often electronic data provides only explicit relationships. The importance of implicit or social ties is critical to the study of social behaviour and thus central to social network analysis. As it is easier to collect data of explicit ties, it makes sense to attempt to infer the implicit ties from the observed explicit ties. We term this

process *social network construction* and discuss it in the next section.

## ELECTRONIC SOCIAL NETWORK CONSTRUCTION

The aim of social network construction is to process an electronic data set to derive a social network perspective of the same dataset. Figure 1 shows a schematic diagram of the construction process. The four boxes enclosed in the red square are the processes that are required for network construction.

The best way to understand the steps involved in this process is by using an example. Consider a dataset of phone call logs from a mobile phone company. The reason for constructing the social network varies by application and by domain. A sociologist might want to infer a social network from phone call data to understand and model the intricacies in patterns of human communication. A mobile phone company might want to understand the underlying social network so that based on the understanding of the network the company can predict future phone calls, predict new mobile phone adoption or predict customers leaving the network (churn). An intelligence officer working in drug enforcement might be interested in the pattern of communication to trace information passing through the network to identify suppliers in the chain.

The first process in constructing a network is to associate each phone number to an individual. A person can have more than one phone number therefore it is important to map each phone number to a network actor. This process is called *actor identification*.

The second challenge is to understand whether a particular phone communication does in fact represent a relationship relevant to the research question. In the case of phone call data, one would typically want to ignore advertising phones calls, answering machine callbacks, or calls to a wrong number. The stage of identifying ties between actors is called *tie inference*.

Once the existence of a tie is established one may want to understand the strength of the tie. Does the tie represent a strong tie between the two actors or a weak tie? This stage is called *tie strength measurement*.

In Figure 1 we notice that there are arrows linking the 3 main processes of actor identification, tie inference, and tie strength measurement. The reason for the multi-directional arrows between the processes is that each process can make use of information derived from the other processes. Specifically, the actor inference process can make use of the network structure to improve the identification of actors, for example by identifying actors with a similar name and having the same neighbours as the same actor. Likewise, there is a strong link between tie inference and tie strength measurement as the relevant ties to a network can be determined based on their strength, or tie type.

Irrespective of the application, the steps in creating the network are the same, yet the most appropriate network for a task is dependent on the application. The network construction process is the process that tries to come up with the best parameters that define a particular network. How long should the duration of a phone call be in an emotional support network? How often do calls have to be observed to determine the presence of an emotional support tie? Should unreciprocated phone calls be included in an intelligence network? These are the types of questions that the processes of network construction try to answer.

In the following section we will explain the different methods that are currently available to construct social networks from electronic data. We will also look at different ways the networks can be validated to ensure that, if possible, the derived network is the best network for the application under study.

## Actor Identification

An essential step in constructing a network is identifying the actors of the network. Often in electronic data sources actors are identified by a unique identifier such as a record id, username, email address or phone number. Although this is quite common, not all data sources have this information. Even when data sources contain a unique identifier, the unique identifier might not necessarily point to a single person, or a single person might have more than one identifier. If one were to take an example from an email dataset, it is not uncommon for the same person to have more than one email address. Also, group email addresses or a common addresses shared by multiple people (e.g. a department email address) will not uniquely identify a person.

The problem of identifying multiple records referring to the same single entity was recognised more than six decades ago by H. L. Dunn (Dunn, 1946) who used the term *record linkage* to define the problem. The seminal paper by Fellegi and Sunter (Fellegi & Sunter, 1969) formally defined record linkage building on prior work by Newcombe (Newcombe, Kennedy, Axford, & James, 1959), and the approaches outlined by Fellegi and Sunter are still used today. Although the problem has been around for a long time, it is still considered as one of data mining's grand challenges (Piatetsky-Shapiro et al., 2006).

In computer science, the same problem spans many different research communities, under different names. In the database and KDD communities the problem is often called *merge/purge*, *data cleansing* or *duplicate elimination* (HernÃ¡ndez & Stolfo, 1998). In this context, the aim is to identify which tuples within the same table, or different tables, correspond to the same real world object. Computer scientists and AI practitioners call the problem *entity resolution*. In computer vision, the term *correspondence problem (Scharstein & Szeliski, 2002)* is used to describe the identification of features belonging to the same object in two different images. The problem has also been studied in Natural Language Processing, under the term *coreference resolution* (Hirschman & Chinchor). The application of entity resolution has been applied and documented in several domains including medical data (Churches, Christen, Lim, & Zhu, 2002), national statistics (Winkler, 1999), direct marketing (HernÃ¡ndez & Stolfo, 1998), meta search engines (Bilenko, Basu, & Sahami) and identifying airline customers (Farrugia & Quigley, 2010).

A typical entity resolution solution is divided in five stages (Christen, Churches, & Hegland, 2004). First the data needs to be cleaned and consistently divided into separate fields that are used in the following stages of entity resolution. After the cleaning stage the data is typically divided into blocks to reduce the number of comparisons between potential duplicates. Next, field comparisons measure the similarity between pairs of records which are then classified as either being identical or not. Finally, the output of the classification is evaluated to measure the quality of the whole process. Elmagarmid et al. (Elmagarmid, Ipeirotis, & Verykios, 2007) document the progress and advancements in entity resolution in a comprehensive survey paper which describes the state of the art throughout the various stages of Entity Resolution.

The traditional approach to entity resolution has been to use attribute information of the records to compare the similarity between the records. The same problem has been formulated in different ways (Benjelloun et al., 2006) some of which exploit the nature of the data to infer more information than the attributes alone contain. One such approach is to use relational information such as child-parent relationships and co-authorship links between paper authors to add information and improve the accuracy of the classification process.

The early relational entity resolution techniques treated relational information as another attribute in the comparison vector. While these approaches still used a pairwise comparison process, relational information was added to improve the accuracy of this process. In one such approach, Ananthakrishna et al (Ananthakrishna, Chaudhuri, & Ganti) describe a database centric approach that exploits data hierarchies in the database as additional relational information. This information is also used to reduce the number of comparisons during the entity resolution process. Bhattacharya and Getoor (Bhattacharya & Getoor, 2007) describe a more complete relational model with their collective entity resolution approach. They define the entity resolution problem as a clustering problem where each cluster represents a unique entity. Clusters are merged based on their similarity which is calculated with a similarity measure that combines relational similarities and attribute similarities. The authors have shown that this approach improves both on attribute based entity resolution and on techniques that treat relationships as additional attributes.

The actor identification task is often required when constructing co-authorship networks. Authors in co-authorship datasets are not uniquely identified and sometimes an author's name is spelled differently, abbreviated or there might be more than one author with the same name. When constructing co-authorship networks, Newman (Newman, 2001) created two different networks with different rules for determining same authors.

Kang et al (Kang, Getoor, Shneiderman, Bilgic, & Licamele, 2008) describe a visual analytical system called D-dupe to assist with the process of actor identification in co-authorship networks.

## Tie Inference

In sampling network data, as with any sampling task, ensuring that a representative sample of the underlying population is gathered is a primary concern. In network sampling, we are faced not only with the problem of obtaining a sample of the actors in the network, but also must gather the tie information that defines their social network. Sometimes, it may be trivial to obtain the complete set of relationships, given the actors, but when the data collection process is difficult, incomplete, ambiguous or dangerous, we cannot assume that complete tie information has been obtained, and tie inference becomes an important tool.

In the computer science literature, the tie inference problem can be framed in many different ways and has been directly or indirectly tackled in different computing problems. A recent comprehensive survey by (Lu & Zhou, 2010) outlines the different techniques and processes of tie prediction in the context of complex networks. Tie inference has been called different names including, *link prediction, link discovery, relationship identification* and *link inference*. The same problem can be seen in information retrieval where the problem can be formulated as predicting the links between words and documents, recommender systems where the problem is to predict a link between a person being linked to a product in a bipartite network, and also entity resolution, or actor identification.

Tie inference can be applied in different ways to a static network (single network snapshot), and to a dynamic network. In the static network case, we may perform tie inference in order to fill out the incomplete social network obtained from data collection (L. A. Adamic & Adar, 2003; Popescul & Ungar). In a dynamic network case, where network ties change over time, we may further

wish to infer which relationships are likely to be formed in future. The problem is typically formulated as a predictive task to predict what will happen in future time steps, specifically given a static network as observed at time $t_n$ what is the probability that either a new tie, or an already existing tie appears in the network observed at time $t_{n+1}$. Most approaches to predict future ties (Liben-Nowell & Kleinberg, 2007; O'Madadhain, et al., 2005; Tylenda, Angelova, & Bedathur) use previous static snapshots of the network to predict future ties. An interesting approach to incorporating a temporal perspective is taken by (Huang & Lin, 2009). Rather than making inferences using a single snapshot in time, they model each tie in the network as a discrete time series, where the value at each point in time corresponds to the number of times that tie occurred in the previous time interval.

An interesting observation in the context of our discussions on network construction, is that the actor identification problem can in fact be formulated as a link prediction problem. When identifying the same actors using a relational approach, one is effectively computing the similarity between two nodes. The measures of network similarity in this respect can give indications as to which nodes might be referring to the same actor.

The various approaches to tie inference can be classified into two general categories – machine learning techniques and statistical. In machine learning, tie inference is often formulated as a binary classification problem: for any 2 nodes $i$ and $j$ in the dataset, determine if there is a link in which case $l_{ij} = 1$ or else there is no link $l_{ij} = 0$. Feature vectors that compute a measure of attribute and linkage similarity between two nodes are formed and used to provide input to a general-purpose classification algorithm such as SVM (Support Vector Machines). The difference between traditional machine learning classification and graph based machine learning classification is that in traditional learning, each data element is treated independently of the other elements. In graph based learning, the relationships between the data elements are considered important for determining the classification result. This distinction parallels the distinction between traditional statistical analysis and social network analysis in the social sciences.

Liben-Nowell and Klienberg (Liben-Nowell & Kleinberg, 2007) try to understand which network measures are the best at making the most accurate predictions, based solely on the information that can be extracted from the network topology. As intuitively expected, they find that network connection features do contain information about possible future (or missing) connections. Having said this however, basing predictions only on network topology results in low overall prediction since factors outside the network topology are not considered. An interesting result from this work is the fact that relatively indirect measures of similarity involving the sum over paths based calculations, such as Katz's measure (Katz, 1953) and its variants, often outperform more direct measures such as shortest path measures and shared neighbours.

In order to classify the instances various traditional 'off-the-shelf' classifiers can be used to learn how to predict the nodes. Adar and Adamic (Adar & Adamic) use Support Vector Machines (SVM) to predict diffusion of information through the blogosphere. O'Madadhain et al (O'Madadhain, et al., 2005) use a logistic regression classifier to obtain good efficiency at classifying large datasets.

In contrast to machine learning, statistical approaches to tie prediction use stochastic models of the graph in order to predict the existence of missing or future ties. The statistical approach amounts to fitting the observed data to the model and using the fitted model to make predictions. While these approaches have the potential to provide more accurate predictions, they are limited in their scalability and much research is focused on developing computationally tractable algorithms to fit the models. A good survey of statistical network models is provided in (Goldenberg, Zheng, Fienberg, & Airoldi, 2009).

When trying to infer links, the problem of dealing with an unbalanced dataset is often encountered. This problem is exacerbated when attempting to learn links in graphs as the total number of possible links is $O(n^2)$, where n is the number of actors in the network. The number of actual links is typically much smaller $O(n)$ in real-world sparse graphs, so that the balance between negative and positive samples may be very skewed. Provisions to counteract this are often required when training and testing the algorithms.

## Tie Strength Measurement

The importance of determining the strength of a social tie became a key concept in social science following the seminal paper by Granovetter (Granovetter, 1973) on the importance of weak ties. Granovetter described four properties that characterize tie strength; the duration, emotional intensity, intimacy and reciprocal services.

These properties and the others proposed later on by other researchers (Blumstein & Kollock, 1988; Marsden & Campbell, 1984) are often referred to as *indicators* of tie strength, in that they are aspects that define and make up tie strength. These properties can be distinguished from *predictors* of tie strength, which are properties which increase the likelihood that a strong tie exists between two actors without being a component of the tie. Predictors can include properties such as social status, gender, common interests, kinship and physical proximity. The principle behind predictors of tie strength is related to the concept of homophily (McPherson, Smith-Lovin, & Cook, 2001) which claims that people who are similar are more likely to form ties together, or as the common saying goes, 'birds of a feather flock together'.

Although the concept of tie strength is extensively used in social networks, there have been comparatively few studies that attempt to measure tie strength. Granovetter himself postponed this task for future work while he focused on the manifestation of different tie strength and their respective importance, rather than actually measuring of tie strength. Marsden (Marsden & Campbell, 1984) took up the task and in a paper called "Measuring tie strength" measured the best indicators of tie strength. From this work closeness was identified as the best indicator of tie strength, while the temporal aspects of tie strength, namely frequency and duration, were found to be lesser indicators in the 3 different datasets studied.

Recently, Petroczi et al (Petróczi, Nepusz, & Bazsó, 2006) attempt to measure tie strength in an online environment by measuring tie strength in forums. They use a similar experimental setup in an online context by using questionnaires to ask active members of a forum questions about the ties with other forum members. The results show similar patterns to the studies in real networks with allowances for specific characteristics of user forums, such as seeking help and desire to meet in person.

The importance of tie strength was recognized almost four decades ago but perhaps today, with the prevalence and widespread use of social media, this principle is more important and relevant than ever. In most social networking sites, all relationships are considered equal yet this is clearly not the case in reality. A person cannot possibly have the same type of relationship between hundreds or even thousands of acquaintances, even in an online environment.

Using tie strength to distinguish between this mixture of heterogeneous ties has several practical applications in this context. These applications can include improved user experience to promote broadcasting to and displaying activities from people with whom one has stronger ties, improved search facilities, enhancement or automation of privacy settings based on tie strength and the improvement of visualisation tools to give more visual prominence to actors with stronger ties (Gilbert & Karahalios; Xiang, Neville, & Rogati).

The measuring of tie strength in social media has been recently explored in two separate studies by Xiang et al (Xiang, et al.) and by Gilbert and Karahlios (Gilbert & Karahalios). Xiang et al develop an unsupervised statistical model to estimate tie strength based on the interaction profile (tie indicators) and user similarity profile (tie predictors). In this work, the proposed model derives a continuous quantitative figure for the tie strength as opposed to the more often binary approach of classifying ties into strong and weak ties. While the notion of a continuous variable of tie strength might have limited relevance to sociology, particularly when this enables ties of the same type to be ranked and possibly cause misunderstandings in a social context, a continuous tie weight can be useful from a computer science and algorithmic perspective. Applications such as recommender systems, link classifiers and link inference algorithms can make use of such information.

Gilbert and Karahalios (Gilbert & Karahalios) also tackle the issue of modeling tie strength in social media by considering relationships on Facebook. The authors attempt to construct a model to predict tie strength based on a large vector set of features from Facebook interaction and profile similarities measures. They use 70 numeric indicators grounded on established theoretical concepts of tie strength from sociology such as, intensity, intimacy, duration, reciprocity, emotional support, shared interests and social distance. These variables are also complemented with measures of site usage. They model tie prediction using a linear model combining the tie prediction variables, interactions between these variables and a vector representing the network structure.

The authors take a very empirical and interesting approach to validate the derived model. Instead of hiding part of the data and comparing the result with the hidden data, the authors collect information from a number of participants by embedding a questionnaire on the Facebook profile page of the respondent's friend in a controlled laboratory setting. In the questionnaire they pose 5 questions on different aspects of tie strength that the respondent can answer by sliding a slider control.

In the study the authors find a parallel in the results with Marsden where the intimacy variable indicators on the site provide the best predictors of tie strength (32.8% of the model's predictive capacity). In contrast with Marsden however the authors find that intensity also contributes to the model's predictive power. Arguably this has to do with the medium and the context of the study where the selection of possible alternatives is much higher than in Marsden's case.

## Validation

As discussed throughout the chapter, the social network construction process involves design decisions that influence the resultant network. A natural question in this respect is how to validate the network to determine that it is the most appropriate network. In this section we discuss different aspects of network validation and compare techniques for manual and electronic data.

### Impact of Measurement Instrument

A central question in network construction is 'what is the impact of the measurement instrument on the resultant network'? Sociologists recognise that the different design decisions taken when designing the measurement instruments lead to different resultant networks. Bernard et al (Bernard et al., 1990) describe this problem and compare four methods for measuring personal social networks. Feld and Carter (Feld & Carter, 2002) evaluate the impact of over reporting and under reporting of interviewees on the actor degree in the network. They also study the impact this will have on general properties of the network such as size and density. Kossinets (Kossinets, 2006) evaluates the impact of boundary decisions, lack of survey response and the decision to limit the actor degree in questionnaires on a scientific

collaboration network. These effects of missing information impact the resultant network properties such as actor degrees, clustering coefficient, network size, path length and size of the largest connected component.

While researchers using manual data collection recognise the impact of network construction on the resultant network, few researchers using electronic data sets have looked at this issue. One notable exception is the study by Chouhury and Watts (De Choudhury, et al.) who derive different networks from two email communication datasets using different tie definitions. They demonstrate the difference in network structure depending on the selected tie definitions.

In his study on scientific collaborations, Newman (Newman, 2001) recognises that different networks can be derived if the name of the same author is spelled differently or abbreviated. To control for this effect two different versions of the networks are constructed and studied.

### Recall Reliability

The reliability of reported data during interviews was questioned by Bernard et al (Bernard, et al., 1984) in an annual survey paper where they comprehensively document the problem of informant accuracy. The authors describe studies from different areas such as recall of child behaviour, health seeking behaviour and recall of social interactions, and find convincing evidence that people are not good at recalling events. They conclude that there is usually a big discrepancy (up to 50%) between real data and what is reported by the interviewee. In a series of 7 experiments on different aspects of informant accuracy relevant to social networks, the main conclusion was; "what people say about their communications bears no useful resemblance to their behaviour".

Following the original accuracy reports by BKS, other researchers evaluated whether respondents are more likely to recall certain types of events than others. This refined the question so that researchers asked why certain events are more likely to be recalled than others. When studying this question, Freeman et al (Freeman, Romney, & Freeman, 1987) found that events are more likely to be reported if they have happened recently. Feld et al (Feld & Carter, 2002) investigated the biases underlying the under-reporting or over-reporting of the number of alters. More recently, Marin (Marin, 2004) studied the possibility of biases towards reporting stronger ties, alters with more overall connections, and alters with whom the respondent tends to interact more.

## Ground Truth

Any study on network data reliability relies on the fact that there is a known true network dataset, the *ground truth*, against which comparisons can be made to determine the reliability of the network construction process. The ground truth is an objectively true data source against which the constructed network is compared for validation. It is of paramount importance that the ground truth is an independent data source from the one being tested.

Obtaining or collecting a ground truth is not always easy. A common approach to collect ground truth data is to use a known alternative data source for the information that was manually collected during a study. For instance, if a study involves interviewing patients about treatment they got in hospital, the ground truth can be the doctor's official medical records (Cannell, Marquis, & Laurent, 1977).

Sometimes to collect the ground truth, two different data collection processes of the same data but using different methods, are used. For instance, Conrath et al (Conrath, Higgins, & McClean, 1983) use diaries as a ground truth to compare results from questionnaires. Respondents are asked to keep a daily diary of communication events in an organisation and at a later date they were asked about those same interactions. The results from the questionnaires were then compared against the daily diary accounts.

In manual data collection, the information collected from one participant can be compared with the same information from another participant. For instance, when collecting ego centric data, information on alters can be validated either by asking the alters themselves, or by validating the information from other neighbours of the same alters.

Earlier on in this chapter, in the section on understanding network ties, we differentiated between explicit ties that are observable and quantifiable, and implicit ties that are difficult to identify from observations. Most of the reliability studies discussed previously study the recall of events or communications that can be explicitly observed and quantified. When studying networks, one needs to closely consider the research question to determine whether explicit ties or implicit ties are more appropriate to answer the research question.

If the network of interest is a network of explicit ties, then a possible solution for obtaining a ground truth is to use electronic data that proves the existence of a tie. From a recall perspective, electronic data is hugely more reliable, as opposed to human memory. In this respect, there is an argument for proposing electronic records as a ground truth for comparing quantitative answers from human recall.

If electronic data on human interactions is being used as a ground truth and therefore by definition established as the better data source, can we rely on electronic data alone for deriving the social networks?

When it comes to electronic data, the question of validity is reversed. The reason for validating electronic data is not recall but relevance. Electronic data often has extra ties that are not relevant to the research question and which act as noise in the data. If the meaning of ties in a network is important, then electronic data should be carefully validated to ensure that the appropriate ties are selected when constructing the network.

When the network task is to understand a possibly abstract or ill defined relationship such as friendship or any other semantic relationship, then the most intuitive way to determine the validity of a tie is to manually ask for that information from the appropriate sources. Unfortunately this is not always practical particularly because of the issues of scale associated with electronic data. Yet there are few studies that follow this process.

One notable study is the study by Eagle et al (Eagle, et al., 2009) who construct social networks from electronic data collected in the MIT reality study. They validate this network with manually collected self reports for the same population of 94 subjects. Firstly they investigate if there is recency bias (memory is biased towards more recent events) and salience bias (memory is biased towards more vivid events) in recalling proximity to other people. Secondly, they try to predict the implicit relationship of friendship from observations of proximity, location and time. They find that they are accurately able to predict over 95% of implicit friendship ties from the explicit behavioural data they observe in the electronic data.

Another study where manual data is collected to validate electronically inferred data is the study by Gilbert et al (Gilbert & Karahalios) on predicting tie strength with social media. In this study, the authors first derive a model to predict tie strength and then they ask a sample of the population to actually quantify the tie strength using self reports.

When the network task for inferring the network is related to prediction or modelling, the ground truth is typically a sub sample from the original data. When evaluating prediction algorithms, researchers often hide part of the data (referred to as the training) when learning and designing the algorithm and then test the prediction accuracy on the rest of the data (the test data). A cross-validation approach is often used, in which several rounds of partitioning of the data

into training and test sets are performed, with the performance measures averaged over the rounds.

## Measuring Validation

To compare different algorithms, measures of classification performance can be applied. First, take a 'positive' classification to mean a correct identification of a network component from the ground truth test set. Next, take a confusion matrix of the classified data which contains four sets, two of which – the true positives and true negatives – consist of samples that were correctly classified as belonging to or not belonging to the test set, respectively; and two of which – the false positives and false negatives – consist of samples that were incorrectly identified as belonging to (respectively not belonging to) the test set. Various measures are used in the literature to compute performance based on the relative sizes of these sets. Two common measures are precision and recall, defined as:

*precision = # true positives*

*#true positives + # false positives*

*recall = # true positives*

*#true positives + # false negatives*

Often decisions depend on a threshold value, such that, for example, a network component is predicted to exist if the prediction measure is above the chosen threshold value. To get a full picture of the algorithm performance, the number of false positives as a fraction of the total number of predictions can be plotted against the fraction of true positives, as the threshold value is varied. The resulting curve, is called a Receiver Operator Characteristic (ROC) curve and the area under the ROC curve – the AUC - can be used as a measure of performance, with perfect performance obtained when AUC=1. The ROC curve can be used to select the best threshold value.

## CONCLUSION

In this chapter we reviewed different methods of social network construction while differentiating between manual and electronic approaches, to network construction. In the text we attempted to highlight the advantages of each approach and also potential areas for improvement. The advantages that electronic data provides in the form of increased availability, lower cost, increase in scale and longitudinal data should not be discounted. Researchers in the social sciences might want to explore more of the possibilities and benefits that electronic network datasets provide.

On the other hand, computational scientists should be more cognisant of the impact that decisions taken during network construction have on the final network. This can be reflected by conducting more empirical studies on the choice of parameters affecting network construction, and also by documenting the different considerations taken during the process of network construction. In this respect, more research is required into the issue of validating social networks. In the section on validation, the interplay between manual data collection and electronic data collection was discussed. Combining the two approaches efficiently for validating the network is a technique worth researching further.

With the increase in size of electronic data sets, it is important to have scalable algorithms and measures that are able to handle millions of actors. Traditional network measures were developed in a time where data sets were still relatively small and consequently some measures and algorithms are too computationally intensive to work on large data sets.

In this respect, there is scope for the development of new network measures that are more appropriate for larger scale networks. Also, when designing new algorithms, the issue of scale needs to be taken into consideration.

Apart from the increase in scale, electronic data sets provide accessible longitudinal network data that was previously not easily available. Social networks are naturally dynamic systems and understanding the evolution and dissolution of ties is a key analytical task whose importance is being increasingly recognised. Techniques, measures, models and tools for analysing dynamic networks are all open areas of research in network sciences.

Each individual network data source provides insight on a narrow perspective of one's social network. The actual social network however is made up of many different layers, each built on different levels and types of interaction. Currently most studies use networks of a single type studied in isolation. It would be beneficial if different types of networks are combined together to get a more complete perspective of one's social connections. Imagine the richness of information that can be obtained by combining one's phone, messaging, email and Facebook networks into one network.

The possibility of combining multiple data sources draws to attention the issues of privacy, ethics and data protection. Most of these aspects are still misunderstood by the general public, yet with advances in network science, the information that can be extracted from the data is becoming more powerful. Naturally, this information can be abused and constitute a risk if it falls into the wrong hands. Designing better policies related to privacy, standardisation of policies across countries, enforcement of regulations related to ethical practices and data protection, and most importantly educating both the public and the scientist, are all areas open to improvement.

This is a very interesting time to be studying networks as there are many advantages for the scientist interested in social networks. All the advantages that electronic data provides, along with the advances in the field, provide a healthy environment for research. Along with this, there are many open challenges and opportunities for further development.

# REFERENCES

Adamic, L. A., & Adar, E. (2003). Friends and neighbors on the web. *Social Networks, 25*(3), 211–230. doi:10.1016/S0378-8733(03)00009-1

Adamic, L. A., & Glance, N. (2005). *The political blogosphere and the 2004 U.S. election: divided they blog.* Paper presented at the Proceedings of the 3rd international workshop on Link discovery.

Adar, E., & Adamic, L. A. (2005). *Tracking information epidemics in blogspace.* Paper presented at the Web Intelligence, 2005. Proceedings. The 2005 IEEE/WIC/ACM International Conference on.

Akoglu, L., & Dalvi, B. (2010). *Structure, tie persistence and event detection in large phone and SMS networks.* Paper presented at the Proceedings of the Eighth Workshop on Mining and Learning with Graphs.

Albert, R., & Barabasi, A. L. (2002). Statistical mechanics of complex networks. *Reviews of Modern Physics, 74*(1), 47–97. doi:10.1103/RevModPhys.74.47

Ananthakrishna, R., Chaudhuri, S., & Ganti, V. (2002). *Eliminating fuzzy duplicates in data warehouses.* Paper presented at the Proceedings of the 28th international conference on Very Large Data Bases.

Bainbridge, W. S. (2007). The Scientific Research Potential of Virtual Worlds. [http://dx.doi.org/10.1126/science.1146930]. *Science, 317*(5837), 472–476. doi:10.1126/science.1146930

Barabasi, A. L., & Albert, R. (1999). Emergence of scaling in random networks. *Science, 286*(5439), 509. doi:10.1126/science.286.5439.509

Benjelloun, O., et al. (2006). *Generic Entity Resolution in the SERF Project.*

Bernard, H. R., Johnsen, E. C., Killworth, P. D., McCarty, C., Shelley, G. A., & Robinson, S. (1990). Comparing four different methods for measuring personal social networks. *Social Networks, 12*(3), 179–215. doi:10.1016/0378-8733(90)90005-T

Bernard, H. R., Killworth, P., Kronenfeld, D., & Sailer, L. (1984). The problem of informant accuracy: The validity of retrospective data. *Annual Review of Anthropology, 13*, 495–517. doi:10.1146/annurev.an.13.100184.002431

Bhattacharya, I., & Getoor, L. (2007). Collective entity resolution in relational data. [http://dx.doi.org/http://doi.acm.org/10.1145/1217299.1217304]. *ACM Trans. Knowl. Discov. Data, 1*(1), 5. doi:10.1145/1217299.1217304

Bilenko, M., Basu, S., & Sahami, M. (2005). *Adaptive Product Normalization: Using Online Learning for Record Linkage in Comparison Shopping.* Paper presented at the ICDM '05: Proceedings of the Fifth IEEE International Conference on Data Mining.

Blumstein, P., & Kollock, P. (1988). Personal relationships. *Annual Review of Sociology, 14*, 467–490. doi:10.1146/annurev.so.14.080188.002343

Boyd, D. M., & Ellison, N. B. (2008). Social Network Sites: Definition, History, and Scholarship. *Journal of Computer-Mediated Communication, 13*(1), 210–230. doi:10.1111/j.1083-6101.2007.00393.x

Burt, R. S. (1984). Network items and the general social survey. *Social Networks, 6*(4), 293–339. doi:10.1016/0378-8733(84)90007-8

Cannell, C. F., Marquis, K. H., & Laurent, A. (1977). A summary of studies of interviewing methodology. *Vital and health statistics. Series 2, Data evaluation and methods research, 69*(69).

Carrington, P., & Scott, J. (2011). *The Sage Handbook of Social Network Analysis*. London: SAGE Publications.

Cebrian, M., Pentland, A., & Kirkpatrick, S. (2010). Disentangling Social Networks inferred from Call Logs. *Arxiv preprint arXiv:1008.1357, pre-print*, pre-print.

Christen, P., Churches, T., & Hegland, M. (2004). Febrl – A Parallel Open Source Data Linkage System. In H. Dai, R. Srikant & C. Zhang (Eds.), *Advances in Knowledge Discovery and Data Mining* (Vol. 3056, pp. 638-647): Springer Berlin / Heidelberg.

Churches, T., Christen, P., Lim, K., & Zhu, J. X. (2002). Preparation of name and address data for record linkage using hidden Markov models. *BMC Medical Informatics and Decision Making, 2*(1), 9. doi:10.1186/1472-6947-2-9

Conrath, D. W., Higgins, C. A., & McClean, R. J. (1983). A comparison of the reliability of questionnaire versus diary data. [http://dx.doi.org/. *Social Networks, 5*(3), 315-322. DOI: 10.1016/0378-8733(83)90031-X]

Dasgupta, K., Singh, R., Viswanathan, B., Chakraborty, D., Mukherjea, S., Nanavati, A. A., & Joshi, A. (2008). *Social ties and their relevance to churn in mobile telecom networks*. Paper presented at the EDBT '08: Proceedings of the 11th international conference on Extending database technology.

De Choudhury, M., Mason, W. A., Hofman, J. M., & Watts, D. J. (2010). *Inferring relevant social networks from interpersonal communication*. Paper presented at the Proceedings of the 19th international conference on World wide web.

Dorogovtsev, S. N., & Mendes, J. F. F. (2002). Evolution of networks. *Advances in Physics, 51*(4), 1079–1187. doi:10.1080/00018730110112519

Dunn, H. L. (1946). Record linkage. *American Journal of Public Health, 36*(12), 1412. doi:10.2105/AJPH.36.12.1412

Eagle, N., Pentland, A. S., & Lazer, D. (2009). Inferring friendship network structure by using mobile phone data. *Proceedings of the National Academy of Sciences of the United States of America, 106*(36), 15274. doi:10.1073/pnas.0900282106

Elmagarmid, A. K., Ipeirotis, P. G., & Verykios, V. S. (2007). Duplicate Record Detection: A Survey. [http://dx.doi.org/http://dx.doi.org/10.1109/TKDE.2007.9]. *IEEE Transactions on Knowledge and Data Engineering, 19*, 1–16. doi:10.1109/TKDE.2007.250581

Farrugia, M., & Quigley, A. (2010). Actor Identification in Implicit Relational Data Sources. In I. II. Ting, H.-J. Wu & T.-H. Ho (Eds.), *Mining and Analyzing Social Networks* (Vol. 288, pp. 67-89): Springer Berlin / Heidelberg.

Feld, S. L., & Carter, W. C. (2002). Detecting measurement bias in respondent reports of personal networks. *Social Networks, 24*(4), 365–383. doi:10.1016/S0378-8733(02)00013-8

Fellegi, I. P., & Sunter, A. B. (1969). A theory for record linkage. *Journal of the American Statistical Association, 64*, 1183–1210. doi:10.2307/2286061

Freeman, L. C., Romney, A. K., & Freeman, S. C. (1987). Cognitive structure and informant accuracy. *American Anthropologist, 89*(2), 310–325. doi:10.1525/aa.1987.89.2.02a00020

Garton, L., Haythornthwaite, C., & Wellman, B. (1997). Studying online social networks. *Journal of Computer-Mediated Communication, 3*(1).

Getoor, L., & Diehl, C. P. (2005). Link mining: a survey. *ACM SIGKDD Explorations Newsletter, 7*(2), 3–12. doi:10.1145/1117454.1117456

Gibson, D., Kleinberg, J., & Raghavan, P. (1998). *Inferring Web communities from link topology.* Paper presented at the Proceedings of the ninth ACM conference on Hypertext and hypermedia.

Gilbert, E., & Karahalios, K. (2009). *Predicting tie strength with social media.* Paper presented at the Proceedings of the 27th international conference on Human factors in computing systems.

Goldenberg, A., Zheng, A. X., Fienberg, S. E., & Airoldi, E. M. (2009). A survey of statistical network models. *Foundations and Trends in Machine Learning, 2*(2), 129–233. doi:10.1561/2200000005

Gomez Rodriguez, M., Leskovec, J., & Krause, A. (2010). *Inferring networks of diffusion and influence.* Paper presented at the Proceedings of the 16th ACM SIGKDD international conference on Knowledge discovery and data mining.

Granovetter, M. S. (1973). The strength of weak ties. *American Journal of Sociology, 78*(6), 1360–1380. doi:10.1086/225469

Hern, Ã¡ndez, M. A., & Stolfo, S. J. (1998). Real-world data is dirty: Data cleansing and the merge/purge problem. *Data Mining and Knowledge Discovery, 2*(1), 9–37. doi:10.1023/A:1009761603038

Hirschman, L., & Chinchor, N. (1997). *MUC-7 Coreference Task Definition - Version 3.0.* Paper presented at the Proceedings of MUC.

Huang, Z., & Lin, D. K. J. (2009). The Time-Series Link Prediction Problem with Applications in Communication Surveillance. *INFORMS Journal on Computing, 21*(2), 286–303. doi:10.1287/ijoc.1080.0292

Kang, H., Getoor, L., Shneiderman, B., Bilgic, M., & Licamele, L. (2008). Interactive entity resolution in relational data: a visual analytic tool and its evaluation. *IEEE Transactions on Visualization and Computer Graphics, 14*, 999–1014. doi:10.1109/TVCG.2008.55

Katz, L. (1953). A new status index derived from sociometric analysis. *Psychometrika, 18*(1), 39–43. doi:10.1007/BF02289026

Kawale, J., Pal, A., & Srivastava, J. (2009). *Churn Prediction in MMORPGs: A Social Influence Based Approach.* Paper presented at the Computational Science and Engineering, 2009. CSE '09. International Conference on.

Kirke, D. M. (1996). Collecting peer data and delineating peer networks in a complete network. *Social Networks, 18*(4), 333–346. doi:10.1016/0378-8733(95)00280-4

Kossinets, G. (2006). Effects of missing data in social networks. *Social Networks, 28*(3), 247–268. doi:10.1016/j.socnet.2005.07.002

Kossinets, G., & Watts, D. J. (2006). Empirical analysis of an evolving social network. *Science, 311*(5757), 88. doi:10.1126/science.1116869

Krebs, V. (2000). Working in the connected world book network. *International Association for Human Resource Information Management Journal, 4*(1), 87–90.

Lazer, D., Pentland, A., Adamic, L., Aral, S., Barabási, A.-L., & Brewer, D. (2009). Computational Social Science. *Science, 323*(5915), 721–723. doi:10.1126/science.1167742

Leskovec, J., & Horvitz, E. (2008). *Planetary-scale views on a large instant-messaging network.* Paper presented at the Proceeding of the 17th international conference on World Wide Web.

Lewis, K., Kaufman, J., Gonzalez, M., Wimmer, A., & Christakis, N. (2008). Tastes, ties, and time: A new social network dataset using Facebook.com. *Social Networks, 30*(4), 330–342. doi:10.1016/j.socnet.2008.07.002

Liben-Nowell, D., & Kleinberg, J. (2007). The link-prediction problem for social networks. *Journal of the American Society for Information Science and Technology, 58*(7), 1019–1031. doi:10.1002/asi.20591

Licoppe, C., & Smoreda, Z. (2005). Are social networks technologically embedded?: How networks are changing today with changes in communication technology. *Social Networks, 27*(4), 317–335. doi:10.1016/j.socnet.2004.11.001

Lu, L., & Zhou, T. (2010). A Survey. In *Submission, In Submission*. Link Prediction in Complex Networks.

Marin, A. (2004). Are respondents more likely to list alters with certain characteristics?: Implications for name generator data. *Social Networks, 26*(4), 289-307.

Marsden, P. V. (1990). Network data and measurement. *Annual Review of Sociology, 16*, 435–463. doi:10.1146/annurev.so.16.080190.002251

Marsden, P. V. (2005). Recent developments in network measurement. In J. S. S. W. Peter J. Carrington (Ed.), *Models and methods in social network analysis*: Cambridge University Press.

Marsden, P. V., & Campbell, K. E. (1984). Measuring tie strength. *Social Forces, 63*(2), 482–501.

Matzat, U., & Snijders, C. (2010). Does the online collection of ego-centered network data reduce data quality? An experimental comparison. [http://dx.doi.org/*Social Networks, 32*(2), 105-111. DOI: 10.1016/j.socnet.2009.08.002].

Mayer, A., & Puller, S. L. (2007). The old boy (and girl) network: Social network formation on university campuses. *Journal of Public Economics, 92*(1-2), 329–347. doi:10.1016/j.jpubeco.2007.09.001

McPherson, M., Smith-Lovin, L., & Cook, J. M. (2001). Birds of a feather: Homophily in social networks. *Annual Review of Sociology, 27*, 415–444. doi:10.1146/annurev.soc.27.1.415

Newcombe, H. B., Kennedy, J. M., Axford, S. J., & James, A. P. (1959). Automatic linkage of vital and health records. *Science, 130*, 954–959. doi:10.1126/science.130.3381.954

Newman, M. E. J. (2001). Scientific collaboration networks. I. Network construction and fundamental results. *Physical Review E: Statistical, Nonlinear, and Soft Matter Physics, 64*(1), 16131. doi:10.1103/PhysRevE.64.016131

O'Madadhain, J., Hutchins, J., & Smyth, P. (2005). Prediction and ranking algorithms for event-based network data. *SIGKDD Explorations Newsletter, 7*, 23–30. doi:10.1145/1117454.1117458

Onnela, J. P., Saramäki, J., Hyvönen, J., Szabó, G., Lazer, D., & Kaski, K. (2007). Structure and tie strengths in mobile communication networks. [http://dx.doi.org/10.1073/pnas.0610245104]. *Proceedings of the National Academy of Sciences of the United States of America, 104*(18), 7332–7336. doi:10.1073/pnas.0610245104

Petróczi, A., Nepusz, T., & Bazsó, F. (2006). Measuring tie-strength in virtual social networks. *Connections, 27*(2), 39–52.

Piatetsky-Shapiro, G., Djeraba, C., Getoor, L., Grossman, R., Feldman, R., & Zaki, M. (2006). What are the grand challenges for data mining. *KDD-2006 Panel Report. SIGKDD Explorations, 8*(2), 70–77. doi:10.1145/1233321.1233330

Popescul, A., & Ungar, L. H. (2003). *Statistical relational learning for link prediction*. Paper presented at the IJCAI03 Workshop on Learning Statistical Models from Relational Data.

Scharstein, D., & Szeliski, R. (2002). A taxonomy and evaluation of dense two-frame stereo correspondence algorithms. *International Journal of Computer Vision, 47*(1), 7–42. doi:10.1023/A:1014573219977

Scott, J. (2000). *Social Network Analysis: A Handbook*. SAGE Publications.

Szell, M., & Thurner, S. (2010). Measuring social dynamics in a massive multiplayer online game. [http://dx.doi.org/DOI: 10.1016/j.socnet.2010.06.001]. *Social Networks, 32*(4), 313-329.

Torenvlied, R., & VanSchuur, H. (1994). A procedure for assessing large-scale 'total' networks using information from key informants. *Connections*, *17*(2), 56–60.

Tylenda, T., Angelova, R., & Bedathur, S. (2009). *Towards time-aware link prediction in evolving social networks.* Paper presented at the Proceedings of the 3rd Workshop on Social Network Mining and Analysis.

Vehovar, V., Lozar Manfreda, K., Koren, G., & Hlebec, V. (2008). Measuring ego-centered social networks on the web: Questionnaire design issues. *Social Networks*, *30*(3), 213–222. doi:10.1016/j.socnet.2008.03.002

Wasserman, S., & Faust, K. (1994). *Social network analysis: Methods and applications.* Cambridge Univ Press.

Watts, D. J., & Strogatz, S. H. (1998). Collective dynamics of 'small-world' networks. *Nature*, *393*(6684), 440–442. doi:10.1038/30918

Wellman, B., & Haythornthwaite, C. A. (2002). *The Internet in everyday life*: Wiley-Blackwell.

Winkler, W. E. (1999). The state of record linkage and current research problems.

Xiang, R., Neville, J., & Rogati, M. (2010). *Modeling relationship strength in online social networks.* Paper presented at the Proceedings of the 19th international conference on World wide web.

# Chapter 10
# Dynamics and Evolutional Patterns of Social Networks

**Yingzi Jin**
*The University of Tokyo, Japan*

**Yutaka Matsuo**
*The University of Tokyo, Japan*

## ABSTRACT

*Previous chapters focused on the models of static networks, which consider a relational network at a given point in time. However, real-world social networks are dynamic in nature; for example, friends of friends become friends. Social network research has, in recent years, paid increasing attention to dynamic and longitudinal network analysis in order to understand network evolution, belief formation, friendship formation, and so on. This chapter focuses mainly on the dynamics and evolutional patterns of social networks. The chapter introduces real-world applications and reviews major theories and models of dynamic network mining.*

## INTRODUCTION

Real-world social networks are dynamic in nature; for example, friends of friends become friends. Social network research has, in recent years, paid increasing attention to dynamic and longitudinal network analysis to understand network evolution, belief formation, friendship formation, and so on. We can define a simple static network as $G = (V, E)$, where $V$ is the finite set of vertices and $E$ is the finite set of edges, each being an unordered pair of distinct vertices. If we let $f$ be a function defined on the vertex set as $f: V \rightarrow N$ and $g$ be the function defined on the edge set as $g: E \rightarrow N$, a fully weighted graph can be represented as $G = (V, E, f, g)$. Dynamic graphs, that is, graphs that change with time, include four kinds of graphs: node-dynamic graphs (in which the vertex set $V$ varies with time—some nodes may be added or removed, and when nodes are removed, the edges or arcs incident with them are also eliminated); edge-dynamic graphs (in which the edge set $E$ varies with time); node-weighted dynamic graphs (in

DOI: 10.4018/978-1-61350-513-7.ch010

which the node weight function *f* varies with time); and edge-weighted dynamic graphs (in which the edge weight function *g* varies with time) (Harary & Gupta, 1997). In this chapter, we first introduce data collection approaches for dynamic networks and describe real-world applications of dynamic networks; we then review the major theories and models of dynamic network mining.

## DATA COLLECTION FOR DYNAMIC NETWORKS

The data for dynamic network mining have usually been collected by means of questionnaires, observations, self-reporting, and simulations. For example, Nordle and Newcomb housed together 17 University of Michigan students who were initially unknown to each other. Each person was asked to rank each of his fraternity members with regard to positive feeling. Rankings were recorded each week and continued for a period of 15 weeks (Newcomb, 1961; Nordle, 1958). Some studies generate small sets of synthetic data to validate their dynamic frameworks (Lin, Chi, Zhu, Sundaram, & Tseng, 2010; Tantipathananandh, Berger-Wolf, & Kempe, 2007). With the increasing accessibility of digitized data through electronic databases and the Internet, researchers have collected longitudinal social network data on a large scale from e-mail interaction records (Carley & Skillicorn, 2005; Freeman, 1979), Digital Bibliography and Library Project (DBLP) citation data (Huang, Zhuang, Li, & Giles, 2008), protein interaction records (Ratmann, Wiuf, & Pinney 2009; Wagner, 2001), online social networks (Falkowski, 2009; Kumar, Novak, & Tomkins, 2006), and Web blogs (Lin et al., 2010). Furthermore, some studies attempt to automatically collect dynamic networks for given entities from news articles or from the entire Web through natural language processing (NLP) and machine learning (ML) techniques (Bernstein, Clearwater, Hill, Perlich, & Provost, 2002; Hu, Xu, Shen, & Fukushima, 2009; Ma,

Pant, & Sheng, 2009, Tetlock, Saar-Tsechansky, & Macskassy, 2008). For example, Bernstein et al. use name co-occurrence frequency to calculate relational strength between companies, and extract inter-company network from public news; Ma et al. observed that a company is more likely to co-occur with its competitors on Web pages than with noncompetitors; Hu et al. use publishing time in news articles to extract temporal company networks from the Web. Other description of the sample data of dynamic social networks can be found in Goldenberg, Zhang, Fienberg, and Airoldi (2009).

## REAL-WORLD APPLICATIONS OF DYNAMIC NETWORK MINING

In this section, we present applications of mining in real-world dynamic networks. We introduce representative works on the evolution of collaboration networks, dynamic community identification, friendship formation networks, the evolution of organizational networks, dynamic biological networks, and so on.

### Evolution of Collaboration Networks

The evolution of collaboration networks and, in particular, of scientific collaboration networks has been studied in the literature (Huang et al., 2008; Liben-Nowell & Kleinberg, 2007; Newman, 2001). Newman (2001) studied empirically the time evolution of scientific collaboration networks in physics and biology. He found that the probability of scientists collaborating increases with the number of collaborators they have in common, and that the probability of a particular scientist acquiring new collaborators increases with the number of his or her past collaborators. Liben-Nowell and Kleinberg (2007) treated the inference of the addition of edges in a future coauthorship collaboration network as a link-prediction problem, and they compared various predictors such as graph distance, common neighbors, and Jaccard, an index of different scientific collaboration datasets. Huang et al. (2008) analyzed the evolution of a scientific collaboration network by different scale levels of analysis; for example, they characterized the pattern of network evolution using various network statistics and predicted future collaboration between individuals based on their local neighborhood structure.

## Dynamic Community Identification

Most communities tend to evolve gradually over time due to changes in social interactions, organizational structures, or more abstract means of interactions such as hyperlinks or similarity. Falkowski (2009) detected and tracked the evolution of community structures from dynamic social networks. Using a macroscopic view (i.e., defining a community as a cluster of similar community instances that are observable over time), they detected communities by a hierarchical edge betweenness clustering algorithm and matched the snapshots of clusters. In addition, using a microscopic view (i.e., defining a community as a dense subgraph that evolves over time), they proposed a density-based clustering approach to analyze incremental cluster updates. Lin et al. (2010) proposed the *FacetNet* framework in which the community structure at a given time step *t* is determined both by the networked data at *t* and by the historical community evolution patterns. Tantipathananandh et al. (2007) proposed to use dynamic programming, maximum matching, and greedy heuristics to find the valid community interpretation. Backstrom, Huttenlocher, Lan, and Kleinberg (2006) considered two ways in which communities grow over time—at the individual level in which individuals make decisions to join communities, and at the global level in which a community evolves in both membership and content. More works, such as those investigating interaction patterns among dynamic communities (Berger-Wolf & Saia, 2006), the evolution of com-

munities within large online social networks like Flickr and Yahoo360° (Kumar et al., 2006), and dynamic communication structures in open source software teams (Wiggins, Howison, & Crowston, 2008), also focus on identifying dynamic communities having different types of network data.

## Friendship Formation Networks

In real life, people may meet new friends and interact with each other, and hence their friendships change over time. Understanding the formation and selection of friendships over time has been a research interest in social literature. Researchers have investigated friendship formation in universities (Newcomb, 1961), in summer camps (Savin-Williams, 1979), and among preschool children (Schaefer, Light, Fabes, Hanish, & Martin, 2010). Van de Bunt, Van Duijn, and Snijders (1999) used an actor-oriented dynamic statistical network model to represent relational choice at the individual level that maximizes the expected amount of utility (i.e., the preference function). Burk, Steglich, and Snijders (2007) investigated the co-evolution of friendship networks and delinquent behaviors in a longitudinal sample of Swedish adolescents with the goal of simultaneously assessing selection and influence processes. Schaefer et al. (2010) examined preschool children's friendship formation using observational data on children's interactions in 11 preschool classrooms over the course of a school year. They investigated several fundamental processes of relationship formation, including reciprocity, popularity, and triadic closure effects, and found that these mechanisms "cascade" or emerge over time in direct relation to their complexity. Mercken, Snijders, Steglich, Vartiainen, and de Vries (2010) studied the mutual influence of smoking behavior and friendship selection in adolescence in order to test for social influence and social selection processes in interdependent dynamics.

## Evolution of Organizational Networks

Over time, social and organizational networks evolve. In addition, the organizational constraint influences relationship formation. De Klepper, Sleebos, van de Bunt, and Agneessens (2010) studied causation of similarity in friendship relations in an organizationally constrained environment. On the basis of their investigation of first-year Royal Netherlands Naval College officer students, they argued that in a setting of organizational constraints (where social collaboration is crucial and friendship choices are more constrained), influence might be the main reason for the similarity found among friends. Carley and Prietula (2001) analyzed organizational networks, focusing on different classes of agents (i.e., using a multi-agent model), and suggested that organizational change lies in socio-cognitive quantum mechanics. A review of merging network paradigms such as social capital, embeddedness, and knowledge management in organizational research can be found in Borgatti and Foster (2003). Brass, Galaskiewicz, Greve, and Tsai (2004) reviewed the antecedents and consequences of networks at interpersonal, interunit, and interorganizational levels of analysis.

## Dynamic Biological Networks

Many biological networks have been introduced, and the topology and evolution of such networks have attracted the interest of researchers. Among these networks, which have been studied extensively, are neural networks (Eguíluz, Chialvo, Cecchi, Baliki, & Apkarian, 2005), metabolic reaction networks (Wagner & Fell, 2001), protein-protein interaction networks (Ratmann et al., 2009; Wagner, 2001), and food networks (Montoya & Sol, 2002). For instance, the structure and evolution of the protein interaction network of the yeast *Saccharomyces cerevisiae* is analyzed by Wagner (2001), who found that the protein contact network is similar to a random graph and that the number of interactions per protein follows a power-law degree distribution. Ratmann et al. (2009) concluded that duplication and divergence have played a larger role in the network evolution of the eukaryote *P. falciparum* than in the prokaryote *H. pylori*, and they emphasized (at least for the eukaryote) the potential importance of subfunctionalization in network evolution.

Other interesting applications of dynamic network mechanisms include investigating the evolution and effects of international networks (Maoz, 2010), estimating social network change detection (McCulloh & Carley, 2009), mining evolution of structural properties of market graph data (Boginski, Butenko, & Pardalos, 2006), and other applications in computer science (Harary & Gupta, 1997).

## THEORIES AND MODELS OF DYNAMIC NETWORKS

Methods for the analysis of network data over time have long appeared in the social science literature (Carley, 2003; Holland & Leinhardt, 1977; Katz & Proctor, 1959; Leenders, 1995; Snijders, 1997; Wasserman, 1980). Modeling dynamic and longitudinal network data is quite complicated because models of the social network must represent the dependencies of the network effects and often require continuous records of network changes, which are difficult to collect. With the emergence of online networks, more data are available for dynamic analysis, and hence interest in dynamic modeling has grown. Kolaczyk (2009) provides an overview of methods and models for the statistical analysis of network data. This section introduces the dominant methods of longitudinal social network analysis of pseudo-dynamic models, Markov chain models, and multi-agent simulation models.

## Pseudo-dynamic Models

The Endös-Rényi-Gilbert random graph model, preferential attachment model, and small-world models are not pure dynamic models, since they model a single, static snapshot of the network, as opposed to multiple snapshots recorded at different time steps. However, they also contain processes for link addition and modification, which is a dynamic process that may have generated the observed graph; therefore, these models are considered to be pseudo-dynamic models (Goldenberg et al., 2010).

## Random Graph Model

The Endös-Rényi-Gilbert random graph model, $G(N,p)$, describes an undirected graph that begins with $N$ vertices and randomly links two nodes with a probability of $p$. This can be viewed as a dynamic model; that is, start from the graph $N$ unconnected nodes at time 0, and then at each subsequent time step, add a different edge to the network with probability $p = E / \binom{N}{2}$. The model assumes that edges (and nodes) are not removed once they are added. The degree distribution of $G(N, E)$ is binomial. To illustrate, the probability of having exactly $k$ neighbors is given by

$$p_k = \binom{n}{k} p^k (1-p)^{(N-k)} \qquad (1)$$

As the number of nodes $N$ goes to infinity, the degree distribution approximates a Poisson distribution. For different values of $p$, the largest connected components and the degree distributions in dynamic random graphs are different. For smaller values of $p$, the sizes of the components are relatively close to each other, and the components have a finite mean size. These components follow an exponential degree distribution. With higher values of $p$, a giant connected component appears in the graph with $O(N)$ vertices. The rest of the vertices in the graph follow an exponential degree distribution. Between these two states, which are dependent on the choice of $p$, lies a phase transition point found at $p = 1/N$.

## Preferential Attachment Model

The Endös-Rényi-Gilbert model is simple and easy to study, but it does not address many issues that are present in real network dynamics. One of the major reasons is that it does not produce a scale-free network, that is, the resulting node degree distribution does not follow a power law. Barabási and Albert (1999) introduced the concept of dynamic preferential attachment (PA) that was specifically designed to generate scale-free networks. The model starts out with $N_0$ unconnected nodes at time 0. At each subsequent time step, a new node is added with $m \leq N_0$ edges. The probability $p_i$ that a new node connects to an existing node $i$ depends proportionally on the degree of node $i$, that is, $p_i = k_i / \Sigma_j k_j$, where $k_i$ denotes the (undirected) degree of node $i$. The node degree distribution of a network with this model evolves into a power-law distribution whose exponent is empirically determined to be $\gamma_{BA} = 2.9 \pm 0.1$.

Many extensions of the PA model and alternative graph generation mechanisms have been proposed, such as the initial attachment model (Barabási, 2002), the fitness model (Ergün & Rodgers, 2002), the R-MAT model (Chakrabarti, Zhan, & Faloutsos, 2004), the winners don't take all model (Gary, Flake, Lawrence, Glover, & Giles, 2002), the forest fire model (Leskovec, Kleinberg, & Faloutsos, 2007), the butterfly model (McGlohon, Akoglu, & Faloutsos, 2008), and the RTG model (Akoglu & Faloutsos, 2009). For example, the fitness model (Ergün & Rodgers, 2002) supposes that each node has an inherent competitive factor, for example, an upper bound on the number of friends. In these models, a fitness parameter that does not change over time is attached to each node. A new node can still attract others (i.e., gather more edges) if its associated fitness value is high.

## Small-World Model

Watts and Strogatz (1998) proposed a small-world model, which begins with a ring lattice with $N$ nodes and $k$ edges per node and randomly rewires each edge with probability $p$. This model interpolates between an ordered finite-dimensional lattice and an Endös-Rényi-Gilbert random graph to produce local clustering and triadic closures. As the probability $p$ in the model goes from 0 to 1, the construction moves toward an Endös-Rényi-Gilbert model. This model is not dynamic, although it is often used to describe networks that evolve over time; thus, it can be thought of as a pseudo-dynamic model.

Some variations on the small-world model have been introduced (Kleinberg, 2001; Sandberg & Clarke, 2006). Kleinberg (2001) proposed to add random edges to a fixed grid. The shortcut edges are added to an underlying finite-dimensional grid. The probability that two nodes are connected by a long edge depends on the distance between them in the grid. Sandberg and Clarke (2006) introduced different rewiring schemes in order to make the network more amenable to statistical analysis.

## Duplication-Attachment Model

A duplication-attachment model was proposed to study the World Wide Web as a directed graph (Kleinberg, Kumar, Raghavan, Rajagopalan, & Tomkins, 1999). This model introduces new nodes in the graph as time evolves, which captures the fact that the Web changes over time. Denote the graph at time $t$ as $G_t = (N_t, E_t)$. At each step, say $t + 1$, one new node $N$ is added to $G_t$. The new node is connected to a prototype node $m$, chosen uniformly at random among these $N_t$. Then $d$ out-links are added to node $N$. The $i$-th out-link is chosen with probability $\alpha$; the destination node

is chosen uniformly at random among those in $N_t$, and with probability $1 - \alpha$. The destination node is taken to be the $i$-th out-link of the prototype node $m$. This generates a constant degree graph with two parameters $(\alpha, d)$. The edges in this model are statistically dependent on each other, and those chosen do not result in the statistics (e.g., the degree distribution) observed on the Web (Kumar et al., 2000). Leskovec et al. (2007) extended this model such that fractions of both out-links and in-links of the prototype node $m$ are copied by the newly added node $N$. Duplication-attachment models are also useful in modeling protein-protein interaction networks (Ratmann et al., 2009).

## Discrete Time Markov Models

One way to simplify a statistical model for social networks is to make a Markov assumption on the network from one time step to the next. In this section, we introduce three dynamic network models operating in the discrete time domain that have the Markov property and represent the likelihood as a sequence of factored conditional probabilities.

$$\Pr(Y^1, Y^2, ..., Y^T) =$$

$$\Pr(Y^T | Y^{T-1}) \Pr(Y^{T-1} | Y^{T-2}) \cdots \Pr(Y^2 | Y^1), \qquad (2)$$

where $\{Y^1, Y^2, ..., Y^T\}$ is a sequence of T observed snapshots of the network (see also Robins & Pattison, 2001).

## Discrete Markov ERGM Model

The Discrete Markov ERGM model proposed by Hanneke and Xing (2007) is an extension of the exponential random graph models (ERGM) (Wasserman & Philippa, 1996) in the discrete Markov domain. The potential function in this model involves the statistics of two consecutive configurations of the network:

$$\Pr(\mathrm{y}^t \mid \mathrm{y}^{t-1}) = \frac{1}{Z} \exp\{\beta_k s_k(\mathrm{y}^t, \mathrm{y}^{t-1})\} . \qquad (3)$$

The following are some examples of network statistics defined on pairs of network snapshots.

- Density of edges:

$$s_1 = (\mathrm{y}^t, \mathrm{y}^{t-1}) = \frac{1}{(n-1)} \Sigma_{ij} y_{ij}^t$$

- Stability:

$$s_2 = (\mathrm{y}^t, \mathrm{y}^{t-1}) = \frac{1}{(n-1)} \Sigma_{ij} \left[ y_{ij}^t y_{ij}^{t-1} + (1 - y_{ij}^t)(1 - y_{ij}^{t-1}) \right]$$

- Reciprocity:

$$s_3 = (\mathrm{y}^t, \mathrm{y}^{t-1}) = n\Sigma_{ij} y_{ij}^t y_{ij}^{t-1} / \Sigma_{ij} y_{ij}^{t-1}$$

- Transitivity:

$$s_4 = (\mathrm{y}^t, \mathrm{y}^{t-1}) = n\Sigma_{ijk} y_{ik}^t y_{ij}^{t-1} y_{jk}^{t-1} / \Sigma_{ijk} y_{ij}^{t-1} y_{jk}^{t-1}$$

The basic model can be extended to allow for multiple relations, node attributes, and $K$-th order Markov dependencies of the form. Maximum likelihood parameter estimates may be computed via any numerical approximation technique like the Newton-Raphson method. Computation of the gradient and Hessian requires the mean and covariance of the sequence network statistics, which are exactly computable for a pair of networks, but require Gibbs sampling in the $K$-sequence case (Hanneke and Xing, 2007). The likelihood is that this model is well behaved if the minimum sufficient statistics involve only dyads; however, similar to its static counterpart, the fully dynamic ERGM is prone to likelihood degeneracy.

## Dynamic Latent Space Model

Sarkar and Moor (2005) extended the latent space model of Hoff, Raftery, and Handcock (2002) in the time domain. In the static latent space model, the log odds ratio of a link between nodes $i$ and $j$ depends on the distance between their latent positions $z_i$ and $z_j$. The dynamic latent space model allows the latent positions to change over time in Gaussian-distributed random steps:

$$Z_t \mid Z_{t-1} : N(Z_{t-1}, \sigma^2 I). \qquad (4)$$

The modified latent space link probability $p_{ij}^L$ is given as follows:

$$p_{ji}^L := P^L(y_{ij} = 1) = \frac{1}{1 + \exp(d_{ij} - r_{ij})}, \qquad (5)$$

where $d_{ij}$ is the Euclidean distance between $i$ and $j$ in latent space, and $r_{ij}$ is a radius of influence defined as $c \times (max(\delta_i, \delta_j) + 1)$ ($\delta_i$ and $\delta_j$ being the degrees of nodes $i$ and $j$ respectively). The link probability $p_{ij}$ is defined as a mixture between the $p_{ij}^L$ and a noise probability $\rho$, that is, $p_{ij} = \kappa(d_{ij}) p_{ij}^L K(d_{ij}) + (1 - \kappa(d_{ij})) \rho$. The idea is that pairs of nodes that are outside of each other's radii have only a low noise probability of establishing a link, while nodes within each other's radii follow the probability $p_{ij}^L$.

The full observation model is then

$$\Pr(Y^t \mid Z^t) = \prod_{i \sim j} p_{ij} \prod_{i \neq j} (1 - p_{ij}), \qquad (6)$$

where $i \sim j$ denotes the presence of and edge from $i$ to $j$. The latent space positions $Z^t$ are estimated in sequence for $t = 1 \ldots T$ by maximizing the likelihood of the observed $Y^t$:

$$Z^t = \mathrm{argmax}_Z \Pr(Y^t | Z) \Pr(Z | Z^{t-1}). \qquad (7)$$

This model is applied to the Neural Information Processing Systems (NIPS) paper co-authorship dataset, and the dynamics of the researchers' latent positions allow for insight into the evolution of the machine learning community. An extended model by Sarkar, Siddiqi, and Gordon (2007) allowed for the representation of two-mode networks, for example, a words-authors network. This line of work offers an explanation of the network at every time step, and it enables accurate and efficient prediction of the state of the network at a future time step. The proposed inference procedures enabled network modeling to scale of large dynamic collections of data. The drawback of this approach is the lack of an explicit mechanism to explain the dynamics behind the real networks.

## Dynamic Contextual Friendship Model

The dynamic contextual friendship model (DCFM) proposed by Goldenberg and Zheng (2006) represents an attempt to explain several aspects of the complexity of the evolution of real social networks over time. In a real-life friendship network, people may meet and interact with each other under different contexts (e.g., school, work projects, social outings, etc.), and the strength of interpersonal relationships changes over time on the basis of these interactions. DCFM offers a mechanism for network evolution where edges have weights that indicate the strength of the relationship, and each node is given a distribution over social interaction spheres (contexts). Context is defined to be any activity where people may interact with each other. At each given time step, each node chooses a random context according to the node's distribution over contexts. Nodes that appear in the same context update the weights of the links between them. The probability of a weight increase (or decrease) depends on whether the pair had a chance to meet and on the "friendliness" parameter of the individuals involved. The possibility of both positive and negative weight updates allows for edge birth and death over time. An extension of the model also allows for the addition and deletion of nodes. The underlying dynamics are captured by a first-order Markov chain model. There are four parameters that denote context distribution, "friendliness," rate of

growth, and decay of edge weight, respectively, for each node $i$. All of these parameters have conjugate priors, which are estimated through Gibbs sampling (Zheng & Goldenberg, 2006).

One drawback of DCFM is its lack of identifiability; without additional knowledge, it is impossible to tell whether an individual formed many friendships because he frequently changes contexts and is very friendly or because the contexts themselves tend to be large. Moreover, weighted network data are hard to obtain, and thus pseudo-weights must often be used.

## Continuous Time Markov Models

Holland and Leinhardt (1977) and Wasserman (1977) proposed to use continuous Markov processes to model dynamic networks, and Snijders (1997) extended the model. In the continuous Markov process model, network edges are taken to be binary, and evolution occurs one edge at a time. More extensions allowed for multiple edges changing at the same time (Mayer, 1984) and for the case where not all edge modifications are observed (Koskinen & Snijders, 2007).

For a continuous Markov process, define $\{Y(t)|t \in T\}$ to be a stochastic process, where $Y(t)$ has a finite outcome space $Y$, and $T$ is a continuous time interval. Suppose that a Markov condition holds as follows: for any possible outcome $\tilde{y} \in Y$ and any pair of time points $\{t_a < t_b \,|\, t_a, t_b \in T\}$,

$$\Pr\{Y(t_b) = \tilde{y} \,|\, Y(t) = y(t), \forall t: t \le t_a\} = \Pr\{Y(t_b) = \tilde{y} \,|\, Y(t_a) = y(t_a)\}. \tag{8}$$

If the above probability depends only on $t_a - t_b$, then one can prove that $Y(t)$ has a stationary transition distribution, and the transition matrix

$$\Pr(t_b - t_a) := \Pr\{Y(t_b) = \tilde{y} \,|\, Y(t_a) = y\}_{y,\tilde{y} \in Y} \tag{9}$$

can be written as a matrix exponential

$$\Pr(t) = e^{tQ}, \tag{10}$$

where $Q$ is known as the intensity matrix with elements $q(y,\tilde{y})$. The elements $q(y,\tilde{y})$ can be thought of as the slope (rate of change) of the probability of state change as a function of time, that is, $\Pr\{Y(t+\varepsilon) = \tilde{y}\,|\,Y(t) = y\} \approx \varepsilon q(y,\tilde{y})$. The diagonal elements $q(y,y)$ are negative and are defined so that the rows of $Q$ sum to zero.

When modeling a social network, the outcome space $Y$ is taken to be all possible edge configurations of an $N$-node network, and an individual configuration $y \in Y$ is taken to be a binary vector of length $\binom{N}{2}$. We use the shorthand $q_{ij}(\mathbf{y})$ to denote the propensity for the edge between nodes $i$ and $j$ to flip to its opposite value under configuration $y$. The function $q_{ij}(\mathbf{y})$ completely specifies the dynamics of the network model. The following variants of CMPM differ only in their definitions of $q_{ij}(\mathbf{y})$.

- *Independent Arc Model*: $q_{ij}(\mathbf{y}) = \lambda_{yij}$, that is, $Y_{ij}$ changes from 0 to 1 at rate $\lambda_0$, and from 1 to 0 at rate $\lambda_1$. In this model, a modification to one edge does not depend on the setting of the other edges. Maximum likelihood parameter estimation for this model was discussed in Snijders and Van Duijn (1997).
- *Reciprocity Model*: $q_{ij}(\mathbf{y}) = \lambda_{yij} + \mu_{yij}y_{ji}$, that is, the rate of change in $y_{ij}$ depends only on the reciprocal edge $y_{ji}$. Thus, if no link currently exists between nodes $i$ and $j$, then the propensity for addition of either directed edge is $\lambda_0$; if one directed edge exists, then the reciprocal edge is added with propensity $\lambda_0 + \mu_0$. If one directed edge exists, then it is deleted at rate $\lambda_1$. If both edges exist, then the deletion propensity for either is $\lambda_1 + \mu_1$. The transition matrix $\Pr(t)$ can be derived, but it has a complicated form (Leenders, 1995).
- *Popularity Model*: $q_{ij}(\mathbf{y}) = \lambda_{yij} + \pi_{yij}y_{+j}$ defines the change rate for edge $y_{ij}$ to be de-

pendent only on the in-degree of node $j$ (i.e., $y+j$).
- *Expansiveness Model*: $q_{ij}(\mathbf{y}) = \lambda_{yij} + \pi_{yij}y_{i+}$ defines the change rate for edge $y_{ij}$ to be dependent only on the out-degree of node $i$ (i.e., $y_{i+}$).

Snijders, Steglich, and van de Bunt (2010) outline two categories of transition dynamics: edge-oriented and node-oriented. In both categories, the continuous time process is split into two subprocesses; the first operating in the continuous time domain and dictating when a change should occur, and the second dealing with the probability of the discrete event of individual edge flips. Both dynamics can be interpreted as stochastic optimizations of a potential function $f(y)$ on the network configuration. The difference between them is that in the edge-oriented case, $f$ is based on global statistics of the network, whereas in the node-oriented case, $f$ is defined for each node's local neighborhood. Moreover, the choice of which edge to flip differs between the two formulations. The potential function $f(\mathbf{y})$ is usually defined as a linear combination of network statistics. For the edge-oriented function, the potential function is $f(\mathbf{y}) = \Sigma_k \beta_k s_k(\mathbf{y})$, where possible effects $s_k(\mathbf{y})$ represent aspects of network structure and dyadic properties, and the importance of each effect is represented by the $\beta_k$ parameters. For example:

- The number of directed arcs (i.e., $s_1(\mathbf{y}) = \Sigma_{ij}\, y_{ij}$),
- The number of reciprocated arcs (i.e., $s_2(\mathbf{y}) = \Sigma_{ij}\, y_{ij}\, y_{ji}$),
- The number of paths of length two (i.e., $s_3(\mathbf{y}) = \Sigma_{ijk}\, y_{ij}\, y_{jk}$).

For the node-oriented function, the potential function is $f_i(\mathbf{y}) = \Sigma_k \beta_k s_{ik}(\mathbf{y})$, where possible effects $s_{ik}(\mathbf{y})$ represent aspects of network structure and individual attributes; whereas the $\beta_k$ parameters represent the importance of each effect. For example:

- The number of directed arcs of $i$ (i.e., $s_{i1}(\mathbf{y}) = \Sigma_j\, y_{ij}$),
- The number of reciprocated arcs of $i$ (i.e., $s_{i2}(\mathbf{y}) = \Sigma_j\, y_{ij}\, y_{ji}$),
- The number of transitive patterns in $i$'s ties (i.e., $s_{i3}(\mathbf{y}) = \Sigma_{ik}\, y_{ij}\, y_{ik}\, y_{jk}$).

As in Snijders (1996) and Snijders et al. (2010), the actor-oriented models can include arbitrary network effects; in such models, all actors are assumed to have full knowledge of the present state of the network, and, given this state, to behave independently. In parameter estimation, the CPCM models use MCMC on simulated networks to obtain expected values (Stephens, 2000). For more details of the parameter estimation procedure, refer to Koskinen and Snijders (2007).

## Multi-Agent Models

Another stream of dynamic network models is the stream of multi-agent models (also called evolutionary models), which are notably represented by Carley (2003) and Doreian (1983). Agents in the multi-agent models can learn, take part in events, and perform tasks to model organizational and social change. Node-level behavior can drive group behavior. The dynamic social network emerges from these actions. These models often combine multi-agent modeling, machine learning, and a meta-matrix approach to network representation. Carley (1991, 1995, 2003) uses multi-agent technology in which the agents use these mechanisms, learn, take part in events, and perform tasks to model organizational and social change. The dynamic social network emerges from these actions. The set of networks linking people, knowledge, tasks and other groups or organizations co-evolves, and nodes in the model have the ability to learn and adapt. These models are proposed for understanding the dynamics of terrorism. For example, DyNet (Carley & Prietula, 2001) is described and used to examine various isolation strategies. The authors use simple learn-ing mechanisms dynamically to adjust networks as the agents in them attend events, acquire new information, or are removed from the network. In DyNet, which is described herein, additional mechanisms that center on agent isolation are also considered. A wide range of applications can be seen from http://www.casos.cs.cmu.edu/.

## CONCLUSION

This chapter focused on dynamics and evolutional social networks and gave a brief introduction to data collection; it also described real-world applications and reviewed the major theories and models of dynamic network mining. Interested readers can further refer to recent trends in studies on social networks dynamics in the *Journal of Social Networks'* special issues on Network Dynamics.

## REFERENCES

Akoglu, L., & Faloutsos, C. (2009). RTG: A recursive realistic graph generator using random typing. *Data Mining and Knowledge Discovery*, *19*(2), 194–209. doi:10.1007/s10618-009-0140-7

Backstrom, L., Huttenlocher, D., Lan, X., & Kleinberg, J. (2006). Group formation in large social networks: Membership, growth, and evolution. In *Proceedings of the 12th ACM SIGKDD International Conference on Knowledge Discovery and Data Mining*(SIGKDD'06).

Barabási, A. L. (2002). *Linked: The new science of networks*. Cambridge, MA: Perseus Publishing.

Barabási, A. L., & Albert, R. (1999). Emergence of scaling in random networks. *Science, 286*, 509–512. doi:10.1126/science.286.5439.509

Berger-Wolf, T. Y., & Saia, J. (2006). A framework for analysis of dynamic social networks. In *Proceedings of the 12th ACM SIGKDD International Conference on Knowledge Discovery and Data Mining (KDD '06)*, Philadelphia, USA (pp. 523-528).

Bernstein, A., Clearwater, S., Hill, S., Perlich, C., & Provost, F. (2002). Discovering knowledge from relational data extracted from business news. In *SIGKDD-2002 Workshop on Multi-Relational Data Mining*.

Boginski, V., Butenko, S., & Pardalos, P. M. (2006). Mining market data: A network approach. *Computers & Operations Research*, *33*(11), 3171–3184. doi:10.1016/j.cor.2005.01.027

Borgatti, S. P., & Foster, P. C. (2003). The network paradigm in organizational research: A review and typology. *Journal of Management*, *29*, 991–1013.

Brass, D. J., Galaskiewicz, J., Greve, H. R., & Tsai, W. (2004). Taking stock of networks and organizations: A multilevel perspective. *Academy of Management Journal*, *47*, 795–817. doi:10.2307/20159624

Burk, W. J., Steglich, C. E. G., & Snijders, T. A. B. (2007). Beyond dyadic interdependence: Actor-oriented models for co-evolving social networks and individual behaviors. *International Journal of Behavioral Development*, *31*, 397–404. doi:10.1177/0165025407077762

Carley, K. M. (1991). A theory of group stability. *American Sociological Review*, *56*(3), 331–354. doi:10.2307/2096108

Carley, K. M. (1995). Communication technologies and their effect on cultural homogeneity, consensus, and the diffusion of new ideas. *Sociological Perspectives*, *38*(4), 547–571.

Carley, K. M. (2003). Dynamic network analysis. In R. Breiger, K. Carley, & P. Pattison (Ed.), *Dynamic social network modeling and analysis: Workshop summary and papers* (pp. 133-145). Committee on Human Factors, National Research Council.

Carley, K. M., & Prietula, M. (2001). *Computational Organization Theory*. Hillsdale: Lawrence Erlbaum Associates.

Carley, K. M., & Skillicorn, D. (2005). Special issue on analyzing large scale networks: The enron corpus. *Computational & Mathematical Organization Theory*, *11*, 179–181. doi:10.1007/s10588-005-5376-1

Chakrabarti, D., Zhan, Y., & Faloutsos, C. (2004). R-MAT: A recursive model for graph mining. In *Proceedings of the 4th SIAM International Conference on Data Mining*.

de Klepper, M., Sleebos, E., van de Bunt, G., & Agneessens, F. (2010). Similarity in friendship networks: Selection or influence? The effect of constraining contexts and non-visible individual attributes. *Social Networks*, *32*, 82–90. doi:10.1016/j.socnet.2009.06.003

Doreian, P. (1983). On the evolution of group and network structures II: structures within structure. *Social Networks*, *8*, 33–64. doi:10.1016/S0378-8733(86)80014-4

Eguíluz, V. M., Chialvo, D. R., Cecchi, G. A., Baliki, M., & Apkarian, A. V. (2005). Scale-free Brainfunctional networks. *Physical Review Letters*, *94*(1), 018102. doi:10.1103/PhysRevLett.94.018102

Ergün & Rodgers, G. J. (2002). Growing random networks with fitness. *Physica A. Statistical Mechanics and Its Applications*, *303*, 261–272. doi:10.1016/S0378-4371(01)00408-3

Falkowski, T. (2009). Community Analysis in Dynamic Social Networks. Unpublished dissertation, University Magdeburg, Germany.

Freeman, L. C. (1979). Centrality in social networks: Conceptual clarification. *Social Networks, 1*, 215–239. doi:10.1016/0378-8733(78)90021-7

Gary, D. P., Flake, G. W., Lawrence, S., Glover, E. J., & Giles, C. L. (2002). Winners don't take all: Characterizing the competition for links on the web. *Proceedings of the National Academy of Sciences of the United States of America, 99*, 5207–5211. doi:10.1073/pnas.032085699

Goldenberg, A., Zhang, A., Fienberg, S. E., & Airoldi, E. (2009). A survey of statistical network models. *Foundations and Trends in Machine Learning, 2*(2), 129–233. doi:10.1561/2200000005

Goldenberg, A., & Zheng, A. (2006). Exploratory study of a new model for evolving networks. In *Proceedings of the 2006 Conference on Statistical Network Analysis*, ICML'06, (pp. 75-89)., Berlin: Springer-Verlag.

Hanneke, S., & Xing, E. P. (2007). Discrete temporal models of social networks. In *Proceedings of the 2006 Conference on Statistical Network Analysis*, ICML'06, 115–125, Berlin: Springer-Verlag.

Harary, F., & Gupta, G. (1997). Dynamic graph models. *Mathematical and Computer Modelling, 25*(7), 79–87. doi:10.1016/S0895-7177(97)00050-2

Hoff, P. D., Raftery, A. E., & Handcock, M. S. (2002). Latent space approaches to social network analysis. *Journal of the American Statistical Association, 97*(460), 1090–1098. doi:10.1198/016214502388618906

Holland, P., & Leinhardt, S. (1977). A dynamic model for social networks. *The Journal of Mathematical Sociology, 5*, 5–20. doi:10.1080/0022250X.1977.9989862

Hu, C., Xu, L., Shen, G., & Fukushima, T. (2009). Temporal Company Relation Mining from the Web. In *Proceedings of the Joint International Conferences on Advances in Data and Web Management* (APWeb/WAIM'09), Suzhou, China, (pp. 392-403).

Huang, J., Zhuang, Z., Li, J., & Giles, C. L. (2008). Collaboration over time: Characterizing and Modeling network evolution. In *Proceedings of the 1st ACM International Conference on Web Search and Data Mining* (WSDM).

Katz, L., & Proctor, C. H. (1959). The configuration of interpersonal relations in a group as a time-dependent stochastic process. *Psychometrika, 24*, 317–327. doi:10.1007/BF02289814

Kleinberg, J. (2001). Small-world phenomena and the dynamics of information. *Advances in Neural Information Processing Systems, 14*, 2001.

Kleinberg, J. M., Kumar, R., Raghavan, P., Rajagopalan, S., & Tomkins, A. S. (1999). The Web as a graph: Measurements, models, and methods. In *Proceedings of the International Conference on Combinatorics and Computing*, (pp. 1-18).

Kolaczyk, E. D. (2009). *Statistical analysis of network data: Methods and models.* New York: Springer-Verlag.

Koskinen, J. H., & Snijders, T. A. B. (2007). Bayesian inference for dynamic social network data. *Journal of Statistical Planning and Inference, 137*(12), 3930–3938. doi:10.1016/j.jspi.2007.04.011

Kumar, R., Novak, J., & Tomkins, A. (2006). Structure and evolution of online social networks. In *Proceedings of the 12th ACM International Conference on Knowledge Discovery and Data Mining* (KDD), Philadelphia, USA, (pp. 611-617).

Kumar, R., Raghavan, P., Rajagopalan, S., Sivakumar, D., Tomkins, A., & Upfal, E. (2000). Stochastic models for the web graph. In *Proceedings of the 41th Annual Symposium on Foundations of Computer Science*, 57-65.

Leenders, R. T. A. J. (1995). Models for network dynamics: A markovian framework. *The Journal of Mathematical Sociology*, *20*, 1–21. doi:10.1080/0022250X.1995.9990149

Leskovec, J., Kleinberg, J., & Faloutsos, C. (2007). Graph evolution: Densification and shrinking diameters. *ACM Transactions on Knowledge Discovery from Data, 1*(1).

Liben-Nowell, D., & Kleinberg, J. (2007). The link-prediction problem for social networks. *Journal of the American Society for Information Science and Technology*, *58*(7), 1019–1031. doi:10.1002/asi.20591

Lin, Y. R., Chi, Y., Zhu, S., Sundaram, H., & Tseng, B. L. (2010). Analyzing communities and their evolutions in dynamic social networks. *ACM Transactions on Knowledge Discovery from Data*, *3*(2), 1–31. doi:10.1145/1514888.1514891

Ma, Z., Pant, G., & Sheng, O. R. L. (2009). A network-based approach to mining competitor Relationships from online news. In *Proceedings of 8th IEEE/ACIS International Conference on Computer and Information Science* (ICIS), Shanghai, China.

Maoz, Z. (2010 in press). *Networks of nations: The evolution, structure, and impact of international networks, 1816-2001*. New York: Cambridge University Press.

Mayer, T. F. (1984). Parties and networks: Stochastic models for relationship networks. *The Journal of Mathematical Sociology*, *10*, 51–103. doi:10.1080/0022250X.1984.9989958

McCulloh, I., & Carley, K. M. (2009). *Longitudinal dynamic network analysis. Casos technical Report*. Center for the Computational Analysis of Social and Organizational Systems.

McGlohon, M., Akoglu, L., & Faloutsos, C. (2008). Weighted graphs and disconnected components: Patterns and a generator. In *Proceedings of the 14th ACM SIGKDD International Conference on Knowledge Discovery and Data Mining*, KDD '08, (pp. 524–532). New York, ACM.

Mercken, L., Snijders, T. A. B., Steglich, C., Vartiainen, E., & de Vries, H. (2010). Dynamics of adolescent friendship networks and smoking behavior. *Social Networks*, *32*, 72–81. doi:10.1016/j.socnet.2009.02.005

Montoya, J. M., & Sol, R. V. (2002). Small world patterns in food webs. *Journal of Theoretical Biology*, *214*(3), 405–412. doi:10.1006/jtbi.2001.2460

Newcomb, T. M. (Ed.). (1961). *The acquaintance process*. New York: Holt, Rinehart, and Winston. doi:10.1037/13156-000

Newman, M. E. J. (2001). The structure of scientific collaboration networks. *Proceedings of the National Academy of Sciences of the United States of America*, *98*(2), 404–409. doi:10.1073/pnas.021544898

Nordle, P. G. (1958). A longitudinal study of interpersonal attraction in a natural group setting. Unpublished Ph.D. dissertation, Department of Psychology, University of Michigan.

Ratmann, O., Wiuf, C., & Pinney, J. W. (2009). From evidence to inference: Probing the evolution of protein interaction networks. *HFSP Journal*, *3*(5), 290–306. doi:10.2976/1.3167215

Robins, G., & Pattison, P. (2001). Random graph models for temporal processes in social networks. *The Journal of Mathematical Sociology*, *25*, 5–41. doi:10.1080/0022250X.2001.9990243

Sandberg, O. &. Clarke, I. (2006). *The evolution of navigable small-world networks*. Department of Computer Science and Engineering Technical Report 2007:14, Chalmers University of Technology.

Sarkar, P., & Moore, A. W. (2005). Dynamic social network analysis using latent space models. *SIGKDD Exploration Newsletter*, *7*, 31–40. doi:10.1145/1117454.1117459

Sarkar, P., Siddiqi, S. M., & Gordon, G. J. (2007). A latent space approach to dynamic embedding of co-occurrence data. In *Proceedings of the 11th International Conference on Artificial Intelligence and Statistics* (AI-STATS'07).

Savin-Williams, R. C. (1979). Dominance hierarchies in groups of early adolescents. *Child Development*, *59*, 923–935. doi:10.2307/1129316

Schaefer, D. R., Light, J. M., Fabes, R. A., Hanish, L. D., & Martin, C. L. (2010). Fundamental principles of network formation among preschool children. *Social Networks*, *32*, 61–71. doi:10.1016/j.socnet.2009.04.003

Snijders, T. A. B. (1996). Stochastic actor-oriented models for network change. *Journal of Mathematical Sociology*, *21*, 149-172. Also published in Doreian and Stokman (1997).

Snijders, T. A. B. (1997). Models for longitudinal network data. In Carrington, P., Scott, J., & Wasserman, S. (Eds.), *Models and methods in social network analysis* (pp. 148–161). New York: Cambridge University Press.

Snijders, T. A. B., Steglich, C. E. G., & van de Bunt, G. G. (2010). Introduction to actor-based models for network dynamics. *Social Networks*, *32*, 44–60. doi:10.1016/j.socnet.2009.02.004

Snijders, T. A. B., & Van Duijn, M. A. J. (1997). Simulation for statistical inference in dynamic Network models. In R. Conte, R. Hegselmann, & P. Terna (Eds.), *Simulating social phenomena*, 493-512. Berlin: Springer.

Stephens, M. (2000). Bayesian analysis of mixtures with an unknown number of components—An alternative to reversible jump methods. *Annals of Statistics*, *28*(1), 40–74. doi:10.1214/aos/1016120364

Tantipathananandh, C., Berger-Wolf, T., & Kempe, D. (2007). A framework for community Identification in dynamic social networks. In *Proceedings of the 13th ACM SIGKDD International Conference on Knowledge Discovery and Data Mining* (KDD), San Jose, California, USA, (pp. 717-726).

Tetlock, P. C., Saar-Tsechansky, M., & Macskassy, S. (2008). More than words: Quantifying language to measure firms' fundamentals. *The Journal of Finance*, *63*(3), 1437–1467. doi:10.1111/j.1540-6261.2008.01362.x

Van de Bunt, G. G., Van Duijn, M. A. J., & Snijders, T. A. B. (1999). Friendship networks through time: An actor-oriented statistical network model. *Computational & Mathematical Organization Theory*, *5*, 167–192. doi:10.1023/A:1009683123448

Wagner, A. (2001). The yeast protein interaction network evolves rapidly and contains few redundant duplicate genes. *Molecular Biology and Evolution*, *18*(7), 1283–1292.

Wagner, A., & Fell, D. A. (2001). The small world inside large metabolic networks. *Proceedings. Biological Sciences*, *268*(1478), 1803–1810. doi:10.1098/rspb.2001.1711

Wasserman, S. (1977). Stochastic models for directed graphs. Unpublished Ph.D. dissertation, Department of Statistics, Harvard University.

Wasserman, S. (1980). Analyzing social networks as stochastic processes. *Journal of the American Statistical Association*, *75*, 280–294. doi:10.2307/2287447

Wasserman, S., & Philippa, P. (1996). Logit models and logistic regressions for social networks: I. an introduction to markov graphs and p\*. *Psychometrika*, *61*(3), 401–425. doi:10.1007/BF02294547

Watts, D., & Strogatz, S. (1998). Collective dynamics of small-world networks. *Nature*, *393*, 440–442. doi:10.1038/30918

Wiggins, A., Howison, J., & Crowston, K. (2008). Social dynamics of floss team communication across channels. In *Proceedings of the Fourth International Conference on Open Source Software* (IFIP 2.13), Milan, Italy.

Zheng, A., & Goldenberg, A. (2006). *A generative model for dynamic contextual friendship networks. CMU-ML-06-107*. Pittsburgh, PA: School of Computer Science. Carnegie Mellon University.

# Chapter 11
# Modeling Customer Behavior with Analytical Profiles

**Jerzy Surma**
*Warsaw School of Economics, Poland*

## ABSTRACT

*Contemporary companies try to build customer relationship management systems based on the customer social relations and behavioral patterns. This is in correspondence with the current trend in marketing that is to move from broadcast marketing operation to a one-to-one marketing. The key issue in this activity is predicting to which products or services a particular customer was likely to respond to. In order to build customer relationship management systems, companies have to learn to understand their customer in the broader social context. The key hypothesis in this approach is that the predictors of behavior in the future are customers behavior patterns in the past. This is a form of human behavioral modeling. The individual customer behavior patterns can be used to build an analytical customer profile. This will be described in section "Introduction" and "Customer profiling". Based on this profile a company might target a specific customer with a personalized message. In section "Critical examples" the authors will focus in particular on the importance of the customer social relations, that reflects referrals influence on the marketing response. In the end in section "Market of analytical profiles" they will discuss the potential business models related to market exchange of analytical profiles.*

## INTRODUCTION

As we live in contemporary world, we leave thousands of digital footprints behind us through usage of mobile phones, credit cards, electronic mail, browsing in social networks etc. Each footprint shows our real actions that we take in given time and place. The analysis of thousands of such footprints on large groups of people allow us to analyze human behavior on an unimaginable before scale in scientific studies concerning psychology and sociology (Lazer et al. 2009). The results of those analysis will have a significant influence on many disciplines such as medical prophylaxis, political elections or contemporary marketing in personalized customer relationship management. In this context it is interesting to look at the summary of

DOI: 10.4018/978-1-61350-513-7.ch011

*Figure 1. Classical marketing based on the customer segmentation: „I have a product, give me a client"*

historical development of customer management by Kumar (2008). It begins with direct relations with individual customers, then entire-market customers, segmented customers and finally the return to the initial idea of personalized service usage of interactive marketing (Deighton et al. 1996). According to Kumar, interactive marketing can be described as follows (Kumar 2008):

1.  The range of decisions: identification of interested customers and assuring on-going relations or relations at proper time.
2.  The range of analysis: elaborating the complete characteristics of the customer.
3.  Value building factor: personalization and adapting proper service at a proper time.

The usage of customer behavior in marketing has a relatively long history. Analytical customer relationship management systems have been used in telecommunications and banking sector since the 90s of the previous century (Shankar, Winer 2006). In this perspective, new type of data about diversified customer behaviors introduces new

opportunities in contemporary marketing. This new potential, related to the development of Business Intelligence systems (Surma 2011), has contributed to the development of personalized marketing concept based on profound analysis of history of contacts with customer[1].

## CUSTOMER PROFILING

### From Segmentation to Personalization

In order to understand properly new analytical opportunities in marketing, it is crucial to differentiate correctly the classic approach based on customer segmentation (see Figure 1) in comparison to personalized approach related to interactive marketing (see Figure 2). In case of segmentation, the division of customers is done usually on the basis of social-demographic characteristics (e.g., sex, age, education, place of residence) and the analysis of the purchase history, using the RFM[2] analysis. In this approach,

*Figure 2. Interactive marketing based on the personalization: „I have a client, give me a product"*

1.

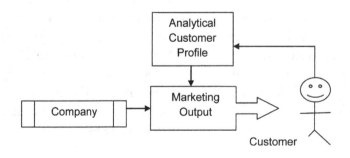

the customer is classified to the segment as a similar object to other members (objects) of the segment[3]. All customers in a given segment, in a given marketing campaign receive the identical message, irrespective of the differences between them. The time and the method of delivering the message is chosen arbitrarily by the manager of marketing campaign and is the same for the whole segment. In this approach we usually don't reflect value changes of customer characteristics in time and we treat the whole segment as static and homogeneous group of objects.

The interactive approach to customer management is significantly different. Customer is treated as an independent person that has specific needs and preferences. The company wants to get to know the characteristics of the customer through conversations, maintaining the relationship (Kumar 2008), as well as collecting and analyzing the digital footprints that customer leaves behind him in different interactions (also with other people). It is well known that customer responds to a given marketing message is not happening in a vacuum. Many factors contributed to this decision, such as psychological variables (motivation, perception, learning, attitude, personality/lifestyle), social influence (family, social class, reference groups, culture), and purchase situation (purchase reason, time, surroundings) (Perreault et al. 2009). However, most factors that contribute directly to customer response cannot be captured and stored in corporate databases. The possible way to reflect these response factors is to relate them to customer behavior patterns. As a result of this pattern analysis, it is possible to create the Analytical Customer Profile (ACP). On the basis of this profile, we can adjust the marketing offer to specific customer needs. The time and the method of delivering the message is determined by the customer preferences. As opposed to segmentation, the contact with customer is activated indirectly by the customer himself through the ongoing process of the prediction of his needs. In

this approach, it is crucial to observe the behavior of the customer in time and to analyze the dynamics of the values of the characteristics represented in the profile. Next we will demonstrate the phases of contact personalization with customer (section "Personalization process") and the idea of the customer analytical profile concept (section "The structure of analytical customer profile").

## Personalization Process

The process of personalization, which is based on the analytical customer profile, is shown on Figure 3. The whole process consist of four phases (Versanen, Raulas 2006):

1. *Processing:* Transform transactional and external client data into analytical customer

*Figure 3. The Process of personalization*

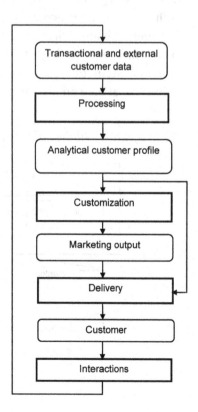

profile. Customer profile is generated based on the econometrical and data mining methods (Chiu, Tavella 2008).

2. *Customization:* Is the production of personalized marketing output due to:

    a. Selection of the proper product/service offer based on the customer needs (*hyle*),

    b. Development of the personalized marketing message, that is adequate to the customer preferences (*morphe*).

3. *Delivery:* Procedure how the personalized marketing output reaches the customer. During this phase an access channel and time of delivery is established. Those parameters are forecasting based on the customer preferences taken from customer profile.

4. *Interactions:* Recognized and registered customer behavior taken from two sources:

    a. *Internal:* response for delivered marketing output, click stream on the company internet portal, personal data deliver into registration forms, contacts with call center, registered purchases, exchange opinion with others customers on the company blog, etc.

    b. *External:* Activities on the external online social networks [4], transactions in the loyalty programs with a business partners, customer data received from external marketing databases, etc.

## The Structure of Analytical Customer Profile

The main aim of personalization process (see Figure 3) is to deliver adequate marketing messages to the customer in proper time. We assume that it is possible to predict customer behavior on the basis of the history of his behaviors and behaviors of similar customers. It is crucial to established which variables describing the customer should be processed and whether there is appropriate transactional data available.

The analytical customer profile is a result of abstraction (generalization[5] and aggregation[6]) of interactions (time series of customer transactional data, as well as other social-demographic data) in order to generate adequate marketing messages[7]. The characteristics (variables) stored in analytical profile generally belong to one of two perspectives (see Figure 4):

- Social-Demographic Perspective: Built on the basis of data declared by customer and received from official contacts with cus-

*Figure 4. The structure of Analytical Customer Profile*

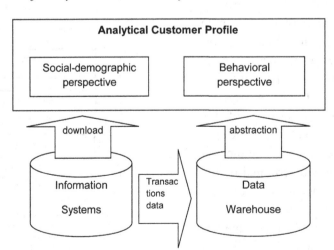

tomer. This data is mainly statistics (e.g., place of birth). However some of them are subject to change in time (e.g., place of residence, education).

- Behavioral Perspective: Build on the basis of behavioral data left by customer during interactions with the company or other customers. This kind of data is dynamic.

The successful prediction of customer behaviors is possible only when analytical profile really reflects motivations and attitudes that determine customer decisions. Those motivations and attitudes result from a human nature of analyzed person and are in reality responsible for her actions (Nisbet, Elder, Miner 2009). The interactions reflected in transactional data can be compared to shadows (σκιά) of Plato in the cave (Plato 2007). If we continue this metaphor, the analytical profile is built on the basis of "shadows" and as defined it is rather imperfect attempt to model human behavior. However, we have to underline three conditions that are favorable to build profiles. First of all, transactional data represents real actions, as opposed to declared information. Secondly, it is the long term, often longstanding abstraction of transactional data that is the key of analytical profile. In this context, the level of credibility of knowledge about customer is increasing according to the length of data collecting period. Finally, the wide range of collected transactional data is also important: from the data available inside the company, through the public data available e.g., on social networks, to data retrieved from customer profiles from other companies (see the discussion in section "Market of analytical profiles").

## Profile Analysis

The business dimension of personalization requires a proper analysis of client profitability in time, i.e., the calculation of profits from sale per customer in comparison to average costs spent on his service. When every customer is unequivo-

cally identified and monitored with the usage of analytical profile, it is possible to calculate the indicator of past customer value and to estimate the indicator of customer lifetime value (Kumar 2008). The indicator of past customer value allows among others the precise monitoring of customer profitability, in which we can compare the positive cash flows earned thanks to the knowledge from analytical profile and the individual costs of building and maintaining the analytical profile. The usage of analytical profile allows us to calculate the indicator of lifetime value, which is related to prediction of future customer margins and future costs (taking into account changes in time value of money). The prediction of emoluments (what and when customer will buy) is in this context a key element[8].

Prediction models determine which characteristics (variables) should be represented in analytical profile. This repertory of variables can differ according to type of products or sector etc. The usage of models that suggest a given customer the most probable purchase and its time allow the personalization management system (after the update of analytical profile) to pass on to customization phase. Afterwards it is possible to activate automatically the phase of delivering the marketing message to customer at proper time[9]. In this context we can talk about the activity of analytical profile whether the process was automatic or was directly monitored by marketing department. In this approach, the analytical profile (as a real customer representation) generates declaration of realization of personalized, 1-to-1 marketing campaign. Everyday management of large volume of unique declarations is a new and nontrivial management problem, i.e., event driven process management.

## CRITICAL EXAMPLES

In this section a three critical example are presented. Those projects were carefully selected in

*Table 1. Critical examples characteristics*

| Example | Customer Social Relations | Customer Profile Management | Source |
|---|---|---|---|
| Proactive CRM | No | Yes | Sun, Li, Zhou (2006) |
| Cyworld | Yes | No | Raghuram, Han, Gupta (2009) |
| Customer refferals | Yes | No | Kumar, Petersen, Leone (2010) |

Source: Author.

order to present the recent research approaches in (see Table 1):

1. Analysis the influence of the customer social relations
2. Usefulness of dynamic customer profiles in real business applications

## Proactive CRM

In the section "Customer profiling" we shown the trend to transform CRM decisions from being campaign-centric (static and ad fashion approach) to being customer-centric, where the company needs to develop detailed customer knowledge, follow the continuous development of customer profile, and adopt CRM interventions that are relevant to the status and preference of each individual customer. In this context, Sun, Li, and Zhou (2006) proposed the framework of proactive CRM based on the adaptive learning. Adaptive learning offers the company the opportunity to learn about customer preferences in an uncertain environment and adapt its strategies in a real-time fashion. Formally they formulate CRM intervention decisions as a solution to a stochastic dynamic control problem under demand uncertainty with built-in customer reactions. The adaptive learning component allows to derive an integrated sequence of CRM decisions about *when* to contact *which* customer with *what* product using which communication channel (*how*). This approach was empirically tested on the cross-selling campaign management for a retail banking services in a national bank (Li, Sun, Montgomery 2005). The

data set consist of monthly account opening and transaction histories, cross-selling solicitations about the type of product promoted, communication channels, and demographic information of a randomly selected sample of 4000 households for 15 financial product groups during a total of 27 month. The effectiveness of a cross-selling campaign was improved from 5,6% to 11,2%. The return on investment on performed campaigns was improved by 40,8%, and demonstrate the increase of long-term profit when the company shifts its cross-selling strategy from campaign centric to customer centric. This research justifies the approach in which the company is able to maximize long-term profit based on the dynamic and customized decisions generated from time series of information about the customer.

## Cyworld

Cyworld[10] is a South Korean social network service operated by SK Communications. With over 18 million users out of a 48 million population (with 33 million Internet users) Cyworld is South Korea's leading social network. Created in 1999 when the online advertising market was not enough to sustain a website, and when valuations of online communities was unheard of, Cyworld had to come up with innovative business models, services and pioneered many functions which are gradually being "rediscovered" elsewhere. Raghuram, Han, and Gupta (2009) performed the research on Cyworld with three questions (a) do friends influence purchases of a user in a social network ? (b) which users are more influenced by social pressure ? and (c) what is the impact of this social influence in sales and revenues. To address these questions they developed a quantitative model that capture the effect of social influence on a member's decision purchase. The transactional (purchasing) data[11] for building the model was taken by monitoring behavior of over 200 users for several months. The final results show that there is a significant and positive impact of friends purchases on the purchase probability of users. They found significant heterogeneity among users. Deep examination reveals differences across three user groups: positive (40%), negative (12%), and zero (48%) social effect. Users who have limited connection to other members are not influenced by friends purchases. Positive social effect, translated into a 5% increase in revenue, was observed in moderately connected users. These users are imitating others behavior. In contrast to this group, highly connected users tend to reduce their purchases of items when they see their friends buying them. This negative social effect reduces the revenue for this group by more than 14%. These empirical results are relevant for social networking sites. The members in high status group have an influence on those in the middle status group for the diffusion of a new product.

## Customer Referrals in Financial Services

The social influence effect investigated in Cyworld social net is recognized currently in the marketing research as a referral marketing. The referral is defined as a situation when a customer enters into transaction with a firm and attributes the motivation for the transaction to a current customer. Kumar, Petersen and Leone (2010) examined the monetary value of word of social relations, referral behavior and their role in consumer decision making and purchase behavior. The main research hypothesis was whether it is possible to predict customer's indirect impact (through referral behavior) on the firm's future profits. This

hypothesis was empirically verified on the basis of data collected from 14160 customers in four years period. The data was obtained from the financial services company (ranks high among the global Fortune 1000 firms), and was related to a wide range of products and services, including banking, insurance, and investments. The data included each customer's own purchase behavior and the estimated marketing costs. The data set included also the findings from a survey given to each of the 14160 customers that provided information on their "willingness to refer" to new customers. In this sample 9492 of customers stated that they are intended to make referrals, however only 4204 actually made attempts at referrals. The efficiency of the performed campaign management was measured by means of CLV (customer lifetime value) and CRV (customer referral value). For CLV, the average in performed experiments in the test group customers was $274 before and $291 after (the same for the control group is significantly lower and was respectively $270 and $271). For CRV, the average in performed experiments in the test group customers was $145 before and $164 after (the same for the control group is significantly lower and was respectively $145 and $146). The results show that each of the performed campaigns was successful in significantly increasing the average customer's CLV and CRV. Based on this research we can see that building a social network can be a long-term competitive advantage for both the customer and the firm because it enables the firm's relationship with each customer to evolve over time (Ganesan 1994).

# MARKET OF ANALYTICAL PROFILES

## Introductory Assumptions

If we assume that we can build customer analytical profiles, we can also ask whether it is possible for other companies to use those customer profiles. In case of complementary products such as airline tickets and hotel rooms, there is a natural business need to exchange information between airlines and hotels[12]. The content of the customer analytical profile is determined by product and sector specifics. However, it seems that it is possible to distinguish the „general characteristics" in the profile, which would be identical irrespective of the activity of the company or the specifics of transactional data. General characteristics contains mainly social-demographic variables (e.g., sex and age) as well as some behavioral variables (e.g., interests).

The class diagram on Figure 5 reflects this idea. The class "Analytical Customer Profile (ACP)" contains general characteristics and „ACP Travel Agency" inherits the variables from general characteristics and adds to them variables related to sector specifics. This approach allows the exchange of information from customer profile between the companies, that products are not directly related. For example the analysis of purchases of a given client in travel agency would allow a FCMG cosmetic company to prepare a special offer for him. In this reasoning there is a hidden assumption about the existence of general customer personality type, which determines consumer behaviors. A good example of it is a lifestyles model VALS elaborated by SRI Consulting[13] in which customers are classified to one of eight behavior groups. If we assume that a customer classified to a given group on the basis of the purchases in travel agency would have the same lifestyle in beauty products purchases, then the exchange of customer profile between travel agency and cosmetic company is economically justified. The possible business models of such profile exchange will be discussed in next section.

## Potential Business Models

The possibility of distinguishing the general characteristics profile allows the trade of customer analytical profiles. We can distinguish the following business models:

- *Local Model*: Standard approach, that can be developed in contemporary used marketing campaign management systems (analytical CRM). The company possess local data warehouse (with precisely defined and relatively poor range of data) and limits profile creation to customer data analysis accepted by law. In this approach the customer is not informed about data processing that concerns him. Customer analytical profile is a property of the company.
- *Open Model (B2C):* Extended local model, in which company (with customer's approval) builds customer analytical profile without restrictions. In exchange for the

*Figure 5. Analytical Customer Profile IS-A hierarchy*

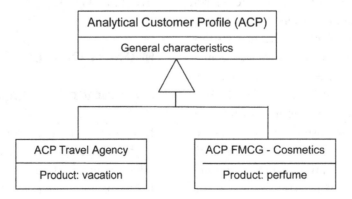

approval for processing behavioral data and delivering additional information, the customer gets benefits from the company e.g., discount or priority in promotions. The level of benefits for a given customer can be estimated by the company on the basis of its lifetime value. The analytical customer profile is a joint property of customer and company.

- *Open Model (B2B)*[14]: Chosen elements of customer profile can be traded between companies. The companies exchange information about customer behaviors[15]. In this approach, the customer is informed about data processing and exchanging and he benefits from loyalty and benefit programs. The analytical customer profile is a joint property of companies participating in the program.

- *Global Model:* The analytical profile is supervised and is a property of a specific person, who can be of course a customer of different companies. The analytical profile is stored and processed by the independent vendor of such service. The customer has full access to his analytical profile and is able to modify it. The customer may release or sell his analytical profile to the company that he works with. Potential value of a new and unknown customer depend on the value of information in his analytical profile.

The key problem of building business models is related with cost estimate of such a profile. It is crucial to answer the question whether the companies are willing to pay for this type of knowledge about the customer. If yes, then we should proceed with the cost estimate. Certainly we can prepare cost estimate post factum, in which we can compare past value of a random group of customers managed with the usage of their analytical profiles and a random group of customers managed without it. On the basis of those studies we can estimate average return on

investment from customer profile, taking into account the cost of its purchase.

## CONCLUSION

In order to build customer relationship management systems companies must learn to understand their customer. The key hypothesis in the presented approach is that the predictors of behavior in the future are customers behavior patterns in the past. This a form of human behavioral modeling. In order to predict the action of customer response we must model human nature based on the available behavior patterns including social relations represented by relational variables. In this context we presented a model of an active analytical customer profile. By means of three critical examples we showed the current research in this field. Additionally based on the concept of customer profile we introduced the idea of general characteristics and consequently an opportunity of creating a variety business models. The presented results are promising but extended empirical evaluation the overall approach is necessary.

## REFERENCES

Broder, A., & Josifovski, F. (2010). *Computational Advertising*. Retrieved November 10, 2010, from http://www.stanford.edu/ class/msande239.

Chiu, S., & Tavella, D. (2008). *Data mining and market intelligence for optimal marketing returns*. Amsterdam: Elsevier.

Deighton, J. (1996). The Future of Interactive Marketing. *Harvard Business Review*, 11–12.

Dokoohaki, N., & Matskin, M. (2008). Personalizing Human Interaction through Hybrid Ontological Profiling: Cultural Heritage Case Study. In M. Ronchetti (Ed.) *1st Workshop on Semantic Web Applications and Human Aspects* (pp 133-140). AIT e-press.

Ganesan, S. (1994). Determinants of Long-Term Orientation in Buyer-Seller Relationship. *Journal of Marketing, 58*, 1–19. doi:10.2307/1252265

Haimowitz, I., & Kohane, I. (1996). Managing temporal worlds for medical trends diagnosis. *Artificial Intelligence in Medicine, 8*(3), 299–321. doi:10.1016/0933-3657(95)00037-2

Kelly, S. (2006). *Customer Intelligence. From Data to Dialoque*. New York: Willey.

Knott, A., Hayes, A., & Neslin, S. (2002). Next-Product-To-Buy Models for Cross-Selling Applications. *Journal of Interactive Marketing, 16*(3), 9–75. doi:10.1002/dir.10038

Kumar, V. (2008). *Managing customers for profits: strategies to increase profits and building loyalty*. New Jersey: Wharton Scholl Publishing.

Kumar, V., Petersen, J., & Leone, R. (2010). Driving Profitability by Encouraging Customer Referrals: Who, When, and How. *Journal of Marketing, 74*, 1–17. doi:10.1509/jmkg.74.5.1

Lazer, D. (2009). Life in the network: the coming age of computational social science. *Science, 6*(323), 721–723. doi:10.1126/science.1167742

Li, S., Sun, B., & Montgomery, A. (2005). *Introducing What Financial Product to Which Customer at What Time - An Empirical Analysis of Customized and Dynamic Cross-selling Campaigns*. Tepper School of Business working paper 2006-E66.

Nisbet, R., Elder, J., & Miner, G. (2009). *Handbook of Statistical Analysis & Data Mining Applications*. Amsterdam: Elsevier.

Pancras, J., & Sudhir, K. (2007). Optimal marketing strategies for a customer data intermediary. *JMR, Journal of Marketing Research, 44*(4), 560–578. doi:10.1509/jmkr.44.4.560

Perreault, J., Cannon, J., & McCarthy, E. (2009). *Essentials of Marketing*. New York: McGraw-Hill.

Plato,. (2007). *The Republic*. New York: Penguin Classics.

Prahalad, C. K., & Krishnan, M. S. (2008). *The New Age of Innovation (Analytics: Insight for Innovation)*. New York: McGraw-Hill.

Raghuram, I., Han, S., & Gupta, S. (2009). *Do Friends Influence Purchases in a Social Network?* Harvard Business School Working Paper, no. 09-123.

Shankar, V., & Winer, R. (2006). When Customer Relationship Management Meets Data Mining. *Journal of Interactive Marketing, 20*(3-4), 2–4. doi:10.1002/dir.20062

Shibo, L., Sun, B., & Wilcox, R. (2005). Cross-Selling Sequentially Ordered Products: An Application to Consumer Banking Services. *JMR, Journal of Marketing Research, XLII*(May), 233–239.

Sun, B., Li, S., & Zhou, C. (2006). "Adaptive" Learning and "Proactive" Customer Relationship Management. *Journal of Interactive Marketing, 20*(3/4), 82–96. doi:10.1002/dir.20069

Surma, J. (2011). *Business Intelligence*. New York: Business Expert Press.

Venkatesan, R., Kumar, V., & Bohling, T. (2007). Optimal Customer Relationship Management Using Bayesian Decision Theory: An Application for Customer Selection. *JMR, Journal of Marketing Research, XLIV*(11), 579–594. doi:10.1509/jmkr.44.4.579

Vesanen, J., & Raulas, M. (2006). Building bridges for personalization: a process model for marketing. *Journal of Interactive Marketing, 20*(1), 5–20. doi:10.1002/dir.20052

Wijsen, J. (2001). Trends in databases: reasoning and mining. *IEEE Transactions on Knowledge and Data Engineering, 13*(3), 426–438. doi:10.1109/69.929900

## ADDITIONAL READING

Attali, J. (2009). *Brief History of the Future: A Brave and Controversial Look at the Twenty-First Century*. Arcade Publishing.

Evans, M., Jamal, A., & Foxall, G. (2009). *Consumer Behaviour*. Chichester, UK: Wiley.

Evans, M., O'Malley, L., & Patterson, M. (2004). *Exploring Direct and Customer Relationship Marketing*. Thompson Learning.

González, M. C., Hidalgo, C. A., & Barabási, A. L. (2008). Understanding individual human mobility patterns. *Nature, 453*, 479–482. doi:10.1038/nature06958

Lace, S. (Ed.). (2005). *The Glass Consumer: Life in a Surveillance Society*. Policy Press, National Consumer Council.

Mitchell, T. M. (2009). Mining Our Reality. *Science, 18*(326), 1644–1645. doi:10.1126/science.1174459

Petland, A. (2008). *Honest Signals. How They Shape our World*. Boston: MIT Press.

Solove, D. (2004). *The Digital Person. Technology and Privacy in the Information Age*. New York: New York University Press.

Tapp, A. (2008). *Principles of Direct and Database Marketing. A Digital Orientation*. Harlow: Prentice Hall.

## KEY TERMS AND DEFINITIONS

**Analytical Customer Profile:** Is a result of abstraction of interactions (time series of customer transactional data, as well as other social-demographic data) in order to generate adequate marketing messages.

**Interactive Marketing:** Is an identification of interested customers and elaborating the complete characteristics of the customer in order to achieve personalization and adapting proper service at a proper time.

**Personalization:** Is a process of analyzing (processing) customer data, customization and delivery of marketing output, and interactions with customers for increasing their lifetime value.

## ENDNOTES

[1] The representative publications in this area are: presentation of the idea of Customer Intelligence (Kelly 2006), introducing N=1 concept by Prahalad and Krishnan (2008) and a series of lectures of Computational Marketing (Advertising) (Broder, Josifovski 2010).

[2] RFM stands for Recency - How recently a customer has purchased ?, Frequency - How often does he purchase ?, Monetary Value - How much does he spend ?

[3] Usually it is segmentation a priori, in which market segments are determined arbitrarily on the basis of expert knowledge. The usage of data exploration methods allows segmentation post-hoc in which thanks to clustering algorithms, it is possible to discover real customer segments on the basis of the analysis of available transactional and social-demographic data.

[4] See as an example functionality of the Open Graph protocol for facebook: developers.facebook.com/docs/opengraph [2010.10.10].

[5] An example of generalization would be defining customer interest on the basis of books purchased and viewed by him. Generalization requires defining and implementing the appropriate ontology model of the chosen field. Exemplary solution is presented in study of Dokoohaki and Matskin (2008).

[6] Aggregation is a standard procedure in data warehouse, it requires performing appropri-

[7] ate procedures on quantitative data such as sum or average.

[7] The idea of abstraction of time series was presented by Haimowitz and Kohan (1996) as well as Wijsen (2001).

[8] Exemplary purchase prediction models are logit models (Knott et al. 2002), probit models (Shibo et al. 2005), or Bayesian models (Venkatesan et al. 2007). The studies of these models have shown that despite the limited access to transactional data, it was possible to achieve statistically accurate improvement of customer purchase prediction compared to expert prediction.

[9] It is also possible to stop delivering message to customer e.g. in case of negative prognosis in analyzed future.

[10] Retrieved November 10, 2010, from: http//:us.cyworld.com.

[11] The cyworld users can decorate their own mini-home pages by purchasing virtual items. In 2007 Cyworld generated $65 million or almost 70% of its revenue from selling these items. The remaining revenue was generated from advertising and mobile services.

[12] Such offers as a static portfolio of services that do not use analytical knowledge about the customer, are already commonly available.

[13] Retrieved November 10, 2010, from http://www.strategicbusinessinsights.com/vals/presurvey.shtml.

[14] Look as an example at Pancras and Sudhir (2007) concept of the Customer Data Intermediary, a firm that collects customer data to offer customer-specific marketing services to marketers.

[15] It is possible to perform when we define standard specifics of customer analytical profile and the protocol of its exchange between the companies. Alternatively, it is possible to build common customer analytical profile management system under the supervision of the third company.

# Chapter 12
# Social Search and Personalization Through Demographic Filtering

**Kamal Taha**
*Khalifa University, UAE*

**Ramez Elmasri**
*University of Texas at Arlington, USA*

## ABSTRACT

*Most existing personalized search systems do not consider group profiling. Group profiling can be an efficient retrieval mechanism, where a user profile is inferred from the profile of the social groups to which the user belongs. The authors propose an XML search system called DemoFilter which employs the concept of group profiling. DemoFilter simplifies the personalization process by pre-defining various categories of social groups and then identifying their preferences. Social groups are characterized based on demographic, ethnic, cultural, religious, age, or other characteristics. DemoFilter can be used for various practical applications, such as Internet or other businesses that market preference-driven products. In the ontology, the preferences of a social group are identified from published studies about the social group. They experimentally evaluate the search effectiveness of DemoFilter and compare it to an existing search engine.*

## INTRODUCTION

With the growth of massive information on the Web, it has become increasingly difficult to search for useful information. As one of the most promising approaches to alleviate this overload, recommender systems have emerged in domains

such as E-commerce, digital libraries, and knowledge management. In general, recommendation systems suggest items or products by analyzing what users with similar tastes have chosen in the past (Herlocker et al., 2002). There are two prevalent approaches to formulate recommendations: collaborative filtering recommendation and content-based recommendation. They depend on the type of items to be recommended and on the

DOI: 10.4018/978-1-61350-513-7.ch012

way that user models (Allen, 1990; Huang et al., 2004) are constructed. In collaborative filtering approach (Dalal, 2007; Herlocker et al., 2004; Hofmann, 2003), information is filtered for a larger group of users. The term collaborative filtering was coined by Goldberg et al. (1992). Collaborative-filtering algorithms aim to identify users that have relevant interests and preferences by calculating similarities and dissimilarities between user profiles. The idea behind this method is that it may be of benefit to one's search for information to consult the behavior of other users who share the same or relevant interests. A content-based approach (Carmine, 2003; Kalles, 2003; Meng, 2002) provides recommendations by comparing an item's content with the content that the user is interested in. In this approach, a model of user ratings is first developed. Then the filtering process is envisioned by computing the expected value of a user prediction given the user's ratings on other items. Content-based algorithms are principally used when documents are to be recommended, such as web pages, publications, or news. The agent maintains information about user preferences either by initial input about user's interests during the registration process or by rating documents. Recommendations are formed by taking into account the content of documents and by filtering in the ones that better match the user's preferences and logged profile.

In this chapter, we propose an XML-based recommender system, called DemoFilter (Demographic Filtering). It is a type of collaborative information filtering system. DemoFilter uses ontology-driven social networks, where nodes represent social groups. A social group is an entity that defines a group based on demographic, ethnic, cultural, religious, age, or other characteristics. For example, people of ethnic group $E_x$; people who follow religion $R_y$; and people who live in neighborhood $N_y$ can all be considered to form various social groups. In the DemoFilter framework, query results are filtered and ranked based on the preferences of the social groups to which the user belongs. If the user belongs to social group $G_x$, results will be filtered based on the preferences of $G_x$ and the preferences of *each* ancestor social group of $G_x$ in the social network. In social communities, it is commonly accepted that people who are known to share a specific background are likely to have additional connected interests (Herlocker et al., 2002). DemoFilter can be used for various practical applications, such as Internet or other businesses that market preference-driven products.

An individual user may belong to more than one social group. Therefore, DemoFilter outputs ranked lists of content items, taking into account not only the initial preferences of the user, but also the preferences of the user's various social groups. Consider for example a Mexican-American user. The user belongs to social groups Mexicans and Americans: the portion of Mexicans living in the USA. The results of a query submitted by this user will be *filtered* and *ranked* based on the union of the interests of social groups "Mexicans" and "Americans". The social groups to which a user belongs usually have *class-subclass* relationships. A subclass social group has its own properties while inheriting the properties of its superclass(es). For example, consider a user who belongs to the ethnic group "Berbers", who lives in the country of "Morocco", which is part of "North Africa". We could have the following representation of the hierarchical relationships between the three social groups: North Africans → Moroccans → Berbers. The Berbers may have their own concerns and preferences, while sharing the concerns and preferences of Moroccans, and more general concerns and preferences of North Africans. Thus, the user's query will be filtered and ranked based on the preferences of "Berbers", "Moroccans", and "North Africans".

In the framework of DemoFilter, the preferences of a social group are identified from published studies about the social group (the availability of such data has had a significant boost with the emergence of the World Wide Web).

DemoFilter helps searchers find what they need faster by trying to put the most relevant results at the top of the result list, a process known as relevance ranking. A demo of the DemoFilter system, running on 1000 MB grocery data and 1000 MB car data, is available at: http://dbse1. uta.edu/~kamal/?action=home.

## BACKGROUND

There have been a number of researches in group-based filtering (Pazzani, 1999; Aimeur et al., 2006; O'Connor, 2008). In these works, members of a group share the same interests on an item. Pazzani (1999) employed text classification for classifying users. For example, the author proposed scanning the contents of users' HTML home pages for determining the interests of the users in a specific item. The key differences between these works and our work are as follows: (1) a user profile in our work is inferred from profiles of groups defined based on ethnic, cultural, religious, etc., (2) a group in these works is formed based on the interest of its members on a single item, while member users of a group in our work may share the same interests on *many* items, and (3) we model the ontological relationships between groups using *entity-based domain ontology* techniques. Most of the algorithms of these works suffer the following limitation. When they determine the users that have similar rating pattern as the active user, the number of these users is usually much less than the actual number. As a result, the interests (preferences) of many users who have similar interests as the active user may be disregarded. The reason is that most of these algorithms consider *only* item features rated by the active user and co-rated by other users, and users usually rate only a *subset* of an item's features. Our work is also different than online group applications such as Yahoo! Groups because a group in these applications is not formed based on the rating patterns of its members.

A number of Collaborative filtering (CF) algorithms have been proposed. There are two major classes of these algorithms, memory-based and model-based approaches. Memory-based CF (Breese et al.1998) predicts a user's preference based on his/her similarity to other users in the database. On the other hand, model-based CF first learns a descriptive model of the user preferences and then uses it for providing item recommendation. The advantage of the memory-based methods over their model-based alternatives is that less parameters have to be tuned. Existing memory-based CF methods, mainly user-based (Breese et al., 1998; Herlocker et al., 1999; Jin et al., 2004) and item-based (Deshpande et al., 2004; Sarwar et al., 2001) methods, predict new ratings by aggregating rating information from either similar users or items. Given an unknown test rating to be estimated, user-based CF measures similarities between test user and other users, and item-based CF measures similarities between test item and other items. Common interactions that take place in a typical recommendation system include ratings, transactions, feedback data etc. Most systems use one of the following for the acquisition of user knowledge and preferences. Some approaches (Liu et al., 2004) first model and gather user's search history to construct a user profile and then construct a general profile based on the ODP (Open Directory Project, 2009) category hierarchy. Other systems ask users for their preferences *explicitly* as the main post-query method for automatically improving the systems' accuracy of users' need. Alternatively, they may use *implicit feedback* techniques. Implicit feedback techniques unobtrusively draw usage data by tracking and monitoring user behavior without explicit user involvement. Systems such as (Keenoy, 2005; Weihua, 2002) obtain data by exploiting previous search history. Other approaches use machine learning to analyze user data (Webb, 2001).

Many systems structure and standardize *individual* users' profiles and web pages through the use of *ontologies*, or *graphs of concepts*.

The system proposed in (Labrou & Finin, 1999) uses *Yahoo!* (YHO, 2008) as an ontology, and it semantically annotates Web pages via the use of *Yahoo! categories* as descriptors of their content; it uses *Telltale* (Pearce & Miller 1997) as its classifier. Telltale computes the similarity between documents using *n*-grams as index terms. Online portals such as Yahoo.com and About.com provide manually-created online subject hierarchies and a set of Web pages manually associated with each subject designed to organize Web content for easy browsing by end-users. In recent studies (Dalal 2007; Meng et al. 2002), personalization is based on meta-searching: the search query is sent to multiple concurrent basic search engines whose results are then aggregated using a preference vector over those search engines. Carmine and Antonio (2003) proposed an approach to enhance the search engines by retrieving the semantic content of a page and by comparing it to the one specified by the user. Weihua (2002) proposed the integration of agent technology and ontology as a technique to significantly impact the effective use of web services. In *most* of these studies, users have to register personal information beforehand or to provide feedback on relevance or irrelevance of previous search results. In order to incorporate personalization into full-scale Web search tools, the researchers studied the behavior of the users as they interacted with information sources. Several approaches applying data mining techniques to extract usage patterns from Web logs have been proposed. In most of these approaches users are asked to construct their individual profile either manually or semi automatically.

## MODELING SOCIAL GROUPS

We use the term "domain" throughout the paper to mean an area of activity, belief, culture, ethnicity, demography, pursuit, or the like. An *Entity of Singular Domain* (*ESD*) is a group of people sharing common domain interests. For example,

people of ethnic group $E_X$ represents an ESD. We now formalize the concept of *ESD*.

*Definition 1- Entity of Singular Domain (ESD):* An ESD is an aggregation $G$ of individual users, where for each $x , y \in G$ ( $x \neq y$ ): $x$ and $y$ share a common and distinctive culture, ethnicity, religion, demography, language, or the like. That is, $x$ and $y$ share the same interests of *only one* domain group.

We introduce another class of social groups called an *Entity of Multiple Domains (EMD)*, whose size is usually smaller than an ESD. The smaller a social group is, the more granular and specific its interests are. An EMD is formed from an aggregation of people sharing common *multi-domain* interests. Thus, an EMD is formed from the *intersection* of two or more ESDs. For example, the *portion* of ethnic group $E_X$ who follow religion $R_Y$ and live in neighborhood $N_Y$ forms an EMD: the intersection of $E_X \cap R_Y \cap N_Y$. The interests of an EMD are the *union* of the interests of the ESDs forming it. Thus, the interests of an EMD are more specific than the interests of each of the ESDs forming it. To fine-grain a user's query results, DemoFilter outputs a filtered and ranked list of items taking into account the preferences of the user's EMD. We now formalize the concept of *EMD*.

*Definition 2- Entity of Multiple Domains (EMD):* Let $S$ be the set of all *ESDs* that exist. An EMD is an aggregation $G$ of individual users, where: $\forall x \in G$ : $x$ shares the same interests of $\exists s \in S : | s | \geq 2$.

ESDs forming an EMD usually have *class-subclass* relationships, where a subclass has its own properties while inheriting the properties of its superclass(s). We model the ontological relationships between ESDs using *ontology-driven* graphical representation, called *Entity of Singular*

*Domain Graph (ESDGraph)*. In this modeling technique, the relationships between ESDs of the same domain are represented by their ontological relationships. For example, in religion-based domain, the ontological relationships between some of the branches of Buddhism are represented as follows: 1. "Buddhists" 2. "Mahayanists" 3. "Zens": "Zens" ESD is a subclass of "Mahayanists" ESD, which is a subclass of "Buddhists" ESD. ESDs of different domains could be related (linked) by an *interoperable* ESD: for example, ESDs of domains $D_i$ and $D_j$ could be linked by an ESD of domain $D_x$ ($D_x \neq D_i, D_j$). We now formalize the ESDGraph concept.

*Definition 3 - Entity of Singular Domain Graph (ESDGraph):* An ESDGraph is a pair of sets *(V, E)*, where *V* is a finite set of vertices representing ESDs and *E*, the set of edges, is a binary relation on *V*, so that $E S_{T_{12}}^{T_1}$ V ∈ V. Let $\pi[u]$ denote the set of vertices representing ESDs that are immediate subclasses of the ESD represented by vertex $u \in$ V. $E$ = {edge (*u, v*): $u \in$ V and v ∈ π [*u*]}.

We model EMDs using a graphical representation of social links called *Entity of Multi Domain Graph (EMDGraph)*. In an EMDGraph, EMDs are represented by vertices and the ontological relationships between them are represented as edges. Each hierarchical level of the graph contains EMDs formed from the *same number* of ESDs. An EMD in level *i* is formed from *i* + 1 ESDs. An EMD $G_x$ in level *j* and an EMD $G_y$ in level *j* + 1 are connected by an edge, if $G_x$ and $G_y$ contain at least one common ESD. We now formalize the EMDGraph concept.

*Definition 4 - Entity of Multi Domain Graph (EMDGraph):* An EMDGraph is an *ontology-driven* graphical representation of social links. It is a pair of sets *(V, E)*, where *V* is a finite set of vertices representing EMDs and *E*, the set of edges, is a binary relation on *V*, so that $E S_{T_{12}}^{T_1}$ V

∈ V. $E$ = {edge( $v_i$, $v_j$ ): $v_i$, $v_j \in V$ *and ESD* $G_x \in$ $v_i$, $v_j$ *and* $v_i$ *in level n and* $v_j$ *in level n + 1*}. That is, there is an edge ( $v_i, v_j$ ) ∈ $E$ if: (1) there exists at least one common ESD in $v_i$ and $v_j$, and (2) $v_i$ and $v_j$ are located in two adjacent hierarchical levels.

The preferences (interests) of an ESD $G_x$ are stored in DemoFilter's database in the form of a *trigger rule*, called TrigRule( $G_x$ ). In response to a user's query, DemoFilter triggers the trigger rules of the ESDs forming the user's EMD. The trigger rules filter the XML tuples, retaining only those satisfying the preferences of the ESDs. The construct of a trigger rule is formed from the "WHERE" clause of XQuery (Chamberlin et al., 2007). That is, a trigger rule contains predicate Boolean conditions and these conditions are the preferences of an ESD. The following is the form of a trigger rule: {\$b $\Delta L \sqcap P$ and/or/not .... \$b $\Delta$ $L \sqcap P$}. The symbol $\Delta$ denotes either an XQuery's child operator '/' or a descendant operator '//'. The symbol $\sqcap$ denotes an XQuery comparison operator. The letter $P$ denotes a *preference* of an ESD corresponding to the *value* contained in an element labeled $L$ in the XML document.

## SYSTEM ARCHITECTURE

We use the term "system administrator" to mean a person employed to maintain and operate the system. The system administrator predefines ESDs, which are usually defined in publications such as: (1) published government's census and statistical studies (e.g., (U.S. Census Bureau, 2006; Minneapolis Census, 2000)), and (2) published studies conducted by specialized centers belonging to universities and organizations (e.g., (Diversitydata.org et al., 2000; Logan, 2002; Lewis Mumford Center, 2001)). Figure 1 shows the system architecture.

*Figure 1. System architecture*

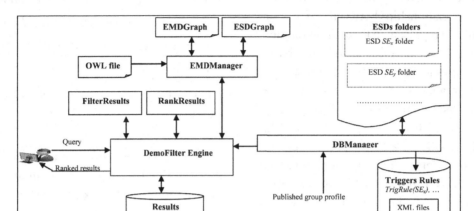

The system administrator inputs an OWL (Bechhofer et al., 2004) file representing a group profile ontology to module *EMDManager*. The module converts the OWL ontologies into an ESDGraph. Using the structure of the ESDGraph, module *EMDManager* determines EMDs and models them in the form of an EMDGraph. Module *DBManager* identifies the preferences of an ESD from published studies. The module will then assign a folder for *each* ESD in a file system database called *ESDs folders*. Each folder contains information such as the name and preferences of an ESD. The preferences of an ESD $SE_x$ are stored in database *Triggers Rules* in the form of trigger rule *TrigRule($SE_x$)*. Database *Triggers Rules* stores also the XML files. Module *FilterResults* filters results *sequentially* by applying the preferences of the ESDs to which the user belongs. After each filtering sequence, the temporary results are stored in *Results Buffer*. Module *RankResults* ranks the filtered results, based on the *weighted* preferences of the user's EMD.

## CONSTRUCTING GROUP PROFILE ONTOLOGY

The creation of group profile ontology is done semi-automatically. DemoFilter prompts the system administrator with two text fields, one representing a class ESD and the other its immediate-subclass. After the system is informed of each two ESDs having class-immediate subclass relationship, it creates a group profile ontology in the form of an OWL ontology (Bechhofer et al., 2004). The OWL file defines the relations between ESDs as ontological classes. Thereafter, DemoFilter converts the OWL file into *ESDGraph*. In an ESDGraph, each ESD in the OWL file is represented by a vertex, and each *class-subClassOf* relation is represented by a directed edge. That is, for each two vertices $u$ and $v$, there is an edge $(u, v)$ in the ESDGraph if $v$ is a subClassOf of $u$ in the OWL file.

DemoFilter internally represents an ESDGraph $=(V, E)$, as a collection of *adjacency lists*. An adjacency-list representation of ESDGraph is an array *Adj*, which consists of $|V|$ lists, one for each vertex in $V$. For each vertex $u \in V$, the adjacency list *Adj[u]* contains all the vertices $v$ such that there is an edge $(u, v) \in E$. The vertices in an adjacency list are typically stored in an *arbitrary order*. DemoFilter constructs an adjacency list from an input OWL file using SPARQL (Prud'hommeaux et al., 2008). SPARQL is a query language for pattern matching against RDF graphs. Variables in the RDF terms will be substituted in the CONSTRUCT part to populate a 2-dimensional array storing the adjacency lists.

*Figure 2. OWL ontology representing USA-based group profile ontology*

```
<owl:Class   rdf:ID = "Ex">
    <rdfs:domain> ethnicity </rdfs:domain>
    <owl:intersecionOf  rdf:parseType = "Collection">
            <owl:Class   rdf:about = "# Nx"/>
            <owl:Class   rdf:about = "# Ny "/>
            <owl:Class   rdf:about = "# Rx "/>
            <owl:Class   rdf:about = "# Ry "/>
      </owl:intersecionOf>
</owl:Class>
<owl:Class   rdf:ID = "Ey">
    <rdfs:domain> ethnicity </rdfs:domain>
    <owl:intersecionOf  rdf:parseType = "Collection">
            <owl:Class  rdf:about = "# Nx"/>
            <owl:Class  rdf:about = "# Ry "/>
      </owl:intersecionOf>
</owl:Class>
<owl:Class   rdf:ID = "MPLS">
       <rdfs:domain> region </rdfs:domain>
       <rdfs:subClassOf  rdf:resource="#MN"/>
</owl:Class>
<owl:Class   rdf:ID = "Nx">
       <rdfs:domain> region </rdfs:domain>
       <rdfs:subClassOf  rdf:resource="#MPLS"/>
</owl:Class>
<owl:Class rdf:ID = "Ny">
       <rdfs:domain> region </rdfs:domain>
       <rdfs:subClassOf  rdf:resource="#MPLS "/>
</owl:Class>
```

*Example 1:* We use as a running example throughout the chapter USA-based ESDs of four domains: (1) *ethnic* groups $E_X$ and $E_Y$, (2) *religious* groups $R_X$ and $R_Y$, (3) *national origin* group $O_X$, (4) *region-based* groups $N_X$ and $N_Y$ (the people living in *neighborhoods* $N_X$ and $N_Y$ respectively), and (5) *region-based* groups *MPLS* and *MN* (the people living in the *city* of Minneapolis and in the state of Minnesota respectively). $N_X$ and $N_Y$ are neighborhoods in *MPLS*. Ethnic group $E_Y$ lives in $N_X$, and follows religion $R_Y$. Part of $E_X$ follows religion $R_X$, and the other follows $R_Y$. Figure. 2 shows an OWL file defining the relationships between the ESDs. Figure 3 shows an ESDGraph constructed from the OWL ontology in Figure 2.

An EMD is denoted by the *set* of the ESDs forming it. DemoFilter analyzes the structure of an ESDGraph to identify *all possible* EMDs that

exist because of the interrelations between ESDs. EMDs are constructed as follows: (1) the intersection of each two ESDs connected by an edge and belonging to different domains forms an EMD, and (2) all unique combinations of the EMDs resulted from construction 1 are enumerated; if a combination does not contain two or more ESDs with the same domain, the intersection of its ESDs forms an EMD. Figure 4 shows an EMDGraph constructed from the ESDGraph in Figure 3.

We built an Algorithm called ConstructEMD-Graph (see Figure 5), which constructs an EMD-Graph. The Algorithm identifies all possible EMDs that exist because of the interrelations between ESDs. The input to the Algorithm is an ESDGraph represented by the adjacency-list *Adj*. The algorithm works as follows. The elements of each set initialized in line 1 are EMDs located in the same

*Figure 3. An ESDGraph depicting the relationships between the USA-based ESDs used in the running example*

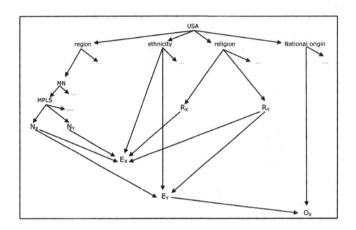

*Figure 4. An EMDGraph constructed from the ESDGraph in Figure 3.*

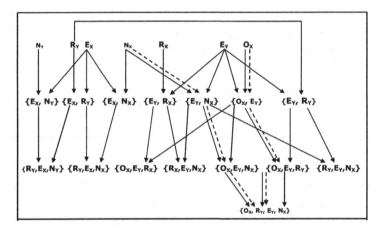

*Figure 5. Algorithm ConstructEMDGraph*

**ConstructEMDGraph {**

1. Initialize to null sets *level$_1$, level$_2$, ...*

2. for each two ESDs $v, u \in Adj$ {    //*Adj* is an adjacency list representing a ESDraph

3.     if ($v \in Adj[u]$)

4.         Insert EMD { $v \cap u$ } in set *level$_1$*

5.     } //end for

6. for each two EMDs $V_i$ , $V_j \in level_1$ {

7.     if (there exist a ESD $S \in V_i, V_j$)

8.         if (each $v \in V_i$, $u \in V_j$ (where $v, u \neq S$) *DifDom* ($v, u$) )

*hierarchical level* of an EMDGraph. Lines 2 - 5: If ESDs $v$ and $u$ are adjacent in the ESDGraph ($v \in$ Adj[$u$]), their intersection forms an EMD, which is located in hierarchical level 1 of the EMDGraph. Lines 6-11: Function *DifDom* takes two ESDs as input and returns true if they belong to different domains. If EMDs $V_i$, $V_j \in$ level$_1$ share a common ESD, and the rest of the ESDs forming them have different domains, then their intersection forms an EMD in level 2. Lines 12-18: lines 6-11 are repeated with the consideration that $V_i, V_j \in$ level$_{2+k}$ (where $k = 0, 1, \ldots$) until no more EMD can be formed.

DemoFilter determines the users' EMDs by *traversing* the paths of the EMDGraph starting from the vertices representing the user's ESDs. The user's smallest EMD is located in the *intersection* of the *longest* paths originated from user's ESDs vertices. If the paths originated from $n$ ESDs vertices, the user's smallest EMD is usually formed from $m$ ESDs, where $m > n$ due to the interrelations between ESDs. We now present example 2 to illustrate how a user's smallest EMD is located.

*Example 2:* Consider a user whose national origin is $O_X$ and lives in neighborhood $N_X$. Using the EMDGraph in Figure 4, DemoFilter can determine that the user's smallest EMD is {$O_X$, $R_Y$, $E_Y$, $N_X$}. The EMD is located in the intersection of the *longest* paths originated from the root vertics $N_X$ and $O_X$ (the paths are marked with dashed arrows in Figure 4). As can be seen, the system started the search using only two ESDs and it could locate an EMD formed from four ESDs.

## DETERMINING THE PREFERENCES OF ESDS

The preferences of an ESD can be obtained from published studies such as: (1) published articles and books, (2) published studies conducted by organizations, and (3) specialized centers belonging to universities. For this study, we collected preference data as follows. We selected 20 US neighborhoods known for their ethnic and religious diversity. Each neighborhood represents a region-based ESD. From the combined residents of the 20 neighborhoods, those who belong to a same ethnicity represent an ethnic-based ESD, and those who have the same religious beliefs represent a religious-based ESD. We obtained the preference data of the ESDs living in the 20 neighborhoods from published studies as follows:

- Cultural and ethnic-driven preferences: preferences could be influenced by culture and ethnic-driven tastes. We collected the ethnic-driven dietary and preference data of the ESDs from publications such as (Anderson, 2005; Harris, 1998; Nabhan, 2004; Bryant et al., 2003; Paul, 1986; Kittler, 1995; TESORO, 2001; Butlersguild, 2008; FAQ Archives, 2008; Fieldhouse, 2005). For example, we identified "spicy flavor" as one of the food ingredient preferences of one of the ethnic groups.

- Religious-driven preferences and restrictions: religion could a determinant of food choices and dietary practices. We collected the religious-driven preferences and restrictions from publications such as (Tesoro, 2001; FAQ Archives, 2008; Kittler, 1995). For example, we identified "no pork-related products" in food ingredients as one one of the religious restrictions of one of the ESDs because the teachings of its religion dictates that.

- Economic-driven preferences: the economic characteristics of a neighborhood, region, or an ethnic group could influence preferences. We collected the median income data of the neighborhoods and ethnicities as well as statistical data of income-based preferences from published studies such as (Minneapolis Census, 2000; U.S. Census Bureau, 2009; Diversitydata.org and Harvard School of Public Health, 2000; Diversitydata.org and Harvard School of Public Health, 2007; Logan, 2002; Logan et al., 2001).

- Weather-driven preferences: preferences could be influenced by a region's dominant weather. We collected this data from publications such as (Weather.com/autos, 2008; HM USA Travel Guide). For example, we identified that the residents of Minnesota State prefers cars with snow-proof features.

First, we need to decide on the number and quality of the publications that we will be using. The more publications used the more accurate results obtained. We also need to select ones issued by reputable sources. For maintaining the integrity of relativity, all rival *item features* and *characteristics* should be rated using the same publications.

- *Notation 1 – An item feature:* We use the term "feature" to refer to the name of a data element in an XML document of preference-driven products. A feature reveals a distinctive and essential aspect of an item.
- *Notation 2 – A feature characteristic:* We use the term "characteristic" to refer to a data item (value) describing a particular data element (item feature) in an XML document. For example, "Ford" is a characteristic of item feature "Make" in the cars XML document. That is, a characteristic is a property which characterizes an item feature.

Preferences on an item's features and characteristics obtained from publications are represented as vectors of weights scaled between 0 and 1. A feature (or a characteristic) is rated based on the *consensus* of publications on its importance to the ESD. Let $f_n$ be a feature and $c_x$ be one of its characteristics. The overall preference weight on characteristic $c_x$ is computed based on: (1) the

ratio of the weight of $f_n$ to the weights of the other features, and (2) the ratio of the weight of $c_x$ to the weights of the other characteristics of $f_n$. Equation 1 computes the normalized preference weight $\bar{w}_{c_x}$ of characteristic $c_x$.

$$\bar{w}_{c_x} = w_{f_n} \times w_{c_x} \qquad (1)$$

$$w_{f_n} = \frac{p_{f_n}}{\sum_{f_i \in F} p_{f_i}} \text{ and } w_{c_x} = \frac{p_{c_x}}{\sum_{c_{x'} \in f_n} p_{c_{x'}}}$$

$w_{f_n}$ - the weight of feature $f_n$ with respect to other features.

$w_{c_x}$ - the weight of characteristic $c_x$ with respect to the other characteristics of feature $f_n$.

$p_{f_n}$ - the percentage of publications recommending feature $f_n$

$F$ - the set of all features.

$p_{c_x}$ - the percentage of publications recommending characteristic $c_x$.

$p_{c_{x'}}$ - the percentage of publications recommending a characteristic $c_{x'}$ of feature $f_n$.

The preferences of an ESD are the characteristics whose weights are equal to or greater than $\frac{n^p}{n}$, where: $n$ is the number of all characteristics and $p$ is a parameter that can be set to a value in the range 0 to 1. These preferences will be stored in the database in the form of trigger rules.

*Example 3*: Consider the XML document fragment in Figure 6. Let us determine the *car* preferences of the residents of neighborhood $N_x$

(recall Figure 3). While some of the preferences of $N_x$ are specific to the neighborhood, others are shared with the people living in the state of MN. According to published surveys, 68% of Minnesotans prefer cars with snow-proof features[1] and 61% prefer fuel-efficient cars[2]. Another survey shows that 76% of the residents of $N_x$ prefer cost-efficient cars[3]. The *characteristics* of these

three features are recommended by publications, as follows:

- *Snow-proof feature*: 25 automobile publications (e.g., (Casagrande, 2000)), recommend the following snow-proof characteristics:

*Figure 6. A fragment of cars.xml document*

```
<cars>

    <car  ID = 10520>

        <make> Ford </make>

        <body-style> SUV</body-style>

        <color> black </color>

        <year> 2007</year>

        <price> 19000</price>

        <fuel-type> ethanol flexible-fuel </fuel>

        <MPG> 34< /MPG>

        <safety-feature>ABS  brakes </safety-feature>

        <wheel-drive> 4WD </wheel-drive>

    </car>

    <car  ID = 10884>

        <make> Chevrolet </make>

        <body-style> SUV</body-style>

        <color> red </color>

        <year> 2008</year>

        <price> 21000</price>

        <fuel-type> gasoline </fuel-type>

        <MPG> 34< /MPG>

        <safety-feature>automatic break</safety-feature>
```

*Table 1. Preference weights on car characteristics for neighborhood $N_x$*

| Characteristic | ESC | 4WD | Price $\leq$ **$18000** | Price range from $18000 to $24000 | ethanol flexible-fuel | hybrid-electric | MPG > 34 |
|---|---|---|---|---|---|---|---|
| $w_{f_n}$ | 0.33 | 0.33 | 0.37 | 0.37 | 0.30 | 0.30 | 0.30 |
| $w_{c_x}$ | 0.63 | 0.38 | 0.70 | 0.30 | 0.50 | 0.14 | 0.36 |
| $\overline{w}_{c_x}$ | 0.21 | 0.12 | 0.26 | 0.11 | 0.15 | 0.04 | 0.11 |

- ◦ 13 of the publications recommend cars with Electronic Stability Control (ESC).
- ◦ 5 of the publications recommend four-wheel drive (4WD) cars.
- ◦ 7 of the publications recommend both ESC and 4WD.

Thus, 80% of the publications recommend ESC and 48% recommend 4WD.

- *Cost-efficient feature:* According to published census surveys (e.g., (Minneapolis census, 2000)), the median income of neighborhood $N_x$ is $60000. Seven consumer and economic surveys (e.g., (Alwitt, 1996)) found that people prefer buying cars that cost equal or less than 30% of their median income. Accordingly, most of the residents of $N_x$ would prefer buying cars that cost $18000 or less. However, other three different surveys found that people prefer buying cars that cost between 30% and 40% of their median income. Accordingly, most of the residents of $N_x$ would prefer buying cars that cost between $18000 and $24000.

Thus, the residents of $N_x$ would prefer cars that cost $18000 or less according to 70% of the surveys, and would prefer cars that cost $18000-$24000 according to 30% of the surveys.

- *Fuel-efficient feature:* 30 fuel-economy guides (e.g., (U.S. Department of Energy, 2007)) recommend the following characteristics for fuel efficiency:
- ◦ 12 of the guides recommend ethanol flexible-fuel cars.
- ◦ 5 of the guides recommend hybrid-electric cars.
- ◦ 7 of the guides recommend cars whose Mileage per Gallon (MPG) is higher than 34.
- ◦ 6 of the guides recommend *both* ethanol flexible-fuel cars and cars whose MPG is higher than 34.

Thus, 60% of the guides recommend ethanol flexible-fuel cars, 43% recommend cars whose MPG is higher than 34, and 17% recommend hybrid-electric cars.

Table 1 shows the preference weights ($\overline{w}_{c_x}$) on the 7 characteristics after applying Equation 1. The characteristics whose weights $\geq \dfrac{n^p}{n}$ (by

*Figure 7. CarTrigRule($N_x$)*

```
CarTrigRule(Nx) {    $b/safety-feature = "ESC"    and    $b/Price < = 18000    }
```

*Figure 8. (a) Algorithm FilterResults (b) Subroutine RefineSelection*

```
FilterResults (Q, V_Y)  {
1.    SItems ← GetInitialResults(Q)
2.    for each ESD G_x ∈ V_Y
3.        SItems ← RefineSelection(G_x , SItems)
    }
                          (a)
RefineSelection(G_x , SItems) {
1.    for (i = 1 → | SItems |)  {
2.        CurrentID ← SItems [i]
3.        for      $b in doc("xml doc")//item
4.        where    $b/@ID = CurrentID  and  TrigRule (G_x)
6.        return   string ($b/@ID)  }
    }
                          (b)
```

setting $p$ to 0.1), which are considered preferences of neighborhood $N_x$ are: (1) ESC, and (2) price $\leq \$16200$. These preferences will be stored in the database in the form of trigger rule CarTrigRule($N_x$) as shown in Figure 7.

## ANSWERING QUERIES

In response to a user's query, DemoFilter first constructs an equivalent XQuery query (Chamberlin et al., 2007). Then, it identifies the user's EMD. Finally, it filters and ranks the initial results based on the preferences of the user's EMD.

### Identifying the User's EMD

To identify the user's smallest EMD, DemoFilter needs to identify at least one of the ESDs to which the user belongs. The more ESDs identified, the smaller in size an EMD can be identified by the system. DemoFilter adopts the following approaches for identifying users' ESDs: (1) it employs lookup databases provided by (IP2Location, 2008; Maponics, 2008) to *implicitly* identify *all* region-based ESDs (by translating users' IP addresses to US zip codes, neighborhoods, cities, and states), (2) it encourages (but does *not* require) users to reveal some of their *non region-based* ESDs, and (3) it identifies some of the users'

non region-based ESDs *implicitly*, by analyzing the structure of the ESDGraph[4]. After identifying the ESDs, DemoFilter determines the users' EMDs using the technique described previously in subsection Modeling EMDs.

## Filtering and Ranking Results

DemoFilter uses Algorithm *FilterResults* (see Figure 8-a) to filter results based on the preferences of the user's EMD. The Algorithm employs recursive querying (*rule-chaining* mechanism) to sequentially optimize (filter) results. In each optimization sequence, the results are filtered based on the preferences of one of the ESDs forming the user's EMD. That is, in each optimization sequence the Algorithm triggers trigger rule *TrigRule($G_x$)*, where $G_x$ is one of the ESDs forming the user's EMD. Recursive querying allows a query to query the results produced by a previous application of itself and allows the computation of *transitive closure* of an XML document.

The inputs to Algorithm *FilterResults* are query $Q$ (which represents the user's initial preferences) and the user's EMD $V_Y$. In line 1 of the Algorithm, function *GetInitialResults* uses an XQuery search engine to return the *IDs* of the items, which satisfy the conditions of query $Q^5$. These *IDs* will be stored in a set called *SItems*. Line 3 filters the *IDs* in set *SItems* recursively by

*Figure 9. A fragment of groceries.xml document*

```
<groceries>
    <grocery  ID = "200004">
        <Type> soup </Type>
        < brand> Progresso </ brand>
        <flavor> spicy </flavor>
        <ingredients>  vegetables, rice, pork  </ingredients>
    </grocery>
    <grocery  ID = "200015">
        <Type> soup </Type>
        < brand> Campbell </brand>
        <flavor> regular </flavor>
        <ingredients>vegetables, rice, no pork-related products</ingredients>
    </grocery>
    <grocery   ID = "200027">
        <Type> soup </Type>
        < brand> Campbell </ brand>
        <flavor> spicy </flavor>
        <ingredients>vegetables, rice, no pork-related products</ingredients>
```

calling subroutine *RefineSelection* (see Figure 8-b). Only the *IDs* of the items satisfying the preferences of ESD $G_x \in V_y$ are retained in *each* recursion. Line 1 of subroutine *RefineSelection* iterates over the *IDs* in set *SItems*. In each iteration, line 2 stores one of the *IDs* in a variable called *CurrentID*. Lines 3-6 are XQuery's FLWOR expressions. The "where" clause searches for items in the XML document, which satisfy the following two conditions: (1) their *IDs* match the *ID* in variable *CurrentID*, and (2) they satisfy the preferences that are triggered by trigger rule *TrigRule(Gₓ)*.

After result items are *filtered*, they will be *ranked* based on the rated *scores* of the preference vector *D* of the user's EMD. The score of an item is defined as the summation of the normalized weights of vector *D* on the features of the item. Thus, the score $T_x$ of an item is defined as: $T_x = \sum_{i=1}^{N} d_i$, where $d_i \in D$, $D = \{d_1, d_2, ..., d_N\}$, and *N* is the number of weighted features. Items whose scores are high are ranked higher.

We now present example 4 to illustrate Algorithm *FilterResults*. The example simulates an online grocery system targeting the USA-based ESDs of our running example. The grocery system uses the fragment of XML document shown in Figure 9.

*Example 4:* Consider that a user is looking for canned soup of brand Campbell. DemoFilter would construct an equivalent XQuery query *Q* as shown

*Figure 10. (a): Query Q. (b) and (c) Subroutine RefineSelection after the first and second calls respectively*

```
Q:                                              RefineSelection(E_Y, SItems) {
for $b in                                       1. for (i = 1; i >= 3; i++) {
        doc("grocery.xml")//grocery             2.    CurrentID = SItems[i]
where    $b/Type = "soup"                        3.    for $b in doc("grocery.xml")//grocery
  and    $b/brand ="Campbell"                    4.    where    $b/@ID = CurrentID
return   string ($b/@ID)                         5.      and    $b/ flavor = "spicy"
                                                 6.    return    string ($b/@ID)
                                                      }
                                                 }                        (b)
                        (a)
```

```
    RefineSelection(Rx, SItems)  {
1. for (i = 1;  i >= 2; i++) {
2.    CurrentID  =  SItems[i]
3.    for       $b in doc("grocery.xml")//grocery
4.    where   $b/@ID = CurrentID
5.      and contains($b/ingredients, " no pork- related products")
6.    return    string ($b/@ID)
      }
}                                               (c)
```

in Figure 10 (a) Consider that DemoFilter identified the user's EMD as $\{E_y, R_x\}$. Line 1 of Algorithm *FilterResults* would return the following set of canned soups' IDs: *SItems* = {200015, 200027, 200044, 200058, 200063}. Line 3 will call subroutine *RefineSelection* two times, as follows:

- *First call*: The inputs to the subroutine are ESD $E_y$ and set *SItems*. The WHERE clause will trigger *FoodTrigRule(E_y)* (see Figure 11). After the substitutions, the subroutine will become as shown in Figure 10-b. From the IDs in set *SItems*, the subroutine will return the subset: *SItems* = {200027, 200058, 200063}.

- *Second call*: The inputs to the subroutine are ESD $R_x$ and set *SItems*. The WHERE clause will trigger *FoodTrigRule(R_x)* (see Figure 12). After the substitutions, the subroutine will become as shown in Figure 10-c. From the IDs in set *SItems*, the subroutine will return the subset: *SItems* = {200027, 200058}.

*Figure 11. FoodTrigRule(E_y)*

```
FoodTrigRule(E_y) { $b/flavor = "spicy"  }
```

*Figure 12. FoodTrigRule(R_x)*

```
FoodTrigRule(R_x) {contains ($b/ingredients, "no pork-

related products")
```

## EXPERIMENTAL RESULTS

We implemented DemoFilter in Java and ran it on an Intel(R) Core(TM)2 Dup CPU processor, with a CPU of 2.1 GHz and 3 GB of RAM, under Windows Vista. A demo of the DemoFilter system, running on 1000 MB grocery data and 1000 MB car data, is available at: http://dbse1.uta.edu/~kamal/?action=home. We asked 18 students at the University of Texas-Arlington to evaluate the DemoFilter grocery demo system. The students belong to two different ethnic backgrounds and three ancestry of origins. Some of them consider religion is irrelevant and the others follow two different religions. We asked each of them to give us two lists of items. The first containing a list of 10 canned food items (from the brands used by DemoFilter) ranked based on the subject's own preferences. The second containing the top 10 canned food items ranked by DemoFilter based on the preferences of the subject's ethnic, religious, and/or national origin groups.

### Search Effectiveness Evaluation

Users usually want to know *only* the initially retrieved elements (at lower ranks). We evaluated the search effectiveness of DemoFilter on initially retrieved elements, by comparing it with Google Base (Google Base Protocol; Google Base Data Feed) and with Oracle XML DB (Oracle). Our objective is to have knowledge of DemoFil-

ter's *extent* of improvement over Google Base and Oracle XML DB as a result of considering group profiling. We generated 1000 MBs grocery.xml document using ToXgene (ToXgene, 2005). We also generated grocery queries to be run against the grocery.xml document (see Table 2 for a sample of the queries and how they were constructed). We ran all of the grocery queries against the document, using DemoFilter, Google Base, and Oracle XML DB. We computed the *Mean Average Precision (MAP)* at variable ranks for each of the three systems. For each query submitted to DemoFilter, we revealed to the system some of the ESDs of the subject (student), for whom the query was constructed[6]. Let $\{t_1, t_2, ..., t_{k_n}\} \in S$ be the set of relevant items for a subject need[7]. Let $R_{nm}$ be the set of ranked retrieval results[8] from the top result until item $t_m$. Then, MAP can be computed as shown in Equation 3.

$$MAP(S) = \frac{1}{|S|} \sum_{n=1}^{|S|} \frac{1}{k_n} \sum_{m=1}^{k_n} \text{Precision}(R_{nm})$$

(3)

We computed MAP at ranks 5 (top 5 answers), 10, and 15. Table 3 shows the overall MAPs. As the table shows, DemoFilter achieved much higher precision, especially at rank 5. The table shows also that the MAPs of the three search engines decrease as the rank increases.

*Table 2. The type of information collected from the subjects and the queries simulating their initial preferences*

| Subject # | Ethnicity | Ancestry Origin | Religion | Subject's weights on features' characteristics ranged from 1-10. **Flavor, ingredient** | Query constructed from basic features of canned food to simulate the subject's initial preferences |
|-----------|-----------|-----------------|----------|------------------------------------------------------------------------------------------|-----------------------------------------------------------------------------------------------------|
| 1 | ... | ... | ... | Chili pepper (8) no meat (10) rice starch (4) | Looking for 15.25 ounce canned soup brand Healthy Choice |
| 2 | ... | ... | ... | Organic spices (5) no pork (10) | Looking for 10.75 ounce canned soup brand Progresso |

*Table 3. MAPs using the grocery queries*

| Rank | DemoFilter | Google Base | Oracle XML DB |
|---|---|---|---|
| 5 | 0.68 | 0.23 | 0.26 |
| 10 | 0.57 | 0.14 | 0.19 |
| 15 | 0.34 | 0.10 | 0.09 |

## User Evaluation of Search Effectiveness

We measured the average *distance* between the two lists obtained from each of the students using the Euclidean distance measure shown in Equation 2.

$$d(\sigma_u, \sigma_s) = \sum_{x \in X} |\sigma_u(x) - \sigma_s(x)| \qquad (2)$$

$\sigma_u \in [0,1]^{|X|}$ - the list of items ranked by subject $u$.

$\sigma_s \in [0,1]^{|X|}$ - the list of items ranked by Demo-Filter.

$X$ - the set of items.

$\sigma_u(x)$ and $\sigma_s(x)$ - the *position* of item $x \in X$ in the lists $\sigma_u$ and $\sigma_s$ respectively (a ranking of a set of $n$ items is represented as a permutation of the integers 1, 2,. . ., $n$).

Figure 13 shows the distances. The average distance is 12.5, which indicates "closeness" between the lists ranked by the subjects and the lists ranked by the DemoFilter system.

## CONCLUSION

We presented a novel approach to XML search that leverages group information to return more relevant query answers for users. We proposed an XML-based recommender system, called DemoFilter. It is a type of collaborative information filtering system, and is based on the combination of search-by-query and recommendations. In the framework of DemoFilter, a user profile is inferred from the profile of the social groups to which the user belongs. Social groups are characterized based on demographic, ethnic, cultural, religious, age, or other characteristics. DemoFilter simplifies the personalization process by: (1) pre-defining and identifying the preferences of various categories of social groups, and (2) filtering and ranking results

*Figure 13. Distances between the lists ranked by the subjects and the lists ranked by DemoFilter*

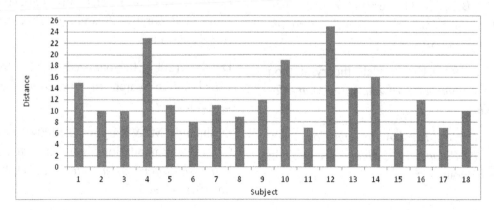

based on the preferences of the social groups to which the user belongs. DemoFilter can be used for various practical applications, such as Internet or other businesses that market preference-driven products.

We experimentally evaluated the search effectiveness of DemoFilter by comparing it with Google Base (Google Base Protocol; Google Base Data Feed) and with Oracle XML DB (Oracle). The experimental results showed that DemoFilter achieved much higher precision than the two search engines on initially retrieved elements. We also conducted user evaluation to measure the closeness of DemoFilter's recommendations to users' preferences. Results showed significant "closeness" between item lists ranked by subjects and lists ranked by the DemoFilter system.

To the best of our knowledge, inferring a user profile from profiles of groups defined based on ethnic, cultural, religious, etc. was never researched in any recommendation-based study. It is an area that could further simplify personalized search and enhance search results. We demonstrated in this study that the methods we propose can be effective and efficient retrieval mechanisms. In future work, we will investigate the acquisition of user characteristics (e.g., user profile) dynamically and implicitly without involving the user.

## REFERENCES

Aimeur, E., Brassard, G., Fernandez, J., & Mani Onana, F. (n.d) *Privacy preserving demographic filtering*. In Proc. SAC'06.

Allen, R.B., (1990). User models: theory, method and Practice. *International Journal of Man–Machine Studies*.

Alwitt, L. (1996). *The Low-Income Consumer: Adjusting the Balance of Exchange*. New York: Sage Publications, Inc.

Anderson, E. (2005). *Everyone eats: understanding food and culture*. New York: New York University Press.

Archives, F. A. Q. (2008). *Religion and Dietary Practices*. Available: http://www.faqs.org/nutrition/Pre-Sma/Religion-and-Dietary-Practices.html

Bechhofer, S., Harmelen, F., Hendler, J., & Patel-Schneider, P.(2004). OWL Web Ontology Language Reference, W3C Recommendation.

Breese, J., Heckerman, D., & Kadie, C. (1998). Empirical analysis of predictive algorithms for collaborative Filtering. In *Proc. the 14th Conference on Uncertainty in Artificial Intelligence*, pp. 43–52.

Bryant, C., & Dewait, K. (2003). *The Cultural Feast: An Introduction to Food and Society*. CA: Thomson Wadsworth.

Butlersguild (2008). *Food Restrictions*. The International Guild of Professional Butlers, Netherlands. Available: http://www.butlersguild.com/ index. php?subject=103

Carmine, C., Antonio, P.(n.d). An Intelligent Search Agent System for Semantic Information Retrieval on the Internet. *WIDM'03*

Casagrande, K. (2000). *Recipes for Car Care: Guide to Auto Health*. Delmar Cengage Learning.

Chamberlin, D., Fankhauser, P., Florescu, D. & Robie, J.(2007). *XML Query Use Cases, W3C Working Draft 2007*.

DALAL. M. (2007). Personalized Social & Real-Time Collaborative Search. *In Proceedings of WWW*, Canada.

Dalal, M. (2007). Personalized Social & Real-Time Collaborative Search. *In Proceedings of WWW*, Canada, 2007.

Deshpande, M., & Karypis, G. (2004). Item-based top-n recommendation algorithms. *ACM Transactions on Information Systems*, 22(1), 143–177. doi:10.1145/963770.963776

DiversityData.org & Harvard School of Public Health (2000). *Exposure to Neighborhood Median Income by Race/Ethnicity and Income*

DiversityData.org & Harvard School of Public Health (2007). *Profiles by Metro Area.* Available: http://diversitydata.sph.harvard.edu/index.jsp

Fieldhouse, P. (2005). *Food, Justice, and the Baha'i Faith.* PhD Dissertation. Available: http://bahai-library.com/ file.php5?file=fieldhouse_food_justice&language=

Goldberg, D., Nichols, D., Oki, B. M., & Terry, D. (1992). Using collaborative filtering to weave an information tapestry. *Communications of the ACM, 35*(12), 61–70. doi:10.1145/138859.138867

Google Base Data Feed. (n.d.) Available: http://base.google.com/ support/bin/answer.py?answer=59461&hl=en

Google Base Protocol.(n.d) Available: http://code.google.com/ apis/base/docs/2.0/ developers_guide_protocol.html

Harris, M. (1998). *Good to Eat: Riddles of Food and Culture.* Long Grove, IL: Waveland Press.

Herlocker, J., Konstan, J. A., Terveen, L., & Riedl, J. (2004). Evaluating Collaborative Filtering Recommender Systems. *ACM Transactions on Information Systems, 22*(1). doi:10.1145/963770.963772

Herlocker, J. L., Konstan, J., Borchers, A., & Riedl, J. (1999). *An algorithmic framework for performing collaborative filtering.* In Proc. of SIGIR.

Herlocker, J. L., Konstan, J. A., & Riedl, J. (2002). *Explaining Collaborative Filtering Recommendations.* Proc. of the ACM Conference on Computer Supported Cooperative Work, 2002

HM USA TRAVEL GUIDE. (n.d) *Weather per state.* Available: http://www.hm-usa.com/ climate/index.html

Hofmann, T. (2003). *Collaborative filtering via Gaussian probabilistic latent semantic analysis.* Proceedings of the 26th International ACM SIGIR Conference on Research and Development in Information Retrieval

Huang, Z., Chung, W., & Chen, H. (2004). A graph model for e-commerce recommender systems. *Journal of the American Society for Information Science and Technology, 55*(3), 259–274. doi:10.1002/asi.10372

Jin, R., Chai, J., & Si. (2008). L. *An automatic weighting scheme for collaborative filtering.* In Proc. of SIGIR'04. IP2Location. User manual, Java component. http://www.ip2location.com/docs/IP2Location_ Java_User_Manual.pdf

Kalles, D., Papagelis, A., & Zaroliagis, C. (2003). *Algorithmic aspects of web intelligent systems. Web Intelligence* (pp. 323–345). Berlin: Springer.

Keenoy, K., & Levene, M. (2005). Lecture Notes in Computer Science: *Vol. 3169. Personalization of Web Search* (pp. 201–228). doi:10.1007/11577935_11

Kittler, P. (1995). *Food and culture in America: A nutrition handbook.* Redding, CA: West Publishing.

Labrou, Y., & Finin, T. (1999). Yahoo! As an Ontology – Using Yahoo! Categories To Describe Documents. In *Proceedings of the 8th International Conference on Information Knowledge Management (CIKM), 180-187.*

Lewis Mumford Center. (2001). *Ethnic Diversity Grows, Neighborhood Integration Lags Behind.* Lewis Mumford Center, University at Albany.

Liu, F., Yu, C., & Meng, W. (2004). *Personalized Web Search For Improving Retrieval Effectiveness.* IEEE TKDE.

Liu, F., Yu, C., & Meng, W. (2004). *Personalized Web Search For Improving Retrieval Effectiveness.* IEEE TKDE.

Logan, J. Stowell, J. & Vesselinov, E. (2001). *From Many Shores: Asians in Census 2000*. Lewis Mumford Center, University at Albany.

Logan, J.(October 2002). *Separate and Unequal: The Neighborhood Gap for Blacks and Hispanics in Metropolitan America*. Lewis Mumford Center, University at Albany.

Maponics (2008). *Neighborhood to ZIP Code Correlation Data*. Available: http://www.maponics.com/ Neighborhood_ZIP_Codes/ neighborhood_zip_codes.html

Meng, W., Yu, C., & Liu, K. L. (2002). Building Efficient and Effective Metasearch Engines. [CSUR]. *ACM Computing Surveys, 34*(1), 48–89. doi:10.1145/505282.505284

Meng, W., Yu, C., & Liu, K. L. (2002). Building Efficient and Effective Metasearch Engines. *ACM Computing Surveys, 34*(1), 48–89. doi:10.1145/505282.505284

Minneapolis Census. (2000). *Selected Economic Characteristics by Neighborhood, city of Minneapolis*. Available: http://www.ci.minneapolis.mn.us/ citywork/planning/Census2000/ maps/economic/

Nabhan, G. (2004). *Why Some Like It Hot: Food, Genes, and Cultural Diversity*. Washington, D.C.: Island Press.

O'Connor, P., Höpken, W., & Gretzel, U. Dynamic Packaging using a Cluster-based Demographic Filtering Approach. In *Proc. the International Conference in Innsbruck, Austria, 2008*. Oracle: Oracle XML DB. (n.d) Retrieved from: //www.oracle.com/technology/ tech/xml/xmldb/index.html

Open Directory Project. (2009). Available: http://dmoz.org.

Paul, F. (1986). *Food and Nutrition: Customs and Culture*. London: Croom Helm.

Pazzani, M. (1999). A Framework for Collaborative, Content-Based and Demographic Filtering. *Artificial Intelligence Review, 13*(5-6), 393–408. doi:10.1023/A:1006544522159

Pearce, C., & Miller, E. (1997). The TellTale dynamic hypertext environment: Approaches to scalability. In *Advances in Intelligence Hypertext, Lecture Notes in Computer Science. Springer-Verlag, 1326, 109-130*.

Prud'Hommeaux, E. & Seaborne, A. (2008). *SPARQL Query Language for RDF W3C Recommendation 2008*.

Sarwar, B., Karypis, G., Konstan, J., & Riedl, J. Item-based collaborative filtering recommendation algorithms. In *Proc. of the WWW Conference, 2001*.

Tesoro, E. (2001). *Religious Determinants of Food Choices*. Available: http://www.eat-online.net/english/ education/religion_and_food/ religious_determinants.htm#References

ToXgene (2005). *ToXgene - the ToX XML Data Generator*

U.S. Census Bureau (2006). *USA Counties*

U.S. Census Bureau. (2009). State & County QuickFacts. Available: http://quickfacts.census.gov/ qfd/states/48/4827000.html

U.S. Department of Energy (2007). *Fuel Economy Guide*.

U.S. Department of Energy (2008). *State & Federal Incentives & Laws*

Weather.com/Autos (2008). *Consumer reviews: Passenger Car weather performance* . Available: http://www.weather.com/outlook/ driving/drivingsafety/autoadvisor/ consumerreview?start_index=0&vehicle_type= passenger&review_type=n&cond=snow&make=all

Webb, G. I., & Pazzani, M. (2001). Machine learning for user modeling. *User Modeling and User-Adapted Interaction, 11*(1), 19–29. doi:10.1023/A:1011117102175

Weihua, L. (n.d) Ontology Supported Intelligent Information Agent. *International IEEE Symposium On Intelligent Systems '02*

YHO. (2008). *Yahoo!*. Retrieved from: http://www.yahoo.com

## ENDNOTES

[1]  Due to the very snowy winter in MN.

[2]  Which is due, in part, to the fact that the government of MN offers sales tax break incentive for buying fuel-efficient cars (e.g., (U.S. Department of Energy, 2008)).

[3]  Due to the fact that $N_x$ is a middle-class neighborhood (e.g., (Minneapolis census, 2000)).

[4]  E.g., by analyzing the structure of the ESD-Graph in Figure 3, the system can identify implicitly that the user belongs to ethnic group $E_Y$ and national origin $O_X$, if the user lives in neighborhood $N_X$ and follows religion $R_Y$.

[5]  Assuming that each item in the XML document has an attribute labeled *ID*.

[6]  Recall that each query represents the initial preferences of one of the subjects (students).

[7]  The set is constructed based on the weights on item features provided by the subject.

[8]  The set returned by DemoFilter, Oracle XML DB, or Google Base.

# Section 3
# Applications and Case Studies in Social Networks Mining and Analysis

# Chapter 13
# Mining Organizations' Networks:
## Multi–Level Approach[1]

**James A. Danowski**
*University of Illinois at Chicago, USA*

## ABSTRACT

*This chapter presents six examples of organization-related social network mining: 1) interorganizational and sentiment networks in the Deepwater BP Oil Spill events, 2) intraorganizational interdepartmental networks in the Savannah College of Art and Design (SCAD), 3) who-to-whom email networks across the organizational hierarchy the Ford Motor Company's automotive engineering innovation: "Sync® w/ MyFord Touch", 4) networks of selected individuals who left that organization, 5) semantic associations across email for a corporate innovation in that organization, and 6) assessment of sentiment across its email for innovations over time. These examples are discussed in terms of motivations, methods, implications, and applications.*

## OVERVIEW

When you think of social network analysis you probably visualize individuals as nodes. This is quite natural, given the "social" aspect, and more specifically because the origins of social network analysis, going back some 89 years (Freeman, 1996), are in the relations among individuals. Nevertheless, 'social' is also considered at levels of analysis in which the focal nodes are groups, subunits of organizations, organizations, or more

macro-level human systems. In this chapter I center on organizational social network analysis, focusing on interorganizational, organizational, departmental, and also individuals as they communicate with organizations.

After this overview I will discuss why such a focus is desirable in light of the literature. First, however, let me point out that this chapter also includes mining for and automatic identification of an organization's networks at several levels based on textual elements of documents available on the web such as news story databases, blogs, reports, and other electronic text content, and also

DOI: 10.4018/978-1-61350-513-7.ch013

available from internal organization documents, such as email, or other kinds of electronic text accessible in real time or as archived internally or in the clouds.

Imbedded in electronic texts are layers of social networks that can be unpeeled with the miner's tools. The highest-order type of network mining I focus on is identification of *interorganizational* networks. This has been an area of research that previously used manual procedures other than mining (Scott, 1988, 1991, 2000; Galaskiewicz, & Shatin, 1981; Galaskiewicz, 1985; Mizruchi, 1996). Here I use an automated procedure based on the co-appearance of organizations across a corpus of web documents. In particular, each time a focal organization appears together with another organization within a proximity window in a document, the pair of organizations is automatically counted. Taking the aggregated collection of pairs, I network analyze them. This enables indexing the organizations' positions in the network and computation of various network structure measures common to social network analysis (SNA). Moreover, by slicing the collection of documents into time segments one can analyze the network structure as a time series. Time-sequenced associations are one of the necessary conditions for establishing possible causal relationships among variables. For example, we could also measure the sentiment expressed in the documents about the organizations and identify any synchronous or lagged associations between sentiment and network structure (Danowski & Cepela, 2010). As an example of this, Noah Cepela and I measured the organizational networks among U.S. presidents' cabinets over time, from Nixon through G.W. Bush, automatically indexing co-appearance of cabinet members in documents. We examined the time-lagged relationships between the presidents' centrality in the administrative network and the link between news sentiment and job approval as measured by the Gallup polls. We tailored the time slicing to the frequency of the Gallup polls for each presidency. This shows how one can build

some of the necessary conditions for causality evidence: identify a sequence of networks, index its attributes, and add measures of other attributes of the organizational actors and contextual factors of theoretical interest. What remains is ruling out rival explanations for observed time-ordered associations.

In this chapter my first several examples illustrate such a new approach to interorganizational social network analysis and data mining. I compile a list of organizations of interest and search across large text corpora for the co-appearance of pairs of organizations in news documents, blogs, reports, and related venues. In the first example I mine for an interorganizational network. I also slice time segments across the larger mining time frame to enable time-series analysis of these network structures. The example examines the interorganizational networks associated with coverage of the Deepwater BP Gulf Oil Spill of 2010. I then examine the relationship between news story sentiment about the most central organization, BP, and its position in the network overtime using a new network-based sentiment measuring approach, based on average shortest paths from BP to each of several thousand possible sentiment words, generating theoretically interesting findings about the sequencing of sentiment and centrality.

A second kind of organizational network mining is for the departments within an organization that co-appear across news stories and other text documents. For example, consider the departments within a university. In many cases the departments are proxies for disciplines. By identifying each pair of departments co-mentioned across a corpus of news and/or blog content about the university one can automatically map the representation of the collaborative network of the university's departments over time in the mining corpora. My example is from the Savannah College of Art and Design (SCAD) that was under accreditation review in 2009 and needed evidence of collaborative networks across departments, surrogates for disciplines.

Third, one may wish to measure the networks of individuals associated with the organization. Based on individuals' co-appearance in organizational documents, one could measure the structural properties of the network at the macro level, such as its size, density, and centralization, and also measure the network positions of the individuals, for example their flow betweenness centrality (Freeman, Borgatti, & White, 1991). The mapping of presidential cabinet networks is an example of this level of organizational analysis.

A fourth kind of organizational text mining is to exact semantic networks from intra-organizational documents, such as email, reports, or other textual materials. There are many ways one could peel the intraorganizational network onion, besides the interdepartmental level network analysis. For example, here I demonstrate mapping the network of individuals based on who sends email to whom, mining email captured automatically in the engineering function of the Ford Motor Company as they work on development of a cluster of innovations for vehicles, referred to as the "Sync® w/ MyFord Touch" product. I consider this as one variation of semantic network analysis because we mine for individuals' names, which are words.

Other research, although not numerous, has measured networks from email for various purposes (Danowski & Edison-Swift, 1985; Gloor, 2006; Gloor and Zhao, 2006; Diesner, Frantz, and Carley, 2005). Based on work with my colleagues Ken Riopelle and Julia Gluesing and I, with associates within the Ford Motor Company, I show how one can make two new uses of organizational email network analysis. One use is representing the network across levels of the organizational hierarchy in terms of the number of steps in the chain of command from the CEO on down. A second use, overlaid onto who-to-whom email hierarchical networks, is to examine the network structures of individuals who have left the organization. This can be useful for management to inform replacement individuals with whom they will be expected to communicate in what kind of

pattern. After management reviews this network and approves of particular links, they can give the recruit a detailed overview of their predecessor's ego-centric network, specifying the names of particular persons with whom it is probably important to communicate.

The other kind of semantic analysis I demonstrate is of the words (other than people's names) that are associated with one of the innovations of "Sync® w/ MyFord Touch." We sliced the networks into weekly intervals to track the evolution of the meanings associated with a cluster of innovations for use of the automobile driver. Here, however, given space constraints, I will show the semantic network of the earliest time slice, and for only one of the innovation concepts, the cockpit.

In sum, by considering the examples of mining for organizational networks at different levels of analysis I hope through this chapter to illuminate your thinking about ways in which you might conceptualize related analyses, or new clusters of links among your conceptual light bulbs, or shall we say 'semantic nodes.'

My intent is to clarify how one can test hypotheses about organizations at various levels or to develop management applications for strategic public relations, intelligence functions, and business analytics. You will also likely think of future directions for development of organizational mining methods and analysis, sparking new ideas about applying and evolving the techniques. In sum, the examples will trigger new thoughts at both the conceptual and methodological levels.

## Overview of Social Network Analysis Organizational Mining Literature

Let's put into context organizational social network mining in terms of the populations of related studies in the literature about data mining and social network analysis combined with various interorganizational, organizational, and intraorganizational terms using Google Scholar.

The first pattern of note is that SNA has exploded in number of studies conducted (Borgatti & Foster, 2003; Borgatti, & Molina, 2003) since its beginnings 89 years ago (Freeman, 1996). On January 13, 2011 Google Scholar (http://scholar.google.com) returns 38,500 hits on for the phrase 'social network analysis.' Combining 'data mining' and 'social network analysis' results in 5,300 hits, or 14% of the total pool of SNA hits. Most of the prior research on SNA studies individuals as nodes in a network. In contrast, SNA using organizations as nodes, or using sub-organization units larger than the individual yields 14,000 hits, although many of these use individuals as nodes within organizations as they conceptualize or measure organizational social networks (Scott, 1988, 1991, 2000).

When adding 'data mining' to the 'organization' and 'social network analysis' terms there are 1,320 hits. 'Interorganizational' coupled with 'social network analysis' returns 3,580 hits and when both are coupled with 'data mining' in only 128 hits.

Consider that many of these hits are not directly about using methods of data mining and SNA in interorganizational or organizational contexts but these terms are mentioned somewhere in the Google Scholar records. These search results show that there is a not much literature about interorganizational networks and data mining, while there are more hits about 'organizations' and 'social network analysis' (Tichy, Tushman, & Fombrun, 1979) and 'data mining,' although most of the studies use individuals as nodes in the organizational network. The primary data mined is electronic mail, much of it with a single corpus, from Enron. When considering 'semantic networks' in the 'organization' and 'data mining' there are 1,320 hits, while adding 'social network analysis' returns only 128.

In short, given only this simple search of the literature, there is evidence for the need for more focus on interorganizational, organizational, and organizational subunit levels with respect to SNA and data mining. There is also need for more attention to semantic networks in organizations using SNA approaches. A more lengthy review of the literature is not within the scope of this chapter.

## Example 1: Interorganizational Networks Associated with the Deepwater BP Oil Spill

In thinking of what example to use to illustrate interorganizational network analysis and data mining, it occurred to me that organizations were one of the main focal points of much news coverage about the 2010 Deepwater BP Gulf Oil Spill. In particular, along with the three major private sector organizations, federal, state, and local government organizations appeared to be active during this period.

I decided to examine the interorganizational networks from a particular vantage point, that of the White House. Accordingly, I went to the website http://www.whitehouse.gov/deepwater-bp-oil-spill/ and copied the names of organizations listed as working on the problems. Some of the links on the web site were to pages of states in the affected areas of the Gulf: Louisiana, Mississippi, Alabama, and Florida, so I extracted as well the names of any organizations appearing on those related web sites. My final list, shown in Table 1, consisted of 81 organizations, approximately half of them being various volunteer organizations.

I used one of the features of WORDij 3.0 (http://wordij.net) (Danowski, 2010), the specification of a string conversion of n-grams to unigrams, and therefore converted the multi-word names of the organizations to a single acronym to aid in the display of the networks. This avoided the problems resulting from many of the governmental organizations having long names that would make difficult visual comprehension of network graphs.

Many applications of natural language processing to large textual corpora, particularly in information retrieval, but in other areas as well, use a

*Table 1. Unigrams Key for Organizations in Figure 2, Figure 4, Figure 5, Figure 6, Figure 7, and Figure 8*

| |
|---|
| ALa Americorp Louisiana |
| ACS Adventist Community Services |
| AGOFBCI Governor's Office of Faith-Based and Community Initiaties |
| AlAC Alabama AmeriCorps |
| ARC American Red Cross |
| ASHFA America's Second Harvest/Feeding America |
| BP BP, British Petroleum |
| CathC Catholic Charities |
| CCA Christian Contractors Association, Inc. |
| CCC Caribbean Conservation Corporation |
| CCST Community Crisis Support Team |
| CDR Christian Disaster Response |
| CNCS Corporation for National and Community Service |
| COH Convoy of Hope |
| CompAll Compassion Alliance |
| CRWRC Christian Reformed World Relief Committee |
| CWS Church World Service |
| DHS Department of Homeland Security |
| DOD Department of Defense |
| DOF Defenders of Wildlife |
| DOI Department of the Interior |
| DOIFWS Department of the Interior's Fish and Wildlife Service |
| DOINPS Department of the Interior's National Park Service |
| DOL Department of Labor |
| EPA Environmental Protection Agency |
| ERD Episcopal Relief and Development |
| ESF15 Emergency Support Function 15 |
| FAFB Florida Association of Food Banks |
| FarmSh Farm Share |
| FAud Florida Audubon |
| FAVC Florida Association of Volunteer Centers |
| FBDR Florida Baptist Disaster Relief |
| FCaCon Florida Catholic Conference |
| FCSDA Florida Conference of Seventh-Day Adventists |
| FDEA Florida Department of Elder Affairs |
| FGCVCS Governor's Commission on Volunteerism and Community Service |
| FIND Florida Interfaith Networking in Disaster |
| FIRST Florida Immediate Response Stress Team |
| FJC Florida Jaycees |
| FLVOAD Florida Voluntary Organizations Active in Disasters |

*continued on following page*

*Table 1. Continued*

| |
|---|
| FSERT Florida State Emergency Response Team |
| FUMC Florida United Methodist Conference |
| GCCF Gulf Coast Claims Facility |
| Halli Halliburton |
| HON Hands On Network |
| HumSoc Humane Society of the United States |
| KFB Keep Florida Beautiful |
| LDCRT Louisiana Department of Culture, Recreation, and Tourism |
| LDR Lutheran Disaster Response |
| LOF Lions of Florida |
| LSC Louisiana Serve Commission |
| MCVS Mississippi Commission for Volunteer Service |
| MDS Mennonite Disaster Service |
| NatComm National Commission on the BP Deepwater Horizon Oil Spill and Offshore Drilling |
| NDR Nazarene Disaster Response |
| NFG Network for Good |
| NOAA National Oceanic and Atmospheric Administration |
| NRMCS Night Runners Mobile Crisis Services, Inc. |
| OpBless Operation Blessing |
| OSHA National Institute for Occupational Safety and Health |
| PDA Presbyterian Disaster Assistance |
| PFC National Pollution Fund Center |
| POLI Points of Light Institute |
| RAla Ready Alabama |
| RTG RestoreTheGulf. gov |
| SBA Small Business Administration |
| SBCDR Southern Baptist Convention Disaster Relief |
| SERVOF State Emergency Responders and Volunteers of Florida |
| SNAT Service Nation |
| SVM Scientology Volunteer Ministers |
| TEWF The Eagles Wings Foundation |
| TransO Transocean |
| TSA The Salvation Army |
| UCCDRM United Church of Christ Disaster Response Ministries |
| UMCR United Methodist Committee Relief |
| USCG U.S. Coast Guard |
| UW The United Way |
| UWaySMS United Way of South MS |
| VolFLA Volunteer Florida |
| VolLA Volunteer Louisiana |
| VolMS Volunteer Mississippi |

*Figure 1. Document Sources in the Lexis-Nexis Text Collection*

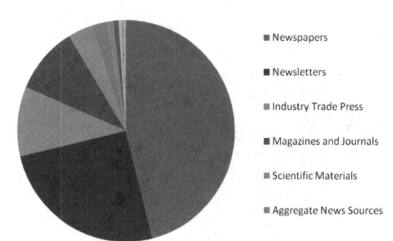

- ■ Newspapers
- ■ Newsletters
- ■ Industry Trade Press
- ■ Magazines and Journals
- ■ Scientific Materials
- ■ Aggregate News Sources

stop word list 'stoplist' to drop frequent function words that appear quite uniformly across documents. In English the most common words at the top of a stop list are: 'the, of, that, and,' and other such grammatical function words that do not carry a large field of social meaning. WORDij has an option to use a stoplist or droplist of words, but for the current example, we make use of the opposite, an *include list*. WORDij enables one to specify a list of words, in this case organization name unigrams, for analysis of their cooccurrences. All other words not on the include list are removed from the analysis. This enables an efficient means of mapping highly-focused networks, in this case, the networks among organizations mentioned in news stories about the oil spill.

Another feature of WORDij is the TimeSlice procedure that allows for taking a larger time frame and dividing the textual corpus into smaller equal time intervals. In this example, the larger time span ran from April 20, 2010 to when this chapter was written in first week of January, 2011. We experimented with setting a weekly or bi-weekly time interval and found that the weekly interval had portions of the span that were sparse in numbers of organizations. A two-week interval was chosen for illustrative purposes. The TimeSlice function prepares the textual corpus so that the

basic WordLink co-occurrence counter quickly runs through each time interval producing the same output files for each slice.

I collected a corpus of 4,728 documents in Lexis-Nexis Academic from the *New York Times, Washington Post, USA Today, Baton Rouge Advocate* (Louisiana), *St. Petersburg Times* (Florida), *Birmingham News* (Alabama), and the *Jackson Clarion-Ledger* (Mississippi). Figure 1 shows the breakdown of the kind of documents in the corpus.

TimeSlice divided the overall corpus into 38 two-week intervals. WORDij WordLink produced the network output file with the optional .net Pajek format (Batagelj & Mrvar, 1998) for each interval and I input this network file to UCINET 6 for conversion to its own format.

This enabled me to run computations of flow betweenness centrality (Freeman, Borgatii, & White, 1991) for each time period, producing centrality scores for each organization as well as providing an overall centralization score for the whole network. Borgatti (2005) has pointed that while betweenness centrality (Freeman, 1979) is most often used in SNA, almost all such uses are inappropriate because the assumptions of the measure do not fit well with the nature of the data. Betweenness centrality assumes that each link has the same strength. Betweenness is

*Figure 2. Interorganizational BP Oil Spill Network Aggregated Across Time*

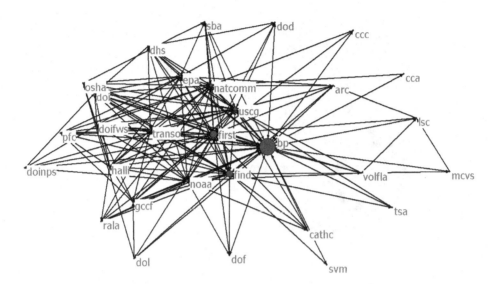

computed on dichotomized, linked/not-linked relationships. Our data are continuous and highly varying. Flow Betweenness (Freeman, Borgatti, & White, 1991) eliminates the need for binarizing the network, which discards valuable variance on link strengths. Betweenness also assumed is that messages flow between nodes based on the single shortest possible path. Nevertheless, in actual communication situations there are varying link strengths, such as based on the frequency of communication. Nodes can also send messages to multiple nodes, varying in path lengths, perhaps even avoiding the node with highest betweenness centrality. Flow betweenness centrality (Freeman, Borgatti, & White, 1991) has assumptions which best meet these conditions. If one is using news stories, email, or other forms of communication as input texts, then it is more appropriate to use it rather than betweenness centrality.

Conversion to UCINET format was also useful to produce NetDraw graphic depictions of each network, which works with the UCINET system files. WORDij has a network visualization function, VISij, which animates the time-series of network structures, but it is not possible to present a network movie in a printed chapter. NetDraw

has more options than VISij for displaying the network in terms of sizes of nodes, labels, links, and sizing nodes and links by variables. For node sizing we chose the closest centralization measure to flow betweenness available in NetDraw, classic betweenness centrality. Figure 2 shows the network of organizations aggregated over time.

For other computations, shown in Figure 3 we used flow betweenness for overall network centralization. Looking at this graph one sees that the lowest centralization in the first half of the time series is for the first time slice. A peak is reached at the sixth slice, followed by a drop to a local low at the ninth slice. The next peak occurs at the fifteenth slice with the lowest in the final slice, the nineteenth one. As a result I thought it would be informative to display the network graphs for each of these noteworthy slices, shown in Figure 4 and Figure 8.

An interesting question with theoretical implications is how is the sentiment expressed in the documents associated with the network structure? To explore this question, I used the same two-week time-slice interval but this time used no include list of organizations when running WordLink, as a result analyzing the full-text of

*Figure 3. Interorganizational Centralization Over Time*

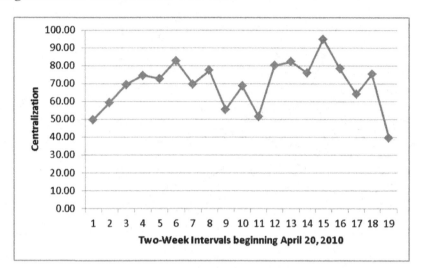

*Figure 4. Period 1/Interval 1: Low Centralization*

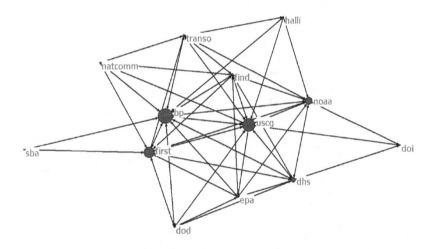

the documents' for semantic networks. After that I input the word pair files to a shortest path network analysis program in WORDij, OptiCommReport. This program allows the specification of a seed word, in this case BP, and then traces the shortest paths from the seed to each of 3,457 lexical variants of positive and negative words taken from the Linguistic Inquiry and Word Count (LIWC) (Pennebaker, Booth, & Francis, 2007). LIWC is a dictionary-based content analysis software package that indexes the occurrences of some 72 categories of words. I took their dictionary entries for two of the categories: positive emotion and negative emotion. There are 266 positive emotion word stems and 346 negative emotion stems. To build a more robust sentiment analysis system I expanded these word stems to all lexical inflected forms of each using the AGID comprehensive list of inflected forms of words on Kevin Atkinson's Word List Page (http://wordlist.source-forge.net/). As a result, I have 1,219 positive words and 2,238 negative words. My OptiCommReport

*Figure 5. Period 1/Interval 6: High Centralization*

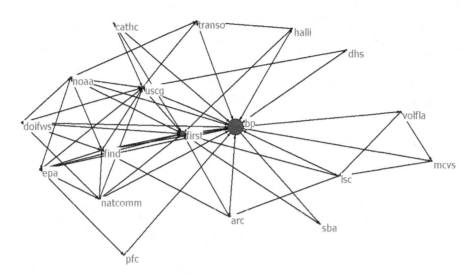

*Figure 6. Period 1/Interval 9: Low Centralization*

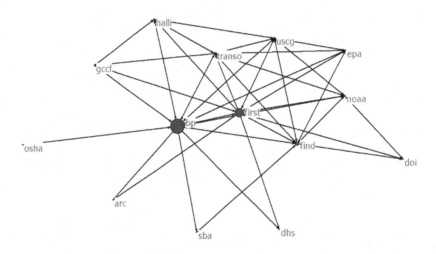

program identifies the shortest weighted path from the seed word to each of the semantic target words in each of the word pair output files. I then compute from the results the total normalized link strengths for the shortest path to each of the positive words and divide by the total link strengths for the shortest path to each of the negative words, and divide the positive by the negative normalized strengths to produce a ratio of positive to negative network threads. This is the positivity index.

For the current example, so you could effectively see the plot of the centrality of BP in relation to positivity for BP, I multiplied the positivity ratio by a constant of 50 to scale it close to the centrality score range. Figure 9 shows the BP centrality values over time as the top line and the positivity ratio as the lower line in the graph. In doing further statistical analysis, I first examined the autocorrelation of the variables in SPSS Forecasting and found that there was no significant autocorrelation

*Figure 7. Period 1/Interval 13: High Centralization*

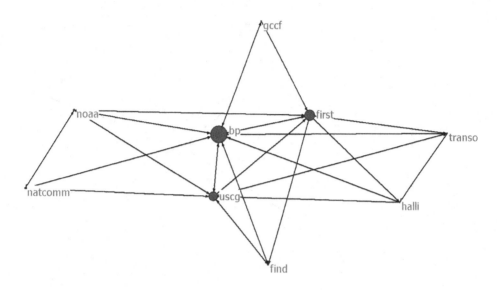

*Figure 8. Period 2/Interval 19: Low Centralization*

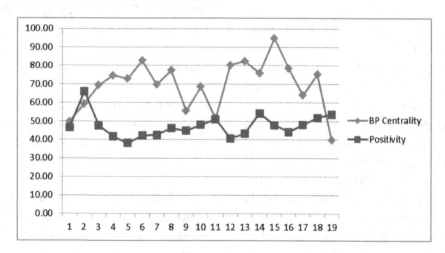

at any lag. It was therefore appropriate to compute the Pearson correlation across the time-series for the two variables. The correlation was r = -.42 (p < .04). This indicates that when BP is in a less central position in the network, the sentiment is more positive, and conversely when BP is in a more central position the sentiment is more negative. Theoretically, it is valuable to examine in future research the generalizability of this centrality/ negativity association and to what extent it is

generalizable and more importantly, under what conditions, and why.

Consider that here at the interorganizational level, in the context of news documents, there is an association between network centrality and sentiment that differs from the general findings at the ego-centric network level. As individuals' networks are more centralized there is more of an instrumental focus and less of an emotional focus suggested by Granovetter (1973) and Burt (1995). In our case, however, centralization around

*Figure 9. Interorganizational Centralization & Positivity Over Time*

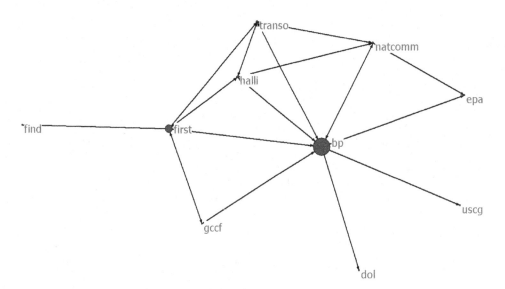

BP is associated with more negative sentiment while less centralization is associated with more positive sentiment. This pattern is probably different from the individual level because of the context of news documents being different from that of individual-level social network behaviors. There are institutional-level factors for journalism related to the macro-level societal functions of news that privilege negative news for societal surveillance purposes. The most noteworthy implication of these findings is that one should be cautious when attempting to generalize associations across network levels. As the level of analysis shifts there may be contextual changes that render cross-level generalization more complex than the core associations subject to potential generalization. In other words, what happens in networks where the individuals are nodes may be quite different than where organizations are nodes. I will leave further contemplation of the implications of this analysis to you and move on to the second example.

## Example 2: Identifying COINs at the Inter-Departmental Level

### Overview

Collaborative Innovation Networks (COINS) (Gloor, 2006) are typically defined using individuals as nodes (Cross, Borgatti, & Parker, 2002; Cross, & Parker, 2004). This is a bias of the social network literature more generally, as we discussed at the beginning of this chapter. Departments in organizations or higher order social units can, however, be considered as forming COINs of interest.

My goal here is to demonstrate the basic techniques of doing a type of automatic social network analysis at the interdepartmental level. The application goal was to produce data on interdisciplinary/interdepartmental collaboration as evidence in support of an accreditation review for the Savannah College of Art and Design (SCAD).

There are four key points this example makes: 1) collaborative innovation often takes place in organizational settings with resources and constraints shaped by system components at levels higher than individuals; 2) The individual level of analysis used in most COINS research ignores the departmental level in organizations, where departments are often considered by participants as the key collaborating units; 3) The betweenness centrality measures used in most COINS research to identify innovative groups of individuals are not appropriate given the assumptions that such collaborations involve communication processes in which messages need not always flow through the shortest path, can be distributed through more than one path either synchronously or asynchronously, and may be increased in frequency of communication by the social actors.

As Borgatti (2005) points out, betweenness centrality is inconsistent with these assumptions because it is based on finding one shortest path linking each pair of actors, treats links as present or absent rather than having valued strengths, and assumes one message is disseminated down each shortest path. Instead, flow betweeenness is the measure that is consistent with the theoretical and practical assumptions about communication discussed in the previous example. This is the measure for identifying COINs used in this research; and 4) How media represent collaborations can be important both for mapping COINs and for observing how these are portrayed in media. Theoretically interesting audience loops back to the COINs may communicate perceptions that influence both the participants and their social observers, communicate changes in resources, or impose constraints on the innovation.

## Methods

A list of the department names in the Savannah College of Art and Design was obtained from college personnel. My approach to assembling corpora for mining was to search Lexis/Nexis Academic to identify stories about the college from 2005 to 2008. I obtained every story containing the college's full name or acronym (SCAD), resulting in a census of the relevant text universe.

I then aggregated all of these files into one text file and used the TimeSlice utility in WORDij 3.0 to segment the file into four annual files. Each of the four text files I automatically analyzed using WORDij 3.0's WordLink program to measure the co-occurrence of the department names.

As I pointed out in example 1, WORDij was originally designed to analyze large numbers of co-occurring words to create semantic networks. Nevertheless, social actors' names are indeed words and mining for their co-occurrence is no different. WORDij 3.0 not only has a stop-word list or droplist, it also has its opposite, an 'include list' that will map the network only among words on it. For this example, using WORDij 3.0's string replacement and include list functions, all aliases I created for each department's name were converted to a single unigram of letters and I then computed proximity-based co-occurrences in WordLink.

## Automatic Link Coding with Proximities not with 'Bag of Words'

A key point I saved until now is that proximity co-occurrence indexing (Danowski, 1982, 1993a, 1993b, 2009, Diesner & Carley, 2004) avoids the problems of the simplistic 'bag of words' approaches common from Information Science and Information Retrieval. While word bags are useful for document retrieval they blur social meaning by ignoring the relationships of social units within the texts, whether these units are words, people, or other entities. It is more analytically precise, however, to use a proximity criterion in defining relationships among entities network analyzed. I used a three-word window, based on empirical testing of window size and network strucrture validity (Danowski, 1993b) operating on the text file after all words except the names of departments were automatically removed by the use of the WordLink 'include list' of department names. Table 2 shows an example of a portion of a larger include file.

*Table 2. Examples of String Replacement*

| |
|---|
| Department of Advertising and Design->Advert_Design |
| Dept. of Advertising and Design->Advert_Design |
| Dept of Advertising and Design->Advert_Design |
| Advertising and Design Department->Advert_Design |
| Advertising and Design Dept. ->Advert_Design |
| Advertising and Design Dept->Advert_Design |
| Advertising and Design->Advert_Design |
| Department of Accessory Design->Accessory |
| Dept. of Accessory Design->Accessory |
| Dept of Accessory Design->Accessory |
| Accessory Design->Accessory |
| Accessory Design Department->Accessory |
| Accessory Design Dept. ->Accessory |
| Accessory Design Dept->Accessory |

## Post-Processing of Link Data for Centrality Measures

As you recall from the first example, the WORDij 3.0 program has the option of producing a network file in the. net Pajek (Batagelj & Mrvar, 1998) format. This is one of the import file types that UCINET (Borgatti, Everett, & Freeman, 2002) accepts and converts to its system files. I chose UCINET because it is widely accepted in the social network analysis community and I wished to use common validated centrality indices to profile the structures. Given the status of UCINET and the ease of output importing I have felt no need to incorporate centrality measures into WORDij.

## Combining Visualization with Statistical Network Centrality of Actors

A fundamental tenet of data analysis is to first visualize it. WORDij 3.0 has VISij for creating static or time-series movies of changes in network composition and structure. My interest in this example is in profiling the aggregate networks of departments, year by year, therefore a series of static representation results. While VISij has

time-series animated visualizations that NetDraw does not have, NetDraw has more options for rendering static networks such as having larger circles for more central nodes. I used eigenvector centrality (Bonacich, 2007) to visually render the nodes' network position in the graphs, because the NetDraw program does not compute flow betweenness, while UCINET does. For link strength I used the maximum available range of thickness of links, from 0 to 12. The larger array of strengths was converted to this scale.

Although visualizing data is essential to help place further statistical analysis in context, it has its limitations, beyond the lack of rules for analysts to use in assessing network visualizations. Spring-embedded layout procedures may present the analyst with a different vantage point on the network each time it is run on the same data, because the stable structure can rotate as a whole, which can result in differing interpretations. Using statistical information following visual inspection of networks affords the analyst with the best of each mode.

While when there are small numbers of social actors visualization may have sufficient face validity to support action with respect to the network, it becomes increasingly less useful as the number of nodes and links increases above 30. How intensively and extensively greater numbers of nodes are linked can add to visual information overload, rendering interpretation of networks of questionable validity. It is difficult to make effective interpretations when the network looks like a cross-cultural accident of a big bowl of spaghetti with jambalaya on top, as is usually the case with visual output from semantic network analysis programs such as Crawdad (Corman, Kuhn, McPhee, & Dooley, 2002), rather than like a plate of sushi.

## Results

There were 1,946 full text documents from Lexis/Nexis Academic for 2005 through 2008 for the college. Table 3 shows departmental flow betweenness centrality on a yearly interval. Figures 10-13 show the interdepartmental networks by year. Figure 14 is the network aggregated across the four years.

## Interpretation

This example focused on showing an additional variation of a new method for identifying the social network structures that emerge in analyzing co-occurrences of organizational departments in news stories using automated text mining. The method used and described in this example appears to have face validity for their accreditation review according to college officials and is worthy of further refinement

Future research of potential interest would be simultaneous mapping of concepts and objects (tools, resources, places, etc.) along with the interdepartmental links, representing all of these in the same network. In this way, one could observe large numbers of social networks automatically viewing the word-networks with which the social actors are associated and with what objects and geographic locations they are linked. Some scholars (LaTour, 2005; Diesner & Carley, 2008) prefer to treat as nodes in the same network the social units, the words they use or are used to describe them, place names, and other proper nouns. WORDij 3.0 also enables this kind of 'actor network theory' mixture of nodes in the same networks identified. Further research might find exploration of these features valuable.

## Example 3: Mining Email for Analysis of Intraorganizational Innovations

Email networks within organizations has been studied by researchers such as Danowski and Edison-Swift (1985), Diesner, Frantz, and Carley (2005), and Gloor and Zhang (2006). Example 4 was conducted among the Ford Motor Company's product engineering staff across its global network as it developed the "Sync® w/ MyFord Touch"

innovation. This was a package of six new products with a single overall name that were created to be new vehicle control features for drivers across a range of the company's vehicles. The number of engineers involved was approximately 1,900.

Communication about the innovations occurred in a variety of modes but the most tractable was email about the innovation. Monitoring all relevant electronic mail over time overcomes limitations of cross-sectional, self-report data which include considerable error introduced by respondents' memory processes and their ability to report only gross summary features of their communication messages about an innovation. To avoid such problems, this study created a procedure by which the over time email content of individuals was monitored both historically and in real time over a two-year period. The organization exclusively used Microsoft Outlook for email with approximately 400 servers with up to 4,000 users each. The first step in establishing the monitoring procedure was to create a new Outlook rule that a participant would apply once on their Windows pc so that it would search all historical emails stored by individuals for key words associated with the innovations and forward these emails to a dedicated researchers' server, and also forward all relevant emails in real time during the course of the study, from January 2005 to December 2007.

A major discussion about deploying this procedure was among the executives and corporate attorneys to ensure confidentiality, respect for the personal privacy of the participants, and compliance with the legal systems of employees from different countries, particularly the Eurpoean ones. After an in-depth review by the company's lawyers from multiple countries the process was approved as an opt-in choice, an approach more characteristic of Europe than the USA. In all cases, participation was voluntary and employees could stop participating at any time. Participants were asked to run rules in Microsoft Outlook to enable automatic forwarding of email to a 'dummy email

*Table 3. Interdepartmental Normalized Flow Betweenness by Year\* c8v9*

| 2005 | |
|---|---|
| | nFlowBtn |
| | ----------- |
| | Mean 2. 23 |
| | Std Dev 3. 99 |
| Network Centralization Index = 10.8% | |
| | nFlowBtn |
| | ----------- |
| | fashion 12.62 |
| | animation 12.54 |
| | interior 11.89 |
| | filmtv 5.05 |
| | architec 3.62 |
| | performing 3.62 |
| | painting 2.56 |
| | print 1.81 |
| | sequential 0.92 |
| | photog 0.58 |
| | illus 0.40 |
| 2006 | |
| | nFlowBtn |
| | ----------- |
| | Mean 1.41 |
| | Std Dev 3.10 |
| Network Centralization Index 10.3% | |
| | nFlowBtn |
| | ----------- |
| | painting 11.22 |
| | teaching 9.34 |
| | performing 4.86 |
| | photog 2.28 |
| | animation 0.85 |
| | writing 0.78 |
| | foundation 0.13 |
| | fashion 0.06 |
| | jewelry 0.06 |
| 2007 | |
| | nFlowBtn |
| | ----------- |
| | Mean 3.78 |

| | Std Dev 5.67 |
|---|---|
| Network Centralization Index 14. 04% | |
| | nFlowBtn |
| | ----------- |
| | painting 17.25 |
| | fashion 15.60 |
| | animation 14.42 |
| | performing 12.40 |
| | interior 11.72 |
| | architec 7.32 |
| | print 6.97 |
| | filmtv 3.35 |
| | jewelry 1.69 |
| | urban 1.38 |
| | writing 1.28 |
| | accessory 0.95 |
| | teaching 0.18 |
| 2008 | |
| | nFlowBtn |
| | ----------- |
| | Mean 4.87 |
| | Std Dev 7.89 |
| Network Centralization 23.9% | |
| | nFlowBtn |
| | ----------- |
| | photog 27.82 |
| | painting 26.39 |
| | interior 17.50 |
| | performing 10.67 |
| | architec 10.25 |
| | teaching 9.83 |
| | fashion 4.16 |
| | sequential 3.56 |
| | animation 3.05 |
| | filmtv 2.89 |
| | jewelry 2.49 |
| | foundation 1.74 |
| | urban 1.25 |
| | sculpture 0.16 |

*Figure 10. 2005 Interdepartmental Network*

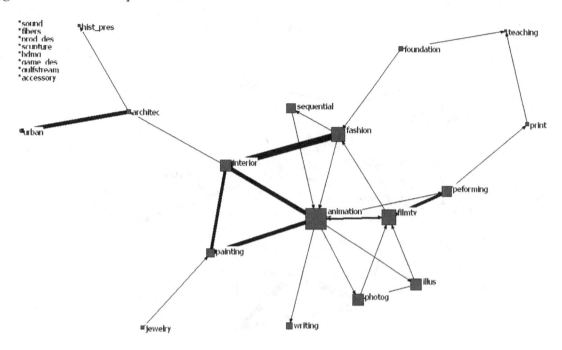

*Figure 11. 2006 Interdepartmental Network*

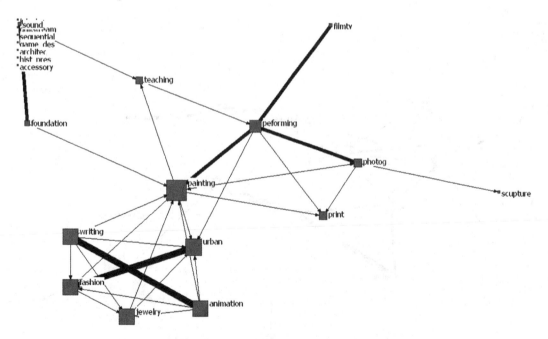

*Figure 12. 2007 Interdepartmental Network*

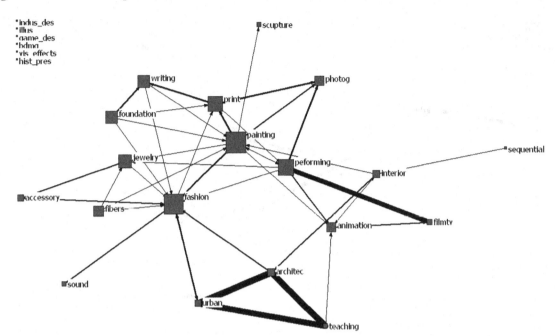

*Figure 13. 2008 Interdepartmental Network*

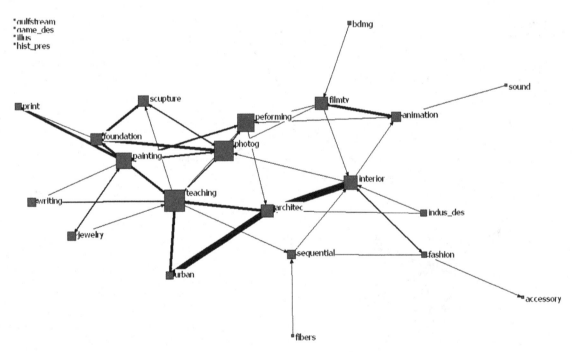

*Figure 14. Aggregate Interdepartmental Network*

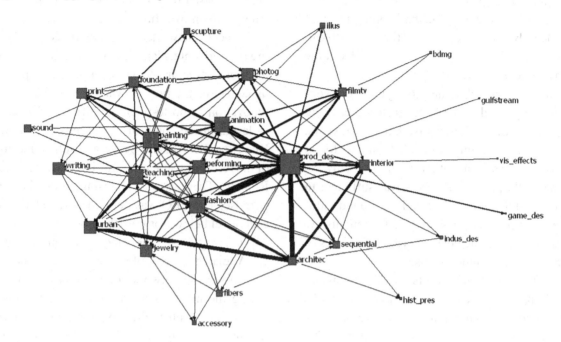

address' on a secure server designated to store the study data.

Once the email data collection process was approved, the academic researchers for this National Science Foundation grant received IRB approval from the two universities at which the PI (Jullia Gluesing at Wayne State University and Co-PI Ken Riopelle also at WSU), and I as Co-PI at the University of Illinois at Chicago were located. I based the protocol on a procedure to protect privacy used in an email network analysis study by Danowski and Edison-Swift (1985).We converted all names in the emails to numbers whose key was known only to the corporate staff who collaborated in this anonymizing activity. While the corporate research team knew the identities of all named individuals in the emails, the academic researchers had no knowledge of these identities. IRB applications were submitted for Exempt status for the research, meaning that because no identifying information was known to the academic researchers, the research was approved as exempt from the need to obtain informed consent.

The first analysis step was to deploy the Outlook rule to the project manager's email going back 9 years. The academic researchers then conducted a network analysis of the who-to-whom network from these emails to identify the most central individuals. The Negopy network analysis program (Richards, 1985) found one large group, evidence of a negentropic center/periphery structure. Because Negopy computes the geodesic distance scores among all pairs of nodes in each group, in this case one, comparable centrality information was available for all nodes in the network. This information was presented to the corporate researchers who used this information along with other considerations to choose 298 target individuals for the email harvesting.

The 298 targets were initially sent an email requesting their participation and application of the Outlook rules. Thirty eight chose to voluntarily participate, for a participation rate of 13%. Follow-up by project staff noted that potential users did not wish to have their email monitored in this fashion because of uncertainty around what it would find and how it would be used, even though most were aware that all corporate email was legally monitored in real time for 'illegal' activity words, as authorized by the Electronic Communication Privacy Act in the U.S. Nevertheless,. Forwarding and Replying were very extensively used in this organization, creating long chains of email going back over two years. Because of this mining of threaded email we found that capturing all innovation emails from only 1% of the 1,900 project engineers was sufficient to capture emails of approximately 1,900 individuals exchanging approximately 45,000 emails. As a result we constructed a two-year time series of emails about the innovations.

There were many facets to the automated email analysis, tracking the semantic networks associated with innovations over time, measuring the who-to-whom networks in relation to this message content, and the four examples shown here: 1) overlaying the who-to-whom email network on the formal organizational hierarchy; 2) highlighting the networks of people who left to provide communication training data for replacement people; 3) semantic associations to an innovation in the organization; and 4) sentiment analysis based on ratios of positive to negative email content over time.

Typically networks in organizations are shown in a flat horizontal plane, ignoring the formal organizational structure. In our example the corporate managers of the project wanted to see how the innovation's who-to-whom email network related to levels in the chain of command. Colleagues Ken Riopelle, Andrew Seary, and Julia Gluesing of the research team used MultiNet (Seary, 2005; Riopelle, Danowski, & Gluesing, 2008) for this purpose. The CEO was defined as 'level 1" and each level below, for the 100 most active nodes, was indexed down to level 9, as is seen in Figure 15. A related interest of the corporate managers was to see the networks of those who had left during the previous downsizing, to help orient new replacements to their expected communication networks. Figure 16 shows one example for four individuals who left, showing levels ranging from 3 down to 15.

## Active Nodes

To show an example of semantic analysis of innovations from the content of the emails, we

*Figure 15. Email Communication Who-to-Whom Networks Across Levels: 100 Most*

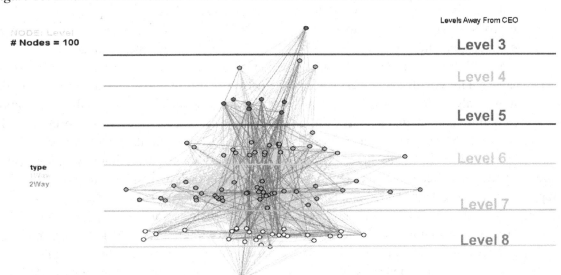

*Figure 16. Who-to-Whom email networks of Some Individuals Who Left the Organization*

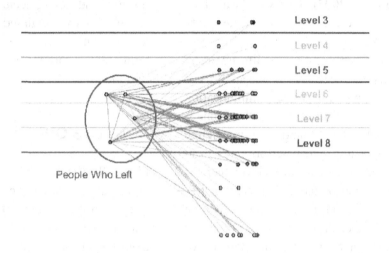

present in Figure 17 one network associated with the concept of automobile 'cockpit,' for which innovations were developing. Several concept labels are redacted

Lastly, we present a graph of the ratio of positive to negative sentiment over time (Danowski, Riopelle, Gluesing, 2008). We indexed sentiment of email texts using the LIWC diction-

*Figure 17. Semantic Network Associated with the 'Cockpit' Innovation*

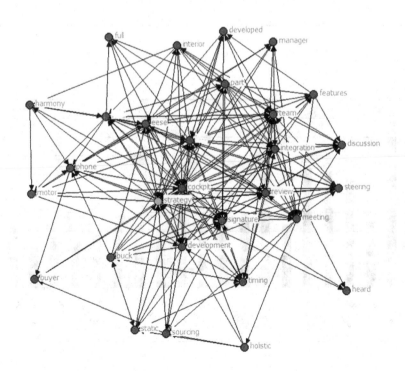

ary-based content analysis software (Pennebaker, Booth, & Francis, 2007). This work was done prior to the later development of the shortest-path netwok analysis of positive and negative inflected forms of sentiment words illustrated by OptiCommReport in example 1. The analysis of the ratio of positive to negative communication is based on the work of Losada (Fredrickson, & Losada, 2005) which has found an optimal range of this ratio for healthy system performance, from 3.0 up to 11.0. Under that ratio level there is likely ineffective performance. This chart in Figure 18 shows the Losada Line graph for all of the engineers working on the innovations. Not shown here is a similar chart for one of the elements of the package of innovations. At one point the positive/negative ratio dropped significantly below the 3.0 level and stayed low over the next six months. We did not have a chance to share this information with corporate executives, but six months later they decided that the unit was not

meeting project objectives and terminated its innovation and the engineers. After seeing our results the executives exclaimed that they wished they had known of them because they could have terminted six months earlier and saved millions of dollors.

## CONCLUSION

I have illustrated in this chapter six examples of organization-related social network mining: 1) interorganizatinal networks in the Deepwater BP Oil Spill events and sentiment analysis over time, 2) intraorganizational interdepartmental networks in the Savannah College of Art and Design (SCAD) over time, 3) who-to-whom email networks across the Ford Motor Company hierarcy in an automative engineering function, 4) networks of selected individuals who left that organization, 5) semantic associations across email for a corporate innova-

*Figure 18. Positive/Negative Email Sentiment Ratio Over Time*

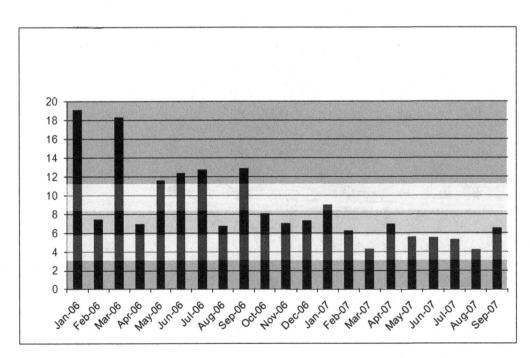

tion the "Sync® w/ MyFord Touch" product, and 6) assessment of sentiment across its email for innovations over time.

I have attempted to give you sufficient detail on the motivations for these examples, their methods, and possible scientific and management applications to stimulate your own ideas along these or other lines of research. While much social network analysis mining uses individuals as nodes, the first two examples use organizations as nodes. The third and fourth examples makes use of formal organizational structure in relation to mining communicatioin networks among individuals. Examples 5 and 6 analyze words as nodes mined from organizational email. This array of organizational mining examples may stimulate you to pursue your own.

## ACKNOWLEDGMENT

This research was supported in part by the National Science Foundation's Human and Social Dynamics (HSD) Award #SES-527487: Accelerating the diffusion of innovations: A "digital diffusion dashboard" methodology for global networked organizations.

Special thanks to Julia Gluesing and Ken Riopelle of the Department of Industrial and Manufacturing Engineering at Wayne State University, Detroit, Michigan, USA for their management of researchers at the Ford Motor Company.

## REFERENCES

Batagelj, V., & Mrvar, A. (1998). Pajek - Program for large network analysis. *Connections, 21*(2), 47–57.

Bonacich, P. (2007). Some unique properties of eigenvector centrality. *Social Networks, 29*(4), 555–564. doi:10.1016/j.socnet.2007.04.002

Borgatti, S. P. (2002). *NetDraw: Graph visualization software*. Harvard, MA: Analytic Technologies.

Borgatti, S. P. (2005). Centrality and network flow. *Social Networks, 27*, 55–71. doi:10.1016/j.socnet.2004.11.008

Borgatti, S. P., Everett, M. G., & Freeman, L. C. (2002). *UCINET for windows: Software for social network analysis*. Harvard, MA: Analytic Technologies.

Borgatti, S. P., & Foster, P. C. (2003). The network paradigm in organizational research: A review and typology. *Journal of Management, 29*(6), 991–1013.

Borgatti, S. P., & Molina, J. L. (2003). Ethical and strategic issues in organizational social network analysis. *The Journal of Applied Behavioral Science, 20*(10), 1–13.

Burt, R. S. (1995). *Structural holes: The social structure of competition*. Cambridge, MA: Harvard University Press.

Carley, K. M., Diesner, J., Reminga, J., & Tsvetovata, M. (2007). Toward an interoperable dynamic network analysis toolkit. *Decision Support Systems, 43*(4), 1324–1347. doi:10.1016/j.dss.2006.04.003

Chaffee, S. H., & Metzger, M. J. (2001). The end of mass communication? *Mass Communication & Society, 4*(4), 365–379. doi:10.1207/S15327825MCS0404_3

Corman, S., Kuhn, R., Mc, T., Phee, R. D., & Dooley, K. J. (2002). Studying complex discursive systems: Centering Resonance Analysis of communication. *Human Communication Research, 28*(2), 157206. doi:10.1093/hcr/28.2.157

Cross, R., Borgatti, S. P., & Parker, A. (2002). Making invisible work visible: Using social network analysis to support strategic collaboration. *California Management Review, 44*(2), 25–46.

Cross, R., & Parker, A. (2004). *The hidden power of social networks*. Boston, MA: Harvard Business School Press.

Danowski, J. A. (1982). A network-based content analysis methodology for computer-mediated communication: An illustration with a computer bulletin board. In Bostrom, R. N. (Ed). *Communication Yearbook, 6*, 904-925. New Brunswick, NJ: Transaction Books.

Danowski, J. A. (1988). Organizational infographics and automated auditing: Using computers to unobtrusively gather and analyze communication. In G. Goldhaber & G. A. Barnett (Eds.) *Handbook of Organizational Communication*, (pp. 335-384). Norwood, NJ: Danowski, J. A. (1993a). *Automatic narrative generation via statistical content analysis of large-scale textual collections*. Paper presented at Conference on Computing for the Social Sciences, National Center for Supercomputing Applications, University of Illinois at Urbana-Campaign, May 18-21.

Danowski, J. A. (1993b). WORDij 3.0: A word-pair approach to information retrieval. *Proceedings of the DARPA/NIST TREC Conference*, Washington, DC.

Danowski, J. A. (1993c). Network analysis of message content. In Rice, R. E., Richards, W., & Barnett, G. (Eds.), *Progress in communication sciences XII* (pp. 197–222). Norwood, NJ: Ablex.

Danowski, J. A. (2007). *Comparing semantic network analysis approaches*. Paper presented to the International Association for Social Network Analysis, Sunbelt XXVII annual meetings Corfu, Greece, May.

Danowski, J. A. (2009). Inferences from word networks in messages. In Krippendorff, K., & Bock, M. A. (Eds.), *The content analysis reader* (pp. 421–429). Sage Publications.

Danowski, J. A. (2010). *WORDij 3.0. [Computer program]*. Chicago, IL: University of Illinois at Chicago.

Danowski, J. A., & Cepela, N. (2010). Automatic mapping of social networks of actors from text corpora: Time series analysis. *Annals of Information Systems, 12*, 31–46. doi:10.1007/978-1-4419-6287-4_3

Danowski, J. A., & Edison-Swift, P. (1985). Crisis effects on intraorganizational computer-based communication. *Communication Research, 12*, 251–270. doi:10.1177/009365085012002005

Danowski, J. A., & Edison-Swift, P. (1985). Crisis effects on intraorganizational computer-based communication. *Communication Research, 12*(2), 251–270. doi:10.1177/009365085012002005

Danowski, J. A., Gluesing, J., & Riopelle, K. (2009). *ICT's effects on diffusion curves, email networks, and semantic networks in an organization: The emergence of herding, bandwagons, and information cascades with less interpersonal communication*. Paper presented to the Communication and Technology Division of the International Communication Association, Chicago, May 21-25.

Danowski, J. A., Riopelle, K., & Gluesing, J. (2008). *Using network analysis of who-to-whom email networks to structure semantic network analysis of email content and manage it in innovation contexts*. Paper presented at annual meetings of the International Network for Social Network Analysis, Sunbelt XXVIII annual meetings, St. Pete Beach, FL, January, 2008.

Diesner, J., & Carley, K. M. (2004). *Using network text analysis to detect the organizational structure of covert networks*. Pittsburg, PA: CASOS, Carnegie-Mellon. Available from: http://www.contrib.andrew.cmu.edu/~jdiesner/publications/NAACSOS_2004_Diesner_Carley_Detect_Covert_Networks.pdf

Diesner, J., & Carley, K. M. (2004). *AutoMap 1.2: Extract, analyze, represent, and compare mental models from texts.* Pittsburg, PA: CASOS, Carnegie-Mellon University. Available from: http://reports-archive.adm.cs.cmu.edu/ anon/anon/usr/ftp/isri2004/ CMU-ISRI-04-100.pdf

Diesner, J., & Carley, K. M. (2008). Conditional random fields for entity extraction and ontological text coding. *Computational & Mathematical Organization Theory, 14*(3), 248262. doi:10.1007/s10588-008-9029-z

Diesner, J., Frantz, T. L., & Carley, K. M. (2005). Communication networks from the Enron email corpus 'it's always about the people. Enron is no different'. *Computational & Mathematical Organization Theory, 11*(3), 201228. doi:10.1007/s10588-005-5377-0

Fredrickson, B. L., & Losada, M. F. (2005). Positive affect and the complex dynamics of human flourishing. *The American Psychologist, 60*(7), 678–686. doi:10.1037/0003-066X.60.7.678

Freeman, L. C. (1979). Centrality in social networks: Conceptual clarification. *Social Networks, 1,* 215–239. doi:10.1016/0378-8733(78)90021-7

Freeman, L. C. (1996). Some antecedents of social network analysis. *Connections, 19*(1), 39–42.

Freeman, L. C., Borgatti, S. P., & White, D. R. (1991). Centrality in valued graphs: A measure of betweenness based on network flow. *Social Networks, 13*(2), 141–154. doi:10.1016/0378-8733(91)90017-N

Galaskiewicz, J. (1985). Professional networks and the institutionalization of a single mindset. *American Sociological Review, 50,* 639–658. doi:10.2307/2095379

Galaskiewicz, J., & Shatin, D. (1981). Leadership and networking among neighborhood human service organizations. *Administrative Science Quarterly, 26,* 434–4. doi:10.2307/2392516

Gloor, P. (2006). *Swarm creativity: Competitive advantage through collaborative innovation networks.* Oxford University Press US.

Gloor, P., & Zhao, Y. (2006). *Analyzing actors and their discussion topics by semantic social network analysis.* Tenth International Conference on Information Visualization, 5-7 July 2006, 130-135. London, England. Available from: http://www.ickn.org/documents/IV06_G2341_Gloor.pdf

Granovetter, M. S. (1973). The strength of weak ties. *American Journal of Sociology, 78*(6), 1360–1380. doi:10.1086/225469

Latour, B. (2005). *Reassembling the social: An introduction to Actor-Network-Theory.* London: Oxford University Press.

Mizruchi, M. S. (1996). What do interlocks do? An analysis, critique, and assessment of research on interlocking directorates. *Annual Review of Sociology, 22,* 27129. doi:10.1146/annurev.soc.22.1.271

Monge, P. R., & Eisenberg, E. M. (1987). Emergent communication networks. In Jablin, F. M., Putnam, L. L., Roberts, K. H., & Porter, L. W. (Eds.), *Handbook of organizational communication: An interdisciplinary perspective* (p. 304342). Newbury Park: Sage.

Pennebaker, J. W., Booth, R. J., & Francis, M. E. (2007). *Linguistic Inquiry and Word Count 2007 (LIWC2007).* Austin, TX: LIWC, Inc.

Richards, W. D. Jr. (1995). *NEGOPY 4.30 Manual and user's Guide.* Burnaby, Canada: School of Communication, Simon Fraser University.

Riopelle, K., Danowski, J. A., & Bishop, A. (2010). *Expression of sentiment by different node positions in email networks.* Paper presented to annual meetings of the International Network for Social Network Analysts, Riva Del Garda, Italy, June 29-July 4.

Riopelle, K., Danowski, J. A., & Gluesing, J. (2008). *Organizational hierarchy predictors of symmetric and asymmetric dyad and triad distributions in a large global organization.* Paper presented at annual meetings of the International Network for Social Network Analysis, Sunbelt XXVIII annual meetings, St. Pete Beach, FL, January.

Scott, J. (1988). Social network analysis. *Sociology, 22*(1), 109–127. doi:10.1177/0038038588022001007

Scott, J. (1991). Networks of corporate power. *Annual Review of Sociology, 17,* 181203. doi:10.1146/annurev.so.17.080191.001145

Scott, J. (2000). *Social network analysis: A handbook* (2nd ed.). Thousand Oaks: Sage.

Seary, A. J. (2005) *MultiNet: An interactive program for analysing and visualizing complex networks.* Doctoral Dissertation, Burnaby, CA: Simon Frazier University. Available from: http://people.math.sfu.ca/~goddyn/ Theses/searyPhDThesis.pdf

Tichy, N. M., Tushman, M. L., & Fombrun, C. (1979). Social network analysis for organizations. *Academy of Management Review, 4*(4), 507–519.

Valente, T. W. (1996). Social network thresholds in the diffusion of innovations. *Social Networks, 18,* 69–89. doi:10.1016/0378-8733(95)00256-1

# Chapter 14

# Universal Dynamics on Complex Networks, Really?
## A Comparison of Two Real–World Networks that Cross Structural Paths … but Ever so Differently.

**Brigitte Gay**
*University Toulouse, Toulouse Business School, France*

## ABSTRACT

*The complex network approach developed in statistical physics seems particularly well-suited to analyzing large networks. Progress in the study of complex networks has been made by looking for shared properties and seemingly universal dynamics, thus ignoring the details of networks individual nodes, links, or sub-components. Researchers now need to assess the differences in the processes that take place on complex networks. The author first discusses briefly the theoretical understanding of evolutionary laws governing the emergence of these universal properties (small-world and scale-free networks) and recent evolutions in the field of network analysis. Using data on two empirical networks, a transaction network in the venture capital industry and an interfirm alliance network in a major sector of the biopharmaceutical industry, the author then demonstrates that networks can switch from one 'universal' structure to another, but each in its own way. This chapter highlights the need of knowing more about networks, as 'more is different'.*

## INTRODUCTION

Studying relationships among actors, be it individuals or organizations, is essential to the social sciences. Social network analysis, or SNA, has been defined by Breiger (2004; p. 505) as the

"disciplined inquiry into the patterning of relations among social actors, as well as the patterning of relationships among actors at different levels of analysis (such as persons or groups)."

Complexity theory has become instrumental in recent models in social sciences. As part of complexity theory, the 'complex network' approach developed in statistical physics seems to

DOI: 10.4018/978-1-61350-513-7.ch014

be particularly appropriate for the analysis of the macro environments, whether technical, social, or natural, into which entities are embedded (Frenken, 2006; Pyka, 2009).

The past decade has indeed witnessed the birth of a new movement of research in the study of complex networks, with the main focus switching from the analysis of small networks to that of networks whose structure is large, irregular, and evolves dynamically in time (Newman, 2003; Boccaletti et al., 2006; Albert and Barabási, 2002). What is also new in network-based research is the availability and exponential growth of computing power that allows handling and managing unprecedented volumes of empirical data.

The literature on complex networks reveals a rapid growth of articles, starting after 2000, which corresponds to the emergence of this new paradigm (Pyka, 2009). Though the notion on networks in general is a shared subject among different disciplines (graph theory in discrete mathematics, philosophy, sociology, anthropology, and more recently economics and strategy (Ahuja et al., 1993; Bollobas, 1998; Degenne and Forse, 1994; Gay, 2005; Jackson, 2007; Scott, 2000; Wasserman and Faust, 1994; West, 1996), statistical analysis is the proper tool for a useful mathematical characterization when studying large scale networks and their complex topologies. The mathematical language of graph theory is thus used to describe these systems and to investigate the formal properties of the interactions defining them.

Although we will highlight the need to combine key network concepts, perspectives, or modeling, spanning from different research traditions, complex networks are therefore conveniently conceptualized here graph-theoretically, i.e. as objects containing nodes and links.

A network is hence described in very general terms as a graph whose nodes identify the elementary constituents of the system, the interconnections between these entities being represented by the linkages in the network. As stated by Madhavan, Koka, and Prescott (1998, p. 441)

*i. A network at a given point in time is a 'snapshot' that shows interactions as they currently exist .... True structural change would be evidenced by significant variation over time in the underlying pattern of relationships that bind a given set of actors*

The first issue that has been faced in statistical physics has been to define new concepts and measures to try to infer the structural properties of large empirical networks. The main outcome has been the identification of a series of unifying principles and statistical properties shared by most of the real-world networks examined.

Real-world networks were in effect found to have statistical regularities that had not been anticipated from the classical random graph theory of Erdös and Rényi (1960). In particular they often have the small-world property (relatively short paths between any two nodes and a large clustering coefficient), and scale-free degree profile (power-law scaling for the probability distribution of the number of links at a node). New models were developed to reproduce the structural properties observed in real topologies. Networks with high clustering coefficient and small average path length can be generated with an evolution by the small-world model of Watts and Strogatz (1998), while networks with power-law degree distribution can be generated with an evolution by the scale-free model of Barabàsi and Albert (1999).

These studies have been motivated by the anticipation that understanding and modeling the structure of complex networks would contribute to a better knowledge of their evolutionary mechanisms, and to a better grasp of their dynamical and functional behavior. However there have been too much specious claims regarding statistical regularities such as universality scaling properties and the functions that they produce. Moreover these claims have been made without testing through periodization of the processes if these functions are truly capable of producing the time-lagged processes. Another common theme is that complex networks are self-organizing and that their character is essentially endogenous. The external environment plays no role; it does not intervene occasionally to stabilize or destabilize networks. We know however that the environment, whether regarding sociopolitics or innovation, etc, is subject to relentless instability.

Though essential, looking for shared properties and seemingly universal dynamics on complex networks holds thus the danger of reductionism as there are more non-trivial structural properties and levels of organization to consider.

Moreover, the onsets and outcomes of growing networks may be very different.

Besides, topological models in statistical physics are so far mainly concerned with link structure. In most cases, the presence of distinct types of nodes is only hypothesized and the type of each node is unknown. Studies need also to examine the interplay between individual agents' behavior and macro networks. Embeddedness in

networks is neither random nor neutral: actors act under the constraints of their environment while they themselves constitute each other's changing environment. Incapacitating embeddedness in cohesive networks can occur. For example, biotech companies can be rapidly stuck in overly cohesive competitive networks while successful companies develop instead diverse portfolios of links to many players in the market (Gay, 2008; Powell et al., 2005; Walker, Kogut, and Shan, 1997). Individual incentives and aggregate network outcomes, including the evolving linkages and competition for interest between different categories of agents, thus need to be captured.

Figure 1 provides an idea of why the study of complex networks is an important issue in SNA. Actors are embedded into macro structures that change, thus disturbing continuously individual positions. Agents are hence constrained by the moves of all actors in a system while they may try at the same time to 'fit in' and possibly control,

*Figure 1. The multi-level aspect of network research. As actors, persons or organizations, are constantly constrained/influenced by moves of others in the system as well as by the dynamics on networks, it is important that they continuously consider how to build effective ego-networks to 'balance' their position and possibly control their environment, be it their immediate neighborhood, the communities into which they operate, and possibly the whole structure.*

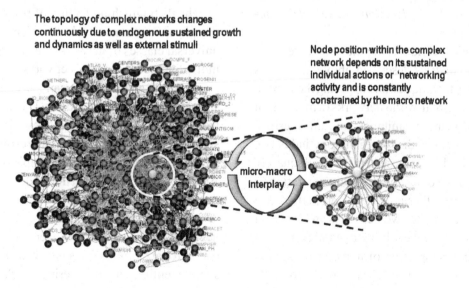

whether partially or totally, the macro structure into which they are embedded.

In this chapter, we will attempt to go beyond what characterizes complex network research, i.e. the search for a few universal principles, by examining whether complex networks contain additional structure which is not captured by the simplest models and how different integrated collective behavior can be.

The chapter will be organized as follows. The first section will sketch out research in complex network analysis that has been fueled by the discovery of *universal structural properties in real-world networks (First section)* and the theoretical understanding of evolutionary laws governing the emergence of these properties (small-world and scale-free networks).

In the second section, we will summarize recent efforts to develop new metrics to escape oversimplifications in the analysis of complex networks and increase our understanding of organizing principles governing complex network dynamics by allowing better descriptions of the hierarchies and organizational architecture of networks. We will briefly describe an occurring shift in research; from systematically looking in statistical physics for universal traits on complex networks to investigating differences in network structures that may epitomize different behaviors and dynamics (*Second section: Universal dynamics and beyond*).

In the third section, using the two models and a set of the metrics described above as well as visualization techniques, and applying them to the analysis of two real-world networks (a transaction network of venture capitalists and an interfirm alliance network in the biotechnology industry), we will seek whether these networks fall squarely under one or the other universal categorization or are defined by other non trivial properties. We will also compare the two networks and focus on the analysis of their evolving dynamics, including from the perspective of hubs. In particular, we will show that networks can switch from one

'universal' structure to another, and each in its own way. Finally, this application will allow us to reveal that social structure may actually rest on central players, or hubs, and the very different power structures that epitomize these networks (*Third section: Complex networks have distinctive signatures and power structure ..... that change*).

As one of the main purposes of the chapter is to highlight the importance of the continuous development of techniques to allow understanding generic as well as discrete evolving architectures in SNA, we'll finally conclude on expected or needed evolutions in the field of network analysis that would further help characterize or understand real-world networks.

## UNIVERSAL STRUCTURAL PROPERTIES IN REAL WORLD NETWORKS

While sociological and psychological work on networks explicitly considers dynamic behavioral effects of different network structures (Heider, 1946; Cartwright and Harary, 1956; Doreian and Stokman, 1997), statistical physics seeks universalities both in the topology of complex networks and in the dynamic processes going on in these networks.

The distinguishing feature of research within the physics community is the identification of universal classes of networks: regardless of their individual details, many networks share certain aggregate properties that can be embodied by simple mathematical models. The implication, from a physicist's point of view, is that very simple models can capture interesting characteristics of even extremely complex networks. Another implication is that the models and metrics developed in this field could be usefully applied in other disciplines as well. Two separate early developments in particular were that by Watts and Strogatz (1998) on small-world networks, supplementing the pioneering work of social psychologist Stanley Milgram (1967), and that by Barabasi and Albert (1999) on scale-free evolving networks. These pioneering studies started an avalanche of research on the properties of these models. Random graphs, small world models that interpolate between highly clustered regular lattices and random graphs, and scale-free models that aim to explain the origin of the power law tails and other non-random degree distributions seen in real-world networks, form today the main classes of modeling paradigms.

## Small-World Networks

When analyzing the architecture of real-world networks, the null hypothesis is that the patterning of links is only determined by chance. Any difference in link structure compared to how a graph originates from a random process in a random null model is then interpreted as a signature of deviation from randomness.

In simple terms, the small-world (SW) concept describes the fact that regardless of their often large size, there is in most real-world networks a relatively short path between any two nodes.

In the SW model by Watts and Strogatz (1998), which has its roots in social systems (Pool and Kochen, 1978; Korte and Milgram, 1979; Milgram, 1967), $N$ nodes form a one-dimensional ring lattice, each node being connected to its two nearest and next-nearest neighbors. With probability $p$, each link is reconnected to a node chosen at random. This process generates long range interactions that decrease the distance between the nodes, leading to a small-world phenomenon. If $p = 1$, the process leads to randomness. Tuning this $p$-parameter produces as a result three different network topologies (regular for $p = 0$, SW for $p$ values between 0 and 1, and random for $p = 1$).

This model thus starts, as is typical of complexity models, from a specification with only one initial parameter, the $p$-parameter, defining the fraction of randomly rewired links.

A SW as defined by Watts and Strogatz (1998) is a structure that has both a short path length as in a random graph and is highly clustered locally as in a regular lattice. It displays this duality for a high range of the rewiring probabilities $p$. Clustering in the model is determined by the clustering coefficient, which quantifies how close the local neighborhood of a node is to being part of a clique, a region of the graph where every node is connected to every other node.

For a ring lattice ($p = 0$), the clustering coefficient is large ($C \sim 3/4$) while, for $p = 1$, it decreases with system size.

In the model also, the scaling from the average shortest path length $L$ between node pairs can change with system size from linear ($p = 0$ for a regular lattice; $L(0) \sim N/2k$) to logarithmically ($p = 1$ for a random network; $L(1) \sim ln(N)/ln(<k>)$, $<k>$ being the average degree of the network).

It was Watts and Strogatz (1998) who first remarked that many real-world networks satisfied the small-world criteria and therefore belonged to a universal class of networks, that is, a family of networks that have in common two aggregate properties regardless of their many idiosyncratic traits.

The SW structure, as defined by these two main metrics, is thought to render large networks extremely efficient in exchanging/diffusing/synchronizing locally and globally all that is contained in networks, be it information, diseases, or coupled oscillators. Only a small amount of randomness is necessary for example for the rapid spreading of epidemics.

Though there is no typical degree in many empirical networks, the SW model follows a Poissonian degree distribution, where the characteristic degree $k$ is the average degree $<k>$ as in a random graph. Thus the topology of SW networks is relatively homogeneous, all nodes having about the same number of links. This means that, as in random graphs or regular lattices, all nodes are topologically equivalent in the SW model.

## Scale Free Networks

The network model described above assumes that we start with a fixed number $N$ of nodes that are then randomly rewired, without varying $N$. This is in sharp contrast with a great majority of real world networks which form open systems that grow by the continuous addition of new nodes.

The Barabasi and Albert algorithm or BA model (1999) uses a basic theme of growth with preferential attachment. In this model, new nodes join the network by attaching $m$ links to other nodes, chosen according to linear preferential attachment. A node obtains one of the new links with a probability proportional to the number of links it already has. In the limit of large graph size, the BA model generates networks with a degree distribution $P(k) = k^\gamma$ with $\gamma = 3$. This model thus leads to networks evolving into scale-invariant states with the probability that a node has $k$ edges following a power-law with a single value $\gamma = 3$ for the distribution exponent.

Because of the preferential attachment, nodes that acquire more connections will increase their connectivity at a higher rate, this process leading overtime to some nodes that are highly connected, or *rich-get-richer* phenomenon.

These networks are thus highly inhomogeneous since they result in the simultaneous presence of a few nodes or *hubs* linked to many other nodes, and a large number of poorly connected entities.

In real-world networks, the power law describes systems of rather different sizes at different stages of their development. The BA model provides a distribution whose main features are independent of time and system size. The network organizes itself into a scale invariant stationary state despite its sustained growth.

Real world networks that are scale-free (SF) include the WWW, Internet, as well as some biological, social, and business networks (Newman, 2001; Jeong et al., 2000; Jeong et al., 2001; Faloutsos et al. 1999; Albert et al., 2000; Adamic and Huberman, 2000). Though the fact that the emergence of the SF behavior takes place in fundamentally different real world networks is in itself striking, the degree exponent $\gamma$ is not universal. Its value is system-dependent (the exponents measured for real networks vary between 1 and 3) and we still do not know what determines the degree exponent $\gamma$.

## UNIVERSAL DYNAMICS AND BEYOND

In essence, to try glimpsing some organizing principle behind these seemingly indecipherable systems, progress in the study of complex networks has first been made by ignoring the details of their individual links and nodes. We now need to probe more fully the subtle dynamics that shape the different systems.

## Extensions or Modifications Intrinsic to Each Model

Variants of the two models have been proposed since (Barthelemy and Amaral, 1999; Dorogovtsev and Mendes, 2000; Newman and Watts, 1999; Bianconi and Barabasi, 2001; Krapivsky and Redner, 2001). For example, the BA model, or *rich get richer* model, ignores the relevance of looking at the knowledge endowment of nodes. Bianconi and Barabasi (2001) have therefore proposed a new model, or *fit get richer*, that accounts for the link between nodes individual differences and their connectivity to determine the rate at which nodes will acquire edges. Each node $i$ is assigned randomly a fitness parameter $\eta_i$. The growth rate in the preferential attachment changes from

$$\Pi(k_i) = k_i \,/\, \Sigma_i \; k_i \quad \text{to} \quad \Pi(\eta_i k_i) = \eta_i k_i \,/\, \Sigma_i \; \eta_i k_i$$

Nodes with large $\eta$ are therefore able to join networks at a later time and overcome older nodes that are or have become less fit.

On the other hand Newman and Watts (1999) have proposed a variant of the SW model in which links are added between randomly chosen pairs of nodes, but no links are removed from the regular lattice. An alternative SW model starts also from the ring lattice (Kasturirangan, 1999). Additional nodes are added in the middle of the lattice and then randomly connected to a large number of nodes chosen randomly on the main lattice. Kleinberg (2000) also presented a generalization of the SW model based on a two-dimensional square lattice. Interestingly, Ozik, Hunt and Ott (2004) introduced a simple evolution model of growing SW networks to try to understand how these models emerge in the first place. In this model, all connections are made locally to geographically nearby sites. In this case, the SW topology is reproduced by combining the concept of preferentially attachment in SF networks with geography. Other SW and SF topologies were generated in a deterministic way rather than stochastically (Zhang et al., 2006; Barabasi, 2001).

## New Contributions on Structural Properties

We've seen that complex systems exhibit characteristic properties that transcend microscopic properties. However, their constituents are heterogeneous and many different types of interactions exist. We must therefore try to understand patterns and regularities of interactions in a way which might make it possible to break complex systems into possible subcomponents.

The characterization of such systems goes far beyond the basic properties described above. The development and use of more metrics has led to the increasing evidence for the presence in networks of motifs, hierarchies when applying for example $k$-core decomposition methods, communities and modular ordering, assortative mixing, patterns of weighted connections, etc that define different classes of heterogeneous complex networks, whose structures vary and extend over

many possible scales (Barrat et al., 2004; Girvan and Newman, 2002; Milo et al., 2002; ; Newman, 2002; Seidman, 1983; Shen-Orr et al., 2002). Community structures are an important property in social networks as tightly connected groups of nodes represent individuals or organizations belonging to social communities. Similarly, eigenvalues direct the influence of the network on a number of other dynamical phenomena and, on the whole, on the emergence of coherent behavior (Motter et al., 2005).

The use of the assortative coefficient is also interesting as correlated graphs can be classified as assortative if nodes tend to connect to their connectivity peers, and as disassortative if nodes with low degree are more likely connected with highly connected ones. All nodes indeed are not created equal. How much the nodes themselves differ in their intrinsic ability to build connections must bear on the interpretation of empirical findings. If the different categories of nodes in a network are identified, the link structure of complex networks may reveal a distinct signature.

Distinguishing between nodes, links, subparts, and using new metrics as they are developed, can help us determine how a complex system depends on its parts, as well as how these parts are linked together, whether different classes of actors operate within or/and outside these parts and how.

## Dynamics on Networks

Structure strongly influences network dynamics. In the context of epidemic spreading, research by Watts and Strogatz (1998) on SW networks and by Barabasi and Albert (1999) and subsequently Pastor-Satorras and Vespignani (2004) on SF networks demonstrated that dynamical processes in complex systems could be strongly influenced by the structure of an underlying network. SF networks for example were shown to lack an epidemic threshold.

Progress that has been made for the study of processes on networks also include network failure, models displaying phase transitions, and dynamical systems like random Boolean networks and cellular automata (see Newman, 2003 for a review).

In reality however, two processes are entwined: the growth and change of an underlying network structure and the dynamics of the processes operating on this structure. Work on network growth is still in its infancy.

## The Interpretation of Empirical Data

Studies of complex empirical networks have generally not extended the exploration of network structure beyond examining whether it fell under one or the other categorization, SW or SF. Moreover, researchers that looked for a SW structure in their empirical data have often taken as a postulate that a high clustering coefficient and a small average path length effectively described a modular structure of weakly connected coupled clusters. Besides, most studies did not bother looking at, or interpreting, the degree distribution.

Another overlooked issue concerns the nodes themselves. Distinguishing between different types of links should also be important to the interpretation of structural characteristics. Links for example can be considered as being either tangible (and therefore capable of transferring information, or material, etc) or symbolic (abstract relations between entities). In particular, stochasticity is a common feature of complex network models that generates SW and SF topologies. New nodes connect to existing nodes in a network using a probabilistic rule. The random placement or addition of links and nodes are not appropriate techniques for tangible networks. In this case, models that lead to SW or SF networks in a deterministic manner would have more practical significance (Comellas and Sampels, 2002; Zhang et al., 2006).

## REAL-WORLD COMPLEX NETWORKS HAVE DISTINCTIVE SIGNATURES AND POWER STRUCTURES ..... THAT CHANGE

To understand the global properties of real-world systems and their dynamics, we need to capture the topology of complex wiring architectures, and figure out how these architectures can behave collectively, and whether they really possess unifying principles and statistical properties.

The focus of recent work in the area of complex empirical networks has been their comparative study from different disciplines, with emphasis on common properties and the mathematical developments that reflect those properties. To show the usefulness of the statistical approaches in practice but also the danger of oversimplification, we compare here two complex networks, an interfirm alliance network in the biopharmaceutical industry and a transaction network in the venture capital industry as venture capitalists invest in the biopharmaceutical industry. We only provide data critical for comparison, the details of the different studies being given elsewhere (Gay, 2010 and 2011). To examine effectively network growth and dynamics, we followed in both cases an event focused approach as advocated by Madhavan, Koka, and Prescott (1998). The timing of industry events allows for a setting in which the length of "windows" or periodization is mechanically determined for the researcher. We expect the ability of organizations to acquire connections to fluctuate with the different events, endogenous and exogenous, that mark the two industry sectors. As our purpose is to compare the two networks and their dynamics, we investigated for statistical tests and each network a whole period as well a four-period analysis, corresponding to major shifts in the power structure, or degree to which an entire network is focused around a few central nodes, of the two organizational networks. We looked at network traits using these time windows and therefore do not use arbitrary time points for analysis.

An interfirm alliance network was constructed for companies, where the nodes are the companies and two nodes are connected if the two companies have signed a formal contractual agreement within a consistent subset of the biopharmaceutical industry, the antibody sector. The definitional focus for the inclusion of actors is based on the actor's participation in the specified exchange. To uncover the topology of this complex graph, we used a unique collaborative agreement dataset compiled by querying specialized internet sites (leading sources for news releases and regulatory filings from companies throughout the world such as Business Wire et PRNewswire, as well as companies' internet site) for alliances made in the antibody sector in the years 1998 to 2007, and employing Perl scripts to collect and parse data (Gay, 2010). Using multiple data sources was indispensable to track effectively alliances made by companies, private or public, and ascertain the accuracy of our database. Major alliance databases are incomplete in that they do not capture all announced alliances and understate heavily the size of the industry (Schilling and Phelps, 2009), particularly regarding private or "young" companies. Our sample contains 443 firms. Major shifts in degree centrality occurred in periods 2000-2001, 2002-2003, 2004-2005, and 2006-2007 which were thus selected for analysis.

Venture capital consists in a formal and professionally managed pool of capital raised for the purpose of making actively-managed direct equity investments in promising private ventures at different stages of their development, and with a well defined exit strategy. Transaction networks in the venture capital industry are built up through the extensive use of syndicated investing. Many VC firms involved in syndications invest across a range of start-ups, creating a chain of investments in which the syndications form the links. We define a syndicated deal or syndication as the collection of VCs that invest in a given portfolio company, comprising those investing in a given portfolio company investment round as well as those invest-

ing in subsequent rounds. We have studied the web constructed among Venture Capital (VC) firms in the US biopharmaceutical industry where the ties among them are their co-investments. The time period examined here run from the first quarter of 1988 to the last quarter of 2008. During this time, 1499 biotech companies received venture capital funding in either one round or more and 1158 firms provided venture capital. Major shifts in VC investments with concurrent changes in degree centralization occurred in periods 1993-1996, 1997-2000, 2001-2004, and 2005-2008 which were thus selected for analysis. The data are drawn from VentureXpert, a comprehensive database of venture capital funds, portfolio companies, and deals owned and managed by Thomson Financial and the only database officially endorsed by the National Venture Capital Association. Data from VentureXpert has been used extensively in studies of the venture capital industry (Sorenson and Stuart, 2001; Gans, Hsu and Stern, 2002; Kogut, Urso, and Walker, 2007, Walker, 2008).

We were interested in examining whether the two systems shared global features and organizing principles encoded in their topology and whether the main models we have at our disposal adequately mimic their structural properties and growth.

## Small-World Properties

Both networks display the small-world property, with relatively high clustering as well as small path length. The clustering coefficient $C$ is 0,27 for the antibody network (period 1998-2007) and 0,643 for the VC network (period 1988-2008) while the average path length $L$ is 3,5 and 3 respectively.

In addition the two networks maintained these properties (large $C$ and small $L$) as they continuously expanded (Table 1). At all times, the clustering coefficients of the two networks were at least 10 times (first network) and 30 times (second network) higher than the clustering coefficients of the random graphs.

*Table 1. General characteristics of the two real-world networks, the interfirm alliance network (network 1) and the VC network (network 2), for the different time periods studied. For each network, we indicated the number of nodes, the density d, the average path length $l_{Emp}$, the clustering coefficient $C_{Emp}$, and the γ exponent. We also compared $C_{Emp}$ and $l_{Emp}$ to values of equivalent random and scale-free graphs, $C_{Rand}$, $l_{rand}$, and $C_{SF}$.*

| | | **Period 1** | **Period 2** | **Period 3** | **Period 4** |
|---|---|---|---|---|---|
| N | Network 1 | 80 | 96 | 187 | 218 |
| | Network 2 | 233 | 353 | 423 | 511 |
| d | Network 1 | 0,037 | 0,028 | 0,017 | 0,016 |
| | Network 2 | 0,046 | 0,027 | 0,026 | 0,022 |
| $C_{Emp}$ | Network 1 | 0,239 | 0,208 | 0,27 | 0,404 |
| | Network 2 | 0,634 | 0,636 | 0,676 | 0,672 |
| $C_{Emp}/<k>$ | Network 1 | 0,21 | 0,20 | 0,17 | 0,24 |
| | Network 2 | 0,13 | 0,15 | 0,12 | 0,12 |
| $C_{Rand}$ | Network 1 | 0,025 | 0,018 | 0,017 | 0,015 |
| | Network 2 | 0,023 | 0,013 | 0,013 | 0,011 |
| $C_{SF}$ | Network 1 | 0,034 | 0,028 | 0,020 | 0,018 |
| | Network 2 | 0,017 | 0,012 | 0,011 | 0,009 |
| $l_{Emp}$ | Network 1 | 3,27 | 4,414 | 4,246 | 4,784 |
| | Network 2 | 2,82 | 3,05 | 3,04 | 3,06 |
| $l_{rand}$ | Network 1 | 5,58 | 6,33 | 4,60 | 4,44 |
| | Network 2 | 3,3 | 3,8 | 3,5 | 3,6 |
| γ | Network 1 | 1,11 | 1,46 | 1,6 | |
| | Network 2 | | | | 1,1 |

The clustering coefficient $C_{rand}$ of a random graph is $<k>/N$. Therefore the ratio $C_{rand}/<k>$ decreases as $N^{-1}$. The ratio of the clustering coefficient of the two real networks and their average degree $C_{emp}/<k>$ does not decrease as a function of their size as in random graphs. The two empirical networks clearly do not follow the prediction of random graphs. Instead, as in small-world models, $C_{emp}$ remains large and independent of network size N in both cases.

Also in agreement with the SW model, the average path length in the two real world networks stays small and close to that of a random graph with the same size and average degree.

However, while the value of the clustering coefficient remains almost unchanged for the VC network as would be expected in a SW, it varies for the biotech alliance network. In particular, as the alliance network develops through time, the clustering coefficient ratio rises significantly in the last period. Also, the clustering coefficient of the VC network is always consistently higher than that of the alliance network and close to the value of a regular network ($C(0) \sim ¾$).

## Degree Distribution

The degree distribution of the alliance network is consistent with a power-law with degree exponent

*Figure 2. Scaling behavior of the biotech alliance network (left) and the VC network (right) from period 3 to 4. For the biotech alliance network the distribution is better fitted by a power law ($R^2 = 0,91$) in the first period and by an exponential in the second ($R^2 = 0,95$) while it is the reverse for the VC network ($R^2 = 0,98$ and $0,97$ respectively).*

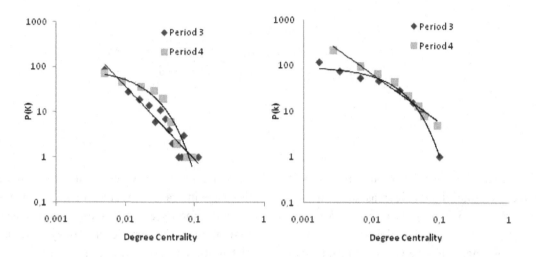

$\gamma = 1,2$ for the whole period analyzed. Contrarily, the degree distribution of the VC network is better fitted by an exponential than by a power-law.

The results are however more nuanced if we look at statistics as the two networks grow. For the first three periods, the degree distribution of the biotech alliance network indicates that the network indeed follows the power law that characterizes scale-free networks. The data also demonstrates the existence of a scaling regime with different exponents (Table 1). The scaling increasingly deviates as time increases and therefore is not constant as in the BA model. However, in the last period, we have an exponential truncation of the degree distribution. Figure 2 shows the change from period 3, as degree distribution shows up as power law, to period 4 when the distribution is exponential.

Interestingly, the VC network behavior is exactly opposite: degree distribution is exponential during the first three periods while the last period shows up as power law (Figure 2).

## Node Typology and the Use of More Network Metrics

Many researchers have proposed modifications of the BA scale-free model that alter its behavior. In the BA model, the clustering coefficient vanishes with system size as $C \sim N^{-0.75}$, a phenomenon clearly not observed in our networks, where $C$ is higher (while being variable in the first network and a constant in the second network) and independent of $N$ (Table 1). Generalizations to reinforce the clustering properties, lacking in the BA scale-free model, have been considered. Different models using different rewiring procedures produce SF distributions as well as a clustering coefficient much larger than in the BA model (Caldarelli, 2007; Cowan and Jonard, 2008).

A simple wrapping up of the analysis can thus be that the first network shifts from a SF (with high clustering coefficient) to a SW topology while the second one operates in reverse, going from a SW structure, with many redundant pathways, to a still cohesive but SF architecture.

Indeed, in the last period, the degree distribution of the antibody alliance network tends towards

*Figure 3. Visual rendering of the biotech alliance network changing architecture. The network switches from a clear SF or hub-dominated structure (left; period 1998- 2003; 202 companies) to a SW topology, marked by cohesive pockets (right; period 2006- 2007; 218 companies).*

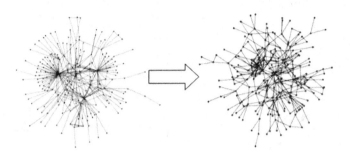

more homogeny as in a SW model, the ratio of $<k>$ over maximal degree decreasing from 14.7 in 2000-2001 to 5.9 in the last period. We must also take into account that the assumption of homogeneity made in the SW model is not exact as, if the mechanism underlying the creation of a network is a search process, the likelihood of forming alliances with non-local partners must decline exponentially with its distance from the firm (Kleinberg, 2000).

For the first network, a shift from a SF to a SW topology thus seems to describe adequately its evolving dynamics and is also corroborated by a visual rendering of the data (Figure 3).

For the VC network, the ratio of $<k>$ over maximal degree is between 11 and 13 at all times. The structural dynamics of this second network could not in effect be interpreted as functioning as with the first network but in 'reverse mode'. For this second network, due to its highly cohesive structure, more metrics were needed to disentangle its structural dynamics.

Salient differences between networks were also that the first network was characterized by a very fast turn-over of links and nodes, including hubs, while the second network was defined by repeat interactions among partners and the presence of a core structure of tightly linked hubs.

To actually figure out the collective behavior of the two networks, we had to resort in both cases to the categorization of hubs.

More specifically, we found that, since its links are in reality directed (firms in- or out- license technologies, processes, or products[1]), the first network is best described by two degree distributions: the distribution of out-going links and the distribution of in-going links. We found that the first period is dominated by the SF distribution of out-going links $P_{out}(k)$. However, in the last period, in-degree links also play a major role; $P_{out}(k)$ still follows a power-law tail while $P_{in}(k)$ is best fitted with an exponential. The first period describes the domination of a few highly innovative biotech players, or 'fittest' hubs, that essentially out-license their technologies to many partners. The next periods are much more competitive, with more biotech companies to challenge the first hubs until finally network control is exerted mostly by pharmaceutical incumbents, or 'richest' nodes, both locally and globally, as in small worlds. These 'richest' firms fundamentally only in-license assets (Gay, 2010).

For the VC network, we could not find an unambiguous SW structure (Figure 4) though it was inherent in the data for the whole period and at least the first three periods (Table 1).

We applied a core decomposition method and found a clear global hierarchical structure, with common $k$-connectivity among major players in the VC industry. We also found using a new community centrality measure (Newman, 2006) that hubs operated within and outside communities.

*Figure 4. Visualization of a subset of the VC transaction network (period 2004-2005). The darker lines indicate the presence of repeat ties between firms. Though the time period considered here is very short, network structure is highly cohesive. However the network does not form a modular architecture of weakly connected clusters as defined in the SW model. The presence of a hierarchical structure of tightly interconnected hubs is also apparent.*

A clustered scale-free structure that could explain this hierarchical structure, takes precedence over the 'SW topology' only in 2005-2008 with the appearance of a large fraction of a population with minimal connectivity and a sudden increase in activity for large players.

Figure 5 shows how major players of the VC industry timely operate within the core layer of the network. The figure also reveals that two different types of hubs are involved and are interconnected, generalists or experts in the biopharmaceutical industry. In particular, specialized hubs intervene primarily after 2000, when the sequencing of the human genome engaged market mechanisms and created a financial bubble.

Therefore, despite the fact that the VC network has apparent SW features and that the Watts and Strogatz model assumes that the average degree is bounded by a constant $K$, results strongly support the view that VC hubs represent the most influential elements of the network.

*Figure 5. Temporal graph visualization of hubs dynamics operating within the VC firms' transaction network using the VisuGraph algorithm (Gay, and Loubier, 2009).*

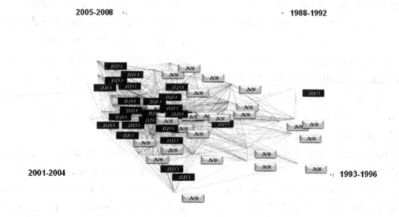

## CONCLUSION

The resolution of complex networks structure still presents a substantial and empirical challenge. In particular, the links between micro- and macro-behavior and their dynamics are understudied as well as the dynamics of interconnected or entangled complex networks.

Searching for universality is one of the most pursued endeavors in physics, particularly in statistical and nonlinear physics. However care must be exercised when claiming universal features of networks.

The statistical approach however is unavoidable for large networks and represents an exciting research field. Though the first models in statistical physics were in fact not suitable as models of complex social networks because the claims in the original models used to generate networks were not necessarily plausible and therefore could not replicate as such (a number of) features of real-world networks, contributions of the main network modeling approaches have been essential to SNA.

However, the fact that research goes for universal laws can easily, despite their success, become a corollary of reductionism. Classical physics for example treats problems at a microscopic scale. The collective behavior of complex systems cannot nevertheless be understood in terms of a simple extrapolation of the elementary features of a few nodes.

Instead, at each level of complexity, completely novel properties appear and each level may require a new conceptual structure (Anderson, 1972). The rapid progression in different disciplines, including within the field of statistical physics, must therefore be taken into account. Active research is ongoing that will benefit all fields tackling the challenge of analyzing networks at different scales.

A possible explanation of the so-called universality (the sharing of properties) has been to suppose a common formation mechanism acting in different cases. Though growing networks share properties, networks maintain many differences, including regarding their onset and outcomes. Accordingly, the graphs produced can be of very different kinds.

We performed a statistical analysis on two real world networks to search for unifying or other principles and statistical properties. The two networks both possess nontrivial properties. We have discussed models that generate SF or SW topologies in the light of the present analysis of these two networks. We have first analyzed the behavior in time of some average network metrics such as the clustering coefficient and the shortest average path length. When dealing with the two networks as 'SW networks only', we impede a realistic modeling of their topology and of their growth and evolution. More clear-cut characterization of the networks topological properties was given by additionally looking at the degree distribution $P(k)$. However, we found that even when large scale-correlations, witnessed by the appearance of power-law distributed frequency for the degree for example, were present in both systems they corresponded to extremely different mechanisms. Moreover the systems were not shaped by self-organization.

In addition, the analysis of many real world networks has been based on the analysis of their static topological properties. We demonstrate that understanding networks evolution and dynamics must be considered a fundamental goal. We show that the two networks analyzed in this study, deploy timely very dissimilar architectures. The topological properties of the two networks have not settled to well-defined stationary states but instead follow altogether extremely different dynamical regimes.

In the first system, we first found a clear power-law behavior $P(k) \sim k^{-\gamma}$. The power law exponent $\gamma$ was nevertheless not scale invariant and not interpretable by the preferential attachment hypothesis. The network finally went from a SF to a SW structure.

On the contrary, the second network evolved from a SW to a SF structure. A unique finding was that networks could switch from one 'universal' structure to another. Still, though the evolution of the two networks seemed to run in reverse, we could not use a backward approach to interpret the structure of the second network. Several other metrics, such as nodes' hierarchy, correlation between degrees, communities in graphs, etc., as well as the use of specific algorithms for dynamic network visualization were instead needed to construe how this network functioned and its dynamics. In this second network, a large contribution to the growth was given by the appearance of links with already existing nodes. Growth was strongly driven by the need for redundancy wiring and external 'demand shocks'.

Overall, nodes were not equal and looking for distinctive categories of nodes and evolving power structures was also essential. A hierarchical structure could be traced out in both systems but different types of hubs operated differently in each system (asymmetrical evolving from the *fittest* to the *richest* in one case; a cohesive core of two entwined categories of hubs, specialized or not, in the second case).

We think the results reported here are relevant for more realistic modeling and empirical study of complex networks growth and evolution. A detailed discussion of different models or work within different disciplines was beyond the scope of the present chapter. However we advocate that to develop a science on complex networks and their dynamics a high interdisciplinary synthesis of newer and older analytical techniques and models, using distinct concepts at different levels and combining the macro perspective on links with individual details, is needed.

# REFERENCES

Adamic, L. A., & Huberman, B. A. (2000). Power-law distribution of the World Wide Web. *Science, 287*, A2115. doi:10.1126/science.287.5461.2115a

Ahuja, R. K., Magnanti, T. L., & Orlin, J. B. (1993). *Network Flows: Theory, Algorithms, and Applications*. Upper Saddle River, NJ: Prentice Hall.

Albert, R., & Barabási, A. L. (2002). Statistical mechanics of complex networks. *Reviews of Modern Physics, 74*, 47–97. doi:10.1103/RevModPhys.74.47

Albert, R., Jeong, H., & Barabási, A. L. (2000). Error and attack tolerance of complex networks. *Nature, 406*, 378–382. doi:10.1038/35019019

Anderson, P. W. (1972). More is different. *Science, 177*, 393–396. doi:10.1126/science.177.4047.393

Barabási, A. L., & Albert, R. (1999). Emergence of scaling in random networks. *Science, 286*, 509–512. doi:10.1126/science.286.5439.509

Barabási, A. L., Ravasz, E., & Vicsek, T. (2001). Deterministic scale-free networks. *Physica A, 299*, 559–564. doi:10.1016/S0378-4371(01)00369-7

Barrat, A., Barthélemy, M., Pastor-Satorras, R., & Vespignani, A. (2004). The architecture of complex weighted networks. *Proceedings of the National Academy of Sciences of the United States of America, 101*(11), 3747–3752. doi:10.1073/pnas.0400087101

Barthelemy, M., & Amaral, L. A. N. (1999). Small world networks: evidence for a crossover picture. *Physical Review Letters, 82*, 3180–3183. doi:10.1103/PhysRevLett.82.3180

Bianconi, G., & Barabási, A. L. (2001). Competition and multiscaling in evolving networks. *Europhysics Letters, 54*, 436–442. doi:10.1209/epl/i2001-00260-6

Boccaletti, S., Latora, V., Moreno, Y., Chavez, M., & Hwang, D. U. (2006). Complex networks: Structure and dynamics. *Physics Reports, 424*(4-5), 175–308. doi:10.1016/j.physrep.2005.10.009

Bollobas, B. (Ed.). (1998). *Modern Graph Theory*. New York, NY: Springer.

Breiger, R. L. (1999). The analysis of social networks. *Physical Review Letters*, *82*, 505–526.

Caldarelli, G. (2007). *Scale-Free Networks*. Oxford: Oxford University Press. doi:10.1093/acprof:oso/9780199211517.001.0001

Cartwright, D., & Harary, F. (1956). Structural balance: A generalization of Heider's. theory. *Psychological Review*, *63*, 277–293. doi:10.1037/h0046049

Comellas, F., & Sampels, M. (2002). Deterministic small-world networks. *Physica A*, *309*, 231–235. doi:10.1016/S0378-4371(02)00741-0

Cowan, R., & Jonard, N. (2008). If the alliance fits …: innovation and network dynamics. In Baum, J., & Rowley, T. J. (Eds.), *Network Strategy: Advances in Strategic Management* (pp. 427–455). Oxford, UK: JAI/Elsevier.

Degenne, A., & Forse, M. (1994). *Introducing Social Networks*. London: Sage.

Doreian, P., & Stokman, F. (1997). *Evolution of Social Networks*. New York: Gordon and Breach.

Dorogovtsev, S. N., & Mendes, J. F. F. (2000). Exactly solvable small-world network. *Europhysics Letters*, *50*, 1–7. doi:10.1209/epl/i2000-00227-1

Erdos, P., & Renyi, A. (1960). On the evolution of random graphs. *Publications of the Mathematical Institute Hungarian Academy of Sciences*, *5*, 17–61.

Faloutsos, M., Faloutsos, P., & Faloutsos, C. (1999). On power-law relationships of the Internet topology. *Computer Communication Review*, *29*, 251–262. doi:10.1145/316194.316229

Frenken, K. (2006). *Innovation, evolution and complexity theory*. Cheltenham & Northampton, MA: Edward Elgar.

Gans, J., Hsu, D., & Stern, S. (2000). When does start-up innovation spur the gale of creative destruction? *The Rand Journal of Economics*, *33*, 571. doi:10.2307/3087475

Gay, B. (2008). Firm dynamic governance of global innovation by means of flexible networks of connections. *Journal of Innovation Economics*, *2*, 63–83. doi:10.3917/jie.002.0063

Gay, B. (2010). *Innovative network in transition: From the fittest to the richest*. Available from http://papers.ssrn.com/ abstract=1649967.

Gay, B. (2011). *Venture Capital Firms: Birds of a Feather that Flock Together, Really?* Paper presented at the international Sunbelt Social Network conference, St. Pete Beach, FL.

Gay, B., & Dousset, B. (2005). Innovation and network structural dynamics: Study of the alliance network of a major sector of the biotechnology industry. *Research Policy*, *34*, 1457–1475. doi:10.1016/j.respol.2005.07.001

Gay, B., & Loubier, E. (July, 2009). *Dynamics and evolution patterns of business networks*. Paper presented at the international conference on Advances in Social Network Analysis and Mining (ASONAM), Athens, Greece.

Girvan, M., & Newman, M. E. J. (2002). Community structure in social and biological networks. *Proceedings of the National Academy of Sciences of the United States of America*, *99*, 7821–7826. doi:10.1073/pnas.122653799

Heider, F. (1946). Attitudes and cognitive organization. *The Journal of Psychology*, *21*, 107–112. doi:10.1080/00223980.1946.9917275

Jackson, M. O. (2007). The study of social networks. In Rauch, J. E. (Ed.), *The missing links: formation and decay of economic networks* (pp. 19–43). London, UK: Russell Sage Foundation.

Jeong, H., Mason, S., Barabási, A. L., & Oltvai, Z. N. (2001). Lethality and centrality in protein networks. *Nature*, *411*, 41–42. doi:10.1038/35075138

Jeong, H., Tombor, B., Albert, R., Oltval, Z. N., & Barabasi, A. L. (2000). The large-scale organization of metabolic networks. *Nature*, *407*, 651–654. doi:10.1038/35036627

Kasturirangan, R. (1999). *Multiple scales in small-world graphs*. In MIT AI Lab Memo 1663., cond-mat/9904055.

Kleinberg, J. M. (2000). Navigation in a small world—it is easier to find short chains between points in some networks than others. *Nature, 406*, 845. doi:10.1038/35022643

Kogut, B., Urso, P., & Walker, G. (2007). Emergent properties of a new financial market: American venture capital syndication, 1965-2005. *Management Science, 53*, 1181–1198. doi:10.1287/mnsc.1060.0620

Korte, C., & Milgram, S. (1970). Acquaintance linking between white and Negro populations: application of the small world problem. *Journal of Personality and Social Psychology, 15*, 101–118. doi:10.1037/h0029198

Krapivsky, P. L., & Redner, S. (2001). Organization of growing random networks. *Physical Review E: Statistical, Nonlinear, and Soft Matter Physics, 6306*, 066123. doi:10.1103/PhysRevE.63.066123

Madhavan, R., Koka, B. R., & Prescott, J. E. (1998). Networks in transition: how industry events (re)shape interfirm relationships. *Strategic Management Journal, 19*(5), 439–459. doi:10.1002/(SICI)1097-0266(199805)19:5<439::AID-DIA952>3.0.CO;2-2

Milgram, S. (1967). The small world problem. *Psychology Today, 2*, 60–67.

Milo, R., Shen-Orr, S., Itzkovitz, S., Kashtan, N., Chklovskii, D., & Alon, U. (2002). Network motifs: simple building blocks of complex networks. *Science, 298*, 824–827. doi:10.1126/science.298.5594.824

Motter, A. E., Zhou, C., & Kurths, J. (2005). Enhancing complex-network synchronization. *Europhysics Letters, 69*, 334–340. doi:10.1209/epl/i2004-10365-4

Newman, M. E. J. (2001). The structure of scientific collaboration networks. *Proceedings of the National Academy of Sciences of the United States of America, 98*, 404–409. doi:10.1073/pnas.021544898

Newman, M. E. J. (2002). Assortative mixing in networks. *Physical Review Letters, 89*, 208701. doi:10.1103/PhysRevLett.89.208701

Newman, M. E. J. (2003). The structure and function of complex networks. *SIAM Review, 45*(2), 167–256. doi:10.1137/S003614450342480

Newman, M. E. J. (2006). Finding community structure in networks using the eigenvectors of matrices. *Physical Review E: Statistical, Nonlinear, and Soft Matter Physics, 74*, 036104. doi:10.1103/PhysRevE.74.036104

Newman, M. E. J., & Watts, D. J. (1999). Scaling and percolation in the small-world network model. *Physical Review E: Statistical Physics, Plasmas, Fluids, and Related Interdisciplinary Topics, 60*, 7332–7342. doi:10.1103/PhysRevE.60.7332

Ozik, J., Hunt, B., & Ott, E. (2004). Growing networks with geographical attachment preference: emergence of small worlds. *Physical Review E, 69*, 026-108.

Pastor-Satorras, R., & Vespignani, A. (2004). *Evolution and structure of the Internet: A statistical physics approach*. Cambridge, UK: Cambridge Univ. Press. doi:10.1017/CBO9780511610905

Pool, IdeS., & Kochen, M. (1978). Contacts and influence. *Social Networks, 1*, 1–48.

Powell, W. W., White, D. R., Koput, K. W., & Owen-Smith, J. (2005). Network dynamics and field evolution: the growth of interorganizational collaboration in the life sciences. *American Journal of Sociology, 1104*, 1132–1206. doi:10.1086/421508

Pyka, A., & Scharnhorst, A. (2009). *Innovation networks. New approaches in modelling and analyzing*. Berlin: Springer-Verlag.

Schilling, M., & Phelps, C. C. (2007). Interfirm collaboration networks: The impact of large-scale network structure on firm innovation. *Management Science*, *53*(7), 1113–1126. doi:10.1287/mnsc.1060.0624

Scott, J. (2000). *Social Network Analysis: A Handbook*. London: Sage.

Seidman, S. (1983). Internal cohesion of LS sets in graphs. *Social Networks*, *5*, 97–107. doi:10.1016/0378-8733(83)90020-5

Shen-Orr, S. S., Milo, R., Mangan, S., & Alon, U. (2002). Network motifs in the transcriptional regulation network of *Escherichia coli*. *Nature Genetics*, *31*, 64–68. doi:10.1038/ng881

Sorensen, O., & Stuart, T. (2001). Syndication networks and the spatial distribution of venture capital investments. *American Journal of Sociology*, *106*, 1546–1588. doi:10.1086/321301

Walker, G. (2008). The rise of Ecommerce as an epidemic in the small world of venture capital. *Network Strategy*, *25*, 3–29. doi:10.1016/S0742-3322(08)25001-1

Walker, G., Kogut, B., & Shan, W. (1997). Social capital, structural holes and the formation of an industry network. *Organization Science*, *8*, 109–125. doi:10.1287/orsc.8.2.109

Wasserman, S., & Faust, K. (1994). *Social Network Analysis: Methods and Applications*. Cambridge, UK: Cambridge Univ. Press.

Watts, D. J., & Strogatz, S. H. (1998). Collective dynamics of 'small-world' networks. *Nature*, *393*, 440–442. doi:10.1038/30918

Zhang, Z., Rong, L., & Guo, C. (2006). A deterministic small-world network created by edge iterations. *Physica A*, *363*, 567–572. doi:10.1016/j.physa.2005.08.020

## KEY TERMS AND DEFINITIONS

**Centralization:** It is a network-level, macro structural measure that quantifies how 'dispersed' the centralities of the actors are. When the measure is large, it means that few actors are highly central and the remaining actors occupy much less central positions in the network. Conversely, if network centralization is low, it means that the network is populated by actors who occupy similarly central positions.

**Clustering Coefficient:** The clustering coefficient $C$ is defined as follows. If a node $v$ has $k_v$ neighbors, then at most $k_v (k_v-1)/2$ edges can exist between them when every neighbor of v is connected to every other neighbor of $v$. $C_v$ denotes the fraction of these allowable edges that actually exist and $C$ or $C(p)$ is actually defined as the average of $C_v$ over all $v$.

**Degree Centrality:** Centrality is a node-level construct that measures the importance of a node in a network relative to others and in relation to the whole network structure, and therefore its position and the reach of its network. Degree centrality $D_c$ only counts the number of paths of length one that emanate from a node.

**K-Core:** The $k$-core decomposition is based on a recursive pruning of the least connected nodes and where $k$ stands for degree. The nodes displayed in the most internal shell of the network are those forming the central core of the network. Applying a $k$-core decomposition method allows to identify the inherent layer structure of a network, and thus gain information on its hierarchical structure and the placement of hubs (globally central if in the innermost $k$-cores and locally central if hubs are merely members of the outer k-cores).

**Network:** A network is described in very general terms as a graph whose nodes identify the elementary constituents of the system, the interconnections between these entities being represented by the linkages in the network.

**Path Length:** The characteristic path length, defined as the average shortest path length between node pairs, reflects the overall network connectivity.

**Scale-Free Network:** Scale-free networks are a class of graphs that follow power laws in the degree distribution, where the degree $k$ is the number of edges incident upon a given node; they have no characteristic scale and some nodes (hubs) are linked to many others while a large number of nodes are simultaneously poorly connected. In the scale-free model, new nodes join the network by attaching $m$ links to other nodes, chosen according to linear preferential attachment. A node obtains one of the new links with a probability proportional to the number of links it already has.

**Small-World Network:** High clustering and low characteristic path length are the defining features of small worlds. A network with $N$ nodes and $m$ links is a small-world network if it has a similar path length but greater clustering of nodes than an equivalent random graph with the same $m$ and $N$.

## ENDNOTE

[1]    Alliances in our database are mainly of two types: licensing agreements (about 50%), by which firms sells or acquire the rights to others' assets, these in the biopharmaceutical industry being generally target sourcing, or basic techniques, or biological materials that have application to more than one end product. These agreements mostly translate in annual user fees for access to proprietary assets. The second type of agreement or so-called collaboration (about 40%) consists in fact, for most biotech companies, in partnering through licensing agreements that include a milestone structure in compliance with cooperation phases and defines adaptable responses for positive and negative events which may occur in correlation with a milestone or to changed development or business needs.

Chapter 15

# A Social Network Model for Understanding Technology Use for Knowledge-Intensive Workers

**Kon Shing Kenneth Chung**
*University of Wollongong, Australia*

## ABSTRACT

*This chapter presents a theoretical model based on social network theories and the social influence model for understanding how knowledge professionals utilise technology. In particular, the association between egocentric network properties (structure, position and tie) and information and communication technology (ICT) use of individuals in knowledge-intensive and geographically dispersed settings is explored. A novel triangulation methodology is adopted where in-depth interviews and observation techniques were utilised to develop constructs for the conceptual model which were then vetted by domain-level experts. A reliable and validated social network-based questionnaire survey is also developed to operationalise the model. Results show that task-level ICT use is significantly associated with degree centrality and functional tie-diversity; and communication-level ICT use is negatively associated with efficiency. The implications of these associations for knowledge-intensive work mean that it is important to consider the professional social network characteristics of potential users of the technology for designing ICT-enabled organisations.*

## INTRODUCTION

Traditional information systems, management and organisation science literature have documented the implementation and use of technology as being crucial for accomplishing organisational goals es-

DOI: 10.4018/978-1-61350-513-7.ch015

pecially when there exists a good task-technology fit. With rapid developments in technology, there exists a secondary effect of technology use in that information can now traverse spatial, structural and temporal boundaries thus redefining work structures and communication patterns (Sproull & Kiesler, 1991). Consequently, information science and information systems researchers have sought to understand the social processes that influence the use of such information and communication technologies (ICT). While there are competing models and theories that explain technology use such as the technology acceptance model (Davis et al., 1989) and the social influence model (Fulk et al., 1990), only a few have focused on the significance of social structure, social position and social ties that constitute the influence (Sykes et al., 2009; Chung & Hossain, 2010). A key tenet in this study is that understanding the relationship between social network properties and ICT use of individuals is fundamental to the design of an effective information based organisation. In this study, the motivating questions are: at the individual level, (1) what forms of network structure are conducive to ICT use at the task and sociological levels? (2) what network position influences ICT use for task and communication purposes? (3) does personal experience or geographical co-location of peers shape ICT use more so than an individual's social network property in distributed work settings? (4) how does one account for social factors that are important for designing and implementing ICT for enhanced performance?

A theoretical framework is developed based on the theory of structural holes, strength of weak tie theory and the social influence model for understanding how individuals in knowledge-intensive work use ICT for task and communication purposes. The framework is guided by the question that if the social influence model is based on the precept that people act towards things based on the meanings that the things have for them, and that the meaning of these things is derived out of social interaction with others and is always changing, then a subsequent question is what form of social structures and positions constitute these interactions that influences the meaning of things?

In attempting to answer this question, the model is operationalised in the context of individuals whose work is both knowledge-intensive and geographically isolated, and where the uptake of ICT has been of considerable governmental inter-

est recently. In the following sections, I highlight the need for a social networks perspective into understanding ICT use by reviewing literature on social networks and current models for explaining ICT use along with justified hypotheses. I then describe the domain for this research followed by results and discussion.

## CONCEPTUAL FOUNDATIONS

The revolution of technology and internet means that the entire communication environment has taken on a virtual dimension. Personal relations are no longer conducted face-to-face only and various forms of ICT are currently available for various purposes (e.g. blogs, wikis, social networking sites like Facebook, Linkedin and so on). Thus, personal networks not only shape the ICT for communication, but the patterns and frequency of ICT use are also shaping personal networks and re drawing social boundaries.

### Models of ICT Use

In light of the above discussion, there have been several theories and models that propose to conceptualise ICT use. Drawing on structuration theory as an analytic perspective to view the use of ICT, Orlikowski (1992) presented a model of interaction among institutional properties, technology, and human action. Her argument is that technology is an outcome of human action, which is sustained by ICT use, which in turn mediates human action by facilitating or constraining performance. Furthermore, human action, in using technology acts upon the institutional properties of an organisation such as structure, which can, for example, be described in terms of professional ties that link information workers together. In sum, human actions in ICT use shape and are shaped by such structural properties.

Other scholars attempted to conceptualise ICT use based on the factors contributing to individual usage of ICT such as the technology acceptance model (Davis, 1989), the social information processing model (Salancik & Pfeffer, 1978) and the social influence model (Fulk et al., 1990). There is also a long tradition of research on impacts of ICT which examines how individuals experience information systems and technologies (Igbaria & Tan, 1997; Mukhopadhyay et al., 1997). As this study is concerned with the network effects of ICT use at the individual level, Sproull and Kiesler's (1991) categorisation of the effects of ICT use as efficiency (task-level) and social (communication-structure) effects is most relevant. Their work captures the two forms of effect of ICT use at both the task level and at the communication structural level. Efficiency effects are about productivity gains and social effects are about the changes instigated in the work and communication processes as a result of frequency and patterns of ICT use. Therefore, in this study, by ICT use, the focus is on the *use* of *information* and *communication* technologies in a professional context for achieving a certain set of tasks as well as for the purpose of communication to obtain information for accomplishing the task(s).

## Communication Structure and Sociology

Sproull and Kiesler's (1991) categorisation of social system effect is in line with Orlikowski's (1992) conceptualisation of technology in that the recursive process of dual change occurs at both the individual and technological level and affects each other over time. Change at the technological level can be grouped into two categories in terms of providing sources of information: *relational* and *non-relational*. As an example of the former, with developments in the Internet, individuals can now seek advice, information, collaborate and communicate overcoming temporal and spatial barriers as well as offer new modes of communication (synchronous and asynchronous) (Wellman et al., 1996). Furthermore, they also cross hierarchical and departmental barriers, change standard operating procedures and reshape work norms (Sproull & Kiesler, 1991; Rice, 1994). Abundant studies have reported on how communication technologies have extended information reach and enabled acquisition of useful information for individuals (Constant et al., 1994) and occupational communities (Pickering & King, 1995) through weak ties, despite lack of personal connections with others (Constant et al., 1996). Furthermore, individuals tap into online communities and portals where benefits of social support, influence and information advantages are plenty (Butler, 2001). Such online communities and other artefacts within the online space also serve as a *non-relational* source of information. Internet-based discussion groups and listservs providing summaries of communications to its members via email digests is one such example. Furthermore, company newsletters, online databases, journal repositories and online search engines such as Google also provide readily available information matching almost the same credibility and quality as from a relational source (Henry & Butler, 2001; Zimmer & Henry, 2007).

While the study anticipates that those who use both relational and non-relational sources of information will enhance performance and coordination, it is equally important to understand the factors that are conducive or contradictory to the relationship between ICT use and social structure. In other words, what forms of network structure at the individual level are conducive to ICT use at the task and sociological levels? Alternatively, does the uptake and use of ICT foster change in network structures at both task and sociological levels? To this end, there are various theories that have been postulated. For instance, the rational choice model explains that individuals choose to use technology based on the best match between the kind of technology available and the task at hand along with a whole set of factors such as media accessibility, usage experience, personal preference, time and cost advantages. In particular, media use theory, a proponent of the rational choice model, argues that individuals choose media through a matching process. This matching involves assessing the requirements of the particular communication task at hand and selecting a medium with communication capabilities that match the requirements (Williams, 1979). Along the same lines of the rational choice model, social presence theorists argue that individuals choose media based on social presence, which is the degree to which the medium facilitates awareness of the other person and interpersonal relationships during the interaction (for example, on a scale from high to low social presence, face-to-face is highest and print media has lowest social presence) (Short et al., 1976). Yet another alternative view of the rational choice model is the information richness theory whereby communication media are arrayed along a continuum of "information richness" based on four factors: the degree to which the source is personal enough, speed of feedback, types of channels used for communication and the richness of the communication (Daft & Macintosh, 1981). However, the social influence model is a more comprehensive model that encapsulates and accounts for the dynamics of social influence in explaining ICT use. While the rational choice model argues that choice of ICT use is objectively rational and that behavior is efficiency-motivated, it fails to explain why certain individuals choose to use ICT although their motivations may not be efficiency-motivated. For example, when various forms of ICT are introduced, there is consistently growing literature that demonstrates social influence as potent predictors of use (Fulk et al., 1990). In case of introducing new ICT in organisations, strong ties are useful predictors for its use (Haythornthwaite, 2002). The phenomena in such cases are beyond explanations of the rational choice model.

The social influence model (Fulk et al., 1990) starts with the basic assumption that individuals cognitively process stimuli. It argues that perceptions of ICT are subjective and socially constructed and can be determined to a substantial degree by the attitudes, statements, and behaviours of colleagues. Colleagues exert social influence through overt statements about characteristics of the media or tasks that individuals absorb mentally within their perceptions. The influence may also take place through vicarious learning from observing the experiences of others. Thus, if an individual observes effective behavior by another, the observational learning produces similar behavior by that individual. In sum, the social influence model postulates that for any application, an individual's ICT use is "a function of: (a) media evaluations (perceptions and attitudes); (b) experience and skills; (c) social influence in the form of direct statements by coworkers regarding the application, vicarious learning, group behavioral norms, and social definitions of rationality; (d) tasks evaluations; and (e) situational factors such as individual differences, facilitating factors, and constraints" (Fulk et al., 1990, p. 127).

Given these postulations from the social influence model, it helps to explain why a study in a large insurance firm found similar patterns of usage of voicemail among colleagues occupying the same structural network position (Shook, 1988). Similarly, Rice et. al. (1990) found similar patterns of email adoption among colleagues who were closely connected. In a subsequent study, Rice (1994) found that the amount and network measures of email usage were significantly associated with work and work familiarity networks. Furthermore, as ICT such as email, networked databases, and group decision support systems vastly increase the potential for information sharing amongst individuals such as knowledge-intensive workers also increases. Information seeking in social and work contexts is thus a function of social influence in terms of social or professional network structure (Cross et al., 2001) and tie diversity (Cummings, 2004). Therefore, for individuals in knowledge-intensive work, I hypothesise the following:

*H1a: The number of professional ties, rather than number of co-located colleagues or experience, of an individual is positively associated with use of ICT for task-level activities in knowledge-intensive work*

*H1b: The number of professional ties, rather than number of co-located colleagues or experience, of an individual is positively associated with use of ICT for professional communication activities in knowledge-intensive work*

## Understanding ICT Use through Social Networks

Both the technology acceptance model (Davis, 1989) and the social influence model (Fulk et al., 1990) emphasise the significance of social influence and norms in affecting ICT use. These models however, do not clearly indicate the kind of social structures or relations that are conducive or detrimental to the adoption or use of ICT. On the contrary, social network studies have linked the process of innovation-diffusion (e.g. medical and technological) to social processes such as how information is disseminated through social ties and structure.

## Strength of Weak Ties Theory

In a seminal work by Grannovetter (1973), it was demonstrated that individuals obtain new and novel information from *weak* ties rather than *strong* ties within the individual's group structure. The argument rests on the assumption concerning the homophilous nature of actors in a social system, where strong ties tend to bond similar people to each other, and that these similar people tend to cluster together such that they all become mutually connected. As such, information that originate and circulate at a high velocity amongst strongly tied cliques or clusters tend to become obsolete or redundant in a short amount of time. Such network-clusters or cliques of people bound together by strong ties are therefore are not conducive to channels of innovation. That is, such networks are closed networks and are not well receptive of new information. Granovetter (1973, p. 10653) suggests that the influx of new and novel information must therefore come from weak ties (hence, the theory of the strength of weak ties), which serves as a *bridge* to a different cluster of people from where the new information originates. This theory helped delineate Coleman's classical study on how physicians adopted an innovation – a new medical drug (Coleman et al., 1957) and on how individuals found jobs (Granovetter, 1995). Weak ties also account for the diversity of information which is useful for innovation diffusion and knowledge sharing (Cummings & Cross, 2003; Cummings, 2004). More recently, Obstfeld (2005) and Tortoriello and Krackhardt (2010) have similarly argued about the nature of diversity of ties that affect the generation of innovations through the existence of the relationship of the "third who joins". Formally stated:

*H2: Tie diversity is positively associated with ICT use at both the task and communication levels*

## Structural Holes Theory

A criticism of the weak tie theory is that it implies that the more individuals "bridge" weak ties, the better they are in receiving novel information or adopting new adoptions. Burt (1992) however criticises the theory in that weak ties are just "the chasm spanned and the chasm itself" and that the chasm itself provides opportunities for information benefit and control. Burt's (1992) theory on structural holes offers a novel and interesting perspective in explaining why some individuals perform better and others do not. For example, it extends Coleman et. al.'s (1957) study by offering an explanation of why social processes such as innovation diffusion may occur faster from a structural positional point of view rather than from a relational perspective. The theory is linked to personality theory suggesting that personal attributes (such as locus of control, leadership skills, ability to perform well) of an individual is associated with structural autonomy – an optimal situation where an individual benefits from non-redundant information benefits. Burt (1992) argues that the structural configuration of an individual's social network which provides an optimised "brokerage" position is what dictates structural advantages such as information novelty and control. The bridging of connection to others provides opportunities; the lack of connections among those others is the holes in the structure (and therefore, structural holes). Individuals who attain structural autonomy are those who bridge all structural holes while the groups to whom the individual is connected to are surrounded by structural holes. Therefore, individuals who are well connected to groups who are themselves not well connected are considered efficient because the structural holes offers brokerage opportunities such as information about new technologies. Conversely, individuals who are connected to those clusters of individuals in a way that it leads

back to the same contact are said to be highly constrained. Therefore, I hypothesise:

*H3: Efficiency is positively associated with ICT Use at both the task and communication levels*

*H4: Constraint is negatively associated with ICT Use at both the task and communication levels*

## Towards a Social Networks Model for ICT Use

A fundamental assumption of most social networks research is that individual outcome such as coordination or performance is influenced by the interplay of both network structure and tie correlates, autonomous of the medium that conduct the relations. Most studies pertaining to social networks and performance have either focused on the impact of network structure or on the effect of differing tie strengths within organisational contexts. However, most of these network studies have been conducted isolating the fact that contemporary information and communication (ICT) media play

*Figure 1. Social Networks Model for Understanding ICT Use*

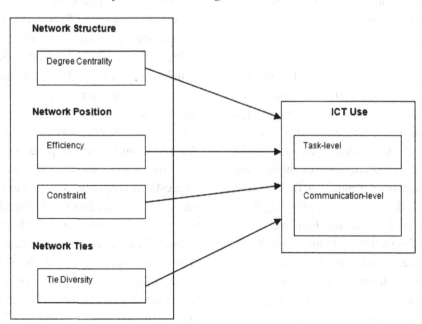

no significant role in the creation and maintenance of social ties – the fundamental relations that connect individuals spanning geographical distances. While most studies have assumed relations being conducted face-to-face, another criticism is that the studies formally emphasise on the focus of one strand of tie – often work relations, therefore neglecting the multiplex character of personal networks, which tend precisely to intersect several social relations (Licoppe & Smoreda, 2005). Furthermore, individuals often work within a network of informal links that fits into a larger social structure. Such ties are generally geographically dispersed, specialised and connected by ICTs that facilitate communication and information transfer. This study is an attempt to address part of the gap and therefore outline the conceptual model.

## METHODOLOGY AND CONTEXT OF STUDY

The domain for the study is the rural general practitioners (GPs) in New South Wales (NSW), Australia. Rural GPs are considered knowledge intensive workers because of their extensive medical expertise, high patient to GP ratio, provision of diverse healthcare services and so on (Humphreys & Rolley, 1998). In knowledge-intensive work, knowing where and whom to obtain information from is crucial for performance. Yet, problems such as obsolescence with modern technology, lack of association with professional peers, and isolation from community hinder performance. In the past years, the Australian government initiated the "practice incentive programs" that fund doctors up to $10,000 AUD each for computerizing their practices (Strasser et al., 2000). However, little is known about the factors and value of ICT use in such cases. These issues provide justification for the rural GPs as knowledge-intensive work subjects for this study (Choudhry et al., 2005) and make it potentially important as well.

A triangulation methodology consisting of two major phases of data collection was used for the study. Firstly, qualitative interviews were held with seven GPs, some who had dual job functions such as university honorary associates and lecturer. The qualitative interviews were semi-structured and held for at least an hour with each of the interviewees at appointed times over a two month period. The qualitative interviews were useful for exploring validity and relevance of ICT and social network constructs used in the study. The interviews were audio-recorded, transcribed and summarised as contact summary notes. Pattern-coding and memo-ing techniques were used to analyze the data. The analysis was used in conjunction with the existing literature to develop a conceptual model for the study.

Following on, an initial questionnaire survey was developed and pre-piloted amongst a group of 5 students within the research laboratory. Ten copies of the survey were then sent out to rural GPs, with only three who responded. With low response rates, experts in the domain of general practice, including former president of a rural doctor's association in Australia, professor and head of discipline of general practice in a renowned university, and rural GPs were consulted about the survey instrument. Subsequently, the research design and theoretical constructs were further refined. The experts also vetted the instrument, which was then pre-tested for comprehension and ease-of-use. The general response from them was that the design of the network component in the survey was visually complex and confounding. As this not only deters response rates but also add cognitive load to survey completion, advice and suggestions from the experts were accepted and the survey was modified accordingly. The second version of the survey was designed to cater for improved ease of comprehension and completion. Attribute items such as asking whether the GPs were trained overseas or locally were included. Other items to determine whether they were accredited with fellowships from the RACGP (Royal

Australian College of General Practitioners) and ACRRM (Australian College of Rural and Remote Medicine) were also included in order to allow for cross demographic comparisons (although not shown in this study). The survey was piloted to 136 rural GPs practising in two different divisions of rural general practice over the months of December 2006 to February 2007. 56 agreed to fill out the survey thus achieving a response rate of about 41%. The survey was mostly personally administered in order to allow for capturing of survey duration, respondent reaction and errors in the survey. Only one was administered through telephone and five others through postal mail.

After making cosmetic refinements, a final questionnaire was posted out to 1488 GPs in the remaining fifteen divisions of rural general practice in NSW. Telephone calls were made to the practices two weeks in advance to gauge GPs' likelihood of survey response before the actual mail-out. Follow-up calls were made reminding those who agreed to do the survey two weeks after the mail-out. A total of 110 rural GPs participated in the study achieving a response rate of 7.8%.

## Semi-Structured Interview Questions

In keeping with the direction of the constructs of the study, semi-structured interviews were conducted with a sample of GPs for the conceptual development of the theoretical model. There were three major categories of questions. The first entailed generic questions about the GP's demographics (e.g. professional background and history; information about current practice; the daily workflow of a rural GP, etc.). The second category related directly to questions about social and professional networks of the GP interviewed. The questions are listed below and it is to be noted that they served as a guide in the semi-structured interview process (the reader will note this in the form of italicised statements) as opposed to a rigid structure:

1. From time to time, you may come across difficulties in your practice as a GP. Do you seek help in professional matters from other people? (*Professional matters need to be explained to the GP as discussing about activities or information that are related to the provision of medical and preventative health care*).

2. Who are the people whom you consider important for the provision of your medical practice and service? These people may be professional (e.g. nurses, other GPs, Specialists, etc.) or non-professionals (e.g. family, relatives, friends).

3. In your opinion, are social networks an important requirement in terms of task-based activities or contextual-based activities?

The third category of questions related to the use of ICT by the GP for both work practice and communication for work purposes. The questions are listed as below:

Information and Communication technologies are defined in this study as the technology that facilitates the transfer of information and communication to and from the General Practice. Video conferencing, satellite communications, PDAs, Email and so on are examples of ICT. *ICT is also to be defined more narrowly.*

1. What mediums of ICT are used in the practice? *Identify which ones are most useful in context of their workflow.*

2. Are the ICTs usually used for administrative and functional tasks (e.g. patient record keeping, clinical decision systems) or for social tasks (e.g. email, discussion forums, searching for information from the internet)?

3. In your opinion, do you feel that ICTs are beneficial for the performance of your work? (*Relate this to the context of the workflow they described*).

4. Are ICTs important for establishing and maintaining a sense of connectedness especially in rural communities?

## Egocentric Network Measures

I utilised the egocentric approach for collecting network data because of its practicality and feasibility. In this approach, the actor of interest is referred to as the "ego" and the actors referred to by the "ego" as his affiliate, advisor, friend, or relative, are known as "alters" (Scott, 2000). Name generators are used in order to elicit alters' names. In this study, I used the following name generator to elicit names from a GP's professional network:

"By 'professional network', we mean professional people whom you associate, interact or work with for the provision of care to patients (e.g. nurses, admin staff, specialists, pathologists, doctors etc.) Looking back over the last six months, please identify people (up to 15 maximum) who are important in providing you with information or advice for providing care to patients."

Name interpreter questions are also commonly asked to elicit some attribute data about the alters and ties. In this case, I requested GPs to indicate the occupational code (e.g. nurse, practice manager, specialist, etc.) as well as the geographical location (e.g. same practice, other practice, etc.) of each alter. The strength of each tie, measured by "time known the person", "frequency of interaction", "type of relationship", and "degree of closeness" (Marsden & Campbell, 1984) was also solicited. Attribute data about the frequency of interaction via email, telephone, and video conferencing were also included in the instrument to segregate face-to-face and ICT media interactions.

To determine the relationship between elicited alters in order to complete the network structure, I asked GPs to determine how the members of their professional network relate to each other based on a five point degree of closeness scale ranging from 'especially close' to 'do not know each other'. That is, for each alter nominated,

the GP would determine a closeness scale for every other alter. Although this approach has been criticised in the past for its recall reliability and accuracy (Bernard et al., 1985), later studies confirmed that people also remembered long-term or typical patterns of interaction with other people rather well (Freeman et al., 1987). Furthermore, the free recall method elicits a richer data on the social networks of people whereas the fixed choice method influences people to elicit accurate information on the most important relationships (i.e. strong ties) (Hammer, 1984).

## Efficiency and Constraint

Effective size is a measure of the number of alters minus the average degree of alters within the ego network, not counting ties to the ego (Burt, 1992, p. 55). Effective size of an actor's (ego) network is thus:

$$\sum_j \left[ 1 - \sum_q p_{iq} m_{jq} \right], q \neq i, j$$

where $i$ is the ego, actor $j$ is a primary contact, and actor $q$ is also a primary contact who has strong ties with the ego $i$ (represented by strong tie - $p_{iq}$) and actor $j$ (represented by marginal tie - $m_{jq}$). *Efficiency* is measured by dividing the effective size by the number of alters in the ego's network.

Ego *constraint* measures the opportunities held back by the extent to which the ego has invested time and energy in relations with alters that lead back to a single contact (Burt, 1992, p. 55). In other words, it measures the extent to which the ego's connections are to others who are connected to one another. Constraint on an actor's network is defined as:

$$\left( p_{ij} + \sum_q p_{iq} p_{qj} \right)^2, q \neq i, j$$

where $i$ is the ego, actor $j$ is a primary contact, and actor $q$ is also a primary contact who has strong ties with the ego $i$ (represented by $p_{iq}$) and actor $j$ (represented by $p_{qj}$).

## Degree Centrality

Degree centrality ($C_D$) is measured as the count of the ties (a) to the ego ($p_k$) (Freeman, 1978). In graph theoretical terms:

$$C_D(p_k) = \sum_{i=1}^{n} a(p_i, p_k)$$

where $a(p_i, p_k) = 1$ if and only if and are connected by a line, 0 otherwise.

## Tie Diversity

Diversity is measured using an entropy-based diversity index developed by Teachman (1980):

$$H = -\sum_{i=1}^{s} P_i(\ln P_i)$$

where if there are $N$ possible states in which the system can be, $P_i$ is the probability that the system will be found in state $i$, the only exception being when the a state is not represented in the case of which the value is 0 (Ancona & Caldwell, 1992). Tie Diversity in this study is measured in terms of functional (occupational) and geographical diversity. Therefore, if a GP has ties to professionals from diverse occupations, her functional diversity would be high. Similarly, if a GP has ties to professionals who are from differing cities and towns, her occupational diversity would be considered high.

## ICT Use Items

ICT use has been primarily ascertained by measuring the attitudes of individual users in terms of tasks for which it is used, the frequency of use, and perceived ease and comfort of use. Such attitudes of individual users towards ICT are quite important, mainly because a positive attitude is usually indicative of technology acceptance (Mahmood et al., 2000), which in turn allows the user to believe that using the ICT would enhance his or her performance (Davis et al., 1989). The premise of measuring attitudes stems from the theory of reasoned action which describes an attitude as a "predisposition to respond favorably or unfavorably to an object, person, event, institution, or another discriminable aspect of the individual's world" (Ajzen, 1988). Therefore, this study argues that attitude towards behavior is a direct determinant of the behavioral intention to perform the behavior.

In this study, ICT includes computers, technological software applications and systems such as Medical Director (a customised medical practice software popular among GPs), email, video conference and so on. Based on Sproull and Kiesler's (1991) categorisation of the effects of ICT use as efficiency (task-level) and social (communication-structure) effects, ICT use in this case was divided into *context-specific ICT use* (or task-level activities – e.g. clinical tasks) and *internet-related ICT use* (communication and task-level activities). Task-level measures were based on the reliable and valid item sets used by Western et al (2001). Internet-related ICT use items were adapted from Andrews et al's (2004), developed by the University of Kentucky's Department of Family Practice in a project supported by the Agency for Healthcare Research and Quality (AHRQ) in the US (see Table 1).

*Table 1. ICT Use Items*

| Task-level ICT Use | Internet-related ICT use |
|---|---|
| Generating health summaries | Accessing medical journals (e.g. BMJ) |
| Recording progress notes | Accessing databases (e.g. PUBMED) |
| Using decision support functions to help you solve diagnostic problems or make decisions about dispensing or treatments | Accessing clinical guidelines |
| Writing prescriptions | Accessing evidence-based medicine related information (e.g. InfoPOEMS) |
| Accessing educational material for patients | Communicating with professional associations (including email) |
| Receiving or storing information electronically such as pathology results and reports | Continuing medical education (CME) |
| Preparing referral letters for patients | Professional development |
| Running a recall system to remind patients to return for routine tests | Finding information to help patients |
| | Email with colleagues |
| | Communicating with special interest groups |

ICT use was measured on a 5 point Likert scale ranging from "daily use" to "never". Both the eight task-level ICT use (Cronbach's $\alpha$ = 0.942) and ten internet-level ICT use items (Cronbach's $\alpha$ = 0.900) items demonstrated high reliability.

## RESULTS

The results of the study are broken down into two phases: (i) results from the interviews and (ii) results from the survey questionnaire.

### Qualitative Results: Semi-structured Interviews

In terms of the workflow of general practice, there was wide consensus amongst the interviewees about the processes, activities and flow of work. In sum, it is listed as below and is consisted with the general practice literature (Usherwood, 1999):

1. Patients book an appointment
2. In exceptional cases, patients walk in
3. When patient gets called, the doctor pulls up the patient's file or creates a new one.
4. GPs consult with the patient for an average of 10-15 minutes. Sometimes, it is 30-40 minutes in rare cases.
5. According to the nature of the consultation, the payment(s) are made by the patient.
6. After the consultation, the GP records the details into paper (or electronic records (although very seldom)).
7. If drugs are ordered, the prescription will be given to the patient.
8. In some cases, patients are referred to the specialists (e.g. Pathology labs).
9. Investigations are then faxed or electronically faxed to the surgery (or medical centre).

When asked about the topic of the importance of social and professional networks in their practice, there appears to be a consistent notion of the importance of collegial peers, friends and to some extent even families in supporting their work, especially given the context of rural practice where most GPs practice in isolation. Although GPs don't often have the chance to meet in rural areas, they highlight the importance of rural GP conferences, meetings and even social gatherings for the purpose of medical information and knowledge updates. As one GP puts it,

*"Because the senior GPs have practised for over 37 years, they know anyone who walks in the*

*door…so I look forward to getting help from the two senior GPs in my practice and also from the practice manager….*

*…GPs usually have a monthly regional meeting where updates are provided. Most of them come to meet their own fellow GPs and have a chat in the evening. At the same time they get a dose of continuous medical education. So that kind of social network is important and I think that it will give rise to an improvement of their performance to some extent because they would have had a talk with their specialist or fellow GP. Sometimes, I also remember things (that are useful) that I chat to my friends when I meet."*

In terms of ICT use, there is also a general consensus that ICT and task based activities do not seem to be as streamlined nor well fit with each other. For instance, in one of the projects called the "Skin Cancer Project" for rural areas, most of the doctors do not use coding and use free-text to enter notes. The records are entered in the progress notes section and although it is possible to access them by SQL, the access is restricted and encrypted by password. Coding of the records using medical codes will streamline data retrieval and also allow for analysis later on. Furthermore, ICT is under-utilised for the purpose for which it was designed for. For example, pathology reports are still being handled and delivered physically although the MD program (or "Medical Director", a computer software program for GPs) can download them electronically. The pathology reports are still being handled physically. A GP commented that *"The specialist will have to invariably type the letter on a computer and print it and send the letter…just because the hospital is not computerised, although the same service can be provided to use MD."* While most GPs commented on the best feature of MD in its ability to check for drug interactions, most also agree that they do not use computer-based resources for connecting to their social and professional

networks, with the exception of email. The following comments highlight the importance of ICT use not just for work practice but for connecting to social and professional networks for information and knowledge updates:

*"Without ICT, you cannot practice! My view is biased in that to be updated in medicine, you need to read a journal paper every three minutes. Even then, you are 8-10 years behind of the medical advances and developments. I don't think it is possible to practise without ICT; the patients expect you to be updated in medical know-how."*

*"Doctors will be isolated (in rural areas). I think the rural GPs should be given not only computers but at least video conferencing facilities. This is because if they need to call another doctor, they need to be able to just dial and talk to them (through video-conference). I believe this is quite important otherwise they will be practicing in isolation."*

Some even identify the importance of both relational sources and non-relational sources of information in their work practice. This is consistent with literature (Henry & Butler, 2001). Relational information sources include both social and professional networks of peers, colleagues, friends and families. Non-relational sources of information include books, journals, magazines and electronic resources such as websites, online discussion forums, blogs, community portals, and so on. In the words of a GP,

*"When GPs are in doubt regarding a diagnosis or a problem, they always refer to specialist or their colleagues or the hospital. The other thing that I would certainly do (and wish others would do) is refer to some electronic resources. For example, there is the ciap.health.nsw.gov.au website which is the most fantastic site I have ever seen. In there, you can read most of the electronic journals and medical textbooks for free….I have seen 60-70% of the medical textbooks online and it is free for*

*Table 2. Demographics (n=110)*

|  | Mean | Std. Dev | Min | Max |
|---|---|---|---|---|
| Years in Rural Practice | 20.24 | 10.44 | 1 | 50 |
| Years in Current Practice | 13.63 | 10.37 | 1 | 43 |
| No of GPs in Current Practice | 4.54 | 4.11 | 0 | 25 |

*all doctors. This includes books about detailed prescriptions and also the website provides you external resources as well such as PubMed."*

## Quantitative Results: Survey & Social Network Analysis

Results from the respondents surveyed indicate that the typical rural GP has been in rural practice for 20.24, with 13.63 years in the current practice (Table 2). Although there are solo-practices (a one doctor-only practice), the typical rural GP, as indicated by the results, works with at least 4 colleague GPs in the same practice. Furthermore, 90 (or 81.8%) are male and 20 (or 18.2%) are female, and 85 (or 77.3%) have hospital appointments.

Table 3 lists the descriptive statistics for the variables of interest (network structure, position, ties, and ICT use).

Given that there were no clear outliers in the data distribution of all variables and that the histograms of the ICT use variables were fairly normal, I examined Pearson's product-moment correlations indices. From Table 4, it is evident that high numbers of colleagues working in the same practice is not significantly associated with extent of task-level ICT use. Also, there is a significant negative association between experience in terms of years in current practice and task-level ICT use $(r=-.288, p<.01)$.

Hypothesis H1a and H1b also tests whether ICT use at the task-level and communication-level respectively is associated with number of professional ties (degree centrality). While there is clearly no support for H1b, the t-test was adopted to test (H1a) for differences between the groups of high task-level ICT use and low task-level ICT use on the continuous variable – degree centrality. In order to group respondents into high

*Table 3. Descriptive Statistics*

|  | Mean | Median | Std. Dev. | Min | Max |
|---|---|---|---|---|---|
| Network Structure |  |  |  |  |  |
| Degree | 8.77 | 8.0 | 3.94 | 1.00 | 15.0 |
| Network Position |  |  |  |  |  |
| Constraint | .402 | .35 | .197 | .078 | 1.00 |
| Efficiency | .475 | .40 | .297 | .067 | 1.00 |
| Relations (Ties) |  |  |  |  |  |
| Geographic Diversity | .700 | .67 | .367 | .000 | 1.71 |
| Functional Diversity | .799 | .86 | .447 | .000 | 1.58 |
| ICT Use |  |  |  |  |  |
| Task level ICT Use | 30.37 | 35 | 10.9 | 8.00 | 40.0 |
| Communication related ICT Use | 26.52 | 28.0 | 8.45 | 10.0 | 45.0 |

*Table 4. Pearson's Product Moment Correlation (n=110)*

| | (1) | (2) | (3) | (4) | (5) | (6) | (7) | (8) |
|---|---|---|---|---|---|---|---|---|
| No of GPs in Current Practice (1) | | | | | | | | |
| Years in Current Practice (2) | -.038 | | | | | | | |
| Degree (3) | .056 | -.091 | | | | | | |
| Constraint (4) | .130 | .185 | -.72 (**) | | | | | |
| Efficiency (5) | -.145 | -.146 | -.18 | -.296 (**) | | | | |
| Task level ICT Use (6) | .015 | -.288 (**) | .241 (*) | -.182 | -.047 | | | |
| Comm- related ICT Use (7) | -.011 | -.021 | .131 | -.003 | -.216 (*) | .538 (**) | | |
| Geo- Diversity (8) | -.003 | -.137 | .207 (*) | -.286 (**) | .053 | .106 | -.088 | |
| Functional Diversity (9) | -.040 | -.230 (*) | .301 (**) | -.285 (**) | -.044 | .322 (**) | .004 | .422 (**) |

** Correlation is significant at the 0.01 level (2-tailed).

* Correlation is significant at the 0.05 level (2-tailed).

and low users, the dataset was sorted in ascending order based on the task-level ICT use score. The median *(Md=35)* was selected as the cut-point to divide the two groups. GPs with a task-level ICT use score higher or equal to 35 were classified as "high task-level ICT use group", all else being the "low task-level ICT use group". If the "degree" means across the two groups differ significantly, then there is evidence that task-level ICT use is significantly associated with number of professional ties in knowledge-intensive work. The direction of the association (i.e. positive or negative) can be evidenced in the mean score of the groups by examining which group has a higher mean. Results from the t-test (table not shown) reveal significant difference in the degree centrality of high task-level ICT users *(M=9.625, SD=4.16, n=56)* and low task-level ICT users *(M=7.86, SD=3.51, n=53); t (105.62) = -2.384, p=.019 (two-tailed)*. The magnitude of the differences in the means *(mean difference = -1.757, 95% CI: -3.218 to -.295)* was small *(eta squared =.05)*. Given these results, I find support for H1a.

Regarding hypothesis H2 which positively associates tie diversity with ICT use at both the task and communication levels, Table 4 confirms a very significant and positive correlation between functional tie diversity and task-level ICT use *(r=.322, p<.01)*. The t-test was also used to test for differences in the functional diversity scores of high task-level ICT user groups and low task-level ICT user groups. The results confirm significant difference in the functional diversity of high task-level ICT users *(M=.9247, n=56)* and low task-level ICT users *(M=.6674, n=53); t (107) = -3.120, p = .002 (two-tailed)*. The magnitude of the difference in the means *(mean difference = .08247, 95% CI: -.4207 to -.0938)* was moderate *(eta squared = .08)*. Clearly, high task-level ICT users have a higher mean in functional diversity score *(M=.9257)* than low task-level ICT users *(M=.6674)*. Given these results, there is thus partial support for H2, none in terms of geographical diversity.

There was no support for the network-position hypotheses - H3 and H4. It is interesting however to note that for H3, efficiency is negatively correlated with communication-related ICT use, *r=-.216, p<.05.*

Of the variables that have shown to be associated with task-level ICT use, we were curious to examine which one(s) best explain the variance in the relationship with task-level ICT use controlling for any effects that other independent variables may bear on the relationship. In order to effectively reduce the number of possible explanatory variables to a smaller set in a single regression analysis, I used the stepwise multiple regression technique with forward selection. Preliminary analyses were conducted to ensure no violation of the assumptions of normality, linearity, multicollinearity and homoscedasticity occurred.

The regression analysis identified two models of significance. In the first model, the only predictor is functional diversity, which explains 9.5% of the variance (R Square = .095 in Model 1) in task-level ICT use. The second model shows the entry of another variable – RACGP (a professional fellowship accreditation), the total variance explained by the model as a whole being 15.1% (R Square = .151). That is, RACGP explained an additional 6.3% (R Square change = .063 in model 2 in Table 5) of the variance in task-level ICT use, after controlling for functional diversity, F change (1, 106) = 8.051, *p < .01*. From the ANOVA table, it is clear that models 1 [*F (1, 107) = 12.350, p=.001*] and 2 [*F (2, 106) = 10.607, p=.000*] are quite significant.

In the final model (model 2), functional diversity and FRACGP were statistically significant with functional diversity recording a higher beta value (beta = .280, p < .01) than FRACGP (beta = .225, p < .01). Therefore, one may conclude that among variables – of professional accreditation (FRACGP), network structure (degree centrality) and network ties (functional diversity), functional tie diversity makes the largest unique contribution to explaining the variance in task-level ICT use.

## DISCUSSION AND CONCLUSION

The findings from the study provide further insight into the social influence model for explaining ICT use by using concepts from social network studies as a theoretical and analytical perspective. In doing so, it has highlighted the importance of the intrinsic but not so visible relationship between social network structure, technology use and work roles (Barley, 1990). The results confirm that in knowledge-intensive work, personal characteristics such as professional experience and number of co-located colleagues do not contribute towards ICT use. Rather, network properties of degree centrality and functional tie diversity are more conducive towards ICT use at the task-level with functional diversity being the most potent predictor. This contribution is novel and extends previous theoretical and domain-level studies which document older GPs being prone to technology obsolescence and low usage of task-level ICT (Fulk et al., 1990; Choudhry et al., 2005). Also interesting is the negative correlation between ego-network efficiency and communication-level ICT use. The general idea from current literature is that as individuals adopt more ICTs for professional communication, they have greater propensities to reach out to different groups or individuals beyond temporal, spatial and organisational barriers. However, results show no support for this hypothesis (H3). There are two possible conjectures at this point – (1) that the rural GPs who use high levels of communication-related ICTs are reaching out to the same group of people where the group themselves are well connected, thereby decreasing ego-network efficiency; (2) that the rural GPs already knows where to obtain information from through their professional network within the community and therefore does not need to rely solely on communication-related ICT. Therefore, the highly *efficient* GP is not likely to use the Internet media for communication especially where relational sources are readily known

*Table 5. Regression Model for FRACGP, Degree Centrality and Functional Diversity on Task-level ICT use*

| ANOVA(c) | | | | | | |
|---|---|---|---|---|---|---|
| Model | | Sum of Squares | df | Mean Square | F | Sig. |
| 1 | Regression | 1336.47 | 1 | 1336.47 | 12.350 | .001(a) |
| | Residual | 11579.64 | 107 | 108.22 | | |
| | Total | 12916.12 | 108 | | | |
| 2 | Regression | 2153.85 | 2 | 1076.92 | 10.607 | .000(b) |
| | Residual | 10762.26 | 106 | 101.53 | | |
| | Total | 12916.12 | 108 | | | |

a Predictors: (Constant), Functional Diversity
b Predictors: (Constant), Functional Diversity, Fellow of RACGP (Royal Australian College of General Practitioners accreditation)
c Dependent Variable: Task level ICT Use

| Model Summary(c) | | | | | | | | | |
|---|---|---|---|---|---|---|---|---|---|
| Model | $R$ | $R^2$ | Adjusted $R^2$ | Std. Error | $R^2$ Change | F Change | df1 | df2 | Sig. F Change |
| 1 | .322(a) | .103 | .095 | 10.40293 | .103 | 12.350 | 1 | 107 | .001 |
| 2 | .408(b) | .167 | .151 | 10.07625 | .063 | 8.051 | 1 | 106 | .005 |

a Predictors: (Constant), Functional Diversity
b Predictors: (Constant), Functional Diversity, Fellow of RACGP (Royal Australian College of General Practitioners accreditation)
c Dependent Variable: Task level ICT Use

| Excluded Variables(c) | | | | | |
|---|---|---|---|---|---|
| Model | | Beta In | t | Sig. | Partial Correlation |
| 1 | Years in Rural Practice | -.174(a) | -1.902 | .060 | -.182 |
| | Years in Current Practice | -.225(a) | -2.453 | .016 | -.232 |
| | Fellow of ACRRM | .182(a) | 1.976 | .051 | .188 |
| | Fellow of RACGP | .255(a) | 2.837 | .005 | .266 |
| | Degree | .159(a) | 1.668 | .098 | .160 |
| 2 | Years in Rural Practice | -.102(b) | -1.077 | .284 | -.105 |
| | Years in Current Practice | -.172(b) | -1.849 | .067 | -.178 |
| | Fellow of ACRRM | .169(b) | 1.887 | .062 | .181 |
| | Degree | .124(b) | 1.329 | .187 | .129 |

a Predictors in the Model: (Constant), Functional Diversity
b Predictors in the Model: (Constant), Functional Diversity, Fellow of RACGP (Royal Australian College of General Practitioners accreditation)
c Dependent Variable: Task level ICT Use

| Coefficients(a) | | | | | | |
|---|---|---|---|---|---|---|
| Model | | Unstandardized Coefficients | | Standardized Coefficients | t | Sig. |
| | | B | Std. Error | Beta | | |
| 1 | (Constant) | 24.086 | 2.048 | | 11.762 | .000 |
| | Functional Diversity | 7.863 | 2.237 | .322 | 3.514 | .001 |
| 2 | (Constant) | 22.639 | 2.048 | | 11.054 | .000 |
| | Functional Diversity | 6.838 | 2.197 | .280 | 3.112 | .002 |
| | Fellow of RACGP | 5.667 | 1.997 | .255 | 2.837 | .005 |

a Dependent Variable: Task level ICT Use

and accessible; and this finding is supported in literature (Henry & Butler, 2001).

In conclusion, the study addresses an important gap in the literature concerning understanding social processes that influence ICT use. As the technology acceptance and the social influence models lack empirical evidence from a networks perspective, this research shows that rather than the strength of ties which functions as a conduit of novel ideas and information, it is the functional tie diversity within individual professionals networks that increase ICT use at the task-level. A limitation concerning this study is that data from only 110 general practitioners in rural NSW medical practices were collected. This is attributed to the extreme difficulty in accessing the rural doctor population in addition to their patient overload and tight consultation turnaround and schedule. As such, it is important that the results and findings be interpreted within the scope of the sample. Although the results are not obviously generalisable to the larger population and the possibility of a selection bias or skewed results may be present, the findings however, allow us useful insights into exploring, as first step, the interplay between social network structure and patterns and frequency of ICT use of knowledge-intensive work and in geographically distributed settings. This is evidenced in the response collated from the qualitative interviews. Therefore, for knowledge-workers, it is important to consider the professional social network characteristics of potential users of the technology for designing ICT-enabled organisations. The greater the number and diversity of peers individuals interact with translates into more opportunities to use ICT for context-specific tasks. Results from this study also show that individuals who tend to isolate themselves from peers tend to be slow adopters or low users of ICT. Thus, implementing ICT in such contexts would be faced with much resistance. A possible strategy could be to introduce ICT through opinion leaders of influential colleagues rather than by doing so bureaucratically

or authoritatively. Thus, an understanding of how network structure inter-relates with technology and its users would go a long way in reaping benefits required at the organisational (macro) and individual (micro) levels.

## REFERENCES

Ajzen, I. (1988). Attitude Structure and Behavior Relations. In Partkanis, A. R., Berckler, S. T., & Greenwald, A. G. (Eds.), *Attitude Structure and Function*. Hillsdale, NJ: Erlbaum.

Ancona, D. G., & Caldwell, D. F. (1992). Demography and Design: Predictors of New Product Team Performance. *Organization Science, 3*(3), 321–341. doi:10.1287/orsc.3.3.321

Andrews, J. E., Pearce, K. A., Sydney, C., Ireson, C., & Love, M. (2004). Current State of Information Technology Use in a US Primary Care Practice-based Research Network. *Informatics in Primary Care, 12*(1), 11–18.

Barley, S. R. (1990). The Alignment of Technology and Structure through Roles and Networks. *Administrative Science Quarterly, 35*(1), (Special Issue: Technology, Organizations, and Innovation) 61-103.

Bernard, H. R., Killworth, P. D., Kronenfeld, D., & Sailer, L. (1985). On the Validity of Retrospective Data. *Annual Review of Anthropology, 13*, 495–517. doi:10.1146/annurev.an.13.100184.002431

Burt, R. S. (1992). *Structural Holes: The Social Structure of Competition*. Massachusetts: Harvard University Press.

Butler, B. S. (2001). Membership Size, Communication Activity, and Sustainability: A Resource-Based Model of Online Social Structures. *Information Systems Research, 12*(4), 346–362. doi:10.1287/isre.12.4.346.9703

Choudhry, N. K., Fletcher, R. H., & Soumerai, S. B. (2005). Systematic Review: The Relationship between Clinical Experience and Quality of Health Care. *Annals of Internal Medicine, 142*(4), 260–283.

Chung, K. S. K., & Hossain, L. (2010). Towards a Social Network Model for Understanding Information and Communication Technology use for General Practitioners in Rural Australia. *Computers in Human Behavior, 26*(4), 562–571. doi:10.1016/j.chb.2009.12.008

Coleman, J. S., Katz, E., & Menzel, H. (1957). The Diffusion of an Innovation among Physicians. *Sociometry, 20*(4), 253–270. doi:10.2307/2785979

Constant, D., Kiesler, S., & Sproull, L. (1994). What's Mine is Ours, or Is It? A Study of Attitudes about Information Sharing. *Information Systems Research, 5*(4), 400–421. doi:10.1287/isre.5.4.400

Constant, D., Sproull, L., & Kiesler, S. (1996). The Kindness of Strangers: The Usefulness of Electronic Weak Ties for Technical Advice. *Organization Science, 7*(2), 119–135. doi:10.1287/orsc.7.2.119

Cross, R., Rice, R. E., & Parker, A. (2001). Information Seeking in Social Context: Structural Influences and Receipt of Information Benefits. *IEEE Transactions on Systems, Man and Cybernetics. Part C, Applications and Reviews, 31*(4), 438–448. doi:10.1109/5326.983927

Cummings, J. N. (2004). Work Groups, Structural Diversity, and Knowledge Sharing in a Global Organization. *Management Science, 50*(3), 352–364. doi:10.1287/mnsc.1030.0134

Cummings, J. N., & Cross, R. (2003). Structural Properties of Work Groups and their Consequences for Performance. *Social Networks, 25*(3), 197–210. doi:10.1016/S0378-8733(02)00049-7

Daft, R. L., & Macintosh, N. B. (1981). A Tentative Exploration into the Amount and Equivocality of Information Processing in Organizational Work Units. *Administrative Science Quarterly, 26*(2), 207–224. doi:10.2307/2392469

Davis, F. D. (1989). Perceived Usefulness, Perceived Ease of Use, and User Acceptance of Information Technology. *Management Information Systems Quarterly, 13*(3), 319–340. doi:10.2307/249008

Davis, F. D., Bagozzi, R. P., & Warshaw, P. R. (1989). User Acceptance of Computer Technology: A Comparison of Two Theoretical Models. *Management Science, 35*(8), 982–1003. doi:10.1287/mnsc.35.8.982

Freeman, L. C. (1978). Centrality in Social Networks: Conceptual Clarification. *Social Networks, 1*(3), 215–239. doi:10.1016/0378-8733(78)90021-7

Freeman, L. C., Romney, A. K., & Freeman, S. C. (1987). Cognitive Structure and Informant Accuracy. *American Anthropologist, 89*(2), 311–325. doi:10.1525/aa.1987.89.2.02a00020

Fulk, J., Schmitz, J., & Steinfield, C. (1990). A Social Influence Model of Technology Use. In Fulk, J., & Steinfield, C. (Eds.), *Organizations and Communication Technology* (pp. 117–140). Newbury Park, CA: Sage.

Granovetter, M. (1995). *Getting a Job: A Study of Contacts and Careers.* Chicago: University of Chicago Press.

Granovetter, M. S. (1973). The Strength of Weak Ties. *American Journal of Sociology, 78*(6), 1360–1380. doi:10.1086/225469

Hammer, M. (1984). Explorations into the Meaning of Social Network Interview Data. *Social Networks, 6*(4), 341–371. doi:10.1016/0378-8733(84)90008-X

Haythornthwaite, C. (2002). Strong, Weak, and Latent Ties and the Impact of New Media. *The Information Society*, *18*(5), 385–401. doi:10.1080/01972240290108195

Henry, R. M., & Butler, B. S. (2001, August 3-8). *Is it Who You Know or Where You Go: A Comparison of Relational and Non-Relational Information Sources.* Paper presented at the Academy of Management Conference, Washington, DC.

Humphreys, J. S., & Rolley, F. (1998). A Modified Framework for Rural General Practice: The Importance of Recruitment and Retention. *Social Science & Medicine*, *46*(8), 939–949. doi:10.1016/S0277-9536(97)00212-8

Igbaria, M., & Tan, M. (1997). The Consequences of Information Technology Acceptance on Subsequent Individual Performance. *Information & Management*, *32*(3), 113–121. doi:10.1016/S0378-7206(97)00006-2

Licoppe, C., & Smoreda, S. (2005). Are Social Networks Technologically Embedded?: How Networks are Changing Today with Changes in Communication Technology. *Social Networks*, *27*(4), 317–335. doi:10.1016/j.socnet.2004.11.001

Mahmood, M. A., Burn, J. M., Gemoets, L. A., & Jacquez, C. (2000). Variable affecting Information Technology End-user Satisfaction: A Meta-analysis of the Empirical Literature. *International Journal of Human-Computer Studies*, *52*(4), 751–771. doi:10.1006/ijhc.1999.0353

Marsden, P., & Campbell, K. E. (1984). Measuring Tie Strength. *Social Forces*, *63*(2), 482–501.

Mukhopadhyay, T., Rajiv, S., & Srinivasan, K. (1997). Information Technology Impact on Process Output and Quality. *Management Science*, *43*(12), 1645–1659. doi:10.1287/mnsc.43.12.1645

Obstfeld, D. (2005). Social Networks, the Tertius Iungens Orientation, and Involvement in Innovation. *Administrative Science Quarterly*, *50*(1), 100–130.

Orlikowski, W. (1992). The Duality of Technology: Rethinking the Concept of Technology in Organizations. *Organization Science*, *3*(3), 398–427. doi:10.1287/orsc.3.3.398

Pickering, J. M., & King, J. L. (1995). Hardwiring Weak Ties: Interorganizational Computer-mediated Communication, Occupational Communities, and Organizational Change. *Organization Science*, *6*(4), 479–486. doi:10.1287/orsc.6.4.479

Rice, R. E. (1994). Relating Electronic Mail Use and Network Structure to R&D Work Networks and Performance. *Journal of Management Information Systems*, *11*(1), 9–29.

Rice, R. E., Grant, A., Schmitz, J., & Torobin, J. (1990). Individual and Network Influences on the Adoption and Perceived Outcomes of Electronic Messaging. *Social Networks*, *12*(1), 27–55. doi:10.1016/0378-8733(90)90021-Z

Salancik, G. R., & Pfeffer, J. (1978). A Social Information Processing Approach to Job Attitudes and Task Design. *Administrative Science Quarterly*, *23*(2), 224–253. doi:10.2307/2392563

Scott, J. (2000). *Social Network Analysis: A Handbook*. London: SAGE Publications.

Shook, D. E. (1988). *A Structural Equivalence and Contingency Theory Perspective on Media Usage and Communication Performance: The Case of Voice Messaging*. Los Angeles, California: University of Southern California.

Short, J., Williams, E., & Christie, B. (1976). *The Social Psychology of Telecommunications*. London: John Wiley.

Sproull, L., & Kiesler, S. (1991). *Connections: New Ways of Working in the Networked Organization*. Cambridge: MIT Press.

Strasser, R. P., Hays, R. B., Kamien, M., & Carson, D. (2000). Is Australian Rural Practice Changing? Findings from the National Rural General Practice Study. *The Australian Journal of Rural Health*, *8*(4), 222–226. doi:10.1046/j.1440-1584.2000.00305.x

Sykes, T. A., Venkatesh, V., & Gosain, S. (2009). Model of Acceptance with Peer Support: A Social Network Perspective to Understand Employees' System Use. *Management Information Systems Quarterly, 33*(2), 371–393.

Teachman, J. D. (1980). Analysis of Population Diversity: Measures of Qualitative Variation. *Sociological Methods & Research, 8*(3), 341–362. doi:10.1177/004912418000800305

Tortoriello, M., & Krackhardt, D. (2010). Activating Cross-Boundary Knowledge: The Role of Simmelian Ties in the Generation of Innovations. *Academy of Management Journal, 53*(1), 167–181. doi:10.5465/AMJ.2010.48037420

Usherwood, T. (1999). *Understanding the Practice: Evidence, Theory and Practice*. Buckingham: Open University Press.

Wellman, B., Salaff, J., Dimitrova, D., Garton, L., Gulia, M., & Haythornthwaite, C. (1996). Computer Networks as Social Networks: Collaborative Work, Telework, and Virtual Community. *Annual Review of Sociology, 22*, 213–238. doi:10.1146/annurev.soc.22.1.213

Western, M., Dwan, K., Makkai, T., Mar, C. d., & Western, J. (2001). Measuring IT use in Australian General Practice. Retrieved 11th October, 2004, from http://www.gpcg.org/publications/ docs/ projects2001/GPCG_Project24_01.pdf

Williams, E. (1979). Experimental Comparisons of Face-to-Face and Mediated Communication: A Review. *Psychological Bulletin, 84*(5), 963–976. doi:10.1037/0033-2909.84.5.963

Zimmer, J. C., & Henry, R. M. (2007). *Antecedents to Relational and Nonrelational Source Use: An Exploratory Investigation*. Paper presented at the 40th Annual Hawaii International Conference on System Sciences (HICSS'07), Hawaii.

# Chapter 16

# Social Recommendations:
## Mentor and Leader Detection to Alleviate the Cold-Start Problem in Collaborative Filtering

**Armelle Brun**
*Nancy Université, France*

**Sylvain Castagnos**
*Nancy Université, France*

**Anne Boyer**
*Nancy Université, France*

## ABSTRACT

*Recommender systems aim at suggesting to users items that fit their preferences. Collaborative filtering is one of the most popular approaches of recommender systems; it exploits users' ratings to express preferences. Traditional approaches of collaborative filtering suffer from the cold-start problem: when a new item enters the system, it cannot be recommended while a sufficiently high number of users have rated it. The quantity of required ratings is not known a priori and may be high as it depends on who rates the items.*

*In this chapter, the authors propose to automatically select the adequate set of users in the network of users to address the cold-start problem. They call them the "delegates", and they correspond to those who should rate a new item first so as to reliably deduce the ratings of other users on this item.*

*They propose to address this issue as an opinion poll problem. The authors consider two kinds of delegates: mentors and leaders. They experiment some measures, classically exploited in social networks, to select the adequate set of delegates.*

*The experiments conducted show that only 6 delegates are sufficient to accurately estimate ratings of the whole set of other users, which dramatically reduces the number of users classically required.*

DOI: 10.4018/978-1-61350-513-7.ch016

## INTRODUCTION

With the democratization of the Internet, users often need to be assisted in their search of information or search of items. Recommender systems have been proposed in the beginning of the 90's (Goldberg *et al*, 1992), with the aim to fulfill this need. Indeed, the volume of items that users can access is now so huge that they cannot get the information they want within a small amount of time; users are thus unsatisfied. This consequence can be dramatic for e-commerce services for example, that aim at increasing their sales and at developing customers' loyalty. As a consequence, recommender systems are increasing in popularity and are no more of secondary importance; they are becoming mandatory in many e-services.

Recommender systems are not simple information delivery systems; they recommend and display personalized information or pertinent items to users. They are a way to cope with the classical "one size fits all" characteristic of many information delivery systems, such as classical search engines (Allan *et al.*, 2003).

Recommender systems take into consideration the users' specific characteristics, represented under the form of users' profile (Adomavicius & Tuzhilin, 2005). An item is the minimal unit that a recommender system can manage. For example, an item can be a book, a movie, a web page, etc. Recommender systems are now exploited in many application domains, such as e-commerce (Paolino *et al.*, 2009), e-learning (Zhuhadar *et al.*, 2009), restaurants (Hosseini-Pozveh *et al.*, 2009), news (Tintarev & Masthoff, 2006), etc.

Recommender systems generally fall into three categories: content-based systems which compute recommendations from the semantic content of items (Pazzani & Billsus, 2007); knowledge-based systems where recommendations rely on the knowledge about the domain, the users and pre-established heuristics (Burke *et al*, 1996); and at last collaborative filtering systems (Adomavicius & Tuzhilin, 2005) which compute recommendations by examining users' preferences on items.

The users' preferences managed by a collaborative filtering (CF) system are often expressed under the form of ratings and stored in users' profiles. The structure of such a system can be represented under the form of a graph, with nodes being the users and links being the similarity of preferences among them. This graph can be viewed as a social network (Brun & Boyer, 2010), where the links are not social relations but preference relations. To compute recommendations for an active user *a,* a classical CF system exploits the known preferences of the users linked to *a* in the social network, as well as the values of the links.

In CF, *a* implicitly requests the preferences from his like-minded users about some items: he asks them for some recommendations. The ratings of the items *a* has not rated yet are then inferred from these recommendations. The items with the highest ratings are then recommended to *a*.

A collaborative filtering recommender system is thus a social process: not only the active user is involved in the recommendation process; other users are also. In CF, *a*'s like-minded users are called his neighbors. Two main approaches are used to select *a*'s neighbors: the memory-based approach and the model-based approach. In the memory-based approach, the set of neighbors is specific to each user; in the model-based approach, the set of neighbors can be specific to each class of users.

The search of the best set of neighbors has attracted much attention in the literature (Breese *et al*, 1998, Herlocker *et al*, 2004, Kim & Yang, 2007, Castagnos & Boyer, 2007). Classically the number of neighbors required to get high quality recommendations is about several dozens (Shardanand & Maes, 1995, Brun *et al*, 2009).

In the literature, the set of neighbors is only selected according to their similarity with the active user. These neighbors are then used as recommenders. However, we argue that these neighbors may be bad recommenders despite their similarity with the active user, since we do not consider their predictive capacity. As an example, they may be unable to recommend items that have not been rated by the active user $a$, if they have not rated them either. Thus, we claim that the use of the similarity as the only criterion for selecting neighbors is not sufficient.

In this book chapter, we propose a new approach of collaborative filtering: the delegate-based collaborative filtering. This approach has the following characteristics:

- A subset of users, called the delegates, is defined by the system. A delegate is a reliable user who provides high quality recommendations to other users.

- Users do not ask anymore for some recommendations to their neighbors, but to the delegates.

- The set of delegates is small.

- In the traditional approach, each user has a relatively large number of neighbors and chooses who are his neighbors. In the delegate-based approach, the set of neighbors is defined by the system; it is the set of delegates. As the set of delegates is small, users ask recommendations to a smaller number of users, compared to the traditional approach.

- A delegate does not recommend his preferences to all the other users, only to a subset of users: his community. A delegate is a reliable and representative user of the users in his community. As a delegate recommends his opinions to many other users, he can be viewed as a mentor or a leader within his community.

- The recommendation process is still collaborative: the system recommends items to an active user by exploiting the preferences of other users: the delegates.

The delegate-based approach has thus two main advantages. First, as users get some recommendations from only the delegates, the knowledge of the preferences of only the small set of delegates is required. Second, the set of delegates are reliable users; they are chosen for their capacity to accurately recommend some items, based on another criterion than similarity. The quality of the resulting recommendations will be high, while managing the ratings of few users.

Classical collaborative filtering systems face the new item cold-start problem (Schein *et al*, 2002). When a new item enters the system, a CF system cannot recommend this new item while the number of users who have rated this new item is small.

In this paper, we focus on the cold-start problem in CF. We propose to exploit the delegate-based CF with the aim to alleviate this problem. The delegate-based CF asks first the delegates to rate a new item. The set of delegates can be viewed as the editorial committee in a newspaper: they give their opinion on each new article (here item) to be potentially published. Once these ratings are known, as the delegates are reliable and representative users, each user can get some recommendations from them. The cold-start problem is thus alleviated.

The challenge of the delegate-based approach is to find the adequate set of delegates. To efficiently alleviate the cold-start problem, this set has to be as small as possible, while being representative of as many users as possible. From a general point of view, the question is: what is the minimal set of users from which the preferences of the whole population can be deduced?

We point out here that this problem is similar to opinion poll problems: which subset of people from a population has to be polled, in order to reliably deduce the preferences of the whole population? The problem we face is thus: how to choose the people to poll and how many of these people should be polled. As in standard opinion polls, all the users of the systems cannot be polled, as it would be too time consuming. Moreover, in

CF, once the opinion of each user is known, the recommender system becomes useless.

Many of the polling methods propose to partition the population into groups of users. However, in the end, these methods select randomly the users to be polled. In our approach, the people to be polled should be representative users: the delegates. To accurately choose the delegates, we propose to focus on mentors and leaders and the way they are defined and exploited in the literature.

This paper is organized as follows. In the first section, collaborative filtering and the way neighbors are classically chosen are introduced. The next two sections present related works linked to the approach we propose. The first one introduces opinion polls and sampling methods, whereas the second one is interested in mentors and leaders. The following section presents our delegate-based collaborative filtering. Next, the evaluation protocol is presented and some experiments are conducted to evaluate the performance of the delegate-based approach. Last, we conclude and present some perspectives.

## COLLABORATIVE FILTERING

### Collaborative Filtering in General

Given a set of items $I = \{i_1, \cdots, i_m\}$ and a set of users $U = \{u_1, \cdots, u_n\}$, the input data of a CF system is the set of ratings that users $u \in U$ have assigned to some items $i \in I$. Most of the time these ratings are chosen in a non binary rating scale (for example, from *1* to *5* (Grcar *et al*, 2005)). This set is stored under the form of a rating matrix $R = U \times I$.

Let *a* be the active user. To make recommendations to *a*, the CF system first estimates, for each item *i* that *a* has not rated, the rating $r^*(a,i)$ that *a* would assign to the item *i* if he rated it. Second, given this set of estimated ratings, the system recommends the items with the highest

rating values. In the literature, "making recommendations" is equivalent to estimating the user's ratings for unrated items.

To estimate $r^*(a,i)$, the system adopts a collaborative or social approach. The underlying principle behind CF is to use *a*'s like-minded users, who rated *i*, to estimate $r^*(a,i)$. CF first computes the similarity between each pair of users. The resulting social network represents the users linked by their similarities of preference. Second, it exploits the ratings of the users linked to *a* in the network and that have rated *i*. These two steps are now further detailed.

## Computation of the Similarity Between Users

The similarity between two users is a similarity of ratings; it measures how the two users rate (appreciate) similarly items. This similarity is classically instantiated by the Pearson correlation, presented in Equation (1).

$$corr(a, u) = \frac{\sum_{j \in I_{a \cap u}} (r(a, j) - \overline{r(a)}) \times (r(u, j) - \overline{r(u)})}{\sqrt{\sum_{j \in I_{a \cap u}} (r(a, j) - \overline{r(a)})^2} \times \sqrt{\sum_{j \in I_{a \cap u}} (r(u, j) - \overline{r(u)})^2}}$$

(1)

This correlation is computed on $I_{a \cap u}$, the set of items commonly rated by users *a* and *u*. $r(u,i)$ is the rating that user *u* has assigned to item *i*, $\overline{r(u)}$ is the average rating of user *u*. (Candillier *et al*, 2007) presents other equations to compute user similarities.

Once these similarities are computed, the ratings of *a* on the item *i* can be estimated.

### Estimation of Ratings

One classical way to estimate a rating $r^*(a,i)$ is presented in Equation (2).

$$r^*(a,i) = \overline{r(a)} + \frac{\sum_{u \in U_{a,i}} sim(a,u) \times (r(u,i) - \overline{r(u)})}{\sum_{u \in U_{a,i}} |sim(a,u)|}$$

$$(2)$$

where $U_{a,i}$ is the set of users linked to $a$ in the network and who rated the item $i$: $a$'s neighbors. $sim(a,u)$ represents the similarity between users $a$ and $u$. Equation (1) can be used to represent the similarity between two users.

The estimated rating is the weighted average of the absolute difference between the ratings the other users assigned to the item $i$ and their average rating, added to the average rating of user $a$. The more a user is similar to $a$, the higher his weight in the estimation of $r^*(a,i)$ is. (Candillier *et al*, 2007) also presents an overview of other equations and approaches to estimate this rating.

## The Neighbor Selection

In Equation (2), only $a$'s neighbors are actually used to estimate $r^*(a,i)$. The choice of the neighbors (and their number) highly influences three main features in a CF system: the computation time, the accuracy of the estimated ratings and the coverage. There are basically two approaches to implement neighbor selection: respectively the memory-based approach and the model-based approach. These approaches both exploit the similarity between users to select the neighbors.

*The memory-based approach*, also called direct neighbor selection, keeps among the users linked to $a$ in the network (with a non-null similarity value) and that have rated $i$, those users that comply with a given criterion. This criterion can be a threshold value (Amati *et al*, 2007, Herlocker *et al*, 1999): all users with a similarity or link value with the active user $a$ above a predefined threshold are selected as neighbors of $a$. The resulting community is user-centered. Thus, the neighbors are specific to each user and are usually different from one user to the other.

This neighbor selection criterion can also be an integer value $K$. The $K$ nearest neighbors (KNN) of $a$, that have rated $i$, are kept; $K$ being fixed *a priori* (Herlocker *et al*, 1999).

One main drawback of the memory-based approach is scalability. For example, on the MovieLens database, (Castagnos & Boyer, 2006) showed that the memory-based approach is very time-consuming when the number of users exceeds tens of thousands.

In addition, the choice of $K$ or of the threshold value is tricky. At last, KNN is not robust to data sparsity: it is unable to form reliable neighborhoods in case of high sparsity level (Grcar *et al*, 2005).

*The model-based approach*, computes a model of the data. The two most popular model-based approaches respectively rely on Bayesian networks and clustering. Systems based on Bayesian networks, similarly to the memory-based approach, face a scalability problem when learning for the structure of the directed acyclic graph associated (Castagnos, 2008).

The clustering-based approach computes groups or clusters of users (Castagnos & Boyer, 2006), by exploiting the similarity between users. These clusters are computed offline. This approach identifies groups of users with similar preferences (Breese *et al*, 1998), *i.e.* who have high link values in the network. As a result, the neighbors of a user $a$ are the users who belong to the same cluster than $a$.

There are typically three kinds of clustering methods: partitioning (Mobasher *et al*, 2006), hierarchical (Castagnos & Boyer, 2006), and fuzzy clustering (Teran & Meier, 2010). Most of the time, CF relies on a partitioning algorithm since it allows considering that each user belongs to exactly one cluster (O'Connor & Herlocker, 1999), (Ungar & Foster, 1998). For example, the well-known $K$-means algorithm (Mobasher *et al*, 2006), computes $K$ clusters so that the average pair-wise similarity between users within clusters is maximized.

## The Cold-Start Problem

Recommender systems based on CF face the new item cold-start problem, also called the latency problem (Schein et al, 2002). When a new item enters the system, while the number of ratings on this item is low, it cannot be recommended to users. More specifically, while none of $a$'s neighbors has rated this item, none of them can recommend it to $a$.

The minimal number of ratings required by the system to recommend a new item cannot be defined beforehand. Indeed, according to who rates this item, it can be recommended or not to other users. For example, if the users who rate this item are neighbors of no or few users, the item cannot be recommended to other users. Let us notice that users generally do not devote much time to express regularly their preferences about new items (Sollenborn & Funk, 2002).

To alleviate the cold-start problem, four main solutions have been proposed in the literature: content-based filtering, ontology-based filtering, advertising and modification of the similarity. We present here an overview of these three solutions.

*Content-based filtering* is one of the three main techniques of recommender systems (see the Introduction section) (Lang, 1995), (Billsus & Pazzani, 2000). This technique relies on the analysis of the content of the items to generate recommendations. An item is recommended to the active user if its content similarity with the other items that $a$ has liked, is high. For example, a user who has liked some items about "genetics" will be recommended some items related to this area.

Content-based filtering does not suffer from the cold-start problem. Indeed, a new item can be recommended to any user since the analysis of its content can be performed. However, content-based filtering has one main weakness: it suffers from overspecialization of its recommendations, also called novelty problem. The recommended items are similar or identical to those appreciated by the user before. Thus, the other items with a different content are neglected and are never integrated in recommendation lists suggested to this user. The analysis of the content of items can help to bridge the gap from existing items to new items, by inferring similarities among them.

In the context of solving the cold-start problem, content-based and collaborative filtering are often combined resulting in hybrid recommender systems (Good *et al*, 1999), (Melville *et al*, 2002). In these hybrid systems, the content-based algorithm aims at facing the cold-start problem, while the collaborative filtering algorithm guarantee the introduction of novel recommendations.

*Ontology-based filtering* has also been suggested as a solution to the cold-start problem of CF (Pan *et al*, 2010). Ontologies are used to automatically build knowledge bases and extract semantic profiles of items (Ruiz & Aldana, 2009). Semantic similarities between items can thus be computed. Two examples of ontology-based recommender systems are Quickstep-Foxtrot (recommending research papers) (Middleton *et al*, 2004) and Entree (recommending restaurants) (Burke, 2002).

The main problem regarding such a solution is the requirement of the availability of a ontology. However, no limit to this computation appears in the case of new items. Thus this approach can also be used by a CF system to cope with the cold-start problem (Schickel & Faltings, 2007).

*Getting some ratings for new items.* The last solution is mainly adopted by e-commerce websites: advertising the new items. For example, a floating banner may be displayed at the homepage of the website, presenting this new item. As a result, some users will rate these items. However, users may perceive this solution as a recommendation, despite the fact that this banner is not personalized. This may result in a reduction of acceptance and adoption rates of the system. In other words, some users who do not like the new item may feel unsatisfied and leave the website (Jones, 2010).

*Modifying the computation of the similarity.* With the objective of reducing the cold-start problem, (Ahn, 2008) proposed a new similarity measure, so that it can be computed on a small number of ratings. This measure, that exploits proximity, impact and popularity of users, has been devoted to the new user problem, but can be easily transposed to the new item problem.

To alleviate the cold-start problem, the approach we propose is close to the last method: it asks some users to rate new items. The opinion of the whole population is then deduced from these ratings. Thus, the question we raise is: what could be this set of users? At the opposite of the last approach, these users are not those that visit the website.

We propose to take inspiration of opinion polls to perform this task. In the following section, we define opinion polls and present some well-known sampling techniques.

## OPINION POLLS AND SAMPLING

Opinion polls are usually conducted with the aim to get the opinion of a whole population in the case either all the people cannot be polled or it would take too much time or be expensive to poll everybody. A sampling of the population is made and this sample is polled. The objective is to get the opinions of that sample that are as close as possible from the opinions that would have been obtained if it had been possible to interview all of the people.

Sampling is used in many application domains, such as agriculture (Pedigo & Buntin, 1994), politics (Baddie, 2010), image analysis (Wang *et al*, 2005), etc. Sampling is also the fundamental basis for all polling research.

The classical sampling methods are: simple random sampling, systematic sampling, stratified sampling, cluster sampling, proportional to size sampling, etc. (Groves *et al*, 2009, Fuller, 2009). We present here the three most popular ones: simple random sampling, stratified sampling and cluster sampling.

*The simple random sampling* is the most basic method. The population is not subdivided nor partitioned, the sample is randomly selected; thus each person of the population has an equal probability of selection. The advantage of this technique is that it does not require any additional information about the population except the complete list of members. Although simple, this method is vulnerable to sampling errors. Indeed, the randomness of the selection may result in a sample that does not reflect the whole population.

*Stratified sampling* segments the population into mutually exclusive sub-groups, also called strata. The grouping criterion can be whatever attribute the system has about the people in the population: age, sex, profession, etc. Then, a subset of users is randomly selected within each of the strata. As a result, the sample is made of people from all the strata of the population.

One of the advantages of the stratified sampling is that it improves the accuracy of the estimations compared to the simple random sampling. In addition, it allows drawing inferences about specific strata and the selection criterion can be different from one stratum to the other. However, stratified sampling requires the selection of relevant stratification variables, which may be difficult.

*Cluster sampling* also groups people into groups, called clusters. At the opposite of stratified sampling, sampling is not performed on the whole set of clusters. Only a subset of clusters is chosen, but each person within the chosen clusters is polled. In other words, the sample is made up of all the people from a subset of clusters. Cluster sampling assumes that the distribution of the population within one cluster is similar to the one of the whole population. However, this may be not true.

Usually the clusters used are "natural" clusters from the population. For example, a cluster may be made up of people located in a geographical area so that all people of a chosen cluster can be studied with minimal costs (when pollsters have to meet people).

Cluster sampling also improves the accuracy of estimations compared to the simple random sampling. In case of a large variation in size of the clusters, one can perform selection with probability proportional to size: the selection probability of one cluster is proportional to its size.

The two last polling and sampling techniques presented in this section form groups of people and, in the end, select randomly the people to be polled. In our case, the delegates exploited by our method should be reliable and representative users. Selecting them randomly could not lead to high quality estimations. To select these delegates, we propose to take advantage of notions used in social networks. More specifically, we focus on mentors and leaders. In the following section we present how mentors and leaders are defined and the way they are used in the literature.

## MENTORS AND LEADERS

### Mentors

A mentor can be a trusted friend, a counselor or a teacher. A mentor is often defined with the following characteristics: wise, trusted, experienced, expert. A mentor is also a person who likes to transfer his knowledge. The student of a mentor is called mentee, or *protégé*.

Mentoring, which can be interpreted as a social relationship, is used in several domains. The most popular one is education. The concept of mentoring has entered the business domain as well.

### Mentors in Collaborative Filtering

In collaborative filtering, the terms mentor and neighbor are usually used interchangeably. A mentor often simply refers to a user with similar interests, *i.e.* a like-minded user, which is equivalent to the definition of neighbors (see section The Neighbor Selection). Within this context, the mentors are in fact some neighbors (Bohnert *et al*,

2008, Aggarwal *et al*, 1999, Greening, 1997, Shardanand & Maes, 1995) selected with the Pearson correlation (see Equation (1)), as neighbors are. However, based on the straight definition above and according to (Paulson & Tzanavari, 2003), a mentor in collaborative filtering should be a user with high expertise or knowledge.

Some works exploit mentors as defined above. For example, in (Brun & Boyer, 2010), the choice of mentors is based on the connectivity of the users. The higher a neighbor of *a* is connected to other neighbors of *a*, the most representative this user is. Such a user is thus a mentor. In this work, the similarities of preferences are not considered. In (Chandrashekhar & Bhasker, 2007), mentors are selected based on their predictability in place of the classical similarity. The predictability results from the examination of the relationship between the mentor and *a* at each of the rating levels. In reciprocal recommender systems (Pizzato *et al*, 2010), the system recommends people to people. Reciprocal recommenders are mainly applied in the education domain where some mentors (users) are recommended to students. Mentors are selected based on their level of knowledge and on their willingness to be a mentor (Vassileva *et al*, 2003).

### Leaders

Leaders are "the individuals who are likely to influence other persons in their immediate environment" (Elihu & Lazarsfeld, 1955). In the literature, leaders are usually associated with opinion leaders (Goyal *et al*, 2008, Keller & Berry, 2003).

### Application Domains

Leadership and influence propagation have been much studied in the area of marketing, social sciences and recently social networks analysis (Goyal *et al*, 2008). They tend to understand how communities start, what are their properties, how they evolve, what are the roles of their members and how influencers and opinion leaders can be detected through these communities.

In the area of *marketing* (viral marketing), influence propagation is often linked to the word-of-mouth phenomenon and its effects on the success of new products (Domingos & Richardson, 2001). The most important challenge in marketing is how to find a small segment of the population (influencers or leaders) that can influence the other segments by their positive or negative opinions regarding products and services (Watts & Dodds, 2007).

With the development of the Internet, leaders and influencers do not only use traditional word-of-mouth. They can also propagate their opinions based on interactive exchanges through blogs, forums, wikis, and various social network platforms. Indeed, nowadays, social networks have become the most important medium for propagating information, innovation and opinions. As an example, there were approximately 500 millions active Facebook accounts in November 2010. This is almost a third of the 1.73 billions Internet users.

## Identifying Leaders

In the frame of social networks, some studies (Barabasi *et al*, 2002, Newman, 2003) emphasize the role of highly connected nodes called also hubs, in information dissemination. (Malcolm, 2000, Agarwal *et al*, 2008, Keller & Berry, 2003) confirm that highly connected nodes have an important influence on their neighbors.

Leaders can also be defined as active users. For example, this criterion has been used to identify active and non active influential bloggers (Agarwal *et al*, 2008). Recently, Chang defines leaders as users that are not only highly connected (often interact with others), these connections being of high quality but also active users (Chang, 2010).

## Leaders in Recommender Systems

To our knowledge, in the context of recommender systems and CF, the detection of leaders and influencers has been examined in few studies. (Cheon & Lee, 2005) present a recommendation system that uses a fuzzy inference system exploiting a marketing method called RFM (Recency, Frequency, Monetary) to detect leaders. (Rashid *et al*, 2005) define several metrics to measure the influence of users in rating based recommender systems. They propose a metric that measures the influence of users by removing some users' ratings while computing predictions and observing the effect of this removal on the recommendation results. If the difference is high, the user is detected as influential.

## Mentors vs. Leaders

From the previous sections, we can say that mentor and leader are two highly similar terms, used in different contexts. However, one can see a slight difference between these two terms.

A mentor is a user who knows something that a mentee does not know, and who passes his knowledge to the mentee.

In the definition of leaders the notion of influence is important: a leader influences his neighbors.

Thus a mentor is somebody who knows more than the mentee and "teaches" him what he knows, whereas a leader is somebody who influences others. The knowledge or the decision of a user will thus be different according to the fact that he exploits the opinion of a mentor or of a leader. If he exploits the opinion of a mentor, his deduced opinion will be the one of the mentor, whereas if he exploits the opinion of a leader, it will be different from the one of the leader (although influenced by his opinion).

## The Delegate-Based Collaborative Filtering

To alleviate the cold-start problem that traditional Collaborative Filtering faces, we propose a new approach: the delegate-based Collaborative Filtering.

To implement this new approach, we propose to take inspiration from opinion polls. When a new item *ni* enters the system, an opinion poll about this item is conducted. The polled users "recommend" their ratings (opinions) on *ni* to other users. The ratings *r\*(u,ni)* of each user *u* in the whole population on *ni* is then deduced from the opinions of the polled users. The system then recommends *ni* to a user *u* if the estimated rating *r\*(u,ni)* is high.

Of course, the set of polled users has to be chosen carefully so that the exploitation of their ratings results in high quality recommendations. We propose to poll reliable users from who the system can deduce the opinion of the whole population; these polled people are called delegates. In this paper, delegates will be instantiated by the mentors and the leaders within the population of users.

The smaller this set, the more the cold-start problem is avoided. As a consequence, when a new item *ni* enters the system, the delegate-based CF requires a few number of ratings on *ni* (only those from delegates). In addition, as the set of delegates in a population of users is pre-computed, the number of ratings required is known beforehand. At the opposite, the classical CF did not control the number of ratings required to deduce the opinion of the whole population.

As in classical opinion polls, a sampling method has to be chosen.

## The Sampling Method

The simple random sampling though simple, often leads to a lower performance compared to the stratified and cluster samplings. The latter two sampling methods exploit pieces of information about the people in the population to orient the choice of the persons to poll. Concretely, these pieces of information are used to form groups of people. Cluster sampling selects a sample of clusters and all the people within these selected clusters are polled. This clustering is usually used to minimize the polling cost. However, in case the selected clusters do not have the same distribution than the one of the whole population, it may also lead to a bad performance.

Stratified sampling does not have this distribution problem and is more appropriate in the CF context, where clusters of users are usually disjointed. Moreover, it generally leads to high-quality deductions. Thus we decide to exploit the stratified sampling that selects a sample of people within each group.

The only information the delegate-based CF has about the users is their ratings on some items. At the opposite of groupings used in polling techniques, groups cannot be formed based on a single attribute: the rating on one item. Thus we propose to group users according to their similarity in terms of ratings, resulting in groups of like-minded users. The resulting strata (or groups) will be noted $S = \{s_1, \cdots s_l\}$.

So as to group users according to this similarity criterion, we propose to use a clustering algorithm, such as the classical k-means (McQueen, 1967) or PAM (Kaufman & Rousseeuw, 1987) algorithms. Each group is made up of users who have similar preferences among themselves. These algorithms are partitioning algorithms, thus each user $u \in U$ belongs to exactly one group.

Let us recall that the k-means algorithm is classically used in the model-based CF to group users (Ungar & Foster, 1998, Kim & Yang, 2007) (see Section about neighbor selection).

As in stratified sampling, user sampling is performed within each stratum; we have to focus on the way we propose to select the users within each stratum, *i.e.* the delegates.

## Defining the Delegates

In classical stratified sampling, the choice of people to poll in each group or stratum is performed randomly. Despite this randomness, the system aims at selecting the people who represent the best the group they belong to.

In collaborative filtering, the system has the social network that represents users and their preference relations. This network has already been used to group users. We propose to exploit it once again in order to guide the selection of delegates within groups.

In our approach, the delegates will be instantiated by mentors or by leaders. Let $D = \{D_1, \cdots, D_l\}$ be the set of delegates. $D_j = \{d_{j1}, \cdots, d_{jk}\}$ is the set of delegates of the stratum $j$. Each delegate $d_{jk}$ is the delegate of all the users in his stratum. We note $d(u)$ the function that gives the set of delegates of the user $u$ in parameter.

To decide which users may be selected as delegates, we propose to exploit measures from social networks.

First, we propose to exploit the two measures classically used to detect leaders: *connectivity* and *activity*, as presented in section about leaders.

Second, we propose to exploit the *distance centrality* measure (Wasserman & Faust, 1994), used in social networks, that measures the position of a node within a graph. This measure considers the distance of a node to all other nodes in the group; the nodes with short paths to most or all nodes have high closeness. In our network, the users with the lowest distance with other users of the group are thus considered as central users, thus delegates. Centrality has not been much used in collaborative filtering. For example (Cantador *et al*, 2009) exploits nodes centrality with the aim of recommending tags.

## Inferring Ratings

Once the delegates are defined, the opinion of the whole group can be deduced.

This deduction depends on if a delegate is considered as a mentor or as a leader.

If the selected delegates are viewed as mentors, the deduction is instantiated by a strict equality. The estimated rating of a user is computed as the average rating of all his mentors, as presented in Equation (3).

$$r^*(a, i) = \frac{\sum_{u \in d(a)} r(u, i)}{|d(a)|} \qquad (3)$$

If the selected users are viewed as leaders, we propose to instantiate the deduction by a function depending on the relationship between the leader and the user. This relationship is the similarity between the two users. The estimated rating is computed as in classical CF, by adapting Equation (2), where we substitute delegates for neighbors.

$$r^*(a, i) = \overline{r(a)} + \frac{\sum_{u \in d(a)} sim(a, u) \times (r(u, i) - \overline{r(u)})}{\sum_{u \in d(a)} |sim(a, u)|} \qquad (4)$$

## EVALUATION PROTOCOL

### Corpus

To evaluate the delegate-based CF approach, we used the state-of-the-art MovieLens database (http://www.movielens.org). This movie database is made up of user preferences on movies. These preferences are expressed under the form of ratings: integer values between 1 and 5, where 1 means that the user did not like the movie and 5 means that he really liked it.

The database contains 1682 users, 943 items and 100k preferences. We divided the set of items into 2 subsets: the training items and the test items. The set of training items is made up of 80% of the items and the test items represent the 20% remaining ones. The test items represent the new items.

The training corpus *Tr* contains the triplets <user,item,rating> that represent the ratings of the users on the training items and the test corpus *Te* contains the triplets <user,item,rating> that represent the ratings of the users on the test items. In the experiments, we aim at retrieving the ratings of the users on the new items (*i.e.* test items) from the training corpus.

## Evaluation

The training of the groups and the choice of the delegates is made only on the training corpus. Once the delegates are selected, their ratings are extracted from the test corpus (in order to simulate the fact that they rate the new items) and are used to deduce the ratings of other users on the same items.

The quality of the deduced ratings is evaluated in terms of MAE (Mean Absolute Error). MAE computes the mean error on the ratings estimated by the system, as presented in Equation (5). The lower the MAE, the lower the error. Thus we aim at minimizing the MAE value.

$$MAE = \frac{\sum_{(u,i) \in Te} |\, r(u,i) - r^*(u,i)\,|}{|\,Te\,|} \qquad (5)$$

## The Clustering Algorithms

To evaluate the delegate-based approach, we tested two clustering algorithms.

The first algorithm is the well-known k-means algorithm (McQueen, 1967). This algorithm builds groups of users so that the Euclidean distance between the gravity center (centroid) and the users of the class is minimized. This algorithm is usually used in CF to build classes of users.

*Figure 1. Example of class with the centroid and the medoid being far from each other*

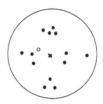

The second algorithm is the PAM (Partitioning Around Medoids) algorithm (Kaufman & Rousseeuw, 1987). At the opposite of k-means that uses gravity centers, PAM exploits medoids, *i.e.* the centers of the classes are real users. Figure 1 presents an example of class of users, where full circles are users, the cross is the centroid of the class and the empty circle is the medoid of the class. We can see that the medoid is far from the centroid, which may highly influence the results of the experiments conducted.

In these two algorithms, the number of classes has to be defined *a priori*. However, we do not know the optimal number of classes. Thus, in our experiments the number of classes varies from 1 to 15.

In addition, as PAM and k-means are dependent on the initialization values (that are chosen randomly), the MAE values presented in the experiments are average values from 20 executions.

## EXPERIMENTS

### Intra-Class Average Distance

In this section, we present the evolution of the average intra-class distances (between the centroid or the medoid and other users), according to the number of classes and the partitioning algorithm; these average distances are presented in Figure 2.

We can first notice that the average distance between the center and other users of the class in the k-means algorithm is lower than the one ob-

*Figure 2. Average intra-class distances according to the partitioning algorithm and the number of classes*

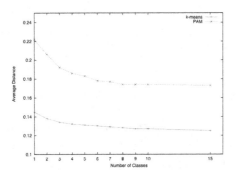

*Figure 3. MAE according to the partitioning algorithm, the number of classes and the type of delegates, with delegates selected according to their connectivity.*

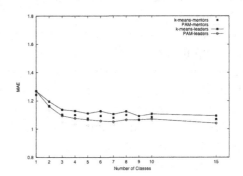

tained with PAM. This difference was expected as k-means exploits the iso-barycenter as the center of the class. However, this lower average distance does not mean that k-means leads to better estimations.

As expected too, the average distance decreases asymptotically with the number of classes. The asymptote is reached with 8 classes, for both partitioning algorithms. Once more, this asymptote does not mean that the optimal number of classes is 8.

In the following sections, we present the MAE values according to several criteria: the choice of the delegates, the number of classes, the partitioning algorithm and the way delegates are viewed (mentors or leaders). As the number of delegates has to be as small as possible, we decide to select only one delegate per class.

## The Most Connected Users

In this section, the selection of the delegates is performed according to users' connectivity. In each class, the user with the highest connectivity is considered as a delegate. Figure 3 presents the resulting MAE values.

In Figure 3 dashed lines represent the experiments that exploit mentors; solid lines represent the leaders. The squares on the lines refer to the

use of the k-means algorithm as partitioning algorithm, and circles show the use of PAM.

When selecting the most connected users as delegates, their exploitation as mentors leads to a better performance compared to their exploitation as leaders, whatever is the partitioning algorithm.

In addition, the PAM algorithm leads on average to a lower MAE, compared to the k-means algorithm. The lowest MAE of the PAM algorithm is 1.02 and is reached when exploiting mentors, with a number of 6 classes. We consequently have reached the optimum before the asymptote in Figure 2.

## The Most Active Users

In this section, the selection of delegates is performed according to the activity of the users: the most active user in each class is viewed as a delegate. Figure 4 presents the MAE values.

The first conclusion that can be drawn from this figure is that when delegates are selected based on their activity, the lowest MAE value is reached with 4 classes; this number is smaller than the one deduced from the previous selection criterion.

However, the corresponding MAE is larger: 1.08, which corresponds to an increase of about 6%.

*Figure 4. MAE according to the partitioning algorithm, the number of classes, and the type of delegates, when delegates are selected according to their activity*

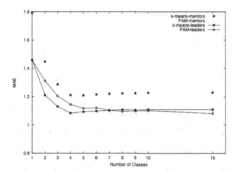

*Figure 5. MAE according to the partitioning algorithm, the number of classes and the type of delegates, when delegates are selected according to their centrality distance*

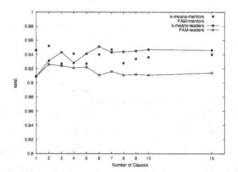

In addition, the lowest MAE is not reached by the same configuration than in the previous section. Here the best MAE is reached with the k-means algorithm and delegates viewed as leaders.

The PAM algorithm with mentors, which corresponds to the best configuration from the previous experiment, leads to a similar MAE (1.09) but with 8 classes. Thus the number of delegates required is twice larger than with the optimal configuration.

## Users with the Lowest Distance Centrality

In this section, users at the center of the classes are selected as delegates. Figure 5 presents the evolution of the MAE according to the number of classes.

We would like to mention that in this figure, the range of the y-axis is different from the 2 previous figures, to have a more precise view of the evolution of the MAE.

First of all, we can notice that the MAE values are on average lower when selecting delegates based on their centrality. Thus, this criterion seems to be more appropriate than the 2 previous ones.

In addition, the k-means partitioning algorithm leads to a higher MAE compared to PAM. This can be easily explained by the way the classes are

formed. Indeed, the selected delegates are users at the center of each class, which corresponds exactly to the criterion used to form classes with PAM.

Here again, the selection of mentors with PAM leads to the best MAE value. The optimal value is reached with 10 classes (0.870); but the MAE reached with 6 classes is not statistically different from this one (0.874).

As a consequence, the optimal value is reached when 6 classes are formed.

The three previous experiments show that partitioning the set of users into 6 classes with the PAM algorithm, then extracting one delegate within each class, based on his centrality, and exploiting him as a mentor leads to the best performance. The corresponding MAE is about 0.87, which corresponds to an improvement of almost 20% compared to the activity-based criterion.

## How to Choose the 6 Best Delegates?

In the previous section, we have shown that the optimal number of delegates is 6; these delegates being viewed as mentors. However, in these previous experiments, the number of delegates per class was fixed to 1. We propose to study the evolution of the MAE when these 6 delegates are selected from a varying number of classes, which remains

*Table 1. MAE with 6 delegates, selected according to their centrality distance, and depending on the number of classes.*

| # of Classes | # of Delegates per Class | Mentors | Leaders |
|---|---|---|---|
| 1 | 6 | 0.890 | 0.838 |
| 2 | 3 | 0.885 | 0.886 |
| 3 | 2 | 0.879 | 0.899 |
| 6 | 1 | 0.874 | 0.911 |

lower than the number of delegates (cf. Section "Opinion polls and sampling"). For example, the 6 delegates may be selected as the 6 most central users when 1 class is formed, or selected as the 2 most central users when 3 classes are formed, etc.

Table 1 presents the MAE corresponding to the various number of classes used to select the 6 delegates. In addition, these delegates are viewed either as mentors or as leaders.

Table 1 shows that, when the delegates are viewed as mentors, the best way to select the delegates is by forming 6 classes of users, and select in each class, the user who is the most at the center of the class. At the opposite, when the delegates are viewed as leaders, the best choice is building only 1 class and selects the 6 users at the center of the class.

Moreover, at the opposite of the conclusions drawn from the previous experiments; the best MAE value is reached when delegates are viewed as leaders. Intuitively this result is coherent: mentors aim at passing the knowledge (only one mentor is sufficient to impose the optimal rating for the new item), while leaders only tend to influence users (several leaders are required to pull users toward the optimal rating).

In addition, we checked the statistical significance of the decrease of the MAE when selecting delegates based on their centrality, relatively to the previous delegate selection methods. In order to do that, we chose the best configuration for each selection method, i.e. PAM-mentors for the connectivity-based method, k-means-leaders for the activity-based method, and PAM-mentors for

the centrality-based method. On one hand, the difference of performance between connectivity-based and activity-based methods is marginally significant on average, according to Student's T-test (p=0.0651). On the other hand, the decrease in MAE of the centrality-based is significant at 0.99 level on average compared to, respectively, the connectivity-based method (p=1.01e-06) and the activity-based method (p=9.98e-06). We can conclude that the centrality-based method is the most suitable selection criterion, since it got the lowest MAE values for each number of classes.

We also compared the performance of the centrality-based method with a baseline MAE value, that is computed based on the estimation of new items' ratings for each user $u$ as an average of $u$'s ratings. This baseline is independent on the number of classes and the resulting MAE is 0.94. This result is surprisingly equivalent to the MAE of our centrality-based method when all users are considered in the same class (number of class = 1). However, our method resulted in a lower MAE when the number of classes is increased: 0.874, and this is significant at 0.99 level (p = 3.27e-05).

## CONCLUSION AND DISCUSSION

This paper focused on the alleviation of the cold-start problem that classical collaborative systems face. In the standard approach, the number of ratings required to estimate reliably the ratings of some users on new items is not known *a priori*; it highly depends on which users rate the new items. This number may be high, specifically if the users who rate the new items are neighbors of few or no user.

We proposed a new approach of collaborative filtering: the delegate-based approach. This approach is based on the exploitation of delegate users. A delegate user is a reliable, experienced and trustworthy user. The knowledge of the rating of a delegate on one item allows the system deducing the rating of a large number of other users on this item. To alleviate the cold-start problem, the system first asks the delegates to rate the new item, which just entered the system. Then, the rating of all the users in the population on this item is deduced. The set of delegates has to be as small as possible and representative of as many users as possible to alleviate the cold-start problem.

We have proposed to take inspiration of opinion polls and have proposed several methods to select the delegates, based on measures from social networks. In addition, we have proposed to consider these delegates either as mentors or as leaders; the deduced rating of a given user depends on if her delegate is viewed as a mentor or as a leader. If the delegate is viewed as a mentor, the estimated rating of a user is equal to that of the delegate. If the delegate is viewed as a leader, the estimated rating is function of the value of the link between the user and the delegate.

The experiments have shown that, when the set of neighbors is partitioned into classes with the PAM algorithm, and one delegate is selected in each class, considering delegates as mentors leads to the best performance on the MovieLens database. Similarly, when leaders are used, 6 classes with one leader per class leads to a better performance. As the difference of performance between these two configurations is not statistically significant, we can consider them as equivalent. They both significantly improve the accuracy of new items' predictions in comparison with other models tested in this paper (it improves the MAE of the activity-based approach by 20%). In addition, the baseline performance, which is computed based on the estimation of new items' ratings for each user $u$ as an average of $u$'s ratings, is about 0.94. Our method statistically improves this MAE by 7%.

As a conclusion, in this paper, we have shown that, when a new item enters a collaborative filtering recommender system, the knowledge of the rating of a very small number of delegates on this item is sufficient to deduce the rating of the whole set of other users, with a high quality. This work constitutes a preliminary survey that acts as a proof-of-concept. In MovieLens, only 6 delegates were required. These 6 delegates may either be viewed as mentors and selected as the 6 most central users when 1 class is formed, or be viewed as leaders and selected as the most central user of each class when 6 classes are formed. These optimal values for the numbers of classes and delegates are obviously strongly dependent from the corpus. Nevertheless, we expect to have similar results as regards the other properties, whatever the corpus is.

Based on these conclusions, several questions can be raised. The users who are detected by the systems as being mentors or leaders may be overwhelmed by the number of items they are asked to rate. Indeed, each time a new item enters the system, they are asked to rate it. As a consequence, delegates may sooner or later refuse to rate items. As a consequence, it may be appropriate to detect several delegates (those with the highest quality) within each group and ask each of them rating in turn so as to not solicit them too frequently. The overall quality of the system may be slightly decreased as some of the delegates may have a lower quality but this strategy may guarantee the persistence of the approach.

Another question that may be raised is the stability of delegates over time. Does a user, who is a delegate at a given time, remains a delegate later? Similarly, delegates may be topic-dependent delegates; it could be interesting to take into account the topics associated to the items so that to refine the way to detect delegates.

In addition, we can ask how to automatically detect if a delegate is a mentor or a leader, based on the characteristics of her link within the network.

Thus, as a first perspective, we plan to extend our experiments to other databases such as Netflix or Jester. This should confirm the efficiency of our delegate selection method, combined with the PAM clustering algorithm. If so, this theory and our model will be easily transposable in a real industrial context. In the other case, we will have to identify patterns that characterize corpuses and explain the differences of performances. Then, we will be able to propose the model adapted to a specific situation. We would also like to study the way to automatically deduce if a given delegate should be viewed as a mentor or as a leader, in order to improve the performance.

Among other perspectives, we aim at introducing a fourth selection method for delegates, in addition to connectivity, activity and distance centrality. We propose to exploit the criterion defined in (Chang, 2010) in the frame of social networks. In this work, the influence of a user is a combination of his centrality, expertise and activeness.

Finally, we plan to study the performance of the system, when delegates do not rate the new items. What is the resulting performance if a delegate with a lower quality, rates the new items?

## REFERENCES

Adomavicius G., Tuzhilin A. (2005). Toward the Next Generation of Recommender Systems: A Survey of the State-of-the-Art, *IEEE transactions on knowledge and data engineering*, vol. 17, n° 6, p. 734-749.

Agarwal, N., Liu, H., Tang, L., and Yu, P. S. (2008). Identifying the influential bloggers in a community. In *Proceedings of the international conference on Web search and web data mining (WSDM'08)* (New York, NY, USA, 2008), ACM, pp. 207–218.

Aggarwal, C.C., Wolf, J., Wu, K.L. and Yu, P.S. (1999). Horting hatches an egg: a new graph-theoretic approach to collaborative filtering. *Proceedings of the fifth ACM SIGKDD international conference on Knowledge discovery and data mining.*

Ahn, H.J. (2008) A new similarity measure for collaborative filtering to alleviate the new user cold-starting problem. *Information Sciences* 178, pp 37–51.

Allan, J., Aslam, J., Belkin, N., Buckley, C., Callan, J., & Croft, B. A. (2003). Challenges in information retrieval and language modeling. *Report of a workshop held at the center for intelligent information retrieval*, University of Massachusetts Amherst, september 2002. ACM SIGIR Forum, 37(1).

Amati G., Carpineto C., Romano G. (2007). An Effective Threshold-Based Neighbor Selection in Collaborative Filtering, *European Conference on Information Retrieval* (ECIR 2007), pp. 712-715.

Baddie E. R. (2010). The Practice of Social Research, *vol. 12th edition, Cengage learning, chapter The Logic of Sampling.*

Barabasi, A. L., Jeong, H., Neda, Z., Ravasz, E., Schubert, A., & Vicsek, T. (2002). Evolution of the social network of scientific collaboration. *Physica A 311*, 3-4, 590–614.

Billsus, D., & Pazzani, M. (2000). User modeling for adaptive news access. *User-Modeling and User-Adapted Interaction 10*, 2-3, 147–180.

Bohnert, F., Zukerman, I., Berkovsky, S., Baldwin, T. & Sonenberg, L. (2008). Using Collaborative Models to Adaptively Predict Visitor Locations in Museums. *In Proceedings of the 5th International Conference on Adaptive Hypermedia and Adaptive Web-Based Systems*, Hanover, Germany, pp. 42-51

Breese J., Heckerman D., Kadie C. (1998). Empirical Analysis of Predictive Algorithms for Collaborative Filtering, *Proc. of UAI-98*, 1998.

Brun, A. & Boyer, A. (2010). Linking Collaborative Filtering and Social Networks: Who Are My Mentors? Proceedings of the International Conference on Advances in Social Networks Analysis and Mining (ASONAM), pp 409-410.

Brun A., Castagnos S., Boyer A. (2009). A positively directed mutual information measure for collaborative filtering, 2nd International Conference on Information Systems and Economic Intelligence (SIIE'09), p. 943-958.

Burke, R. (2002). Hybrid recommender systems: Survey and experiments. *User Modeling and User-Adapted Interaction 12*, 4, 331–370.

Burke, R., Hammond, K., Cooper, E. (1996). Knowledge-based navigation of complex information spaces. *In Proceedings of the 13th National Conference on Artificial Intelligence*, Menlo Park, Canada (1996) 462–468

Candillier L., Meyer F., Boullé M. (2007). Comparing State-of-the-Art Collaborative Filtering Systems, *Proc. of 5th International Conference on Machine Learning and Data Mining in Pattern Recognition*, MLMD'07, p. 548-562.

Cantador I., Vallet D., Jose J., (2009) Measuring Vertex Centrality in Co-occurrence Graphs for Online Social Tag Recommendation, *9th European Conference on Machine Learning and Principles and Practice of Knowledge Discovery in Databases*, ECML PKDD 2009 Discovery Challenge, 2009.

Castagnos S., Boyer A. (2006). A Client/Server User-Based Collaborative Filtering Algorithm: Model and Implementation, *17th European Conference on Artificial Intelligence (ECAI 2006), in the 4th Prestigious Applications of Intelligent Systems special section (PAIS).*

Castagnos S., Boyer A. (2007). Personalized Communities in a Distributed Recommender System, *Proc. of the European Conference on Information Retrieval*, p. 343-355.

Castagnos S. (2008). Modélisation de comportements et apprentissage stochastique non supervisé de stratégies d'interactions sociales au sein de systèmes temps réel de recherche et d'accès à l'information. *PhD Thesis Manuscript*, University Nancy 2, France.

Chandrashekhar, H. & Bhasker, B. (2007). Collaborative Filtering Based on the Entropy Measure. *Proceedings of the International Conference on E-Commerce Technology and the 4th IEEE International Conference on Enterprise Computing, E-Commerce and E-Services*, pp 203-210.

Chang E. (2010). AdHEat - A New Influence-based Social Ads Model and its Tera-Scale Algorithms, *Proceedings of the Workshop on Algorithms for Modern Massive Data Sets* (MMDS2010).

Cheon, H., & Lee, H. (2005). *Opinion Leader Based Filtering*, vol. 3815/2005 of *Lecture Notes in Computer Science*. Springer Berlin/Heidelberg.

Domingos, P.,& Richardson, M. (2001). Mining the network value of customers. In *KDD'01: Proceedings of the seventh ACM SIGKDD international conference on Knowledge discovery and data mining* (New York, NY, USA), ACM, pp. 57–66.

Elihu, K., & Lazarsfeld, P. F. (1955). *Personal Influence; the Part Played by People in the Flow of Mass Communications*. Free Press.

Fuller W. (2009) *Sampling Statistics*. Wiley.

Goldberg D., Nichols D., Oki B., Terry D. (1992). Using collaborative filtering to weave an information tapestry. *Communications of the ACM*, 35 (12), p. 61-70.

Good, N., Schafer, J. B., Konstan, J. A., Borchers, A., Sarwar, B., Herlocker, J., & Riedl, J. (1999). Combining collaborative filtering with personal agents for better recommendations. In *Proceedings of the sixteenth national conference on Artificial intelligence and the eleventh Innovative applications of artificial intelligence conference innovative applications of artificial intelligence (AAAI'99/IAAI'99)* (Menlo Park, CA, USA), American Association for Artificial Intelligence, pp. 439–446.

Goyal, A., Bonchi, F., & Lakshmanan, L. V. (2008). Discovering leaders from community actions. *In Proceeding of the 17th ACM Conference on Information and Knowledge Management* (CIKM'08) (New York, USA), ACM, pp. 499–508.

Grcar M., Fortuna B., Mladenic D. (2005). kNN Versus SVM in the Collaborative Filtering Framework, *Proceedings of the WebKDD'05 conference.*

Greening, D. (1997). Building Consumer Trust with Accurate Product Recommendations. *LikeMinds White Paper* LMWSWP-210-6966.

Groves R. M., Fowler F., Couper M., Lepkowski J., Singer E., Tourangeau R. (2009). *Survey Methodology*, vol. 2nd edition, Wiley, 2009.

Herlocker J., Konstan J., Borchers A., Riedl J. (1999). An algorithmic framework for performing collaborative filtering, *Proc. of the SIGIR conference*, p. 230-237.

Herlocker J., Konstan J., Terveen L., Riedl J. (2004). Evaluating collaborative filtering recommender systems, *ACM Transactions on Information Systems* (TOIS).

Hosseini-Pozveh, M., Nematbakhsh, M., and Movahhedinia, N. (2009). A multidimensional approach for context-aware recommendation in mobile commerce. *International Journal of Computer Science and Information Security*, 3(1).

Jones, N. (2010). U*ser Perceived Qualities and Acceptance of Recommender Systems: The Role of Diversity.* PhD Thesis Manuscript, EPFL, Lausanne, Switzerland.

Kaufman L., Rousseeuw P. J. (1987). *Statistical Data Analysis Based on the L1Norm*, North Holland/ Elsevier, chapter Clustering by means of medoids, p. 405-416.

Keller, E., & Berry, J. (2003). *The influentials*. Simon and Schuster Ed..

Kim T., Yang S. (2007). Advances in Information Retrieval, vol. 4425/2007, Lecture Notes in Computer Science - Springer, chapter *An Effective Threshold-Based Neighbor Selection in Collaborative Filtering*.

Lang, K. (1995). Newsweeder: Learning to filter netnews. In *Proceedings of the 12th International Conference on Machine Learning (ICML95)*, pp. 331–339.

Malcolm, G. (2000). *The Tipping Point: How Little Things Can Make a Big Difference*. Little Brown, New York.

Mc Queen J. (1967). Some methods for classification and analysis of multivariate observations, *Proceedings of the 5th Symposium on Math, Statistics and Probability*, p. 281-297.

Melville, P., Mooney, R.J. & Nagarajan, R. (2002). Content-Boosted Collaborative Filtering for Improved Recommendations. *Proceedings of the Eighteenth National Conference on Artificial Intelligence* (AAAI), pp. 187-192

Middleton, S.E., Shadbolt, N. R., & Roure, D. D. (2004). Ontological user profiling in recommender systems. *ACM Trans. Inf. Syst. 22*, 1, 54–88.

Mobasher, B., Burke, R., Sandvig, J. (2006). Model-based collaborative filtering as a defense against profile injection attacks. *In Conference of the American Association for Artificial Intelligence* (AAAI2006).

Newman, M. (2003). The structure and function of complex networks. *SIAM Review 45*, 167–256.

O'Connor M., Herlocker J. (1999) « Clustering Items for Collaborative Filtering », *Proc. of the SIGIR Conference (SIGIR99).*

Pan, P.Y., Wang, C.H., Horng, G.J. & Cheng, S.T. (2010). The Development of An Ontology-based Adaptive Personalized Recommender System. *Proceedings of the 2010 International Conference on Electronics and Information Engineering* (ICEIE 2010), pp 76-80.

Paolino, L., Sebillo, M., Tortora, G., Martellone, A., Tacconi, D., & Vitiello, G. (2009). Dynamic user modeling for personalized advertisement delivery on mobile devices. *In Third International United Information Systems Conference* (UNISCON 2009), pages 508–513.

Paulson, P. & Tzanavari, A. (2003). *Combining Collaborative and Content-Based Filtering Using Conceptual Graphs.* Words: Learning, Fusion, and Reasoning within a Formal Linguistic Representation Framework, LNAI 2873, Springer–Verlag Berlin Heidelberg 168–185.

Pazzani, M., Billsus, D. (2007). Content-Based Recommendation Systems. In: *The Adaptive Web. Springer Berlin / Heidelberg,* 325–341

Pedigo L., Buntin G. (1994). Handbook of sampling methods for arthropods in agriculture, CRC Press.

Pizzato, L., Rej, T., Chung, T., Yacef, K., Koprinska, I. & Kay, J. (2010). Reciprocal Recommenders, *in Proc. 8th Workshop on Intelligent Techniques for Web Personalization and Recommender Systems, held in conjunction with the 18th International Conference on User Modeling, Adaptation and Personalization* (UMAP'2010), 20-24 June 2010, Hawaii, USA.

Rashid, A., Katypis, G., & Riedl, J. (2005). Influence in ratings-based recommender systems: An algorithm-independent approach. *Proceedings of the Fifth SIAM International Conference on Data Mining.*

Ruiz-Montiel, M. & Aldana-Montes, F. (2009). Semantically Enhanced Recommender Systems. *Proceedings of the OTM 2009 conference, workshop on The Move To Meaningful Internet Systems. LNCS.*

Schein, A., Popescul, A., Ungar, L. H., & Pennock, D. M. (2002). Methods and metrics for cold-start recommendations. In *Proceedings of the 25th annual international ACM SIGIR conference on Research and development in information retrieval (SIGIR '02)* (New York, USA), ACM, pp. 253–260.

Schickel-Zuber, V., & Faltings, B. (2007). Using Hierarchical Clustering for Learning the Ontologies used in Recommendation Systems. In *Proceedings of 13th International Conference on Knowledge Discovery and Data Mining (KDD '07)* (San Jose, California, USA), pp. 599–608.

Shardanand U., Maes P. (1995). Social Information Filtering: Algorithms for Automating "Word of Mouth", *Proc. of CHI-95.*

Sollenborn, M., & Funk, P. (2002). Category-based filtering and user stereotype cases to reduce the latency problem in recommender systems. In *Proceedings of the 6th European Conference on Advances in Case-Based Reasoning (ECCBR '02)* (London, UK), Springer-Verlag, pp. 395–420.

Teran, L., Meier, A. (2010). A fuzzy recommender system for eelections. In: *Proc. of the International Conference on Electronic Government and the Information Systems Perspective* (EGOVIS'10). pp. 62–76.

Tintarev, N. & Masthoff, J. (2006). Similarity for news recommender systems. *In Proceedings of the AH'06 Workshop on Recommender Systems and Intelligent User Interfaces.*

Ungar L., Foster D. (1998). Clustering Methods for Collaborative Filtering, *AAAI Workshop on Recommendation Systems*.

J. Vassileva, G. Mccalla,& J. Greer. (2003). Multi-agent multi-user modeling in i-help. *User Modeling and User-Adapted Interaction*, 13(1-2),179_210.

Wang, S., Manoranjan, D., & Liang-Tien, C. (2005). Efficient sampling: Application to image data. *In Proceedings of the Pacific-Asia conference on advances in knowledge discovery and data mining* (PAKDD'05), pages 452–563.

Wasserman S., Faust K. (1994). *Social Network Analysis: Methods and Applications*, Cambridge University Press.

Watts, D. J., & Dodds, P. S. (2007). Influentials, networks, and public opinion formation. *Journal of Consumer Research 34*, 4, 441–458.

Zhuhadar, L., Nasraoui, O., Wyatt, R., & Romero, E. (2009). Multi-model ontology-based hybrid recommender system in e-learning domain. *In Workshop of the 2009 IEEE/WIC/ACM International Conference on Web Intelligence and Intelligent Agent Technology*, pages 91–95.

# Chapter 17
# Capturing Market Mavens among Advergamers:
## A Case of Mobile–Based Social Networking Site in Japan

**Shintaro Okazaki**
*Universidad Autónoma de Madrid, Spain*

**Jaime Romero**
*Universidad Autónoma de Madrid, Spain*

**Sara Campo**
*Universidad Autónoma de Madrid, Spain*

## ABSTRACT

*The objective of this chapter is to identify a market maven segment among advergamers on a mobile-based social networking site (SNS). A real online campaign with a multiplayer game is designed for Procter & Gamble's Pringles, after which online surveys are conducted via mobile device. Finite mixture models are employed to identify clusters. The estimation results suggest four clusters. The majority group belongs to Clusters 1 (67%) and 2 (21%), while Clusters 3 (6.8%) and 4 (4.8%) exhibit the propensity of market mavens. Specifically, the members of Cluster 3 are likely to have been actively engaged in information search, purchased the sponsor brand, and disseminated their brand knowledge of the brand, mainly through personal conversation after the game play. By contrast, the members of Cluster 4 are unlikely to have sought information, nor to have purchased the brand after the game, but are very likely to have spread their brand knowledge through word-of-mouth. Furthermore, they did so via not only personal conversation but also SNS functions (i.e., messaging, blog, and discussion board). Given this, Clusters 3 and 4 could be labeled as traditional and innovative market mavens, respectively. Our findings suggest that online marketers should identify and incentivize market mavens by branded entertainment so that they can then disseminate information, encourage followers, and generate a viral chain of word-of-mouth.*

DOI: 10.4018/978-1-61350-513-7.ch017

## INTRODUCTION

The objective of this research is to identify a market maven segment among advergamers on a mobile-based social networking site (SNS). Advergaming refers to "a form of branded entertainment that features advertising messages, logos, and trade characters in a game format" (Mallinckrodt & Mizerski, 2007). It is a practical use of interactive gaming technology to deliver explicit or implicit advertising messages to the consumer (Winkler & Buckner 2006), in which brand-related images or themes are embedded within it. Technically, advergames can be offline or online, but the majority are presented to the general public via websites (Deal, 2005).

Our assumption is that there is a "market maven" segment: that is, a small group of people who are genuinely interested in helping others' consumption needs. They are likely to play the advergame and to engage in some kind of brand-related activities. For example, after playing the game, market mavens may seek information about the sponsor brand, visit a shop to purchase it, and disseminate their brand knowledge through word-of-mouth (WOM). Prior research confirms these behavioral assumptions (Nelson 2004).

In this article, we describe a case study that uses a real promotional campaign of Procter & Gamble. More specifically, we use, as a stimulus, an advergame that was designed as an integrated part of a cross-media campaign for their potato chips brand, Pringles. In this campaign, the game is embedded on the largest mobile SNS, Mobag-eTown in Japan, and the subsequent diffusion of the game within the network is observed. The focus of the study is mainly descriptive and exploratory, and we attempt to present a preliminary picture of advergamers' demographic, attitudinal, and behavioral patterns.

Despite the inherent limitations of a case study with a single-product, single-game situation, this research sets out to make significant contributions to the literature, in three ways. First, advergames were quickly converted into one of the merging 'jargons' in online marketing, although empirical evidence is still scarce. Most published studies are experimental, and hardly provide a clear picture of how advergames are used in an actual situation. In particular, advergame players' profiles have rarely been considered. However, in developing effective business-to-consumer branded entertainment, how do online marketers or advertisers identify their target segment, without knowing their profiles? An effort to classify advergame players based on specific attributes may therefore help them to achieve this goal.

Second, advergames are often embedded on SNS, because they generate a 'stickiness' factor that stimulates word-of-mouth (WOM). However, prior research does not report the magnitude of this effect. This study addresses a basic question: to what extent do people spread the word after playing the game? This includes not only personal conversation, but also a diverse range of SNS functions. For example, would SNS users use messaging, chat, or post comments on their experience in SNS after playing an advergame? Or, would they personally seek information about the sponsor brand in a shop? These questions are important, because the ultimate purpose of advergaming is to increase branding effectiveness and purchase intention.

Third, this study employs finite mixture models, one of the data mining techniques that have been used in clustering consumer segments. Data mining is a technique that describes the process of trawling through data in the hope of identifying statistical patterns (Hand, 1998). When applied to our dataset, finite mixture models can provide useful information for managers because they identify behavioral patterns that examine customer responsiveness in a probabilistic manner, thus avoiding the general arbitrariness of traditional cluster analysis.

In what follows, we first review the literature on advergames as the background of the study. Then, we establish our theoretical framework and formulate research questions. Next, we describe the methodology in detail, explain the primary statistical treatment, and report the results. Finally, we draw theoretical and managerial implications, while recognizing important limitations of the study.

## BACKGROUND

Advergames have gained increasingly popularity in recent years, because traditional online advertising has not been as effective as marketers had expected (Deal, 2005). Deal (2005) explains the major benefits of advergames, compared with other forms of online advertising.

First, in an advergame, an advertising message is inserted within the game, which implies that players are required to expose themselves to that message. Second, an advergame has a longer exposure time (6 to 35 minutes, compared with 30-60 seconds in traditional advertising). Finally, advergames entertain the player, and this may improve attitude towards the brand, and create greater preference, recall, and purchase intention (Batra & Raj, 1986; Biel, 1990; Mackezie et al., 1986; Shimp, 1981). Furthermore, Hudson & Hudson (2006) point out that advergames could increase the proactive involvement of the player, as opposed to the passive involvement in traditional advertising, while enabling marketers to target specific consumer segments with longer shelf-life.

Prior research on advergames focuses mainly on brand recall, brand recognition, and attitudinal variables, according to the three levels of brand integration (Chen & Ringel, 2001; Hudson & Hudson, 2006; Winkler & Buckner, 2006). In the low level of integration, the product or brand is linked to a particular feature of the game. In the med level, the product itself plays a significant role in the game play. In the high level, there is a demonstrative integration, in which players actually feel the product and experience it in the gaming environment.

In the low and med levels of brand integration, advergames are often viewed as an extension of product placement. However, prior research indicates that the former differs from the latter, because of the interactive nature of advergames (Nicovich 2005). In the high level of brand integration, i.e. demonstrative integration, advergames are found to generate stronger brand recall, and more favorable attitudes towards the game, and towards the brand (Hudson & Hudson, 2006).

Nelson (2002) conducted two experiments with university students, using car-racing games containing numerous background billboard ads, which is the med level of brand integration. In the first experiment, seven out of 20 participants aged 18-25 remembered at least one brand placed in the game, while almost 30% of the brands were recalled in the second experiment. Using a similar car-racing game, Schneider and Cornwall (2004) found that a prominent placement (rated on a combination of size, color, position, and attractiveness) was remembered better than a subtle placement, and that previous game experience positively affected recall. Similarly, Chaney et al. (2004) found that an advergame of low brand integration led to a low recall of the sponsor brand, while game experience had no impact on either brand recall or purchase intention. Wise et al. (2008) used 40 adult participants in an experimental study that examined their preferences for high (travel-related) and low (non-travel-related) thematic connection advergames sponsored by an online travel company. They found that those who played the high thematic connection games showed a stronger positive relationship between attitude toward the advergame and attitude toward the brand.

Winkler & Buckner (2006) examined brand recall in three sports games with different integration levels. They conducted quantitative research on a sample of 80 players (mostly men aged 20-29). Their findings suggest that, although brand recall was high, it also depended on the game type to which the respondents were exposed. In the demonstrative integration, attitude towards the brand increased. By contrast, game complexity negatively affected brand recall: in simpler games, where the brand was clearly advertised, brand recall was greater (Schneider & Cornwall, 2005). In more complex games, the players could not remember the advertising message (Chaney et al., 2004). Hudson & Hudson (2006) found that advergames work better for well-known consumer brands.

In the most recent exploration, Cauberghe and De Pelsmacker (2010) examined the impact of in-game brand exposure strength on the advertising effects of brand prominence and game repetition. Their results indicate that brand prominence positively affected brand recall, without influencing brand attitude. Interestingly, however, repeated play of an identical game had no influence on brand recall, but a negative impact on brand attitude. Chaney et al. (2004) and Hudson & Hudson (2006) both found that some demographic and cultural factors influence attitude toward the ad, advergame acceptance, and the response to the sponsor brand. For instance, from children's perspectives, Mallinckrodt and Mizerski (2006) found that the older children who played the advergame exhibited a significantly greater preference for the brand.

## Social Exchange Theory

To establish a conceptual framework for assessing the structure of advergame players, this study draws on social exchange theory. Formally defined, a social exchange network consists of (1) a set of actors (either individuals or firms), (2) a distribution of valued resources among those actors, (3) for each actor, a set of exchange opportunities with other actors in the network, (4) a set of historically developed and utilized exchange opportunities called exchange relations, and (5) a set of network connections linking exchange relations into a single network structure (Cook et al. 1983).

Social exchange theory posits that relationships evolve over time into trusting, loyal, and mutual commitments, by conforming to certain 'rules' of exchange. Rules of exchange form a 'normative definition of the situation that forms among or is adopted by the participants in an exchange relation' (Emerson, 1976, pp. 351), which then convert into 'the guidelines' of exchange processes. In this theory, social behavior is the outcome of an exchange process, whose primary purpose is to maximize benefits and minimize costs. Thus, the relationship grows when the potential benefits outweigh the risks of social relationships; otherwise, people will terminate or abandon that relationship. In the marketing literature, social exchange theory has been recognized as a useful theoretical base, and its explanatory value has been felt mainly in the two areas of relationship marketing (Bagozzi, 1975; Crosby et al., 1990; Morgan & Hunt, 1994) and industrial marketing (Frazier, 1983; Luo, 2002).

In our study context, users of an SNS can be viewed as 'actors' who are engaged in social behavior as an outcome of the exchange process. Valued resources are distributed within the SNS, where the users seek to maximize their benefits from the network structure. In this light, advergames, along with other forms of entertainment, serve as an agent to strengthen the linkage between the users and the sponsor brand, because the users receive emotional benefits (such as enjoyment, excitement, curiosity, or thrill) from game play. In exchange, the users return reciprocal rewards—a favorable attitude toward the sponsor brand.

This study posits that this social exchange can be led by a small group of users, or market mavens, whose primary functions are (1) early trial of "hot topics" related to the sponsor brand, (2) engagement in some brand-related activities, and (3) post-game WOM activities. First, market mavens have been said to be the catalysts of the diffusion of innovation. They are willing to find, and to try to understand, new information, and are thus more knowledgeable about market trends.

The faster the information acquisition, the more likely they are to accept, partake of, and assess the advergame before any SNS users (Hudson & Hudson, 2006): the longer the playing time, the greater the exposure to the sponsor brand (Wise et al. 2008). Second, participation in the advergame determines the level of brand favorability and recognition, which may lead to an ultimate brand purchase. For example, market mavens may try to seek more information, obtain product samples, or visit an outlet to redeem discount coupons. Third, market mavens are eager to transmit their brand experience, and to try to engage in direct or indirect WOM on the game and/or sponsor brand.

## Research Questions

Taken together, this study formulates research questions, rather than formal hypotheses, because of the scarcity of relevant research on advergamers' profiles. Without prior information related to the key exploratory variables, it is extremely difficult to postulate directional hypotheses about advergamers' behavior. Furthermore, because of the study's positioning as a case study, the generalization of the results is not our goal. Instead, this study sets out to provide initial snapshot profiles of actual advergamers, by exploring their behavioral patterns. To this end, we formally put forward the following research questions:

*RQ1: How many clusters exist among advergame players in an SNS? What are the primary socio-demographic characteristics of each cluster? How about their prior knowledge of the sponsor brand and actual gaming experience?*

*RQ2: What kind of subsequent activities can be observed after the game play? Are they actually engaged in eWOM, or do they transmit the brand/game information to others? How about their information search and purchase intention regarding the sponsor brand?*

## METHODOLOGY

To address these research questions, we conducted a study on one of the popular advergames. The site of this study was Japan, a country with a high penetration of mobile SNS, which is a necessary condition to make our research realistic.

## Mobile Social Networking Site

In designing the study, we searched the industry for potential collaborators in the fast-moving consumer goods (FMCG) sector, where brands frequently use advergaming (Hudson & Hudson, 2006; Nelson, 2002). Two companies supported our data collection. First, a well-known consumer goods manufacturer, Procter & Gamble (P&G) Japan, agreed to use its popular potato chip brand, Pringles, as a campaign stimulus. Second, this advergaming campaign involved one of the largest mobile SNS in Japan, MobageTown, which has gained more than 10 million subscribers since 2006. MobageTown offers an ideal context for the study, because it is a game-based SNS where registered users can freely download online games. Site users can exchange information through three main applications: mini-email, diary, and circle. Mini-email allows users to send private messages directly to other users on the site. In the diary, users update their personal activities, opinions, pictures, and videos in a small size blog, for access by their network friends only. The circle is essentially an online bulletin board, on which any user may freely post, circulate, and read comments.

## Advergaming Development

The principal game character, Shaberings, is a penguin-like, imaginary creature whose beak is made of potato chips. The word 'shaberu' is the verb 'to talk' in Japanese. Field pretests with general consumers proved this character to fit well with Pringles' brand image. The game consisted of a 'match' between a Shabering (the

*Figure 1. Advergame 'Shaberings'*

participant) and MobageTown's original character, Yubizo ('Finger monster' in Japanese), in which the one who first hits a pole on the ring can gain a point. Game winners automatically entered a sweepstake to win Shaberings' avatars as a prize. When the game was uploaded to MobageTown, simultaneous cross-media campaigns promoted the advergaming campaign. Figure 1 shows Shaberings' screen images.

## Survey

Three days after the end of the campaign, we conducted a questionnaire survey, by sending an invitation email to the registered SNS users. This invitation to participate was linked directly to a mobile Website: if they agreed to participate in the survey and click the link, it automatically directed participants to the survey website where the questionnaire appeared. Responders browsed the questionnaire item by item. Because only one question appears onscreen at a time, they did not need to scroll down. To avoid incomplete data, we created a system that required respondents to complete each question before proceeding to

the next one. In total, we obtained 1174 usable responses, an approximate response rate of 25%.

The questionnaire consisted of two parts: (1) items related to the five primary concerns of this study: a. perceived brand image, b. SNS usage, c. advergaming usage, d. brand behavior, and e. post-game WOM; and (2) questions related to demographic information (sex, age, and occupation).

### Respondents' Profiles

Table 1 summarizes the demographic characteristics of the game participants and nonparticipants in terms of frequency of SNS usage. As is clearly seen, the demographic patterns of participants and nonparticipants are generally similar. With regard to gender, female users outnumber male users in both groups. In terms of age, more than 75% of the SNS users are under 30, regardless of their advergame participation: only 6% and 5% are older than 40 among participants and nonparticipants, respectively. More than 40% of the respondents are office workers or self-employed. In terms of the frequency of SNS usage, most of the advergaming participants are heavy to medium users: more than 40% of them use SNS more than 10 times per day, much more than the 20% of advergaming nonparticipants.

## FINITE MIXTURE MODEL

This study employs a descriptive data mining technique—finite mixture models. Our finite mixture model identifies behavioral patterns according to the SNS users' responsiveness to the advergame, and assumes that there are a number of clusters among them. The users in a given cluster share similar responses to a set of variables ($x = x1, x2, ..., xJ$). However, such cluster membership cannot be directly observed and thus must be inferred from the users' response patterns. Thus, their responses are treated in a probabilistic fashion. The probability of observing some specific values in a set

*Table 1. Respondents' profile (%)*

| Demographics | Total Participants[1] | | SNS Usage Frequency[2] | | | | | | | |
|---|---|---|---|---|---|---|---|---|---|---|
| | | | > 10 times per day | | 1-9 times per day | | 1-6 times per week | | Few times a month | |
| Total | 100 | (100) | 40.3 | (20.2) | 52.0 | (50.4) | 6.4 | (2.9) | 1.2 | (14.6) |
| Gender | | | | | | | | | | |
| Male | 47.1 | (47.7) | 40.5 | (22.4) | 52.7 | (46.5) | 6.1 | (3.4) | 0.8 | (16.0) |
| Female | 52.9 | (52.3) | 40.1 | (18.1) | 51.5 | (54.0) | 6.8 | (2.4) | 1.7 | (13.4) |
| Age | | | | | | | | | | |
| 19 > | 43.3 | (40.3) | 42.4 | (25.5) | 51.0 | (50.0) | 6.2 | (3.1) | 0.4 | (12.2) |
| 20-29 | 35.1 | (36.6) | 37.6 | (18.5) | 56.4 | (53.4) | 4.5 | (2.2) | 1.5 | (12.9) |
| 30-39 | 15.3 | (17.9) | 38.4 | (14.9) | 53.5 | (47.1) | 7 | (4.6) | 1.2 | (21.8) |
| 40-49 | 4.6 | (4.1) | 46.2 | (5.0) | 34.5 | (50.0) | 19.2 | (0.0) | 0 | (15.0) |
| 50 < | 1.6 | (1.0) | 44.4 | (20.0) | 22.2 | (20.0) | 11.1 | (0.0) | 22.2 | (40.0) |
| Occupation | | | | | | | | | | |
| High school students | 22.6 | (23.5) | 37 | (25.4) | 54.3 | (49.2) | 8.7 | (2.6) | 0 | (13.1) |
| University and other students | 8.9 | (7.8) | 38 | (15.8) | 58.0 | (63.2) | 2 | (5.3) | 2 | (5.2) |
| Office workers and self-employed | 40.1 | (46.3) | 39.1 | (17.3) | 52.8 | (45.8) | 6.7 | (3.6) | 1.3 | (20.0) |
| Housewives | 8.4 | (7.2) | 42.6 | (20.0) | 51.1 | (57.1) | 4.2 | (0.0) | 0 | (0.0) |
| Unemployed | 20.0 | (15.2) | 46.4 | (23.0) | 45.5 | (56.8) | 6.3 | (1.4) | 0 | (13.1) |

Notes: The left-hand number in each column indicates those who played the advergame (n = 557), and the right-hand number with parenthesis in each column indicates those who did not play the advergame (n = 486).

[1] Sum to 100% vertically in each demographic category.

[2] Sum to 100% horizontally in each row.

of J variables $(x_i = x_{1i}, x_{2i}, \ldots, x_{Ji})$ for a respondent i is expressed as

$$P(x_i) = \sum_{1}^{C} P(x_i \mid c) \times P(c_i) \qquad (1)$$

where $P(x_{is} \mid c)$ is the probability of observing some specific values in the J variables conditional of respondents belonging to cluster c, and $P(c_i)$ is the probability of respondent i belonging to cluster c. Under the assumption that the J variables are independent, E-1 becomes

$$P(x_i) = \sum_{c=1}^{C} \prod_{j=1}^{J} P(x_{ji} \mid c) \times P(c_i) \qquad (2)$$

Our primary objective here is to classify behavioral responses to advergaming—$P(x_{ji} \mid c)$—in terms of post-game brand behavior, and in particular (1) information search, (2) actual purchase, and (3) WOM. With regard to (3), we further identified whether advergamers participated in (1) WOM via direct contact (i.e., face-to-face), (2) WOM via mini-mail, or (3) WOM via diary or circle. These response variables are modeled through binomial logistic regressions. We also attempt to model cluster membership—$P(c_i)$—as a logistic regression, in which the explanatory variables are perceived brand image, SNS usage, and advergame participation. With regard to perceived brand image, prior research by practitioners in the campaign team identified three primary dimensions of Pringles: sharedness, enjoyment, and popularity.

Finite mixture models are estimated in the following way:

1. The model is estimated assuming that there are one and two clusters among respondents.
2. Both solutions are compared using an information criterion. This criterion provides a trade-off between the goodness of fit and the complexity of the model, thus indicating which solution is better. If the one-cluster solution is the better one then the estimation process stops. In the case of selecting the two-cluster solution, a new model assuming the existence of three clusters must be estimated and compared again with the previous one.
3. The estimation process stops when adding a new cluster to the model (and therefore increasing its complexity) does not compensate for the improvement in goodness of fit. To find this threshold point, we use AIC3 as information criterion (e.g., Rust & Verhoef 2005; Dias & Vermunt 2007; Wieringa & Verhoef 2007). According to Andrews and Currim (2003), AIC3 performs better than the other cluster retention criteria that are typically used with finite-mixture models (such as AIC, BIC, and CAIC).
4. According to AIC3, there are 4 behavioral patterns in our dataset. Clusters 1, 2, 3, and 4 represent approximately 64.0%, 23.9%, 7.2% and 4.9% of respondents, respectively.

## RESULTS

In this section, we describe each cluster membership, employing the following variables collectively: (1) demographics (Table 3), (2) perceived image of the sponsor brand (Figure 2), (3) SNS usage and advergame participation (Figure 2), (4) post-game brand behavior (Figure 3), and (5) types of WOM (Figure 4).

### Cluster 1

Cluster 1 constitutes the majority group, and it accounts for 67% of the total respondents. Females outnumber males by 7.8%, which is consistent with national-level mobile usage data. More than 77% are under 29 years old, and within this the largest proportion is the 20-29 age-block, although almost the same proportion consists of office workers and self-employed.

In terms of the perceived image of the sponsor brand, as well as use of SNS and advergame, this Cluster exhibits the lowest levels overall—in sharedness, enjoyment, and popularity. By the same token, with regard to brand behavior, they are unlikely to have sought information, or to have purchased, or recommended, the brand after the game play. Hence, post-game WOM is not a probable result.

*Table 2. Segment Membership*

|  | Cluster 1 | | Cluster 2 | | Cluster 3 | |
|---|---|---|---|---|---|---|
| Intercept | 6.36 | *** | 1.22 | n.s. | -23.28 | *** |
| Sharedness | -0.94 | n.s. | 0.26 | n.s. | 3.63 | ** |
| Enjoyment | -2.28 | *** | -1.52 | ** | 0.13 | ns |
| Popularity | 0.75 | n.s. | 1.88 | ** | 1.69 | ns |
| Advergame usage | -0.49 | ** | 0.03 | n.s. | 2.23 | *** |
| Social network usage | -0.81 | n.s. | 0.11 | n.s. | 5.34 | ** |
| ** $p<.05$. *** $p<.001$, n.s. = non-significant; segment 4 is normalized to zero. | | | | | | |

*Table 3. Demographic profiles (%)*

| Demographic variables | Cluster 1 (n=373) | | Cluster 2 (n=119) | | Cluster 3 (n=38) | | Cluster 4 (n=27) | | Total (n=557) | |
|---|---|---|---|---|---|---|---|---|---|---|
| Gender | | | | | | | | | | |
| Male | 46.1 | | 47.1 | | 55.3 | | 70.4 | | 48.1 | |
| Female | 53.9 | | 52.9 | | 44.7 | | 29.6 | | 51.9 | |
| Age | | | | | | | | | | |
| < 19 | 34.3 | | 39.5 | | 29.0 | | 40.7 | | 35.4 | |
| 20-29 | 43.2 | | 32.8 | | 36.8 | | 29.6 | | 39.8 | |
| 30-39 | 17.4 | | 21.9 | | 23.7 | | 11.1 | | 18.5 | |
| 40-49 | 3.7 | | 5 | | 7.9 | | 18.5 | | 5 | |
| > 50 | 1.3 | | 0.8 | | 2.6 | | 0 | | 1.3 | |
| Occupation | | | | | | | | | | |
| High school students | 17.7 | | 21.8 | | 13.2 | | 22.2 | | 18.5 | |
| University and other students | 12.9 | | 7.6 | | 7.9 | | 3.7 | | 10.9 | |
| Office workers and self-employed | 46.6 | | 40.3 | | 47.4 | | 44.4 | | 45.3 | |
| Housewives | 7.0 | | 11.8 | | 5.3 | | 14.8 | | 8.3 | |
| Unemployed | 15.8 | | 18.5 | | 26.4 | | 14.8 | | 17 | |
| Total | 100 | | 100 | | 100 | | 100 | | 100 | |

*Figure 2. Brand image, SNS, and advergame usage*

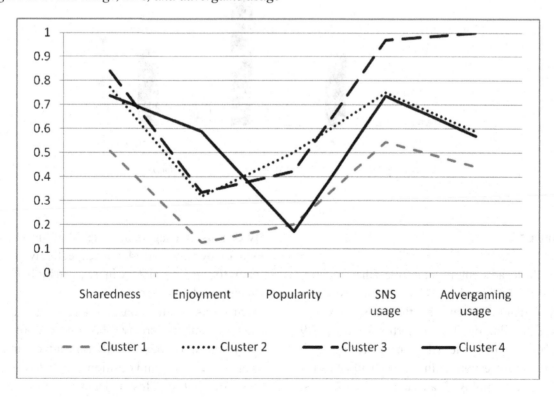

*Figure 3. Post-game brand behavior*

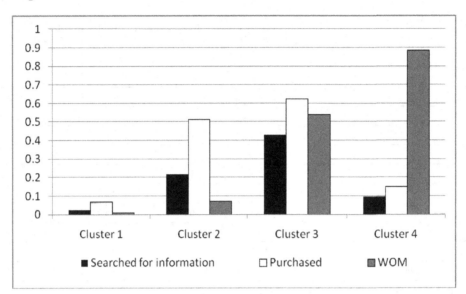

*Figure 4. Types of WOM*

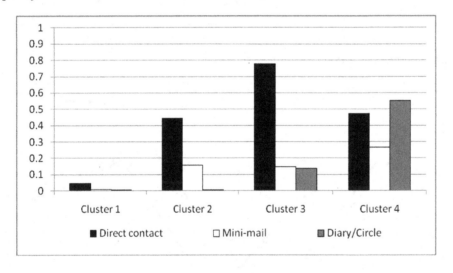

## Cluster 2

This Cluster accounts for slightly less than a quarter of the total respondents. Gender composition is very similar to Cluster 1, but there are differences in age distribution. The proportion of the 20-29 age-block is 10.4% less than in Cluster 1, which appears to correspond to the drops in office workers and self-employed, and university students.

By contrast, teenagers and the 30-39 age-block increase by 5.2% and 14.5%, respectively, which seems to coincide with the increase in high school students and housewives.

In terms of the sponsor brand image, these Cluster members perceive sharedness more than enjoyment and popularity. SNS and advergaming usage is "regular," and positioned in between the two extremes (i.e., Clusters 1 and 3). In contrast to

Cluster 1, there is a fair chance of having purchased the sponsor brand after the game (the probability is approximately .50), while the likelihood of engaging in an active information search is less likely (the probability is approximately .20). Nor are they likely to have recommended the brand after the game play.

## Cluster 3

Cluster 3 is one of the remaining two minority groups, and accounts for 6.8% of total respondents. Contrary to Clusters 1 and 2, males outnumber females by 10.6%. Also, there is an important difference in age: among the four clusters, the proportion of the 30-39 year-old block is highest (23.7%), while that of teenagers is the lowest (40.7%). These differences are also reflected in the occupational patterns: the proportion of high school students is lowest, and that of office workers and self-employed is the highest amongst the clusters. Also, there is a notable increase in unemployed, which reaches its highest figure amongst the four.

In terms of sponsor brand image, Cluster 3 exhibits the greatest level of sharedness, while general perceptual tendencies are very similar to Cluster 2. The SNS and advergaming usage is substantially greater in this cluster than in the others. Furthermore, there is an equally strong likelihood of post-game information search, purchase, and WOM behavior. In particular, the probability of post-game information search is substantially greater than in the other clusters. With regard to WOM, the propensity to use direct contact is the highest amongst the four, while that to use mini-mail or other SNS functions is low.

## Cluster 4

Probably the most notable difference in this cluster is the proportion of males, which is the highest (70.4%) amongst the four. Age-wise, teenagers represent the majority group, while the 20-29 year-old block is the smallest amongst the four, and the 30-39 year-old block is smaller than Clusters 2 and 3, but larger than Cluster 1. To our surprise, the proportion of the 40-49 year-old block is much larger than in any of the other clusters. Reflecting these patterns, the proportions of high school students and housewives are the largest amongst the four. However, the proportion of unemployed is the lowest.

This cluster tends to perceive enjoyment more strongly, compared with the other clusters, while the perception of sharedness is almost equal to Clutters 2 and 3. However, the perception of popularity was the lowest amongst the four. The usage of SNS and advergaming is very similar to Cluster 2.

This cluster has the highest propensity to use WOM amongst the four, but neither post-game information search nor purchase is a likely consequence. The further break-down of WOM reveals that this cluster tends to employ more electronic media, in particular, SNS functions (i.e., mini-mail, diary, and circle), than the other clusters. At the same time, the likelihood of using direct contact WOM is almost equal to that of Cluster 2.

## LIMITATIONS

Before drawing important implications, three limitations should be recognized, to make our study findings more objective. First and foremost, this study is a case study that used a single campaign for one brand. Our findings should be regarded as an on-the-spot report of real advergame players, which may be particularly useful for online marketing practitioners. Second, given the limitations inherent in the use of mobile-based surveys, the majority of scale items were dichotomous or categorical. While certain benefits were warranted (quickness and accuracy), there was less variance in the results, compared with interval scale. Future studies should overcome these limitations in order to obtain more generalizable results. Third, the study we presented in this article takes place in a mobile device. While the specifics of this medium are not our main focus, it should be noted that, in Japan, Internet connection via mobile device exceeds that via PC, and SNS access is thus becoming more ubiquitous. In this light, firms could combine location-based functions and entertainment, to enable users to enjoy spontaneous fun at the right place at the right time.

## DISCUSSION

In this case study, we try to paint preliminary profiles of advergaming participants in an SNS, using their post-game brand behaviors. Despite a study based on a single-product, single-game case, we were able to note several important implications.

### Theoretical Implications

Our study identified two small clusters that may be market mavens: Clusters 3 and 4. However, their behavior seems very distinct. Cluster 3 consists mainly of young adults, teenagers, and mature adults (in order of importance), who are likely to purchase and actively investigate the sponsor brand, and to transmit their knowledge via WOM after playing the advergame. However, their WOM is likely to occur mainly through direct personal contact. On this basis, Cluster 3 can be considered the traditional market maven. By contrast, Cluster 4 consists mainly of teenagers, young adults, and middle-aged adults (in order of importance), with little propensity to brand purchase but heavy involvement in WOM through SNS as well as direct contact. Thus, Cluster 4 seems to act as the innovative market maven.

This typology is by no means conclusive. However, it does seem to make sense that there is a group of people within an SNS that actively disseminates information to the others. Furthermore, they do so more actively in an online environment. Perhaps this pattern of behavior is accentuated

because 40% of Cluster 4 consists of high school students—a reason why many are unlikely to have sought information on, or purchased, the sponsor brand, although they may have spoken a lot about the brand to others in all media (i.e., direct contact, mini-mail, diary, and circle). In this light, Cluster 3 seems to lead the other clusters, because this group complies with the necessary behavior patterns of what we define as a market maven: information search, purchasing behavior, and knowledge dissemination.

These characteristics of Cluster 3 are also consistent with social exchange theory, which posits certain 'rules' of exchange. Users' behavior in SNS can be seen as the outcome of an exchange process, which must be activated by some leaders. These leaders try to disseminate information to maximize the benefits for their peers, friends, or families, and this seems to be a necessary condition of maintaining one's social network. In the case of Pringles' advergaming campaign, Cluster 3 seems to consist of such leaders, who are actively engaged in social behavior as an outcome of the exchange process.

### Managerial Implications

The findings of this study seem to provide online marketers with the important lesson that SNS could be an important marketing tool, if we can effectively create the stickiness factor. In this light, the mere insertion of ads or links on a site—a typical practice in many SNSs—no longer seems to work, because consumers may view it as an extension of traditional promotion. Given the universal trend of the increasing popularity of online games, the creation of advergames seems to be a practical solution that involves users in an entertaining brand experience. Our study provides a snapshot of this mechanism.

Perhaps the most important recommendation for online firms is to integrate advergames with some kind of incentives. Prior research on sales promotion suggests that not only hedonic but also utilitarian motives are key in making consumers "act" (Chandon et al., 2002). Thus, firms could offer a redeemable coupon (perhaps in a digital form), or a product sample that is closely connected to the advergame. Furthermore, this integration must be programmed as an attraction of the SNS. For example, a "tell-a-friend" type of promotion could be planned—when an advergamer convinces someone to play the game, he or she will receive a prize. One of the recommendations we may have is to directly link the brand purchase and the advergame. For example, many Japanese firms employ a two-dimensional industrial barcode or QR (quick response) code in cross-media promotions. QR codes, which store a URL to the game, can be printed in the product package or promotional leaflets. Consumers can scan the code using a camera-equipped mobile device with the correct reader software, and be redirected to the programmed URL. This could work as a more direct incentive to brand purchase, as opposed to an indirect "post-game" incentive.

Furthermore, if this QR code is transferable, we could propose a combination of advergames and incentives as a "reason to talk," thus activating a viral chain of WOM. This would provide firms with twofold benefits. First, the brand's sales may increase because of the attractive and entertaining purchase incentive. Second, the viral marketing may generate a chain-reaction of "me too" sales. An implicit managerial implication may be that traditional segmentation may not be a cost-effective tool, if firms are still trying to identify and incentivize all segments. In an era of online community, it would make more sense to use segmentation to identify the market maven—a small number of people who lead the market trend and disseminate information. Firms should probably use or invest their limited resources to provide the market maven with sufficient motivations to serve as the market catalyst.

## ACKNOWLEDGMENT

This research was funded by a grant from the Spanish Ministry of Science and Innovation (National Plan for Research, Development and Innovation EC02008-01557).

## REFERENCES

Andrews, R. L., & Currim, I. S. (2003). A Comparison of Segment Retention Criteria for Finite Mixture Logit Models. *JMR, Journal of Marketing Research*, *40*(4), 235–243. doi:10.1509/jmkr.40.2.235.19225

Bagozzi, R. P. (1975). Marketing as an Exchange. *Journal of Marketing*, *39*(4), 32–39. doi:10.2307/1250593

Batra, R., & Ray, M. (1986). Affective Responses Mediating Acceptance of Advertising. *The Journal of Consumer Research*, *13*(2), 234–250. doi:10.1086/209063

Biel, A. L. (1990). Love the Ad. Buy the Product? *ADMAP*, *26*(9), 141–154.

Chandon, P., Wansink, B., & Laurent, G. (2000). A Benefit Congruency Framework of Sales Promotion Effectiveness. *Journal of Marketing*, *64*(October), 65–81. doi:10.1509/jmkg.64.4.65.18071

Chaney, I. M., Lim, K. H., & Chaney, J. (2004). The Effect of Billboards within the Gaming Environment. *Journal of Interactive Advertising*, *5*(1), 1–11.

Chen, J., & Ringel, R. (2001). *Can Advergaming be the Future of Interactive Advertising?* White paper, Fast Forward. Retrieved from: http://www.locz.com.br/ loczgames/advergames.pdf. (accessed on March 1, 2010).

Cook, K. S., Emerson, R. M., & Gillmore, M. R. (1983). The Distribution of Power in Exchange Networks: Theory and Experimental Results. *American Journal of Sociology, 89*(2), 275–305. doi:10.1086/227866

Crosby, L. A., Evans, K. R., & Cowles, D. (1990). Relationship Quality in Services Selling: An Interpersonal Influence Perspective. *Journal of Marketing, 54*(3), 68–81. doi:10.2307/1251817

Deal, D. (2005). The Ability of Branded Online Games to Build Brand Equity: An Exploratory Study. *Proceedings of DIGRA 2005 Conference: Changing Views–Worlds in Play* (pp. 1-7), Vancouver, Canada.

Dias, J.G.& Vermunt. J.K. (22007). Latent Class Modeling of Website Users' Search Patterns: Implications for Online Market Segmentation. *Journal of Retailing and Consumer Services, 14*(6), 359–368.

Emerson, R. M. (1976). Social Exchange Theory. *Annual Review of Sociology, 2*, 335–362. doi:10.1146/annurev.so.02.080176.002003

Frazier, G. L. (1983). Interorganizational Exchange Behavior in Marketing Channels: A Broadened Perspective. *Journal of Marketing, 47*(4), 68–78. doi:10.2307/1251400

Hand, D. J. (1998). Data Mining: Statistics and More? *The American Statistician, 52*(2), 112–118. doi:10.2307/2685468

Hudson, S., & Hudson, D. (2006). Branded Entertainment: A New Advertising Technique or Product Placement in Disguise? *Journal of Marketing Management, 22*, 489–504. doi:10.1362/026725706777978703

Luo, X. (2002). Trust Production and Privacy Concerns on the Internet: A Framework Based on Relationship Marketing and Social Exchange Theory. *Industrial Marketing Management, 31*(2), 111–118. doi:10.1016/S0019-8501(01)00182-1

Mackenzie, S., Lutz, R., & Belch, G. (1986). The Role of Attitude toward the Ad as a Mediator of Advertising Effectiveness: A Test of Competing Explanations. *JMR, Journal of Marketing Research, 23*(2), 130–144. doi:10.2307/3151660

Mallinckrodt, V., & Mizerski, D. (2007). The Effects of Playing and Advergame on Young Children's Perceptions, Preferences, and Requests. *Journal of Advertising, 36*(2), 87–100. doi:10.2753/JOA0091-3367360206

Morgan, R. M., & Hunt, S. D. (1994). The Commitment-Trust Theory of Relationship Marketing. *Journal of Marketing, 58*(3), 20–38. doi:10.2307/1252308

Rust, R. T., & Verhoef, P. C. (2005). Optimizing the Marketing Interventions Mix in Intermediate-Term CRM. *Marketing Science, 24*(3), 477–489. doi:10.1287/mksc.1040.0107

Shimp, T. (1981). Attitude toward the Ad as a Mediator of Consumer Brand Choice. *Journal of Advertising, 10*(2), 9–17.

Wieringa, J. E., & Verhoef, P. C. (2007). Understanding Customer Switching Behavior in a Liberalizing Service Market: An Exploratory Study. *Journal of Service Research, 10*(2), 174–186. doi:10.1177/1094670507306686

Winkler, T., & Buckner, K. (2006). Receptiveness of Gamers to Embedded Brand Messages in Advergames: Attitudes towards Product Placement. *Journal of Interactive Advertising, 7*(1), 1–9.

Wise, K., Bolls, P. D., Kim, H., Venkataraman, A., & Meyer, R. (2008). Enjoyment of Advergames and Brand Attitudes: The Impact of Thematic Relevance. *Journal of Interactive Advertising, 9*(1), 27–36.

## ADDITIONAL READING

Cauberghe, V., & De Pelsmacker, P. (2010). Advergames: the Impact of Brand Prominence and Game Repetition on Brand Responses. *Journal of Advertising*, *39*(1), 5–18. doi:10.2753/JOA0091-3367390101

Grigorovici, D., & Constantin, C. (2004). Experiencing Interactive Advertising beyond Rich media: Impacts of AD type and presence on brand effectiveness in 3D gaming immersive virtual Environments. *Journal of Interactive Advertising*, *5*(Fall). available at www.jiad.com accessed July 8, 2010.

Mau, G., Silberer, G., & Gödecke, J. (2010). Game outcome and in-game advertising effects. In R. Terlutter, S. Diehl & S. Okazaki (eds.), *Advances in Advertising Research (Vol. 1): Cutting edge international research* (pp. 159-170), Heidelberg: Springer-Gabler Verlag.

Okazaki, S. (2011). *Fundamentals of Mobile Marketing: Theories and practices*. NY: Peter Lang.

Yang, M., Roskos-Ewoldsen, D. R., Dinu, L., & Arpan, L. M. (2006). The effectiveness of 'in-game' advertising. *Journal of Interactive Advertising*, *35*(4), 143–152.

## KEY TERMS AND DEFINITIONS

**Advergaming:** A form of branded entertainment that features advertising messages, logos, and trade characters in a game format.

**Market Maven:** Consumers who have up-to-date information about products, places to shop, and different markets.

**Social Exchange Network:** A theory that explains how relationships evolve over time into trusting, loyal, and mutual commitments, by conforming to certain 'rules' of exchange.

**Word-of-Mouth:** Interpersonal transmission of commercial or noncommercial message.

# Chapter 18
# Semantic–Awareness for a Useful Digital Life

**Johann Stan**
*Alcatel-Lucent Bell Labs, France*

**Myriam Ribière**
*Alcatel-Lucent Bell Labs, France*

**Jérôme Picault**
*Alcatel-Lucent Bell Labs, France*

**Lionel Natarianni**
*Alcatel-Lucent Bell Labs, France*

**Nicolas Marie**
*Alcatel-Lucent Bell Labs, France*

## ABSTRACT

*In this book chapter the authors address two main challenges for building compelling social applications. In the first challenge they focus on the user by addressing the issue of building dynamic interaction profiles from the content they produce in a social system. Such profiles are key to find the best person to contact based on an information need. The second challenge presents their vision of "object-centered sociality", which allows users to create spontaneous communities centered on a digital or physical object. In each case, proof-of-concept industrial prototypes show the potential impact of the concepts on the daily life of users. The main contribution of this chapter is the design of conceptual frameworks for helping users to take maximum advantage from their participation in online communities, either in the digital web ecosystem or real-life spontaneous communities.*

## INTRODUCTION

With Web 2.0 practices such as collaborative tagging, social networking and bookmarking, where users are able to easily generate content and make it immediately available for others, users were

supposed to increase their social connectedness, as those practices related to content sharing allow them to be permanently aware of others' activities, thoughts, plans and preoccupations. However, this participation requires effort, but there is rarely an added-value for users, as in current systems there is no seamless way to access content relevant to a specific information need. This often leads to

DOI: 10.4018/978-1-61350-513-7.ch018

a phenomenon called "social network fatigue"[1], i.e. the situation where users have lots of connections and thus lots of corresponding notifications that are not relevant to their current information needs (information overload). One possible consequence is that users will not participate as much as before in the life of the virtual community, as the added-value is constantly low compared to the effort needed to share interesting and quality content with others. In order to avoid this issue, and increase the motivation of users to be active members of online communities, social applications should have the ability of better analyzing social activities of users (in particular interactions), in order to recommend them the right people or communities at the right moment as information providers for their current information needs.

In this book chapter, we aim at providing a framework for the implementation of compelling social applications, intended to facilitate the access of users to the right information in real time, depending on their current information needs. Our approach is based on an analysis of the constituents of online communities, namely users and "objects" (i.e. user-generated content or any resource) and to exploit each of them as two directions to leverage the semantics of user interactions within communities: (1) focusing on the user constituent of communities, how to better understand their interactions through their social streams and recommend appropriate people of the same community to interact with? In order to do that, we propose to study how to build dynamic user interaction profiles from user content production and sharing; and (2) focusing on the "objects", how to build paths between the communities these objects are creating, so that users can easily move cross different communities; i.e. more specifically, how to use object-centered sociality as a paradigm for user communication making possible the interlinking of communities.

Thus, the next section introduces these two pillars of social applications – users and objects. Users are characterized by a profile, activities,

connections, whereas objects are characterized by annotations that users put and that serve as starting point for interactions between users. Then, we explain how the need of awareness of people interactions motivates the two challenges for social applications we are addressing in this chapter: first, discovering new connections based on the semantic similarity of social awareness streams, and second, enable seamless and dynamic links between communities. The following section introduces how to build dynamic user interaction profiles. We present the specificities of dynamic user interaction profiles compared to usual user profiles, how to build such profiles from social streams and how to use them to recommend the best people to interact with in order to maximize successful communications. We illustrate the usefulness of such profiles through an application called the "Social Adviser". Then, we propose to look at social networks through the angle of objects. Therefore, we introduce and define object-centered social networks (OCSN) and how to make people participate in pertinent communities by the semantic interlinking of those kinds of communities. This social network paradigm is illustrated by an example of application, the sBook. Finally, as conclusion we present a set of remaining challenges to make this vision and concepts real.

## THE SOCIAL WEB ECOSYSTEM

In this section we present an upper-view of the social web ecosystem. We first discuss online communities and its main pillars. Finally, we examine the nature of content productions in these communities and corresponding challenges to extract knowledge from it.

## Online Communities

As mentioned before, online communities are the building blocks of almost any social system. Community is a term that continuously evolves over the change of the technologies and human behaviour. The concept of community exists in sociology and is defined as a group of interacting people, living in a common location and organized around common values. Since the advent of the Internet, the concept of community has no longer geographical limitations. People can now virtually gather in online communities, forming virtual communities where they can share common interests regardless of physical location. Since its beginning in the 70s', the Internet technologies in its early forms, like bulletin board systems (BBS), Internet Relay Chat (IRC), Usenet and forums were strongly bound to the community concept. Historically, the Well (The Whole Earth 'Lectronic Link), a computer conferencing system that enables people around the world to carry on public conversations and exchange private electronic mail (e-mail) in 1985 appears as the first real online community. At this early stage, online-communities were used to describe persons using Internet to make online discussions on a communication space that we used to call "the cyberspace". The term of virtual communities was used for the first time in 1993 by Howard Rheingold in the book "The Virtual Community" (Rheingold, 1993) and described people connected online and having long public discussions that formed personal relationships. Since this period, user-generated content and social interactions in virtual spaces all over the world start to characterize the main form of interactions. Social networks like Facebook or LinkedIn are commonly known as the most successful and visible part of online-communities. Today, with the development of mobility, real-time Web and pervasive computing online interactions are more and more transient and opportunistic.

The Web today is more and more organized around user-generated content produced by online-communities. For example, popular web sites like Wikipedia or Delicious are well known by the feature they propose such as knowledge access and content sharing but less as a commu-

nity structure they have behind. Rheingold gives a representation of the social web by proposing a classification of major online communities in: (i) social communities where people are connected to share interests and activities (Facebook, MySpace), (ii) mobile communities, (iii) Social Bookmarking communities that store, recommend and share links of internet sites (Delicious, Diigo), (iv) Social blogging and micro-blogging communities where people post and broadcast their activities and interests (Twitter, Yammer, Posterous), (v) Social shopping communities where members are involved in shared shopping experiences (Tipper, Groupon, SocialShopper) and finally, (vi) Crowd sourcing communities where people share knowledge and experience (Wikipedia). Meta communities are umbrella of inter-connected online communities where single ones can be managed, collected and maintained (SocialUrl, Ning).

## Pillars of Online Communities

In this section, we study what we call the two main pillars of Online Communities. Online communities are formed by their users and the objects representing the intermediations of users' interactions. We describe the different characteristics of the users such as user explicit profile, their activities, their connections, and how trust is applied between users in communities. Then, we propose a concrete definition of an object, study the different types of annotations on objects, and introduce research issues in studying semantics of annotations.

### Users

Any social platform is composed of a set of users. In a given social platform, a user is characterized by a profile, his/her activities and his/her connections:

- *User profile:* The profile generally includes basic personal information, like name, email and address, as well as information about the interests of the user. The role of user profile is essential in online communities as pointed out in (Berlanga *et al.*, 2009). Generally user profiles are different from one application to another, as users present themselves differently based on the targeted population of the given application (which are sometimes very specific). Thus, a user profile in a social networking system where the user has mostly friends will probably include more information about the hobbies and social activities. On the contrary, in a system targeted for professional networking, the profile will include information about the professional interests of the user, like technical skills, jobs and future plans. More generally, a user can be a member of multiple social platforms and have different identity facets in each of them. An identity facet is a subset of the user's profile, targeted for a well-defined community. Even in the case of strangers, the social platform allows to view fragments of user profiles, which can show if the user can be trusted in the given domain.

- *Activities*: Another dimension of users is represented by the activities they perform in the social platform. This includes content sharing, media uploading and content description (such as photo tagging). In order to better understand the behavior of users in online communities, it is necessary to take into account some statistics about their activities and the amount of time spent performing them. According to the *"Edison Arbitron Internet and Multimedia Study"* (year 2010)[2], based on 2000 telephone interviews conducted in February 2010 in the United States, 48% of the interviewees possess a public profile in at least one social platform. This was 34% in 2009, and only 24% in 2008. The increase seems to accelerate as more and more applications are available.

Another important observation is the fact that social network usage becomes a daily habit, as 30% of interviewees access their online accounts several times a day. Initially the use of such application was considered only for fun and for young people, but now the report clearly indicates a significant modification in the perception of such activities. Indeed, it switched to an activity of socialization and social-awareness, as 25% of users are 18-25 years old and 23% 25 to 34. The most widespread shared content on social networking websites are status messages, i.e. short content that users post to express their current activity, interests or mood or to share a resource they consider interesting for their community. 72% of frequent social networkers post such a message frequently and 55% of less avid users. 35% of users update their status several times a day.

- *Social connections*: Finally, the third dimension of the user is represented by their social connections. Users are members of different communities, belonging to different social spheres (e.g. friends, family, co-workers). Depending on the nature and scope of the social platform, a connection can be undirected, i.e. the result of a mutual agreement between two users in the platform, or directed, i.e. when a user follows the activities of another, but the inverse relation is not true.

- *Trust:* Another important characteristic of users is related to trust. Indeed, the different applications allow users to be closer to their communities and to follow the activities and opinions of peers. This brings new dimensions to trust and allows users to have higher confidence in others recommendations, suggestions and sentiment. This tendency is also confirmed by the Socialnomics report[3] as friends' recommendations are much more trusted than recommendations from brand websites, consumer forums, television or newspapers. The increase of trust in this category of recommendations is due to the consumer generated content and the reliance on word of mouth (i.e. propagation of conversations in a community) in the decision making process, either from friends or followers or from people that are just simple participants in the community.

As a summary, a user can be defined as an entity in online communities with a set of corresponding community-dependent faceted profiles, activities and connections, regulated by communication processes, like trust, that influence their participation in the community.

## Objects and Annotations

As said before shared content is influencing interactions between users. This observation led to the object-centered sociality principle. An *object* is a common interest focal point, the "*reason why people affiliate with each specific other and not just anyone*" (Engeström, 2005). An object has a concrete and perceptible, physical and/or numeric, manifestation. It is a coherent whole, indivisible, which triggers specific activities. Some objects are the source of conversational interactions and keepers of collective attention. They constitute a conversation support. We will focus on them. On the Web, objects are accessible through their URI. In our actual numeric context objects are mainly multimedia ones as articles (Wordpress, Wikipedia), videos (Youtube, Dailymotion), pictures (Flickr, Picasa), consists of annotations produced by users to describe different artefacts such as Web pages, online media content, opinions, moods, activities etc. It can be divided into structured (i.e. semantic annotations), semi-structured (i.e. social tags) and unstructured (i.e. free text, also called social awareness streams or status updates). The manipulation of object involves tasks like description, retrieval, reuse, presentation and search. All these tasks need a prior knowledge layer, which is represented by the annotations. In the case of

automatic annotation, the system automatically extracts features from the object (e.g. relevant descriptors for an image, keywords from a textual document etc.) and uses them as annotations. In the case of semi-automatic annotation, the system generally extracts the annotations from the resource, but asks the user to validate them. In the case of manual annotations, the user's cognitive capacity to interpret the meaning of an object is leveraged. In this case, the user has generally two possibilities for annotation: (i) the system gives the user complete freedom in choosing the term they intend to use in the annotation (the case of social tagging and free-text annotations), (ii) the system uses a vocabulary of terms and the user can choose a term from the vocabulary for the annotation (the case of semantic annotations and also some cases of social tagging). This second option gives users less freedom, but allows having a stable, convergent vocabulary that allows better retrieving documents, as the description of resources will not suffer from synonyms, spelling errors or discrepancies in granularity.

- *Structured Annotations:* In this case, the terms employed in the annotation are regulated by a common domain vocabulary that must be used by the members of the system. These types of annotations are currently not used in the majority of social platforms because a domain vocabulary that contains the necessary terms for the annotations is needed. Although such an approach has many advantages (e.g. absence of synonyms, absence of differences in pronunciation), this is not the natural way to describe resources in web 2.0 platforms, as the domain is not well-defined and therefore it is very difficult to build such vocabularies and to establish a consensus for each term used. In the same time, the use of semantic annotations would be cumbersome for people, as it is time-consuming and requires an additional cognitive effort to select concepts from existing domain ontologies.

Also, semantic annotations work well in systems where the domain is well-defined (e.g. a system for sharing knowledge about human genes), in social platforms this is not the case, as the shared content is generally very heterogeneous (i.e. covers multiple domains with no regularities and relations).

- *Semi-Structured Annotations:* On the contrary, semi-structured annotations, such as *social tags,* are widely used in social platforms for photo tagging and bookmarking (e.g. the annotation of a web page). These annotations are generally freely selected keywords without a vocabulary in the background. However, we consider them as semi-structured, as they represent an intermediate approach between semantic annotations (i.e. annotations that are based on concepts from domain ontologies) and free-text annotations. Also, such collections of tags converge to a structured data organization, called a folksonomy (Mathes *et al.,* 2004). This consists of a set of users, a set of free-form keywords (called tags), a set of resources, and connections between them. As folksonomies are large-scale bodies of lightweight annotations provided by humans, they are becoming more and more interesting for research communities that focus on extracting machine-processable semantic structures from them. These underlying data clouds of collaborative tagging systems enable Internet users to annotate or search for resources using custom labels instead of being restricted by pre-defined navigational or conceptual hierarchies (e.g. ontologies).
- *Unstructured Annotations:* Finally, a more recent form of User Generated Content is represented by *free text annotations*, also called *social awareness streams or status updates* (Naaman *et al.,* 2010). This can be found in the majority of social networks and microblogging systems and primarily consists of free text in the form of short messages describing a resource, a finding, an impression, a feeling, a recent activity, mood or future plan. The limitations of this practice from the viewpoint of information retrieval and knowledge management are similar to that of social tagging, as users have complete freedom in the formulation of these messages. It is important to mention that in social awareness streams, the produced content contains often the described resource itself, in the form of URLs. A common practice is either to express an opinion about the resource (e.g. web page) or to provide a short summary of it for the community (an activity similar to bookmarking). (Naaman *et al.*, 2010) propose a classification of such awareness streams.

Considering this description of the pillars of online communities, the following problems arise:

- Are explicit user profiles sufficient to understand how to make new connections, and how to help the user by suggesting new contacts through recommendation?
- How to benefit from user activities to better understand users' interests?
- How systems can increase trust when proposing some recommendation of new contacts?

We think that to answer those questions, we need to identify research issues related to the extraction of semantics from annotations.

## Research Issues in Studying Semantics of Annotations

While social tagging is certainly easier for end-users, this kind of practice has lots of limitations in the case of future exploration of the shared content. This includes ambiguity, lack of synonymy relations between tags and discrepancies in granularity. An ambiguous word, e.g. apple, may refer to the

*Figure 1. Analysis of social awareness streams in Twitter. The lower curve represents for each user, the amount of messages that contain named entities or URLs.*

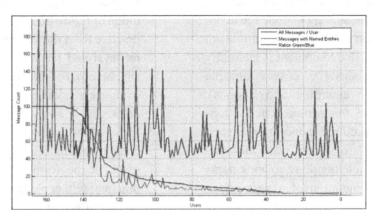

fruit or the computer company and this in practice can make the user retrieve undesired results for a certain query. Synonyms like lorry and truck, or the lack of consistency among users in choosing tags for similar resources, e.g., NYC and New York City, make it impossible for the user to retrieve all the desired resources unless he/she knows all the possible variants of the tags that may have been used. Different levels of granularity in the tags may also be a problem: documents tagged with a specific keyword, like java may be too specific for some users, but documents tagged programming may be too general for others.

Our study of more than 40 000 messages in Twitter also confirms that users have different objectives when sharing content: an important user population shares messages about their current context. Such messages generally do not contain entities (e.g. people, technology names, location names etc.) or resources. In Figure 1, we represented the total number of messages for each user (blue curve) and messages that contain either URLs or named entities (green curve). On the contrary, there is a significant user population in the IS category (users sharing messages containing only URLs or messages containing named entities). However, most users do both, as their messages can be divided into those that describe an activity, mood (in this case the mes-

sage does not contain named entities, URL) and messages where the user shares an information about a resource (the message contains named entities or URLS).

As mentioned before, one of the key motivations of our work is to extract structured knowledge from these different types of annotations. Only such an additional knowledge layer on shared content allows efficiently performing this task, as it is very difficult to reason on raw data. Based on the category of the shared content (such as structured, semi-structured and completely unstructured), different operations are needed for knowledge extraction. In the case of structured annotations, the concepts from the associated domain ontology can be directly injected into the user profile, as the presence of the ontology (or some kind of knowledge base) solves issues like disambiguation and granularity. The case of semi-structured annotations is somewhat more complicated, as these are freely selected keywords. The necessary step in this case is the disambiguation, i.e. the selection of the most relevant concept from a knowledge base and the association of the annotation to this concept. Finally, the case of textual annotations is the most difficult. For textual annotations, the first step is the extraction of named entities and keywords from the text and then the disambiguation. In each case, a final operation can be performed, called semantic expansion, which allows including concepts that are semantically related to the initial concept (e.g. Paris - France).

## Challenges for Social Applications

As identified in the previous section, users and objects are the pillars of online communities. In this chapter we would like to make an emphasis on the capacity of such application to create connections between people based on the semantic similarity of their social activities. We have two objectives in providing a representation of the semantic awareness of people interactions:

- From the user perspective it is the capability to discover new connections based on the semantic similarity of corresponding social awareness streams. We propose for this to study the building of dynamic user interaction profiles, in order to compute similarities between profiles and suggest connections when needed.

- From online communities' perspective, it is the capability to rethink the structure of

*Figure 2. General view of the Framework for Social Network Analysis*

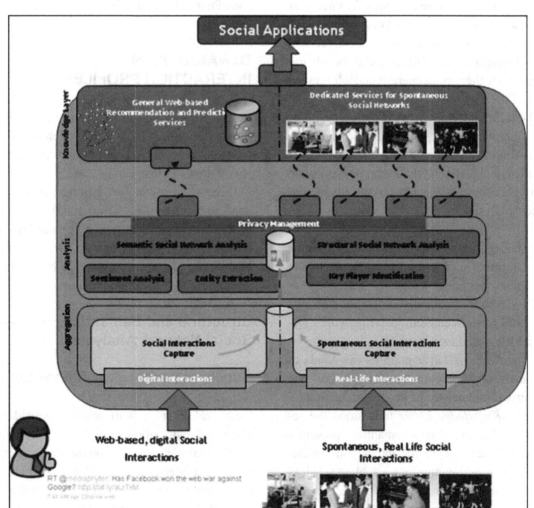

social networks around objects and use the semantic awareness of such "object-centered social networks" to enable seamless and dynamic links between communities, enabling cross-community user discovery experiences.

Semantic awareness of people and object-centered social networks activities would considerably increase the motivation of users to be active members of online communities, by making them informed of other members' interests, or of about what is going on around related objects. More formally, the objective of this component is to reduce the gap between the user's physical life, characterized for example by an information need (e.g. the user moved recently to a new city and needs help in finding a good doctor), and digital life, characterized by a set of connections to people and contents (objects) that do not always correspond to the current interests and information needs of the user.

The following framework (Figure 2) exposes the different layers needed to extract semantic information from social awareness streams and activities in object-centered social networks and to provide social applications taking advantages of such analysis:

- The *Aggregation Layer* is dedicated to the capture of social interactions from existing social networks (such as Facebook or Twitter) or spontaneous social interactions from object-centered social networks (real-life social interactions).
- The *Analysis Layer* exposes two kinds of analysis, the semantic analysis and the structural analysis of people interactions.
- The *Knowledge Layer* transforms the result of analysis into semantic representations such as dynamic interaction profiles of users or communities, enabling services such as people recommendations or cross community discovery experiences.

In the next section, we propose to address the building of dynamic user interaction profiles, and how this work benefit from related work in semantic social network analysis and structural social network analysis. We present (1) the issues in using people production of content to better recommend new connections, (2) a proposal for building profiles and (3) potential applications. Then we propose to study the value of objects in generating adequate communities and how the semantic analysis of people interactions (represented as dynamic community interaction profile) in such social structure can enable opening dynamic paths between communities. In this section we also propose one a social reading application implementing the concept of object-centered social network around the e-book object.

## DYNAMIC USER INTERACTION PROFILES

In this section we introduce the notion of user interaction profile, which is, as described in the previous section, a key enabler for advanced social applications.

First we present the different strategies to analyze communities: (i) structural analysis (i.e. analysis of the structure) and (ii) semantic analysis (i.e. analysis of shared content). Then we are presenting issues and a proposition to build valuable dynamic user interaction profiles.

### Structural and Semantic Social Network Analysis

#### Structural Social Network Analysis

Structural social network analysis considers the statistical distribution of nodes and links in the network in order to extract communities of strongly connected users, understand the mathematical (statistical or probabilistic) functions that govern the distribution of connections and predict the evolution of the network. A common property of many large networks is that the vertex connectivity follows a scale-free power-law distribution (Newman et al., 2006). This feature was found to be a consequence of two generic mechanisms: (i) networks expand continuously by the addition of new vertices, and (ii) new vertices attach preferentially to existing ones that are already well connected. More concretely, the probability with which a new vertex connects to the existing vertices is not uniform, as there is a higher probability that it will be linked to a vertex that already has a large number of connections. A vertex that acquires more connections than another one will increase its connectivity at a higher rate. Thus, an initial difference in the connectivity between two vertices will increase further as the network grows.

A second property of such networks, the 6 degrees of separation principle shows that the network is organized in small strongly connected communities (small worlds) and nodes that connect these communities (called key players). It is theoretically possible to connect any two nodes in the network with a path composed of, at most, 6 nodes according to the Milgram experiment (Blass, 2004). The analysis of the network structure is generally done to suggest new friends, identify a key-player or a community. There is an increasing investment in this area in different social platforms. This can be explained by the need for very representative individuals (e.g. for marketing needs). A conclusion about structural analysis could be also that this is certainly useful for researchers, but compelling applications that demonstrate the practical usefulness of the scientific results for the end user are still missing.

## Semantic Social Network Analysis

The majority of social platforms consider a structural analysis of the underlying community. The other interesting dimension, which has started to attract research communities as well as industries, is the integration of semantic technologies, both on the modeling and content exploration level. There is a growing interest in the exchanged content inside the social interactions in social networks. This can help to better understand users' expectations. From a pragmatic perspective, the content may also help in solving some research problems related to the understanding of social networks structure. The only platforms that focus on this dimension are platforms involving a heavy research investment and which build an additional layer of services for the user/service provider, like search and marketing. The most important issue for social platform providers is certainly how to make money from their "social capital".

The previously mentioned social awareness streams represent the most common forms of shared content in social networks. This does not exclude tags, as the majority of social networks now include the capability to tag uploaded photos. Semantic analysis of social networks proposes different strategies to analyses such streams and to build different recommendation services that leverage knowledge extracted from social awareness streams. Lately, the analysis of such streams receives increased attention from different communities (user modeling, data mining and semantic web) for two main reasons: (i) nowadays, such messages represent the most frequent form of interaction in social platforms and (ii) the understanding of such messages is a valuable source for building advanced recommendation strategies that have up-to-date information about the current needs and preoccupations of an individual or a community. An important observation is also the fact that shared content provides a richer representation of an online community at a given time, as it changes more rapidly than the topology (e.g. connections). The most important semantic analysis strategies that can be performed on social awareness streams to extract additional knowledge include: (i) *Sentiment Analysis* (i.e. also called Opinion Mining, is the extraction of the sentimental polarity of a message) and (ii) *Entity/Keyword Extraction* (i.e. the extraction of named entities or keywords from a message and their disambiguation). In the case of social awareness streams, the main difficulty consists in the fact that there are few contextual cues to correctly disambiguate a named entity, as the messages are generally very short and completely unstructured (e.g. 140 characters allowed in Twitter).

## Definition of User Interaction Profiles

In our case, the main difference between the user profiles we consider and "traditional" user profiles are the fact that our primary objective is to model the interactivity. This can be defined as the motivation of the user to interact about a given concept (e.g. to answer a question). Therefore the source of data used to profile users is quite different from traditional approaches of profiling: instead of being interested on consumed content, we base our profiling approach on social awareness streams as this is the most popular form of content production (e.g. 55 millions new updates each day in Twitter).

Formally, any user model is represented by a set of concepts and associated weights. We consider U the domain of all users involved in the social platform. CU represents the set of concepts correlated with user u, i.e. CU = {c | $P(c, u)>0$}. Therefore, user u and concept c are correlated when $P(c, u) > 0$, P being the weight of concept c in the profile. In our case the weight represents the interactivity score associated to a given concept and is composed of semantic and statistical measures on the interaction involving the given concept.

## Linked-Data Based Profile Construction

The main difficulty with social awareness streams used to build interaction profiles is the absence of structure and contextual cues due to the small size and lack of common vocabulary, which is a considerable drawback for machine-learning based algorithms that attempt to extract rules about the meaning of the message and make predictions for categories of keywords. For this reason, it is necessary to integrate in the analysis semantic web technologies, such as Linked Data (Heath *et al.*, 2009) in order to better disambiguate such interactions. The most mature and biggest knowledge base for Linked Data was produced by the Semantic Web community and is called DBPedia (Auer *et al.*, 2007). The objective is to extract Wikipedia content and transform it into RDF triples. This knowledge base can be used for semantic expansion, disambiguation or computation of similarities between the profiles. The following operations are needed to transform social awareness streams into user interactions profiles (Figure 3):

- Entity-extraction
- Disambiguation
- Semantic expansions
- Sentiment analysis

*Figure 3. Toolkit for User Profile Construction*

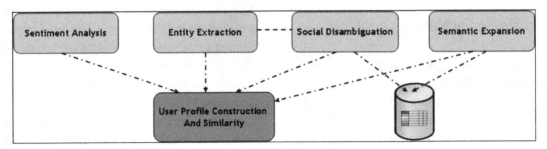

- Statistical content analysis

Entity extraction, disambiguation and semantic expansion form a first chain of operations that aims at transforming an interaction to a set of meaningful concepts. The other operations (sentiment analysis, statistical content analysis) attempt to provide an insight into the quality of a message and the interactivity level of the user related to concepts in the given message. For example, in a social system, a message that expresses strong sentiment reflects more interest for interaction from the person who shared it.

## From Social Streams to Ontological Concepts

In the profiling process, the first phase consists in extracting and detecting relevant concepts from social streams. Concepts can be either come from named entities or from pertinent keywords that appear in social streams. In our approach, this is done through several functions: entity extraction enables to extract concept related to named entities, disambiguation consist in determining the concept associated to a keyword in a given context and semantic expansions enable to broaden the concept to related ones. These processes are summarized above.

## Entity and Keyword Extraction

Entity Extraction corresponds to the effort of extracting entities, such as people's names, technologies, places and institutions from text. The most important difficulty in entity extraction is the issue of name variations. Common types of name variations include: (i) lexical (e.g. organization, organization), (ii) orthographic (e.g. Rocky 2, Rocky II), (iii) structural (day of birth, birthday) and (iv) morphological (plural, singular variations, like mouse – mice). Also, a common problem is represented by ambiguous meanings (e.g. Calvin: theological or comics figure? or Apple: company

name or fruit?). Entity Extraction techniques generally perform a text-pre-processing that includes the splitting of text into sentence boundaries, tokenization and word stemming (e.g. Porter stemming). As social awareness stream messages are generally short, it is important to note that issues like anaphora (an element in the text which depends for its reference on the reference of another element) and metonymy (a figure of speech consisting of the use of the name of one thing for that of another) are rare. After the pre-processing, several techniques can be applied to extract named entities (Nadeau *et al.*, 2007): (i) lexicon-based (e.g. the comparison of keywords to terms in a lexicon), (ii) regular expressions (the definition of rules that specify the syntax of company names, people names, locations etc.), (iii) statistical classifier-based, like boundary window and sliding window token and (iv) finite state machines.

In addition, concepts in the profile can be based on extracted keywords. However, basic keyword extraction techniques are not enough, as they do not solve the problem of semantic ambiguity. Therefore, for a given annotation, after the removal of stop words, each remaining keyword and entity can be expanded vertically and horizontally. Vertical expansion of a concept means the retrieval of the associated concept hierarchy (i.e. generalization relations). Horizontal expansion refers to the retrieval of neighboring concepts (i.e. any concept that is connected to the given concept). The expansion of each concept allows having more contextual cues, essential for the disambiguation process. The result of the expansion is the fact that we transform the original message with few contextual cues into a tag cloud, where tags are connected with properties. The second step is to retrieve from the knowledge base the list of potential concepts that contain the keywords or entities in the message in their label or description. For each potential meaning we also make the two expansions. The final step is to rank potential meanings based on the similarity of their expanded tag cloud to the expanded concepts in the message. In this case, a co-occurrence based similarity measure is used. It is important to note that before the expansion of concepts in the message, for each word that is not a stop word, we apply a windowing in an attempt to learn if two words form together meaningful concepts or not (e.g. Gran Torino is a meaningful concept, being the title of a movie, but separately Gran and Torino have completely different meanings). It is currently under investigation how to combine statistical classifiers with knowledge bases to improve the disambiguation in the case of short messages.

A special case for disambiguation is represented by new terms introduced by users that do not appear in the knowledge base. The case of special hash tags that are used to group together messages that describe the same object, neologisms or other kinds of special terms all belong to this category. Considering entities or keywords in their context that are present in the knowledge base can disambiguate such terms. Their disambiguation allows including such words in the user profile, which is an additional contextual element for finding similarities.

## Semantic Expansion

Whenever possible, a concept, say c that is included in the user profile must be linked to an external knowledge base that can be either relational, graph or ontology-based. The transformation of a keyword to concepts is the disambiguation process, which consists in selecting the concept from the knowledge base (K) with the closest meaning.

The result of the disambiguation process is the creation of a link between the concept c and the knowledge base K. Using the knowledge base, further concepts can be included in the user profile that we call related concepts. The two most important categories of related concepts are represented either by the semantic neighborhood of the concept c in the knowledge base ($SN_k(C)$), or the hierarchy tree of concept c. The formal

definition of the semantic neighborhood of a given concept c in knowledge base K is the following:

$$SN_K(c) = \left\langle \quad \forall c_{rel} \in K, \exists p_{j=1,\ldots n} \in P \ / \ p(c, c_{rel}). \quad \right\rangle$$

The hierarchy tree $T_k(C)$ of concept c is represented by the set of concepts that are more general. Based on the knowledge base, different properties are used for the establishment of such relationships (e.g. isA relation or relations from the SKOS vocabulary, such as *skos:broader, skos:subject*). Consider m(c) the meaning of concept c. Then, $T_k(C)$ can be defined as follows:

$$T_K(c) = \left\langle \quad \forall c_{rel} \in K, m(c) \subseteq m(c_{rel}) \right\rangle$$

These two sets are valuable resources for a better approximation of the user's topics of interest. The main reason for this is that social awareness streams are short messages and does not offer the user a full expressive power. As an example, a user who watches a movie might only share that she liked it. However, it is clear, that this positive sentiment probably propagates to other concepts related to the movie: its actors, its script, places in the movie, producers etc. The propagation of weights is however not trivial, as it must take into consideration the initially shared content. The property that connects the two concepts (c and $cr_{el}$) is a factor that certainly plays a key role in the propagation of the weight.

Concepts in hierarchy trees are used for the classification in the user profile into categories. A category of concepts represents a set of concepts that are in a close semantic field. For example, Twitter and Facebook are both Web 2.0 technologies; therefore belong to the same category. A corresponding function needs to compute for each new concept the closest category. A concept can belong to several categories, with a corresponding weight. A second use of concept hierarchy is the computation of similarities. Without knowing that both Twitter and Facebook are Web 2.0 technologies, it would be very difficult to know that interactions containing them belong to the same semantic field.

Finally, as the profile is composed of disambiguated concepts linked to an RDF knowledge base, the computation of similarity between concepts can also benefit from the links in the base. Therefore, in order to compute similarity between concepts e.g. in a question asked by a user and interaction profiles existing in the system, we can retrieve the taxonomical paths that exist in the knowledge base between the concepts on both sides (in the question and in each interaction profile) and compute their length (number of vertices). The second step is to rank the top k most similar profiles according to the interactivity scores associated to the concepts that have the minimum taxonomical path length. The selection of most relevant interaction profiles is further improved as profiles are clustered and the representative of each cluster stores the most important concepts in the cluster (i.e. signature of the cluster). Therefore, a first step is to select the closest representative (e.g. centroid) to the concepts in a question and then to continue the search in the profiles that are inside the cluster.

## Weighting Concepts

Once concepts have been identified, a weight indicating their importance in the user profile w.r.t. Interactivity has to be set. In order to do so, we are investigating several methods, which are bringing different dimensions w.r.t. Interactivity.

### Sentiment Analysis

Sentiment analysis consists in extracting the sentiment score associated to a message. This is based on keywords that express subjective feelings that can be generally found near named entities (e.g. like, hate etc.). In the case of interaction profiles, our intuition is the fact that an interaction express-

ing strong sentiment reflects higher motivation for the user to further discuss about its topic. An interesting resource for sentiment analysis is the SentiWordNet vocabulary, which associates to WordNet synsets the corresponding sentiment polarity. This vocabulary was built using a semi-supervised method (Esuli and Sebastiani, 2006). The main difficulty in using such a dictionary is the fact that a given term may appear in different synsets. Therefore, the right meaning must be selected before retrieving the sentiment polarity of the word. The most important problem in the case of entity extraction and sentiment analysis is the fact that these techniques were mostly designed for documents that have a well-defined structure. However, as mentioned before, social awareness streams are short with very little structure in terms of syntax. Therefore a corresponding research challenge is to establish how these methods must be modified or completely redesigned to work well also in the case of such micro-documents. Also, the above analysis clearly shows that semantic analysis and modeling is becoming an important preoccupation in research communities (some online social platforms, e.g. Swotti -sentiment analysis- and Ubervu -sentiment analysis, entity extraction- already integrate such features). Still, a unified approach to integrate the different analysis techniques is still missing.

Our current implementation of the system uses the SentiWordNet vocabulary for sentiment analysis. The main difficulty in this case is also the disambiguation, i.e. the selection of the right synset for an adjective (a synset represents synonyms grouped together). A good example for this is the word like, which can express either a comparison (Google is not like Apple) or a sentiment (I like Clint Eastwood). However in this case, the fact that messages are short is positive, as the size of the message limits the vocabulary for the expression of sentiments. Thus, such communities use a limited set of adjectives and often other signs, like smileys to express sentiment. Part-of-Speech (POS) tagging is used to annotate the grammatical category of words in the message. Based on such grammatical patterns, we select the synset from the vocabulary, which has the same grammatical category, associated. Although this approach is basic, results are satisfactory because of the small size of the vocabulary. For computing the sentiment of a message, we consider the average of the individual sentiment values that are associated to each synset in the SentiWordNet vocabulary.

As currently our approach is highly vocabulary-dependent, we investigate semi-supervised learning methods for sentiment analysis of short messages. Although existing algorithms in sentiment analysis and entity extraction are promising, there is still significant progress to be made in the case of short, unstructured messages. In the next section we present our approach for user modelling, which uses the output of the entity extraction and disambiguation as input. On the other hand, sentiment analysis is used as a measure of expertise and interactivity, together with a set of statistical measures.

## Statistical Measures of Interactivities

The basic form of weighting schema is frequency-based and measures how frequently the user shared or consumed content w.r.t. the given concept. Formally, this is an adapted tf-idf (Salton and McGill, 1983) measure used in information retrieval. The weighting schema must take into account (i) concepts that better describe user u and (ii) those concepts which better distinguish him from the other users. The first provides quantification of intra-user similarity, while the second inter-user dissimilarity. Inter-user dissimilarity is quantified by measuring the inverse of the frequency of a concept c among all users. This factor is therefore called Inverse User Frequency (IUF) factor. Concept Frequency is the number of times concept c occurs in the profile of user u. In our model, this is equivalent to FF (u, c) = P (u, f) =, e.g. the number of interactions (I) involving the user u that contain concept c.

The User Frequency UF(c) is the number of users in which concept c occurs at least once. Finally, the Inverse User Frequency IUF(c) can be calculated from UF(c) as follows (|U| is the total number of users):

$$IUF(c) = \log \frac{|U|}{UF(c)}$$

The IUF score for a concept if low if the concept occurs in many users' profiles and high if in only few. The final weight for a given concept is thus a combination of FF and IUF:

W (u, c) = FF (u, c)*IUF(c)

Additionally, we consider other factors in order to better infer the interactivity of a user w.r.t. a given concept. For this purpose, we first consider content-based factors involving the quality of user interactions w.r.t. the given concept. The most basic form of quality measure is the length of the interaction, meaning the number of words. More advanced forms for measuring the quality of an interaction are the following: comment informativeness, number of named entities / hyperlinks/ tags and sentiment (e.g. the underlying sentiment –positive, neutral or negative in the interaction). We use a combination of such measures to understand the potential expertise level of the user in the given concept and her interactivity. Interaction complexity refers to the entropy of words in the interaction. The entropy of words measures the disorder of word, similarly to disorder in a thermodynamic system. For an interaction involving $\lambda$ words, with frequency of occurrence pi for each word, the entropy is calculated in the following way:

$$entropy(i) = \frac{1}{\lambda} \sum_{i=1}^{n} p_i [\log(\lambda) - \log(p_i)]$$

*Figure 4. Dynamic User Interaction Profile extracted from social awareness streams (colors represent the associated sentiment score, size of entities represent the overall inveractivity score)*

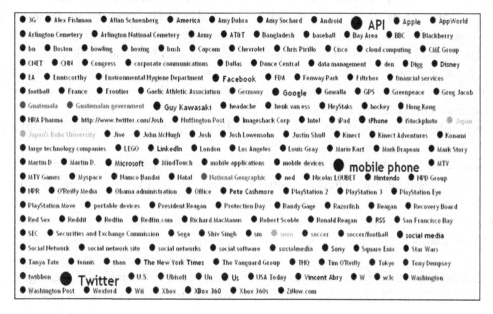

The number of named entities is also a basic measure, which allows inferring the potential usefulness of the comment for the community and the user's expertise level. Also, it is clear that an interaction that expresses either high or low sentiment potentially indicates the user's cognitive involvement w.r.t. the given concept, but also the probable expertise level.

A high level formal interpretation of the user profile is that of a graph, with nodes being the concepts and vertices the relations between concepts. In the case of nodes, there are two categories: (i) primary nodes – representing nodes that come from shared content and (ii) secondary nodes that come from the expansion of primary nodes. Also, there are category nodes that group primary and secondary nodes into clusters. A secondary node can become primary with the condition that there is at least one piece of shared content that contains the concept represented by the node. Relations can either represent connections between two concepts or a generalization relation (i.e. a relation to a concept that has a more general meaning). Figure 4 shows an example of

dynamic user interaction profile, extracted from the social awareness streams of a user (as it can be seen, highest interactivity scores were attributed to API, mobile phone, Twitter concepts). Colors in the image represent the computed sentiment score (green for positive, red for negative and black for neutral).

## Weight Propagation

Any user profile is a set of concepts with corresponding weights. In our case, as the profile contains also Any user profile is a set of concepts with corresponding weights. In our case, as the profile contains also additional concepts, not directly shared by the user, the weights must propagate. As mentioned before, we consider the property that connects the two concepts as a factor for weight propagation. Thus, the weight attributed to a concept in $SN_C(K)$ has the following weight:

$$w_{c_{rel}} = w_{old_{c_{rel}}} + p_{c,c_{rel}} * w_{new_c}$$

If $c_{rel}$ is a new concept in the user profile, its weight will inherit that of the related concept, multiplied with a factor that depends on the property that links them together. This factor is in the interval $[0, 0.5]$, meaning that a propagation should divide the weight by at least two. Any modification of the weight of a concept will be transmitted to related concepts. The relaxation parameter for the propagation is in the interval $[0, 0.5]$. Respectively, the different dimensions to compute interactivity must be weighted in order to get a global score. The weights need to adjusted for each application, according to the specificities of the community (e.g. if little sentiment is shared, more weight must be given to the quality measures).

## Profile Exposure in Multiple Spheres

Additionally, the semantic expansion allows controlling the level of granularity of a concept. More concretely, a given level in the hierarchy can be associated to a social sphere. People belonging to that social sphere will have access only to that specific level of granularity of the given concept. Since users have different preferences for concepts that belong to different categories, such association rules between levels in the hierarchy and social spheres will be different for each cluster. For example, the user will probably expose more details about her interests in sports and movies to friends, but less detail about her working schedule. The opposite might be true for coworkers. We call such an association between a taxonomy (e.g. hierarchy of concepts) and social spheres a social taxonomy, or socionomy. In the given example, we consider a situation where the user interacts about the term Facebook. The corresponding concept hierarchy retrieved from DBPedia using *skos:subject* and *skos:broader* properties are *Facebook ≤Web 2.0 ≤ WWW ≤ Internet ≤Computing ≤ Hypertext*. As the user does not want to expose the fact that e.g. she is interested in Facebook to her family, she associates the level Web 2.0 to this social category. Further on, strangers will only see WWW or an even more general concept, like Internet. This kind of approach attempts to simulate the case of real world objects: closer we are to an object, more details we see. An underlying learning mechanism extracts user habits and will predict the probable socionomy for a new concept, by associating it to the cluster that is semantically the closest.

## Proof of Concept: the Social Adviser

Our first implementation of the semantic-awareness framework is a people recommendation service called Social Adviser. The main idea is to consider the currently viewed webpage of the user as a query to the social network. This is achieved by the extraction of entities and keywords from the webpage, their disambiguation using DBPedia and the construction of a first semantic tag cloud from the data (i.e. the query). Each disambiguated concept is expanded, both horizontally and vertically using DBPedia. This expanded tag cloud is further compared to the interaction profiles of users in the social network and the top 5 most similar users are shown. In this specific application, interactivity is modeled only with sentiment. Thus, users who in their interactions relevant to the query expressed strong sentiment (positive or negative) will be shown first. The user has then several options: (i) check the interactions of the recommended user or (ii) contact her (e.g. phone call or IM). Also, a summarized view of the recommended users is shown in the form of a graph, with distances based on the semantic similarity to the query concept and colors represent the sentiment. This application is an add-on to the Firefox navigator. The example in Figure 5 shows a scenario where the user is checking the webpage of the Gran Torino movie. The concept Gran Torino is the most frequent term in the webpage, thus this concept receives the highest weight in the query. It can be seen that 4 friends shared. Carla has positive sentiment about the movie, Bob negative, and the others neutral. Bob is identified as the person with highest interactivity, followed by Alice.

*Figure 5. Example of dynamic user interaction profile and corresponding web application*

We are currently developing an additional feature to this service, where the user will be able to manually formulate a question, instead of automatically constructing it from web navigation data. Further on, we intend to combine web navigation data with the manually formulated question, as navigation data can be an additional context source for disambiguation. This is based on the assumption that users generally search on the web for information before asking a question. Also, a feature under development consists in generating meaningful explanations for users to further motivate them to interact based on the concept-path in DBPedia between the topic of the question or generated query and the concepts in the user's interaction profile. From preliminary tests, users liked the fact that such an application can bring closer their digital and physical worlds as they could seamlessly access people relevant to their current activity on the web and interact with them. We currently investigate how to manage interruptions, i.e. how to provide users with a mechanism that allows them to set when they can be interrupted with a question of a specific topic. Indeed some users prefer to be interrupted during working hours with topics related to their work. On the contrary, such topics should be avoided during other situations (e.g. at home, during travel etc.).

## Conclusion

The construction of a pertinent user interaction profile raised several issues for the capture of relevant concepts and their weighting. We suggested in this section several techniques and criteria that we aimed at testing and validating in further developments. Behind the goal of solving raised issues, our objective was also to provide adequate applications of such profiles. Exposing such profiles normally dedicated to recommendation systems can contribute to the activity awareness of people, and increase trust among community members. Finally, using them to recommend on the fly contacts in order to get recommendations or information is of high value, and can be embedded in many usages, such as browsing activities.

## OBJECT-CENTERED SOCIAL NETWORKS

In order to go further and provide the user with a real experience of seamless access to any relevant community at a given time, we propose a definition of object-centered social networks (OCSN), and how the semantic awareness of the community activity around an object in a dedicated OCSN management framework can help to link communities between them.

### Intuition

Human is well-known as a social animal because of his natural propensity to socialize with others and form communities to share interest, ideas, goals and relationships. Since the emergence of the Internet and communication technologies, all usual daily-life social connections such as working, learning and meeting are more and more digitalized. This digitalization of our social connections is now forming new online-communities, from where our interactions are organized, structured and stored on the Internet.

People speak to or connect with others through "something" they have in common. For instance, people present in the same bar or cinema, people reading the same book or wanting to buy the same furniture create de facto a form of implicit social structure, based on a context which is common to all of them. However, nowadays, those people are not necessary aware of this common link, therefore do not benefit from applications or services resulting from the fact of sharing this common context. This context is central to interactions: it constitutes the *primary object of the interactions* between people who do not know each other a priori, either because interactions relate to it or because it enables them.

The recent popularity of the term "social networks" was brought by the success of social network sites like Facebook, Myspace or Linkedin. Despite their huge adoption and popularity, these sites lead to some confusion about how the sociality is built. Mainly, these social network sites, also called people-centered or ego-centered social networks, are used to connect people to each other. They are based on users' profiles and status to generate topics to connect with friends. Users check friends' content and share their thoughts, exchange messages or leave comments to strengthen their friendship. Some recent studies have been performed to explore the range of socialization that can occur in Facebook and highlight the user-centered characteristics of this network. For instance, some studies (Lampe *et al.*, 2006) concluded that Facebook primary usage is to maintain existing offline connections in order to keep in touch with friends that users have met socially offline. This leads to a situation where discussions and conversations are multiple, heterogeneous and not focused on a specific subject. Moreover, if these social sites have the advantage to tie friends with physical and social activities, they are often limited to connect people who you already know.

In our approach, we believe that social interactions and real life activities will form the future of our communications. We think that our everyday life is full of artifacts or social objects (e.g. books, films, paintings, places) that can serve as enablers for social communication. We envision that rather just being connected simply through online social network relationships, people will be bound together through social objects of common interest.

In the literature, some close concepts have been studied, approaching the mediation and communication around objects. Among them, boundary object (Star & Griesemer, 1989) is a concept of object that serves as interface between different communities. They are commonly described as information spaces where participant gather to exchange information, coordinate activities and create knowledge. Another approach using social objects is proposed in Activity theory (Engeström, Y., 1987), a derivation of Soviet Activity theory of (Vygotsky, 1978) and (Leont'ev, 1978). Activity consists of a subject and an object, mediated by a tool. A subject can be an individual or a group. For our approach we adopt the concept of "object-centered sociality" (Knorr-Cetina, 1997) which consists in considering the object as the central element in social interactions. This theory was baked in field of Internet and computer science by influent people like Jyri Engeström who argued that the objects are "the reason people connect and socialize with each other". He theorized about the social networks sites design and explained that longevity of these sites is proportional to their "object-centered of sociality" (Engeström, 2005). Popular social content sharing sites are mainly designed around objects like photos on Flickr, videos on Youtube or bookmarks in Delicious. For example, on Flickr, people can use classic web 2.0 conversations tools, they can annotate, comment, tag or connect with the community of the photography, but in any case, content is at the center of the mediation process. People instead of being connected through an explicit online relationship and expecting to boost their number of friends, are bound together through the object of a common interest. Media sharing sites have mainly proposed rich commenting and annotation features before to be turned into a social network-ing platform; the main purpose has always been content sharing. In Youtube and Flickr people can't connect for a particular purpose in mind, a common objective or activity. Instead, they use friendship mechanisms to connect or to browse other's content, to be aware of the last uploaded video or to be authorized to put a comment on a video. They provide neither tools nor means to leverage user interactions that occurred around a single posted video or photo.

In our approach, we believe that social networks build around discrete and identifiable objects is fundamental to connect people over something that is meaningful. Recently, more and more of commercial solutions proposed concepts close to true object-centered sociality paradigm. They start from general concepts like travel, music, events and allow their users to create a social network instance for each of these concepts. For instance: in Dopplr (www.dopplr.com) the trip itself is turned to social object, in Soundcloud (soundcloud.com) the music track itself is turn into a social object, Upcoming (www.upcoming.com) or Plancast (plancast.com) consider an event as a discrete object that can be socially shared. Similar approaches are observed in the Internet–of–Things domain where the generalization of object identification techniques like RFID, QR code, etc. companies implement and offer services to socialize around physical objects. Among them, Stickibit (http://www.stickybits.com), Tales of Thing (http://talesofthings.com), Itizens (http://itizen.com), WideTag (http://www.widetag.com), Thingd (www.thingd.com) or more recently Bump (bump.com) that allow to build a social network around car plates. To summarize, if today many projects implement and leverage the concept of object-centered social network, none of them propose to study the impact of linking and making interdependent all these social networks. Object-centered social networks are already present on the web, but there is so far no way for providing the user with a cross-media and furthermore a cross-community experience. Each social application is built as a silo for multimedia content (video, image, sound) and for other types of objects such as an event, an activity. In our approach we believe that each object's community is not used in isolation. If these objects are social, by definition they tend to be connected to each other, forming an heterogeneous ecosystem.

## Towards Cross-Media and Cross-Community Discovery Experiences

Getting the right information at the right moment has been a challenge for many years. The Web is bringing us closer by making available lots of information, but getting to the right information through Web search is still a challenge. Social networks help to build relationships and to get trusted information from network's people. They change the information retrieval paradigm, the information is behind a person and the new challenge is to retrieve the relevant person.

Current approaches about social networking are too much global and user-centered, and therefore do not really include objects (places, multimedia content, goals, etc.) as a way to connect people. In our research, we propose a paradigm shift compared to current approaches dealing with social networks: we aim at developing object-centered social structure and associated services/applications based on the interactions between those object-connected people, in order to serve them in various tasks. Such networks would be used to better extract and build knowledge around the object, create dynamic links between communities and provide an eco-system of socially-enabled objects.

An object-centered representation of social structure enables (1) to obtain information about the object, as interactions between people and the object (object annotations); (2) to see the community of the object and interact with this community (conversations between people triggered by annotations or directly on the object); (3) to build knowledge from conversations by transforming conversations into individual or collective object annotations; (4) to get a semantic representation of the object through the different types of interactions (annotations and conversations); (5) to establish dynamic links with other object-centered social structures enabling a cross-community discovery experience.

## Definitions

We previously introduced the concept of objects. In this section we present some definitions that help defining the Object-Centered Social Net-

work (OCSN) paradigm. Those definitions are statements related to our analysis and could not constitute general reusable definitions outside the scope of this study.

- *Definition of "object-centered sociality"*: It represents the social interactions about and on an object. It includes for example functions such as annotation, conversation and sharing.
- *Definition of an "interaction"*: Interactions encompass annotations or conversations (see below)
- *Definition of a "conversation"*: A conversation is an informal interchange of thoughts or information between people on a particular annotation, or on the object itself.
- *Definition of "object-centered social network" (OCSN)*: A *object-centered social network* is a dynamic network composed of people that do not know each other *a priori* and that are participating on a same object (event, content, place, intention) through dedicated functionalities (presence, annotation, conversation, information management). The main properties of these social networks are:
  - *ad-hoc involvement* (i.e. no explicit account creation) triggered by the location, the object or a common intention. Having a personal and simplified authentication mechanism, such as Open-ID[4], Sxip[5], WebID[6], OAuth[7] or some other single-sign-on mechanism, allowing not to repeat the registration or authentication process each time user entering in an OCSN may help;
  - *links between people are mediated by a object*: there are a priori no direct links between people (unless they preexist because they already know each other), the object is the key con-

*Figure 6. Pervasive Sociality Ontology*

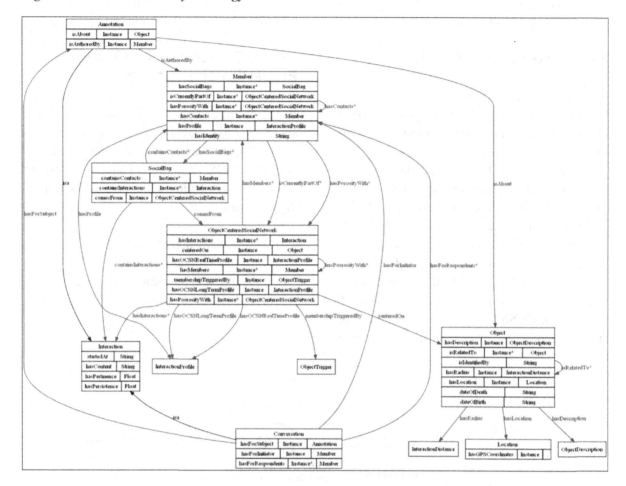

nector. New links can be created between people through their conversations around the object.

Conceptually, an OCSN can be seen as a kind of contextualized social network bundled with a set of tools and services (i.e. a kind of framework) to handle easily interactions within the OCSN between (1) users; and (2) one user and the resource and exploit them to provide participants of the network with advances added-values services to support and enhance interactions.

- *Definition of "perception summary":* Perception generally refers to the process of senses' information collection and

analysis or awareness resulting of it. In our approach, interactions are the results of OCSN members' perceptions. We are calling *perception summary* a representation describing in an aggregated manner the interactions that occurred during a given time window in the network.

- *Definition of "pervasive sociality":* Communication paradigm based on exploitation of heterogeneous OCSN ecosystem. The pervasive sociality aspires to provide a "close to context and need" oriented interactions via objects. In this ecosystem OCSN are bounded through semantic and physical proximity links and allow users to navigate in this new communication field. Usage perspectives are multiple.

## Pervasive Sociality Ontology

We have formalized the concept of "object-centered social network" through an ontology (Figure 6) which links together most of the terms defined in the previous section.

As described on Figure 6, an object-centered social network is characterized by several main properties: it is centered on an object (which is defined by an URI, a semantic description, relationship with other objects, eventually a location, etc.), it has a fluctuating number of members, whose membership is triggered by a specific trigger (presence in location, click on a link, etc). In addition the OCSN contains a number of interactions, which can be either annotations or conver-

sations. It may also have some dynamic links with other OCSNs, as explained in the next section.

## Object-Centered Social Networks Properties and Functions

Based on this comparison with existing forms of social networks, we can clarify key characteristics of OCSNs, the functions and services they should provide to OCSN members. Thus, we envision a framework which aims at supporting the following functions:

- Ad-hoc user management
- Information management
- Perception management
- Porosity management

*Figure 7. OCSN management framework*

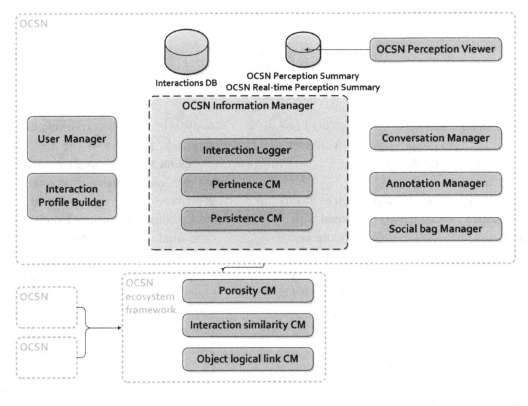

The following sections explain the role of each of these functions and propose some initial ideas to address the research challenges that are central to them.

## Ad-hoc User Management

In an OCSN, users should not have to explicitly connect to a "system" to be part of the network. Instead, the contact (physical or virtual) with the object which constitutes the kernel of the network shall trigger the registration or the identification/authentication to be logged in (this part must be handled by the Profile Manager Module in Figure 7). Depending on the object which the OCSN is centered to, this seamless connection can be hard to achieve because it may require specific hardware, e.g. active RFID badges such as in (Alani *et al.*, 2009) or advanced techniques (fingerprint or face recognition, etc.).

## Information Management

One of the main interests of focusing on the OCSN paradigm is to better manage information that is available in social networks. In our view, managing information inside a OCSN consists in exploiting the information sources to provide users with pertinent information, as well as making this information available to the user, even from outside of the network.

*Information Sources:* In an OCSN, available information originates from various types of interactions that can exist in such social structure (see Conversation and Annotation Manager Modules in Figure 7):

- Interaction between the object and a person, we call those interactions *annotations*.
- Interactions between people, we call those interactions *conversations*. We distinguish two types of conversations:
  ○ Conversations related to the object;
  ○ Conversations related to someone's annotation (such as comments).

*Exploitation of information sources:* Different exploitations of these information sources may be envisioned, for example:

- *Exploitation of collective intelligence* of the collection of annotations for services specific to the object. Examples of such services are presented later in this chapter into the sBook application.
- *Classification of interactions* to identify groups of interests inside the OCSN. This could help to filter interactions so that people receive or have access only to pertinent information.
- *Transforming conversations into knowledge pieces.* For instance, if an interaction of type conversation is rated high by the community (from explicit or implicit feedback), then this interaction can be transformed into a new annotation and considered as a knowledge piece for the object. In the same way a thread of interactions, if high rated, can be transformed into a collective annotation.

*Pertinence and persistence:* In order to provide valuable knowledge, it is necessary to have some metrics that characterizes the usefulness of interactions. In particular, what is a "good" interaction? In an automatic system, how to trust an annotation? And, when the number of interactions increases over time, what kind of information should be retained? How to forget about less relevant interactions in the network?

We have identified two axes to characterize interactions: *pertinence* and *persistence* of interactions (see Pertinence and Persistence Computation Module, Figure 7).

The *pertinence* of an interaction can be measured by taking into account several parameters, such as:

- Computation of the semantic distance between the interaction and the subject of the interaction (object, annotation). For example when the subject of the conversation is not anymore about the object, but a personal interaction because of the opportunity to be there at the same time, then the pertinence of the interaction is low.
- Computation of the pertinence through implicit/explicit relevance feedback (must be computed dynamically).
- Social roles in the interaction. For example when the author of an annotation within an object is the creator or editor of this object and not a simple member, then the pertinence of the annotation may be considered higher.

The *persistence* of an interaction is function of its pertinence and the date of first appearance (it may include for example a decay factor (Koychev & Schwab, 2000)). For example if an annotation has a low pertinence and is relatively old, then this annotation will no longer be displayed to users.

*Personal object-associated memory:* The individual persistence also called *social bag* (see Social Bag Manager Module in Figure 7) is the set of contacts, interactions and potentially new contents, a user has generated or gathered during his/her involvement with the OCSN. It represents the user activity within the OCSN. This functionality of the OCSN enables people to leave the OCSN with a "trace" of their activity, which allows for example to include their new contacts into their favourite web people-centered social network such as Facebook or LinkedIn. This is also a way to keep this activity as a personal memory within what we call a *social bag*.

## Perception Summary Management

Interactions around the object are the best information to give a perception of what the object is and what the behaviors of people around this object are. The perception of the interactions of the social network are described by a public dynamic interaction profile (as described earlier in this chapter) built from annotations and conversations of all OCSN members during an adapted time window (see Interaction Profile Builder Module in Figure 7). This dynamic interaction profile may be represented visually (e.g. as a tag cloud, see OCSN Perception Viewer, Figure 7) as the perception an external user can get from the OCSN. We distinguish two types of perception summary:

- Lifelong perception summary: this summary uses only annotations and represents a summary of all users' annotations since the birth of the OCSN. This summary evolves over time since new annotations will be added and some will disappear (see the notion of interaction persistence). It can be presented to external people in order to identify if they have some interest in participating to this community and if they have something to bring or to learn from this community. This summary could help to identify durable semantic links between OCSNs, by measuring the similarity between two different OCSN perception summaries.
- Real-time perception summary: this summary uses annotations and conversations; it represents a summary of interactions inside a predefined time window. This summary is pertinent to understand what is going on in real time inside a OCSN; it gives a real time visibility to the OCSN e.g. by highlighting some useful conversations about the object that are linked to an ephemeral phenomenon such as an event.

Each perception summary gives an overview of the "life" of this object, and can become a factor to augment the visibility of this object and its community.

## Porosity Management

Enhancing the user experience with a cross community and cross media experience is possible if all OCSNs could be linked in some ways, opening paths from one to another. As defined earlier, an object is defined by its own properties and the annotations of OCSN members. Logical links can be deduced from the object properties such as causality, temporality, closeness (location-based) and semantic similarity. Those links establish stable relationships between OCSNs, but we think that they are not sufficient and do not take into account the perception of people about an object.

Thus, we propose to build pertinent links between objects and their communities by creating paths computed both from the logical links and the similarities of interactions between communities. Those paths can help to join related OCSNs. The decision to join must be taken by the user based on a pertinent metric. We introduce the notion of *porosity* between two OCSNs as a metric that characterizes how users from $OCSN_i$ can be aware of interactions from $OCSN_j$ (see Porosity Computation Module in the OCSN eco-system framework, Figure 7).

We saw in the previous section that there is a possibility to distinguish a lifelong perception summary and a real time perception summary. In order to give a better explanation of the porosity level between two communities, the same distinction in the computation (sources and time window) can be applied, so that the user will have propositions about joining other OCSNs based on a lifelong porosity metric and real-time porosity metric.

In a generic way, the degree of porosity between two OCSNs can be computed as follows:

$$Porosity(OCSN_i, OCSN_j) = a*sim(\{Inter.\}_{OCSNi}, \{Inter.\}_{OCSNj}) + b*logicalLink(obj(OCSN_i), obj(OCSNj_i))$$

Where

- Sim is a similarity measure
- $\{Inter.\}_{OCSNi}$ and $(\{Inter.\}_{OCSNj}$ is the representation of the set of interactions respectively from $OCSN_i$ and $OCSN_j$
- logicalLink is a similarity measure between the logical and semantic properties of both objects
- *a* and *b* are variable enabling to balance the weight of the object logical link and the similarity between OCSNs users' perceptions. This balance must be based on the nature of the object.

This porosity metric could also be applied individually, e.g. to indicate to a particular user a list of objects communities (with associated porosity metric) as potential communities to join. The computation of the porosity would be defined as follows:

$$Porosity(u, OCSN_j) = a*sim(\{i\}_{u,OCSNi}, \{Inter.\}_{OCSNj}) + b*logicalLink(obj(OCSN_i), obj(OCSNj_i))$$

where

- *u* is a user that belongs to $OCSN_i$ and $\{i\}_{u,OCSNi}$ is the set of interactions of *u* within $OCSN_i$.

From the end-user perspective, the personal measure of porosity can be exploited to suggest what the most relevant communities to join are. However, it may happen that there are still too many possible relevant OCSNs, which demands additional filtering. That is the reason why several additional parameters can be taken into account to adapt the computation of the porosity metric, such as the location of the user, or information resulting from some form of collaborative filtering (Resnick & Varian, 1997) – for example based on the similarity of interaction profiles between the user and interaction profiles of others members, based on the assumption that similar users from the point of view of interactions are more likely to be part of the same other OCSNs. In a more subtle version, it may be possible to compare patterns of OCSNs memberships between several other members of the user's OCSN to better predict relevant OCSN for that user.

## Challenges

We have proposed a formal representation of an object-centered social network and its ecosystem. This proposal is being tested through the implementation of a "sBook" prototype (see next section). Nevertheless, we already identified some challenges linked to our proposal such as:

- *Identification of Objects*: In order to link objects together and to let users move from one OCSN to another one, it is needed that there are identified (URIfication), described semantically (for example is a typology of objects needed?, how to express potential relationship between objects such as inclusion?)
- *Object Life Cycle*: Some objects may be only ephemeral; some other may change over time or may be represented by several different instances (e.g. the various e-versions on a book).
- *Finding OCSNs*: In order to propose users with relevant OCSNs to join, objects should be stored in a form of repository. Which form should it take? Shall it be centralized or decentralized?
- *User Engagement and Incentive*: Annotations and conversations between people may be very sparse in some environments. How to stimulate them or how to cope with that?
- *Specificity of Objects:* Although it is possible to define a high level model of OCSN and have a quite generic approach to define a number of required functions and

modules, the detail of many of them must be fine-tuned based on the specificities of the objects. For example, many of the information management computation metrics have to be adapted to the nature of the object.

## A First Instance of OCSN: the sBook

In order to better develop the paradigm of object-centered social networks, we have started to work on one specific instance: the sBook. At school and universities, e-books are starting to be objects more and more used in order to sustain students' learning activities. E-books constitute one of the few objects already digitalized and were a natural starting point to make them the center of a social network. However, these objects are still quite static and do not provide as much interactions as they could. Thus, there is a need to reinvent the interactions students have with the books, by making them more social.

Thus, we have built the sBook (Ribière *et al.*, 2010), which is the first instance of an object-centered social network, and which consists in enriching an e-book with a set of associated tools to create, develop and sustain social interactions. The benefits are potentially huge - in particular for people having learning reading goals - leading potentially to a wide range of new services: faster access to information, possibility to interact with people sharing similar concerns or able to provide relevant explanations, determining most interesting areas in a book, or even helping users accessing faster the information that will make them progress in their learning curve.

In order to make this OCSN real, we started with the implementation of an advanced e-reader social platform, letting students connect easily, put annotations and share them. These annotations - when shared - become the support of students' conversations, as they provide the *right context* for readers, i.e. people and semantic context linked to a specific book section. Given the importance of the

*Figure 8. Heat map display, darker paragraphs/chapters are the most annotated paragraphs*

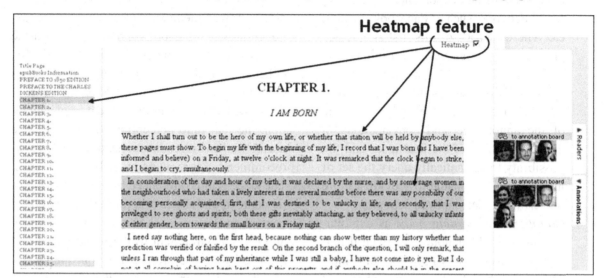

annotations with respect to an e-book 'object', we have investigated different kinds of annotations, in particular *semantic* and *symbolic* annotations.

- *Semantic (or free text) annotation* represents the user's interpretation of the content element, e.g. an analysis or a summary of their understanding; it is expressed through free text (natural language).
- *Symbolic annotation* can help the user to identify points of interest in the content, or points of difficulties. It consists of a simple annotation the user generally does during his first reading: underlining, highlighting text, use symbols to mark an interest or a difficulty about a highlighted text.

In the first prototype we are developing, we are focusing on a few of the functions of the OCSN evoked previously. The first research and developments on the sBook are mainly concentrating in *providing information management functions* in this OCSN, in particular the exploitation of collective intelligence coming from the large number of annotations and conversations resulting from social interactions enabled by our platform. This collective knowledge can be used to provide useful information or related content to OCSN members.

Thus, we have envisioned many added-value services exploiting the various types of annotations described above, which are currently being implemented, among which the following ones:

- *Heat maps* as exploitation of collective semantic annotations to help OCSN members in their readings to find appropriate information and learn in a more efficient way. The *heat map* is a service helping readers to identify key paragraphs within the book. The interest is to offer students a mean to relieve the pain to read all the content for getting important information and knowledge from the book. In a first instance of the heat map, the collection of symbolic annotations denoting an interest for paragraphs are used to compute a statistical value for each chapter and each paragraph. This value corresponds to the proportion of annotations of this chapter/paragraph w.r.t the entire book (Figure 8). Amazon's Kindle e-reader has a similar heat map feature, letting users bookmark book sections and export them to existing social networks such as Facebook, Twitter, etc. The drawback of this first simple approach is the consensus of the result. People do not have the same goals while reading, and especially students. The integration of the notion of pertinence and persistence of the annotations and conversations in the computation of the heat map, and the possibility to semantically query the set of interactions will enable to provide a more powerful and personalized *heat map*.

- *Collaborative learning paths* as exploitation of symbolic annotations: Even if features such as *heat maps* provide some indications on what could be of general interest to the student, it does not take into account past things he learnt, and the fact that by nature, learners are diverse (Smith & McGreggor, 1992), have personal needs of information and that each student has his own *learning path* that we are trying to accompany. We assume that users sharing a similar reading sequence are more likely to share same questions, goals and intentions about the e-book. We focus in particular on symbolic annotations, classified into two big classes: *questions* (misunderstanding, etc.) and *explanations* (comments, remarks, interpretations, etc.). When a user starts to put some symbolic annotations in the e-book: "?" when he does not understand a paragraph, "!" when it is of particular relevance. The system finds users of the social network of the book that have annotations in common with him. Then it analyzes sequences of annotations of those people, compares them with the sequence of annotations the user did, and at the end, and suggests possible next steps within the book, in terms of contact opportunities or reading opportunities.

In addition, we have started investigating the notion of cross-media and cross-community experience through some forms of *porosity* between the OCSN associated to one e-book and other OCSNs, either associated to similar objects (other e-books) or to other objects, such as OCSNs of videos.

In the latter case, in the current implementation, the real time perception summary of one user (based on his reading context) is exploited to recommend videos on an available Web source. The video is thus referenced by the user's semantic context, and the text is referenced as related content on the video. The next step will provide an OCSN environment to the object video and the user would be proposed to join the OCSN of videos which are semantically related. Future versions will also take into account the interactions on the video in order to totally implement the porosity management of an OCSN.

In further work, we are aiming at providing pertinent added-value services around e-book annotations to enhance the learning experience of users, and go further in the exploitation of other OCSN to augment the discovery experience of students.

The set of ideas about the future of e-books we have presented in this section are currently being addressed in the scope of a collaborative project between Alcatel-Lucent Bell Labs, Abilene Christian University (ACU) and Cambridge University Press (CUP). The goal of this project (which runs until 2013) is to develop an application to facilitate cross-media and cross-community information discovery. The project has started with the implementation of an advanced e-reader platform, letting students be logged in the social network of the book, put annotations and share them with different granularity levels (friends, groups etc.), plus the semantic heat map feature. We shall thank here the sBook team from Alcatel-Lucent Bell Labs composed of Olivier Durécu, Hebbar Abdelkrim, Julien Robinson, Sylvain Squedin for their work on the prototype, and Natalie Ebenreuter (Bell Labs), Robert McKelvain and Daniel Connell (ACU) for their work on the experimentation inside this project.

## CONCLUSION

In this book chapter we propose a general framework for the construction of social applications based on semantic analysis of people interactions. Finding the right information at the right moment cannot be overcome only through information retrieval techniques. Social Networks have shown the benefits of maintaining connections in the digital eco-system and how people can be the aggregators of relevant and meaningful information. In this chapter we proposed to leverage the semantics of interactions to propose two different ways to be directed to the relevant information through the right person:

- Dynamic user interaction profiles are the vector to suggest new relevant contacts based on an information need, but also an efficient way to summarize user social activities by exposing the user profile to his/her multiple social spheres. In this work we studied the issues in building user profiles from user interactions streams compared to state-of-the-art in this domain. We proposed methods to extracts concepts from social streams and metrics to weight each concept. We also proposed a social application called *social adviser* illustrating the use of dynamic user interaction profiles.
- A formalisation of Object-Centered Sociality through the definition of object-centered social networks (OCSNs). In this work, we made an emphasis on the use of semantic analysis of interactions to overcome the well-known problem of wall garden illustrated in existing web social networks. Making possible to open paths between communities by measuring the porosity of two communities through the

logical links existing between the objects of the communities and the similarity of interactions between the two OCSNs. This second proposal makes use of the dynamic interaction profiles to propose the notion of perception summary of an OCSN. We presented an application called *sBook* to illustrate how an object like an e-book can be changed into a social network of readers, transforming the reading experience into a social experience.

In our view, a motivation for users to be active members in online communities is to discover hidden links, i.e. links beyond explicitly declared friendship relations, based on shared interests.

Several open questions are related to the framework of Figure 2:

- *What is the right privacy management in social applications?*

We presented in this chapter an approach based on the granularity of concepts, where the level of granularity of a concept can be linked with a social sphere. A sharing schema can be learned for each cluster of concepts in the user profile. Whether this approach will be accepted by users is still under investigation and large-scale experimentations are needed for this.

- *How to combine structural and semantic analysis for recommendation ranking?*

Even if in this chapter we focused on semantic analysis, it is clear that it should be combined with structural analysis to refine recommendations. This can be achieved in several ways. We are currently working on the exploration of connections in the networks, to rank recommendations based on social proximity. The underlying idea is that users will better trust a recommendation where not only the shared interest, but also the social path can be explained. In other words, a recommendation from a friend of a friend will be more trusted, than a recommendation from a stranger, even if sentiment and quality of shared content is lower.

- *What is the right strategy for knowledge extraction from textual annotations?*

In this chapter we showed the main steps for knowledge extraction for different kinds of annotations. The objective of this chapter was not to analyse in details this issue, but to give professionals some basic principles. It is however clear, that further investigation is required and current content analysis techniques need to be adapted to work well in the case of social awareness streams. A first idea for this is to transform a message into a document. This can be achieved, e.g. by retrieving previous messages from the user that potentially related (e.g. shared in a close time interval, semantically related, same hashtags). Messages from friends who participated in the same event can also help. Additionally, perspectives of this work include large-scale experimentations of the recommendation strategies and further connections with the user modelling community in order to find the right semantic representation for the user profiles and integrate a relevance feedback mechanism.

- *Proposing new properties of objects into OCSN?*

Our next challenge concerning Object-centered networks is to get information from users behaviors into the OCSN ecosystem. In fact we can perform a better recommendation and user experience by considering the people attention distribution. To achieve this challenge we will introduce new concepts such as the gravity and the stickiness of an OCSN:

- The gravity is the potential of an OCSN to attract users in the ecosystem. This proper-

ty can be linked to the porosity metric and measure the propensity to enter into some network based on collective behaviors in using path between OCSNs. We can imagine that someone who is near to the Louvre OCSN will probably enter the Joconde one soon.

- The stickiness is an OCSN capacity to hold user attention. When someone is proposed to join an OCSN through porosity, he can see shared content and decide to not contribute or, at the opposite, declare an explicit and persistent link with the community. The time spent into the network will be used to calculate such capacity. Jyri Engeström used the term of "snack-size sociality: *"People incrisingly snacking on content"* (Engeström, 2008)".

## REFERENCES

Alani, H., Szomszor, M., Cattuto, C., Van den Broeck, W., Correndo, G., Barrat, A. (2009). *Live Social Semantics*, ISWC 2009.

Auer, S., Bizer, C., Kobilarov, G., Lehmann, J., Cyganiak, R., & Ives, Z. (2007). DBpedia: a nucleus for a web of open data. In *Proceedings of the 6th international the Semantic Web and 2nd Asian Conference on Asian Semantic Web Conference* (Busan. Korea & World Affairs, (November): 11–15.

Berlanga, A., Rusman, E., Bitter-Rijpkema, M., & Sloep, P. (2009). Guidelines to Foster Interaction in Online Communities. In Koper, R. (Ed.), *Learning Network Services For Professional Development*. New York: Springer Verlag. doi:10.1007/978-3-642-00978-5_3

Blass, Thomas. (2004). *The Man Who Shocked the World: The Life and Legacy of Stanley Milgram.*

Engeström, J. (2005). *Why some social network services work and others don't – Or: the case for object-centered sociality.* Jyri Engestrom's web blog (www.zengestrom.com/blog).

Engeström, J. (2008). *People incrisingly snacking on content.* http://www.slideshare.net/jyri/snack-size-sociality.

Engeström, Y. (1987). *Learning by Expanding: an Activity-Theoretical Approach to Developmental Research.* Helsinki, Finland: Orienta-Konsultit, OY.

Esuli, A., & Sebastiani, F. (2006). *Determining term subjectivity and term orientation for opinion mining.* In *Proceedings of EACL-06, 11th Conference of the European Chapter of the Association for Computational Linguistics, Trento, IT.*

Heath, T., Hepp, M., & Bizer, C. (2009). Linked Data - The Story So Far. Special Issue on Linked Data. *International Journal on Semantic Web and Information Systems (IJSWIS).* Retrieved from: http://linkeddata.org/ docs/ijswis-special-issue

Knorr-Cetina, K. (1997). Sociality with Objects: Social Relations in Post-social Knowledge Societies. *Theory, Culture & Society, 14*(4), 1–30. doi:10.1177/026327697014004001

Koychev, I., & Schwab, I. (2000). *Adaptation to Drifting User's Interests.* In Workshop on Machine Learning in New Information Age (MLNet 2000) at the 11th European Conference on Machine Learning (ECML 2000), pp. 39–45, Barcelona, Spain.

Lampe, C., Ellison, N., & Steinfield, C. (2006). *A face(book) in the crowd: social Searching vs. social browsing.* Proceedings of the 2006 20th Anniversary Conference on Computer Supported Cooperative Work, Alberta, Canada.

Leont'ev, A. N. (1978). *Activity, Consciousness and Personality.* Englewood Cliffs, NJ: Prentice-Hall.

Mathes, A. (2004). *Folksonomies - Cooperative Classification and Communication Through Shared Metadata. Technical report.* Graduate School of Library and Information Science, University of Illinois Urbana-Champaign.

Naaman, M., Boase, J., & Lai, C. (2010). *Is it really about me?: message content in social awareness streams.* In Proceedings of the 2010 ACM Conference on Computer Supported Cooperative Work, Savannah, Georgia, USA.

Nadeau, D., Sekine, and Satoshi. (2007). A survey of named entity recognition and classification. *Linguisticae Investigationes, 30*(1), 3–26. doi:10.1075/li.30.1.03nad

Newman, M., Watts, D., & Barabási, A.-L. (2006). *The Structure and Dynamics of Networks.* Princeton University Press.

Resnick, P., & Varian, H. (1997). Recommender Systems. *Communications of the ACM, 40*(3), 56–58. doi:10.1145/245108.245121

Rheingold, H. (1993). *The virtual community: Homesteading on the electronic frontier.* Reading, MA: Addison Wesley.

Ribière, M., Picault, J., & Squedin, S. (2010). The sBook: towards social and personalized learning experiences. In *Proceedings of the third workshop on Research advances in large digital book repositories and complementary media* (BooksOnline '10). New York: ACM, 3-8.

Salton, G., & McGill, M. J. (1983). *Introduction to modern information retrieval.* McGraw-Hill.

Smith, B. L., & MacGregor, J. T. (1992). *What Is Collaborative Learning?* National Center on Postsecondary Teaching, Learning, and Assessment at Pennsylvania State University.

Star, S. L., & Griesemer, J. R. (1989). Institutional ecology, 'translations' and boundary objects: amateurs and professionals in Berkeley's museum of vertebrate zoology, 1907-1939. *Social Studies of Science, 19*, 387–420. doi:10.1177/030631289019003001

Vygotsky, L. S. (1978). *Mind and Society*. Cambridge, MA: Harvard University Press.

## KEY TERMS AND DEFINITIONS

**Object-Centered Social Network:** A social structure formed by people interacting, in an opportunistic way or in the long term, on a common social object through dedicated functionalities (online presence, comments, rates, reviews, etc.).

**Semantic Web:** The Semantic Web refers to technologies and standards, allowing to represent content generated in the Web in a common, interoperable format and to perform advanced reasoning on top of it.

**Social Object:** A social object has a concrete and perceptible, physical and/or numeric, manifestation. It is a coherent whole, indivisible, which triggers specific activities. Some objects are the source of conversational interactions and keepers of collective attention. They constitute a conversation support. In the case of the Social Web, social objects are also called user generated content (UGC).

**Social Platform:** We consider a Social Platform' any system that allows its members to share some kind of content and have interactions with some kind of virtual communication process (e.g. rating, commenting, status updating).

**Social Web:** We define the Social Web as a component of the World Wide Web composed of systems that allow their users to share content and engage in conversations related to it. Such systems include social networking sites (SNS), such as Facebook, microblogging sites, such as Twitter, or more general social web platforms, such as Flickr for photo annotation.

**User Interaction Profile:** A user profile constructed from the content productions of the user in the Social Platform.

## ENDNOTES

[1] Online Blog Post - http://blog.jonudell.net/2007/02/06/critical-mass-and-social-network-fatigue – visited Nov. 2010.
[2] http://www.edisonresearch.com – visited 2010
[3] http://socialnomics.net - visited 2010
[4] http://openid.net/
[5] http://www.sxip.com/
[6] http://esw.w3.org/WebID
[7] http://oauth.net/

Chapter 19

# The Comparability of Event-Related and General Social Support

**Valentina Hlebec**
*University of Ljubljana, Slovenia*

**Maja Mrzel**
*University of Ljubljana, Slovenia*

**Tina Kogovšek**
*University of Ljubljana, Slovenia*

## ABSTRACT

*Some studies (e.g., Kogovšek & Hlebec, 2008, 2009) have shown that the name generator and the role relation approaches to measuring social networks are to some extent comparable, but less so the name generator and the event-related approaches (Hlebec, Mrzel, & Kogovšek, 2009). In this chapter, the composition of the social support network assessed by both the general social support approach and the event-related approach (support during 15 major life events) is analyzed and compared. In both cases, the role relation approach is used. In addition, in both approaches a more elaborate (16 possible categories ranging from partner, mother, father, friend to no one) and a more simple (6 possible categories ranging from family member, friend, neighbor to no one) response format is applied and compared. The aim of the chapter is to establish, in a controlled quasi-experiment setting, whether the different approaches (i.e. the general social support and the event-related approach) produce similar social networks regardless of the response format (long vs. short).*

## INTRODUCTION

Social support networks can be measured in many different ways. Each approach has specific advantages and disadvantages and each may be useful and appropriate for specific research pur-

poses. It could be argued that the name generator approach produces the most complete, broad ranging and substantively rich data about one's social network. It asks a respondent to directly name actual persons in his/her network. Usually a broad range of other information is also collected about the obtained network members (e.g., type

DOI: 10.4018/978-1-61350-513-7.ch019

of relationship, strength of tie, network members' personal characteristics and so on). Therefore, relatively accurate estimates and interpretively rich information about network characteristics such as network composition, structure etc. are made possible. Yet such network data collection may be quite burdensome for the respondents, especially in the case of relatively large networks. In contrast the role relation approach, whereby network members are represented only as role relationships and typically only the first two important persons are obtained and with the help of a showcard the possible role relations are listed, is cheaper, simpler to administer and less burdensome for respondents. However, owing to the specific response format less precise information on network members is obtained and therefore the estimation of the different network characteristics is limited. Third, many studies in the field of social support (e.g., Cutrona & Russell, 1990; Hobfoll, 1985; Keinan, 1997; Thoits, 1985) show that the effectiveness of a certain type of support provided and the mechanisms through which the support works are often highly dependent on the specific situation requiring support. For instance, emotional support may be provided in a situation (e.g., an accident) where the affected person needs or expects help of a more practical kind. If an unsuitable type of support is provided this may thus cause additional stress, dissatisfaction, feelings of being misunderstood, controlled or alienated. Therefore, the context of a specific situation influences how effective a certain type of support can be. Since all of these approaches are often used in large cross-national substantive studies (e.g., International Social Survey Programme, General Social Survey, Generations and Gender Programme, European Quality of Life Survey), this raises a number of questions about the comparability of results, biases, limitations and so on among such studies. In addition, there are differences among the approaches in terms of the costs and benefits, respondent burden, measurement instrument characteristics and complexity

of implementation which are, again, important issues in large cross-national studies.

Various conceptualizations of social support frequently stress the difference between actually received (enacted) social support and the subjective appraisal of social support or perceived[1] support (Burleson, Albrecht, Goldsmith, & Sarason, 1994; Knipscheer & Antonucci, 1990; Laireiter & Baumann, 1992; Sarason, Pierce, & Sarason, 1990; Vaux, 1988, 1992). In most models social support resources or social support network are part of the definition.

Sarason, Sarason, and Pierce (1990a, 1990b, 1994a; Sarason, Pierce, & Sarason, 1990) define *received (enacted) social* support as help people receive from others in specific stressful situations. Received support depends on the availability of support (whether or not respondents have a social network), the individual's coping skills and the degree of severity of the stress perceived by others (potential providers of support). *Perceived support* refers to a person's belief that social support is available if needed, but without it necessarily being actually taken up. One can further distinguish between (Sarason, Pierce, & Sarason, 1990) the availability of support and the adequacy of the available support, as well as global and specific measures of perceived support. The third dimension of social support is a social support network. Events that stimulate the provision of social support are divided along several dimensions such as minor-major, simple-complex, and stressful-nonstressful (Sarason, Sarason, & Pierce, 1994a, pp. 93-95).

Two main hypotheses regarding the role of social support can be distinguished with regard to the distinction between stressful and non-stressful events. The hypothesis about the *buffering effects* of social support states that social support is only effective during stressful events (e.g., death of a close family member, divorce, retirement, moving to another place etc.). The *main effect* hypothesis holds that social support is related to well-being in non-stressful situations. We can say that these two alternative hypotheses are related to the concept of the event-related approach (support during stressful events) and to the concept of the general support approach given in everyday life situations (main effects). Empirical evidence can be found for both models (e.g., Franks & Stephens, 1996).

A variety of measures of perceived support (Vaux, 1988, pp. 33-59) focusing on individual perceptions of support availability and adequacy has been developed. Further, measures developed after Weiss' (1974) and Cobb's (1976) theoretical models primarily focus on the affective aspects of social support such as the perception of being loved and accepted by others, the sense of belonging, enhancing of one's self-esteem etc. Although several of these measures have been presented as general measures of social support, they most often only assess emotional support (Bolger & Eckenrode, 1991; Cohen & Towbes, 1988; Procidano & Heller, 1983; Sarason, Levine, Basham, & Sarason, 1983).

Social context factors (Vaux, 1988, pp. 76-87) such as stressors, family, social roles and settings, housing and community, social network stressors and network vulnerability mediate the transactional processing of social support. Social ties are often a source of stress as well as support.

A previous study (Hlebec, Mrzel, & Kogovšek, 2009) has shown a correspondence between perceived support network and enacted support network, although it is not at a high level; there is a tendency of a larger discrepancy between the two approaches when non-family segments are called for support during stressful events. Two possible explanations for this were offered. The observed differences were the result of the approaches used or, alternatively, the main effects and the buffering hypothesis work differently and people actually rely on different segments of their overall support network.

Since there were several methodological differences in the mentioned study (Hlebec, Mrzel, & Kogovšek, 2009), the aim of this chapter is to compare the network composition (% of kin,

friends etc.) of the general social network and the event-related support network approaches, both measured by the role relation approach and perceived support.

The role of general social networks was assessed with questions measuring four social support dimensions varying from emotional support to financial support. The role of social support during stressful events was assessed in such a way that a list of stressful events was given to respondents (Holmes & Rahe, 1967) and both received as well as perceived social support were assessed in a very simple way using the role relation approach.

In addition, two different role relation response formats were used:

- The short response format (also used in the European Quality of Life Survey [EQLS]) that has a very limited number of choices for support providers (family member, co-worker, good friend, neighbor, other, no one); and
- The long response format (also used in the International Social Survey Programme [ISSP]) that has a larger set of available roles (husband/wife/partner, mother, father, daughter, son, sister, brother, grandmother/father, granddaughter/son, other kin – my family, other kin – partner's family, good friend, neighbor, co-worker, other, no one).

Examples of the questionnaires are given in the appendix.

The chapter aims to compare the network composition (% of kin, friends etc.) of the general social network measured by the role relation approach and the event-related support network as measured by two different response formats.

## DATA AND METHODS

Our experiment was conducted on a convenience quota sample of 987 respondents involving personal interviewing by students of the Faculty of Social Sciences and the Faculty of Arts at the University of Ljubljana in October and November 2009. Each student filled in the questionnaire him/herself and five additional respondents of his/her own choosing. Each student participated in 4 hours of fieldwork training during a methodology course. The quotas were designed so that half the respondents had to be male and half female, and within these two groups there had to be one in each of the three age groups (20-29, 30-49 and 50+ years of age). A split-ballot design was used whereby respondents were distributed into two groups: students at the Faculty of Arts used the role relation short format (EQLS short list; N=621), while students at the Faculty of Social Sciences used the role relation long format (ISSP long list; N=366). At both faculties general social support and event-related support were measured. The collected dataset was edited for out-of-range responses, simple consistency and checked for logic errors.

Both questionnaires had two parts:

1.  The first part consisted of questions about general social support (ISSP version): seven questions related to different social support needs were asked, and each respondent chose two people from his/her social network to which he/she first turns to in that particular situation.
2.  The second part of the questionnaire included questions about stressful events (EQLS version): 15 different stressful events in an individual's life were introduced, and for each of such events a respondent chose one person who helps him/her the most when such an event happens.

In the short response format respondents could choose among six different role relations (family, friends, neighbors, co-workers, other, no one) and in the long response format respondents could choose among 16 different role relations (husband/

wife/partner, mother, father, daughter, son, sister, brother, grand-mother/father, grand-daughter/son, other kin – my family, other kin – partner's family, good friend, neighbor, co-worker, other, no one).[2]

In order to make these two parts of the questionnaire as comparable as possible, in the analysis we only took into account the first person (and not the second) who was identified by the respondent in the general social support part of the questionnaire. Thus, for each respondent we obtained two different social networks – first, the general social support network and, second, the social network at the time of a stressful event. Our goal is to compare the network composition (i.e., percentages of family, friends, neighbors etc. in the network) of the general social support and the event-related approaches and, in addition, to compare the network composition in the short and the long response formats. Moreover, we intend to determine the differences in network composition between these two approaches and the reasons these differences occur.

## RESULTS

### Frequency Distributions

In the first part of our analysis we compared the overall network composition of the general social support (all seven general social supports together) with the overall network composition of stressful events (all 15 stressful events together). There are two different aspects of the comparison: first, between the approaches and, second, between the response formats.

Table 1 shows quite a big difference between the approaches in the percentage of kin when the long response format is used. The percentage of kin seems to be "underestimated" in the general social support approach (76.9% compared to 81.6% in the event-related approach). In more detail, the difference comes largely from the lower percentage of husband/wife/partner in the general

*Table 1. Network Composition (%), the Long Response Format*

| | General social support | Event-related approach |
|---|---|---|
| Husband/wife/partner | 39.8 | 53.3 |
| Mother | 10.6 | 12.7 |
| Father | 7.7 | 4.4 |
| Daughter | 6.4 | 1.7 |
| Son | 4.0 | 0.9 |
| Sister | 4.4 | 4.0 |
| Brother | 2.3 | 1.8 |
| Grand-mother/father | 0.2 | 0.3 |
| Grand-daughter/son | 0.3 | 0.2 |
| Other kin – my family | 1.0 | 1.7 |
| Other kin – partner's family | 0.2 | 0.6 |
| Family total | 76.9 | 81.6 |
| Good friend | 12.9 | 11.2 |
| Neighbor | 0.8 | 0.2 |
| Co-worker | 8.4 | 5.8 |
| Other | 1.1 | 1.4 |

social support (39.8% compared to 53.3% in the event-related approach), although this is slightly compensated for by somewhat larger percentages of father, daughter and son.

Table 2 demonstrates that a less detailed list of offered response categories produces smaller differences between the general social support and the event-related approaches – the frequency distribution of roles is practically the same in both approaches. If Tables 1 and 2 are compared, we see that in the short response format the role of the family is "underestimated" (63.3/63.4% compared to 76.9/81.6% in the long response format)

and all other roles are "overestimated" (especially with the friend category, the difference is almost double) in comparison to the long response format.

Next, calculations of the frequency distributions of the general social support approach and the event-related approach were made for each support and each event separately. All calculations were made separately for the short and for the long response questionnaire formats. As a result, four tables were produced:

•   Two for the long response format:

*Table 2. Network Composition (%), Short Response Format*

| | General social support | Event-related approach |
|---|---|---|
| Family | 63.3 | 63.4 |
| Friend | 21.8 | 21.0 |
| Neighbor | 1.6 | 0.9 |
| Co-worker | 9.7 | 9.5 |
| Other | 3.7 | 5.2 |

*Table 3. Comparison of Supports/Events on the Basis of the Most Important Support Providers, Short Response Format*

| General social support approach | vs. | Event-related approach |
|---|---|---|
| Borrowing money<br>Problems with partner<br>Depression<br>Advice | vs. | Great changes in financial state<br>Death of a close friend<br>Pregnancy<br>Great personal injustice or disease<br>Great changes in living conditions<br>Great changes in health/behavior of family members<br>Wedding<br>Death of a close family member<br>Living changes (moving, renovation of a home) |
| Help in the household<br>Illness | vs. | Birth of a new family member |

○ Table 7x16 (seven supports and 16 role relations from which a respondent chose one);

○ Table 15x16 (15 events and 16 role relations from which a respondent chose one);

• Two for the short response format:

○ Table 7x6 (seven supports and six role relations from which a respondent chose one);

○ Table 15x6 (15 events and six role relations from which a respondent chose one).

The sum of all relations (16 or 6 relations) together within a single support/event is 100%.

Since the tables are relatively large they are included in Appendix 3 and only two summary tables (Tables 3 and 4) are presented in the text. The network composition of the general support network and of the social network during stressful events was compared. We focused on the distribution of the main (important) providers of general support and of support during stressful events. A role was marked as important if it represented at least 10% of an individual's support network. Next, the distribution of important roles in the general support network was compared to the distribution of important roles in the social net-

*Table 4. Comparison of Supports/Events on the Basis of the Most Important Support Providers, Long Response Format*

| General social support approach | vs. | Event-related approach |
|---|---|---|
| Borrowing money | vs. | Great changes in financial state |
| Depression | vs. | Death of a close friend |
| Illness<br>Advice | vs. | Pregnancy<br>Great personal injustice or disease<br>Great changes in living conditions<br>Birth of a new family member<br>Death of a close family member<br>Great changes in health/behavior of family members |
| Problems at work | vs. | Difficulties with a boss<br>Change at the workplace |
| Help in the household | vs. | Living changes (moving, renovation of a home) |

work during stressful events. For instance, let us take support/event in the long version (Table 4) where the most important roles are as an example the husband/wife/partner, mother and father. The combination of these three most important roles can be found in borrowing large sums of money (general social support) and in great changes in the financial state (support during stressful events). If certain roles are important for providing specific support and if those same roles are important in a specific stressful event, it may be concluded that the underlying reason for this is probably that these are similar or comparable situations where these roles provide the most important assistance to the individual.

A comparison of Table 3 and Table 4 reveals that the correspondence in support providers is much more distinct in the long response format. The general social support types seem substantively logically "paired up" with specific events, for instance, borrowing money with great changes in one's financial state; problems at work with difficulties with a boss and change at the workplace. The substantive correspondence is much more difficult to see in the short response format (Table 3).

The comparison of the results of the general social support and event-related approaches thus indicates that, in the short response format, there are two and, in the long response format, there are five different groups of support/events that can be differentiated. As an individual's support network is mostly defined by family support, it is not surprising to observe the more distinct patterns in the long response format. The most evident result of this analysis is the mapping of the first three groups in the long response format to just one group in the short response format. The first group in the short response format is defined by the help of the family and friends, and it breaks up into three groups in the long response format that each have their own specifics regarding which part of the family offers important support in these specific situations.

## Multiple Classification Analysis

In the final stage of our analyses we wanted to compare the network composition of general social support and support during stressful events controlled for method and demographic variables. Multiple Classification Analysis [MCA] was used for this purpose (Andrews, Morgan, Sonquist, & Klem, 1973). MCA is a multivariate method used for analyzing the relationships between multiple independent variables (or predictors) and a dependent variable. It is similar to a multiple regression but has the advantage that nominal measurement level variables need not be dichotomized.

Multiple classification analysis yields the following information:

- The overall (grand) mean and group means of the dependent variable for each combination of categories of predictors;
- Tests of the significance of the effects of individual predictors as well as the interactions between them;
- The effect of each predictor is shown by parameter $\beta$ which tells us the effect of the predictor if other predictors are held constant; the rank order of $\beta$s shows the relative importance of an individual predictor for explaining the dependent variable;
- Deviations from the grand mean of the dependent variable for each category of a predictor (therefore, how much would the grand mean of the dependent variable increase or decrease as a result of the effect of a certain predictor); and
- The percentage of explained variance for all predictors included in the analysis ($R^2$).

In our case, the dependent variables were the network composition indicators (i.e., percentages of each role in the support network) and the independent variables were the response format (short, long), gender (male, female), age (18-29, 30-49, 50+) and marital status (has a partner, other).

*Table 5. Summary of the MCA Analyses*

| | General social support approach | | | | Event-related approach | | | |
|---|---|---|---|---|---|---|---|---|
| Family | long r.f. | female | 50+ | has partner | long r.f. | female | 50+ | has partner |
| | $R^2=14.7\%$ | | | | $R^2=20.4\%$ | | | |
| Friend | short r.f. | (male) | 18-29 | no partner | short r.f. | (male) | 18-29 | no partner |
| | $R^2=12.4\%$ | | | | $R^2=15.6\%$ | | | |
| Neighbor | (short r.f.) | (male) | 50+ | no partner | short r.f. | male | 50+ | no partner |
| | $R^2=4.7\%$ | | | | $R^2=5.3\%$ | | | |
| Co-worker | short r.f. | (male) | 30-49 | has partner | (short r.f.) | male | 30-49 | (has partner) |
| | $R^2=11.2\%$ | | | | $R^2=7.2\%$ | | | |
| Other | short r.f. | (male) | (50+) | (no partner) | short r.f. | (male) | (30-49) | (no partner) |
| | $R^2=2.9\%$ | | | | $R^2=4.4\%$ | | | |

\* Non-statistically significant predictors are in brackets.

Altogether, ten MCA analyses were conducted, five for each approach. The roles included were: family, friend, neighbor, co-worker and other.[3]

Again, since there are many tables the detailed MCA results are presented in Appendix 4 and only a summary table (Table 5) is presented here. First, let us explain how the table should be read. For instance, regarding the percentage of family in the network (the first row in Table 5), this percentage is higher in the long response format, for women, for respondents older than 50 and for respondents who have a partner. This pattern is the same regardless of which approach – general social support or event-related – is used. The effects of all predictors are statistically significant. Where the effect is not statistically significant, the characteristic is put in brackets, for example, it can be seen that regarding the percentage of friends in the network men tend to have a higher percentage than women, but overall the effect of gender is not statistically significant.

If we take the broader picture into account, for four out of five roles the choice of method and the age of the respondent produce statistically significant effects on the percentage share of a particular role in an individual's support network. Method is the most important predictor in six of the ten MCA analyses, mainly in the event-related approach. The least important is the gender of the respondent. In the long response format, the percentage of family in an individual's support network is "overestimated" (in both approaches) and all other roles are underestimated, which confirms the observations made when we compared the frequency distributions of roles in Section Frequency distributions. The same can be said for the subgroup of women. Older respondents rely more on family and neighbors for support, while young adults rely more on friends. Co-workers are most important for the working-age group (30-49). Friends, neighbors and others are more important to those who are single.

Another interesting outcome of this analysis, when comparing the general social support and event-related approaches, is the behavior of predictors in the MCA analyses. Indeed, the statistical significance of predictors varies between the two approaches. Yet, apart from this, there is only one difference (others/age) between these two, in principle, very different approaches. The chief difference between the two approaches is the percentage of explained variance, which is greater in the event-related approach for all roles except co-worker. Thus, the variability of the support network composition can be better explained by the event-related approach than by the general social support approach.

## DISCUSSION

If the findings of this experiment are summarized, it could be argued that larger differences occur in the long response format than in the short response format. It seems that the long version »favors« family over other roles, regardless of the approach used. The main reason is probably the greater availability of specific family roles which prompts respondents' memory to name a larger number and more diverse types of family members rather than just one overall family category in the short version, therefore producing a greater percentage of family in the overall support network. One particular difficulty or at least ambiguity might be posed by the partner role since several interviewers reported some respondents' dilemmas regarding in which category the partner should be placed in the short response format (in most cases they hesitated between "family" and "friend"). Another characteristic which could cause the differences is the term used for friends in both approaches. Namely, in the long response format the term "good friend" was used, whereas in the short response format the term "friend" was used. The former probably has a substantively much narrower and stricter meaning than the latter. If nothing else, this shows one must be careful when using the role relation approach to network measurement since particular role relations tend to be highly context-sensitive, whether individually or collectively. For instance, how respondents interpret the above mentioned role of a (good) friend may highly widely among individuals as well as among cultures or even generations (e.g., the specific meaning of a "Facebook friend" among the young generation).

Looking at the frequency distributions of role relations in more detail, it seems that the long version in the general social support approach "underestimates" the partner and family total within a network and "overestimates" co-workers and children in comparison to the event-related approach. It therefore seems that with the general

support approach the "help tasks" seem to be more widely distributed among different role relationships within people's networks. In contrast, the event-related approach seems to mainly tap into the family part of people's networks. This result would go together well with arguments that normative role expectations may be different with regard to (close) family on the one hand and other roles on the other hand (e.g., van der Poel, 1993). It may well be that when people are confronted with very specific and highly demanding life situations (such as the events used in this study) an implicit normative role "guideline" would be to turn to family rather than friends, neighbors and so on. For instance, when needing help in the case of a serious long term illness or asking for a large sum of money, most people would be reluctant to burden friends with such demands, but expect family to help. It is also possible that respondents name persons they feel they "should" name as opposed to naming actual supportive people. Again, the reason behind such responses may be implicit cultural norms, which "prescribe" whom should we (or whom it is not "decent") to ask for help. This is not to say that one approach is superior to the other, but that one has to be aware that the kind of network obtained depends partly on the approach used and one has to carefully consider which of the two is more appropriate for a specific research question. Social support does seem to be perceived (or even functions) differently if it is considered from a more general perspective as a kind of general "sense of support" and if it is also considered with regard to the specific life situations in which it actually occurs.

With regard to comparing the method effect with other possible effects on network composition indicators we found a similar pattern of effects in the MCA for the general social support and event-related approaches (regardless of the quite different network generator questions). Method (short/long response format) seems to especially affect the percentage of family (higher in the long version) and other in both (a smaller percentage in the long version) the event-related and general social support approaches. Method is also the most important predictor of the percentage of friends and co-workers in the event-related approach (all lower in the long version). Thus the MCA method confirms what we have already seen with the simple frequency distributions of roles in both response formats. It seems that in this case the difference between the short and the long versions are more important than the differences between the approaches (the general social support approach versus the event-related approach). The differences between them mainly arise from the family roles which are much more elaborated in the long version than in the short one.

Generally, age along with marital status seem to be the most important predictors among the demographic variables, which can probably be explained by "the life cycle hypothesis" of social support.

However, in terms of this experiment one also has to bear in mind that we have only analyzed the first named person, which is an important limitation and very relevant since at least in the EQLS study this is how support network is actually measured. It is true that social support networks tend to be generally quite small but, for the majority of people, they are larger than one. Therefore, a possibility for further research could involve studying what happens to both approaches and both response formats if more network members are taken into account. One could hypothesize that the differences in the proportion of family in the network would level out if respondents have the possibility to name more persons.

## REFERENCES

Andrews, F. M., Morgan, J. N., Sonquist, J. A., & Klem, L. (1973). *Multiple Classification Analysis. A Report on a Computer Program for Multiple Regression Using Categorical Predictors*. Ann Arbor: The Institute for Social Research, University of Michigan.

Bolger, N., & Eckenrode, J. (1991). Social relationships, personality, and anxiety during a major stressful event. *Journal of Personality and Social Psychology*, *61*(3), 440–449. doi:10.1037/0022-3514.61.3.440

Burleson, B. R., Albrecht, T. L., Goldsmith, D. J., & Sarason, I. G. (1994). The communication of social support. In Burleson, B. R., Albrecht, T. L., & Sarason, I. G. (Eds.), *Communication of Social Support: Messages, Interactions, Relationships, and Community* (pp. 11–30). Thousand Oaks: Sage Publications.

Cobb, S. (1976). Social support as moderator of life stress. *Psychosomatic Medicine*, *38*, 300–314.

Cohen, L. H., & Towbes, L. C. (1988). Effects of induced mood on self-reported life events and perceived and received social support. *Journal of Personality and Social Psychology*, *55*(4), 669–674. doi:10.1037/0022-3514.55.4.669

Cutrona, C. E., & Russell, D. (1990). Type of Social Support and Specific Stress. Toward a Theory of Optimal Matching. In Sarason, B. R., Sarason, I. G., & Pierce, G. R. (Eds.), *Social Support: An Interactional View* (pp. 319–366). New York: Wiley.

Franks, M. M., & Stephens, M. A. P. (1996). Social support in the context of caregiving: Husbands' provision of support to wives involved in parent care. *Journals of Gerontology. Psychological Science*, *51*, 43–52.

Hlebec, V., Mrzel, M., & Kogovšek, T. (2009). Social support network and received support at stressful events. *Metodološki zvezki*, *6*(2), 155-171.

Hobfoll, S. E. (1985). Limitations of social support in the stress process. In Sarason, I. G., & Sarason, B. R. (Eds.), *Social Support: Theory, Research and Applications* (pp. 391–414). Dordrecht: Martinus Nijhoff Publishers.

Holmes, T. H., & Rahe, R. H. (1967). The social readjustment rating scale. *Journal of Psychosomatic Research, 11*(2), 213–218. doi:10.1016/0022-3999(67)90010-4

Keinan, G. (1997). Social Support, Stress and Personality: Do All Women Benefit from Their Husband's Presence during Childbirth? In Pierce, G. R., Lakey, B., Sarason, I. G., & Sarason, B. R. (Eds.), *Sourcebook of Social Support and Personality* (pp. 93–106). New York: Plenum Press.

Knipscheer, C. P. M., & Antonucci, T. C. (1990). *Network Research: Substantive Issues and Methodological Questions.* Amsterdam: Swets & Zeitlinger.

Kogovšek, T., & Hlebec, V. (2008). Measuring ego-centered social networks: do cheaper methods respondent burden provide good estimates of network composition? *Metodološki zvezki, 5*(2), 127-143.

Kogovšek, T., & Hlebec, V. (2009). Stability of typologies produced on the basis of repeated measurement with the role relationship and the name generator approach. *Metodološki zvezki, 6*(2), 85-97.

Laireiter, A., & Baumann, U. (1992). Network structures and support functions - Theoretical and empirical analyses. In Veiel, H. O. F., & Baumann, U. (Eds.), *The Meaning and Measurement of Social Support* (pp. 33–56). New York: Hemisphere Publishing Corporation.

Procidano, M. E., & Heller, K. (1983). Measures of perceived social support from friends and from family: Three validation studies. *American Journal of Community Psychology, 11*(1), 1–24. doi:10.1007/BF00898416

Sarason, B. R., Pierce, G. R., & Sarason, I. G. (1990). Social support: The sense of acceptance and the role of relationships. In Sarason, B. R., Sarason, I. G., & Pierce, G. R. (Eds.), *Social Support: An Interactional View* (pp. 97–128). New York: Wiley.

Sarason, B. R., Sarason, I. G., & Pierce, G. R. (1990a). *Social Support: An Interactional View.* New York: John Wiley & Sons.

Sarason, B. R., Sarason, I. G., & Pierce, G. R. (1990b). Traditional views of social support and their impact on assessment. In Sarason, B. R., Sarason, I. G., & Pierce, G. R. (Eds.), *Social Support: An Interactional View* (pp. 9–25). New York: Wiley.

Sarason, I. G., Levine, H. M., Basham, R. B., & Sarason, B. R. (1983). Assessing social support: The social support questionnaire. *Journal of Personality and Social Psychology, 44*, 127–139. doi:10.1037/0022-3514.44.1.127

Sarason, I. G., Sarason, B. R., & Pierce, G. R. (1994a). Relationship-specific social support: Toward a model for the analysis of supportive interactions. In Burleson, B. R., Albrecht, T. L., & Sarason, I. G. (Eds.), *Communication of Social Support: Messages, Interactions, Relationships, and Community* (pp. 91–112). Thousand Oaks: Sage Publications.

Sarason, I. G., Sarason, B. R., & Pierce, G. R. (1994b). Social support: Global and relationship-based levels of analysis. *Journal of Social and Personal Relationships, 11*(2), 295–312. doi:10.1177/0265407594112008

Thoits, P. A. (1985). Social Support and Psychological Well-Being: Theoretical Possibilities. In I. G Sarason & B. R. Sarason (Eds.), *Social Support: Theory, Research and Applications* (51-72). Dordrecht: Martinus Nijhoff Publishers.

Van der Poel, M. G. M. (1993). *Personal Networks.* Lisse: Swets and Zeitlinger.

Vaux, A. (1988). *Social Support: Theory, Research, and Intervention.* New York: Praeger.

Vaux, A. (1992). Assessment of social support. In Veiel, H. O. F., & Baumann, U. (Eds.), *The Meaning and Measurement of Social Support* (pp. 193–216). New York: Hemisphere.

Weiss, R. S. (1974). The provisions of social relationships. In Rubin, Z. (Ed.), *Doing unto Others* (pp. 17–26). Englewood Cliffs: Prentice-Hall.

## KEY TERMS AND DEFINITIONS

**Social Support Networks:** Vaux (1988, pp. 28-29) defines the social support network as a subset of the larger social network to which ego turns or could turn for assistance. Support networks, that is, social support network resources, are assumed to be stable in terms of size and composition, except in times of developmental transitions or non-normative life changes.

**Support Behaviors:** Support behaviors on the other hand are specific acts generally recognized as intentional efforts to help a person. Not every supportive behavior is helpful. Helpfulness depends on proper timing and mode of support as well as on relationship with the support provider.

**Support Appraisals:** Support appraisals are subjective evaluative assessments of support resources and behaviors. They are primary indicators of how effectively support functions are fulfilled.

**The Name Generator Approach for Measuring Social Support Networks:** It asks of a respondent directly to name actual persons in his/her network. Usually also a broad range of other information is collected about the obtained network members (e.g., type of relationship, strength of tie, network members' personal characteristics and so on).

**The Role Relation Approach for Measuring Social Networks:** Network members are represented only as role relationships and typically, only the first two important persons are obtained and that with the help of a showcard with possible role relations listed, is cheaper, simpler to administer and less burdensome for respondents.

**The Buffering Effects Hypothesis of Social Support:** It states that social support is effective only during stressful events (e.g., death of a close family member, divorce, moving to another place etc.).

**The Main Effect Hypothesis:** It holds that social support also influences behavior and well-being in nonstressful situations.

**Multiple Classification Analysis (MCA):** (Andrews et al., 1973) MCA is a multivariate method by which relationships between multiple independent variables (or predictors) and a dependent variable are analyzed. It is similar to multiple regression, with the advantage that nominal measurement level variables need not be dichotomized.

## ENDNOTES

[1] Perceived support is part of a support appraisal. It refers to the perception that social support is available when needed – it refers to the availability of support, whereas a social support appraisal may include several other evaluative dimensions.

[2] Examples of the question response formats (ISSP short and long version and EQLS short version) are found in Appendix 1, while the question wording for social support provision in the ISSP version is presented in Appendix 2.

[3] To enable comparison within the same model, the long response format had to be adapted to the short response format. Husband/wife/partner, mother, father, daughter, son, sister, brother, grand-mother/father, grand-daughter/son, other kin – my family and other kin – partner's family were pooled into one family category.

## APPENDIX 1

Examples of survey questions:

An example of the general social support approach using the long response format.

*First, we would like to ask you who you would ask for help in some cases, when help is usually needed.*

A1. Some tasks in the apartment or in the garden a person cannot do by him/herself. It may happen that you need someone to hold a ladder for you or help you move furniture.
    A.    Who would you ask for help first?
    B.    Who would you ask for help second?

|  | FIRST | SECOND |
|---|---|---|
| Husband/wife/partner | 01 | 01 |
| Mother | 02 | 02 |
| Father | 03 | 03 |
| Daughter | 04 | 04 |
| Son | 05 | 05 |
| Sister | 06 | 06 |
| Brother | 07 | 07 |
| Grand-mother / father | 08 | 08 |
| Grand-daughter / son | 09 | 09 |
| Other kin – my family | 10 | 10 |
| Other kin – partner's family | 11 | 11 |
| Good friend | 12 | 12 |
| Neighbor | 13 | 13 |
| Co-worker | 14 | 14 |
| Someone else (who) _____ | 15 | 15 |
| No one | 16 | 16 |

An example of the general social support approach using the short response format.

A2. Say you have the flu and have to rest for a few days. You need help with various household tasks such as shopping and similar.
    A.    Who would you ask for help first?
    B.    Who would you ask for help second?

|  | FIRST | SECOND |
|---|---|---|
| Family member | 01 | 01 |
| Co-worker | 02 | 02 |
| Friend | 03 | 03 |
| Neighbor | 04 | 04 |
| Someone else | 05 | 05 |
| No one | 06 | 06 |

An example of the event-related approach using the short response format.

Various things are happening to us in our lives. Which of the listed *life events* have you personally already experienced? For events you have experienced, please indicate *who helped you the most at that time*. If an event has not happened to you yet, think who would help you the most at that time.

(For each event the respondent must choose ONE response)

|  | Family member | Co-worker | Friend | Neighbor | Someone else | No one |
|---|---|---|---|---|---|---|
| Wedding | 1 | 2 | 3 | 4 | 5 | 6 |
| Difficulties with a boss | 1 | 2 | 3 | 4 | 5 | 6 |
| Death of a close family member | 1 | 2 | 3 | 4 | 5 | 6 |
| Change of personal habits | 1 | 2 | 3 | 4 | 5 | 6 |
| Death of a close friend | 1 | 2 | 3 | 4 | 5 | 6 |
| Pregnancy | 1 | 2 | 3 | 4 | 5 | 6 |
| Great changes in health/behavior of family members | 1 | 2 | 3 | 4 | 5 | 6 |
| Great changes in financial state | 1 | 2 | 3 | 4 | 5 | 6 |
| Birth of a new family member | 1 | 2 | 3 | 4 | 5 | 6 |
| Living changes (moving, renovation of a home) | 1 | 2 | 3 | 4 | 5 | 6 |
| Great changes in religious activity | 1 | 2 | 3 | 4 | 5 | 6 |
| Change at the workplace | 1 | 2 | 3 | 4 | 5 | 6 |
| Great personal injustice or disease | 1 | 2 | 3 | 4 | 5 | 6 |
| Great changes in living conditions | 1 | 2 | 3 | 4 | 5 | 6 |
| Retirement | 1 | 2 | 3 | 4 | 5 | 6 |

The event-related approach using the long response format is exactly the same as the short response format except for the long list of answer categories (see the first example).

## APPENDIX 2

Question wording of the general social support network indicators

1. There are some tasks in the apartment or in the garden that a person cannot do by him/herself. It may happen that you need someone to hold a ladder for you or help you move furniture. Who would you ask for help first? Who would you ask for help as a second choice? (instrumental support)

2. Say you have the flu and have to rest for a few days. You would need help with various household tasks such as shopping and similar. Who would you ask for help first? Who would you ask for help as a second choice? (instrumental support)

3. Now imagine you need to borrow a larger sum of money. Who would you ask for help first? Who would you ask for help as a second choice? (instrumental support)

4. Say you have problems in your relationship with your husband/wife/partner – problems you cannot solve on your own. Who would you ask for help first? Who would you ask for help as a second choice? Even if you are not married and do not have a partner, try to answer what you would do in such a case. (emotional support)

5. What about the situation where you feel a little down or depressed and would like to talk to someone about it. Who would you ask for help first? Who would you ask for help as a second choice? (emotional support)

6. Say you need advice with regard to an important life decision, for instance getting a job or moving to another place. Who would you ask for help first? Who would you ask for help as a second choice? (informational support)

7. Say you have a problem at your work, for instance regarding a problem with a work task or a misunderstanding with a co-worker. Who would you ask for help first? Who would you ask for help as a second choice? (work)

# APPENDIX 3

Frequency distributions (network composition)

*Table 6. Long Response Format, General Social Support Approach*

| | N | Husband / wife / partner | Mother | Father | Daughter | Son | Sister | Brother | Grand-mother / father | Grand-daughter / son | Other kin – my family | Other kin – partner's family | Good friend | Neighbor | Co-worker | Other | No one |
|---|---|---|---|---|---|---|---|---|---|---|---|---|---|---|---|---|---|
| Help in the house-hold | 366 | **47** | 7.4 | **18.6** | 2.2 | 9.6 | 3 | 4.6 | 0 | 0.8 | 0.8 | 0 | 3 | 2.2 | 0.3 | 0.3 | 0.3 |
| Illness | 366 | **56.3** | **21.6** | 1.6 | 9.3 | 2.5 | 4.6 | 0.8 | 0.3 | 0.3 | 0.3 | 0 | 1.1 | 0.8 | 0 | 0.3 | 0.3 |
| Bor-rowing money | 366 | **20.8** | **18.9** | **21.9** | 5.2 | 6 | 3.3 | 5.7 | 0.5 | 0 | 2.5 | 0.5 | 8.5 | 0 | 0 | 1.6 | 4.6 |
| Problems with partner | 366 | **18.3** | 7.9 | 1.6 | **10.7** | 2.7 | 9.8 | 1.9 | 0.3 | 0.3 | 1.4 | 0.8 | **37.4** | 0.3 | 0.3 | 0.5 | 5.7 |
| Depres-sion | 366 | **52.2** | 4.6 | 0.3 | 6.6 | 1.4 | 5.7 | 0.5 | 0.3 | 0.3 | 0.3 | 0 | **22.4** | 0.8 | 0.5 | 0 | 4.1 |
| Advice | 366 | **60.9** | **11.5** | 7.1 | 5.2 | 2.2 | 1.4 | 1.6 | 0 | 0 | 0.8 | 0.3 | 6 | 0.3 | 0.8 | 0 | 1.9 |
| Problems at work | 312 | **11.5** | 1.6 | 1.6 | 1 | 0.3 | 2.6 | 0.3 | 0 | 0 | 0.3 | 0 | **10.3** | 0.3 | **64.4** | 4.8 | 1 |
| Gen-eral social support together | 366 | **39.8** | **10.6** | 7.7 | 6.4 | 4 | 4.4 | 2.3 | 0.2 | 0.3 | 1 | 0.2 | **12.9** | 0.8 | 8.4 | 1.1 | * |

* Not considered in calculations.

*Table 7. Long Response Format, Event-Related Approach*

| | N | Husband / wife / partner | Mother | Father | Daughter | Son | Sister | Brother | Grand-mother / father | Grand-daughter / son | Other kin – my family | Other kin – partner's family | Good friend | Neighbor | Co-worker | Other | No one |
|---|---|---|---|---|---|---|---|---|---|---|---|---|---|---|---|---|---|
| Wedding | 366 | **36.3** | 29 | 4.9 | 0.3 | 0 | **10.1** | 2.7 | 0 | 0 | 1.4 | 0.5 | 9.6 | 0 | 1.1 | 1.1 | 3 |
| Difficulties with a boss | 366 | 28.7 | 2.5 | 4.1 | 0.8 | 0 | 1.9 | 1.4 | 0 | 0 | 0.5 | 0 | **12.3** | 0 | **39.3** | 0.8 | 7.7 |
| Death of a close family member | 366 | **56.3** | **16.4** | 1.4 | 2.7 | 1.1 | 4.4 | 3.8 | 0.3 | 0 | 1.9 | 0 | 8.5 | 0 | 0 | 0.5 | 2.7 |
| Change of personal habits | 366 | **50.5** | 5.5 | 1.1 | 2.7 | 1.1 | 2.7 | 0.8 | 0.3 | 0.3 | 1.4 | 0.3 | **16.1** | 0.3 | 0 | 1.4 | **15.6** |
| Death of a close friend | 366 | **57.9** | 5.2 | 0 | 0.5 | 0.5 | 4.1 | 1.1 | 0 | 0 | 0.5 | 0 | **23.2** | 0.5 | 0.3 | 0.8 | 5.2 |
| Pregnancy | 366 | **53** | 23.2 | 1.9 | 0.3 | 0 | 4.4 | 0.3 | 0 | 0 | 1.4 | 2.7 | 6.6 | 0 | 0 | 1.6 | 4.6 |
| Great changes in health/behavior of family members | 366 | **52.5** | 16.9 | 1.9 | 3 | 1.1 | 6.3 | 1.1 | 0.3 | 0.3 | 2.7 | 0.3 | 9 | 0 | 0.5 | 0.3 | 3.8 |
| Great changes in financial state | 366 | **40.2** | 12.3 | 20.2 | 0.5 | 1.9 | 3 | 2.5 | 0.8 | 0 | 2.7 | 0.8 | 8.2 | 0 | 0.5 | 0.5 | 5.7 |
| Birth of a new family member | 366 | **58.5** | 23 | 1.4 | 0 | 0.3 | 4.6 | 1.4 | 0.5 | 0 | 2.2 | 1.4 | 3 | 0.3 | 0 | 0.3 | 3.3 |
| Living changes (moving, renovation of a home) | 365 | **58.9** | 4.4 | **14** | 0.8 | 1.9 | 2.5 | 3.3 | 0.3 | 0 | 1.6 | 1.4 | 9 | 0.5 | 0 | 0.5 | 0.8 |
| Great changes in religious activity | 365 | **27.1** | 5.8 | 1.4 | 1.4 | 0.5 | 2.7 | 0.8 | 0.8 | 0 | 0.5 | 0.8 | 9.3 | 0.3 | 0.5 | 3.6 | **44.4** |
| Change at the workplace | 366 | **31.7** | 1.6 | 2.7 | 0.5 | 0 | 2.5 | 1.1 | 0 | 0 | 1.6 | 0 | **15.3** | 0.3 | **32.8** | 2.2 | 7.7 |
| Great personal injustice or disease | 366 | **60.9** | 15 | 2.5 | 2.7 | 0.8 | 2.2 | 1.1 | 0 | 0.5 | 1.1 | 0 | 8.2 | 0 | 0.3 | 1.4 | 3.3 |
| Great changes in living conditions | 366 | **57.9** | 12.6 | 3.6 | 1.9 | 1.1 | 2.5 | 1.9 | 0.5 | 0 | 2.5 | 0 | 7.9 | 0.3 | 0.3 | 1.1 | 6 |
| Retirement | 366 | **65.3** | 1.1 | 0.8 | 3.6 | 0.8 | 1.6 | 0.8 | 0 | 0.8 | 0.5 | 0 | 6.6 | 0 | 2.5 | 1.6 | **13.9** |
| Support during stressful events together | 365 | **53.3** | 12.7 | 4.4 | 1.7 | 0.9 | 4 | 1.8 | 0.3 | 0.2 | 1.7 | 0.6 | **11.2** | 0.2 | 5.8 | 1.4 | * |

* Not considered in calculations.

*Table 8. Short Response Format, General Social Support Approach*

| | N | Family | Friends | Neighbors | Co-workers | Other | No one |
|---|---|---|---|---|---|---|---|
| Help in the household | 621 | **86.8** | 7.6 | 3.9 | 0.5 | 0.5 | 0.8 |
| Illness | 621 | **91.8** | 3.9 | 1.6 | 0 | 1.6 | 1.1 |
| Borrowing money | 621 | **71.5** | **14.7** | 0.5 | 1.9 | 7.1 | 4.3 |
| Problems with partner | 621 | **30.4** | **53.6** | 0.8 | 1.4 | 4.5 | 9.2 |
| Depression | 621 | **47.7** | **39.3** | 1.3 | 1.9 | 4.3 | 5.5 |
| Advice | 621 | **75.4** | **15.3** | 0.5 | 1.9 | 2.6 | 4.3 |
| Problems at work | 479 | 8.6 | **13.6** | 0.4 | **73.3** | 3.3 | 0.8 |
| General social support together | 620 | **63.3** | **21.8** | 1.6 | 9.7 | 3.7 | * |

* not considered in calculations

*Table 9. Short Response Format, Event-Related Approach*

| | N | Family | Friends | Neighbors | Co-workers | Other | No one |
|---|---|---|---|---|---|---|---|
| Wedding | 605 | **74.2** | **19.7** | 0.3 | 0.3 | 0.8 | 4.6 |
| Difficulties with a boss | 609 | **16.3** | **12.6** | 0 | **57.6** | 2.1 | **11.3** |
| Death of a close family member | 616 | **76.8** | **17.5** | 2.3 | 0.3 | 1.3 | 1.8 |
| Change of personal habits | 615 | **43.7** | **30.4** | 1 | 0.7 | 6.8 | **17.4** |
| Death of a close friend | 612 | **52.5** | **38.9** | 1 | 0.7 | 3.1 | 3.9 |
| Pregnancy | 608 | **73.8** | **14.1** | 0.7 | 0.7 | 5.1 | 5.6 |
| Great changes in health/behavior of family members | 610 | **59.2** | **25.9** | 1 | 0.5 | 9 | 4.4 |
| Great changes in financial state | 611 | **71.2** | **13.9** | 0.5 | 0.8 | 5.6 | 8 |
| Birth of a new family member | 615 | **85.7** | 7.2 | 0.5 | 0.7 | 1 | 5 |
| Living changes (moving, renovation of a home) | 617 | **66.1** | **24.6** | 2.8 | 1.3 | 2.1 | 3.1 |
| Great changes in religious activity | 605 | **30.6** | **18.2** | 0 | 0.2 | 12.7 | **38.3** |
| Change at the workplace | 608 | **20.4** | **11.7** | 0 | **56.9** | 2 | 9 |
| Great personal injustice or disease | 613 | **72.3** | **17.5** | 0.2 | 0.5 | 6.2 | 3.4 |
| Great changes in living conditions | 611 | **69.4** | **19.6** | 0 | 0.7 | 4.4 | 5.9 |
| Retirement | 600 | **56.5** | **12.8** | 0.7 | **10.7** | 5.2 | **14.2** |
| Support during stressful events together | 620 | **63.4** | **21** | 0.9 | 9.5 | 5.2 | * |

* not considered in calculations

# APPENDIX 4

## Multiple Classification Analyses

*Table 10. MCA, Percentage of Family in the Network*

| Family | | \multicolumn{6}{c|}{Social support} | | | | | | \multicolumn{6}{c|}{Stressful events} | | | | | |
|---|---|---|---|---|---|---|---|---|---|---|---|---|---|---|
| | | \multicolumn{3}{l}{Mean = 68.36} | Predicted Mean | Deviation | | \multicolumn{3}{l}{Mean = 70.13} | Predicted Mean | Deviation | |
| | | N | Eta | Beta | Adjusted for Factors | Adjusted for Factors | | N | Eta | Beta | Adjusted for Factors | Adjusted for Factors | |
| Method | ISSP | 366 | 0.298 | 0.292 | **76.76** | 8.40 | *** | 365 | 0.390 | 0.379 | **81.19** | 11.05 | *** |
| | EQLS | 617 | | | 63.38 | -4.98 | | 617 | | | 63.60 | -6.54 | |
| Gender | Male | 487 | 0.046 | 0.065 | 66.90 | -1.46 | ** | 485 | 0.051 | 0.077 | 68.40 | -1.74 | *** |
| | Female | 496 | | | **69.79** | 1.43 | | 497 | | | **71.83** | 1.70 | |
| Age | 18 - 29 | 334 | 0.217 | 0.208 | 63.87 | -4.49 | *** | 335 | 0.169 | 0.137 | 66.31 | -3.82 | *** |
| | 30 - 49 | 319 | | | 66.56 | -1.80 | | 319 | | | 70.38 | 0.24 | |
| | 50 + | 330 | | | **74.64** | 6.28 | | 328 | | | **73.80** | 3.67 | |
| Marital status | Has a partner | 718 | 0.132 | 0.091 | **69.58** | 1.22 | *** | 717 | 0.200 | 0.150 | **72.18** | 2.04 | *** |
| | Other | 265 | | | 65.05 | -3.31 | | 265 | | | 64.60 | -5.53 | |
| Multiple R² | | | | 0.147 | | | | | | 0.204 | | | |

*Table 11. MCA, Percentage of Friends in the Network*

| Friend | | \multicolumn{6}{c|}{Social support} | | | | | | \multicolumn{6}{c|}{Stressful events} | | | | | |
|---|---|---|---|---|---|---|---|---|---|---|---|---|---|---|
| | | \multicolumn{3}{l}{Mean = 18.48} | Predicted Mean | Deviation | | \multicolumn{3}{l}{Mean = 17.31} | Predicted Mean | Deviation | |
| | | N | Eta | Beta | Adjusted for Factors | Adjusted for Factors | | N | Eta | Beta | Adjusted for Factors | Adjusted for Factors | |
| Method | ISSP | 366 | 0.228 | 0.224 | 12.99 | -5.49 | *** | 365 | 0.257 | 0.246 | 11.45 | -5.86 | *** |
| | EQLS | 617 | | | **21.74** | 3.26 | | 617 | | | **20.78** | 3.47 | |
| Gender | Male | 487 | 0.010 | 0.029 | **19.04** | 0.55 | | 485 | 0.012 | 0.042 | **18.09** | 0.78 | |
| | Female | 496 | | | 17.94 | -0.54 | | 497 | | | 16.55 | -0.76 | |
| Age | 18 - 29 | 334 | 0.256 | 0.239 | **24.38** | 5.90 | *** | 335 | 0.254 | 0.213 | **22.45** | 5.14 | *** |
| | 30 - 49 | 319 | | | 17.46 | -1.03 | | 319 | | | 16.26 | -1.05 | |
| | 50 + | 330 | | | 13.51 | -4.98 | | 328 | | | 13.09 | -4.22 | |
| Marital status | Has a partner | 718 | 0.149 | 0.077 | 17.60 | -0.88 | ** | 717 | 0.233 | 0.166 | 15.46 | -1.85 | *** |
| | Other | 265 | | | **20.88** | 2.39 | | 265 | | | **22.32** | 5.01 | |
| Multiple R² | | | | 0.124 | | | | | | 0.156 | | | |

*Table 12. MCA, Percentage of Neighbors in the Network*

| Neighbor | | Social support | | | | | | Stressful events | | | | | |
|---|---|---|---|---|---|---|---|---|---|---|---|---|---|
| | | Mean = 1.27 | | | Predicted Mean | Deviation | | Mean = 0.609 | | | Predicted Mean | Deviation | |
| | | N | Eta | Beta | Adjusted for Factors | Adjusted for Factors | | N | Eta | Beta | Adjusted for Factors | Adjusted for Factors | |
| Method | ISSP | 366 | 0.057 | 0.046 | 0.86 | -0.41 | | 365 | 0.122 | 0.116 | 0.21 | -0,40 | *** |
| | EQLS | 617 | | | **1.52** | 0.24 | | 617 | | | **0.85** | 0,24 | |
| Gender | Male | 487 | 0.029 | 0.039 | **1.54** | 0.27 | | 485 | 0.057 | 0.062 | **0.78** | 0,17 | ** |
| | Female | 496 | | | 1.00 | -0.27 | | 497 | | | 0.45 | -0,16 | |
| Age | 18 - 29 | 334 | 0.168 | 0.183 | -0.09 | -1.36 | *** | 335 | 0.176 | 0.184 | 0.09 | -0,51 | *** |
| | 30 - 49 | 319 | | | 0.98 | -0.29 | | 319 | | | 0.48 | -0,13 | |
| | 50 + | 330 | | | **2.93** | 1.66 | | 328 | | | **1.26** | 0,66 | |
| Marital status | Has a partner | 718 | 0.100 | 0.130 | 0.73 | -0.54 | *** | 717 | 0.048 | 0.075 | 0.49 | -0,12 | ** |
| | Other | 265 | | | **2.74** | 1.47 | | 265 | | | **0.94** | 0,33 | |
| Multiple R² | | | | 0.047 | | | | | | 0.053 | | | |

*Table 13. MCA, Percentage of Co-Workers in the Network*

| Co-worker | | Social support | | | | | | Stressful events | | | | | |
|---|---|---|---|---|---|---|---|---|---|---|---|---|---|
| | | Mean = 9.14 | | | Predicted Mean | Deviation | | Mean = 8.14 | | | Predicted Mean | Deviation | |
| | | N | Eta | Beta | Adjusted for Factors | Adjusted for Factors | | N | Eta | Beta | Adjusted for Factors | Adjusted for Factors | |
| Method | ISSP | 366 | 0.069 | 0.076 | 8.29 | -0.85 | ** | 365 | 0.248 | 0.249 | 5.77 | -2.38 | |
| | EQLS | 617 | | | **9.65** | 0.51 | | 617 | | | **9.55** | 1.41 | |
| Gender | Male | 487 | 0.027 | 0.022 | **9.34** | 0.19 | | 485 | 0.091 | 0.091 | **8.82** | 0.68 | *** |
| | Female | 496 | | | 8.96 | -0.19 | | 497 | | | 7.48 | -0.66 | |
| Age | 18 - 29 | 334 | 0.318 | 0.312 | 9.75 | 0.61 | *** | 335 | 0.049 | 0.045 | 7.96 | -0.18 | *** |
| | 30 - 49 | 319 | | | **12.18** | 3.04 | | 319 | | | **8.61** | 0.47 | |
| | 50 + | 330 | | | 5.59 | -3.55 | | 328 | | | 7.87 | -0.27 | |
| Marital status | Has a partner | 718 | 0.094 | 0.074 | **9.54** | 0.39 | ** | 717 | 0.011 | 0.009 | **8.18** | 0.04 | |
| | Other | 265 | | | 8.09 | -1.06 | | 265 | | | 8.03 | -0.11 | |
| Multiple R² | | | | 0.112 | | | | | | 0.072 | | | |

*Table 14. MCA, Percentage of Others in the Network*

| Other | | \multicolumn{6}{c}{*Social support*} | | \multicolumn{6}{c}{*Stressful events*} | |
|---|---|---|---|---|---|---|---|---|---|---|---|---|---|
| | | \multicolumn{3}{c}{Mean = 2.74} | Predicted Mean | Deviation | | \multicolumn{3}{c}{Mean = 3.80} | Predicted Mean | Deviation | |
| | | N | Eta | Beta | Adjusted for Factors | Adjusted for Factors | | N | Eta | Beta | Adjusted for Factors | Adjusted for Factors | |
| Method | ISSP | 366 | 0.152 | 0.149 | 1.10 | -1.64 | *** | 365 | 0.203 | 0.201 | 1.39 | -2.41 | *** |
| | EQLS | 617 | | | **3.71** | 0.97 | | 617 | | | **5.23** | 1.43 | |
| Gender | Male | 487 | 0.048 | 0.051 | **3.18** | 0.44 | | 485 | 0.010 | 0.013 | **3.92** | 0.12 | |
| | Female | 496 | | | 2.31 | -0.43 | | 497 | | | 3.69 | -0.11 | |
| Age | 18 - 29 | 334 | 0.056 | 0.061 | 2.08 | -0.65 | | 335 | 0.045 | 0.050 | 3.19 | -0.62 | |
| | 30 - 49 | 319 | | | 2.81 | 0.07 | | 319 | | | **4.27** | 0.47 | |
| | 50 + | 330 | | | **3.33** | 0.59 | | 328 | | | 3.98 | 0.17 | |
| Marital status | Has a partner | 718 | 0.028 | 0.036 | 2.55 | -0.19 | | 717 | 0.018 | 0.020 | 3.69 | -0.11 | |
| | Other | 265 | | | **3.24** | 0.51 | | 265 | | | **4.11** | 0.30 | |
| Multiple R² | | | | 0.029 | | | | | | 0.044 | | | |

[1] Perceived support is part of a support appraisal. It refers to the perception that social support is available when needed – it refers to the availability of support, whereas a social support appraisal may include several other evaluative dimensions.

[2] Examples of the question response formats (ISSP short and long version and EQLS short version) are found in Appendix 1, while the question wording for social support provision in the ISSP version is presented in Appendix 2.

[3] To enable comparison within the same model, the long response format had to be adapted to the short response format. Husband/wife/partner, mother, father, daughter, son, sister, brother, grand-mother/father, grand-daughter/son, other kin – my family and other kin – partner's family were pooled into one family category.

# Compilation of References

Abbasi, R., Chernov, S., Nejdl, W., Paiu, R., & Staab, S. (2009). *Exploiting Flickr Tags and Groups for Finding Landmark Photos.* In proceedings of the 31st European Conference on Information Retrieval Research. Springer-Verlag, Berlin, Heidelberg, pp. 654-661.

Ackland, R. (2005). *Estimating the Size of Political Web Graphs.* Retrieved from http://acsr.anu.edu.au/ staff/ackland /papers/ political webgraphs.pdf.

Ackland, R. (2005b). *Mapping the U.S. Political Blogosphere: Are Conservative Bloggers More Prominent?* Retrieved from http://acsr.anu.edu.au/ staff/ackland/ papers/ polblogs.pdf.

Ackland, R., & Gibson, R. (2004). Mapping Political Party Networks on the WWW. *Australian Electronic Governance Conference*, April 14-15, Melbourne, Australia.

Adamic, L. A., & Adar, E. (2003). Friends and neighbors on the web. *Social Networks, 25*(3), 211–230. doi:10.1016/S0378-8733(03)00009-1

Adamic, L. A., & Huberman, B. A. (2000). Power-law distribution of the World Wide Web. *Science, 287*, A2115. doi:10.1126/science.287.5461.2115a

Adamic, L. A., & Glance, N. (2005). *The political blogosphere and the 2004 U.S. election: divided they blog.* Paper presented at the Proceedings of the 3rd international workshop on Link discovery.

Adar, E., & Adamic, L. A. (2005). *Tracking information epidemics in blogspace.* Paper presented at the Web Intelligence, 2005. Proceedings. The 2005 IEEE/WIC/ACM International Conference on.

Agarwal, N., & Liu, H. (2009). *Modeling and Data Mining in Blogosphere* (Vol. 1). Morgan & Claypol Publishers. A · eur, E., Brassard, G., Fernandez, J., & Mani Onana, F. (2006). Privacy preserving demographic filtering. *Proceedings of the ACM Symposium on Applied Computing (SAC'06),* (pp. 872-878).

Agell, N., Rovira, X., & Ansotegui, C. (2000). Homogenising references in orders of magnitude spaces: An application to credit risk prediction. In *Proceedings of International Workshop on Qualitative Reasoning* (pp. 1-8).

Ahuja, R. K., Magnanti, T. L., & Orlin, J. B. (1993). *Network Flows: Theory, Algorithms, and Applications.* Upper Saddle River, NJ: Prentice Hall.

Aimeur, E., Brassard, G., Fernandez, J., & Mani Onana, F. (n.d) *Privacy preserving demographic filtering.* In Proc. SAC'06.

Ajzen, I. (1988). Attitude Structure and Behavior Relations. In Partkanis, A. R., Berckler, S. T., & Greenwald, A. G. (Eds.), *Attitude Structure and Function.* Hillsdale, NJ: Erlbaum.

Akoglu, L., & Faloutsos, C. (2009). RTG: A recursive realistic graph generator using random typing. *Data Mining and Knowledge Discovery, 19*(2), 194–209. doi:10.1007/s10618-009-0140-7

Akoglu, L., & Dalvi, B. (2010). *Structure, tie persistence and event detection in large phone and SMS networks.* Paper presented at the Proceedings of the Eighth Workshop on Mining and Learning with Graphs.

Alani, H., Dasmahapatra, S., O'Hara, K., & Shadbolt, N. (2002). Identifying communities of practice through ontology network analysis. *IEEE Intelligent Systems, 18*(2), 18–25. doi:10.1109/MIS.2003.1193653

Albert, R., A. L. (2002). Statistical mechanics of complex networks. *Reviews of Modern Physics, 74*(1), 47–97. doi:10.1103/RevModPhys.74.47

Albert, R., Jeong, H., & Barabási, A. L. (2000). Error and attack tolerance of complex networks. *Nature, 406*, 378–382. doi:10.1038/35019019

Aliakbary, S., Abolhassani, H., Rahmani, H., & Nobakht, B. (2009). Web page classification using social tags. *IEEE International Conference on Computational Science and Engineering, 4* (pp. 588-593. Vancouver, BC, Canada. IEEE Computer Society 2009. Crammer, K., & Singer, Y. (2002). On the algorithmic implementation of multi-class kernel-based vector machines. *Journal of Machine Learning Research, 2*, 265–292.

Allen, R.B., (1990). User models: theory, method and Practice. *International Journal of Man–Machine Studies.*

Alwitt, L. (1996). *The Low-Income Consumer: Adjusting the Balance of Exchange*. New York: Sage Publications, Inc.

Amer-Yahia, S., Lakshmanan, L., & Yu, C. (2009). Social-Scope: Enabling Information Discovery on Social Content Sites. *CIDR'09: Proceedings of the biennial Conference on Innovative Data Systems Research.*

Ananthakrishna, R., Chaudhuri, S., & Ganti, V. (2002). *Eliminating fuzzy duplicates in data warehouses.* Paper presented at the Proceedings of the 28th international conference on Very Large Data Bases.

Ancona, D. G., & Caldwell, D. F. (1992). Demography and Design: Predictors of New Product Team Performance. *Organization Science, 3*(3), 321–341. doi:10.1287/orsc.3.3.321

Anderson, E. (2005). *Everyone eats: understanding food and culture*. New York: New York University Press.

Anderson, P. W. (1972). More is different. *Science, 177*, 393–396. doi:10.1126/science.177.4047.393

Andrews, J. E., Pearce, K. A., Sydney, C., Ireson, C., & Love, M. (2004). Current State of Information Technology Use in a US Primary Care Practice-based Research Network. *Informatics in Primary Care, 12*(1), 11–18.

Andrews, R. L., & Currim, I. S. (2003). A Comparison of Segment Retention Criteria for Finite Mixture Logit Models. *JMR, Journal of Marketing Research, 40*(4), 235–243. doi:10.1509/jmkr.40.2.235.19225

Archives, F. A. Q. (2008). *Religion and Dietary Practices.* Available: http://www.faqs.org/nutrition/ Pre-Sma/Religion-and-Dietary-Practices.html

Backstrom, L., Huttenlocher, D., Lan, X., & Kleinberg, J. (2006). Group formation in large social networks: Membership, growth, and evolution. In *Proceedings of the 12th ACM SIGKDD International Conference on Knowledge Discovery and Data Mining*(SIGKDD'06).

Badia, A., & Kantardzic, M. M. (2005). Link analysis tools for intelligence and counterterrorism. In *Proceedings of IEEE International Conference on Intelligence and Security Informatics* (pp. 49-59).

Bagga, A., & Baldwin, B. (1998). Entity-based cross-document coreferencing using the vector space model. In *Proceedings of Annual Meeting of Association for Computational Linguistics*, (pp. 79-85).

Bagozzi, R. P. (1975). Marketing as an Exchange. *Journal of Marketing, 39*(4), 32–39. doi:10.2307/1250593

Bainbridge, W. S. (2007). The Scientific Research Potential of Virtual Worlds. [http://dx.doi.org/10.1126/science.1146930]. *Science, 317*(5837), 472–476. doi:10.1126/science.1146930

Barabasi, A. L., & Albert, R. (1999). Emergence of scaling in random networks. *Science, 286*(5439), 509. doi:10.1126/science.286.5439.509

Barabási, A. L. (2002). *Linked: The new science of networks*. Cambridge, MA: Perseus Publishing.

Barabási, A. L., Ravasz, E., & Vicsek, T. (2001). Deterministic scale-free networks. *Physica A, 299*, 559–564. doi:10.1016/S0378-4371(01)00369-7

Barley, S. R. (1990). The Alignment of Technology and Structure through Roles and Networks. *Administrative Science Quarterly, 35*(1), (Special Issue: Technology, Organizations, and Innovation) 61-103.

Baroni, M., Matiasek, J., & Trost, H. (2002). Unsupervised discovery of morphologically related words based on orthographic and semantic similarity. In *Proceedings of the ACL-02 workshop on Morphological and phonological learning* (pp. 48-57).

Barrat, A., Barthélemy, M., Pastor-Satorras, R., & Vespignani, A. (2004). The architecture of complex weighted networks. *Proceedings of the National Academy of Sciences of the United States of America, 101*(11), 3747–3752. doi:10.1073/pnas.0400087101

Barthelemy, M., & Amaral, L. A. N. (1999). Small world networks: evidence for a crossover picture. *Physical Review Letters, 82,* 3180–3183. doi:10.1103/PhysRevLett.82.3180

Batagelj, V., & Mrvar, A. (1998). Pajek - Program for large network analysis. *Connections, 21*(2), 47–57.

Batchelder, E. (2002). Comparing three simultaneous measurements of a sociocognitive network. *Social Networks, 24*(3), 261–277. doi:10.1016/S0378-8733(02)00007-2

Batra, R., & Ray, M. (1986). Affective Responses Mediating Acceptance of Advertising. *The Journal of Consumer Research, 13*(2), 234–250. doi:10.1086/209063

Bechhofer, S., Harmelen, F., Hendler, J., & Patel-Schneider, P. (2004). OWL Web Ontology Language Reference, W3C Recommendation.

Benevenuto, F., Magno, G., Rodrigues, T., & Almeida, V. (2010). *Detecting spammers on Twitter, Collaboration, Electronic messaging.* Anti-Abuse and Spam Conference, CEAS, July.

Benjelloun, O., et al. (2006). *Generic Entity Resolution in the SERF Project.*

Berger-Wolf, T. Y., & Saia, J. (2006). *A framework for analysis of dynamic social networks.* In Proceedings of the 12th ACM SIGKDD International Conference on Knowledge Discovery and Data Mining (KDD '06), Philadelphia, USA (pp. 523-528).

Bernard, H. R., Johnsen, E. C., Killworth, P. D., McCarty, C., Shelley, G. A., & Robinson, S. (1990). Comparing four different methods for measuring personal social networks. *Social Networks, 12*(3), 179–215. doi:10.1016/0378-8733(90)90005-T

Bernard, H. R., Killworth, P., Kronenfeld, D., & Sailer, L. (1984). The problem of informant accuracy: The validity of retrospective data. *Annual Review of Anthropology, 13,* 495–517. doi:10.1146/annurev.an.13.100184.002431

Bernard, H. R., Killworth, P. D., Kronenfeld, D., & Sailer, L. (1985). On the Validity of Retrospective Data. *Annual Review of Anthropology, 13,* 495–517. doi:10.1146/annurev.an.13.100184.002431

Bernstein, A., Clearwater, S., Hill, S., Perlich, C., & Provost, F. (2002). *Discovering knowledge from relational data extracted from business news.* In SIGKDD-2002 Workshop on Multi-Relational Data Mining.

Berry, M. W., & Castellanos, M. (Eds.). (2008). *Survey of Text Mining II: Clustering, Classification, and Retrieval.* New York: Springer.

Bertot, J. C., Jaeger, P. T., Munson, S., & Glaisyer, T. (2010). Social Media Technology and Government Transparency. *IEEE Computer Society, 43*(11), 53–59.

Bhattacharya, I., & Getoor, L. (2007). Collective entity resolution in relational data. [http://dx.doi.org/http://doi.acm.org/10.1145/1217299.1217304]. *ACM Trans. Knowl. Discov. Data, 1*(1), 5. doi:10.1145/1217299.1217304

Bianconi, G., & Barabási, A. L. (2001). Competition and multiscaling in evolving networks. *Europhysics Letters, 54,* 436–442. doi:10.1209/epl/i2001-00260-6

Biel, A. L. (1990). Love the Ad. Buy the Product? *ADMAP, 26*(9), 141–154.

Bilenko, M., Mooney, R., Cohen, W., Ravikumar, P., & Fienberg, S. (2003). Adaptive name matching in information integration. *IEEE Intelligent Systems, 18*(5), 16–23. doi:10.1109/MIS.2003.1234765

Bilenko, M., Basu, S., & Sahami, M. (2005). *Adaptive Product Normalization: Using Online Learning for Record Linkage in Comparison Shopping.* Paper presented at the ICDM '05: Proceedings of the Fifth IEEE International Conference on Data Mining.

Blumstein, P., & Kollock, P. (1988). Personal relationships. *Annual Review of Sociology, 14,* 467–490. doi:10.1146/annurev.so.14.080188.002343

Boccaletti, S., Latora, V., Moreno, Y., Chavez, M., & Hwang, D. U. (2006). Complex networks: Structure and dynamics. *Physics Reports*, *424*(4-5), 175–308. doi:10.1016/j.physrep.2005.10.009

Bodon, F. (2003). A fast apriori implementation. *Proceedings of the IEEE ICDM Workshop on Frequent Itemset Mining Implementations (FIMI'03), volume 90 of CEUR Workshop Proceedings*. Melbourne, Florida, USA.

Boginski, V., Butenko, S., & Pardalos, P. M. (2006). Mining market data: A network approach. *Computers & Operations Research*, *33*(11), 3171–3184. doi:10.1016/j.cor.2005.01.027

Boll, S. (2007). Multitube-where web 2.0 and multimedia could meet. *IEEE MultiMedia*, *14*(1), 9–13. doi:10.1109/MMUL.2007.17

Bollobas, B. (Ed.). (1998). *Modern Graph Theory*. New York, NY: Springer.

Bolton, R., & Saxena-Iyer, S. (2009). Interactive services: a framework, synthesis and research directions. *Journal of Interactive Marketing*, *23*(1), 91–104. doi:10.1016/j.intmar.2008.11.002

Bonacich, P. (2007). Some unique properties of eigenvector centrality. *Social Networks*, *29*(4), 555–564. doi:10.1016/j.socnet.2007.04.002

Boongoen, T., & Shen, Q. (2010). Nearest-neighbor guided evaluation of data reliability and its applications. *IEEE Transactions on Systems, Man and Cybernetics. Part B*, *40*(6), 1622–1633.

Boongoen, T., Shen, Q., & Price, C. (2010). Disclosing false identity through hybrid link analysis. *AI and Law*, *18*(1), 77–102.

Boongoen, T., Shang, C., Iam-On, N., & Shen, Q. (2011) Extending data reliability measure to a filter approach for soft subspace clustering. To appear in *IEEE Transactions on Systems, Man and Cybernetics, Part B: Cybernetics*.

Boose, J. H. (1986). *Expertise Transfer for Expert System Design*. Amsterdam: Elsevier.

Borgatti, S. P., & Foster, P. C. (2003). The network paradigm in organizational research: A review and typology. *Journal of Management*, *29*, 991–1013.

Borgatti, S. P. (2005). Centrality and network flow. *Social Networks*, *27*, 55–71. doi:10.1016/j.socnet.2004.11.008

Borgatti, S. P., Everett, M. G., & Freeman, L. C. (2002). *UCINET for windows: Software for social network analysis*. Harvard, MA: Analytic Technologies.

Borgatti, S. P., & Foster, P. C. (2003). The network paradigm in organizational research: A review and typology. *Journal of Management*, *29*(6), 991–1013.

Borgatti, S. P., & Molina, J. L. (2003). Ethical and strategic issues in organizational social network analysis. *The Journal of Applied Behavioral Science*, *20*(10), 1–13.

Borgatti, S. P. (2002). *NetDraw: Graph visualization software [computer program]*. Harvard, MA: Analytic Technologies.

Bourdieu, P. (1989). *The Logic of Practice*. Cambridge: Polity.

Boyd, D. M., & Ellison, N. B. (2008). Social Network Sites: Definition, History, and Scholarship. *Journal of Computer-Mediated Communication*, *13*(1), 210–230. doi:10.1111/j.1083-6101.2007.00393.x

Brass, D. J., Galaskiewicz, J., Greve, H. R., & Tsai, W. (2004). Taking stock of networks and organizations: A multilevel perspective. *Academy of Management Journal*, *47*, 795–817. doi:10.2307/20159624

Breese, J., Heckerman, D., & Kadie, C. (1998). *Empirical analysis of predictive algorithms for collaborative Filtering*. In *Proc. the 14th Conference on Uncertainty in Artificial Intelligence*, pp. 43–52.

Breiger, R. L. (1999). The analysis of social networks. *Physical Review Letters*, *82*, 505–526.

Breiman, L. (2001). Random forests. *Machine Learning*, *45*(1), 5–32. doi:10.1023/A:1010933404324

Brieman, L., Friedman, J., Olshen, R., & Stone, C. (1984). *Classification and Regression Trees*. Belmont, CA: Wadsworth International Group.

Brin, S. & Page, L. (1998). The anatomy of a large-scale hypertextual Web search engine. *Computer Networks and ISDN Systems*, *30*(1–7), pp. 107–117.

Broder, A., & Josifovski, F. (2010). *Computational Advertising.* Retrieved November 10, 2010, from http://www.stanford.edu/ class/msande239.

Brooks, C., & Montanez, N. (2006). Improved annotation of the blogosphere via auto-tagging and hierarchical clustering. *Proceedings of the Fifteenth International Conference on World Wide Web*, (pp. 625–632). New York.

Brüggen, E., & Dholakia, U. M. (2010). Determinants of participation and response effort in web panel surveys. *Journal of Interactive Marketing, 24*(3), 239–250. doi:10.1016/j.intmar.2010.04.004

Bryant, C., & Dewait, K. (2003). *The Cultural Feast: An Introduction to Food and Society.* CA: Thomson Wadsworth.

Buechi, M., Borthwick, A., Winkel, A., & Goldberg, A. (2003). Cluemaker: A language for approximate record matching. In *Proceedings of Eighth International Conference on Information Quality* (pp. 207-223).

Burk, W. J., Steglich, C. E. G., & Snijders, T. A. B. (2007). Beyond dyadic interdependence: Actor-oriented models for co-evolving social networks and individual behaviors. *International Journal of Behavioral Development, 31*, 397–404. doi:10.1177/0165025407077762

Burt, R. S. (1984). Network items and the general social survey. *Social Networks, 6*(4), 293–339. doi:10.1016/0378-8733(84)90007-8

Burt, R. S. (1995). *Structural holes: The social structure of competition.* Cambridge, MA: Harvard University Press.

Butler, B. S. (2001). Membership Size, Communication Activity, and Sustainability: A Resource-Based Model of Online Social Structures. *Information Systems Research, 12*(4), 346–362. doi:10.1287/isre.12.4.346.9703

Butlersguild (2008). *Food Restrictions* [Online]. The International Guild of Professional Butlers, Netherlands. Available: http://www.butlersguild.com/ index.php?subject=103

Calado, P., Cristo, M., Goncalves, M. A., de Moura, E. S., Ribeiro-Neto, B. A., & Ziviani, N. (2006). Link-based similarity measures for the classification of web documents. *Journal of the American Society for Information Science and Technology, 57*(2), 208–221. doi:10.1002/asi.20266

Caldarelli, G. (2007). *Scale-Free Networks.* Oxford: Oxford University Press. doi:10.1093/acprof:oso/9780199211517.001.0001

Campesato, O. (2004). *Fundamentals of SVG Programming.* Hingham, MA: Charles River Media.

Cannell, C. F., Marquis, K. H., & Laurent, A. (1977). A summary of studies of interviewing methodology. *Vital and health statistics. Series 2, Data evaluation and methods research, 69*(69).

Carley, K. M. (1991). A theory of group stability. *American Sociological Review, 56*(3), 331–354. doi:10.2307/2096108

Carley, K. M. (1995). Communication technologies and their effect on cultural homogeneity, consensus, and the diffusion of new ideas. *Sociological Perspectives, 38*(4), 547–571.

Carley, K. M., & Prietula, M. (2001). *Computational Organization Theory.* Hillsdale: Lawrence Erlbaum Associates.

Carley, K. M., & Skillicorn, D. (2005). Special issue on analyzing large scale networks: The enron corpus. *Computational & Mathematical Organization Theory, 11*, 179–181. doi:10.1007/s10588-005-5376-1

Carley, K. M., Diesner, J., Reminga, J., & Tsvetovata, M. (2007). Toward an interoperable dynamic network analysis toolkit. *Decision Support Systems, 43*(4), 1324–1347. doi:10.1016/j.dss.2006.04.003

Carley, K. M. (2003). Dynamic network analysis. In R. Breiger, K. Carley, & P. Pattison (Ed.), *Dynamic social network modeling and analysis: Workshop summary and papers* (pp. 133-145). Committee on Human Factors, National Research Council.

Carmine, C., Antonio, P.(n.d). An Intelligent Search Agent System for Semantic Information Retrieval on the Internet. *WIDM'*03

Carpenter, C. (2010). The Obamachine: Technopolitics 2.0. *Journal of Information Technology & Politics, 7*(2), 216–225. doi:10.1080/19331681003765887

Carrington, P., & Scott, J. (2011). *The Sage Handbook of Social Network Analysis.* London: SAGE Publications.

Cartwright, D., & Harary, F. (1956). Structural balance: A generalization of Heider's. theory. *Psychological Review*, *63*, 277–293. doi:10.1037/h0046049

Casagrande, K. (2000). *Recipes for Car Care: Guide to Auto Health*. Delmar Cengage Learning.

Cattuto, C., Baldassarri, A., Servedio, V., & Loreto, V. (2008). Emergent Community Structure in Social Tagging Systems. [ACS]. *Advances in Complex Systems*, *11*(04), 597–608. doi:10.1142/S0219525908001817

Cebrian, M., Pentland, A., & Kirkpatrick, S. (2010). Disentangling Social Networks inferred from Call Logs. *Arxiv preprint arXiv:1008.1357, pre-print*, pre-print.

Chaffee, S. H., & Metzger, M. J. (2001). The end of mass communication? *Mass Communication & Society*, *4*(4), 365–379. doi:10.1207/S15327825MCS0404_3

Chakrabarti, D., Zhan, Y., & Faloutsos, C. (2004). R-MAT: A recursive model for graph mining. In *Proceedings of the 4th SIAM International Conference on Data Mining*.

Chamberlin, D., Fankhauser, P., Florescu, D. & Robie, J.(2007). *XML Query Use Cases, W3C Working Draft 2007*.

Chan, S., & Franklin, J. (1998). Symbolic connectionism in natural language disambiguation. *IEEE Transactions on Neural Networks*, *9*(5), 739–755. doi:10.1109/72.712149

Chan, C.-C., & Santhosh, S. (2003). Blem2: Learning Bayes' Rules From Examples Using Rough Sets (pp 187–190). *NAFIPS 2003, 22nd Int. conf. of the North American Fuzzy Information Processing Society*, July 24 – 26, Chicago, Illinois.

Chandon, P., Wansink, B., & Laurent, G. (2000). A Benefit Congruency Framework of Sales Promotion Effectiveness. *Journal of Marketing*, *64*(October), 65–81. doi:10.1509/jmkg.64.4.65.18071

Chaney, I. M., Lim, K. H., & Chaney, J. (2004). The Effect of Billboards within the Gaming Environment. *Journal of Interactive Advertising*, *5*(1), 1–11.

Chawla, N. V., Japlowicz, N., & Kolcz, A. (2004). Editorial: special issue on learning from imbalanced data sets. *SIGKDD Explorations*, *6*(1), 1–6. doi:10.1145/1007730.1007733

Chen, H., Schroeder, J., Hauck, R., Ridgeway, L., Atabakhsh, H., & Gupta, H. (2003). Coplink connect: information and knowledge management for law enforcement. *Decision Support Systems*, *34*(4), 271–285. doi:10.1016/S0167-9236(02)00121-5

Chen, J., & Ringel, R. (2001). *Can Advergaming be the Future of Interactive Advertising?* White paper, Fast Forward. Retrieved from: http://www.locz.com.br/ loczgames/advergames.pdf. (accessed on March 1, 2010).

Chen, W.-C., Battestini, A., Gelfand, N., & Setlur, V. (2009). *Visual Summaries of Popular Landmarks from Community Photo Collections*. In proceedings of the 17th ACM International Conference on Multimedia. New York: ACM, pp. 789-792.

Chi, E. H. (2008). The Social Web: Research and Opportunities. *Computer*, (Sept): 88–91. doi:10.1109/MC.2008.401

Chi, Y., Song, X., Zhou, D., Hino, K., & Tsend, B. (2007a). Evolutionary spectral clustering by incorporating temporal smoothness. *Proceedings of the 13th ACM SIGKDD international conference on Knowledge discovery and data mining*, (pp. 153–162).

Chiu, S., & Tavella, D. (2008). *Data mining and market intelligence for optimal marketing returns*. Amsterdam: Elsevier.

Chopra, K., & Wallace, W. A. (2000). Modeling relationships among multiple graphical structures. *Computational & Mathematical Organization Theory*, *6*(4), 361–379. doi:10.1023/A:1009658313423

Choudhry, N. K., Fletcher, R. H., & Soumerai, S. B. (2005). Systematic Review: The Relationship between Clinical Experience and Quality of Health Care. *Annals of Internal Medicine*, *142*(4), 260–283.

Christen, P., Churches, T., & Hegland, M. (2004). Febrl – A Parallel Open Source Data Linkage System. In H. Dai, R. Srikant & C. Zhang (Eds.), *Advances in Knowledge Discovery and Data Mining* (Vol. 3056, pp. 638-647): Springer Berlin / Heidelberg.

Chung, K. S. K., & Hossain, L. (2010). Towards a Social Network Model for Understanding Information and Communication Technology use for General Practitioners in Rural Australia. *Computers in Human Behavior*, *26*(4), 562–571. doi:10.1016/j.chb.2009.12.008

Church, S. H. (2010). YouTube Politics: You Choose and Leadership Rhetoric During the 2008 Election. *Journal of Information Technology & Politics*, 7(2), 124–142. doi:10.1080/19331681003748933

Churches, T., Christen, P., Lim, K., & Zhu, J. X. (2002). Preparation of name and address data for record linkage using hidden Markov models. *BMC Medical Informatics and Decision Making*, 2(1), 9. doi:10.1186/1472-6947-2-9

Clarke, R. (1994). Human Identification in Information Systems: Management Challenges and Public Policy Issues. *IT and People*, 7(4), 6–37. doi:10.1108/09593849410076799

Clauset, A., J., N. M., & Moore, C. (2004). Finding community structure in very large networks. *Physical Review E: Statistical, Nonlinear, and Soft Matter Physics*, 70(6), 66–111. doi:10.1103/PhysRevE.70.066111

Coleman, J. S., Katz, E., & Menzel, H. (1957). The Diffusion of an Innovation among Physicians. *Sociometry*, 20(4), 253–270. doi:10.2307/2785979

Comellas, F., & Sampels, M. (2002). Deterministic small-world networks. *Physica A*, 309, 231–235. doi:10.1016/S0378-4371(02)00741-0

Conrath, D. W., Higgins, C. A., & McClean, R. J. (1983). A comparison of the reliability of questionnaire versus diary data. [http://dx.doi.org/DOI: 10.1016/0378-8733(83)90031-X]. *Social Networks, 5*(3), 315-322.

Constant, D., Kiesler, S., & Sproull, L. (1994). What's Mine is Ours, or Is It? A Study of Attitudes about Information Sharing. *Information Systems Research*, 5(4), 400–421. doi:10.1287/isre.5.4.400

Constant, D., Sproull, L., & Kiesler, S. (1996). The Kindness of Strangers: The Usefulness of Electronic Weak Ties for Technical Advice. *Organization Science*, 7(2), 119–135. doi:10.1287/orsc.7.2.119

Cook, K. S., Emerson, R. M., & Gillmore, M. R. (1983). The Distribution of Power in Exchange Networks: Theory and Experimental Results. *American Journal of Sociology*, 89(2), 275–305. doi:10.1086/227866

Cooley, R., Mobasher, B., & Srivastava, J. (1997). Web Mining: Information and Pattern Discovery on the World Wide Web. *9th International Conference on Tools with Artificial Intelligence(ICTAI '97)*. New Port Beach, CA, USA, IEEE Computer Society, 558-567.

Corman, S., Kuhn, R., Mc, T., Phee, R. D., & Dooley, K. J. (2002). Studying complex discursive systems: Centering Resonance Analysis of communication. *Human Communication Research*, 28(2), 157206. doi:10.1093/hcr/28.2.157

Couper, M. P., & Miller, P. V. (2008). Web survey methods. *Public Opinion Quarterly*, 72(5), 831–835. doi:10.1093/poq/nfn066

Cowan, R., & Jonard, N. (2008). If the alliance fits ...: innovation and network dynamics. In Baum, J., & Rowley, T. J. (Eds.), *Network Strategy: Advances in Strategic Management* (pp. 427–455). Oxford, UK: JAI/Elsevier.

Crandall, D., Backstrom, L., Huttenlocher, D., & Kleinberg, J. (2009). *Mapping the World's Photos.* In proceedings of the 18th International conference on World Wide Web. ACM, New York, USA.

Crandell, D., Cosley, D., Huttenlocher, D., Kleinberg, J., & Suri, S. (2008). *Feedback effects between similarity and social influence in online communities* (pp. 160–168). ACM.

Crosby, L. A., Evans, K. R., & Cowles, D. (1990). Relationship Quality in Services Selling: An Interpersonal Influence Perspective. *Journal of Marketing*, 54(3), 68–81. doi:10.2307/1251817

Cross, R., Borgatti, S. P., & Parker, A. (2002). Making invisible work visible: Using social network analysis to support strategic collaboration. *California Management Review*, 44(2), 25–46.

Cross, R., & Parker, A. (2004). *The hidden power of social networks*. Boston, MA: Harvard Business School Press.

Cross, R., Rice, R. E., & Parker, A. (2001). Information Seeking in Social Context: Structural Influences and Receipt of Information Benefits. *IEEE Transactions on Systems, Man and Cybernetics. Part C, Applications and Reviews*, 31(4), 438–448. doi:10.1109/5326.983927

Cummings, J. N. (2004). Work Groups, Structural Diversity, and Knowledge Sharing in a Global Organization. *Management Science*, 50(3), 352–364. doi:10.1287/mnsc.1030.0134

Cummings, J. N., & Cross, R. (2003). Structural Properties of Work Groups and their Consequences for Performance. *Social Networks*, 25(3), 197–210. doi:10.1016/S0378-8733(02)00049-7

Daft, R. L., & Macintosh, N. B. (1981). A Tentative Exploration into the Amount and Equivocality of Information Processing in Organizational Work Units. *Administrative Science Quarterly*, *26*(2), 207–224. doi:10.2307/2392469

Dalal, M. (2007). Personalized Social & Real-Time Collaborative Search. *In Proceedings of WWW*, Canada, 2007.

Danowski, J. A., & Cepela, N. (2010). Automatic mapping of social networks of actors from text corpora: Time series analysis. *Annals of Information Systems*, *12*, 31–46. doi:10.1007/978-1-4419-6287-4_3

Danowski, J. A., & Edison-Swift, P. (1985). Crisis effects on intraorganizational computer-based communication. *Communication Research*, *12*, 251–270. doi:10.1177/009365085012002005

Danowski, J. A. (2009). Inferences from word networks in messages. In Krippendorff, K., & Bock, M. A. (Eds.), *The content analysis reader* (pp. 421–429). Sage Publications.

Danowski, J. A. (1993c). Network analysis of message content. In Rice, R. E., Richards, W., & Barnett, G. (Eds.), *Progress in communication sciences XII* (pp. 197–222). Norwood, NJ: Ablex.

Danowski, J. A. (1982). A network-based content analysis methodology for computer-mediated communication: An illustration with a computer bulletin board. In Bostrom, R. N. (Ed). *Communication Yearbook*, *6*, 904-925. New Brunswick, NJ: Transaction Books.

Danowski, J. A. (1988). Organizational infographics and automated auditing: Using computers to unobtrusively gather and analyze communication. In G. Goldhaber & G. A. Barnett (Eds.) *Handbook of Organizational Communication*, (pp. 335-384). Norwood, NJ: Danowski, J. A. (1993a). *Automatic narrative generation via statistical content analysis of large-scale textual collections.* Paper presented at Conference on Computing for the Social Sciences, National Center for Supercomputing Applications, University of Illinois at Urbana-Campaign, May 18-21.

Danowski, J. A. (1993b). WORDij 3.0: A word-pair approach to information retrieval. *Proceedings of the DARPA/NIST TREC Conference*, Washington, DC.

Danowski, J. A. (2007). *Comparing semantic network analysis approaches.* Paper presented to the International Association for Social Network Analysis, Sunbelt XXVII annual meetings Corfu, Greece, May.

Danowski, J. A. (2010). *WORDij 3.0. [Computer program].* Chicago, IL: University of Illinois at Chicago.

Danowski, J. A., Gluesing, J., & Riopelle, K. (2009). *ICT's effects on diffusion curves, email networks, and semantic networks in an organization: The emergence of herding, bandwagons, and information cascades with less interpersonal communication.* Paper presented to the Communication and Technology Division of the International Communication Association, Chicago, May 21-25.

Danowski, J. A., Riopelle, K., & Gluesing, J. (2008). *Using network analysis of who-to-whom email networks to structure semantic network analysis of email content and manage it in innovation contexts.* Paper presented at annual meetings of the International Network for Social Network Analysis, Sunbelt XXVIII annual meetings, St. Pete Beach, FL, January, 2008.

Dasgupta, K., Singh, R., Viswanathan, B., Chakraborty, D., Mukherjea, S., Nanavati, A. A., & Joshi, A. (2008). *Social ties and their relevance to churn in mobile telecom networks.* Paper presented at the EDBT '08: Proceedings of the 11th international conference on Extending database technology.

David, M., & Dale, L. (2000). Repertory grid technique, an interpretive research framework. *European Journal of Marketing*, *34*(7), 816–834. doi:10.1108/03090560010331261

Davis, S. J., Burnett, I. S., & Ritz, C. H. (2009). Using Social Networking and Collections to Enable Video Semantics Acquisition. *IEEE MultiMedia*, *16*(4), 52–61.

Davis, F. D. (1989). Perceived Usefulness, Perceived Ease of Use, and User Acceptance of Information Technology. *Management Information Systems Quarterly*, *13*(3), 319–340. doi:10.2307/249008

Davis, F. D., Bagozzi, R. P., & Warshaw, P. R. (1989). User Acceptance of Computer Technology: A Comparison of Two Theoretical Models. *Management Science*, *35*(8), 982–1003. doi:10.1287/mnsc.35.8.982

De Choudhury, M., Mason, W. A., Hofman, J. M., & Watts, D. J. (2010). *Inferring relevant social networks from interpersonal communication.* Paper presented at the Proceedings of the 19th international conference on World wide web.

De Choudhury, M., Sundaram, M., John, A., & Seligmann, D. D. (2009). *What Makes Conversations Interesting? Themes, Participants, and Consequences of Conversationsin Online Social Media.* In proceedings of the 18th International conference on World Wide Web. ACM, New York, USA.

De Kleer, J., & Brown, J. S. (1984). A qualitative physics based on confluences. *Artificial Intelligence, 24*, 7–83. doi:10.1016/0004-3702(84)90037-7

de Klepper, M., Sleebos, E., van de Bunt, G., & Agneessens, F. (2010). Similarity in friendship networks: Selection or influence? The effect of constraining contexts and non-visible individual attributes. *Social Networks, 32*, 82–90. doi:10.1016/j.socnet.2009.06.003

Deal, D. (2005). The Ability of Branded Online Games to Build Brand Equity: An Exploratory Study. *Proceedings of DIGRA 2005 Conference: Changing Views–Worlds in Play* (pp. 1-7), Vancouver, Canada. Dias, J.G.& Vermunt. J.K. (22007). Latent Class Modeling of Website Users' Search Patterns: Implications for Online Market Segmentation. *Journal of Retailing and Consumer Services, 14*(6), 359–368.

Degenne, A., & Forse, M. (1994). *Introducing Social Networks.* London: Sage.

Deighton, J. (1996). The Future of Interactive Marketing. *Harvard Business Review*, 11–12.

Deshpande, M., & Karypis, G. (2004). Item-based top-n recommendation algorithms. *ACM Transactions on Information Systems, 22*(1), 143–177. doi:10.1145/963770.963776

Dewey, J. (1910). *How We Think.* Boston: Heath. doi:10.1037/10903-000

Dewey, J. (1911). Causation. In P. Monroe (Ed.), *A Cyclopedia of Education (Dewey Middle Works 6)* (pp. 38). New York: The Macmillan company.

Dhar, V., & Chang, E. A. (2009). Does chatter matter? The impact of user-generated content on music sales. *Journal of Interactive Marketing, 23*(4), 300–307. doi:10.1016/j.intmar.2009.07.004

Dhillon, I., Guan, Y., & Kulis, B. (2007). Weighted graph cuts without eigenvectors: A multilevel approach. *IEEE Transactions on Pattern Analysis and Machine Intelligence*, 1944–1957. doi:10.1109/TPAMI.2007.1115

Diesner, J., & Carley, K. M. (2008). Conditional random fields for entity extraction and ontological text coding. *Computational & Mathematical Organization Theory, 14*(3), 248262. doi:10.1007/s10588-008-9029-z

Diesner, J., Frantz, T. L., & Carley, K. M. (2005). Communication networks from the Enron email corpus 'it's always about the people. Enron is no different'. *Computational & Mathematical Organization Theory, 11*(3), 201228. doi:10.1007/s10588-005-5377-0

Diesner, J., & Carley, K. M. (2004). *Using network text analysis to detect the organizational structure of covert networks.* Pittsburg, PA: CASOS, Carnegie-Mellon. Available from: http://www.contrib.andrew.cmu.edu/~jdiesner/publications/NAACSOS_2004_Diesner_Carley_Detect_Covert_Networks.pdf

Diesner, J., & Carley, K. M. (2004). *AutoMap 1.2: Extract, analyze, represent, and compare mental models from texts.* Pittsburg, PA: CASOS, Carnegie-Mellon University. Available from: http://reports-archive.adm.cs.cmu.edu/ anon/anon/usr/ftp/isri2004/ CMU-ISRI-04-100.pdf

DiversityData.org & Harvard School of Public Health (2000). *Exposure to Neighborhood Median Income by Race/Ethnicity and Income*

DiversityData.org & Harvard School of Public Health (2007). *Profiles by Metro Area* [Online]. Available: http://diversitydata.sph.harvard.edu/index.jsp

Dokoohaki, N., & Matskin, M. (2008). Personalizing Human Interaction through Hybrid Ontological Profiling: Cultural Heritage Case Study. In M. Ronchetti (Ed.) *1st Workshop on Semantic Web Applications and Human Aspects* (pp 133-140). AIT e-press.

Doreian, P. (1983). On the evolution of group and network structures II: structures within structure. *Social Networks, 8*, 33–64. doi:10.1016/S0378-8733(86)80014-4

Doreian, P., & Stokman, F. (1997). *Evolution of Social Networks.* New York: Gordon and Breach.

Dorogovtsev, S. N., & Mendes, J. F. F. (2002). Evolution of networks. *Advances in Physics, 51*(4), 1079–1187. doi:10.1080/00018730110112519

Dorogovtsev, S. N., & Mendes, J. F. F. (2000). Exactly solvable small-world network. *Europhysics Letters, 50*, 1–7. doi:10.1209/epl/i2000-00227-1

Dourisboure, Y., Geraci, F., & Pellegrini, M. (2007). Extraction and classification of dense communities in the Web. *WWW'07: Proceedings of the 16th international conference on World Wide Web*, pp. 461-470.

Drummond, C., & Holte, R. C. (2003). C4.5, class imbalance, and cost sensitivity: why under-sampling beats over-sampling. *Workshop on Learning from Imbalanced Data Sets II, ICML*, Washington DC.

Dunn, H. L. (1946). Record linkage. *American Journal of Public Health*, *36*(12), 1412. doi:10.2105/AJPH.36.12.1412

Eagle, N., Pentland, A. S., & Lazer, D. (2009). Inferring friendship network structure by using mobile phone data. *Proceedings of the National Academy of Sciences of the United States of America*, *106*(36), 15274. doi:10.1073/pnas.0900282106

Earl, P. E. (1986). *Lifestyle Economics: Consumer Behavior in a Turbulent World*. New York: St. Martin's Press.

Egan, J. P. (1975). *Signal detection theory and ROC analysis. Series in Cognition and Perception*. New York: Academic Press.

Eguíluz, V. M., Chialvo, D. R., Cecchi, G. A., Baliki, M., & Apkarian, A. V. (2005). Scale-free Brainfunctional networks. *Physical Review Letters*, *94*(1), 018102. doi:10.1103/PhysRevLett.94.018102

Elmagarmid, A. K., Ipeirotis, P. G., & Verykios, V. S. (2007). Duplicate Record Detection: A Survey. [http://dx.doi.org/http://dx.doi.org/10.1109/TKDE.2007.9]. *IEEE Transactions on Knowledge and Data Engineering*, *19*, 1–16. doi:10.1109/TKDE.2007.250581

Elmer-DeWitt, P. (2010). *Apple's Ping is a spam magnet, CNN Money.com*. Retrieved September 2010 from http://tech.fortune.cnn.com/2010/ 09/03/apples-ping-is-a-spam-magnet/

Emerson, R. M. (1976). Social Exchange Theory. *Annual Review of Sociology*, *2*, 335–362. doi:10.1146/annurev.so.02.080176.002003

Erdos, P., & Renyi, A. (1960). On the evolution of random graphs. *Publications of the Mathematical Institute Hungarian Academy of Sciences*, *5*, 17–61.

Ergün & Rodgers, G. J. (2002). Growing random networks with fitness. *Physica A. Statistical Mechanics and Its Applications*, *303*, 261–272. doi:10.1016/S0378-4371(01)00408-3

Falkowski, T. (2009). Community Analysis in Dynamic Social Networks. Unpublished dissertation, University Magdeburg, Germany.

Faloutsos, M., Faloutsos, P., & Faloutsos, C. (1999). On power-law relationships of the Internet topology. *Computer Communication Review*, *29*, 251–262. doi:10.1145/316194.316229

Fang, X., & Sheng, O. R. L. (2005). Designing a Better Web Portal for Digital Government: A Web-Mining Based Approach. *Proceedings of the 2005 National Conference on Digital Government Research*, May 15-18, Atlanta, pp. 277-278.

Farrugia, M., & Quigley, A. (2010). Actor Identification in Implicit Relational Data Sources. In I. H. Ting, H.-J. Wu & T.-H. Ho (Eds.), *Mining and Analyzing Social Networks* (Vol. 288, pp. 67-89): Springer Berlin / Heidelberg.

Feld, S. L., & Carter, W. C. (2002). Detecting measurement bias in respondent reports of personal networks. *Social Networks*, *24*(4), 365–383. doi:10.1016/S0378-8733(02)00013-8

Feldman, R., & Sanger, J. (Eds.). (2007). *The Text Mining Handbook: Advanced Approaches in Analyzing Unstructured Data*. Cambridge: Cambridge University Press.

Fellegi, I., & Sunter, A. (1969). Theory of record linkage. *Journal of the American Statistical Association*, *64*, 1183–1210. doi:10.2307/2286061

Fieldhouse, P. (2005). *Food, Justice, and the Baha'i Faith*. PhD Dissertation [Online]. Available: http://bahai-library.com/ file.php5?file=fieldhouse_food_justice&language=

Flake, G., Lawrence, S., & Giles, C. (2000). Efficient identification of Web communities. *KDD'00: Proceedings of the sixth ACM SIGKDD international conference on Knowledge discovery and data mining*, pp. 150-160.

Foot, K., Schneider, S., Dougherty, M., Xenos, M., & Larsen, E. (2003). Analyzing Linking Practices: Candidate Sites in the 2002 U.S. Electoral Web Sphere. *Journal of Mediated Communication*, *8*(4). Retrieved from http://jcmc.indiana.edu/ vol8/issue4/foot.html.

Forbus, K. (1996). *Qualitative Reasoning. CRC Handbook of Computer Science and Engineering.* CRC Press.

Fortun, M., & Bernstein, H. J. (1998). *Muddling Through: Pursuing Science and Truths in the 21st Century.* Washington: Counterpoint.

Fouss, F., Pirotte, A., Renders, J. M., & Saerens, M. (2007). Random-walk computation of similarities between nodes of a graph with application to collaborative recommendation. *IEEE Transactions on Knowledge and Data Engineering, 19*(3), 355–369. doi:10.1109/TKDE.2007.46

Frazier, G. L. (1983). Interorganizational Exchange Behavior in Marketing Channels: A Broadened Perspective. *Journal of Marketing, 47*(4), 68–78. doi:10.2307/1251400

Fredrickson, B. L., & Losada, M. F. (2005). Positive affect and the complex dynamics of human flourishing. *The American Psychologist, 60*(7), 678–686. doi:10.1037/0003-066X.60.7.678

Freeman, L. C., Romney, A. K., & Freeman, S. C. (1987). Cognitive structure and informant accuracy. *American Anthropologist, 89*(2), 310–325. doi:10.1525/aa.1987.89.2.02a00020

Freeman, L. C. (1979). Centrality in social networks: Conceptual clarification. *Social Networks, 1*, 215–239. doi:10.1016/0378-8733(78)90021-7

Freeman, L. C. (1996). Some antecedents of social network analysis. *Connections, 19*(1), 39–42.

Freeman, L. C., Borgatti, S. P., & White, D. R. (1991). Centrality in valued graphs: A measure of betweenness based on network flow. *Social Networks, 13*(2), 141–154. doi:10.1016/0378-8733(91)90017-N

Freeman, L. C. (1978). Centrality in Social Networks: Conceptual Clarification. *Social Networks, 1*(3), 215–239. doi:10.1016/0378-8733(78)90021-7

Freeman, L. C., Romney, A. K., & Freeman, S. C. (1987). Cognitive Structure and Informant Accuracy. *American Anthropologist, 89*(2), 311–325. doi:10.1525/aa.1987.89.2.02a00020

Frenken, K. (2006). *Innovation, evolution and complexity theory.* Cheltenham & Northampton, MA: Edward Elgar.

Fu, X., Boongoen, T., & Shen, Q. (2010). Evidence directed generation of plausible crime scenarios with identity resolution. *Applied Artificial Intelligence, 24*(4), 253–276. doi:10.1080/08839511003715154

Fu, X., & Shen, Q. (2010). Fuzzy compositional modeling. *IEEE Transactions on Fuzzy Systems, 18*(4), 823–840. doi:10.1109/TFUZZ.2010.2050325

Fu, X., & Shen, Q. (2011). Fuzzy complex numbers and their application for classifiers performance evaluation. *Pattern Recognition, 44*(7), 1403–1417. doi:10.1016/j.patcog.2011.01.011

Fuhse, J. A. (2009). The meaning structure of social networks. *Sociological Theory, 27*(1), 51–73. doi:10.1111/j.1467-9558.2009.00338.x

Fulk, J., Schmitz, J., & Steinfield, C. (1990). A Social Influence Model of Technology Use. In Fulk, J., & Steinfield, C. (Eds.), *Organizations and Communication Technology* (pp. 117–140). Newbury Park, CA: Sage.

Gaines, B. R. (1994). The collective stance in modeling expertise in individuals and organizations. *International Journal of Expert Systems, 7*(1), 21–51.

Gaines, B. R. (2006). The learning curves underlying convergence. *Technological Forecasting and Social Change, 57*(1-2), 7–34. doi:10.1016/S0040-1625(97)00078-4

Gaines, B. R. (2009). Designing visual languages for description logics. *Journal of Logic Language and Information, 18*(2), 217–250. doi:10.1007/s10849-008-9078-1

Gaines, B. R. (2010). Human rationality challenges universal logic. *Logica Universalis, 4*(2), 163–205. doi:10.1007/s11787-010-0019-9

Gaines, B. R., Chen, L. L.-J., & Shaw, M. L. G. (1997). Modeling the human factors of scholarly communities supported through the Internet and World Wide Web. *Journal of the American Society for Information Science American Society for Information Science, 48*(11), 987–1003. doi:10.1002/(SICI)1097-4571(199711)48:11<987::AID-ASI3>3.0.CO;2-Y

Gaines, B. R., & Shaw, M. L. G. (1993a). Basing knowledge acquisition tools in personal construct psychology. *The Knowledge Engineering Review, 8*(1), 49–85. doi:10.1017/S0269888900000060

Gaines, B. R., & Shaw, M. L. G. (1993b). Eliciting knowledge and transferring it effectively to a knowledge-based systems. *IEEE Transactions on Knowledge and Data Engineering*, 5(1), 4–14. doi:10.1109/69.204087

Gaines, B. R., & Shaw, M. L. G. (1995). Concept maps as hypermedia components. *International Journal of Human-Computer Studies*, 43(3), 323–361. doi:10.1006/ijhc.1995.1049

Gaines, B. R., & Shaw, M. L. G. (1997). Knowledge acquisition, modeling and inference through the World Wide Web. *International Journal of Human-Computer Studies*, 46(6), 729–759. doi:10.1006/ijhc.1996.0122

Gaines, B. R. (2003). Organizational knowledge acquisition. In Holsapple, C. W. (Ed.), *Handbook on Knowledge Management: 1* (pp. 317–347). Berlin: Springer.

Gaines, B. R. (1995). Porting interactive applications to the web *4th International World Wide Web Conference Tutorial Notes* (pp. 199-217). Sebastopol, CA: O'Reilly.

Gaines, B. R., & Shaw, M. L. G. (1989). Comparing the conceptual systems of experts *Proceedings of the Eleventh International Joint Conference on Artificial Intelligence* (pp. 633-638). San Mateo, California: Morgan Kaufmann.

Gaines, B. R., & Shaw, M. L. G. (1994). Using knowledge acquisition and representation tools to support scientific communities *AAAI'94: Proceedings of the Twelfth National Conference on Artificial Intelligence* (pp. 707-714). Menlo Park, California: AAAI Press/MIT Press.

Gaines, B. R., & Shaw, M. L. G. (2007). *WebGrid evolution through four generations 1994-2007* (No. TR-2007-WG): http://cpsc.ucalgary.ca/ ~gaines/reports/.

Gaines, B. R., & Shaw, M. L. G. (2009). *Rep 5 Manuals*: Centre for Person-Computer Studies, http://repgrid.com.

Gaines, B. R., & Shaw, M. L. G. (2010). Computer aided constructivism. In P. Caputi & L. Viney (Eds.), *Constructivist Methods* (pp. to appear). New York: Wiley.

Galaskiewicz, J. (1985). Professional networks and the institutionalization of a single mindset. *American Sociological Review*, 50, 639–658. doi:10.2307/2095379

Galaskiewicz, J., & Shatin, D. (1981). Leadership and networking among neighborhood human service organizations. *Administrative Science Quarterly*, 26, 434–4. doi:10.2307/2392516

Gale, W. A., Church, K. W., & Yarowsky, D. (1992). A method for disambiguating word senses in large corpora. *Computers and the Humanities*, 26, 415–439. doi:10.1007/BF00136984

Ganesan, S. (1994). Determinants of Long-Term Orientation in Buyer-Seller Relationship. *Journal of Marketing*, 58, 1–19. doi:10.2307/1252265

Gans, J., Hsu, D., & Stern, S. (2000). When does start-up innovation spur the gale of creative destruction? *The Rand Journal of Economics*, 33, 571. doi:10.2307/3087475

Gao, W., Tian, Y., Huang, T., & Yang, Q. (2010). Vlogging: A Survey of Video Blogging Technology on the Web. *ACM Computing Surveys*, 42(4), 1–57. doi:10.1145/1749603.1749606

Garton, L., Haythornthwaite, C., & Wellman, B. (1997). Studying online social networks. *Journal of Computer-Mediated Communication*, 3(1).

Gary, D. P., Flake, G. W., Lawrence, S., Glover, E. J., & Giles, C. L. (2002). Winners don't take all: Characterizing the competition for links on the web. *Proceedings of the National Academy of Sciences of the United States of America*, 99, 5207–5211. doi:10.1073/pnas.032085699

Gay, B. (2008). Firm dynamic governance of global innovation by means of flexible networks of connections. *Journal of Innovation Economics*, 2, 63–83. doi:10.3917/jie.002.0063

Gay, B., & Dousset, B. (2005). Innovation and network structural dynamics: Study of the alliance network of a major sector of the biotechnology industry. *Research Policy*, 34, 1457–1475. doi:10.1016/j.respol.2005.07.001

Gay, B. (2010). *Innovative network in transition: From the fittest to the richest.* Available from http://papers.ssrn.com/ abstract=1649967.

Gay, B. (2011). *Venture Capital Firms: Birds of a Feather that Flock Together, Really?* Paper presented at the international Sunbelt Social Network conference, St. Pete Beach, FL.

Gay, B., & Loubier, E. (July, 2009). *Dynamics and evolution patterns of business networks.* Paper presented at the international conference on Advances in Social Network Analysis and Mining (ASONAM), Athens, Greece.

Getoor, L., & Diehl, C. P. (2005). Link mining: a survey. *ACM SIGKDD Explorations Newsletter, 7*(2), 3–12. doi:10.1145/1117454.1117456

Gibson, R. K. (2009). New Media and the Revitalisation of Politics. *Representation, 45*(3), 289–299. doi:10.1080/00344890903129566

Gibson, D., Kleinberg, J., & Raghavan, P. (1998). Inferring Web communities from link topology. *HYPERTEXT '98: Proceedings of the ninth ACM conference on Hypertext and hypermedia: links, objects, time and space--structure in hypermedia systems,* pp. 225-234.

Gibson, R. K., & Mcallister, I. (2009). Crossing the Web 2.0 Frontier? Candidates and Campaigns Online in the Australian Federal Election of 2007. *Paper presented at the 2009 ECPR General Conference,* Potdam, Germany.

Gilbert, M. (1992). *On Social Facts.* Princeton, N.J.: Princeton University Press.

Gilbert, E., & Karahalios, K. (2009). Predicting tie strength with social media. *Proceeding of the 27th international conference on Human factors in computing systems* (pp. 211-220). New York: ACM.

Gilbert, E., & Karahalios, K. (2009). *Predicting tie strength with social media.* Paper presented at the Proceedings of the 27th international conference on Human factors in computing systems.

Ginter, F., Boberg, J., Jarvinen, J., & Salakoski, T. (2004). New techniques for disambiguating in natural language and their application to biological text. *Journal of Machine Learning Research, 5,* 605–621.

Girvan, M., & Newman, M. (2002). Community structure in social and biological networks. *Proceedings of the National Academy of Sciences of the United States of America, 99*(12), 7821–7826. doi:10.1073/pnas.122653799

Gloor, P. (2006). *Swarm creativity: Competitive advantage through collaborative innovation networks.* Oxford University Press US.

Gloor, P., & Zhao, Y. (2006). *Analyzing actors and their discussion topics by semantic social network analysis.* Tenth International Conference on Information Visualization, 5-7 July 2006, 130-135. London, England. Available from: http://www.ickn.org/documents/IV06_G2341_Gloor.pdf

Goldberg, S. (2010). *Relying on Others: An Essay in Epistemology.* Oxford: Oxford University Press.

Goldberg, D., Nichols, D., Oki, B. M., & Terry, D. (1992). Using collaborative filtering to weave an information tapestry. *Communications of the ACM, 35*(12), 61–70. doi:10.1145/138859.138867

Goldenberg, A., Zheng, A. X., Fienberg, S. E., & Airoldi, E. M. (2009). A survey of statistical network models. *Foundations and Trends in Machine Learning, 2*(2), 129–233. doi:10.1561/2200000005

Goldenberg, A., & Zheng, A. (2006). Exploratory study of a new model for evolving networks. In *Proceedings of the 2006 Conference on Statistical Network Analysis,* ICML'06, (pp. 75-89)., Berlin: Springer-Verlag.

Golder, S., & Huberman, B. A. (2006). The structure of collaborative tagging systems. *Journal of Information Science, 32*(2), 198–208. doi:10.1177/0165551506062337

Gomez Rodriguez, M., Leskovec, J., & Krause, A. (2010). *Inferring networks of diffusion and influence.* Paper presented at the Proceedings of the 16th ACM SIGKDD international conference on Knowledge discovery and data mining.

Google Base Data Feed. (n.d.) Available: http://base.google.com/ support/bin/answer.py?answer=59461&hl=en

Google Base Protocol. (n.d) Available: http://code.google.com/ apis/base/docs/2.0/ developers_guide_protocol.html

Gower, J. C. (1966). Some distance properties of latent root and vector methods used in multivariate analysis. *Biometrika, 53,* 325–338.

Gower, J. C., & Dijksterhuis, G. B. (2004). *Procrustes Problems.* Oxford: Oxford University Press. doi:10.1093/acprof:oso/9780198510581.001.0001

Granovetter, M. S. (1973). The strength of weak ties. *American Journal of Sociology, 78*(6), 1360–1380. doi:10.1086/225469

Granovetter, M. (1995). *Getting a Job: A Study of Contacts and Careers.* Chicago: University of Chicago Press.

Granovetter, M. S. (1973). The Strength of Weak Ties. *American Journal of Sociology, 78*(6), 1360–1380. doi:10.1086/225469

Greenfield, S. (2008). *I.D.: The Quest for Meaning in the 21st Century.* London: Hodder & Stoughton.

Grier, C., Thomas, K., Paxson, V., & Zhang, M. (2010). @spam; the underground on 140 characters or less, *CCS '10, Proceedings of the 17th ACM conference on Computer and Communications Security* (pp. 27 – 37), October 4 – 8, 2010, Chicago, Illinois.

Griffiths, T. L., Steyvers, M., & Firl, A. (2007). Google and the mind. *Psychological Science, 18*, 1069–1076. doi:10.1111/j.1467-9280.2007.02027.x

Gullati, G. J. J., & Williams, C. B. (2010). Congressional Candidates' Use of YouTube in 2008: Its Frequency and Rationale. *Journal of Information Technology & Politics, 7*(2), 93–109. doi:10.1080/19331681003748958

Haase, P., Siebes, R., & van Harmelen, F. (2004). Peer selection in peer-to-peer networks with semantic topologies. *Bouzeghoub, M., ed.: Proc. of the Int. Conf. on Semantics in a Networked World (ICNSW'04). Volume 3226 of Lecture Notes in Computer Science., Springer-Verlag*, pp. 108–125.

Hagen, L., & Kahng, A. (1992). New spectral methods for ratio cut partitioning and clustering. *IEEE Transactions on Computer-Aided Design of Integrated Circuits and Systems, 11*(9), 1074–1085. doi:10.1109/43.159993

Haimowitz, I., & Kohane, I. (1996). Managing temporal worlds for medical trends diagnosis. *Artificial Intelligence in Medicine, 8*(3), 299–321. doi:10.1016/0933-3657(95)00037-2

Hall, M., Frank, E., Holmes, G., Pfahringer, B., Reutemann, P., & Witten, I. H. (2009). The WEKA Data Mining Software: An Update. *SIGKDD Explorations, 11*(1). doi:10.1145/1656274.1656278

Hammer, M. (1984). Explorations into the Meaning of Social Network Interview Data. *Social Networks, 6*(4), 341–371. doi:10.1016/0378-8733(84)90008-X

Hand, D. J. (1998). Data Mining: Statistics and More? *The American Statistician, 52*(2), 112–118. doi:10.2307/2685468

Hanneke, S., & Xing, E. P. (2007). Discrete temporal models of social networks. In *Proceedings of the 2006 Conference on Statistical Network Analysis*, ICML'06, 115–125, Berlin: Springer-Verlag.

Hao, Q., Cai, R., Wang, X. J., Yang, J. M., Pang, Y., & Zhang, L. (2009). *Generating Location Overviews with Images and Tags by Mining User-generated Travelogues.* In proceedings of the 17th ACM International Conference on Multimedia. New York: ACM. pp. 801-804.

Harary, F., & Gupta, G. (1997). Dynamic graph models. *Mathematical and Computer Modelling, 25*(7), 79–87. doi:10.1016/S0895-7177(97)00050-2

Harris, M. (1998). *Good to Eat: Riddles of Food and Culture.* Long Grove, IL: Waveland Press.

Hattiangadi, J. N. (1987). *How is Language Possible?: Philosophical Reflections on the Evolution of Language and Knowledge.* La Salle: Open Court.

Haythornthwaite, C. (2002). Strong, Weak, and Latent Ties and the Impact of New Media. *The Information Society, 18*(5), 385–401. doi:10.1080/01972240290108195

He, H., & Garcia, E. A. (2009, September). Learning from imbalanced data. *IEEE Transactions on Knowledge and Data Engineering, 21*(9), 1263–1284. doi:10.1109/TKDE.2008.239

Heerwegh, D., & Loosveldt, G. (2008). Face-to-face versus web surveying in a high-Internet-coverage population. *Public Opinion Quarterly, 72*(5), 836–846. doi:10.1093/poq/nfn045

Heider, F. (1946). Attitudes and cognitive organization. *The Journal of Psychology, 21*, 107–112. doi:10.1080/00223980.1946.9917275

Heine, K. (2009). Using personal and online repertory grid methods for the development of a luxury brand personality. *Electronic Journal of Business Research Methods, 7*(1), 25–38.

Hendrickson, B., & Leland, R. W. (1995). *A multi-level algorithm for partitioning graphs.* Supercomputing.

Henry, R. M., & Butler, B. S. (2001, August 3-8). *Is it Who You Know or Where You Go: A Comparison of Relational and Non-Relational Information Sources*. Paper presented at the Academy of Management Conference, Washington, DC.

Herlocker, J., Konstan, J. A., Terveen, L., & Riedl, J. (2004). Evaluating Collaborative Filtering Recommender Systems. [TOIS]. *ACM Transactions on Information Systems, 22*(1). doi:10.1145/963770.963772

Herlocker, J. L., Konstan, J., Borchers, A., & Riedl, J. (1999). *An algorithmic framework for performing collaborative filtering*. In Proc. of SIGIR.

Herlocker, J. L., Konstan, J. A., & Riedl, J. (2002). *Explaining Collaborative Filtering Recommendations*. Proc. of the ACM Conference on Computer Supported Cooperative Work, 2002

Hern, Ã¡ndez, M. A., & Stolfo, S. J. (1998). Real-world data is dirty: Data cleansing and the merge/purge problem. *Data Mining and Knowledge Discovery, 2*(1), 9–37. doi:10.1023/A:1009761603038

Herrera, F., & Herrera-Viedma, E. (2000). Linguistic decision analysis: steps for solving decision problems under linguistic information. *Fuzzy Sets and Systems, 115*, 67–82. doi:10.1016/S0165-0114(99)00024-X

Herrera-Viedma, E., & Pasi, G. (2006). Soft Approaches to Information Retrieval and Information Access on the Web: An Introduction to the Special Topic Section. *Journal of the American Society for Information Science and Technology, 57*(4), 511–514. doi:10.1002/asi.20305

Heymann, P., Koutrika, G., & Garcia-Molina, H. (2008). Can social bookmarking improve web search? *WSDM '08: Proceedings of the international conference on Web search and web data mining* (pp. 195-206). New York: ACM.

Hiro, K., Wu, H., & Furugori, T. (1996). Word-sense disambiguation with a corpus-based semantic network. *Journal of Quantitative Linguistics, 3*, 244–251. doi:10.1080/09296179608599631

Hirschman, L., & Chinchor, N. (1997). *MUC-7 Coreference Task Definition - Version 3.0*. Paper presented at the Proceedings of MUC.

HM USA TRAVEL GUIDE. (n.d) *Weather per state* [Online]. Available: http://www.hm-usa.com/ climate/ index.html

Hoff, P. D., Raftery, A. E., & Handcock, M. S. (2002). Latent space approaches to social network analysis. *Journal of the American Statistical Association, 97*(460), 1090–1098. doi:10.1198/016214502388618906

Hoffman, D. L., & Novak, T. P. (2009). Flow online: lessons learned and future prospects. *Journal of Interactive Marketing, 23*(1), 23–34. doi:10.1016/j.intmar.2008.10.003

Hofmann, T. (2003). *Collaborative filtering via Gaussian probabilistic latent semantic analysis*. Proceedings of the 26th International ACM SIGIR Conference on Research and Development in Information Retrieval

Holland, P., & Leinhardt, S. (1977). A dynamic model for social networks. *The Journal of Mathematical Sociology, 5*, 5–20. doi:10.1080/0022250X.1977.9989862

Holzer, R., Malin, B., & Sweeney, L. (2005). Email alias detection using social network analysis. In *Proceedings of International Workshop on Link Discovery* (pp. 52-57).

Hong, G. H., & Lee, J. H. (2005). Designing an Intelligent Web Information System of Government Based on Web Mining. *Lecture Notes in Computer Science, 3614*, 1071–1078. doi:10.1007/11540007_138

Hong, T. P., Wu, Y. Y., & Wang, S. L. (2009). An effective mining approach for up-to-date patterns. *Expert Systems with Applications, 36*, 9747–9752. doi:10.1016/j.eswa.2009.02.029

Hou, J., & Zhang, Y. (2003). Effectively finding relevant web pages from linkage information. *IEEE Transactions on Knowledge and Data Engineering, 15*(4), 940–951. doi:10.1109/TKDE.2003.1209010

Hoyt, D. R., & Babchuk, N. (1983). Adult kinship networks: The selective formation of intimate ties with kin. *Social Forces, 62*(1), 84–101.

Hsiung, P., Moore, A., Neill, D., & Schneider, J. (2005). Alias detection in link data sets. In *Proceedings of International Conference on Intelligence Analysis*.

Hsu, C.-W., & Lin, C.-J. (2002). A comparison of methods for multi-class support vector machines. *IEEE Transactions on Neural Networks, 13*(2), 415–425. doi:10.1109/72.991427

Hu, C., Xu, L., Shen, G., & Fukushima, T. (2009). Temporal Company Relation Mining from the Web. In *Proceedings of the Joint International Conferences on Advances in Data and Web Management* (APWeb/WAIM'09), Suzhou, China, (pp. 392-403).

Huang, Z., & Lin, D. K. J. (2009). The Time-Series Link Prediction Problem with Applications in Communication Surveillance. [http://dx.doi.org/10.1287/ijoc.1080.0292]. *INFORMS Journal on Computing, 21*(2), 286–303. doi:10.1287/ijoc.1080.0292

Huang, Z., Chung, W., & Chen, H. (2004). A graph model for e-commerce recommender systems. [JASIST]. *Journal of the American Society for Information Science and Technology, 55*(3), 259–274. doi:10.1002/asi.10372

Huang, J., Zhuang, Z., Li, J., & Giles, C. L. (2008). Collaboration over time: Characterizing and Modeling network evolution. In *Proceedings of the 1st ACM International Conference on Web Search and Data Mining* (WSDM).

Hudson, S., & Hudson, D. (2006). Branded Entertainment: A New Advertising Technique or Product Placement in Disguise? *Journal of Marketing Management, 22,* 489–504. doi:10.1362/026725706777978703

Hume, D. (1888). *A Treatise of Human Nature.* Oxford: Clarendon Press.

Humphreys, J. S., & Rolley, F. (1998). A Modified Framework for Rural General Practice: The Importance of Recruitment and Retention. *Social Science & Medicine, 46*(8), 939–949. doi:10.1016/S0277-9536(97)00212-8

Igbaria, M., & Tan, M. (1997). The Consequences of Information Technology Acceptance on Subsequent Individual Performance. *Information & Management, 32*(3), 113–121. doi:10.1016/S0378-7206(97)00006-2

Imafuji, N., & Kitsuregawa, M. (2002). Effects of maximum flow algorithm on identifying Web community. *WIDM'02: Proceedings of the Fourth International Workshop on Web Information and Data Management,* pp. 43-48.

Ino, H., Kudo, M., & Nakamura, A. (2005). Partitioning of Web Graphs by Community Topology. *WWW '05: Proceedings of the 14th international conference on World Wide Web.*

Internet Multimedia Mining. (2009). *The 1st International Workshop on Internet Multimedia Mining in conjunction with IEEE International Conference on Data Mining.* December 6, Miami, Florida.

Irani, Z. Al-Sebie, & M., Elliman, T. (2006). Transaction Stage of e-Government Systems: Identification of its Location & Importance. *Proceedings of the 39th Hawaii International Conference on System Sciences,* January 4-7, Hawai, USA.

Jackson, N., & Lilleker, D. (2009). Building an Architecture of Participation? Political Parties and Web 2.0 in Britain. *Journal of Information Technology & Politics, 6*(3-4), 232–250. doi:10.1080/19331680903028438

Jackson, M. O. (2007). The study of social networks. In Rauch, J. E. (Ed.), *The missing links: formation and decay of economic networks* (pp. 19–43). London, UK: Russell Sage Foundation.

Jackson, P., & Moulinier, I. (2007). *Natural Language Processing for Online Applications. Text Retrieval, Extraction and Categorization,* 2nd revised edition. John Benjamins Publishing Company, Amsterdam/Philadephia, 2007. ISBN: 978-90-272-49920.

Jaeger, P. T., Paquette, S., & Simmons, S. N. (2010). Information Policy in National Political Campaigns: A Comparison of the 2008 Campaigns for President of the United States and Prime Minister of Canada. *Journal of Information Technology & Politics, 7,* 67–82. doi:10.1080/19331680903316700

Jagersberger, A., & Waldh, K. (2008). Dynamic Packaging using a Cluster-based Demographic Filtering Approach. In P. O'Connor, W. Hken, & U. Gretzel, (eds). *Information and Communication Technologies in Tourism,* 186-197. New York: Springer.

Jaro, M. A. (1995). Probabilistic linkage of large public health data files. *Statistics in Medicine, 14*(5-7), 491–498. doi:10.1002/sim.4780140510

Java, A., Joshi, A., & Finin, T. (2008). Detecting communities via simultaneous clustering of graphs and folksonomies. *Proceedings of the Tenth Workshop on Web Mining and Web Usage Analysis (WebKDD)*. ACM.

Jeh, G., & Widom, J. (2002). SimRank: A measure of structural-context similarity. In *Proceedings of the ACM SIGKDD International Conference on Knowledge Discovery and Data Mining* (pp. 538-543).

Jeong, H., Mason, S., Barabási, A. L., & Oltvai, Z. N. (2001). Lethality and centrality in protein networks. *Nature, 411*, 41–42. doi:10.1038/35075138

Jeong, H., Tombor, B., Albert, R., Oltval, Z. N., & Barabasi, A. L. (2000). The large-scale organization of metabolic networks. *Nature, 407*, 651–654. doi:10.1038/35036627

Ji, R., Xie, X., Yao, H., & Ma, W.-Y. (2009). *Mining City Landmarks from Blogs by Graph Modeling. In proceedings of the 17th ACM international conference on multimedia* (pp. 105–114). New York: ACM.

Jin, Y., Matsuo, Y., & Ishizuka, M. (2009). Ranking Companies on the Web Using Social Network Mining. In Ting, I.-H., & Wu, H.-J. (Eds.), *Web Mining Applications in E-commerce and E-services, Studies in Computational Intelligence 172* (pp. 169–179). Heidelberg, Germany: Springer-Verlag. doi:10.1007/978-3-540-88081-3_8

Jin, R., Chai, J., & Si. (2008). L. *An automatic weighting scheme for collaborative filtering.* In Proc. of SIGIR'04. IP2Location. User manual, Java component. http://www.ip2location.com/ docs/IP2Location_Java_User_Manual.pdf

Jing, F., Zhang, L., & Ma, W.-Y. (2006). *Virtualtour: An Online Travel Assistant Based on High Quality Images. In proceedings of the 14th ACM international conference on multimedia* (pp. 599–602). New York, USA: ACM.

Joachims, T. (1998). Text categorization with support vector machines: Learning with many relevant features. *European Conference on Machine Learning* (pp. 137–142). Berlin: Springer.

Jung, J. J., & Euzenat, J. (2007). Towards semantic social networks. *ESWC'07: Proceedings of the 4th European conference on The Semantic Web: Research and Applications*, pp. 267–280.

Kako-Batt, Y. (2010). *Pharmacy spam: pharmaceutical websites fall into two distinct operations.* Retrieved December 1, 2010, from http://www.symantec.com/connect/blogs/ pharmacy-spam-pharmaceutical-websites- fall-two-distinct-operations

Kalashnikov, D. V., & Mehrotra, S. (2006). Domain-independent data cleaning via analysis of entity-relationship graph. *ACM Transactions on Database Systems, 31*(2), 716–767. doi:10.1145/1138394.1138401

Kalles, D., Papagelis, A., & Zaroliagis, C. (2003). *Algorithmic aspects of web intelligent systems. Web Intelligence* (pp. 323–345). Berlin: Springer.

Kalnes, O. (2009). Norwegian Parties and Web 2.0. *Journal of Information Technology & Politics, 6*(3), 251–266. doi:10.1080/19331680903041845

Kang, H., Getoor, L., Shneiderman, B., Bilgic, M., & Licamele, L. (2008). Interactive entity resolution in relational data: a visual analytic tool and its evaluation. [http://dx.doi.org/http://doi.ieeecomputersociety.org/10.1109/TVCG.2008.55]. *IEEE Transactions on Visualization and Computer Graphics, 14*, 999–1014. doi:10.1109/TVCG.2008.55

Kao, A., & Poteet, S. R. (2007). *Natural Language Processing and Text Mining.* Springer-Verlag, 2007.

Karypis, G., & Kumar, V. (1998). A fast and high quality multilevel scheme for partitioning irregular graphs. *SIAM Journal on Scientific Computing, 20*(1), 359–392. doi:10.1137/S1064827595287997

Kasturirangan, R. (1999). *Multiple scales in small-world graphs.* In MIT AI Lab Memo 1663., cond-mat/9904055.

Katz, L. (1953). A new status index derived from sociometric analysis. *Psychometrika, 18*(1), 39–43. doi:10.1007/BF02289026

Katz, L., & Proctor, C. H. (1959). The configuration of interpersonal relations in a group as a time-dependent stochastic process. *Psychometrika, 24*, 317–327. doi:10.1007/BF02289814

Kawale, J., Pal, A., & Srivastava, J. (2009/#aug.#). *Churn Prediction in MMORPGs: A Social Influence Based Approach.* Paper presented at the Computational Science and Engineering, 2009. CSE '09. International Conference on.

Keenoy, K., & Levene, M. (2005). Lecture Notes in Computer Science: *Vol. 3169. Personalization of Web Search* (pp. 201–228). doi:10.1007/11577935_11

Kelly, G. A. (1955). *The Psychology of Personal Constructs*. New York: Norton.

Kelly, S. (2006). *Customer Intelligence. From Data to Dialoque*. New York: Willey.

Kennedy, L. S., & Naaman, M. (2008). *Generating Diverse and Representative Image Search Results for Landmarks. In proceedings of the 17th international conference on World Wide Web* (pp. 297–306). New York: ACM.

Keppens, J., Shen, Q., & Schafer, B. (2005). Probabilistic abductive computation of evidence collection strategies in crime investigation. In *Proceedings of International Conference on Artificial Intelligence and Law* (pp. 215-224).

Kernighan, B. W., & Lin, S. (1970). An efficient heuristic procedure for partitioning graphs. *The Bell System Technical Journal, 49*(1), 291–307.

Kim, J., Tomasik, B., & Turnbull, D. (2009). Using Artist Similarity to Propagate Semantic Information. *ISMIR'09: 10th International Conference on Music Information Retrieval.*

Kirkcaldy, B., Pope, M., & Siefen, G. (1993). Sociogrid analysis of a child and adolescent psychiatric clinic. *Social Psychiatry and Psychiatric Epidemiology, 28*(6), 296–303. doi:10.1007/BF00795911

Kirke, D. M. (1996). Collecting peer data and delineating peer networks in a complete network. *Social Networks, 18*(4), 333–346. doi:10.1016/0378-8733(95)00280-4

Kittler, P. (1995). *Food and culture in America: A nutrition handbook*. Redding, CA: West Publishing.

Kleinberg, J. (2001). Small-world phenomena and the dynamics of information. [NIPS]. *Advances in Neural Information Processing Systems, 14*, 2001.

Kleinberg, J. M. (2000). Navigation in a small world—it is easier to find short chains between points in some networks than others. *Nature, 406*, 845. doi:10.1038/35022643

Kleinberg, J. (1998). Authoritative sources in a hyperlinked environment. *SODA'98: Proceedings of the ninth annual ACM-SIAM symposium on Discrete algorithms*, pp. 668–677.

Kleinberg, J. M., Kumar, R., Raghavan, P., Rajagopalan, S., & Tomkins, A. S. (1999). The Web as a graph: Measurements, models, and methods. In *Proceedings of the International Conference on Combinatorics and Computing*, (pp. 1-18).

Klink, S., Reuther, P., Weber, A., Walter, B., & Ley, M. (2006). Analysing social networks within bibliographical data. In *Proceedings of International Conference on Database and Expert Systems Applications* (pp. 234-243).

Klotz, R. (2010). The Sidetracked 2008 YouTube Senate Campaign. *Journal of Information Technology & Politics, 7*(2), 110–123. doi:10.1080/19331681003748917

Knott, A., Hayes, A., & Neslin, S. (2002). Next-Product-To-Buy Models for Cross-Selling Applications. *Journal of Interactive Marketing, 16*(3), 9–75. doi:10.1002/dir.10038

Ko, M. N., Cheek, G. P., Shehab, M., & Sandhu, R. (2010). Social-Networks Connect Services. *IEEE Computer Society, 43*(8), 37–43.

Kogut, B., Urso, P., & Walker, G. (2007). Emergent properties of a new financial market: American venture capital syndication, 1965-2005. *Management Science, 53*, 1181–1198. doi:10.1287/mnsc.1060.0620

Kohavi, R. (1998). Data mining with MineSet: what worked, what did not, and what might. In *Workshop on Commercial Success of Data Mining*. Fourth International Conference on Knowledge Discovery and Data Mining.

Kolaczyk, E. D. (2009). *Statistical analysis of network data: Methods and models*. New York: Springer-Verlag.

Korte, C., & Milgram, S. (1970). Acquaintance linking between white and Negro populations: application of the small world problem. *Journal of Personality and Social Psychology, 15*, 101–118. doi:10.1037/h0029198

Kosala, R., & Blockeel, H. (2000). Web Mining Research: A Survey. *ACM, 2*(1), 1–15.

Koskinen, J. H., & Snijders, T. A. B. (2007). Bayesian inference for dynamic social network data. *Journal of Statistical Planning and Inference, 137*(12), 3930–3938. doi:10.1016/j.jspi.2007.04.011

Kossinets, G., & Watts, J. D. (2009). Origins of homophily in an evolving social network. *American Journal of Sociology, 115*(2), 405–450. doi:10.1086/599247

Kossinets, G. (2006). Effects of missing data in social networks. *Social Networks*, *28*(3), 247–268. doi:10.1016/j.socnet.2005.07.002

Kossinets, G., & Watts, D. J. (2006). Empirical analysis of an evolving social network. *Science*, *311*(5757), 88. doi:10.1126/science.1116869

Krackhardt, D. (1987). Cognitive social structures. *Social Networks*, *9*(2), 109–134. doi:10.1016/0378-8733(87)90009-8

Krapivsky, P. L., & Redner, S. (2001). Organization of growing random networks. *Physical Review E: Statistical, Nonlinear, and Soft Matter Physics*, *6306*, 066123. doi:10.1103/PhysRevE.63.066123

Kraut, R., Maher, M. R., Olson, J., Malone, T. W., Pirolli, P., & Thomas, J. C. (2010). Scientific Foundations: A Case for Technology-Mediated Social-Participation Theory. *IEEE Computer Society*, *43*(11), 22–28.

Krebs, V. (2000). Working in the connected world book network. *International Association for Human Resource Information Management Journal*, *4*(1), 87–90.

Kumar, R., Novak, J., Raghavan, P., & Tomkins, A. (2005). On the bursty evolution of blogspace. *World Wide Web (Bussum)*, *8*(2), 159–178. doi:10.1007/s11280-004-4872-4

Kumar, V. (2008). *Managing customers for profits: strategies to increase profits and building loyalty*. New Jersey: Wharton Scholl Publishing.

Kumar, V., Petersen, J., & Leone, R. (2010). Driving Profitability by Encouraging Customer Referrals: Who, When, and How. *Journal of Marketing*, *74*, 1–17. doi:10.1509/jmkg.74.5.1

Kumar, R., Novak, J., & Tomkins, A. (2006). Structure and evolution of online social networks. In *Proceedings of the 12th ACM International Conference on Knowledge Discovery and Data Mining* (KDD), Philadelphia, USA, (pp. 611-617).

Kumar, R., Raghavan, P., Rajagopalan, S., Sivakumar, D., Tomkins, A., & Upfal, E. (2000). Stochastic models for the web graph. In *Proceedings of the 41th Annual Symposium on Foundations of Computer Science*, 57-65.

Labrou, Y., & Finin, T. (1999). Yahoo! As an Ontology – Using Yahoo! Categories To Describe Documents. *In Proceedings of the 8th International Conference on Information Knowledge Management (CIKM), 180-187.*

Langville, A. N., & Meyer, C. D. (2006). *Google's PageRank and Beyond: The Science of Search Engine Rankings*. Princeton, N.J.: Princeton University Press.

Lappas, G. (2008). An Overview of Web Mining in Societal Benefit Areas. *Journal of Online Information Review*, *32*(2), 179–195. doi:10.1108/14684520810879818

Lappas, G., Kleftodimos, A., & Yannas, P. (2010). Greek Parties and Web 2.0. *paper presented at Elections, Campaigning, and Citizens Online Workshop*, Oxford Internet Institute, Oxford, UK, 15-16 September, available at: http:// drupals.humanities.manchester.ac.uk/ ipol/sites/default/files/ ecco/Lappas.pdf.

Latour, B. (2005). *Reassembling the social: An introduction to Actor-Network-Theory*. London: Oxford University Press.

Lawrence, S., Giles, C. L., & Bollacker, K. D. (1999). Autonomous citation matching. In *Proceedings of International Conference on Autonomous Agents* (pp. 392-393).

Lazarfeld, P. F., & Merton, R. K. (1954). A substantive and methodologies analysis. *Freedom and control in modern society, 18*, 66.

Lazer, D., Pentland, A., Adamic, L., Aral, S., Barabási, A.-L., & Brewer, D. (2009). Computational Social Science. [http://dx.doi.org/10.1126/science.1167742]. *Science*, *323*(5915), 721–723. doi:10.1126/science.1167742

Lazer, D. (2009). Life in the network: the coming age of computational social science. *Science*, *6*(323), 721–723. doi:10.1126/science.1167742

Lee, K., Caverlee, J., & Webb, S. (2010). Uncovering social spammers: social honeypots + machine learning. *SIGIR 2010, Special Interest Group on Information Retrieval* (pp. 435 – 422), July 19 – 23, 2010, Geneva, Switzerland.

Leenders, R. T. A. J. (1995). Models for network dynamics: A markovian framework. *The Journal of Mathematical Sociology*, *20*, 1–21. doi:10.1080/0022250X.1995.9990149

Leskovec, J., & Horvitz, E. (2008). *Planetary-scale views on a large instant-messaging network.* Paper presented at the Proceeding of the 17th international conference on World Wide Web.

Leskovec, J., Kleinberg, J., & Faloutsos, C. (2007). Graph evolution: Densification and shrinking diameters. *ACM Transactions on Knowledge Discovery from Data, 1*(1).

Lewis, K., Kaufman, J., Gonzalez, M., Wimmer, A., & Christakis, N. (2008). Tastes, ties, and time: A new social network dataset using Facebook. com. *Social Networks, 30*(4), 330–342. doi:10.1016/j.socnet.2008.07.002

Lewis Mumford Center. (2001). *Ethnic Diversity Grows, Neighborhood Integration Lags Behind.* Lewis Mumford Center, University at Albany.

Li, B., Xu, S., & Zhang, J. (2007). Enhancing clustering blog documents by utilizing author/reader comments. *Proceedings of the 45th Annual Southeast Regional Conference,* (pp. 94–99). New York

Li, S., Sun, B., & Montgomery, A. (2005). *Introducing What Financial Product to Which Customer at What Time - An Empirical Analysis of Customized and Dynamic Cross-selling Campaigns.* Tepper School of Business working paper 2006-E66.

Liben-Nowell, D., & Kleinberg, J. (2007). The link-prediction problem for social networks. *Journal of the American Society for Information Science and Technology, 58*(7), 1019–1031. doi:10.1002/asi.20591

Licoppe, C., & Smoreda, Z. (2005). Are social networks technologically embedded?: How networks are changing today with changes in communication technology. *Social Networks, 27*(4), 317–335. doi:10.1016/j.socnet.2004.11.001

Lilleker, D. G., Pack, M., & Jackson, N. (2010). Political Parties and Web 2.0: The Liberal Democrat Perspective. *Politics, 30*(2), 103–112. doi:10.1111/j.1467-9256.2010.01373.x

Lin, Y. R., Chi, Y., Zhu, S., Sundaram, H., & Tseng, B. L. (2010). Analyzing communities and their evolutions in dynamic social networks. *ACM Transactions on Knowledge Discovery from Data, 3*(2), 1–31. doi:10.1145/1514888.1514891

Lin, Y. R., Sundaram, H., Chi, Y., Tatemura, J., & Tseng, B. L. (2007). Blog community discovery and evolution based on mutual awareness expansion. *Proceedings of the IEEE/WIC/ACM international conference on web intelligence,* 48-56.

Lin, Z., King, I., & Lyu, M. R. (2006). Pagesim: A novel link-based similarity measure for the world wide web. In *Proceedings of IEEE/WIC/ACM International Conference on Web Intelligence* (pp. 687-693).

Liszka, K., Chan, C., Shekar, C., & Wakade, S. (2010). Mining pharmaceutical spam from Twitter. *International Conference on Intelligent Systems and Applications (ISDA 2010),* November 2010, pp. 813-817.

Liu, F., Yu, C., & Meng, W. (2004). *Personalized Web Search For Improving Retrieval Effectiveness.* IEEE TKDE.

Logan, J. Stowell, J. & Vesselinov, E. (2001). *From Many Shores: Asians in Census 2000.* Lewis Mumford Center, University at Albany.

Logan, J. (October 2002). *Separate and Unequal: The Neighborhood Gap for Blacks and Hispanics in Metropolitan America.* Lewis Mumford Center, University at Albany.

Lozano, S., Duch, J., & Arenas, A. (2006). Community detection in a large social dataset of European Projects. *Workshop on Link Analysis, Counterterrorism and Security (SIAM on Data mining).*

Lu, L., & Zhou, T. (2010). A Survey. In *Submission, In Submission.* Link Prediction in Complex Networks.

Luo, X. (2002). Trust Production and Privacy Concerns on the Internet: A Framework Based on Relationship Marketing and Social Exchange Theory. *Industrial Marketing Management, 31*(2), 111–118. doi:10.1016/S0019-8501(01)00182-1

Luo, D., & Huang, H. (2009). *Link Prediction of Multimedia Social Network via Unsupervised Face Recognition.* In ACM Multimedia Proceedings, ACM Press, pp. 805-808.

Luxburg, U. (2007). A tutorial on spectral clustering. *Statistics and Computing, 17*(4), 395–416. doi:10.1007/s11222-007-9033-z

Ma, Z., Pant, G., & Sheng, O. R. L. (2009). A network-based approach to mining competitor Relationships from online news. In *Proceedings of 8th IEEE/ACIS International Conference on Computer and Information Science* (ICIS), Shanghai, China.

Mackenzie, S., Lutz, R., & Belch, G. (1986). The Role of Attitude toward the Ad as a Mediator of Advertising Effectiveness: A Test of Competing Explanations. *JMR, Journal of Marketing Research, 23*(2), 130–144. doi:10.2307/3151660

Madhavan, R., Koka, B. R., & Prescott, J. E. (1998). Networks in transition: how industry events (re) shape interfirm relationships. *Strategic Management Journal, 19*(5), 439–459. doi:10.1002/(SICI)1097-0266(199805)19:5<439::AID-DIA952>3.0.CO;2-2

Mahmood, M. A., Burn, J. M., Gemoets, L. A., & Jacquez, C. (2000). Variable affecting Information Technology End-user Satisfaction: A Meta-analysis of the Empirical Literature. *International Journal of Human-Computer Studies, 52*(4), 751–771. doi:10.1006/ijhc.1999.0353

Mallinckrodt, V., & Mizerski, D. (2007). The Effects of Playing and Advergame on Young Children's Perceptions, Preferences, and Requests. *Journal of Advertising, 36*(2), 87–100. doi:10.2753/JOA0091-3367360206

Manfreda, K. L., Bosnjak, M., Berzelak, J., Haas, I., & Vehovar, V. (2008). Web surveys versus other survey modes: a meta-analysis comparing response rates. *International Journal of Market Research, 50*(1), 79–104.

Mann, G., & Yarowsky, D. (2003). Unsupervised personal name disambiguation. In *Proceedings of International Conference on Computational Natural Language Learning* (pp. 33-40).

Maoz, Z. (2010in press). *Networks of nations: The evolution, structure, and impact of international networks, 1816-2001*. New York: Cambridge University Press.

Maponics (2008). *Neighborhood to ZIP Code Correlation Data*. Available: http://www.maponics.com/ Neighborhood_ZIP_Codes/ neighborhood_zip_codes.html

Marin, A. (2004). Are respondents more likely to list alters with certain characteristics?: Implications for name generator data. [http://dx.doi.org/DOI: 10.1016/j.socnet.2004.06.001]. *Social Networks, 26*(4), 289-307.

Marsden, P. V. (1990). Network data and measurement. *Annual Review of Sociology, 16*, 435–463. doi:10.1146/annurev.so.16.080190.002251

Marsden, P. V., & Campbell, K. E. (1984). Measuring tie strength. *Social Forces, 63*(2), 482–501.

Marsden, P. V. (2005). Recent developments in network measurement. In J. S. S. W. Peter J. Carrington (Ed.), *Models and methods in social network analysis*: Cambridge University Press.

Matzat, U., & Snijders, C. (2010). Does the online collection of ego-centered network data reduce data quality? An experimental comparison. [http://dx.doi.org/DOI: 10.1016/j.socnet.2009.08.002]. *Social Networks, 32*(2), 105-111.

Mayer, A., & Puller, S. L. (2007). The old boy (and girl) network: Social network formation on university campuses. *Journal of Public Economics, 92*(1-2), 329–347. doi:10.1016/j.jpubeco.2007.09.001

Mayer, T. F. (1984). Parties and networks: Stochastic models for relationship networks. *The Journal of Mathematical Sociology, 10*, 51–103. doi:10.1080/0022250X.1984.9989958

McCarthy, K., Zabar, B., & Weiss, G. (2005). Does cost-sensitive learning beat sampling for classifying rare classes? *Proceedings of UBDM 2005*, August 21, Chicago, Illinois, USA, pp. 69 – 77.

McCulloh, I., & Carley, K. M. (2009). *Longitudinal dynamic network analysis. Casos technical Report*. Center for the Computational Analysis of Social and Organizational Systems.

McGlohon, M., Akoglu, L., & Faloutsos, C. (2008). Weighted graphs and disconnected components: Patterns and a generator. In *Proceedings of the 14th ACM SIGKDD International Conference on Knowledge Discovery and Data Mining*, KDD '08, (pp. 524–532). New York, ACM.

McPherson, M., Smith-Lovin, L., & Cook, J. M. (2001). Birds of a feather: Homophily in social networks. *Annual Review of Sociology, 27*(1), 415–444. doi:10.1146/annurev.soc.27.1.415

Mead, G. H. (1934). *Mind, Self & Society From the Standpoint of a Social Behaviorist*. Chicago: University of Chicago Press.

Meng, W., Yu, C., & Liu, K. L. (2002). Building Efficient and Effective Metasearch Engines. [CSUR]. *ACM Computing Surveys, 34*(1), 48–89. doi:10.1145/505282.505284

Mercken, L., Snijders, T. A. B., Steglich, C., Vartiainen, E., & de Vries, H. (2010). Dynamics of adolescent friendship networks and smoking behavior. *Social Networks, 32*, 72–81. doi:10.1016/j.socnet.2009.02.005

Milgram, S. (1967). The small world problem. *Psychology Today, 2*, 60–67.

Miller, G. (1956). The magical number seven, plus or minus two: Some limits on our capacity for information processing. *Psychological Review, 63*(2), 81–97. doi:10.1037/h0043158

Milo, R., Shen-Orr, S., Itzkovitz, S., Kashtan, N., Chklovskii, D., & Alon, U. (2002). Network motifs: simple building blocks of complex networks. *Science, 298*, 824–827. doi:10.1126/science.298.5594.824

Minkov, E., Cohen, W. W., & Ng, A. Y. (2006). Contextual search and name disambiguation in email using graphs. In *Proceedings of International ACM SIGIR Conference on Research and Development in Information Retrieval* (pp. 27-34).

Minneapolis Census. (2000). *Selected Economic Characteristics by Neighborhood, city of Minneapolis.* Available: http://www.ci.minneapolis.mn.us/ citywork/planning/Census2000/ maps/economic/

Mitchell, M. (2006). Complex systems: Network thinking. *Artificial Intelligence, 170*, 1194–1212. doi:10.1016/j.artint.2006.10.002

Mizruchi, M. S. (1996). What do interlocks do? An analysis, critique, and assessment of research on interlocking directorates. *Annual Review of Sociology, 22*, 27129. doi:10.1146/annurev.soc.22.1.271

Moh, T. S., & Murmann, A. (2010). Can you judge a man by his friends? - Enhancing spammer detection on the Twitter microblogging platform using friends and followers. *Information Systems, Technology and Management. Communications in Computer and Information Science, 54*(4), 210–220. .doi:10.1007/978-3-642-12035-0_21

Monge, P. R., & Eisenberg, E. M. (1987). Emergent communication networks. In Jablin, F. M., Putnam, L. L., Roberts, K. H., & Porter, L. W. (Eds.), *Handbook of organizational communication: An interdisciplinary perspective* (p. 304342). Newbury Park: Sage.

Montoya, J. M., & Sol, R. V. (2002). Small world patterns in food webs. *Journal of Theoretical Biology, 214*(3), 405–412. doi:10.1006/jtbi.2001.2460

Morgan, R. M., & Hunt, S. D. (1994). The Commitment-Trust Theory of Relationship Marketing. *Journal of Marketing, 58*(3), 20–38. doi:10.2307/1252308

Mori, J., Tsujishita, T., Matsuo, Y., & Ishizuka, M. (2006). Extracting Relations in Social Networks from the Web Using Similarity Between Collective Contexts. *Lecture Notes in Computer Science, 4273*, 487–500. doi:10.1007/11926078_35

Motter, A. E., Zhou, C., & Kurths, J. (2005). Enhancing complex-network synchronization. *Europhysics Letters, 69*, 334–340. doi:10.1209/epl/i2004-10365-4

Mowbray, M. (2010). The twittering machine. *Journal of Applied Statistics, 17*(2), 211–217.

Mukhopadhyay, T., Rajiv, S., & Srinivasan, K. (1997). Information Technology Impact on Process Output and Quality. *Management Science, 43*(12), 1645–1659. doi:10.1287/mnsc.43.12.1645

Murata, T., & Moriyasu, S. (2008). Link prediction based on structural properties of online social networks. *New Generation Computing, 26*, 245–257. doi:10.1007/s00354-008-0043-y

mxLogic (2004). *Spam classification techniques.* Retrieved October 2010 from http://wp.bitpipe.com/resource/ org_1094140501_975/MX_Logic_Spam%20Classification%20Techniques.pdf

Naamarn, M. (2010). Social Multimedia: highlighting opportunities for search and mining of multimedia data in social media applications. *Multimedia Tools and Applications*, http://www.springerlink.com/ content/v836432078k27014/

Nabhan, G. (2004). *Why Some Like It Hot: Food, Genes, and Cultural Diversity*. Washington, D.C.: Island Press.

Nasir, A. N. M., Selamat, A., & Selamat, M. H. (2009). Web Mining for Malaysia's Political Social Networks using Artificial Immune System. *Lecture Notes in Computer Science, 5465*, 137–146. doi:10.1007/978-3-642-01715-5_12

Newcomb, T. M. (Ed.). (1961). *The acquaintance process*. New York: Holt, Rinehart, and Winston. doi:10.1037/13156-000

Newcombe, H. B., Kennedy, J. M., Axford, S. J., & James, A. P. (1959). Automatic linkage of vital and health records. *Science, 130*, 954–959. doi:10.1126/science.130.3381.954

Newman, M. E. J. (2001). Scientific collaboration networks. I. Network construction and fundamental results. *Physical Review E: Statistical, Nonlinear, and Soft Matter Physics, 64*(1), 16131. doi:10.1103/PhysRevE.64.016131

Newman, M. E. J. (2001). The structure of scientific collaboration networks. *Proceedings of the National Academy of Sciences of the United States of America, 98*(2), 404–409. doi:10.1073/pnas.021544898

Newman, M. E. J. (2002). Assortative mixing in networks. *Physical Review Letters, 89*, 208701. doi:10.1103/PhysRevLett.89.208701

Newman, M. E. J. (2003). The structure and function of complex networks. *SIAM Review, 45*(2), 167–256. doi:10.1137/S003614450342480

Newman, M. E. J. (2006). Finding community structure in networks using the eigenvectors of matrices. *Physical Review E: Statistical, Nonlinear, and Soft Matter Physics, 74*, 036104. doi:10.1103/PhysRevE.74.036104

Newman, M. E. J., & Watts, D. J. (1999). Scaling and percolation in the small-world network model. *Physical Review E: Statistical Physics, Plasmas, Fluids, and Related Interdisciplinary Topics, 60*, 7332–7342. doi:10.1103/PhysRevE.60.7332

Ng, H. T., Wang, B., & Chan, Y. S. (2003). Exploiting parallel texts for word sense disambiguation: an empirical study. In *Proceedings of Annual Meeting of the Association for Computational Linguistics* (pp. 455-462).

Ning, H., Xu, W., Chi, Y., Gong, Y., & Huang, T. (2007). Incremental spectral clustering with application to monitoring of evolving blog communities. *Paper presented at the SIAM International Conference on Data Mining.*

Nisbet, R., Elder, J., & Miner, G. (2009). *Handbook of Statistical Analysis & Data Mining Applications*. Amsterdam: Elsevier.

Noll, M. G., & Meinel, C. (2008b). *The metadata triumvirate: Social annotations, anchor texts and search queries. Web Intelligence and Intelligent Agent Technology* (pp. 640–647). Sydney, Australia: IEEE CS Press.

Noll, M. G., & Meinel, C. (2007). Authors vs. readers: A comparative study of document metadata and content in the WWW. *Proceedings of the 2007 ACM symposium on Document engineering* (pp. 177-186). Winnipeg, Manitoba, Canada: ACM.

Noll, M. G., & Meinel, C. (2008a). Exploring social annotations for web document classification. *Proceedings of the 2008 ACM symposium on Applied computing* (pp. 2315-2320). Fortaleza, Ceara, Brazil: ACM.

Nordle, P. G. (1958). A longitudinal study of interpersonal attraction in a natural group setting. Unpublished Ph.D. dissertation, Department of Psychology, University of Michigan.

Nye, J. (2004). *Soft Power: The Means to Success in World Politics*. New York: Public Affairs.

O'Connor, P., Höpken, W., & Gretzel, U. *Dynamic Packaging using a Cluster-based Demographic Filtering Approach*. In Proc. the International Conference in Innsbruck, Austria, 2008. Oracle: Oracle XML DB. (n.d) Retrieved from://www.oracle.com/technology/tech/xml/xmldb/index.html

O'Hara, K., Alani, H., & Shadbolt, N. (2002). Identifying Communities of Practice: Analysing Ontologies as Networks to Support Community Recognition. *Proc. Conf. Int'l Federation Information Processing (IFIP), World Computer Congress*.

Obstfeld, D. (2005). Social Networks, the Tertius Iungens Orientation, and Involvement in Innovation. *Administrative Science Quarterly, 50*(1), 100–130.

Olmo, C., Sanchez, G., Prats, F., Agell, N., & Sanchez, M. (2007). Using orders of magnitude and nominal variables to construct fuzzy partitions. In *Proceedings of IEEE International Conference on Fuzzy Systems* (pp. 1-6).

Olson, G., Mark, G., Churchill, E., & Rotman, D. (2010). Technology-Mediated Social Participation: New Missions for a Sociotechnical Infrastructure. *IEEE Computer Society*, *43*(11), 37–43.

O'Madadhain, J., Hutchins, J., & Smyth, P. (2005). Prediction and ranking algorithms for event-based network data. [http://dx.doi.org/http://doi.acm.org/10.1145/1117454.1117458]. *SIGKDD Explorations Newsletter*, *7*, 23–30. doi:10.1145/1117454.1117458

Onnela, J. P., Saramäki, J., Hyvönen, J., Szabó, G., Lazer, D., & Kaski, K. (2007). Structure and tie strengths in mobile communication networks. [http://dx.doi.org/10.1073/pnas.0610245104]. *Proceedings of the National Academy of Sciences of the United States of America*, *104*(18), 7332–7336. doi:10.1073/pnas.0610245104

Open Directory Project. (2009). Available: http://dmoz.org.

Orlikowski, W. (1992). The Duality of Technology: Rethinking the Concept of Technology in Organizations. *Organization Science*, *3*(3), 398–427. doi:10.1287/orsc.3.3.398

Ozik, J., Hunt, B., & Ott, E. (2004). Growing networks with geographical attachment preference: emergence of small worlds. *Physical Review E*, *69*, 026-108.

Panagis, Y., Sakkopoulos, E., Tsakalidis, A., Tzimas, G., Sirmakessis, S., & Lytras, M. (2008). Techniques for mining the design of e-government services to enhance end-user experience. *Int. J. Electronic Democracy*, *1*(1), 32–50. doi:10.1504/IJED.2008.021277

Pancras, J., & Sudhir, K. (2007). Optimal marketing strategies for a customer data intermediary. *JMR, Journal of Marketing Research*, *44*(4), 560–578. doi:10.1509/jmkr.44.4.560

Pantel, P. (2006). Alias detection in malicious environments. In *Proceedings of AAAI Fall Symposium on Capturing and Using Patterns for Evidence Detection* (pp. 14-20).

Pastor-Satorras, R., & Vespignani, A. (2004). *Evolution and structure of the Internet: A statistical physics approach*. Cambridge, UK: Cambridge Univ. Press. doi:10.1017/CBO9780511610905

Pasula, H., Marthi, B., Milch, B., Russell, S., & Shpitser, I. (2003). Identity uncertainty and citation matching. *Advances in Neural Information Processing Systems*, *15*, 1425–1432.

Paul, F. (1986). *Food and Nutrition: Customs and Culture*. London: Croom Helm.

Pazzani, M. (1999). A Framework for Collaborative, Content-Based and Demographic Filtering. *Artificial Intelligence Review*, *13*(5-6), 393–408. doi:10.1023/A:1006544522159

Pearce, C., & Miller, E. (1997). The TellTale dynamic hypertext environment: Approaches to scalability. *In Advances in Intelligence Hypertext, Lecture Notes in Computer Science*. *Springer-Verlag*, *1326*, 109-130.

Pennebaker, J. W., Booth, R. J., & Francis, M. E. (2007). *Linguistic Inquiry and Word Count 2007 (LIWC2007)* [Computer program.]. Austin, TX: LIWC, Inc.

Perreault, J., Cannon, J., & McCarthy, E. (2009). *Essentials of Marketing*. New York: McGraw-Hill.

Petróczi, A., Nepusz, T., & Bazsó, F. (2006). Measuring tie-strength in virtual social networks. *Connections*, *27*(2), 39–52.

Piatetsky-Shapiro, G., Djeraba, C., Getoor, L., Grossman, R., Feldman, R., & Zaki, M. (2006). What are the grand challenges for data mining. *KDD-2006 Panel Report. SIGKDD Explorations*, *8*(2), 70–77. doi:10.1145/1233321.1233330

Pickering, J. M., & King, J. L. (1995). Hardwiring Weak Ties: Interorganizational Computer-mediated Communication, Occupational Communities, and Organizational Change. *Organization Science*, *6*(4), 479–486. doi:10.1287/orsc.6.4.479

Piera, N. (1995). *Current trends in qualitative reasoning and applications. Monografia CIMNE*, *33*. Barcelona: International Center for Numerical Methods in Engineering.

Plato,. (2007). *The Republic*. New York: Penguin Classics.

Pool, IdeS., & Kochen, M. (1978). Contacts and influence. *Social Networks*, *1*, 1–48.

Pope, M. L., & Keen, T. R. (1981). *Personal Construct Psychology and Education*. London: Academic Press.

Popescul, A., & Ungar, L. H. (2003). *Statistical relational learning for link prediction.* Paper presented at the IJCAI03 Workshop on Learning Statistical Models from Relational Data.

Poplin, D. E. (1979). *Communities: A Survey of Theories and Methods of Research* (2nd ed.). New York: MacMillan Publishing Co., Inc.

Popp, R. L., & Yen, J. (2006). *Emergent information technologies and enabling policies for counter-terrorism.* Wiley. doi:10.1002/047178656X

Porter, G. (Jan 25, 2008). Crying (iranian) wolf in argentina. *Asia Times Online*

Powell, W. W., White, D. R., Koput, K. W., & Owen-Smith, J. (2005). Network dynamics and field evolution: the growth of interorganizational collaboration in the life sciences. *American Journal of Sociology, 1104*, 1132–1206. doi:10.1086/421508

Prahalad, C. K., & Krishnan, M. S. (2008). *The New Age of Innovation (Analytics: Insight for Innovation).* New York: McGraw-Hill.

Provost, F., & Fawcett, T. (1997). Analysis and visualization of classifier performance: comparison under imprecise class and cost distributions. *Proceedings of the Third International Conference on Knowledge Discovery and Data Mining (KDD 1997)*, Huntington Beach, CA, pp. 43 – 48.

Prud'Hommeaux, E. & Seaborne, A. (2008). *SPARQL Query Language for RDF W3C Recommendation 2008.*

Pyka, A., & Scharnhorst, A. (2009). *Innovation networks. New approaches in modelling and analyzing.* Berlin: Springer-Verlag.

Qi, X., & Davison, B. D. (2009). Web page classification: Features and algorithms. *ACM Computing Surveys, 41*(2), 1–31. doi:10.1145/1459352.1459357

Quinlan, J. R. (1993). *C4.5: Programs for Machine Learning.* San Francisco, CA: Morgan Kaufmann Publishers.

Raghuram, I., Han, S., & Gupta, S. (2009). *Do Friends Influence Purchases in a Social Network?* Harvard Business School Working Paper, no. 09-123.

Raiman, O. (1991). Order of magnitude reasoning. *Artificial Intelligence, 51*(1-3), 11–38. doi:10.1016/0004-3702(91)90107-U

Ramage, D., Heymann, P., Manning, C. D., & Garcia-Molina, H. (2009). Clustering the tagged web. *Proceedings of the Second ACM International Conference on Web Search and Data Mining* (pp. 54-63). Barcelona, Spain: ACM.

Ratmann, O., Wiuf, C., & Pinney, J. W. (2009). From evidence to inference: Probing the evolution of protein interaction networks. *HFSP Journal, 3*(5), 290–306. doi:10.2976/1.3167215

Resnick, L. B., Levinc, J. M., & Teasley, S. D. (1991). *Perspectives on Socially Shared Cognition.* Washington: American Psychological Association. doi:10.1037/10096-000

Reuther, P., & Walter, B. (2006). Survey on test collections and techniques for personal name matching. *International Journal on Metadata. Semantics and Ontologies, 1*(2), 89–99. doi:10.1504/IJMSO.2006.011006

Rice, R. E. (1994). Relating Electronic Mail Use and Network Structure to R&D Work Networks and Performance. *Journal of Management Information Systems, 11*(1), 9–29.

Rice, R. E., Grant, A., Schmitz, J., & Torobin, J. (1990). Individual and Network Influences on the Adoption and Perceived Outcomes of Electronic Messaging. *Social Networks, 12*(1), 27–55. doi:10.1016/0378-8733(90)90021-Z

Richards, W. D. Jr. (1995). *NEGOPY 4.30 Manual and user's Guide.* Burnaby, Canada: School of Communication, Simon Fraser University.

Riedl, R. (2003). Design Principles for E-Government Services. *Proceedings eGov Day*, February 13-14, Vienna, Austria.

Riopelle, K., Danowski, J. A., & Bishop, A. (2010). *Expression of sentiment by different node positions in email networks.* Paper presented to annual meetings of the International Network for Social Network Analysts, Riva Del Garda, Italy, June 29-July 4.

Riopelle, K., Danowski, J. A., & Gluesing, J. (2008). *Organizational hierarchy predictors of symmetric and asymmetric dyad and triad distributions in a large global organization.* Paper presented at annual meetings of the International Network for Social Network Analysis, Sunbelt XXVIII annual meetings, St. Pete Beach, FL, January.

Robertson, S. P., Vatrapu, R. K., & Medina, R. (2009). *The Social Life of Social Networks: Facebook Linkage Patterns in the 2008 U.S. Presidential Election*. In the Proceedings of the 10th International Digital Government Research Conference, Puebla, Mexico, May 17-20, 2009.

Robins, G., & Pattison, P. (2001). Random graph models for temporal processes in social networks. *The Journal of Mathematical Sociology, 25*, 5–41. doi:10.1080/0022250X.2001.9990243

Rubin, S., & Lee, G. (2003). A natural language interface for an intelligent universal situational awareness (USA) system. In *Proceedings of IEEE International Conference on Fuzzy Systems* (pp. 1261-1267).

Rust, R. T., & Verhoef, P. C. (2005). Optimizing the Marketing Interventions Mix in Intermediate-Term CRM. *Marketing Science, 24*(3), 477–489. doi:10.1287/mksc.1040.0107

Sahimi, M., Dumais, S., Heckerman, D., & Horvitz, E. (1998). A Bayesian approach to filtering junk e-mail, *Learning for Text Categorization: Papers from the 1998 Workshop*. AAAI Technical Report WS-98-05.

Salancik, G. R., & Pfeffer, J. (1978). A Social Information Processing Approach to Job Attitudes and Task Design. *Administrative Science Quarterly, 23*(2), 224–253. doi:10.2307/2392563

Sandberg, O. &. Clarke, I. (2006). *The evolution of navigable small-world networks*. Department of Computer Science and Engineering Technical Report 2007:14, Chalmers University of Technology.

Sarkar, P., & Moore, A. W. (2005). Dynamic social network analysis using latent space models. *SIGKDD Exploration Newsletter, 7*, 31–40. doi:10.1145/1117454.1117459

Sarkar, P., Siddiqi, S. M., & Gordon, G. J. (2007). A latent space approach to dynamic embedding of co-occurrence data. In *Proceedings of the 11th International Conference on Artificial Intelligence and Statistics* (AI-STATS'07).

Sarwar, B., Karypis, G., Konstan, J., & Riedl, J. *Item-based collaborative filtering recommendation algorithms*. In Proc. of the WWW Conference, 2001.

Savin-Williams, R. C. (1979). Dominance hierarchies in groups of early adolescents. *Child Development, 59*, 923–935. doi:10.2307/1129316

Scarpi, D. (2010). Does size matter? An examination of small and large web-based brand communities. *Journal of Interactive Marketing, 24*(1), 14–21. doi:10.1016/j.intmar.2009.10.002

Schaefer, D. R., Light, J. M., Fabes, R. A., Hanish, L. D., & Martin, C. L. (2010). Fundamental principles of network formation among preschool children. *Social Networks, 32*, 61–71. doi:10.1016/j.socnet.2009.04.003

Scharstein, D., & Szeliski, R. (2002). A taxonomy and evaluation of dense two-frame stereo correspondence algorithms. *International Journal of Computer Vision, 47*(1), 7–42. doi:10.1023/A:1014573219977

Schilling, M., & Phelps, C. C. (2007). Interfirm collaboration networks: The impact of large-scale network structure on firm innovation. *Management Science, 53*(7), 1113–1126. doi:10.1287/mnsc.1060.0624

Schütz, A. (1943). The problem of rationality in the social world. *Economica, 10*(38), 130–149. doi:10.2307/2549460

Scott, J. (2000). *Social Network Analysis: A Handbook*. SAGE Publications.

Scott, J. (1991). Networks of corporate power. *Annual Review of Sociology, 17*, 181203. doi:10.1146/annurev.so.17.080191.001145

Scott, J. (2000). *Social network analysis: A handbook* (2nd ed.). Thousand Oaks: Sage.

Seary, A. J. (2005) *MultiNet: An interactive program for analysing and visualizing complex networks.* Doctoral Dissertation, Burnaby, CA: Simon Frazier University. Available from: http://people.math.sfu.ca/~goddyn/Theses/searyPhDThesis.pdf

Seidman, S. (1983). Internal cohesion of LS sets in graphs. *Social Networks, 5*, 97–107. doi:10.1016/0378-8733(83)90020-5

Selman, B., Kautz, H., & Shah, M. (1997). Referralweb: Combining social networks and collaborative filtering. *Communications of the ACM*, (March): 1997.

Shamma, D. A., Kennedy, L., & Churchill, E. F. (2009). Tweet the Debates: Understanding Community Annotation of Uncollected Sources. *In proceedings of the 1st SIGMM workshop on Social Media*, ACM, New York, USA, pp 3-10.

Shamma, D. A., Kennedy, L., & Churchill, E. F. (2010). Statler: Summarizing media through short-messages services. *In proceedings of the 2010 ACM conference on Computer Supported Cooperative Work (CSCW 2010).* ACM, New York, USA.

Shankar, V., & Winer, R. (2006). When Customer Relationship Management Meets Data Mining. *Journal of Interactive Marketing, 20*(3-4), 2–4. doi:10.1002/dir.20062

Shaw, M. L. G. (1979). Conversational heuristics for eliciting shared understanding. *International Journal of Man-Machine Studies, 11*, 621–634. doi:10.1016/S0020-7373(79)80012-7

Shaw, M. L. G. (1980). *On Becoming a Personal Scientist: Interactive Computer Elicitation of Personal Models of the World.* London: Academic Press.

Shaw, M. L. G., & Gaines, B. R. (1989). Comparing conceptual structures: consensus, conflict, correspondence and contrast. *Knowledge Acquisition, 1*(4), 341–363. doi:10.1016/S1042-8143(89)80010-X

Shaw, M. L. G. (1985). Communities of knowledge. In Epting, F., & Landfield, A. W. (Eds.), *Anticipating Personal Construct Psychology* (pp. 25–35). Lincoln, Nebraska: University of Nebraska Press.

Shaw, M. L. G. (1978). Interactive computer programs for eliciting personal models of the world. In Fransella, F. (Ed.), *Personal Construct Psychology 1977* (pp. 59–67). London: Academic Press.

Shaw, M. L. G., & Gaines, B. R. (1996). WebGrid: knowledge elicitation and modeling on the web. In Maurer, H. (Ed.), *Proceedings of WebNet96* (pp. 425–432). Charlottesville, VA: Association for the Advancement of Computing in Education. doi:10.1007/978-1-4471-0351-6_21

Shaw, M. L. G., & Gaines, B. R. (1983). A computer aid to knowledge engineering *Proceedings of British Computer Society Conference on Expert Systems* (pp. 263-271). Cambridge: British Computer Society.

Shaw, M. L. G., & Gaines, B. R. (1991a). Extending electronic mail with conceptual modeling to provide group decision support *COCS'91: Proceedings of Conference on Organizational Computing Systems* (pp. 153-158). New York: ACM Press.

Shaw, M. L. G., & Gaines, B. R. (1991b). Supporting personal networking through computer networking *Proceedings of CHI'91: Human Factors in Computing Systems* (pp. 437-438). New York: ACM Publications.

Shen, Q., Keppens, J., Aitken, C., Schafer, B., & Lee, M. (2006). A scenario-driven decision support system for serious crime investigation. *Law Probability and Risk, 5*, 87–117. doi:10.1093/lpr/mgl014

Shen, Q., & Leitch, R. (1993). Fuzzy qualitative simulation. *IEEE Transactions on Systems, Man, and Cybernetics, 23*(4), 1038–1061. doi:10.1109/21.247887

Shen, Q., & Zhao, R. (2011). A credibilistic approach to assumption-based truth maintenance. *IEEE Transactions on Systems, Man, and Cybernetics. Part A, Systems and Humans, 41*(1), 85–96. doi:10.1109/TSMCA.2010.2064298

Shen. Q., & Boongoen, T. (2011) Fuzzy orders-of-magnitude based link analysis for qualitative alias detection. To appear in *IEEE Transactions on Knowledge and Data Engineering.*

Shen-Orr, S. S., Milo, R., Mangan, S., & Alon, U. (2002). Network motifs in the transcriptional regulation network of *Escherichia coli. Nature Genetics, 31*, 64–68. doi:10.1038/ng881

Shi, J., & Malik, J. (2000). Normalized cuts and image segmentation. *IEEE Transactions on Pattern Analysis and Machine Intelligence, 22*(8), 888–905. doi:10.1109/34.868688

Shibo, L., Sun, B., & Wilcox, R. (2005). Cross-Selling Sequentially Ordered Products: An Application to Consumer Banking Services. *JMR, Journal of Marketing Research, XLII*(May), 233–239.

Shimp, T. (1981). Attitude toward the Ad as a Mediator of Consumer Brand Choice. *Journal of Advertising, 10*(2), 9–17.

Shook, D. E. (1988). *A Structural Equivalence and Contingency Theory Perspective on Media Usage and Communication Performance: The Case of Voice Messaging.* Los Angeles, California: University of Southern California.

Short, J., Williams, E., & Christie, B. (1976). *The Social Psychology of Telecommunications.* London: John Wiley.

Simmel, G. (1910). How is Society Possible? *American Journal of Sociology, 16*(3), 372–391. doi:10.1086/211904

Singla, P., & Richardson, M. (2008). Yes, there's a correlation: -from social networks to personal behavior on the web.

Slater, P. (Ed.). (1976). *Dimensions of Intrapersonal Space (Vol. 1)*. London: John Wiley.

Small, H. (1973). Co-citation in the scientific literature: A new measure of the relationship between two documents. *Journal of the American Society for Information Science American Society for Information Science, 24*, 265–269. doi:10.1002/asi.4630240406

Smeulders, A., Worring, M., Santini, S., Gupta, A., & Jain, R. (2000). Content-based Image Retrieval at the End of the Early Years. *IEEE Transactions on Pattern Analysis and Machine Intelligence, 22*(12), 1349–1380. doi:10.1109/34.895972

Smith, G. (2008). *Tagging: people-powered metadata for the social web*. Berkeley, California, United States: New Riders.

Snijders, T. A. B., Steglich, C. E. G., & van de Bunt, G. G. (2010). Introduction to actor-based models for network dynamics. *Social Networks, 32*, 44–60. doi:10.1016/j.socnet.2009.02.004

Snijders, T. A. B. (1997). Models for longitudinal network data. In Carrington, P., Scott, J., & Wasserman, S. (Eds.), *Models and methods in social network analysis* (pp. 148–161). New York: Cambridge University Press.

Snijders, T. A. B. (1996). Stochastic actor-oriented models for network change. *Journal of Mathematical Sociology, 21*, 149-172. Also published in Doreian and Stokman (1997).

Snijders, T. A. B., & Van Duijn, M. A. J. (1997). Simulation for statistical inference in dynamic Network models. In R. Conte, R. Hegselmann, & P. Terna (Eds.), *Simulating social phenomena*, 493-512. Berlin: Springer.

Soon, W. M., Ng, H. T., & Lim, D. C. Y. (2001). A machine learning approach to coreference resolution of noun phrases. *Computational Linguistics, 27*(4), 521–544. doi:10.1162/089120101753342653

Sorensen, O., & Stuart, T. (2001). Syndication networks and the spatial distribution of venture capital investments. *American Journal of Sociology, 106*, 1546–1588. doi:10.1086/321301

Sproull, L., & Kiesler, S. (1991). *Connections: New Ways of Working in the Networked Organization*. Cambridge: MIT Press.

Staab, S., Domingos, P., Mika, P., Golbeck, J., Ding, L., & Finin, T. (1993). Social networks applied. *IEEE Intelligent Systems, 20*(1), 80–93. doi:10.1109/MIS.2005.16

Stephens, M. (2000). Bayesian analysis of mixtures with an unknown number of components—An alternative to reversible jump methods. *Annals of Statistics, 28*(1), 40–74. doi:10.1214/aos/1016120364

Strasser, R. P., Hays, R. B., Kamien, M., & Carson, D. (2000). Is Australian Rural Practice Changing? Findings from the National Rural General Practice Study. *The Australian Journal of Rural Health, 8*(4), 222–226. doi:10.1046/j.1440-1584.2000.00305.x

Stringhini, G., Kruegelm, C., & Vigna, G. (2010). A study on social network spam. *GSWC 2010, The Fifth Annual Graduate Student Workshop on Computing*, (pp. 43 – 44), October 8, 2010, Santa Barbara, California.

Sun, J., Qu, H., Chakrabarti, D., & Faloutsos, C. (2005). Relevance search and anomaly detection in bipartite graphs. *ACM SIGKDD Explorations Newsletter, 7*(2), 48–55. doi:10.1145/1117454.1117461

Sun, B.-Y., Huang, D.-S., Guo, L., & Zhao, Z.-Q. (2004). *Support vector machine committee for classification. Advances in Neural Networks – ISNN 2004* (pp. 648–653). Dalian, China: Springer.

Sun, B., Li, S., & Zhou, C. (2006). "Adaptive" Learning and "Proactive" Customer Relationship Management. *Journal of Interactive Marketing, 20*(3/4), 82–96. doi:10.1002/dir.20069

Surfer Beware. (2010). *Spam filters word list.* Retrieved July 2010 from http://www.surferbeware.com/ spam/ spam-spam-filter.htm

Surma, J. (2011). *Business Intelligence*. New York: Business Expert Press.

Surma, J., & Furmanek, A. (2010). Improving Marketing Response by Data Mining in Social Network, *in Proceedings of the International Conference on Advances in Social Networks Analysis and Mining (ASONAM 2010),* Aug 09-11, Odense, Denmark, pp.446-451, 2010, 2010

Swets, J. (1988). Measuring the accuracy of diagnostic systems. *Science, 240,* 1285–1293. doi:10.1126/science.3287615

Sykes, T. A., Venkatesh, V., & Gosain, S. (2009). Model of Acceptance with Peer Support: A Social Network Perspective to Understand Employees' System Use. *Management Information Systems Quarterly, 33*(2), 371–393.

Szell, M., & Thurner, S. (2010). Measuring social dynamics in a massive multiplayer online game. [http://dx.doi.org/DOI: 10.1016/j.socnet.2010.06.001]. *Social Networks, 32*(4), 313-329.

Tan, F. B., Tung, L.-L., & Xu, Y. (2009). A study of web-designers' criteria for effective business-to-consumer (b2c) websites using the repertory grid technique. *Journal of Electronic Commerce Research, 10*(3), 155–177.

Tantipathananandh, C., Berger-Wolf, T., & Kempe, D. (2007). A framework for community Identification in dynamic social networks. In *Proceedings of the 13th ACM SIGKDD International Conference on Knowledge Discovery and Data Mining* (KDD), San Jose, California, USA, (pp. 717-726).

Teachman, J. D. (1980). Analysis of Population Diversity: Measures of Qualitative Variation. *Sociological Methods & Research, 8*(3), 341–362. doi:10.1177/004912418000800305

Team, N. W. B. (2006). *Network Benchmark Tool.* Retrieved from http://nwb.slis.indiana.edu

Tesoro, E. (2001). *Religious Determinants of Food Choices.* Available: http://www.eat-online.net/english/education/religion_and_food/ religious_determinants.htm#References

Tetlock, P. C., Saar-Tsechansky, M., & Macskassy, S. (2008). More than words: Quantifying language to measure firms' fundamentals. *The Journal of Finance, 63*(3), 1437–1467. doi:10.1111/j.1540-6261.2008.01362.x

Thelwall, M., Wilkinson, D., & Uppal, S. (2010). Data Mining Emotion in Social Network Communication: Gender Differences in MySpace. *Journal of the American Society for Information Science and Technology, 61*(1), 190–199.

This research was supported in part by the National Science Foundation's Human and Social Dynamics (HSD) Award #SES-527487: Accelerating the diffusion of innovations: A "digital diffusion dashboard" methodology for global networked organizations.

Tian, Y., Srivastava, J., Huang, T., & Contractor, N. (2010). Social Multimedia Computing. *IEEE Computer Society, 43*(8), 27–36.

Tichy, N. M., Tushman, M. L., & Fombrun, C. (1979). Social network analysis for organizations. *Academy of Management Review, 4*(4), 507–519.

Ting, I. H., Wu, H. J., & Ho, T. H. (2010). *Mining and Analysing Social Networks.* Heidelberg, Germany: Springer-Verlag.

Ting, I.-H., & Wu, H.-J. (2009). Web Mining Techniques for On-line Social Networks Analysis: An Overview. In Ting, I.-H., & Wu, H.-J. (Eds.), *Web Mining Applications in E-commerce and E-services, Studies in Computational Intellligence 172* (pp. 169–179). Heidelberg, Germany: Springer-Verlag. doi:10.1007/978-3-540-88081-3_10

Tong, H., Faloutsos, C., & Pan, J. Y. (2006). Fast random walk with restart and its applications. In *Proceedings of International Conference on Data Mining* (pp. 613-622).

Torenvlied, R., & VanSchuur, H. (1994). A procedure for assessing large-scale 'total' networks using information from key informants. *Connections, 17*(2), 56–60.

Tortoriello, M., & Krackhardt, D. (2010). Activating Cross-Boundary Knowledge: The Role of Simmelian Ties in the Generation of Innovations. *Academy of Management Journal, 53*(1), 167–181. doi:10.5465/AMJ.2010.48037420

Torvik, V., Weeber, M., Swanson, D. W., & Smalheiser, N. R. (2004). A probabilistic similarity metric for medline records: a model of author name disambiguation. *Journal of the American Society for Information Science and Technology, 56*(2), 140–158. doi:10.1002/asi.20105

ToXgene (2005). *ToXgene - the ToX XML Data Generator*

Trave-Massuyes, L., & Piera, N. (1989). The orders of magnitude models as qualitative algebras. In *Proceedings of International Joint Conference on Artificial Intelligence* (pp. 1261-1266).

Tumasjan, A., Sprenger, T. O., Sandner, P. G., & Welpe, I. M. (2010). Predicting Elections with Twitter: What 140 Characters Reveal about Political Sentiment, in *Proceedings of the 4th International AAAI Conference on Weblogs and Social Media*, pp. 178-185.

Tuomela, R. (2007). *The Philosophy of Sociality: The Shared Point of View*. Oxford: Oxford University Press.

Tylenda, T., Angelova, R., & Bedathur, S. (2009). *Towards time-aware link prediction in evolving social networks.* Paper presented at the Proceedings of the 3rd Workshop on Social Network Mining and Analysis.

U.S. Census Bureau (2006). *USA Counties*

U.S. Census Bureau. (2009). State & County QuickFacts [Online]. Available: http://quickfacts.census.gov/ qfd/ states/48/4827000.html

U.S. Department of Energy (2007). *Fuel Economy Guide.*

U.S. Department of Energy (2008). *State & Federal Incentives & Laws*

UN Global E-Government Readiness Report. (2008). *From E-Government to Connected Governance.* Available on http://www2.unpan.org/ egovkb/global_ reports/08report.htm

Usherwood, T. (1999). *Understanding the Practice: Evidence, Theory and Practice*. Buckingham: Open University Press.

Valente, T. W. (1996). Social network thresholds in the diffusion of innovations. *Social Networks*, *18*, 69–89. doi:10.1016/0378-8733(95)00256-1

Van de Bunt, G. G., Van Duijn, M. A. J., & Snijders, T. A. B. (1999). Friendship networks through time: An actor-oriented statistical network model. *Computational & Mathematical Organization Theory*, *5*, 167–192. doi:10.1023/A:1009683123448

Van Rijsbergen, C. A. (1979). *Information retrieval* (2nd ed.). London: Butterworths.

Vaughn's Summaries. (2010). *Email spam filter word list.* Retrieved July 2010 from http://www.vaughns-1-pagers. com/ internet/spam-word-list.htm

Vehovar, V., Lozar Manfreda, K., Koren, G., & Hlebec, V. (2008). Measuring ego-centered social networks on the web: Questionnaire design issues. *Social Networks*, *30*(3), 213–222. doi:10.1016/j.socnet.2008.03.002

Venkatesan, R., Kumar, V., & Bohling, T. (2007). Optimal Customer Relationship Management Using Bayesian Decision Theory: An Application for Customer Selection. *JMR, Journal of Marketing Research*, *XLIV*(11), 579–594. doi:10.1509/jmkr.44.4.579

Verbrugge, L. M. (1977). The structure of adult friendship choices. *Social Forces*, *56*(2), 576–597.

Vesanen, J., & Raulas, M. (2006). Building bridges for personalization: a process model for marketing. *Journal of Interactive Marketing*, *20*(1), 5–20. doi:10.1002/dir.20052

Wagner, A. (2001). The yeast protein interaction network evolves rapidly and contains few redundant duplicate genes. *Molecular Biology and Evolution*, *18*(7), 1283–1292.

Wagner, A., & Fell, D. A. (2001). The small world inside large metabolic networks. *Proceedings. Biological Sciences*, *268*(1478), 1803–1810. doi:10.1098/rspb.2001.1711

Walker, G. (2008). The rise of Ecommerce as an epidemic in the small world of venture capital. *Network Strategy*, *25*, 3–29. doi:10.1016/S0742-3322(08)25001-1

Walker, G., Kogut, B., & Shan, W. (1997). Social capital, structural holes and the formation of an industry network. *Organization Science*, *8*, 109–125. doi:10.1287/orsc.8.2.109

Wallsten, K. (2010). "Yes We Can": How Online Viewership, Blog Discussion, Campaign Statements, and Mainstrem Media Coverage Produced a Viral Phenomenon. *Journal of Information Technology & Politics*, *7*(2), 163–181. doi:10.1080/19331681003749030

Wang, F.-Y., Carley, K. M., Zeng, D., & Mao, W. (2007). Social Computing: From Social Informatics to Social Intelligence. *IEEE Intelligent Systems*, *22*(2), 79–83. doi:10.1109/MIS.2007.41

Wang, F.-Y., Zeng, D., Hendler, J. A., Zhang, Q., Feng, Z., & Gao, Y. (2010). A Study of the Human Flesh Search Engine: Crowd-Powered Expansion of Online Knowledge, *IEEE. Computers & Society*, *43*(8), 45–53.

Wang, G. A., Chen, H., Xu, J. J., & Atabakhsh, H. (2006). Automatically detecting criminal identity deception: an adaptive detection algorithm. *IEEE Transactions on Systems, Man and Cybernetics. Part A*, *36*(5), 988–999.

Wang, A. (2010). Don't follow me: Twitter spam detection. *Proceedings of 5th International Conference on Security and Cryptography (SECRYPT)*, July 2010, Athens, Greece.

Wang, G. A., Atabakhsh, H., Petersen, T., & Chen, H. (2005). Discovering identity problems: A case study. In *Proceedings of IEEE International Conference on Intelligence and Security Informatics* (pp. 368-373).

Wasserman, S., & Faust, K. (1994). *Social network analysis: methods and applications*. Cambridge, UK: Cambridge University Press.

Wasserman, S., & Faust, K. (1994). *Social network analysis: Methods and applications*. Cambridge Univ Press.

Wasserman, S. (1980). Analyzing social networks as stochastic processes. *Journal of the American Statistical Association*, *75*, 280–294. doi:10.2307/2287447

Wasserman, S., & Philippa, P. (1996). Logit models and logistic regressions for social networks: I. an introduction to markov graphs and p*. *Psychometrika*, *61*(3), 401–425. doi:10.1007/BF02294547

Wasserman, S., & Faust, K. (1994). *Social Network Analysis: Methods and Applications*. Cambridge, UK: Cambridge Univ. Press.

Wasserman, S. (1977). Stochastic models for directed graphs. Unpublished Ph.D. dissertation, Department of Statistics, Harvard University.

Watts, D. J., & Strogatz, S. H. (1998). Collective dynamics of 'small-world' networks. *Nature*, *393*(6684), 440–442. doi:10.1038/30918

WEATHER.COM/AUTOS (2008). *Consumer reviews: Passenger Car weather performance* [Online]. Available: http://www.weather.com/outlook/ driving/drivingsafety/ autoadvisor/ consumerreview?start_index=0&vehicle_type=passenger&review_type=n&cond=snow&make=all

Webb, G. I., & Pazzani, M. (2001). Machine learning for user modeling. *User Modeling and User-Adapted Interaction*, *11*(1), 19–29. doi:10.1023/A:1011117102175

Weber, M. (1968). *Economy and Society: An Outline of Interpretive Sociology*. New York: Bedminster Press.

Weick, K. E. (1995). *Sensemaking in Organizations*. Thousand Oaks, CA: Sage.

Weihua, L. (n.d) Ontology Supported Intelligent Information Agent. *International IEEE Symposium On Intelligent Systems '02*

Weiss, G. M. (2004). Mining with rarity: a unifying framework. *SIGKDD Explorations*, *6*(Issue 1), 7–19. doi:10.1145/1007730.1007734

Wellman, B., Salaff, J., Dimitrova, D., Garton, L., Gulia, M., & Haythornthwaite, C. (1996). Computer Networks as Social Networks: Collaborative Work, Telework, and Virtual Community. *Annual Review of Sociology*, *22*, 213–238. doi:10.1146/annurev.soc.22.1.213

Wellman, B., & Haythornthwaite, C. A. (2002). *The Internet in everyday life*: Wiley-Blackwell.

Western, M., Dwan, K., Makkai, T., Mar, C. d., & Western, J. (2001). Measuring IT use in Australian General Practice. Retrieved 11th October, 2004, from http://www.gpcg.org/ publications/ docs/projects2001/GPCG_Project24_01.pdf

Weston, J., & Watkins, C. (1999). Multi-class support vector machines. Proceedings of the 1999 European Symposium on Artificial Neural Networks (pp. 219-224). Bruges, Belgium: D-Facto.

Wieringa, J. E., & Verhoef, P. C. (2007). Understanding Customer Switching Behavior in a Liberalizing Service Market: An Exploratory Study. *Journal of Service Research*, *10*(2), 174–186. doi:10.1177/1094670507306686

Wiggins, A., Howison, J., & Crowston, K. (2008). Social dynamics of floss team communication across channels. In *Proceedings of the Fourth International Conference on Open Source Software* (IFIP 2.13), Milan, Italy.

Wijsen, J. (2001). Trends in databases: reasoning and mining. *IEEE Transactions on Knowledge and Data Engineering*, *13*(3), 426–438. doi:10.1109/69.929900

Williams, E. (1979). Experimental Comparisons of Face-to-Face and Mediated Communication: A Review. *Psychological Bulletin, 84*(5), 963–976. doi:10.1037/0033-2909.84.5.963

Williams, C. B., & Gulati, G. J. J. (2007). Social Networks in Political Campaigns: Facebook and the 2006 Midterm Elections, *paper presented at the 2009 Annual Meeting of the American Political Science Association*, Chicago, Illinois, August 30- September 2.

Williams, C. B., & Gulati, G. J. J. (2009a). Facebook Grows Up: An Empirical Assessment of its Role in the 2008 Congressional Elections, *paper presented at the 2009 Annual Meeting of the Midwest Political Science Association*, Chicago, Illinois, April 2-5.

Williams, C. B., & Gulati, G. J. J. (2010). *Communicating with Constituents in 140 Characters or Less: Twitter and the Diffusion of Technology Innovation in the United States Congress*. Paper presented at the 2010 Annual Meeting of the Midwest Political Science Association, Chicago, Illinois, April 22-25.

Winkler, T., & Buckner, K. (2006). Receptiveness of Gamers to Embedded Brand Messages in Advergames: Attitudes towards Product Placement. *Journal of Interactive Advertising, 7*(1), 1–9.

Winkler, W. E. (1999). The state of record linkage and current research problems.

Wise, K., Bolls, P. D., Kim, H., Venkataraman, A., & Meyer, R. (2008). Enjoyment of Advergames and Brand Attitudes: The Impact of Thematic Relevance. *Journal of Interactive Advertising, 9*(1), 27–36.

Witten, I. H., & Frank, E. (2005). *Data Mining: Practical Machine Learning Tools and Techniques* (2nd ed.). San Francisco: Morgan Kaufmann Publishers.

Wolff, K. H. (1976). *Surrender and Catch: Experience and Inquiry Today*. Dordrecht: Reidel.

Wordpress, (2010). *Spam words*. Retrieved July, 2010, from http://codex.wordpress.org/ Spam_Words

Wright, R. P., & Cheung, F. K. K. (2007). Articulating appraisal system effectiveness based on managerial cognitions. *Personnel Review, 36*(2), 206–230. doi:10.1108/00483480710726118

Xiang, R., Neville, J., & Rogati, M. (2010). *Modeling relationship strength in online social networks*. Paper presented at the Proceedings of the 19th international conference on World wide web.

Yager, R. R. (1988). On ordered weighted averaging aggregation operators in multi-criteria decision making. *IEEE Transactions on Systems, Man, and Cybernetics, 18*, 183–190. doi:10.1109/21.87068

Yamamoto, D., Masuda, T., Ohira, S., & Nagao, K. (2008). Video Scene Annotation Based on Web Social Activities. *Multimedia. IEEE, 15*, 22–32. doi:10.1109/MMUL.2008.67

Yannas, P., & Lappas, G. (2007). Evaluating Local E-Government: An Analysis of Greek Prefecture Websites. In *Proceedings of the 2nd IEEE International Conference on Digital Information Management (ICDIM 07)*, October 28-31, Lyon, France, pp. 254-259.

Yardi, S., & Romerao, D., Schoenebeck, & G., Boyd, D. (2010). Detecting spam in a Twitter network. *First Monday, 15*(1).

Yeung, C. M. A., Gibbins, N., & Shadbolt, N. (2008). Web search disambiguation by collaborative tagging. *Proceedings of the Workshop on Exploring Semantic Innotations in Information Retrieval at ECIR'08* (pp. 48-61).

YHO. (2008). *Yahoo!* [Online]. Retrieved from: http://www.yahoo.com

Yolum, P., & Singh, M. P. (2003). Dynamic communities in referral networks. *Web Intelligence and Agent Systems, 1*(2), 105–116.

Yoshii, K., Goto, M., Komatani, K., Ogata, T., & Okuno, H. (2006). ISMIR'06: 7th International Conference on Music Information Retrieval, pp. 296-301.

Zafarani, R., & Liu, H. (2009). *Social computing data repository at ASU*. Retrieved from http://socialcomputing.asu.edu.

Zhang, Z., Rong, L., & Guo, C. (2006). A deterministic small-world network created by edge iterations. *Physica A, 363*, 567–572. doi:10.1016/j.physa.2005.08.020

Zheng, A., & Goldenberg, A. (2006). *A generative model for dynamic contextual friendship networks. CMU-ML-06-107.* Pittsburgh, PA: School of Computer Science. Carnegie Mellon University.

Zheng, Y.-T., Zhao, M., Song, Y., Adam, H., Buddermeier, U., Bissacco, A., et al. (2009). *Tour the World: Building a Web-scale Landmark Recognition Engine.* In proceedings of the 2009 IEEE computer society conference on computer vision and pattern recognition, pp. 1085-1092.

Zhou, P., & Le, Z. (2007). A Framework for Web Usage Mining in Electronic Government, *in IFIP International Federation for Information Processing: Vol. 252. Integration and Innovation Orient to E-Society* (pp. 487–496). Boston: Springer.

Zhou, Y., & Davis, J. (2006). Community discovery and analysis in blogspace. *Proceedings of the 15th international conference on World Wide Web* (p. 1018). ACM.

Zimmer, J. C., & Henry, R. M. (2007). *Antecedents to Relational and Nonrelational Source Use: An Exploratory Investigation.* Paper presented at the 40th Annual Hawaii International Conference on System Sciences (HICSS'07), Hawaii.

Zubiaga, A., Fresno, V., & Martínez, R. (2009b). Is unlabeled data suitable for multiclass SVM-based web page classification? *SemiSupLearn '09: Proceedings of the NAACL HLT 2009 Workshop on Semi-Supervised Learning for Natural Language Processing* (pp. 28-36). Morristown, NJ: ACL.

Zubiaga, A., Martínez, R., & Fresno, V. (2009a). Getting the most out of social annotations for web page classification. *DocEng '09: Proceedings of the 9th ACM symposium on Document engineering* (pp. 74-83). New York: ACM.

# About the Contributors

**I-Hsien Ting** is an Assistant Professor in the Department of Information Management, National University of Kaohsiung, TAIWAN from 2008. He received his Ph.D. degree in Computer Science, the University of York, UK in 2008, His research interests are focusing on Data Mining and E-commerce, particular on Web Mining, Social Network Analysis and Decision Support Systems, Web Intelligence, E-commerce, Semantic Web. He used to be a chair in the 1st, 2nd and 3rd International workshop on mining social networks for decision support (MSNDS 2009, 2010, 2011) and 1st and 2nd International workshop on web mining application in E-commerce and E-services (WMEE 2007), and a co-organizer in a special session of ICHIT 2006 conference and he also joined as a member of program committee in several conferences. Furthermore, he is now also a member of editorial advisory board of Online Information Review and as a referee in some academic Journals, such as Journal of Information Science, and in the editorial review board of Journal of Information, CyberPsychology and Behavior, Neurocomputing, Information Technology and Organizations. In additional, he is now editing two journal special issues in Journal of Online Information Review and Journal of Intelligent Information Systems. About academic paper publishing, he published more than twenty conference and journal papers in international journals, such as Journal of Web Engineering, Information Research Journal.

**Tzung-Pei Hong** received his B.S. degree in chemical engineering from National Taiwan University in 1985, and his Ph.D. degree in computer science and information engineering from National Chiao-Tung University in 1992. He was a faculty at the Department of Computer Science in Chung-Hua Polytechnic Institute from 1992 to 1994, and at the Department of Information Management in I-Shou University from 1994 to 2001. Since 2001, he has served as Director of Library and Computing Center, Dean of Academic Affair, and Vice President of National University of Kaohsiung. He is currently a distinguished professor at the Department of Electrical Engineering and the department of Computer Science and Information Engineering in National University of Kaohsiung. His current research interests include machine learning, data mining, soft computing, management information systems, WWW applications and has published more than 300 technical papers.

**Leon S.-L. Wang** received his Ph.D. from State University of New York at Stony Brook in 1984. From 1984 to 1987, he joined the University of New Haven as assistant professor. From 1987 to 1994, he joined New York Institute of Technology as assistant/associate professor. From 1994 to 2002, he joined I-Shou University in Taiwan and served as Director of Computing Center, Director of Library, and Chairman of Information Management Department. In 2002, he joined National University of Kaohsiung, Taiwan. In 2003, he rejoined NYIT. He is now professor and chairman in National University of Kaohsiung, Taiwan. He has published over 150 papers in the areas of data mining and soft computing, and served as a PC member of several national and international conferences. He is a member of the board of Chinese American Academic and Professional Society, USA.

* * *

**Lylia Abrouk** Since 2006, Lylia is associate Professor of Computer Science at at the Le2i CNRS Lab. (Laboratory of Electronics, Computer Science and Image), university of Bourgogne. In 2003, Dr. Abrouk joined, as a research engineer, the Euro-Mediterranean Information System on know-how in the Water sector project. She received her MSc and PhD degree in computer science from the University of Montpellier 2, France in 2003 and 2006 respectively within the area of semantic Web and Information research. Her research interests include documents annotation, ontology construction, and her current research field is community construction in collaborative Web and recommender systems. She is participating in the ANR Neuma project.

**Nitin Agarwal**, assistant professor of Information Science at University of Arkansas at Little Rock, holds a Ph.D. in Computer Science from Arizona State University with outstanding dissertation recognition. His research interests include social computing and behavioral modeling, data mining, knowledge extraction in social media, modeling and evaluation of influence, trust, homophily, and collective intelligence. This expertise is demonstrated through numerous highly cited articles in leading journals and participation in prestigious conferences (including a Best Paper Award), and through the publication of various books on Modeling and Data Mining in Blogosphere and Social Computing in Blogosphere: Challenges, Methodologies, and Opportunities. He has guest edited special issues on Social Computing in Blogosphere for IEEE Internet Computing and Social Computational Systems for the Journal of Computational Science. He currently serves on program and technical committees of several prestigious conferences and Editor-in-chief for the SocialComp 2011. More details can be found at: http://ualr.edu/nxagarwal/.

**Halil Bisgin** is currently a Ph.D. candidate at University of Arkansas at Little Rock. His primary research interests lie in network mining with applications ranging from Social Computing to Bioinformatics and biomedical signal processing in a high performance computing environment. He has published his research at various prestigious venues. He holds a MSE degree in Computational Science and Engineering from Istanbul Technical University, Turkey. His master thesis involved a mix of concepts from machine learning, parallel computing, and signal processing. Specifically, he identified new climate zones for Turkey via parallel k-means clustering algorithm based on an updated multidimensional data. More details on his research can be found at: www.halilbisgin.com.

**Anne Boyer** is professor in computer science in Nancy University, France. Her research focuses on human computer interaction, user modeling, recommender systems for individuals and groups, social networks, trust and computer supported learning. Anne Boyer is co-author of more than 50 publications in these research domains. Anne Boyer is "chargée de mission" at the French ministry of higher education and research. She is in charge of several national projects, such as the National Digital Universities.

**Armelle Brun** is an associate professor in computer science in Nancy University, France. Her research has initially focused on statistical language modeling for speech recognition and now addresses a variety of human-computer interaction issues, including user modeling, new modalities of expressing user preferences, personalization (recommender systems and collaborative filtering), and social networks. She got her PhD in computer science from Nancy University in January 2003. She is co-author of several journal articles, book chapters, and more than 50 articles in conference. She teaches database management, programming and personalization to bachelor and master students in computer science.

**Tossapon Boongoen** is an Assistant Professor with the Department of Mathematics and Computer Science, Royal Thai Air Force Academy, Thailand. Prior to this appointment, he obtained a PhD in artificial intelligence from Cranfield University, UK, and worked as Postdoctoral Research Associate at Aberystwyth University, UK. His research interests include data mining, pattern recognition, natural language processing and medical data analysis. Dr Boongoen's current research focuses on link analysis, data clustering, ensemble methodology and optimization for unmanned aerial vehicle design. He has published over 10 peer-refereed papers in leading international journals, including IEEE Transactions on Systems, Man and Cybernetics, Part B: Cybernetics; IEEE Transactions on Knowledge and Data Engineering; IEEE Transactions on Patter Recognition and Machine Intelligence; Bioinformatics; and Artificial Intelligence and Law.

**Sara Campo** is an Associate Professor of Marketing at Universidad Autónoma de Madrid (Spain), from which she received her Ph.D. in Marketing. She has published in International Journal of Service Industry Management, Tourism Management, Journal of Business to Business Marketing, International Journal of Tourism Research, Tourism Economics, International Journal of Culture, Tourism and Hospitality Research, and Journal of Travel and Tourism Marketing, among others. Her work also appears in many international conference proceedings.

**Sylvain Castagnos** got his Ph.D. degree in Artificial Intelligence from the Nancy University in France. After two years at the Swiss Federal Institute of Technology in Lausanne (EPFL), he joined the KIWI Team in the LORIA Laboratory. His research interests include scalable recommender systems, information retrieval, user modeling, privacy, trust, human/computer interactions, stochastic models for artificial intelligence, multi-agent systems, electronic commerce, collaborative filtering, natural language processing, purchase decision making, economy of attention, automated learning, and social navigation.

**Chien-Chung Chan** received his Ph.D. in computer science from the University of Kansas, Kansas, USA in 1989. He is a professor of the Computer Science department at the University of Akron, Akron, Ohio, USA since 1989. His research areas include rough set theory and its applications to machine learning and data mining, expert systems, and granular computing. He served as the general chair for the 2008 international conference on Rough Sets and Current Trends in Computing (RSCTC) bi-annual conference held at Akron, Ohio.

**Kenneth Chung** is a lecturer at the University of Wollongong. His research interest is in the area of network science, in particular, in social networks and its influence on social and organizational outcomes such as coordination, performance and innovation. His work uses a triangulation of inter-disciplinary theories and methods from social networks, sociology, information systems and management science. Much of his recent work has been published in top-tier conferences & journals such as Computer-

Supported Cooperative Work, European Conference on Information Systems, Human-Computer Interaction, SIG-Management of Information Systems, Interact, Project Management Journal and Computers in Human Behavior.

**James A. Danowski** (Ph.D., Michigan State University, Communication) is a faculty member in the Department of Communication at the University of Illinois at Chicago, where he has taught courses in research methods, organizational communication, and communication technologies. His research has involved automated communication network analysis of words, people, organizations, and nations. He developed the WORDij (http://wordij.net) software. His theoretical interests include how changes in semantic and sentiment networks in social systems are associated with changes in who-to-whom communication networks. He has been a member of the Board of Directors of the International Communication Association. He was in the founding group of the International Network for Social Network Analysis.

**Ramez Elmasri** is Professor of Computer Science and Engineering at the University of Texas at Arlington, USA, since 1990. He was an Assistant Professor (1982-1987) and an Associate Professor (1987-1990) at the University of Houston, Texas, USA. He completed his M.S. and Ph.D. degrees in Computer Science at Stanford University in 1980. He has over 130 refereed publications in journals and conference proceedings. He is a co-author of the textbooks "Fundamentals of Database Systems" (5th edition, Addison-Wesley, 2007) and "Operating Systems: A Spiral Approach" (1st edition, McGraw-Hill Science/Engineering/Math, 2009). His research interests are in Database Systems, XML, Network Management Information Systems, Web Modeling and Ontologies, E-Commerce, Temporal Databases, Conceptual Modeling, Object-Oriented Databases, Distributed Object Computing, Operating Systems, Systems Integration, Database Models and Languages, DBMS System Implementation, Indexing Techniques, and Software Engineering Environments. Dr. Elmasri served on numerous conference and workshop program committees. He is member of IEEE, IEEE Computer Society, and ACM SIGMOD.

**Michael Farrugia** received his B.Sc. degree in computer science from the University of Malta in 2002. He is currently a Ph.D. candidate at University College Dublin. His research interests include information visualisation, large scale social networks, data mining and airline business informatics.

**Victor Fresno** is Assistant Professor at the Department of Lenguajes y Sistemas Informáticos (LSI) at the National Distance Learning University (UNED), in Madrid, Spain. He received the PhD in Computer Science from the Universidad Rey Juan Carlos (Spain) in 2006. Prior to that, he enjoyed a fellowship in the Spanish Council for Scientific Research (Consejo Superior de Investigaciones Científicas - CSIC) and he was teaching assistant of the Computer Science Department at URJC until 2006. His research interests include web page characterization for classification, clustering and Multimedia Information Retrieval, Fuzzy Logic and Natural Language Processing Tools for Text Mining. In these areas, he has published more than 40 papers in national and international journals,conferences and workshops. He has been involved in projects funded by Spanish Goverment with academic and industrial partners.

**Brian R Gaines** is Professor Emeritus at the University of Calgary. He was formerly Killam Memorial Research Professor, Dean of Graduate Studies, Associate Vice President (Research) and Director of the Knowledge Science Institute. His previous positions include Professor of Industrial Engineering at the University of Toronto, Technical Director and Deputy Chairman of the Monotype Corporation, and Chairman of the Department of Electrical Engineering Science at the University of Essex. He received his BA, MA and PhD from Trinity College, Cambridge, and is a Chartered Engineer, Chartered Psychologist, and a Fellow of the Institution of Electrical Engineers, the British Computer Society and the British Psychological Society. He is editor of the International Journal of Human-Computer Studies and Knowledge Acquisition, and of the Computers and People and Knowledge-Based Systems book series. He has authored over 400 papers and authored or edited 10 books on a wide variety of aspects of computer and human systems. His research interests include: the socio-economic dynamics of science and technology; the nature, acquisition and transfer of knowledge; software engineering for heterogeneous systems; and knowledge-based system applications in manufacturing, the professions, sciences and humanities.

**Brigitte Gay** is Professor in Management and Director of the Specialized Master in Biotechnology Management program with Group ESC Toulouse Business School. She is also a researcher in economics at University of Social Sciences (Toulouse I). After a 10-years spell abroad in a big pharmaceutical company as a project team head in Research & Development, she took up full-time research teaching in the field of technology and innovation management working at Group ESC Business School in Toulouse, France. She is also a member of different panels on innovation economics and competitive intelligence. Her areas of research interest include the management of discontinuous innovation, strategies for managing alliance networks, and, more recently, the structure of capital markets.

**David Gross-Amblard.** Since 2006, David is assistant professor at the Le2i CNRS Lab., university of Bourgogne, France. He was previously an assistant professor at Cedric Lab., CNAM-Paris (2001-2006), in the Vertigo database team. He received MSc and PhD degree in computer science from the University of Paris XI, Orsay, France in 1996 and 2000 respectively, and his Research habilitation thesis from Bourgogne university, France, in 2010. His research interests include database watermarking, database complexity, application of finite model theory, and more recently Web-scale database management and social networks. He was part of the ACI SI Tadorne project, and is now participating in the ANR Neuma and ERC WebDam projects.

**Valentina Hlebec** (PhD in sociology at the Faculty of Social Sciences, University of Ljubljana, 1999) is associate professor for sociology at the Faculty of Social Sciences University of Ljubljana. Her research interests cover topics in sociology of ageing, social networks and survey methodology, especially designing and testing survey questionnaires. She has been involved in several national and international project groups in these fields, is co-athor of several books and articles.

**Neil J. Hurley** received an M.Sc. in mathematical science from University College Dublin (UCD), Dublin, Ireland, in 1988. In 1989, he joined Hitachi Dublin Laboratory, a computer science research laboratory at the University of Dublin, Trinity College, from which he received the Ph.D. degree in 1995, for his work in knowledge-based engineering and high-performance computing. He joined the academic staff of UCD in 1999 where his present research activities lie in the areas of large-scale network analysis, robust information retrieval and data-hiding.

**Yingzi Jin** is a postdoctoral researcher at the Graduate School of Engineering, the University of Tokyo. She received her M.S. and PhD. in Information Science and Technology from the University of Tokyo, Japan, in 2006 and 2009, respectively. She was awarded her Research Fellowship for Young Scientists from the Japan Society for the Promotion of Science (JSPS). She visited the IBM T. J. Watson Research Center as a visiting scholar from Jun. 2009 to Apr. 2010. Her research interests are Web Mining, Social Networks, E-commerce, and Artificial intelligence. Currently, she is working on Social Network Extraction from the Web and Cross-organizational Network Analysis.

**Tina Kogovšek** (PhD in sociology at the Faculty os Social Sciences, University of Ljubljana, 2001) is associate professor for social science methodology at the Faculty of Arts and Faculty of Social Sciences University of Ljubljana. Her main research interests are social science methodology (especially measurement and quality of measurement) and social support. She has applied her expertise in social science methodology in various research projects (e.g., quality of measurement of social networks, quality in education, measurement of social capital, social integration of the elderly, political participation of women, intimate lifestyles of the young). She has published papers on social science methodology and on sociology in various publications, predominantly international scientific journals.

**Georgios Lappas** is an Associate Professor of Informatics and the Head of the Public Relations and Communication Department at the Technological Educational Institution (TEI) of Western Macedonia, Greece. His research interests: Multimedia and Web Communication (Web 2.0, Social Media, Semantic Web, Web Marketing, E-Government, Politics and the Web, E-Campaigns), Artificial Intelligence (Pattern Recognition, Neural Networks, Machine Learning), and combination of the above fields (Social Computing, Web Mining, Intelligent Web, Intelligent Multimedia, Social Multimedia Mining). On these topics he published over 60 articles in International Journals and Conference Proceedings and was the editor of two conference proceedings and one Journal Special Issue. He serves as an Editorial Board Member and referee in 6 Journals and as a PC member in over 30 Int. Conferences. He is the Scientific Coordinator of 4 EU Founded Research Projects.

**Damien Leprovost** is a PhD student at the Laboratoire Eléctronique, Informatique et Image (LE2I) CNRS laboratory, University of Bourgogne, France. He received is Msc degree in computer science from the same university in 2009. He is also an MBA student. His research area is the detection of implicit online communities, by analyzing communications between Web users. These studies investigate the importance of semantics in the construction of these communities.

**Kathy Liszka** received her Ph.D. in computer science from the Kent State University, Ohio, USA, in 1993. She is a professor of the Computer Science department at the University of Akron, Akron, Ohio, USA since 1993. Her research areas include software security, sensor networks and their applications. She has been involved in the annual MIT Spam conferences held at MIT, Cambridge, USA, for the past few years, and she served as the general chair for the 2010 Spam conference.

**Nicolas Marie** is a Phd candidate and research engineer in Bell Labs, Alcatel-Lucent, France, since 2010. He is focused on social objects, object centered sociality, object centered social networks in a "next level" context: semantic and pervasive web context. He is also working on the pervasive sociality vision, both conceptual and formal aspect, which aims to bring new ideas in the field of connected communication.

**Raquel Martínez Unanue** is Associate Professor at the Department of Lenguajes y Sistemas Informáticos (LSI) at the National Distance Learning University (UNED), in Madrid, Spain. Her research lines include: Multilingual Text Mining, particularly Multilingual Document Clustering where the use of Named Entities and Cognate are studied, and Corpus alignment. She has been involved in several founded research projects.

**Yutaka Matsuo** is an associate professor at the Institute of Engineering Innovation, the University of Tokyo. He received his B.S., M.S., and PhD. degrees from the University of Tokyo in 1997, 1999, and 2002 (supervised by Prof. Ishizuka). He joined the National Institute of Advanced Industrial Science and Technology (AIST) from 2002 to 2007. His major is Web mining (especially social network mining), text processing, and the semantic Web in the context of artificial intelligence research. He is one of the prominent young researchers in the information technology field in Japan. He has written more than 30 journal papers in Japanese over the past seven years and 60+ international conference papers. He received the Japanese Society for Artificial Intelligence (JSAI) Best Paper Award in 2002, JSAI Anniversary Project Award in 2006, and Information Processing Society of Japan (IPSJ) Nagao Special Researcher Award in 2008. He joined the editorial committee of JSAI in 2004, and currently serves as associate editor-in-chief. He received a Japan Society for the Promotion of Science (JSPS) Postdoctoral Fellowship for Research Abroad in 2005 and stayed for two years at the Center for the Study of Language and Information (CSLI), Stanford University. In 2007, after returning to Japan, he joined the faculty of the University of Tokyo.

**Maja Mrzel** is an undergraduate student of Social Informatics on the Faculty of Social Sciences at the University of Ljubljana. Since 2009 she participated on projects The Quality of Life of Social Groups and Intergenerational Solidarity in Slovenia, both part of the Centre for Welfare Studies on the Faculty of Social Sciences. She is currently finishing her study with a thesis on comparison of single and multiple name generators for measuring social support networks. Her national and international publications mainly cover research in the field of social networks.

**Lionel Natarianni**. Since July 2007 Lionel Natarianni is working as a Research Engineer for Bell Labs in Applications Domain. As member of Social Communication team, is studying ways of building a social graph according to the usage of communication means. More recently he joined the "Real-time Social Life Group" to study how real-time impact the formation of social graph. Prior to Bell Labs, Lionel serves in Alcatel-Lucent Carrier business group in Mobile Access business division as software engineer and architect in WIMAX WAC (Wireless Access Controller) project. He also worked on software development projects for Alcatel-Lucent GSM/GPRS 2.5G access network solutions like Radio Management Systems.

**Shintaro Okazaki** is an Associate Professor of Marketing at the Universidad Autónoma de Madrid (Spain), from which he received his Ph.D. in Marketing. Dr. Okazaki's research focuses on mobile commerce, global branding, and information privacy concerns. His work has appeared in Journal of Advertising, Journal of Advertising Research, International Journal of Advertising, Journal of International Marketing, Journal of Business Research, Journal of World Business, Psychology & Marketing, Information & Management, Online Information Review, Journal of Computer-Mediated Communication, Computers in Human Behavior, and Internet Research, among others. He serves on the editorial boards of Journal of Advertising (Associate Editor), International Journal of Advertising, Journal of Public Policy & Marketing, Journal of Interactive Advertising, Electronic Markets, and Internet Research, among others. Dr. Okazaki is also on the Executive Board of the European Advertising Academy (EAA) and the Spanish Marketing Association (AEMARK), and has been named as the 2008 Best Academic of the Year by the Mobile Marketing Association.

**Diane Payne** is the Director of the Geary Dynamics Lab and a member of the School of Sociology at University College Dublin (UCD). She is appointed Principal Investigator (PI) at the UCD Complex and Adaptive Systems Laboratory (CASL). Dr. Payne's various research interests belong to the field of Computational Social Science and in particular, behavioural models of group processes and collective decision making. She has research expertise in group decision modelling and (formal) social network analysis.

**Jérôme Picault** is a research engineer at Bell Labs, Alcatel-Lucent, France, since 2008. He graduated from the Institut National des Télécommunications, France, in 2001. He is currently working on social networks. Prior to joining Bell Labs, Jérôme spent 8 years as Senior Research Engineer in Motorola Labs where he developed research in agent-based architectures and mobile services, context-awareness, social networks and recommender systems. He is the author of 28 patent applications and 20 publications on intelligent systems, personalization and related topics. He has co-organized several workshops: UbiDeUM (Ubiquitous and Decentralized User Modeling at UM'07) and PRSAT 2010 (Practical Use of Recommender Systems, Algorithms and Technologies at RecSys 2010). He is also a PC member for several conferences or journals (e.g. ESWC'10, ACM Transactions on Intelligent Systems and Technology).

**Aaron Quigley** is the Chair of Human Computer Interaction in the School of Computer Science at the University of St Andrews in Scotland. He is the director of SACHI, the St Andrews Computer Human Interaction research group and his appointment is part of SICSA the Scottish Informatics and Computer Science Alliance. His research interests include surface and multi-display computing, human computer interaction, pervasive and ubiquitous computing and information visualisation. He is the chair of the steering committee for the International Conference series on Pervasive Computing and the Editor-In-Chief for the Journal "Computers". Aaron has had leading roles in over a dozen international conferences and has served on over sixty international conference and workshops program committees. He has published over 110 internationally peer-reviewed publications including edited volumes, journal papers, book chapters, conferences and workshop papers and holds 3 patents. He is a Chartered Fellow of the British Computer Society (BCS), a senior member of the IEEE, a member of the ACM and a recipient of a National Institute of Engineers Australia award for excellence in engineering education.

**Myriam Ribière** is a research engineer at Bell Labs, Alcatel-lucent, France, since 2008. She got her PhD in Artificial Intelligence and Knowledge Representation in 1999 and performed it at the INRIA Sophia-Antipolis laboratory. She is currently working on social networks. Prior to joining Bell Labs, Myriam was a senior research engineer at the Personalization and Knowledge Lab of Motorola in Paris (from 2001 to 2008) and worked before at the SRI (Stanford Research Institute). Her main research interests include the social and semantic web, knowledge representation and management, leveraging collective intelligence from people interactions. She has many patent applications (14) and publications (30) in the domain of knowledge representation, ontologies, semantic web services, cooperative building of ontologies, and conceptual graphs.

**Jaime Romero** is an Associate Professor of Marketing at Universidad Autónoma de Madrid (Spain), from which he received his Ph.D. in Marketing. He has published in International Journal of Market Research, Journal of Marketing Management, and Online Information Review, among others. His work also appears in many international conference proceedings. He is currently Treasurer of the Spanish Marketing Association (AEMARK).

**Mildred L G Shaw** is Professor Emerita at the University of Calgary. She was formerly Industrial Research Chair in Software Engineering and Professor of Computer Science. She received her BSc and MSc from the University of London, and her PhD from Brunel University. She is a Chartered Mathematician and a Fellow of the Institute of Mathematics and its Applications and prior to retirement was a Chartered Psychologist, a Fellow of the British Computer Society and an Associate Fellow of the British Psychological Society. She has authored over 150 papers and authored or edited 5 books on a wide variety of aspects of computer and human systems. Her research interests include: human-computer interaction; the acquisition and transfer of knowledge; software engineering; and knowledge-based system applications.

**Chandra Shekar** received his B.S. in Computer Application from Bangalore University and a Master's degree in Computer Applications from Visveswaraiah Technological University, India. He is completing his Master's degree in Computer Science at the University of Akron. His main interest is in developing iphone applications.

**Qiang Shen** is Head of Department of Computer Science at Aberystwyth University, an Honorary Fellow of the University of Edinburgh and a Fellow of British Computer Society. His current research interests include: computational intelligence, fuzzy and qualitative modelling, reasoning under uncertainty, pattern recognition, data mining, and real-world applications of such techniques for intelligent decision support (e.g. crime detection, consumer profiling, systems monitoring, and medical diagnosis). He is a long-serving associate editor of two IEEE flagship Journals (Systems, Man and Cybernetics, and Fuzzy Systems) and an editorial board member of several other leading international periodicals. He has chaired and given keynote lectures at many prestigious international conferences. He has authored 2 research monographs and over 270 peer-reviewed papers, including one receiving an IEEE Outstanding Transactions Paper Award.

**Johann Stan** is a PhD candidate and research engineer at Bell Labs, Alcatel-Lucent, France, since 2008. He graduadet from the Institut National des Sciences Appliquées de Lyon, France, in 2003. Enrolled also in a PhD programme with Saint-Etienne University. His current research interests are social network analysis and user modeling using semantic web technologies. He is the author of 12 patent applications and 7 publications in these fields (ASONAM, UMAP, Social Computing). He is a PC member of several international workshops (MultiAPro, WIVE, WI&C) and reviewer for several books in the field. Johann is also active in the community as a lecturer at conference tutorials (Caise 2011) and the international CIMET Master research programme, involving universities from France, Norway and Spain.

**Jerzy Surma** is an Assistant Professor at Warsaw School of Economics and a director of executive studies on Business Intelligence. Prior to his teaching positions, he worked as a business consultant in an information management group and was responsible for the design and implementation of business intelligence solutions for international companies. He is a member of the Strategic Management Society and IESE Business School Alumni. Currently, Dr. Surma has been working on applying advanced data mining techniques in reality mining and analytical customer relationship management. Look for details at http://www.surma.edu.pl.

**Kamal Taha** received his M.S. degree in Software Engineering in 2002 from the University of St. Thomas in Minnesota-USA. He completed his Ph.D. degree in Computer Science at The University of Texas at Arlington-USA in 2010. Dr. Taha is currently an Assistant Professor of Computer Engineering at Khalifa University of Science, Technology and Research - UAE. He was an instructor of Computer Science and Engineering at The University of Texas at Arlington from August 2008 to August 2010. He worked as an Engineering Specialist for Seagate Technology (a leading computer disc drive manufacturer in the US) from 1996 to 2005. Dr. Taha authored a book and coauthored three book chapters. In addition, he has 14 refereed publications that have appeared (or are forthcoming) in journals, conferences, and workshops proceedings. His scholarly interests span databases, information retrieval, and data mining. Dr. Taha was selected by Marquis Who's Who to be included in the 2011-2012 (11th) Edition of Who's Who in Science and Engineering, the world-renowned reference directory. He serves as a member of the Program Committee of two international conferences and as a reviewer for a number of conferences and academic journals. He was a GAANN Fellow (US Department of Education Graduate Assistance in Areas of National Need).

**Charalampos E. Tsourakakis** was born in 1984 in the beautiful island of Crete in Greece. Currently, is a Ph.D. candidate in the program of Algorithms, Combinatorics and Optimization at Carnegie Mellon University working under the supervision of Alan M. Frieze. His main research interests include probabilistic combinatorics, efficient algorithm design (sequential and parallel) and machine learning. Algorithmic and mining issues arising in the context of social networks and computational biology act as sources of interesting problems for his research.

**Xiaowei Xu**, a professor of Information Science at the University of Arkansas at Little Rock, received his Ph.D. degree in Computer Science at the University of Munich in 1998. He is a recipient of the prestigious Oak Ridge Institute for Science and Education (ORISE) Faculty award. He holds an adjunct professor position at the National Center for Toxicological Research. He is a visiting professor in Microsoft Research Asia and Chinese University of Hong Kong. He was a senior research scientist in Siemens AG. His major research interests include data mining, machine learning, database systems, bioinformatics and high performance computing. He has published over 50 papers in journals and conference proceedings including IEEE Transactions in Data Engineering, ACM SIGKDD Conference on Knowledge Discovery and Data Mining. His groundbreaking work on density-based clustering algorithms has been widely used in textbooks; and received over 2951 citations based on Google scholar to date.

**Arkaitz Zubiaga** is a PhD student at the Department of Lenguajes y Sistemas Informáticos of the National Distance Learning University (UNED). He is member of the Natural Language Processing and Information Retrieval Group at UNED. His research interests revolve around Data Mining and Information Processing on Social Media. Up to now, his work has focused on getting the most out of social annotations for Information Management tasks. He was member of the program committee for several international workshops and journals.

# Index

## A

absolute order-of-magnitude 81, 86-88, 91

active inquiry 35

Actor Identification 133, 142-144, 152

Advergaming 292, 295-297, 300-303, 305

Agency for Healthcare Research and Quality (AHRQ) 259

analytical CRM 178

Analytical Customer Profile (ACP) 171, 173-174, 178-179, 181

AOM - See absolute order-of-magnitude.

Application Programming Interface (API) 101-102, 104, 106, 321

a priori algorithm 25-26

authority page 58

Automated Text Mining 219

## B

BBS - See bulletin board systems.

Behavioral Perspective 175

Bitstring Creation Command 72

Bitstrings 70-72

BlogCatalog 17, 19, 21-23, 25-26, 28-30, 34

Breadth First Search (BFS) 69

bulk-synchronous parallel model (BSP) 67

bulletin board systems 308

## C

cardinality 81, 86, 89, 92, 94, 129

Centralization 64, 207, 211-216, 239, 248

CF - See Collaborative Filtering.

class-subclass 184, 186

Clustering Coefficient 64, 147, 232, 235, 238-241, 244, 248

CLV - See customer lifetime value

cognitive commonality 36

cognitive observations 141

Cold-start problem 270, 272, 275-276, 279, 284-285

Collaborative Annotations 118

Collaborative Filtering 185, 271, 273-275, 278-281, 284

collaborative filtering recommendation 183, 202

Collaborative Innovation Networks (COINS) 216-217, 229

Collaborative Tagging 117, 127-129, 306, 311

collective stance 51, 54

comparisons of conceptual grids 48

complex empirical networks 238

Complexity Analysis 71

Complex Systems 63, 99, 135, 237, 244

Computational Social Science 135, 153, 180

Concept Network 54, 61

conceptual grid elicitation 35, 39-40, 50, 54

conceptual modeling 35-40, 46, 50, 53, 55

conceptual modeling techniques 36

Connected-Triple (CT) 81, 84, 86, 89, 92, 94, 129

consensual conceptual model 47

Content-based filtering 183, 289

content-based recommendation - See Content-based filtering.

Content Management 62

coreference resolution 82, 100, 143

correspondence problem 143

CT - See cardinality.

cURL 106

customer lifetime value 177

Customer profiling 171-172, 176

customer referral value (CRV) 177

Cyworld 176-177, 182

## D

Data collection -See Data Mining.

Data Mining 19, 21, 86, 131-135, 137-140, 144, 147-148, 150, 157, 165, 223, 256, 295, 340

DCFM - See dynamic contextual friendship model.